John Knox, Thomas Kitchin

A new geographical, historical and commercial grammar and present state of the several kingdoms of the world

Vol. 2, Second Edition

John Knox, Thomas Kitchin

A new geographical, historical and commercial grammar and present state of the several kingdoms of the world
Vol. 2, Second Edition

ISBN/EAN: 9783337274047

Printed in Europe, USA, Canada, Australia, Japan

Cover: Foto ©Andreas Hilbeck / pixelio.de

More available books at **www.hansebooks.com**

A NEW

Geographical, Hiftorical, and Commercial

GRAMMAR;

AND

PRESENT STATE

OF THE SEVERAL

KINGDOMS OF THE WORLD.

CONTAINING

I. The Figures, Motions, and Diftances of the Planets, according to the Newtonian Syftem and the lateft Obfervations.

II. A general View of the Earth confidered as a Planet; with feveral ufeful Geographical Definitions and Problems.

III. The grand Divifions of the Globe into Land and Water, Continents and Iflands.

IV. The Situation and Extent of Empires, Kingdoms, States, Provinces, and Colonies.

V. Their Climate, Air, Soil, vegetable Productions, Metals, Minerals, natural Curiofities, Seas, Rivers, Bays, Capes, Promontories, and Lakes.

VI. The Birds and Beafts peculiar to each Country.

VII. Obfervations on the Changes that have been any where obferved upon the Face of Nature fince the moft early Periods of Hiftory.

VIII. The Hiftory and Origin of Nations: their Forms of Government, Religion, Laws, Revenues, Taxes, naval and military Strength.

IX. The Genius, Manners, Cuftoms, and Habits of the People.

X. Their Language, Learning, Arts, Sciences, Manufactures, and Commerce.

XI. The chief Cities, Structures, Ruins, and artificial Curiofities.

XII. The Longitude, Latitude, Bearings, and Diftances of principal Places from London.

XIII. A General Index.

With a TABLE of the COINS of all Nations, and their
Value in ENGLISH MONEY.

By WILLIAM GUTHRIE, Efq.

ILLUSTRATED WITH

A NEW AND CORRECT SET OF LARGE MAPS,
Engraved by Mr. KITCHIN, Geographer.

THE SECOND EDITION.

VOLUME II.

LONDON:

Printed for J. KNOX, at N°. 148, near Somerfet-Houfe,
in the Strand. M DCC LXXI.

EUROPE.

FRANCE.

HAVING gone over the Britifh ifles, we fhall now return to the continent, beginning with the extenfive and mighty kingdom of France, being the neareft to England; though part of Germany and Poland lies to the northward of France.

SITUATION AND EXTENT.

	Miles.		Degrees.
Length	600	} between {	5 and 8 weft and eaft long.
Breadth	500		42 and 51 north lat.

BOUNDARIES.] It is bounded by the Englifh channel and the Netherlands, on the north; by Germany, Switzerland, and Italy, eaft; by the Mediterranean and the Pyrenean mountains, which divides it from Spain, fouth; and by the Bay of Bifcay, weft.

DIVISIONS.] This kingdom is divided, and the dimenfions of the feveral parts diftinctly fpecified in the following table, by Mr. Templeman.

Countries Names.	Square Miles.	Length	Breadth	Chief Cities.
France.				
Orleannois	22,550	230	180	Orleans
Guienne	12,800	216	120	Bourdeaux
Gafcoigne	8,800	125	90	Aux or Augh
Languedoc	13,175	200	115	Thouloufe
Lyonnois	12,500	175	130	Lyon
Champagne	10,000	140	110	Rheims
Bretagne	9,100	170	105	Rennes
Normandy	8,200	155	85	Rouen
Provence	6,800	95	92	Aix
Burgundy	6,700	150	86	Dijon
Dauphine	5,820	107	90	Grenoble
Ifle of France	5,200	100	85	PARIS
French Compte	4,000	100	60	Befancon
Picardy	3,650	120	87	Amiens
Roufillon	1,400	50	44	Perpignan
Total—	131,095			

The French Netherlands will be found under the title Netherlands.

NAME AND CLIMATE.] France took its name from the Francs, a German nation, who conquered the Gauls, the antient inhabitants. By its fituation, it is the moft compact kingdom perhaps in the world, and well fitted for every pur-pofe both of power and commerce; and fince the beginning of the 15th century, their inhabitants have fully availed them-felves of their natural advantages. The air, particularly that of the interior parts of the kingdom, is in general mild and wholefome; but fome late authors think it is not near fo fa-lubrious as is pretended; and it muft be acknowledged, that the French have been but too fuccefsful in giving the inhabi-tants of Great Britain falfe prepoffeffions in favour of their own country. It muft be owned, that their weather is more clear and fettled than in England. In the northern provinces, however, the winters are more intenfely cold, and the inhabi-tants not fo well fupplied with firing, which in France is chief-ly of wood.

SOIL AND WATER.] France is happy in an excellent foil, which produces corn, wine, oil, and almoft every luxury of life. Some of their fruits have a higher flavour than thofe of England; but neither their pafturage or tillage are comparable to ours. The heats in many parts burn up the ground, fo that it has no verdure, and the foil barely produces as much rye and chefnuts, as ferve to fubfift the poor inhabitants; but the chief misfortune attending the French foil is, that the in-habitants having but a precarious fecurity in their own pro-perty, do not apply themfelves fufficiently to cultivation and agriculture. Nature, however, has done wonders for them, and both animal and vegetable productions are found there in vaft plenty.

The French have of late endeavoured to fupply the lofs arifing from their precarious title to their lands, by inftituting acade-mies of agriculture, and propofing premiums for its improve-ment, as in England; but thofe expedients, however fuccefs-ful they may be in particular inftances, can never become of na-tional utility in any but a free country, where the hufbandman is fure of enjoying the fruit of his labour. It muft at the fame time be admitted, that the French exceed perhaps the Englifh themfelves in the theory of agriculture. No nation is better fupplied than France is with wholefome fprings and water; of which the inhabitants make excellent ufe, by the help of art and engines, for all the conveniencies of life. I fhall afterwards fpeak of their canals and mineral waters.

MOUNTAINS.] The chief mountains in France, or its borders, are, The Alps, which divide France from Italy. The
Pyrenees,

Pyrenees, which divide France from Spain. Vauge, which divides Lorrain from Burgundy and Alsace. Mount Jura, which divides Franche Compte, from Switzerland. The Cevennes, in the province of Languedoc; and Mount Dor, in the province of Auvergne.

RIVERS AND LAKES.] The principal rivers in France are, the Loire, the Rhone, the Garonne, and the Seine. The Loire takes its course north and north-west, being, with all its windings, from its source to the sea, computed to run about 500 miles. The Rhone flows on south-west to Lyons, and then runs on due south till it falls into the Mediterranean. The Garonne rises in the Pyrenean mountains, takes its course, first, north-east, and has a communication with the Mediterranean by means of a canal, the work of Lewis XIV. The Seine, soon after its rise, runs to the north-west, visiting Troyes, Paris, and Rouen, in its way, and falls into the English channel at Havre. To these we may add, the Scane, which falls into the Rhone at Lyons; the Charente, which rises near Havre de Grace, runs in and discharges itself in the Bay of Biscay. The Rhine, which rises in Swisserland, is the eastern boundary between France and Germany, and receives the Moselle and the Sarte in its passage. The Somme, which runs north-west through Picardy, and falls into the English channel below Abbeville. The Var, which rises in the Alps, and runs south, dividing France from Italy, falls into the Mediterranean west of Nice. The Adour runs from east to west, through Gascoigne, and falls into the Bay of Biscay below Bayonne.

The vast advantage, both in commerce and conveniency, which arises to France from those rivers, is wonderfully improved by the artificial rivers and canals which form the chief glory of the reign of Lewis XIV. That of Languedoc was begun in the year 1666, and compleated in 1680 : it was intended for a communication between the ocean and the Mediterranean, for the speedier passage of the French fleet; but though it was carried on at an immense expence, for 100 miles, over hills and vallies, and even through a mountain in one place, it has not answered that purpose. By the canal of Calais, travellers easily pass by water from thence to St. Omer, Graveline, Dunkirk, Yper, and other places. The canal of Orleans is another noble work, and runs a course of 18 leagues, to the immense benefit of the public and the royal revenue. France abounds with other canals of the like kind, which render her inland navigation inexpressibly commodious and beneficial.

Few

Few lakes are found in this country. There is one at the top of a hill near Alegre, which the vulgar report to be bottomlefs. There is another at Iffoire, in Auvergne; and one at La Beffe, in which if you throw a ftone, it caufes a noife like thunder.

MINERAL WATERS AND RE- The waters of Bareges,
MARKABLE SPRINGS. which lie near the borders
of Spain, under the Pyrenean mountains, have of late been preferred to all the others of France, for the recovery of health. The beft judges think, however, that the cures performed by them, are more owing to their accidental fuccefs, with fome great perfons, and the falubrity of the air and foil, than the virtues of the waters. The waters of Sultzbach in Alface, cure the palfey, weak nerves, and the ftone. At Bagueiis, not far from Bareges, are feveral wholefome minerals and baths, to which people refort as to the Englifh baths, at fpring and autumn. Forges in Normandy is celebrated for its mineral waters, and thofe of St. Amand cure the gravel and obftructions. It would be endlefs to enumerate all the other real or pretended mineral wells in France, therefore I muft omit them, as well as many remarkable fprings: but there is one near Aigne in Auvergne, which boils violently, and makes a noife like water thrown upon lime; it has little or no tafte, but has a poifonous quality, and the birds that drink of it die inftantly.

METALS AND MINERALS.] Languedoc is faid to contain veins of gold and filver. Alface has mines of filver and copper, but they are too expenfive to be wrought. Alabafter, black marble, jafper, and coal, are found in many parts of the kingdom. Britany abounds in mines of iron, copper, tin, and lead. At Laverdau, in Cominges, there is a mine of chalk. At Berry there is a mine of oker, which ferves for melting of metals, and for dying, particularly the beft drab-cloths; and in the province of Anjou are feveral quarries of fine white ftone. Some excellent turquoifes (the only gem that France produces) are found in Languedoc; and great care is taken to keep the mines of marble and free-ftone open all over the kingdom.

VEGETABLE AND ANIMAL PRO- France abounds in
DUCTIONS BY SEA AND LAND. excellent roots, which
are more proper for foups than thofe of England. As to all kinds of feafoning and fallads, they are more plentiful, and in fome places better than in England; they being, next to their vines, the chief object of their culture. The province of Gaftmois produces great quantities of faffron. The wines of Champagne, Burgundy, Bourdeaux, Gafcony, and other

provinces

provinces of France, are so well known, that they need only
to be mentioned. It is sufficient to observe, that though they
differ very sensibly in their taste and properties, yet all of them
are excellent, particularly those of Champagne, Burgundy, Bourdeaux, Pontacke, Hermitage, and Frontiniac ;
and there are few constitutions, be they ever so valetudinary,
to which some one or other of them is not adapted. Oak,
elm, ash, and other timber common in England, is found in
France; but it is said, that the internal parts of the kingdom begin to feel the want of fuel. A great deal of salt is
made at Rhee, and about Rochfort on the coast of Saintoign.
Languedoc produces an herb called kali, which when burnt
makes excellent pot-ashes. The French formerly were famous for horticulture, but they are at present far inferior to
the English both in the management and disposition of their
gardens. Prunes and capers are produced at Bourdeaux and
near Toulon.

France contains few animals, either wild or tame, that are
not to be found in England, excepting wolves. Their horses,
black cattle, and sheep, are far inferior to the English ; nor is
the wool of their sheep so fine. The hair and skin of the cha-
mois, or mountain goats, are more valuable than those of
England. We know of no difference between the marine
productions of France and those of England, but that the
former is not so well served, even on their sea-coasts, with
salt-water fish.

FORESTS.] The chief forests of France are those of Orleans, which contain 14,000 acres of wood of various kinds,
oak, elm, ash, &c. and the forest of Fontainbleau near as
large ; and near Morchismoir is a forest of tall, strait timber,
of 4000 trees. Besides these, large numbers of woods, some
of them deserving the name of forests, lie in different provinces ; but too remote from sea carriage to be of national utility.

POPULATION, INHABITANTS, MANNERS, ⎫ If we believe
    CUSTOMS, AND DIVERSIONS.   ⎰ some French
writers, France contains 20,000,000 of inhabitants ; but the
calculation is certainly overstrained by at least 4,000,000, and
of the remainder near 200,000 are ecclesiastics. I shall not
dispute the populousness of France in former times, but it is
certain that the number of her natives, and those too the most
useful to the public, have, during the last and present century,
been greatly reduced, first, by the revocation * of the edict of
Nantes,

---

* In the year 1598, Henry IV. who was a Protestant, and justly stiled the Great,
after fighting his way to the crown of France, passed the famous edict of Nantes, which
                 A 4   secured

Nantes, by Lewis XIV. and other religious persecutions; secondly, by her perpetual wars; thirdly, by her emigrants to her colonies. Some writers make perhaps the numbers too low, when they fix them at 13,000,000. It is evident however that there is a great defect of population in the interior provinces.

The French, in their persons, are rather lower than their neighbours; but they are well proportioned and active, and more free than other nations in general from bodily deformities. The ladies are celebrated more for their sprightly wit than personal beauty; the peasantry in general are remarkably ordinary, and are best described by being contrasted with women of the same ranks in England. The nobility and gentry accomplish themselves in the academical exercises of dancing, fencing, and riding; in the practice of which, they excel all their neighbours in skill and gracefulness. They are fond of hunting; and the gentry have now left off their heavy jack-boots, their huge war-saddle, and monstrous curb-bridle, in that exercise; and accommodate themselves to the English manner. The landlords are as jealous of their game as they are in England, and equally niggardly of it to their inferiors. A few of the French princes of the blood, and nobility, are more magnificent in their palaces and equipages than any of the English; but the other ranks of life are despicable, when compared to the riches, elegance, and opulence, not only of the English nobility and gentry in general, but to the middling people.

The genius and manners of the French are well known, and have been the subject of many able pens. A national vanity is their predominant character, and they are perhaps the only people ever heard of, who have derived great utility from a national weakness. It supports them under misfortunes, and impells them to actions to which true courage inspires other nations. This character, however, is conspicuous only in the higher and middling ranks, where it produces excellent officers, for the common soldiers of France have few or no ideas of heroism. Hence it has been observed, with great justice, of the French and English, that the French officers will lead, if their soldiers will follow, and the English soldiers will follow, if their officers will lead. This same principle of vanity is of admirable use to the government, because

<hr>

secured to the Protestants the free exercise of their religion, but this edict was revoked by Lewis XIV. which, with the succeeding persecution, s drove that people to England, Holland, and other Protestant countries, where they established the silk manufactures, to the great prejudice of their own country.

becaufe the lower ranks, when they fee their fuperiors elated, as in the time of the laft war with England, under the moft difgraceful loffes, never think that they are unfortunate; thence proceeds the paffive fubmiffion of the French under all their calamities.

The French affect freedom and wit, but their converfation is commonly confined to fafhionable dreffes and diverfions. Their diverfions are much the fame with thofe of the Englifh, but their gallantry is of a very different complexion. Their attention to the fair, degenerates into grofs foppery in the men, and in the ladies it is kept up by admitting of indecent freedoms ; but the feeming levities of both fexes are feldom attended with that criminality which, to people not ufed to their manners, they feem to indicate ; nor are the hufbands fo indifferent as we are apt to imagine, about the conduct of their wives. The French are exceffively credulous and litigious ; but of all people in the world, they bear adverfity and reduction of circumftances with the beft grace ; but in profperity they are intolerably infolent, vain, arbitrary and imperious. An old French officer is an entertaining and inftructive companion, and indeed the moft rational fpecies of all the French gentry.

The French may be characterized as being well mannered, rather than well bred. They are indifcriminately complaifant and officious, but they feldom know how to adjuft their behaviour to the fituation and character of thofe they converfe with. All is a repeated round of politenefs, which for want of difcernment becomes affected, often ridiculous, and always difguftful to fentimental people.

The French have been cenfured for infincerity ; but this is a fault which they poffefs in no greater degree than their neighbours, and the imputation is generally owing to their excefs of civility, which throws a fufpicious light upon their candour. The French, in private life, have juft as much virtue as other European nations, and have given as many proofs of generofity, and difintereftednefs ; but this is far from being the character of their government, which has prepoffeffed the Englifh againft the whole nation, and when the French are no longer formidable, they will be no longer thought faithlefs.

It is doing the French no more than juftice to acknowledge that they have given a polifh to the ferocious manners and even virtues of other nations. They have long poffeffed the lead in tafte, fafhion, and drefs, but it feems now to be in the wane, and they begin to think, that the Englifh are not barbarians. This alteration of opinion has not however taken

its

its rife from their wits, their learned men, their courtiers, nor
the middle ranks of life. The fuperior orders of men in
France are of a very different caft from thofe below them.
They fee with indignation the frivoloufnefs of their court, and
however complying they may appear in public, when retired,
they keep themfelves facred from its follies. Independent by
their rank and fortunes, they think and act for themfelves.
They are open to conviction, and examine things to the bottom. They faw during the late war the management of their
armies, their finances and fleets, with filent indignation, and
their refearches were favourable to the Englifh. The conclufion of the late peace, and the vifits which they have fince
paid to England, have improved that good opinion, the courtiers themfelves have fallen in with it, and what fome years
ago would have been thought incredible, people of fafhion in
France now ftudy the Englifh language, and imitate them
in their cuftoms, amufements, drefs, and buildings. They
both imitate and admire our writers; the names of Milton,
Pope, Addifon, Hume, Robertfon, Richardfon, and many
others of the laft and prefent century, are facred among the
French of any education; and to fay the truth, the writings
of fuch men have equally contributed, with our military reputation, to raife the name of Great Britain, to that degree,
in which it has been held of late by foreign nations, and to
render our language more univerfal, and even a neceffary ftudy
among foreign nobility. But we cannot quit this article of
the manners and cuftoms of the French, without giving a
more minute view of fome diftinguifhing peculiarities obferv-
able among that whimfical people in private life, and this from
the remarks of an ingenious and well informed writer of the
prefent age.

The natural levity of the French, fays he, is reinforced by
the moft prepofterous education, and the example of a giddy
people, engaged in the moft frivolous purfuits. A Frenchman
is by fome prieft or monk taught to read his mother tongue,
and to fay his prayers in a language he does not underftand.
He learns to dance and to fence by the mafters of thofe fciences. He becomes a compleat connoiffeur in dreffing hair,
and in adorning his own perfon, under the hands and inftructions of his barber and valet de chambre. If he learns to play
upon the flute or the fiddle, he is altogether irrefiftible. But
he piques himfelf upon being polifhed above the natives of
any other country, by his converfation with the fair fex. In
the courfe of this communication, with which he is indulged
from his tender years, he learns like a parrot, by rote, the
                                                        whole

whole circle of French compliments, which are a set of phrases, ridiculous even to a proverb; and these he throws out indiscriminately to all women without distinction, in the exercise of that kind of address, which is here distinguished by the name of gallantry. It is an exercise, by the repetition of which he becomes very pert, very familiar, and very impertinent. A Frenchman, in consequence of his mingling with the females from his infancy, not only becomes acquainted with all their customs and humours, but grows wonderfully alert in performing a thousand little offices, which are overlooked by other men, whose time hath been spent in making more valuable acquisitions. He enters, without ceremony, a lady's bedchamber, while she is in bed, reaches her whatever she wants, airs her shift, and helps to put it on. He attends at her toilette, regulates the distribution of her patches, and advises where to lay on the paint. If he visits her when she is dressed, and perceives the least impropriety in her coeffure, he insists upon adjusting it with his own hands. If he sees a curl, or even a single hair amiss, he produces his comb, his scissars, and pomatum, and sets it to rights with the dexterity of a professed frizeur. He squires her to every place she visits, either on business or pleasure; and, by dedicating his whole time to her, renders himself necessary to her occasions. In short, of all the coxcombs on the face of the earth, a French *petit maitre* is the most impertinent; and they are all *petite maitres*, from the marquis who glitters in lace and embroidery, to the *garcon barbiere*, (barber's boy) covered with meal, who struts with his hair in a long queue, and his hat under his arm.

A Frenchman will sooner part with his religion than his hair. Even the soldiers in France wear a long queue; and this ridiculous foppery has descended, as I said before, to the lowest class of people. The boy who cleans shoes at the corner of a street, has a tail of this kind hanging down to his rump; and the beggar who drives an ass, wears his hair *en queue*, though, perhaps, he has neither shirt nor breeches.

I shall only mention one custom more, which seems to carry human affectation to the very farthest verge of folly and extravagance: that is, the manner in which the faces of the ladies are primed and painted. It is generally supposed that part of the fair sex, in some other countries, make use of *fard* and vermilion for very different purposes, namely, to help a bad or faded complexion, to heighten the graces, or conceal the defects of nature, as well as the ravages of time. I shall not enquire whether it is just and honest to impose in this manner on mankind; if it is not honest, it may be allowed to be

artful

artful and politic, and shews, at least, a desire of being agreeable. But to lay it on as the fashion in France prescribes to all the ladies of condition, who indeed cannot appear without this badge of distinction, is to disguise themselves in such a manner as to render them odious and detestable to every spectator who has the least relish left for nature and propriety. As for the *fard*, or *white*, with which their necks and shoulders are plaistered, it may be in some measure excusable, as their skins are naturally brown, or sallow; but the *rouge*, which is daubed on their faces, from the chin up to the eyes, without the least art or dexterity, not only destroys all distinction of features, but renders the aspect really frightful, or at least conveys nothing but ideas of disgust and aversion. Without this horrible mask no married lady is admitted at court, or in any polite assembly, and it is a mark of distinction which none of the lower classes dare assume.

DRESS.] The French dress of both sexes is so well known that it is needless to expatiate upon them here; but, indeed, their dress in cities and towns is so variable, that it is next to impossible to describe it. They certainly have more invention in that particular than any of their neighbours, and their constantly changing their fashions is of infinite service to their manufactures. With regard to the English, they possess one capital superiority, which is, that the cloaths of both sexes, and their ornaments, are at least one third cheaper.

When a stranger arrives in Paris he finds it necessary to send for the taylor, peruquier, hatter, shoemaker, and every other tradesman concerned in the equipment of the human body. He must even change his buckles, and the form of his ruffles: and, though at the risk of his life, suit his cloaths to the mode of the season. For example, though the weather should be ever so cold, he must wear his *habit d'été*, or *demi-saison*, without presuming to put on a warm dress before the day which fashion has fixed for that purpose; and neither old age nor infirmity will excuse a man for wearing his hat upon his head, either at home or abroad. Females are, if possible, still more subject to the caprices of fashion. All their sacks and negligees must be altered and new trimmed. They must have new caps, new laces, new shoes, and their hair new cut. They must have their taffaties for the summer, their flowered silks for the spring and autumn, their sattins and damasks for winter. The men too must provide themselves with a camblet suit trimmed with silver for spring and autumn, with silk cloaths for summer, and cloth laced with gold, or velvet for winter; and he must wear his bag-wig *a la pigeon*. This variety
riety

riety of dress is absolutely indispensible for all those who pretend to any rank above the meer vulgar; all ranks, from the king downwards, use powder; and even the rabble, according to their abilities, imitate their superiors in the fripperies of fashion. The common people of the country, however, still retain, without any material deviation, the old fashioned modes of dress, the large hat and most enormous jack-boots, with suitable spurs, and this contrast is even perceivable a few miles from Paris. In large cities, the clergy, lawyers, physicians, and merchants, generally dress in black; and it has been observed, that the French nation, in their modes of dress, are in some measure governed by commercial circumstances.

RELIGION.] The religion of France is Roman Catholic, in which their kings have been so constant, that they have obtained the title of Most Christian; and the pope, in his Bull, gives the king of France the title of Eldest Son of the Church. The Gallican church has more than once attempted to shake off the yoke of the Popes, and made a very great progress in the attempt during the reign of Lewis XIV. but it was defeated by the secret bigotry of that prince, who, while he was bullying the pope, was inwardly trembling under the power of the Jesuits, a set that is now exterminated from that kingdom. Though the French clergy are more exempt than some others from the papal authority, their church confining the pope's power entirely to things relating to salvation, yet they are in general great enemies to any thing that looks like reformation in religion; and possessed as they are of immense property, there must be a thorough coalition in opinion between the king and his parliaments, before any ecclesiastical reformation can take place; a prospect which seems at present very distant, notwithstanding the differences between the pope and his most Christian majesty. In the southern parts of France, the clergy and magistrates are as intolerant as ever, and the persecutions of the protestants, or, as they are called, Hugonots, who are very numerous in those provinces, still continue. In short, the common people of France discover no disposition towards a reformation in religion, which, if ever it takes place, must probably be effected by the spirit of the parliaments. I shall not enter into the antiquated disputes between the Molinists and the Jansenists, nor the different sects of Quietists and Bourignons, that prevail among the Roman Catholics themselves, nor into the disputes that prevail between the parliament and clergy about the bull Unigenitus, which advances the pope's power above that of the crown,

crown. The ftate of religion in France is a ftrong proof of the paffive difpofition of the natives, and the bigotry of their kings, who, in complaifance to the pope, have depopulated their kingdom, as I have already hinted, of its moft ufeful inhabitants. It muft at the fame time be owned, that the Hugonots, while they fubfifted in a manner as a feparate ftate within France, did not fhew any remarkable proofs of their moderation, either in religion or government.

ARCHBISHOPRICS, BISHOPRICS, &c.] In the whole kingdom there are 17 archbifhops, 113 bifhops, 770 abbies for men, 317 abbies and priories for women, befides a great number of leffer convents, and 250 commanderies of the order of Malta; but many of the abbies and nunneries have been lately fuppreffed, and the revenues feized by the king. The ecclefiaftics of all forts are computed at near 200,000, and their revenues at about fix millions fterling. The king nominates all archbifhops, bifhops, abbots, and priors, and can tax the clergy without a papal licence or mandate : accordingly, not many years fince, he demanded the twentieth penny of the clergy, and, to afcertain that, required them to deliver in an inventory of their eftates and incomes; to avoid which, they voluntarily made an offer of the annual fum of twelve millions of livres, over and above the ufual free gift, which they pay every five years.

The archbifhop of Lyons is count and primate of France. The archbifhop of Sens, is primate of France and Germany. The archbifhop of Paris, is duke and peer of the realm; and the archbifhop of Rheims, is duke and peer, and legate of the holy fee.

LANGUAGE.] One of the wifeft meafures of Lewis XIV. was his encouragement of every propofal that tended to the purity and perfection of the French language. He fucceeded fo far as to render it the moft univerfal of all the living tongues, a circumftance that tended equally to his greatnefs and his glory, for his court and nation thereby became the fchool of the arts, fciences, and politenefs. The French language, at prefent, is chiefly compofed of words radically derived from the Latin, with many German derivatives, introduced by the Franks. It is at prefent on the decay, its corner ftones, fixed under Lewis XIV. are as it were loofened; and in the prefent mode of writing and expreffing themfelves, the modern French abandon that grammatical ftandard, which alone can render a language claffical and permanent.

As to the properties of the language, they are undoubtedly greatly inferior to the Englifh, but they are well adapted to

subjects

subjeĉts void of elevation or paſſion. It is well accommodated
to dalliance, compliments, and common converſation.

The Lord's Prayer in French is as follows : *Nôtre Pére qui
is aux cieux, ton nom ſoit ſanĉtifié. Ton regne vienne. Ta vo-
lonte ſoit faite en la terre comme au ciel. Donne nous aujourd'huy
notre pain quotidien. Pardonne nous nos offences, comme nous
pardonnons a ceux qui nous ont offencez. Et ne nous indui point en
tentation, mais nous delivre du mal : car a toi eſt le regne, la
puiſſance, & la gloire aux ſiécles des ſiécles.* Amen.

LEARNING AND LEARNED MEN.] The French, like the
other nations of Europe, were for many centuries immerſed in
barbarity. The firſt learning they began to acquire, was not
of that kind which improves the underſtanding, correĉts the
taſte, or regulates the affeĉtions. It conſiſted in a ſubtle and
quibbling logic, which was more adapted to pervert than to
improve the faculties. But the ſtudy of the Greek and Roman writers, which firſt aroſe in Italy, diffuſed itſelf among
the French, and gave a new turn to their literary purſuits.
This, together with the encouragement which the polite and
learned Francis I. gave to all men of merit, was extremely
beneficial to French literature. During this reign, many
learned men appeared in France, whoſe labours are well known,
and highly eſteemed all over Europe. The two Stephens, in
particular, are names which every real ſcholar mentions with
reſpeĉt. It was not, however, till the ſeventeenth century,
that the French began to write with elegance in their own
language. The Academie Françoiſe was formed for this purpoſe ; and though their labours, conſidered as a body, were
not ſo ſuccesful as might have been expeĉted, ſome particular academicians have done great ſervice to letters. In faĉt,
literary copartnerſhips are ſeldom very ſuccesful. Of this we
have a remarkable example in the preſent caſe. The Academy
publiſhed a diĉtionary for improving the French language :
it was univerſally deſpiſed. Furetieres, a ſingle academician,
publiſhes another : it meets with univerſal approbation.

Lewis XIV. was the Auguſtus of France. The proteĉtion
he gave to letters, and the penſions he beſtowed on learned
men, both at home and abroad, which, by calculation, did
not amount to above 12,000 l. per annum, have gained him
more glory than all the military enterpriſes, upon which he
expended ſo many millions. The learned men who appeared
in France during this reign, are too numerous to be mentioned. Their tragic poets, Racine and Corneille, the firſt
diſtinguiſhed for tendernels, the ſecond for majeſty, and both

for

for the strength and justness of their painting, the elegance of their taste, and their strict adherence to the rules of the drama, are, next to the Greek tragedians, the most perfect masters in this species of writing. Moliere would have exhausted the subjects of comedy, were they not every where inexhaustible, and particularly in France. In works of satire, and in criticism, Boileau, though a close imitator of the antients, is not deficient in genius. But France has not as yet produced an epic poem that can be mentioned with Milton's; nor a genius of the same extensive and universal kind with Shakespeare, equally fitted for the gay and the serious, the humorous and the sublime. In the eloquence of the pulpit and of the bar, the French are greatly our superiors: Bossuet, Bourdaloue, Flechier, and Massillon, have carried pulpit eloquence to a degree of perfection, which we may approach to, but never can surpass. The genius, however, of their religion and government, is extremely unfavourable to all improvements in the most useful branches of philosophy. All the establishments of Lewis XIV. for the advancement of science, were not able to counterbalance the influence of the clergy, whose interest it is to keep mankind ignorant in matters of religion and morality; and the influence of the court and ministry, who have an equal interest in concealing the natural rights of mankind, and every sound principle of government. The French have not therefore so many good writers on moral, religious, or political subjects, as have appeared in Great Britain. But France has produced some great men who do honour to humanity, whose career no obstacle could stop, whose freedom no government however despotic, no religion however superstitious, could curb or restrain. Who is ignorant of Pascal, or the archbishop of Cambray? few men have done more service to religion either by their writings or their lives. As for Montesquieu, he is an honour to human nature: he is the legislator of nations; his works are read in every country and language, and, wherever they go, they enlighten and envigorate the human mind.

In the Belles Lettres and miscellaneous way, no nation ever produced more agreeable writers; among whom we may place D'Argens and Voltaire as the most considerable.

Before the immortal Newton appeared in England, Descartes was the greatest philosopher in modern times. He was the first who applied algebra to the solution of geometrical problems, which naturally paved the way to the analytical discoveries of Newton. Many of the present age are excellent mathematicians; particularly D'Alembert, who,

with

with all the precifion of a geometer, has united the talents of a fine writer.

Since the beginning of the prefent century, the French have vied with the Englifh in natural philofophy. Buffon would deferve to be reckoned among men of fcience, were he not ftill more remarkable for his eloquence than for his philofophy. He is to be regarded as a philofophical painter of nature; and under this view, his Natural Hiftory is the firft work of its kind.

Their painters, Pouffin, Le Brun, and above all Le Sueur, did honour to the age of Lewis XIV. They have none at prefent to compare with them in the more noble kinds of painting; but Mr. Greufe, for portraits and converfation pieces, never perhaps was excelled.

Sculpture is in general better underftood in France than in England, or in any other nation. Their treatifes on fhip-building and engineering ftand unrivalled; but in the practice of both they are outdone by the Englifh. No genius has hitherto equalled Vauban in the theory or practice of fortification. The French were long our fuperiors in architecture, though we now bid fair for furpaffing them in this art.

We fhall conclude this head with obferving, that the French have now finifhed the Cyclopedie, or general dictionary of arts and fciences, which was drawn up in 26 volumes in folio, under the direction of meffieurs D'Alembert and Diderot, and is the moft complete collection of human knowledge we are acquainted with.

Universities and public colleges.] Thefe literary inftitutions have received an irreparable lofs by the expulfion of the jefuits, who made the languages, arts, and fciences, their particular ftudy, and taught them all over France. It is not within my plan to defcribe the different governments and conftitutions of every univerfity or public college in France; but they are in number twenty-eight, as follow; Aix, Angiers, Arles, Avignon, Befançon, Bourdeaux, Bourges, Caen, Cahors, Dol, Douay, Fleche, Montauban, Montpellier, Nantes, Orange, Orleans, Paris, Perpignan, Poitiers, Point Moufon, Richlieu, Rheims, Soiffons, Strafbourg, Touloufe, Tournois, and Valence.

Academies.] There are eight academies in Paris, namely, three literary ones; that called the French Academy, that of Infcriptions, and that of the Sciences; one of painting and fculpture, one of architecture, and three for riding the great horfe and other military exercifes.

Antiquities and curiosities, ⎱ Few countries, if we
   natural and artificial. ⎰ except Italy, can boaft

of more valuable remains of antiquity than France. Some of the French antiquities belong to the time of the Celts, and consequently, compared to them, those of Rome are modern. Father Mabillon has given us a most curious account of the sepulchres of their kings, which have been discovered so far back as Pharamond; and some of them when broken open were found to contain ornaments and jewels of value. At Rheims, and other parts of France, are to be seen triumphal arches; but the most entire is at Orange, erected on account of the victory obtained over the Cimbri and Teutones by Caius Marius and Luctatius Catulus. After Gaul was reduced to a Roman province, the Romans took vast delight in adorning it with magnificent edifices, both civil and sacred, some of which are more entire than any to be met with in Italy itself. The ruins of an amphitheatre are to be found at Chalons, and likewise at Vienne. Nismes, however, exhibits the most valuable remains of ancient architecture of any place in France. The famous Pont du Garde was raised in the Augustan age by the Roman colony of Nismes, to convey a stream of water between two mountains, for the use of that city, and is as fresh to this day as Westminster-bridge: it consists of three bridges, or tires of arches one above another; the height is 174 feet, and the length extends to 723. The moderns are indebted for this, and many other stupendous aqueducts, to the ignorance of the ancients that all streams will rise as high as their heads. Many other ruins of antiquity are found at Nismes, but the chief is the temple of Diana, whose vestiges are still remaining. The amphitheatre, which is thought to be the finest and most entire of the kind of any in Europe; but above all, the house erected by the emperor Adrian, called the Maison Carrie. The architecture and sculpture of this building is so exquisitely beautiful that it enchants even the most ignorant, and it is still entire, being very little affected either by the ravages of time, or the havock of war. At Paris may be seen the remains of the palace of Thermæ, which was built by the emperor Julian, surnamed the Apostate, about the year 356, after the same model as the baths of Dioclesian. The remains of this ancient edifice are many arches, and within them a large salloon. It is fabricated of a kind of mastic, the composition of which is not now known, intermixed with small square pieces of free stone and bricks.

At Arles in Provence is to be seen an obelisk of oriental granite, which is 52 feet high, and 7 feet diameter at the base, and all but one stone. Roman temples are frequent in France. The most particular are in Burgundy and Guienne, and other places befides the neighbourhood of Nifmes, contain magnificent ruins of aqueducts. The paffage cut through the middle of a rock near Briançon in Dauphiny, is thought to be a Roman work, if not of greater antiquity. The round buckler of maffy filver, taken out of the Rhone in 1665, being twenty inches in diameter, and weighing twenty one pounds, containing the ftory of Scipio's continence, is thought to be coeval with that great general. It would be endlefs to recount the different monuments of antiquity to be found in France, particularly in the cabinets of the curious.

I have already mentioned feveral remarkable fprings and mountains which may be confidered as natural curiofities. Some of the modern works of art, particularly the canals, have been already mentioned, and fome fubterraneous paffages and holes, efpecially at St. Aubin in Britany and Niont in Dauphiny, are really ftupendous.

CITIES AND TOWNS.] Thefe are numerous in France, of which we fhall mention only Paris, Lifle, and their principal fea-ports, Breft and Toulon.

Lifle, in French Flanders, is thought to be the moft regular and ftrongeft fortification in Europe, and was the mafterpiece of the famous Vauban. It is generally garrifoned with above 10,000 regulars; and for its magnificence and elegance, it is called Little Paris. Its manufactures of filk, cambrick, and camblets, are very confiderable; and its inhabitants amount to about 100,000. Every reader is acquainted with the hiftory of Dunkirk, which the French have been obliged to demolifh, but is ftill a thorn in the fide of the Englifh, by being a harbour for their fmugglers. The reft of French Flanders, and its Netherlands, abound with fortified towns, which carry on very gainful manufactures.

Moving fouthward, we come to the Ifle of France, the capital of which, and the whole kingdom, is Paris. This city has been fo often defcribed, that it may appear fuperfluous to mention it more particularly, were it not that the vanity of the French has given it a preference, which it by no means deferves, to all the capitals in the world, in every refpect, not excepting even population. Many of the Englifh have been impofed upon in this refpect; and I have already hinted at the reafons, particularly the computing from the births and burials within the bills of mortality, which exclude the moft populous parifhes about London. Another miftake lies in computing from births and marriages. The number of diffenters of all kinds in and about London, who do not regifter the births of their children, is amazing; and many of the poorer fort cannot afford the expence of fuch regiftration. Another

B 2   peculiarity

peculiarity exifting in London is, that moft of the Londoners, who can afford the expence, when they find themfelves con-fumptive, or otherwife indifpofed, retire into the country, where they are buried, and thereby excluded from the bills of mortality. The population of Paris therefore, where the regifters are more exact and acceffible to the poor, and where the religion and.the police are more uniform and ftrict, is far more eafily afcertained than that of London; and by the beft accounts, it does not exceed 7 or 800,000, which is far fhort of the inhabitants of London and the contiguous parifhes.

Paris is divided into three parts; the city, the univerfity, and that which was formerly called the Town. The city is old Paris; the univerfity and the town are the new. Paris contains more works of public munificence than utility. Its palaces are more fhewy, and fome of its ftreets, fquares, hotels, hofpitals, and churches, more fuperbly decorated with a profufion of paintings, tapeftry, images, and ftatues; but Paris, notwithftanding its boafted police, is greatly inferior to London in many of the conveniencies of life, and the folid enjoyments of fociety. Without entering into more minute difquifitions, Paris, it muft be owned, is the Paradife of fplen-dor and diffipation. The tapeftry of the Gobelines * is unequalled for beauty and richnefs. The Louvre is a building that does honour to architecture itfelf; and the inftitution of the French academy far exceeds any thing of the kind in England or elfewhere. The Tuilleries, the Palace of Orleans, or, as it is called, Luxembourg, where a valuable collection of paintings are fhewn, the Royal palace, the King's Library, the Guild-Hall, and the hofpital for invalids, are fuperb to the higheft degree. The city of Paris is faid to be fifteen miles in circumference. The hotels of the French nobleffe at Paris, take up a great deal of room, with their court-yards and gardens; and fo do their convents and churches. The ftreets are very narrow, and the houfes very high, many of them feven ftories. The houfes are built of ftone, and are generally mean, even to wretchednefs, owing partly to their containing a different family on every floor. The river Seine, which runs through the centre of the city, is not half fo large as the Thames at London: it is too far diftant from the fea for the purpofes of navigation, and is not furnifhed, as the Thames, with veffels or boats of any fort: over it are many ftone and wooden bridges, which have nothing to recommend them. The ftreets of Paris are generally crowded, particularly with coaches, which gives that capital the appearance of
wealth

* One *Goblei*, a noted dyer at Rheims, was the firft who fettled in this place; in the reign of Francis I. and the houfe has retained his name ever fince; and here the great Colbert, about the year 1667, eftablifhed that valuable manufactury.

wealth and grandeur; though, in reality, there is more show than substance. The glittering carriages that dazzle the eyes of strangers, are mostly common hacks, hired by the day or week to the numerous foreigners who visit that city; and in truth, the greatest part of the trade of Paris arises from the constant succession of strangers that arrive daily from every nation and quarter of the globe. This ascendency over other nations, is undoubtedly owing to the reputation of their language, their public buildings, the Gobelines, or manufacture of tapestry, their libraries, and collections of paintings, that are open to the public; the cheapness of provisions,. excellency of the French wines, and, above all, the purity of the air and climate in France. With all these advantages, however, Paris, in general, will not bear a comparison with London in the more essential circumstances of a thriving foreign and domestic trade, the cleanness of their streets, elegance of their houses, especially within; the plenty of water, and that of a better quality than the Seine, which it is said disagrees with strangers, as do likewise their small wines. In the houses of Paris, most of the floors are of brick, and have no other kind of cleaning than that of being sprinkled with water, and swept once a day. These brick floors, the stone stairs, the want of wainscotting in the rooms, and the thick party-walls of stone, are, however, good preservatives against fire, which seldom does any damage in this city. Instead of wainscotting, the walls are covered with tapestry or damask. The beds in general are very good, and well ornamented, with tester and curtains; but bugs are here a most intolerable nuisance, which frequently oblige strangers to sleep on the floor during the excessive heat in the summer. Their shops are but poorly stored with goods; nor has their government made the provisions that are ever in its power for the comfort of the inferior ranks; its whole attention seeming to be directed to the conveniency and splendor of the great. The shopkeepers and tradesmen, an indolent loitering people, seldom make their appearance before dinner in any other than a morning dress, of velvet cap, silk night-gown, and Morocco slippers; but when they intend a visit or going abroad, all the punctilios of a courtier are attended to, and hardly the resemblance of a man remains. There is a remarkable contrast between this class of people and those of the same rank in London. In Paris, the women pack up parcels, enter the orders, and do most of the drudgery business of the shop, while the husband loiters about, talks of the great, of fashions and diversions, the invincible force of their armies, and the splendor of the grand monarque. The Parisians, however, as well as the

natives

natives of France in general, are remarkably temperate in their living, and to be intoxicated with liquor is confidered as infamous. Bread, and all manner of butchers meat and poultry, are extremely good in Paris; the beef is excellent; the wine they generally drink, is a very thin kind of Burgundy. The common people, in the fummer feafon, live chiefly on bread, butter, grapes, and fmall wine. The Parifians fcarcely know the ufe of tea, but they have coffee in plenty. The police of Paris is fo well attended to, that quarrels, accidents, or felonies, feldom happen; and ftrangers from all quarters of the globe, let their appearance be ever fo uncommon, meet with the moft polite treatment. The ftreets are patrolled at night by horfe and foot, fo judicioufly ftationed, that no offender can efcape their vigilance. They likewife vifit the publicans precifely at the hour of twelve at night, to fee that the company are gone; for in Paris no liquor can be had after that time. The public roads in France are under the fame excellent regulation, which, with the torture of the rack, prevents robberies in that kingdom; but, for the fame reafons, when robberies do happen, they are always attended with the death of the unfortunate traveller; and indeed this is the general practice in every country of Europe, England and Scotland excepted.

The environs of Paris are very pleafant, and contain a number of fine feats, fmall towns, and villages; fome of them being fcattered on the edges of lofty mountains rifing from the Seine, are remarkably delightful.

The palace of Verfailles, which ftands about 12 miles from Paris, though magnificent and expenfive beyond conception, and adorned with all that art can furnifh, is properly a collection of buildings, each of exquifite architecture, but not forming a whole, agreeable to the grand and fublime of that art. The gardens, however, and water-works (which are fupplied by means of prodigious engines acrofs the Seine at Marli, about three miles diftance) are aftonifhing proofs of the fertile genius of man, and highly worthy of a ftranger's attention. Trianon, Marli, St. Germain en Laye, Meudon, and other royal palaces, are laid out with tafte and judgment; each has its peculiar beauties for the entertainment and amufement of a luxurious court; but fome of them are in a fhameful condition, both as to repairs and cleanlinefs.

Breft is a fmall, but very ftrong town, upon the Englifh channel, with a moft fpacious and fine fortified road and harbour, the beft and fafeft in all the kingdom: yet its entrance is difficult, by reafon of many rocks lying under water. At Breft is a court of admiralty, an academy for fea-affairs, docks, and magazines for all kinds of naval ftores, rope-yards, ftorehoufes,

houfes, &c. infomuch, that it may now be termed the capital receptacle on the ocean for the navy-royal of France, and is admirably well adapted for that end.

Lewis XIV. rendered Toulon, from a pitiful village, a fea-port of great importance. He fortified both the town and harbour, for the reception and protection of the navy-royal. Its old and its new harbour lie contiguous ; and by means of a canal, fhips pafs from the one to the other, both of them having an outlet into the fpacious outer harbour. Its arfenal, eftablifhed alfo by that king, has a particular ftorehoufe for each fhip of war, its guns, cordage, &c. being feparately laid up. Here are fpacious workfhops for blackfmiths, joiners, carpenters, lockfmiths, carvers, &c. Its rope-walk of ftone is 320 toifes in length, with three arched walks. Its general magazine fupplies whatever may be wanting in the particular ftorehoufes, and contains an immenfe quantity of all kinds of ftores, difpofed in the greateft order.

COMMERCE AND MANUFACTURES.] Next to Henry IV. juftly ftiled the Great, the famous Colbert, a Scotfman, minifter to Lewis XIV. may be called the father of the French commerce and manufactures. Under him there was a great appearance that France would make as illuftrious a figure as a trading, as fhe then did as a warlike people ; but the truth is, the French do not naturally poffefs that undaunted perfeverance that is ne-ceffary for commerce and colonization, though no people, in theory, underftand them better. It is to be confidered, at the fame time, that France, by her fituation, by the turn of her inhabitants for certain manufactures, and the happinefs of her foil, muft be always poffeffed of a great inland and neighbour-ing trade, which enriches her, and makes her the moft refpect-able power upon the continent of Europe. I have already enumerated her natural commodities, to which may be added her manufactures of falt-petre, filk, embroidery, filver ftuffs, tapeftry, cambrics, lawns, fine laces, fine ferges and ftuffs, velvets, brocades, paper, brandy which is diftilled from wine, a prodigious variety of toys, and other articles ; many of which are fmuggled into Great Britain, for which they are paid in ready money.

The filk manufacture was introduced into France fo late as the reign of Henry IV. and in the age of his grandfon, Lewis XIV. the city of Tours alone employed 8000 looms, and 800 mills. The city of Lyons then employed 18,000 looms ; but after the impolitic revocation of the edict of Nantes, the expulfion of the proteftants, and the ruinous wars maintained by France, they decreafed to 4000, and their filk manufacture is now rivalled by that of England, where the French pro-

B 4   teftants

teſtants took refuge, and were happily encouraged. On the other hand, the French woollen cloths and ſtuffs, more eſpecially at Abbeville, are ſaid to be now little inferior to thoſe of England and Holland, aſſiſted by the clandeſtine importation of Engliſh and Iriſh wool, and workmen from this country.

I have already mentioned the infinite advantage ariſing to her inland commerce by her rivers and navigable canals.

As to her foreign trade, it may be ſaid to extend all over the globe. It is a doubtful point whether the crown of France was a loſer by its ceſſion of Canada and part of Louiſiana at the late peace. But the moſt valuable part of Hiſpaniola in the Weſt Indies, which ſhe poſſeſſes by the partiality and indolence of Spain, is a moſt improveable acquiſition, and the moſt valuable of all her foreign colonies. In the Weſt Indies ſhe likewiſe poſſeſſes the important ſugar iſlands of Martinico and Guadaloupe, St. Lucia, St. Bartholomew, Deſeada, and Marigalante. Her poſſeſſions in North America ſince the late war, are only a ſmall tract upon the Miſiſſippi.

The French have ſtill poſſeſſions in the Eaſt Indies, of which Pondicherry and Mauritius are the principal; and had their genius been more turned for commerce than war, they might have engroſſed more territory and revenues than are now in poſſeſſion of the Engliſh; but they over-rated both their own power and their courage, and their Eaſt India company ſeems now to be at its laſt gaſp. We cannot anſwer for the conſequences if that trade ſhould be thrown open. They may be more fatal to England than beneficial to France. At preſent, (ſays Mr. Anderſon) " her land trade to Switzerland and Italy is by way of Lyons—To Germany, through Metz and Straſburgh—To the Netherlands, through Liſle—To Spain, (a moſt profitable one) through Bayonne and Perpignan. As for her naval commerce, her ports in the channel, and on the weſtern ocean, are frequented by all the trading nations in Europe, to France's very great advantage, more eſpecially reſpecting what is carried on with England, Holland, and Italy. The trade from her Mediterranean ports (more particularly from Marſeilles) with Turkey and Africa, has long been very conſiderable. The negro trade from Guinea ſupplies her ſugar colonies, beſides the gold, ivory, and drugs got from thence."

In the year 1739, France may be ſaid to have been in the zenith of her commerce. Favoured by Spain, and dreaded by all the reſt of Europe, her fleets covered the ocean, but ſhe truſted too much to her own ſelf-importance. Cardinal de Fleury, who then directed her affairs, took no care to protect her trade by proper naval armaments; ſo that the greater it

was,

was, it became the more valuable prey to the Englifh when war broke out. It is, however, the happinefs of France that her wounds are foon clofed, and it is hard to fay how foon fhe may recover all fhe has loft.

One great difadvantage to the commerce of France is, that the profeffion of a merchant is not fo honourable as in England, and fome other countries, fo that the French nobility think it below them, which is the reafon that the church, the law, and the army, are fo full of that order. A great number of the cities of France have the privilege of coinage, and each of them a particular mark to diftinguifh their refpective pieces, which, however, muft be very embarraffing, efpecially to ftrangers.

PUBLIC TRADING COMPANIES.] The inftitutions of public trading companies to Canada or New France, and the Eaft and Weft Indies, formerly coft the French crown immenfe fums, but we know none of them now fubfifting, tho' no doubt their Weft India trade, which is ftill very confiderable, efpecially in fugar, is under proper regulations, prefcribed by their councils of commerce.

CONSTITUTION AND GOVERNMENT.] The conftitution of France, in feudal times, was very unfavourable to monarchy, but the oppreffions of the great landholders by degrees grew fo irkfome to the fubjects, that they preferred the monarchical to the ariftocratical government. Ariftocracy however ftill fubfifted in fome degree to the beginning of the laft century, chiefly through the neceffity which the Hugonots or proteftants were under to have princes of the blood, and men of great quality for their leaders; but Richlieu, in the time of Lewis XIII. gave it a mortal blow, and all the civil difputes in France fince have been among great men for power and places, and between the kings and their parliaments, but the latter were feldom or never attended with any fanguinary effects.

The prefent parliament of France has no analogy with that of Great-Britain. It was originally inftituted to ferve as a kind of law affiftant to the affembly of the ftates, which was compofed of the great peers and landholders of the kingdom, and ever fince it continued to be a law, and at laft, a money court, and the members have had the courage of late to claim a kind of a negative power to the royal edicts, which they pretend can be of no validity till regiftered by them. His moft chriftian majefty has often tried to invalidate their acts and to intimidate their perfons; but, defpotic as he is, he has never ventured to inflict any farther punifhment than a flight banifhment or imprifonment for their moft provoking acts of difobedience.

26   F R A N C E.

This ridiculous fituation between power and privilege fhews
the infirmity of the French conftitution, as the king dares not
punifh, and his parliament will not obey ; but it difcovers at
the fame time, that the nation in general thinks the parliament
its natural guardian againft the court.

The kingdom of France is divided into thirty governments,
over each of which is appointed a king's lieutenant-general,
a fuperintendant, who pretty much refembles the lord lieuten-
ants in England, but their executive powers are far more extenfive. Diftributive juftice in France is adminiftered by parliaments, chamber of accounts, courts of aid, prefidial courts,
generalities, elections, and other courts. The parliaments
were in number fifteen, thofe of Paris, Touloufe, Rouen,
Grenoble, Bourdeaux, Dijon, Aix, Remes, Pau, Mets, Befançon, Douay, Perpignan, Colmar, and Arras. Several of
thefe parliaments however are now united into one. The
parliament of Paris is the chief, and takes the lead in all
national bufinefs. It is divided into ten chambers. The
grand chamber is appropriated chiefly for the trial of peers.
The Tournelle Civil judges in all matters of property above
the value of 1000 livres. The Tournelle Criminel receives
and decides appeals from inferior courts in criminal cafes. Befides thefe three capital chambers, there are five of requefts
for receiving the depofitions of witneffes, and determining
caufes, pretty much in the fame manner as our bills and anfwers in chancery and the exchequer.

The next court of judicature in France is the chamber of
accounts, where all matters of public finances are examined,
treaties of peace and grants regiftered, and the vaffalages due
from the royal fiefs are received. The chambers are in number
twelve, and held in the cities of Paris, Rouen, Dijon, Nantes,
Montpelier, Grenoble, Aix, Pau, Blois, Lifle, Aire, and
Dole.

The third court of judicature is the court of aid, where all
matters that relate to the royal revenue, and the raifing of
money are determined.

The fourth are the prefidial courts, which are compofed of
judges for determining matters in appeal from magiftrates of
little towns and villages.

The next court are the generalities, who proportion the
taxes to be raifed in their diftricts, according to the fum that
is appointed to be levied. They likewife take cognizance of
matters relating to the crown lands, and certain branches of
the revenue. Thefe courts are in number twenty-three, each
confifting of twenty-three perfons, and they are diftributed
over the kingdom for the more convenient difpatch of bufinefs.

Sub-Sub-

Subject to these generalities are the courts of elections, which settle the smaller proportions of taxes that are to be paid by parishes, and inferior districts, and how much each individual in the same is to pay. This is done by a collector, who returns the assessments to the court of generalities. Besides the above courts, the French have intendants of justice, police, and finances, whose powers, when properly executed, are of great service to the peace of the community. They have likewise provosts, seneschals, bailiffs, and other officers, whom we have no room to enumerate.

After the reader has been told of the excellency of the climate, and fertility of the soil in France; her numerous manufactures, and extensive commerce; her great cities, numerous towns, sea-ports, rivers and canals; the cheapness of provisions, wines, and liquors; the formidable armies and fleets she has sent forth to the terror of Europe; and the natural character of her inhabitants, their sprightliness and gaiety, he will undoubtedly conclude, that France is the most powerful nation, and her people the most opulent and happy in Europe. The reverse, however, appears to be the state of that nation at present; and we do not find that in any former period they were more rich or more happy.

True it is, that in a country so extensive and fruitful, her government finds immense resources in men and money; but, as if the French councils were directed by an evil genius, these resources, great as they are, by a wrong application have proved the ruin of the people. The most obvious causes of this national poverty took their rise from the ambition and vanity of their kings and leading men, which led them into schemes of universal dominion, the aggrandizement of their name, and the enslaving of Christendom. Their wars, which they sometimes carried on against one half of Europe, and in which they were generally unfortunate, led them into difficulties to which the ordinary revenues were inadequate; and hence proceeded the arbitrary demands upon the subject, under various pretences, in the name of loans, free gifts, &c. When these failed, other methods, more despotic and unwarrantable, such as raising and reducing the value of money as it suited their own purposes, national bankruptcies, and other grievous oppressions, were adopted, which gave the finishing blow to public credit, shook the foundations of trade, commerce, and industry, the fruits of which no man could call his own.

When we consider the motives of these wars, a desire to enslave and render miserable the nations around them, that man must be devoid of humanity whose breast is not raised
with

with indignation upon the bare mention of the blood that has been spilt, the miseries and desolations that have happened, and the numerous places that have fallen a sacrifice to their ambition. It appears too plain, from their late attack upon Corsica, that their own misfortunes have not taught them wisdom or humanity, for while they thus grasp after foreign conquest, their own country exhibits a picture of misery and beggary. Their towns, a very few excepted, make a most dismal and solitary appearance. The shops are mean beyond description ; and the passengers, who saunter through a labyrinth of narrow dirty streets, appear to be chiefly composed of priests and devotees, passing to or from mass, hair-dressers, and beggars. That this is the appearance of their towns and many of their cities, we may appeal to the observation of any one who has been in that kingdom. Were it possible to mention a people more indigent than these citizens; we might describe the farmers and peasantry. We have in another place mentioned the natural advantages of France, where the hills are covered with grapes, and most extensive plains produce excellent crops of corn, rye, and barley. Amidst this profusion of plenty, the farmer and his family barely exist upon the gleanings ; and his cattle, which are seldom numerous, pick a subsistence in the summer months from the skirts of his fields. Here the farmer, meagre, dispirited, and depressed, exhibits a spectacle of indigence hardly credible. And to see him plowing the ground with a lean cow, an ass, and a goat yoked together, excites in an English traveller that pity to which human nature is entitled. He forgets the country while he feels for the man.

Many of the taxes and revenues in France are let out for a time to the best bidder, or, as it is there called, farmed ; and these harpies, the farmers general, and their underlings, make no scruple of fleecing the people most unmercifully ; and the residue, if any do remain, goes to satisfy the cravings of a numerous clergy, who in their turn are obliged, as well as the laity, to advance the government immense sums, under the names of tenths and free gifts, exclusive of which, as I have observed elsewhere, they are now taxed with a certain sum, to be paid annually. As oppressions are at present exercised in full vigour, and taxes increasing, there is the greatest probability that the bulk of the French nation will long remain that poor, unhappy, and miserable people we have been representing them, which in truth is a happy circumstance for the liberties and the peace of Europe.

REVENUES.] Nothing certain can be said concerning the revenues of a prince who can command the purses of all his

sub-

FRANCE. 29

subjects. In 1716, the whole specie of France in gold and silver was computed to be about seventeen millions sterling; and though the crown was then doubly a bankrupt, being in debt about 100 millions sterling, or 2,000 millions of livres, yet by laying hold of almost all the current money in the kingdom, and by arbitrarily raising or lowering the value of coins, in four years time the duke regent of France published a general state of the public debts, by which it appeared the king scarcely owed 340 millions of livres. This being done by a national robbery, we can form no idea but that of despotism of the means by which so great a reduction was effected. The French court has not since that time blushed to own, to wit towards the conclusion of the late war, and also in 1769, that their king was bankrupt; and his ministers have pursued measures pretty much similar to those practised by the regent to recruit the royal finances.

Some writers say that the annual revenues of France, ordinary and extraordinary, by the account of their own financiers, (including Lorrain) do not amount to clear six millions sterling, which is equal to the natural revenue of England alone. Though I am apt to think that this calculation of the French revenues is rather too low, and that they may be fixed at seven millions; yet we are not to form our ideas of them from the great armaments, garrisons, and fortifications maintained by the French king, because their expence is inconsiderable to him, compared to what they would be to a king of Great-Britain; and the like observation holds good in all the other departments of public expence in both kingdoms. The French themselves, it is true, magnify the revenues of their crown sometimes to twelve millions sterling, or above; but their natural vanity gives them no right to any credit on such a head; and though it is not at all impossible that the French king, in time of war, may raise such a sum upon his subjects, and discharge it by repaying them with one third of the debt, yet that is not to be accounted as a stated national revenue, and tends only to prove the misery of the subject, and the injustice of the crown.

In France taxes are raised by the taille, or land-tax. The taillon, which the nobility are obliged to pay as well as the commons, is only another land-tax; by aids, which we call customs or merchandize; by gabels, which is a tax upon salt; by a capitation, or poll-tax; by the tenths of estates and employments; by the sale of all offices of justice; by confiscations and forfeitures; and by a tenth, or free gift of the clergy, exclusive of the annual sum of twelve millions of livres, which that body has of late advanced to the king.

MILITARY AND MARINE STRENGTH.] In time of peace, the crown of France maintains about 200,000 men, but, as I have already hinted, at a very fmall expence, the pay of the common men being little more than two pence half penny per day. In the time of war 400,000 have been brought to the field ; but thofe which are raifed from the militia are very indifferent troops. In the reign of Lewis XIV. the French had at one time 100 fhips of the line, which was almoft equal to the marine force of all Europe befides. The French have, however, at fea been generally defeated by the Englifh. The engagement at La Hogue, which happened in 1692, gave a blow to the French marine which it never has recovered. The prefent king, Lewis XV. has more than once made prodigious efforts towards re-eftablifhing his navy, but his officers and feamen are fo much inferior to thofe of England, that he feemed during the late war to have built fhips of force for the fervice of Great-Britain, fo frequent were the captures made by the Englifh. At prefent, viz. 1769, we are told, that including 50 gun fhips, the French navy amounts to fixty-four fhips of the line, and twenty-five frigates, befides fmaller veffels.

ROYAL TITLES, ARMS, } The title affumed by the
NOBILITY, AND ORDERS. } French king, is fimply, King of France and Navarre ; and by way of compliment he is called his Moft Chriftian Majefty. His arms are three fleurs-de-lis, or, in a field argent, fupported by two angels in the habits of Levites, having each of them a banner in his hand, with the fame arms. The motto is *Lilia non laborant neque nent.*

About the year 1349 Hubert the laft count of Dauphiny, being accidentally the occafion of his fon's death, annexed that county to the crown of France, upon condition that the eldeft fon of France fhould be, for the time to come, ftiled Dauphine.

The French nobility are of four kinds ; firft, the princes of the blood ; fecondly, dukes and counts, peers of France ; thirdly, the ordinary nobility ; fourthly, the nobility lately made, or thofe made in the prefent reign. The firft prince of the blood, is the perfon who ftands next to the crown after the king's fons. The knights of the Holy Ghoft are ranked among the higher nobility, as are the governors and lieutenants-general of provinces.

In France there are three orders ; firft, that of St. Michael, inftituted in 1469, and though originally compofed only of thirty-fix knights, was afterwards enlarged to a hundred. A
perfon

perfon muft be a knight of this order before he can enter into
that of (fecondly) the Holy Ghoft, which was founded in 1578,
by Henry III. and is compofed of a hundred perfons, exclufive of the fovereign, and conferred only on princes of the
blood, and perfons of the higheft rank. Thirdly, the order
of St. Lewis, which was inftituted in the year 1693 by
Lewis XIV. merely for military merit, and is worn by almoft
every officer, and even fubalterns.

HISTORY.] The hiftory of no country is better authenticated than that of France, and it is particularly interefting to
a Britifh reader. This kingdom, which was by the Romans
called Tranfalpine Gaul, or Gaul beyond the Alps, to diftinguifh it from Cifalpine Gaul, on the Italian fide of the Alps,
was probably peopled from Italy, to which it lies contiguous.
Like other European nations, it foon became a defirable
object to the ambitious Romans ; and, after a brave refiftance,
was annexed to their empire by the invincible arms of Julius
Cæfar, about forty-eight years before Chrift. Gaul continued in the poffeffion of the Romans till the downfal of that
empire in the fifth century, when it became a prey to the
Goths, the Burgundians, and the Franks, who fubdued, but
did not extirpate the ancient natives. The Franks themfelves,
who gave it the name of France, or Frankenland, were a
collection of feveral people inhabiting Germany, and particularly the Salii, who lived on the banks of the river Sale,
and who cultivated the principles of jurifprudence better than
their neighbours. Thefe Salii had a rule, which the reft of
the Franks are faid to have adopted, and has been by the
modern Francs applied to the fucceffion of the throne, ex-
cluding all females from the inheritance of fovereignty, and is
well known by the name of the *Salic law*.

The Franks and Burgundians, after eftablifhing their power,
and reducing the original natives to a ftate of flavery, parcelled out the lands among their principal leaders; and fucceeding kings found it neceffary to confirm their privileges,
allowing them to exercife fovereign authority in their refpective
governments, until they at length affumed an independency,
only acknowledging the king as their head. This gave rife to
thofe numerous principalities that were formerly in France,
and to the feveral parliaments ; for every province became, in
its policy and government, an epitome of the whole kingdom ;
and no laws were made, or taxes raifed, without the concurrence of the grand council, confifting of the clergy and of the
nobility.

Thus, as in other European nations, immediately after the
diffolution of the Roman empire, the firft government in
France

France feems to have been a kind of mixed monarchy, and the power of their kings extremely circumfcribed and limited by the feudal barons.

The firft Chriftian monarch of the Franks (according to Daniel, one of the beft French hiftorians) was Clovis, who began his reign anno 468, from which period the French hiftory exhibits a feries of great events; and we find them generally engaged in domeftic broils or in foreign wars. The firft race of their kings, prior to Charlemagne, found a cruel enemy in the Saracens, who then over-ran Europe, and retaliated the barbarities of the Goths and Vandals upon their pofterity. In the year 800, Charlemagne, king of France, whom we have often mentioned as the glory of thofe dark ages, became mafter of Germany, Spain, and part of Italy, and was crowned king of the Romans by the pope; he divided his empire by will among his fons, which proved fatal to his family and pofterity. Soon after this, the Normans, a fierce warlike people from Norway, Denmark, and other parts of Scandinavia, ravaged the kingdom of France; and about the year 900, obliged the French to yield up Normandy and Bretagne to Rollo, their leader, who married the king's daughter, and was perfuaded to profefs himfelf a Chriftian. This laid the foundation of the Norman power in France; which afterwards gave a king to England, in the perfon of William duke of Normandy, who fubdued Harold, the laft Saxon king, in the year 1066. This event proved unfortunate and ruinous to France, as it engaged that nation in almoft perpetual wars with England, for whom they were not an equal match, notwithftanding their numbers, and the affiftance they received from Scotland.

The rage of crufading, which broke out at this time, was of infinite fervice to the French crown in two refpects; in the firft place, it carried off hundreds of thoufands of its turbulent fubjects, and their leaders, who were almoft independent of the king: in the next, the king fucceeded to the eftates of numbers of the nobility, who died abroad without heirs.

But paffing over the dark ages of the crufades, their expeditions to the Holy Land, and wars with England, which have already been mentioned, we fhall proceed to that period when the French began to extend their influence over Europe; and this brings us to the reign of Francis I. contemporary with Henry VIII. of England. This prince, though he was brave to excefs in his own perfon, and had defeated the Swifs, whom till then were deemed invincible, was an unfortunate warrior. He was a candidate for the empire of Germany, but loft the imperial crown, Charles V. of the houfe of Auftria,

and

and king of Spain, being chofen. Francis made fome daz-
zling expeditions againft Spain; but fuffered his mother, of
whom he was very fond, to abufe his power; by which he
difobliged the conftable of Bourbon, the greateft of his fubjects, who joined in a confederacy againft him with the emperor and Henry VIII. of England. In a capital e.pedition he
undertook into Italy, he was taken prifoner at the battle of
Pavia, and obliged to agree to difhonourable terms, which he
never meant to perform, to regain his liberty. His non-per-
formance of thofe conditions was afterwards the fource of many
wars between him and the emperor; and he died in 1547.

France, at the time of his death, notwithftanding the
variety of difagreeable events during the late reign, was in a
flourifhing condition. Francis I. was fucceeded by his fon,
Henry II. who upon the whole was an excellent and fortunate prince. He continued the war with the emperor of
Germany to great advantage for his own dominions; and
was fo well ferved by the duke of Guife, that though he loft
the battle of St. Quintin, againft the Spaniards and the Englifh, he retook Calais from the latter, who never fince had
any footing in France. He married his fon, the Dauphin,
to Mary queen of Scots, in hopes of uniting that kingdom to
his crown; but in this fcheme he, or rather his country, was
unfortunate, as may be feen in the hiftory of Scotland. He
was killed in the year 1559, at an unhappy tilting-match, by
the count of Montgomery.

He was fucceeded by his fon, Francis II. a weak, fickly,
inactive prince, whofe power was entirely engroffed by a prince
of the houfe of Guife, uncle to his wife, the beautiful queen
of Scotland. This engroffment of power encouraged the
Bourbon, the Montmorenci, and other great families, to form
a ftrong oppofition againft the government. Anthony, king
of Navarre, was at the head of the Bourbon family; but the
queen-mother, the famous Catharine of Medicis, being obliged to take part with the Guifes, the confederacy, who had
adopted the caufe of Hugonotifm, was broken in pieces, when
the fudden death of Francis happened, in the year 1560.

This event took place while the prince of Condé, brother
to the king of Navarre, was under fentence of death, for a
confpiracy againft the court, but the queen-mother faved him;
to balance the intereft of the Guifes; fo that the fole direction
of affairs fell into her hands, during the minority of her fecond
fon, Charles IX. Her regency was a continued feries of
diffimulation, treachery, and murder. The duke of Guife,
who was the fcourge of the proteftants, was treacheroufly
murdered by one Poltrot, at the fiege of Orleans; and the
murderer was thought to have been inftigated by the famous

Coligni, admiral of France, who was then at the head of the protestant party. Three civil wars succeeded each other. At last the court pretended to grant the Hugonots a very advantageous peace, and a match was concluded between Henry, the young king of Navarre and a protestant, and the French king's sister. The heads of the protestants were invited to celebrate the nuptials at Paris, with the infernal view of butchering them all, if possible, in one night. This project proved but too successful, though it was not completely executed, on St. Bartholomew's day, 1572. The king himself assisted in the massacre, in which the admiral fell; and it is said that about 30,000 protestants were murdered at Paris, and in other parts of France; and this brought on a fourth civil war. Though a fresh peace was concluded in 1573, with the protestants, yet a fifth civil war broke out the next year, when the bloody Charles IX. died without heirs.

His third brother, the duke of Anjou, had, some time before, been chosen king of Poland; and hearing of his brother's death, he, with some difficulty, escaped to France, where he took quiet possession of that crown, by the name of Henry III.

Religion at that time supplied to the reformed nobility of France the feudal powers they had lost. The heads of the protestants could raise armies of Hugonots. The governors of provinces behaved in them as if they had been independent of the crown; and the parties were so equally balanced, that the name of the king alone turned the scale. A holy league was formed for the defence of the catholic religion, at the head of which was the duke of Guise. The protestants, under the prince of Condé, and the duke of Alençon, the king's brother, called in the German princes to their assistance; and a sixth civil war broke out in 1577, in which the king of Spain took the part of the league, in revenge of the duke of Alençon declaring himself lord of the Netherlands. This civil war was finished within the year, by another sham peace. The king, ever since his accession to the crown, had plunged himself into a course of infamous debauchery and religious extravagance. He was entirely governed by his profligate favourites, but he possessed natural good sense. He began to suspect that the proscriptions of the protestants, and the setting aside from the succession the king of Navarre, on account of his religion, which was aimed at by the holy league, was with a view to place the duke of Guise, the idol of the Roman-catholics, on the throne, to which that duke had some distant pretences. A seventh civil war broke out in 1579, and another in the year 1585, both of them to the disadvantage of the protestants, through the abilities of the duke of Guise. The king thought him now so dangerous, that after inviting

him

him in a friendly manner to court, both he and his brother, the cardinal, were, by his majesty's orders, and, in a manner, under his eye, basely assassinated. The leaguers, upon this, declared that Henry had forfeited the crown, and was an enemy to religion. This obliged him to throw himself into the arms of the protestants; but while he was besieging Paris, where the leaguers had their greatest force, he was, in his turn, assassinated by one Clement, a young enthusiastic monk, in 1589. In Henry III. ended the line of Valois.

The readers of history are well acquainted with the difficulties, on account of his religion, which Henry IV. king of Navarre *, head of the house of Bourbon, and the next heir by the Salic law, had to encounter before he mounted the throne. The leaguers were headed by the duke of Main, brother to the late duke of Guise; and they drew from his cell the decrepit cardinal of Bourbon, uncle to the king of Navarre, and a Roman-catholic, to proclaim him king of France. Being strongly supported by the power of Spain and Rome, all the glorious actions performed by Henry, his courage and magnanimity, seemed only to make him more illustriously unfortunate; for he and his little court were sometimes without common necessaries. He was, however, personally beloved; and no objection lay against him but that of his religion. The leaguers, on the other hand, split among themselves; and the French nation, in general, being jealous of the Spaniards, who availed themselves of the public distractions, Henry, after experiencing a variety of good and bad fortune, came secretly to a resolution of declaring himself a Roman-catholic. This was a measure of necessity, as the king of Spain had offered his daughter Isabella Clara Eugenia to be queen of France; and would have married her to the young duke of Guise.

In 1593, Henry went publicly to mass, as a mark of his conversion. This complaisance wrought wonders in his favour; and having, with great difficulty, obtained absolution from the pope, all France submitted to his authority, and he had only the crown of Spain to contend with, which he did for several years with various fortunes. In 1598, he published the famous edict of Nantes, which secured to the protestants the free exercise of their religion; and next year the treaty of Vervins was concluded with Spain. Henry next chastised the duke of Savoy, who had taken advantage of the late troubles in his kingdom; and applied himself, with wonderful attention and success, (assisted in all his undertakings by his minister, the great Sully) to cultivate the happiness of his peo-

ple;

---

* A small kingdom lying upon the Pyrenean mountains, of which Henry's predecessors had been unjustly dispossessed of the greatest part, or Upper Navarre, by Ferdinand, king of Spain, about the year 1512.

ple, by encouraging manufactures, particularly that of silk, the benefit of which France feels at this day. Having re-established the tranquillity, and, in a great measure, secured the happiness of his people, he formed connections with the neighbouring powers for reducing the ambition of the house of Austria; for which purpose, it is said, he had formed great schemes, and collected a formidable army; others say (for his intention does not clearly appear) that he designed to have formed Christendom into a great republic, of which France was to be the head, to drive the Turks out of Europe; while others attribute his preparations to more ignoble motives, that of a criminal passion for a favourite princess, whose husband had carried her, for protection, into the Austrian dominions. Whatever may be in those conjectures, it is certain, that while he was making preparations for the coronation of his queen, Mary of Medicis, and was ready to enter upon his grand expedition, he was assassinated in his coach in the streets of Paris, by one Ravilliac, like Clement, another young enthusiast, in 1610.

Lewis XIII. son to Henry IV. deservedly named the Great, was but nine years of age at the time of his father's death. As he grew up, he discarded his mother and her favourites, and chose for his minister the famous cardinal Richelieu, who put a period, by his resolute and bloody measures, to the remaining liberties of France, and to the establishment of the protestants there, by taking from them Rochelle, though Charles I. of England, who had married the French king's sister, endeavoured, by his fleet and arms, to prevent it. This put an end to the civil wars on account of religion in France. Historians say, that in these wars above a million of men lost their lives; that 150,000,000 livres were spent in carrying them on; and that nine cities, four hundred villages, two thousand churches, two thousand monasteries, and ten thousand houses, were burnt, or otherwise destroyed during their continuance.

Richelieu, by a masterly train of politics, though himself was next to an enthusiast for popery, supported the protestants of Germany, and Gustavus Adolphus, against the house of Austria; and after quelling all the rebellions and conspiracies which had been formed against him in France, he died some months before Lewis XIII. who, in 1643, left his son, afterwards the famous Lewis XIV. to inherit his kingdom.

During that prince's nonage, the kingdom was torn in pieces under the administration of his mother, Anne of Austria, by the factions of the great, and the divisions between the court and parliament, for the most trifling causes, and

upon

upon the moſt deſpicable principles. The prince of Condé
ſtamed like a blazing ſtar, ſometimes a patriot, ſometimes a
courtier, and ſometimes a rebel. He was oppoſed by the
celebrated Turenne, who from a proteſtant had turned papiſt.
The nation of France was involved at once in civil and domeſtic wars ; but the queen-mother having made choice of Mazarine for her firſt miniſter, he found means to turn the arms,
even of Cromwell, againſt the Spaniards, and to divide the
domeſtic enemies of the court ſo effectually among themſelves,
that when Lewis aſſumed the reins of government in his own
hands, he found himſelf the moſt abſolute monarch that had
ever ſat upon the throne of France. He had the good fortune,
on the death of Mazarine, to put the domeſtic adminiſtration
of his affairs into the hands of Colbert, whom I have already
more than once mentioned, and who formed new ſyſtems for
the glory, commerce, and manufactures of France, all which
he carried to a ſurprizing height.

To write the hiſtory of this reign, would be to write that
of all Europe. Ignorance and ambition were the only enemies
of Lewis : through the former he was blind to every patriotic
duty of a king, and promoted the intereſts of his ſubjects only
that they might the better anſwer the purpoſes of his greatneſs :
by the latter, he embroiled himſelf with all his neighbours,
and wantonly rendered Germany a diſmal ſcene of devaſtation.
I have often mentioned his impolitic revocation of the edict of
Nantes, which obliged the French proteſtants to take ſhelter
in England, Holland, and different parts of Germany, where
they eſtabliſhed the ſilk manufactories, to the great prejudice of
their own country. He was ſo blinded by flattery, that he
arrogated to himſelf the divine honours paid to the pagan emperors of Rome. He made and broke treaties for his conveniency, and at laſt raiſed againſt himſelf a confederacy of almoſt
all the other princes of Europe, at the head of which was
king William III. of England. He was ſo well ſerved, that
he made head for ſome years againſt this alliance ; but having
provoked the Engliſh by his repeated infidelities, their arms,
duke of Marlborough, and thoſe of the Auſtrians,
under prince Eugene, rendered the latter part of his life as
miſerable as the beginning of it was ſplendid. His reign, from
the year 1702 to 1711, was one continued ſeries of defeats and
calamities ; and he had the mortification of ſeeing thoſe places
taken from him, which, in the former part of his reign, were
acquired at the expence of many thouſand lives, Germans and
Flemings. Juſt as he was reduced, old as he was, to the
deſperate reſolution of collecting his people, and dying at their
head, he was ſaved by the Engliſh withdrawing from their
allies,

allies, and concluding the peace of Utrecht, in 1713. He
furvived his deliverance but two years, for he died on the firſt
of September 1715, and was ſucceeded by his great grandſon,
Lewis XV. the preſent king.

The partiality of Lewis XIV. to his natural children,
might have involved France in a civil war, had not the regency
been ſeized upon by the duke of Orleans, a man of ſenſe and
ſpirit, and the next legitimate prince of the blood. We have
already ſeen in what manner he diſcharged the national debt
of France ; but having embroiled himſelf with Spain, the
king was declared major in 1722, and the regent on the
ſecond of December that year was carried off by an apoplexy.

The reader is not to expect that I am to follow the affairs of
France through all the inconſiſtent ſcenes of fighting and
treating with the ſeveral powers of Europe, which are to be
found in their reſpective hiſtories. Among the firſt acts of
the king's government was his nominating his preceptor,
afterwards cardinal Fleury, to be his firſt miniſter. Though
his ſyſtem was entirely pacific, yet the ſituation of affairs in
Europe upon the death of the king of Poland more than once
embroiled him with the houſe of Auſtria. The intention of
the French king was to replace his father-in-law Staniſlaus on
the throne of Poland. In this he failed through the interpo-
ſition of the Ruſſians and Auſtrians ; but Staniſlaus enjoyed
the title of king and the revenues of Lorrain during the remainder of his life. The connection between France and
Spain forced the former to become principals in a war with
Great-Britain, in the management of which the latter was ſo
ill ſeconded by her allies, that it was finiſhed by the peace of
Aix la Chapelle in 1748. As to the war, which had the
American conteſt for its riſe, and was ended by the peace of
Fontainbleau, in 1763, the chief events attending it have
been already mentioned, and are too recent to be recapitulated
here *.

* Lewis XV. king of France and Navarre, was born in 1710, ſucceeded his
great-grandfather, Lewis XIV. in 1715, crowned at Rheims in 1722, and married
in 1725, to Maria Leſzinſki, only daughter to Staniſlaus, late king of Poland, duke
of Lorrain, and died in 1768. Their iſſue are,
1. Maria Adelaide, Madame of France, ducheſs of Lorrain and Bar, born 1732.
2. Victoria Louiſa Maria Thereſa, born 1733.
3. Sophia Phillippina Elizabeth Juſtinia, born 1734.
4. Louiſa Maria, born 1737.
Iſſue of Lewis, late Dauphin of France, by the late Maria Joſepha of Saxony.
1. Lewis Auguſtus, Dauphin of France, born 1754, married 1770 to Maria
Antonietta, ſiſter of the emperor of Germany, born 1755.
2. L. Stan. Xavier, count de Provence, born 1755.
3. Charles Philip, count D'Artois, born 1757.
4. Maria Adelaide Clotilda Xaveria, born 1759.
5. Elizabeth Philippa Maria Helena, born 1764.

NETHERLANDS.

THE feventeen provinces, which are known by the name of the Netherlands, were formerly part of Gallia Belgica, and afterwards of the circle of Belgium or Burgundy in the German empire.

EXTENT, SITUATION, AND BOUNDARIES OF THE SEVENTEEN PROVINCES.

Length 300 } between { 49 and 54 north latitude.
Breadth 200 } { 2 and 7 eaft longitude.

They are bounded by the German fea on the north; by Germany eaft; by Lorrain and France fouth; and by the Britifh channel weft.

I fhall, for the fake of perfpicuity, and to avoid repetition, treat of the feventeen provinces under two great divifions: Firft, the northern, which contains the feven United Provinces, ufually known by the name of *Holland:* Secondly, the fouthern, containing the Auftrian and French Netherlands. The United Provinces are, properly fpeaking, eight, viz. Holland, Overiffel, Zealand, Friefland, Utrecht, Groningen, Gelderland and Zutphen; but the two latter forming only one fovereignty, they generally go by the name of the feven United Provinces.

SITUATION AND EXTENT OF THE UNITED PROVINCES.

Length 150 }
Breadth nearly } between { 51 and 54 north latitude.
the fame. } { 3 and 7 eaft longitude.

The following is the moft fatisfactory account we meet with of their geographical divifion, including the Texel, and other iflands.

Countries Names. United Provinces.	Square Miles.	Length	Breadth	Chief Cities.
Overiffel	1,900	66	50	Deventer
Holland	1,800	84	52	AMSTERDAM
Gelderland	986	50	40	Nimeguen
Friefland	810	44	34	Leuwarden
Zutphen	644	37	33	Zutphen
Groningen	540	45	37	Groningen
Utrecht	450	41	22	Utrecht
Zealand	303	29	24	Middleburg
Texel and other iflands	113			
Total —	7,546			

(braced as Calvinifts)

AIR, SOIL, AND SEASONS.] Thefe provinces lie oppofite to England, at the diftance of 90 miles upon the eaft
fide of the Englifh channel, and are only a narrow flip of
low fwampy land, lying between the mouths of feveral great
rivers, and what the induftry of the inhabitants have gained
from the fea by means of dykes, which they have raifed and
ftill fupport with incredible labour and expence. The air of
the United Provinces is therefore foggy and grofs, until it is
purified by the froft in winter, when the eaft wind ufually fets
in for about four months, and their harbours are frozen up.
The moifture of the air caufes metals to ruft, and wood to
mould, more than in any other country, which is the reafon
of their perpetually rubbing and fcouring, and the brightnefs
and cleanlinefs in their houfes fo much taken notice of. The
foil is unfavourable to vegetation, but by the induftry of the
inhabitants in making canals, it is rendered fit for pafture,
and in many places for tillage.

RIVERS AND HARBOURS.] The rivers are an important
confideration to the United Provinces; the chief of which
are the Rhine, one of the largeft and fineft rivers in Europe;
the Maefe, the Scheld, and the Vecht. There are many fmall
rivers that join thefe, and a prodigious number of canals; but
there are few good harbours in the United Provinces; the beft
are thofe of Rotterdam, Helvoetfluys, and Flufhing; that of
Amfterdam, though one of the largeft and fafeft in Europe,
has a bar at the entrance of it, over which large veffels cannot pafs without being lightened.

VEGETABLE AND ANIMAL PRO- } The quantity of grain
  DUCTIONS BY SEA AND LAND. } produced here, is not
fufficient for home confumption; but by draining their bogs
and marfhes, they have many excellent meadows, which
fatten lean German and Danifh cattle to a vaft fize; and they
make prodigious quantities of butter and cheefe. Their country produces turf, madder, tobacco, fome fruit, and iron;
but all the pit-coal, and timber ufed there, and indeed moft
of the comforts, and even the neceffaries of life, are imported.
They have a good breed of fheep, whofe wool is highly valued; and their horfes and horned cattle are of a larger fize
than in any other nation in Europe. It is faid there are fome
wild bears and wolves here. Storks build and hatch on their
chimneys, but, being birds of paffage, they leave the country
about the middle of Auguft, with their young, and return the
February following. Their river fifh is much the fame as
ours, but their fea-fifh is generally larger, owing perhaps to
their fifhing in deeper water. No herrings vifit their coafts,
and they have no oifter-beds. Notwithftanding all thefe
                                                    incon-

inconveniencies, the induſtry of the Hollanders furniſhes as great a plenty of the neceſſaries and commodities of life, and upon as eaſy terms, as they are to be met with in any part of Europe.

POPULATION, INHABITANTS, MAN-} The ſeven Uni-
NERS, CUSTOMS, AND DIVERSIONS. } ted Provinces are perhaps the beſt peopled of any ſpot of the ſame extent in the world. They contain, according to the beſt accounts, 113 cities and towns, 1400 villages, and about two millions of inhabitants ; beſides the twenty-five towns, and the people in what is called the Lands of the Generality, or conquered countries and towns of other parts of the Netherlands. The manners, habits, and even the minds of the Dutch (for ſo the inhabitants of the United Provinces are called in general) ſeem to be formed by their ſituation, and to ariſe from their natural wants. Their country, which is preſerved by mounds and dykes, is a perpetual incentive to labour, and the artificial drains with which it is every where interſected, muſt be kept in perpetual repair. Even what may be called their natural commodities, their butter and cheeſe, are produced by a conſtant attention to laborious parts of life, Their principal food they earn out of the ſea by their herring fiſheries, for they diſpoſe of their moſt valuable fiſhes to the Engliſh, and other nations, for the ſake of gain. Their air and temperature of the climate incline them to phlegmatic, ſlow diſpoſitions, both of body and mind ; and yet they are iraſcible, eſpecially if hea- ted with liquor. Even their virtues are owing to their cold- neſs with regard to every object that does not immediately concern their own intereſts ; for in all other reſpects they are quiet neighbours and peaceable ſubjects. Their attention to the conſtitution and independency of their country is owing to the ſame principle, for they were never known to effect a change of government but when they thought themſelves on the brink of perdition.

The valour of the Dutch becomes warm and active when they find their intereſt at ſtake, witneſs their ſea wars with England, and France. Their boors, though ſlow of under- ſtanding, are manageable by fair means. Their ſeamen are a plain, blunt, but rough, ſurly, and ill-mannered ſort of people, and appear to be inſenſible of public ſpirit and affec- tion for each other. Their tradeſmen are not to be truſted but when they know themſelves to be under the laſh of the law for impoſitions ; and they ſeldom uſe more words than are neceſſary about their buſineſs. Smoking tobacco is prac- tiſed by old and young of both ſexes ; and as they are gene- rally plodding upon ways and means of getting money, no

3   people

people are so unsociable. Though a Dutchman, when drunk, is guilty of every species of brutality; and though they have been known to exercise the most dreadful inhumanities for interest abroad, where they thought themselves free from discovery, yet they are in general quiet and inoffensive in their own country, which exhibits but few instances of murder, rapine, or violence. As to the habitual tippling and drinking charged upon both sexes, it is owing in a great measure to the nature of their soil and climate. In general, all appetites and passions seem to run lower and cooler here than in other countries, that of avarice excepted. Their tempers are not airy enough for joy, or any unusual strains of pleasant humour, nor warm enough for love; so that the softer passions are no natives of this country; and love itself is little better than a mechanical affection, arising from interest, conveniency, or habit; it is talked of sometimes among the young men, but as a thing they have heard of rather than felt, and as a discourse that becomes them rather than affects them.

In whatever relates to the management of pecuniary affairs, the Dutch are certainly the most expert of any people; as to the knowledge of acquiring wealth, they unite the no less necessary science of preserving it. Every man spends less than his income, be that what it will; nor does it enter into the heads of this sagacious people, that the common course of expence should equal the revenue; and, when this happens, they think at least that they have lived that year to no purpose; and the report of it discredits a man among them as much as any vicious or prodigal extravagance does in other countries. In all these particulars, the women exactly resemble the men, especially in their natural indifference as to the warmer passions. No country, therefore, can vie with theirs in the number of those inhabitants, whose lot, if not riches, is at least a comfortable sufficiency; and where fewer failures or bankruptcies occur. Hence, in the midst of a world of taxes and contributions, such as no other country does experience, they flourish and grow rich. From this systematic spirit of regularity and moderation, joined to the most obstinate perseverance, they succeeded in the stupendous works of draining their country of those immense deluges of water that had overflowed so large a part of it during many ages, while at the same time they brought under their subjection and command, the rivers and seas that surround them, by dykes of incredible thickness and strength, and made them the principal bulwarks on which they rely for the protection and safety of their territories against the danger of an enemy. This they have done, by covering their frontiers and cities with

innumerable

innumerable fluices, by means of which, at the fhorteft notice, the moft rapid inundations are let in, and they become in a few hours inacceffible.

From that frugality and perfeverance which attends them at all times, and under the moft intolerable difficulties, they were enabled not only to throw off the Spanifh yoke, but to attack that powerful nation in the moft tender parts, by feizing her rich galeons, and forming new eftablifhments in Africa, the Eaft and Weft Indies, at the expence of Spain, and thereby becoming, from a defpicable province, a moft powerful and formidable enemy.

Equally wonderful was the rife of their military and marine eftablifhments, maintaining, during their celebrated contention with Lewis XIV. and Charles II. of England, not lefs than 150,000 men, and upwards of 80 fhips of the line. The rich traders and mechanics however, begin now to approximate to the luxuries of Englifh and French dreffing and living; and their nobility and high magiftrates, who have retired from trade, rival thofe of any other part of Europe in their table, buildings, furniture, and equipages.

The diverfions of the Dutch differ not much from thofe of the Englifh, who feem to have borrowed from them the neatnefs of their drinking booths, fkittle and other grounds, and fmall pieces of water, which form the amufements of the middling ranks, not to mention their hand organs, and other mufical inventions. They are the beft fkaters upon the ice in the world. It is amazing to fee the crowds in a hard froft upon the ice, and the great dexterity both of men and women, in darting along, or rather flying, with inconceivable velocity.

. DRESS.] Their drefs formerly was noted for the large breeches of the men; and the jerkins, plain mobbs, fhort petticoats, and other oddities of the women; all which, added to the natural thicknefs and clumfinefs of their perfons, gave them a very grotefque appearance. Thefe dreffes now prevail only among the lower ranks.

RELIGION.] The eftablifhed religion here is the Prefbyterian or Calvinifm; none but Prefbyterians are admitted into any office or poft in the government, excepting the army; yet all religions and fects are tolerated, and have their refpective meetings or affemblies for public worfhip, among which the papifts and Jews are very numerous.

LANGUAGE.] The natural language of the United Provinces is Low Dutch, which is a corrupted dialect of the German; but the people of fafhion fpeak Englifh and French. Their Lord's Prayer runs thus: *Onfe Vader, die in de hemelin zyn uwen naam worde geheylight: uw koningkryb ch kome: uwe wille gefchiede gelyck in den hemel zoo ook op den arden, ons dagelicks*

licks broot geef ons heeden ene vergeeft onfe fchulden gelyk ook wy vergeeven onfe fchuldenaaren : ene en laat ons neit in verfoer kinge-maer vertoft on van den hoofen. Amen.

LEARNING AND LEARNED MEN.] Erafmus and Grotius, who were both natives of this country, ftand at the head almoft of learning itfelf, as Boerhaave does of medicine. Haerlem difputes the invention of printing with the Germans, and the moft elegant edition of the claffics came from the Dutch pref-fes of Amfterdam, Rotterdam, Utrecht, Leyden, and other towns. The Dutch have excelled in controverfial divinity, which infinuated itfelf fo much into the ftate, that it had almoft proved fatal to the government, witnefs the ridiculous difputes about Arminianifm, free-will, predeftination, and the like. Befides Boerhaave they have produced excellent wri-ters in all branches of medicine. Grævius and Burmann ftand at the head of their numerous commentators upon the claffics. Nothing is more common than their Latin poems and epigrams ; and later times have produced a Van Haaren, who is poffeffed of fome poetical abilities, and about the year 1747 publifhed poems in favour of liberty, which were ad-mired as rarities chiefly becaufe their author was a Dutchman. In the other departments of literature, the Dutch publications are mechanical, and arife chiefly from their employments in univerfities, church, or ftate.

UNIVERSITIES.] Thefe are Leyden, Utrecht, Groningen, Harderwicke, and Franeker.

ANTIQUITIES AND CURIOSITIES, } The prodigious dykes,
NATURAL AND ARTIFICIAL. } fome of which are faid to be 17 ells in thicknefs, mounds, and canals, con-ftructed by the Dutch, to preferve their country from thofe dreadful inundations by which it formerly fuffered fo much, are ftupendous, and hardly to be equalled. A ftone quarry near Maeftricht, under a hill, is worked into a kind of fubterraneous palace, fupported by pillars twenty feet high. The ftadthoufe of Amfterdam is perhaps the beft building of that kind in the world : it ftands upon thirteen thoufand large piles, driven into the ground ; and the infide is equally convenient and mag-nificent. Several mufeums, containing antiquities and curio-fities, artificial and natural, are to be found in Holland and the other provinces, particularly in the famous univerfity of Leyden ; fuch as the effigies of a peafant of Pruffia, who fwal-lowed a knife of ten inches length, and is faid to have lived eight years after the fame was cut out of his ftomach ; but the truth of this feems to be doubtful. A fhirt made of the entrails of a man. Two Egyptian mummies, being the bodies of two princes of great antiquity. All the mufcles and tendons of

the

the human body curiofly fet up, by profeffor Stalpert Vander-
Weil.

CITIES, TOWNS, FORTS, AND } Amfterdam, which is
OTHER EDIFICES, PUBLIC } built upon piles of wood,
AND PRIVATE. } is thought to contain
241,000 people, and to be, next to London, the moft commercial city in the world ; in this refpect, fome have even
given it the preference to London, though I cannot fee with
what propriety. Its conveniencies for commerce, and the
grandeur of its public works, are almoft beyond defcription.
In this, and all other cities of the United Provinces, the
beauty of the canals, and walks under trees planted on their
borders, are admirable ; but above all, we are ftruck with the
neatnefs and cleanlinefs that is every where obferved within
doors. Rotterdam is next to Amfterdam for commerce and
wealth : its inhabitants are computed at 56,000. The Hague,
though but a village, is the feat of government in the United
Provinces, and is celebrated for the magnificence and beauty
of its buildings, the refort of foreign ambaffadors and ftrangers
of all diftinctions who live in it, the abundance and cheapnefs
of its provifions, and the politenefs of its inhabitants, who are
computed to be about 40,000 : it is no place of trade, but it
has been for many years noted as an emporium of pleafure and
politics. Leyden and Utrecht are known in the annals of literature for the accommodations of the fcholars who attend their
univerfities, and the beauty and conveniences of their public
fchools. Saardam, though a wealthy trading place, is mentioned here as the workfhop where Peter the Great, of Mufcovy, in perfon, ferved his apprenticefhip to fhip-building,
and laboured as a common handicraft. The upper part of
Gelderland is fubject to Pruffia, and the capital city Gelder.

Holland, with all its commercial advantages, is not a defirable country to live in, efpecially to foreigners. Here are
no mountains nor rifing grounds, no plantations, purling
ftreams, cr cataracts. The whole face of the country, when
viewed from a tower or fteeple, has the appearance of a continued marfh or bog, drained at certain diftances by innumerable ditches ; and the canals, which ferve as high roads, are
frequently in a ftate of ftagnation. The ufual way of paffing
from town to town is by tractfcouts or covered boats, dragged
along by horfes at a flow trot. This method of travelling is
cheap, but extremely dull, for there is a famenefs through all
the provinces. In Amfterdam, which is built upon piles, are
no fprings of frefh or wholefome water, which obliges the
inhabitants to preferve the rain water in refervoirs.

COM-

COMMERCE AND MANUFACTURES.] An account of the Dutch commerce, would comprehend that of almoſt all Europe. There is ſcarcely a manufacture that they do not carry on, or a ſtate to which they do not trade. In this they are aſſiſted by the populouſneſs of their country, the cheapneſs of their labour, and, above all, by their water carriage, which, by means of their canals, gives them advantages beyond all other nations. The United Provinces are the grand magazine of Europe ; and goods may be purchaſed here ſometimes cheaper than in the countries where they grow. Their Eaſt-India company have had the monopoly of the fine ſpices for more than a hundred years, and is the moſt opulent and powerful of any in the world. Their capital city in India is Batavia, which is ſaid to exceed in magnificence, opulence, and commerce, all the cities of Aſia. Here the viceroys appear in greater ſplendor than the ſtadtholder; and it is ſaid the Dutch ſubjects in Batavia ſcarcely acknowledge any dependance on the mother country. They have other ſettlements in India, but none more pleaſant, healthful, or uſeful, than that on the Cape of Good-Hope, the grand rendezvous of the ſhips of all nations, outward or homeward bound. When Lewis XIV. invaded Holland with an army of 80,000 men, the Dutch made ſome diſpoſitions to ſhip themſelves off to their ſettlements in India; ſo great was their averſion to the French government. Not to mention their herring and whale fiſheries, which they have carried off from the native proprietors, they excel at home in numberleſs branches of trade, ſuch as their pottery, tobacco-pipes, Delft-ware, finely refined ſalt ; their oil-mills, ſtarch-manufactures ; their improvements of the raw linen thread of Germany ; their hemp, and fine paper manufactures ; their fine linen and table damaſks ; their ſaw-mills for timber, for ſhipping and houſes, in immenſe quantities ; their great ſugar-baking ; their vaſt woollen, cotton, and ſilk manufactures ; wax-bleaching ; leather-dreſſing ; the great quantity of their coin and ſpecie, aſſiſted by their banks, moſt eſpecially by that of Amſterdam ; their Eaſt-India trade ; and their general induſtry and frugality. It is greatly doubted, however, whether their commerce, navigation, manufactures, and fiſheries, are in the ſame flouriſhing ſtate now as they were in the beginning of this century ; and whether the riches and luxury of individuals have not damped the general induſtry of the inhabitants.

PUBLIC TRADING COMPANIES.] Of theſe, the capital is the Eaſt-India, by which formerly the Dutch acquired immenſe wealth, having divided ſixty per cent. and ſometimes forty, about the year 1660 ; at preſent the dividends are much

reduced ;

reduced; but in a hundred and twenty-four years, the proprietors, on an average, one year with another, divided somewhat above twenty-four per cent. So late as the year 1760, they divided fifteen per cent. but the Dutch Weſt-India company, the ſame year, divided no more than two and a half per cent. The bank of Amſterdam is thought to be inexhauſtibly rich, and is under an excellent direction: it is ſaid, by Sir William Temple, to contain the greateſt treaſure, either real or imaginary, that is known any where in the world. What may ſeem a paradox is, that this bank is ſo far from paying any intereſt, that the money in it is worth ſomewhat more than current caſh is in common payments. Mr. Anderſon ſuppoſes, that the caſh, bullion, and pawned jewels in this bank, which is kept in the vaults of the ſtadthouſe, amounts to thirty-ſix (though others ſay only to thirty) millions ſterling.

CONSTITUTION AND GOVERNMENT.] This is a very intricate article; for though the United Provinces ſubſiſt in a common confederacy, yet each province has an internal government or conſtitution independent of the others: this government is called the ſtates of that province, and the delegates from them form the ſtates general, in whom the ſovereignty of the whole confederacy is veſted; but though a province ſhould ſend two, or more delegates, yet ſuch province has no more than one voice in every reſolution; and before that reſolution can have the force of a law, it muſt be approved of by every province, and by every city and republic in that province. This formality, in times of great danger and emergency, has been ſet aſide. Every reſolution of the ſtates of a particular province muſt be carried unanimouſly.

The council of ſtate conſiſts likewiſe of deputies from the ſeveral provinces: but its conſtitution is different from that of the ſtates general: it is compoſed of twelve perſons, whereof Gelderland ſends two; Holland, three; Zealand, two; Utrecht, two; Frieſland, one; Overiſſel, one; and Groningen, one. Theſe deputies, however, do not vote provincially, but perſonally. Their buſineſs is to prepare eſtimates, and ways and means for raiſing the revenue, as well as other matters that are to be laid before the ſtates general. The ſtates of the provinces are ſtiled Noble and Mighty Lords; but thoſe of Holland, Noble and Moſt Mighty Lords; and the ſtates general, High and Mighty Lords, or the Lords the States General of the United Netherlands; or, their High Mightineſſes. Subordinate to theſe two bodies, is the chamber of accounts, which is likewiſe compoſed of provincial deputies,
who

who audit all public accounts. The admiralty forms a feparate board, and the executive part of it is committed to five
colleges in the three maritime provinces of Holland, Zealand,
and Friefland. In Holland, the people have nothing to do
either in chufing their reprefentatives or their magiftrates. In
Amfterdam, which takes the lead in all public deliberations,
the magiftracy is lodged in thirty-fix fenators, who are chofen
for life, and every vacancy among them is filled up by the fur-
vivors. The fame fenate alfo elects the deputies to reprefent
the cities in the province of Holland.

I have mentioned the above particulars, becaufe without a
knowledge of them, it is impoffible to underftand the hiftory
of the United Provinces, from the death of King William to
the year 1747, when the ftadtholderfhip was made hereditary
in the male and female reprefentatives of the family of Orange.
This office in a manner fuperfedes the conftitution I have
already defcribed. The ftadtholder is prefident of the ftates
of every province; and fuch is his power and influence, that
he can change the deputies, magiftrates, and officers, in every
province and city. By this he has the moulding of the affembly of the ftates general, though he has no voice in it; in
fhort, though he has not the title, he has more real power and
authority than many kings; for befides the influence and revenue he derives from the ftadtholderfhip, he has feveral principalities and large eftates of his own. The prefent ftadtholder
is William V. prince of Orange and Naffau. His titles are,
Hereditary Stadtholder, Captain General, and Admiral of the
Seven United Provinces. He is fon of the late ftadtholder,
William-Charles, who married Anne, princefs royal of Great
Britain, and died in 1751. The prefent ftadtholder was
born in 1748, and in 1767 married the princefs Frederica of
Pruffia.

With refpect to the adminiftration of juftice in this country, every province has its tribunal, to which, except in criminal caufes, appeal lies from the petty and county courts;
and it is faid that juftice is no where diftributed with more
impartiality.

REVENUES.] The government of the United Provinces
proportion their taxes according to the abilities of each province or city. Thofe taxes confift of an almoft general excife,
a land-tax, poll-tax, and hearth-money; fo that the public
revenue amounts annually to about two millions and a half
fterling. The province of Holland pays above half of this
revenue. The taxes in thefe provinces are fo heavy, and fo
many, that it is not without reafon that a certain author afferts,
that the only thing that has efcaped taxation there, is the air
they

they breathe. For the encouragement of trade, the duties on goods and merchandize are said to be exceeding low. Notwithstanding the number and greatness of the taxes, every province is said to labour under very heavy debts, especially Holland; and the public credit is not in the most flourishing condition, witness the immense sums in the British funds.

MILITARY AND MARINE STRENGTH.] The number of land forces in the United Provinces is uncertain in time of peace, but they commonly amount to about 40,000; 25,000 of whom serve in garrisons; many of them are Scots and Swiss; and, in time of war, they hire whole regiments of Germans. The chief command of the army is vested in the stadtholder, under whom is the field marshal general. No nation in Europe, England excepted, can fit out a more formidable fleet than the Dutch, having always vast quantities of timber prepared for building of ships; but the present marine force of the United Provinces is small, compared to what it once was, when equal, if not superior, to that of Great-Britain itself.

ARMS.] The ensigns armorial of the Seven United Provinces, or the States of Holland, are, or, a lion, gules, holding with one paw a cutlas, and with the other a bundle of seven arrows close bound together, in allusion to the seven confederate provinces, with the following motto, *Concordia res parvæ crescunt.*

HISTORY.] See the Austrian Netherlands.

AUSTRIAN AND FRENCH NETHERLANDS.

SITUATION AND EXTENT.

Length 200 }
Breadth 200 } between { 49 and 52 north latitude.
{ 2 and 7 east longitude.

BOUNDARIES.] BOUNDED by the United Provinces on the north; by Germany, east; by Lorrain, Champaign, and Picardy, in France, south; and by another part of Picardy, and the English sea, west.

As this country belongs to three different powers, the Austrians, French, and Dutch, we shall be more particular in distinguishing the provinces and towns belonging to each state.

1. Province of BRABANT.

Subdivisions.		Chief towns.	
1. Dutch Brabant. ———		Boisleduc, Breda, Bergen-op-Zoom	N.
		Maestricht, S. E.	
		Grave, N. E.	
		Lillo, Steenbergen	N. W.

Subdivisions.   Chief towns.

2. Austrian Brabant ——
{
Bruffels, E. lon. 4 deg. 6 min.
   N. lat. 50-50.
Louvain
Vilvorden } in the middle.
Landen
}

2. A N T W E R P; and, 3. M A L I N E S, are provinces independant of Brabant, though furrounded by it, and fubject to the
houfe of Auftria.

4. Province of L I M B U R G, S. E.

Chief towns   ——
.
{
Limburg, E. lon. 6-5. N. lat.
   50-37. fubject to Auftria.
Dalem
Fauquemont, or } fubject to the
Valkenburg   Dutch.
}

5. Province of L U X E M B U R G.

Subdivisions.   Chief towns.

Auftrian Luxemburg —— } { Luxemburg, E. lon. 6-8.
                              N. lat. 49-45.

French Luxemburg ——   } { Thionville } S. E.
                            Montmedy }

6. Province of N A M U R, in the middle, fubject to Auftria.

Chief towns   ——   } { Namur, on the Sambre and Maefe,
                          E. lon. 4-50. N. lat. 50-30.
                          Charleroy on the Sambre.

7. Province of H A I N A U L T.

Subdivisions.   Chief towns.

Auftrian Hainault ——
{
Mons, E. lon. 3-33.
   N. lat. 50-30. } in the
Aeth   middle
Enguien
}
French Hainault ——
{
Valenciennes
Bouchain   } S. W.
Conde
Landrecy
}

8. Province of C A M B R E S I S.

Subject to France —— } { Cambray, E. of Arras, E. lon.
                            3-15. N. lat. 50-15.
                          Crevecour, S. of Cambray.

9. Province of A R T O I S.

Subject to France ——
{
Arras, S. W. on the Scarpe,
   E. lon. 2-5. N. lat. 50-20.
St. Omer, E. of Boulogne
Aire, S. of St. Omer
St. Venant, E. of Aire
Bethune, S. E. of Aire
Terouen, S. of St. Omer.
}

10. Province of FLANDERS.

Subdivisions.		Chief towns.
Dutch Flanders		Sluys, N. Axel, N. Hulft, N. Sas van Ghent, N.
Austrian Flanders		Ghent, on the Scheldt, E. lon. 3-36. N. lat. 51. Bruges Oftend } N. W. near the fea. Newport Oudenard on the Scheld. Courtray } on the Lis. Dixmude Ypres, N. of Lifle Tournay on the Scheld Menin on the Lis.
French Flanders		Lifle, W. of Tournay Dunkirk, on the coaft E. of Calais Douay, W. of Arras Mardike, W. of Dunkirk St. Amand, N. of Valenciennes Gravelin, E. of Calais.

AIR, SOIL, AND PRODUCE.] The air of Brabant, and upon the coaft of Flanders, is bad ; that in the interior parts is more healthful, and the feafons more fettled, both in winter and fummer, than they are in England. The foil and its produce are rich, efpecially in corn and fruits. They have abundance of pafture ; and Flanders itfelf has been reckoned the granary of France and Germany, and fometimes of England. The moft barren parts for corn, rear far more profitable crops of flax, which is here cultivated to great perfection. Upon the whole, the Auftrian Netherlands, by the culture, commerce, and induftry of the inhabitants, was formerly the richeft and moft beautiful fpot in Europe, whether we regard the variety of its manufactures, the magnificence and riches of its cities, the amenity of its roads and villages, and the fertility of its land. If it has fallen off in later times, it is owing partly to the neglect of its government, but chiefly to its vicinity to England and Holland ; but it is ftill a moft defirable and pleafant country. There are few or no mountains in the Netherlands : Flanders is a flat country, fcarcely a fingle hill in it. Brabant, and the reft of the provinces, confift of little hills and vallies, woods, inclofed grounds, and champaign fields.

D 2

RIVERS AND CANALS.] The chief rivers are the Maese, Sambre, Demer, Dyle, Nethe, Geet, Sanne, Ruppel, Scheld, Lis, Scarpe, Deule, and Dender. The principal canals are thofe of Bruffels, Ghent, and Oftend.

METALS AND MINERALS.] Mines of iron, copper, lead, and brimftone, are found in Luxemburg, Limburg, and Liege, as are fome marble quarries.

INHABITANTS, POPULATION, MAN- } The Flemings (for
NERS, CUSTOMS, AND DIVERSIONS. } fo the inhabitants
of Flanders and the Auftrian Low Countries are generally called) are thought to be a heavy, blunt, honeft people ; but
their manners are fomewhat indelicate. Formerly they were
known to fight defperately in defence of their country ; at prefent they make no great figure. The Auftrian Netherlands
are extremely populous, but authors differ as to their numbers.
Perhaps we may fix them at a medium at a million and a half.
They are ignorant, and fond of religious exhibitions and
pageants. Their other diverfions are the fame with thofe of the
peafants of the neighbouring countries.

DRESS AND LANGUAGE.] The inhabitants of French
Flanders are mere Frenchmen and women in both thefe particulars. The Flemings on the frontiers of Holland drefs
like the Dutch boors, and their language is the fame ; but
the better fort of people fpeak French, and drefs in the fame
tafte.

RELIGION.] The eftablifhed religion here is the Roman-
catholic ; but proteftants, and other fects, are not molefted.

ARCHBISHOPRICS AND BISHOPRICS.] The archbifhoprics
are Cambray, Maline or Mecklin ; the bifhoprics, Ghent,
Bruges, Antwerp, Arras, Ypres, Tournay, St. Omer,
Namur, and Ruremonde.

LEARNING, LEARNED } The fociety of Jefus has pro-
MEN, AND ARTISTS. } duced the moft learned men in
the Auftrian Low countries, in which they had many comfortable fettlements, which are now upon the decline. Works
of theology, and the civil and canon law, Latin poems and
plays, are their chief productions. Strada is an elegant hiftorian and poet. The Flemifh painters and fculptors have great
merit, and form a fchool by themfelves. The works of Rubens
and Vandyke cannot be fufficiently admired. Fiamingo, or
the Flemings models for heads, particularly thofe of children,
have never yet been equalled ; and the Flemings formerly engroffed tapeftry-weaving to themfelves.

UNIVERSITIES.] Louvain, Douay, and St. Omer.

ANTIQUITIES AND CURIOSITIES, } Some Roman mo-
NATURAL AND ARTIFICIAL. } numents of temples

2   and

and other buildings are to be found in thofe provinces. Many curious bells, churches, and the like, ancient and modern, are alfo found here ; and the magnificent old edifices of every kind, feen through all their cities, give evidences of their former grandeur.

CITIES.] This article has employed feveral large volumes publifhed by different authors, but in times when the Auftrian Netherlands were far more flourifhing than now. The walls of Ghent, formerly the capital of Flanders, and celebrated for its linen and woollen manufactures, contain the circuit of ten miles, but now unoccupied, and great part of it in a manner a void. Bruges, formerly fo noted for its trade and manufactures, but above all for its fine canals, is now dwindled to an inconfiderable place. Oftend is now no more than a convenient harbour for traders ; and Ypres, a ftrong garrifon town. The fame may be faid of Charleroy and Namur, which lie in the Auftrian Hainault.

Louvain, the capital of the Auftrian Brabant, inftead of its flourifhing manufactories and places of trade, now contains pretty gardens, walks, and arbours. Bruffels retains fomewhat of its antient manufactories ; and being the refidence of the governor or viceroy of the Auftrian Netherlands, it is a populous, lively place. Antwerp, once the emporium of the European continent, is now reduced to be a tapeftry and thread lace-fhop, with the houfes of fome bankers, jewellers, and painters adjoining. One of the firft exploits of the Dutch, foon after they threw off the Spanifh yoke, was to ruin at once the commerce of Antwerp, by finking veffels, loaded with ftone, in the mouth of the Scheld ; thus fhutting up for ever, the entrance of that river to fhips of burden. This was the more cruel as the people of Antwerp had been their friends and fellow fufferers in the caufe of liberty.

It may be obferved here, that every gentleman's houfe is a caftle or *chateau* ; and that there are more ftrong towns in the Netherlands than in all the reft of Europe ; but fince the decline of their trade, by the rife of the Englifh and Dutch, thefe towns are confiderably diminifhed in fize, and whole ftreets, particularly in Antwerp, are in appearance uninhabited. In the Netherlands, provifions are extremely good and cheap. A ftranger may dine in Bruffels on feven or eight difhes of meat for lefs than a fhilling Englifh. Travelling is fafe, reafonable and delightful in this luxurious country. The roads are generally a broad caufeway, and run for fome miles in a ftraight line, till they terminate with the view of fome noble buildings.

D 3

COMMERCE AND MANUFACTURES.] The chief manufactures of the French and Auftrian Netherlands, are their beautiful linens and laces; in which, notwithftanding the boafted improvements of their neighbours, they are yet unrivalled, particularly in that fpecies called cambricks, from Cambray, the chief place of its manufacture. Thefe manufactures form the principal article of their commerce.

CONSTITUTION AND GOVERNMENT.] The Auftrian Netherlands are ftill confidered as a circle of the empire, of which the archducal houfe, as being fovereign of the whole, is the fole director and fummoning prince. This circle contributes its fhare to the impofts of the empire, and fends an envoy to the diet, but is not fubject to the judicatories of the empire. It is under a governor-general, appointed by the court of Vienna, who, at prefent, is his ferene highnefs prince Charles of Lorrain, brother to the late, and uncle to the prefent emperor. The face of an affembly, or parliament, for each province, is ftill kept up, and confifts of the clergy, nobility, and deputies of towns, who meet at Bruffels. Each province claims particular privileges, but they are of very little effect; and the governor feldom or never finds any refiftance to the will of his court. Every province has a particular governor, fubject to the regent; and caufes are here decided according to the civil and canon law.

REVENUES.] Thefe rife from the demefne lands and cuftoms; but fo much is the trade of the Auftrian Flanders now reduced, that they are faid not to defray the expence of their government. The French Netherlands bring in a confiderable revenue to the crown.

MILITARY STRENGTH.] The troops maintained here by the emprefs-queen are chiefly employed in the frontier garrifons. Though by the barrier treaty, the Auftrians were obliged to maintain three-fifths of thofe garrifons, and the Dutch two, yet both of them are miferably deficient in their quotas, the whole requiring at leaft 30,000 men, and in time of war above 10,000 more.

ARMS.] The arms of Flanders are, or, a lion fable, and languid gules.

HISTORY.] The feventeen provinces, and that part of Germany which lies weft of the Rhine, was called Belgicæ Galliæ by the Romans. Upon the decline of that empire, the Goths, and other northern people, poffeffed themfelves of thefe provinces firft, as they paffed through them in their way to France, and other parts of the Roman empire; and after being erected into fmall governments, the heads of which were defpotic within their own dominions, they were fwallowed up

by

by the houfe of Burgundy. The emperor Charles V. the heir of that family, ranked them as part of the empire, under the title of the Circle of Burgundy. The tyranny of his fon Philip, who fucceeded to the throne of Spain, made the inhabitants attempt to throw off his yoke, which occafioned a general infurrection. The counts Hoorn, Egmont, and the prince of Orange, appearing at the head of it, and Luther's reformation gaining ground about the fame time in the Netherlands, his difciples joined the malecontents. Whereupon king Philip introduced a kind of inquifition, in order to fupprefs them, and many thoufands were put to death by that court, befides thofe that perifhed by the fword. Count Hoorn and count Egmont were taken and beheaded; but the prince of Orange, whom they elected to be their ftadtholder, retiring into Holland, that and the adjacent provinces entered into a treaty for their mutual defence, at Utrecht, in the year 1579. And though thefe revolters at firft were fo defpicable as to be termed Beggars by their tyrants, their perfeverance and courage was fuch, under the prince of Orange, and the affiftance afforded them by queen Elizabeth, both in troops and money, that they forced the crown of Spain at laft to declare them a free people, about the year 1609; and afterwards they were acknowledged by all Europe to be an independant ftate, under the title of *The United Provinces.* When the houfe of Auftria, which for fome ages ruled over Germany, Spain, and part of Italy, with which they afterwards continued to carry on bloody wars, was become no longer formidable, and when the public jealoufy was directed againft that of Bourbon, which was favoured by the government of Holland, who had difpoffeffed the prince of Orange of the ftadtholderfhip, the fpirit of the people was fuch, that they revived it in the perfon of the prince, who was afterwards William III. king of Great-Britain; and during his reign, and that of queen Anne, they were principals in the grand confederacy againft Lewis XIV. king of France. By their fea wars with England, under Cromwell, and in the reign of Charles II. they acquired the reputation of a formidable naval power; but, as I have already mentioned, their military virtue is on the decline. The Spaniards remained poffeffed of the other ten provinces, or, as they are termed, the Low Countries, until the duke of Marlborough, general of the allies, gained the memorable victory of Ramilies, in the year 1706. After which, Bruffels, the capital, and great part of thefe provinces, acknowledged Charles VI. afterwards emperor of Germany, their fovereign; and his daughter, the emprefs queen, remained poffeffed of them until the war of 1741, when the French made an entire conqueft of them,

except

except part of the province of Luxemburg; and the places retained by the French, by the peace of Aix-la-Chapelle in the year 1748, may be feen in the preceding general table of divifions.

G E R M A N Y.

SITUATION AND EXTENT.

Miles.		Degrees.
Length 600	} between {	5 and 19 eaft longitude.
Breadth 500		45 and 55 north latitude.

BOUNDARIES.] THE empire of Germany, properly fo called, is bounded by the German ocean, Denmark, and the Baltic, on the north; by Poland and Hungary, including Bohemia, on the eaft; by Switzerland and the Alps, which divides it from Italy, on the fouth; and by the dominions of France and the Low Countries, on the weft, from which it is feparated by the Rhine, Mofelle, and the Maes.

GRAND DIVISIONS.] The divifions of Germany, as laid down even by modern writers, are various and uncertain. I fhall therefore ftick to thofe that are moft generally received. Germany formerly was divided into the Upper, or fouthern, and the Lower, or northern. The emperor Maximilian, predeceffor and grandfather to the emperor Charles V. divided it into ten great circles; and the divifion was confirmed in the diet of Nuremberg, in 1552; but the circle of Burgundy, or the feventeen provinces of the Low Countries, being now detached from the empire, we are to confine ourfelves to nine of thofe divifions, as they now fubfift.

Whereof three are in the north, three in the middle, and three in the fouth.

The northern circles —— ——	{	Upper Saxony Lower Saxony Weftphalia
The circles in the middle —— ——	{	Upper Rhine Lower Rhine Franconia
The fouthern circles —— ——	{	Auftria Bavaria Swabia.

1. UPPER SAXONY CIRCLE.

Divifions.	Subdivifions.	Chief towns.
Pomerania, in the North {	Pruffian Pomerania, N. E. {	Stetin, E. lon. 14-50, N. lat. 53-30.
	Swedifh Pomerania, N. W. {	Stralfund

Divisions.	Subdivisions.	Chief towns.
Brandenburg in the middle, subject to its own elector the king of Prussia.	Altmark, west Middlemark Newark, east	Stendel Berlin, Potsdam Francfort, Custrin.
Saxony, Proper, in the south, subject to its own elector.	Duchy of Saxony, N. Lusatia, marq. east. Misnia, marq. south	Wittenburgh Bantzen, Gorlits Dresden, E.lon. 13-36. N. Lat. 51. Missein.
Thuringia, langr. west	—— ——	Erfurtt, subject to the elector of Mentz.
The dutchies of	Saxe Meiningen —— Saxe Zeits —— Saxe Altenburg, S. E. Saxe Weimer, west — Saxe Gotha, west —— Saxe Eisnach, S. W. — Saxe Saalfield ——	*Subject to their own dukes.* Meiningen Zeits Altenburg Weimer Gotha Eisnach Saalfield.
The counties of	Schwartsburg, W. Belchingen, N. Mansfield, N.	Subject to their respective counts	Schwartsburg Belchingen Mansfield.
The dutchies of	Hall, middle, subject to Prussia Saxe Naumberg, subject to its own duke	Hall Naumburg.
The counties of	Stolberg, north-west —— Hohenstein, west — —	Stolberg Northhausen
Principality of	Anhalt, north ——	Dessau, Zerbst Bernberg, Kothen.
Bishopric of —	Saxe Hall, west ——	Hall
	Voigtland, south, subject to the elector of Saxony —	Plowen.
Dutchy of ——	Mersberg, middle, subject to the elector of Saxony — —	Mersberg.

2. Lower SAXONY Circle.

Holstein D. north of the Elbe	Holstein Proper, N. Ditmarsh, west Stormaria, south Hamburgh, a sovereign state Wagerland, east	*Partly sub.to Denmark, and partly to the duke of Holstein Gottorp*	Keil, subject to Holstein Gottorp Meldorp } subject to Glucstat } Denmark. Hamburg, E. L. 10-35. N. L. 54. an imperial city Lubec, an imperial city.
Lawenburg Dutchy, north of the Elbe, subject to Hanover			Lawenburg.
Subject to the duke of Brunswick Wolfembuttle.	D. Brunswic Proper D. Wolfembuttle C. Rheinstein, south C. Blachenberg —	*middle*	Brunsvic, E.L. 10-30. N. Lat. 52-30. Wolfembuttle Rheinstein Blackenburg

Subject

Divisions.	Subdivisions.	Chief towns.
Subject to the elector of Hanover, king of Great Britain.	D. Calenburg —	Hanover
	D. Grubbenhagen —	Grubbenhagen
	Gottengen —	Gottengen
Lunenburg D. sub. to Hanover.	D. of Lunenburg Proper	Lunenburg
	D. Zell	Zell, E. lon. 10. N. lat. 32-52.
Bremen D. and Verden D. sub. to Hanover, north ——	Verden.	Bremen, E. lon. 9. N. lat. 53-30, an imperial city.
Mecklenburg Duchy —	D. Swerin, north, subject to its duke ——	Swerin, E. lon. 11-30. N. lat. 54.
	D. Gustrow, north, subject to its duke ——	Gustrow.
Hildesheim bishopric, in the middle, subject to its bishop —— ——		Hildesheim, an imperial city.
Magdeburg duchy, south-east, subject to the king of Prussia —— ——		Magdeburg.
Halberstat duchy, subject to Prussia, south-east		Halberstat.

3. WESTPHALIA Circle.

North Division	Embden, C. or East Friesland, subject to the king of Prussia	Embden, an imperial city
	Oldenburg, C. ⎫ sub. to the king	Oldenburgh
	Delmonhurst ⎭ of Denmark	Delmonhurst
	Hoye ⎫ subject to Ha-	Hoye
	Diepholt ⎭ nover	Diepholt.
Western Division	Munster B. subject to its bishop	Munster, E. lon. 7-10. N. lat. 52.
	Paderborn B. subject to its bishop	Paderborn
	Osnaburg B. subject to its bishop	Osnaburg
	Lippe, C. sub. to its own count	Lippe, Pyrmont
	Minden D. ⎫ sub. to Prussia	Minden
	Ravensburg C. ⎭	Ravensburg
	Westphalia D. sub. to the elector of Cologn ——	Arensburg
	Tecklenburg C. ⎫ subject to their	Tecklenburg
	Ritberg C. ⎬ respective	Ritberg
	Schawenburg C. ⎭ counts	Schawenburg
Middle Division	Cleves D. subject to the king of Prussia —— ——	Cleef, E. lon. 5-36. N. lat. 51-40.
	Berg. D. ⎫ subject to the elector	Dusseldorf
	Juliers D. ⎭ Palatine	Juliers Aix
	Mark C. subject to Prussia	Ham
	Liege B. subject to its own bishop	Liege, E. lon. 5-36. N. lat. 50-40.
		Huy
	Bentheim C. subject to Hanover	Bentheim
	Steinfort C. subject to its count	Steinfort.

4. Upper RHINE Circle.

Divisions.	Subdivisions.	Chief towns.
Hesse	Hesse Cassel, landg. N. ——	Cassel, E. lon. 9-20. N. lat. 51-20.
	Hesse Marpurg, landg. N. —	Marpurg
	Hesse Darmstadt, landg. —	Darmstadt.

Each of the above subdivisions are subject to their respective landgraves.

	Hesse Hoberg — — —	Homberg
	Hesse Rhinefield — — —	Rhinefield
	Hesse Wanfried — — —	Wonfield

Counties in the Wetteraw south.

Naffau Dillenburg —		Dillenburg
Naffau Diets —		Diets
Naffau Hadamar —		Hadamar
Naffau Kerberg —	Each county subject to its own count of the house of Naffau.	Kerberg
Naffau Siegen —		Siegen
Naffau Idstein —		Idstein
Naffau Weilburg —		Weilburg
Naffau Wisbaden —		Wisbaden
Naffau Bielsteid —		Bielsteid
Naffau Otweiler —		Otweiler
Naffau Usingen —		Usingen

Territory of Frankfort, a sovereign state — Frankfort on the Maine, E. lon. 8-30. N. lat. 50-10. an imperial city.

County of Erpach, subject to its own count — Erpach east.

Bishopric of Spire, a sovereign state — Spire on the Rhine, an imperial city

Duchy of Zwebruggen, or Deuxponts, subject to the duke of Deuxponts — — — Deuxponts in the Palat.

County of Catzenelbogen, subject to Hesse Cassel — Catzenelbogen on the Lhon.

Counties of

Waldec, subject to its own count	Waldec
Solms, subject to its own count	Solms
Hanau, subject to Hesse Cassel —	Hanau
Eyfenberg, sub. to its own count	Eyfenberg
Soyn —	Sayn
Wied —	Wied
Wetgenstein —	Witgenstein
Haizfield —	Hatzfield
Westerberg —	Westerberg.

Abby of Fuld, subject to its abbot — Fuld.
Hirchfield — subject to Hesse Cassel — Hirchfield.

5. Lower RHINE Circle.

Divisions.	Chief towns.
Palatinate of the Rhine, on both sides that river, subject to the elector Palatine	Heidelburg on the Neckar, E. lon. 8-40. N. lat. 49-20. Phillisburg, Manheim, and Frankendal on the Rhine.

Divisions.	Subdivisions.	Chief towns.
Archbishoprics and Electorates of { Cologn, Mentz, Triers	Subject to their respective electors.	Cologne, on the Rhone, E. lon. 6-40. N. lat. 50-50. Bonn, on the Rhine. Mentz, on the Rhine, Aschaffenburg, on the Maine. Triers, on the Moselle.

Bishopric of Worms, a sovereign state — { Worms, on the Rhine, an imperial city.

Duchy of Simmeren, sub. to its own duke — Simmeren.

| **Counties of** { Rhinegravestein, Meurs, subj. to Prussia —, Veldenti, subj. to the elector Palatine — — —, Spanheim ———, Leymingen ——— | { Rhinegravestein, Meurs, Veldents, Creutznach, Leymingen. |

6. FRANCONIA Circle.

Divisions.		Chief towns.
Bishoprics of { Wurtsburg, W., Bemberg, N., Aichstat, S.	Subject to their respective bishops.	{ Wurtsburg, Bemberg, Aichstat.
Marquisates of { Cullenback, north-east, Onspach, S.	Subject to their respective margraves	{ Cullenback, Onspach.

Subdivisions.		Chief towns.
Principality of Henneburgh, N. — —		Henneburgh
Duchy of Coberg, N. subj. to its duke —		Coberg
Duchy of Hilburghausen, subj. to its duke —		Hilburghausen
Burgravate of Nuremburg, S. E. an independent state —		} Nuremburg, an imperial city.
Territory of the great master of the Teutonic order, Mergentheim, S. W. — —		} Mergentheim.

| **Counties of** { Reineck, W. —, Bareith, E. sub. to its own margrave, Papenheim, S. sub. to its own count, Wertheim, W. —, Cassel, middle —, Schwartzenburgh, subject to its own count —, Holach, S. W. — | { Reineck, Bareith, Papenheim, Wertheim, Cassel, Schwartzenburg middle, Holach. |

7. AUSTRIA Circle.

The whole circle belongs to the empress queen of Hungary.

Division.	Chief town.
Archduchy of Austria Proper —	{ Vienna, E. lon. 16-20. N. lat. 48-20. Lints Ens, west.

Division.	Chief towns.
Duchies of { Stira and Cilley, C. Carinthia — — Carniola — — Goritia — —	{ Gratz, Cilley, S. E. Glagenfurt, Lavemund, S. E. Laubach, Zerknits, Trieste, St. Veits, S. E. Gorits, S. E.
County of Tyrol — — —	Infpruck } S. W. on the
Bifhoprics of { Brixen — — Trent — —	{ Brixen } confines of Italy { Trent } and Switzerland.

8. BAVARIA Circle.

Subdivifions.	Chief towns.
Duchy of Bavaria Proper, on the Danube } Subject to the elector of Bavaria Palatinate of Bavaria	{ Munich, E. lon. 11-32. N. lat. 48-5. Landfhut, Ingoldftat, N. W. Dona- wert, [Ratifbon] N. an im- perial city. Amberg, [Sultfbach] N. of the Danube, fubject to the elec- tor Palatine.
Freiffingen, fubject to its bifhop ———	Freiffingen
Bifhopric of Paffau, fubject to its own bifhop ——— }	Paffau, E. on the Danube.
Duchy of Neuberg, fubj. to the elector Palatine ——— ——— }	Neuberg, W. on the Danube.
Archbifhop of Saltfburg, fubject to its own archbifhop ——— }	Saltfburg, S. E. Hallen.

9. SWABIA Circle.

Subdivifions.	Chief towns.
Duchy of Wurtemburg, fub. to the duke of Wurtemburg Stutgard. }	Stutgard, E. lon. 9. } On, or N. lat. 48-40. } near the Tubingen, Hailbron } Neckar.
Marqui-fates of { Baden Baden BadenDourlach } fubject to their own refpective margraves.	{ BadenDourlach } On, or { Baden Weiller } near the Rhine.
Bifhopric of Augfburg, fubject to its own bifhop ——— ———	{ Augfburg, an imperial city, Hockftet, Blenheim, on or near the Danube.
Territory of Ulm, a fovereign ftate	{ Ulm, on the Danube, an im-perial city.
Bifhopric of Conftance, fubject to its own bifhop under the houfe of Auftria	{ Conftance, on the lake of Conftance.
Principa-lities of { Mindelheim Furftemburg Hohenzollern } Subject to their refpec-tive princes.	{ Mindelheim, S. of Augfburg. Furftenburg, S. Hohenzollern, S.
Counties of { Oeting — — Koningfeck — — Hohenrichburg —	{ Oeting, eaft Koneckfeck, fouth-eaft Gemund, north

Baronies of	Waldburg — —	Waldburg, south-east
	Limpurg — —	Limpurg, north.

Abbies of	Kempten — —	Kempten, on the Iller
	Buchaw — —	Buchaw, S. of the Danube .
	Lindaw — —	Lindaw, on the lake of Con-stance, imperial cities.

Imperial cities, or sovereign states —
- Nordlingen, north of the Danube
- Memminghen, east
- Rotwell, on the Neckar, and many more.

Subject to the house of Au-stria
Black forest, N. W.	Rhinefield and Lauffenburg
Rhinefield C.	
Marquisate of Burgaw	—Burgaw, east.
Territory of Brisgow, on the Rhine —	Friburgh and Brisac.

NAME.] Great part of modern Germany lay in antient Gaul, as I have already mentioned; and the word Germany is of itself but modern. Many fanciful derivations have been given of the word; the most probable is, that it is compounded of *Ger*, or *Gar*, and *Man*; which, in the ancient Celtic, signifies a warlike man. The Germans, however, went by various other names, such as Allemanni, Teutones; which last is said to have been their most ancient designation; and the Germans themselves call their country Teuchland.

CLIMATE, SEASONS, AND SOIL.] The climate of Germany, as in all large tracts of country, differs greatly, not only on account of the situation, north, east, south, and west, but according to the improvement of the soil, which has a vast effect upon the climate. The most mild and settled weather is found in the middle of the country, at an equal distance from the sea and the Alps. In the north it is sharp; towards the south it is more temperate.

The soil of Germany is not improved to the full by culture, and therefore in many places it is bare and sterile, though in others it is surprizingly fruitful. Agriculture, however, is daily improving, which must necessarily change the most barren parts of Germany greatly to their advantage. The reasons vary as much as the soil. In the south and western parts they are more regular than those that lie near the sea, or that abound . with lakes and rivers. The north wind and the eastern blasts are unfavourable to vegetation. Upon the whole, there is no great difference between the seasons of Germany and those of . Great-Britain.

MOUNTAINS.] The chief mountains of Germany are the Alps, which divide it from Italy, and those which separate
Saxony,

Saxony, Bavaria, and Moravia from Bohemia. Many other large tracts of mountains, however, are found in different parts of the empire.

FORESTS.] The vaſt paſſion which the Germans have for hunting the wild boar, is the reaſon why perhaps there are more woods and chaſes yet ſtanding in Germany than in moſt other countries. The Heraynian foreſt, which in Cæſar's time was nine days journey in length, and ſix in breadth, is now cut down in many places, or parcelled out into woods, which go by particular names. Moſt of the woods are pine, fir, oak, and beech. There is a vaſt number of foreſts of leſs note in every part of this country ; almoſt every count, baron, or gentleman, having a chace or park adorned with pleaſure houſes, and well ſtocked with game, viz. deer, of which there are ſeven or eight ſorts, as roebucks, ſtags, &c. of all ſizes and colours, and many of a vaſt growth ; plenty of hares, conies, foxes, bears, wolves, and boars. They abound ſo much alſo with wild fowl, that in many places the peaſants leave them and veniſon for their ordinary food.

RIVERS AND LAKES.] No country can boaſt a greater variety of noble large rivers than Germany. At their head ſtands the Danube or Donaw, ſo called from the ſwiftneſs of the current, and which ſome pretend to be naturally the fineſt river in the world. From Vienna to Belgrade it is ſo broad, that, in the wars between the Turks and Chriſtians, ſhips of war have been engaged on it ; and its conveniency for carriage to all the countries through which it paſſes is inconceivable. The Danube, however, contains a vaſt number of cataracts and whirlpools ; its ſtream is rapid, and its courſe, without reckoning turnings or windings, is computed to be 1620 miles. The other principal rivers are the Rhine, Elbe, Oder, Weſer, and Moſelle.

The chief lakes of Germany, not to mention many inferior ones, are thoſe of Conſtance and Bregentz. Beſides theſe are the Chiemſee, or the lake of Bavaria ; and the Zecknitzer-ſee in the dutchy of Carniola, whoſe waters often run off and return again in an extraordinary manner.

Beſides thoſe lakes and rivers, in ſome of which are found pearls, Germany contains large noxious bodies of ſtanding water, which are next to peſtilential, and afflict the neighbouring natives with many deplorable diſorders.

MINERAL WATERS AND BATHS.] Germany is ſaid to contain more of thoſe than all Europe beſides. All Europe has heard of the Spa waters, and thoſe of Pyrmont. Thoſe of Aix la Chapelle are ſtill more noted. They are divided into the Emperor's Bath, and the Little Bath, and the ſprings
of

of both are fo hot, that they let them cool ten or twelve hours before they ufe them. Each of thofe, and many other waters have their partizans in the medical faculty, and if we are to believe all they fay, they cure difeafes internal and cutaneous, either by drinking or bathing. The baths and medicinal waters of Embs, Wifbaden, Schwalbach, and Wildungen, likewife perform their wonders in almoft all difeafes. The mineral fprings at the laft mentioned place are faid to intoxicate as foon as wine, and therefore they are inclofed. Carlfbad and Baden baths have been defcribed and recommended by many great phyficians, and ufed with great fuccefs by many royal perfonages.

After all, many are of opinion that great part of the falutary virtues afcribed to thefe waters is owing to the exercifes and amufements of the patients. It is the intereft of the proprietors to provide for both ; and many of the German princes feel the benefit of the many elegant and polite inftitutions for the diverfion of the public. The neatnefs, cleanlinefs, and conveniency of the places of public refort are inconceivable ; and though at firft they are attended with expence, yet they more than pay themfelves in a few years by the company which crouds to them from all parts of the world ; many of whom do not repair thither for health, but for amufement and converfation.

METALS AND MINERALS.] Germany abounds in both. Bohemia, and many places in the circle of Auftria, and other parts of Germany, contain mines of filver, quickfilver, copper, tin, iron, lead, fulphur, nitre, and vitriol. Salt-petre, falt-mines, and falt-pits are found in Auftria, Bavaria, Silefia, and the Lower Saxony ; as are carbuncles, amethifts, jafper, faphire, agate, alabafter, feveral forts of pearls, turquois ftones, and the fineft of rubies, which adorn the cabinets of the greateft princes and virtuofi. In Bavaria, Tirol, and Liege are quarries of curious marble, flate, chalk, ochre, red lead, allum and bitumen ; befides other foffils. In feveral places are dug up ftones, which to a ftrong fancy reprefent different animals, and fometimes trees of the human form. Many of the German circles furnifh coal-pits, and the *terra figillata* of Mentz, with white, yellow, and red veins, is thought to be an antidote againft poifon.

VEGETABLE AND ANIMAL PRODUCTIONS.] Thefe differ in Germany very little, if at all, from the countries I have already defcribed ; but naturalifts are of opinion, that had the Germans, even before the middle of this century, been acquainted with agriculture, their country would have been the moft fruitful of any in Europe. Even in its prefent, what we

may

may call rude state, provisions are more cheap and plentiful in Germany than in any other country perhaps in the world ; witness the prodigious armies which the most uncultivated part of it maintained during the late war, while many of the richest and most fertile provinces remained untouched.

The Rhenish and the Moselle wines differ from those of other countries in a peculiar lightness and detersive qualities, more sovereign in some diseases than any medicine.

The German wild boar differs in colour from our common hogs. Their flesh, and the hams made of it is preferred by many, even to those of Westmoreland, for flavour and grain. The glutton of Germany is said to be the most voracious of all animals. Its prey is almost every thing that has life, which it can master, especially birds, hares, rabbits, goats, and fawns ; whom they surprize artfully and devour greedily. On these the glutton feeds so ravenously, that it falls into a kind of a torpid state, and not being able to move he is killed by the huntsmen ; but though both boars and wolves will kill him in that condition, they will not eat him. His colour is a beautiful brown, with a faint tinge of red.

Germany yields abundance of excellent heavy horses ; but their oxen and sheep are not comparable to those of England, probably owing to the want of skill in feeding and rearing them. Some parts of Germany are remarkable for fine larks, and great variety of singing birds, which are sent to all parts of Europe.

POPULATION, INHABITANTS, MANNERS, } As the em-
   CUSTOMS, DIVERSIONS, AND DRESS. } pire of Ger-
many is a collection of separate states, each having a different government and police, we can say little with precision as to the number of its inhabitants ; but if they are fixed at twenty millions, the number is perhaps not exaggerated. When the landholders become better acquainted with agriculture and cultivation, population must naturally encrease among them.

The Germans in their persons are tall, fair, and strong built. The ladies have generally fine complexions; and some of them, especially in Saxony, have all the delicacy of features and shape that are so bewitching in some other countries ; but this must be understood of the higher ranks.

Both men and women affect rich dresses, which in fashion are the same as in France and England ; but the better sort of men are excessively fond of gold and silver lace, especially if they are in the army. The ladies at the principal courts differ not much in their dress from the French and English, only they are not so excessively fond of paint, as the former. At some courts they appear in rich furs, and all of them are loaded with jewels, if they can obtain them. The female part of the burghers families, in many of the German towns, dress in a

VOL. II.   E   very

very different manner, and fome of them inconceivably fan-taftic, as may be feen in many prints publifhed in books of travels; but in this refpect they are gradually reforming, and many of them make quite a different appearance in their drefs from what they did thirty or forty years ago; as to the peafan-try and labourers, they drefs as in other parts of Europe, ac-cording to their employments, conveniency, and opulence. The ftoves made ufe of in Germany are the fame with thofe already mentioned, in the northern nations, and are fometimes made portable, fo that the ladies carry them to church. In Weftphalia, and many other parts of Germany, they fleep between two feather-beds, with fheets ftitched to them, which by ufe becomes a very comfortable practice. The moft un-happy part of the Germans are the tenants of little needy princes; who fqueeze them to keep up their own grandeur; but in general the circumftances of the common people are far preferable to thofe of the French.

The Germans are naturally a frank, honeft, hofpitable people, free from artifice and difguife. The higher orders are ridiculoufly proud of titles, anceftry, and fhew. The Ger-mans, in general, are thought to want animation, as their per-fons promife more vigour and activity than they commonly exert, even in the field of battle. But when commanded by able generals, efpecially the Italians, fuch as Montecuculi and prince Eugene, they have done great things, both againft the Turks and the French. The imperial arms have feldom made any remarkable figure againft either of thofe two nations, or againft the Swedes or Spaniards, when commanded by Ger-man generals. This poffibly might be owing to the arbitrary obftinacy of the court of Vienna; for in the two laft wars the Auftrians exhibited prodigies of military valour and genius.

Induftry, application, and perfeverance, are the great cha-racteriftics of the German nation, efpecially the mechanical part of it. Their works of art would be incredible were they not vifible, efpecially in watch and clock-making, jewelry, turnery, fculpture, drawing, painting, and certain kinds of architecture, fome of which I fhall have occafion to mention. The Germans have been charged with intemperance in eating and drinking, and perhaps not unjuftly, owing to the vaft plenty of their country in wine and provifions of every kind. But thofe practices feem now to be wearing out. At the greateft tables, though the guefts drink pretty freely at dinner, yet the repaft is commonly finifhed by coffee, after three or four public toafts have been drank. But no people have more feafting at marriages, funerals, and birth-days.

The German nobility are generally men of fo much honour, that a fharper in other countries, efpecially in England, meets with

with more credit if he pretends to be a German, rather than of any other nation..

The merchants and tradefmen are very civil and obliging. All the fons of noblemen inherit their fathers titles, which greatly perplexes the heralds and genealogifts of that country. This perhaps is one of the reafons why the German hufbands are not quite fo complaifant as they ought otherwife to be to their ladies, who are not entitled to any preeminence at the table ; nor indeed do they feem to affect it, being far from either ambition or loquacity, though they are faid to be fome-what too fond of gaming. From what has been premifed, it may eafily be conceived, that many of the German nobility, having no other hereditary eftate than a high founding title, eafily enter into their armies, and thofe of other fovereigns. Their fondnefs for title is attended with many other incon-veniencies. Their princes think that the cultivation of their lands, though it may treble their revenue, is below their atten-tion ; and that, as they are a fpecies of beings fuperior to labourers of every kind, they would demean themfelves in being concerned in the improvement of their grounds.

The domeftic diverfions of the Germans are the fame as in England ; billiards, cards, dice, fencing, dancing, and the like. In fummer, people of fafhion repair to places of public refort, and drink the waters. As to their field diverfions, befides their favourite one of hunting, they have bull and bear baiting, and the like. The inhabitants of Vienna live luxu-rioufly, a great part of their time being fpent in feafting and caroufing ; and in winter, when the feveral branches of the Danube are frozen over, and the ground covered with fnow, the ladies take their recreation in fledges of different fhapes, fuch as griffins, tygers, fwans, fcollop-fhells, &c. Here the lady fits, dreffed in velvet lined with rich furs, and adorned with laces and jewels, having on her head a velvet cap; and the fledge is drawn by one horfe, ftag, or other creature, fet off with plumes of feathers, ribbons, and bells. As this diver-fion is taken chiefly in the night-time, fervants ride before the fledge with torches, and a gentleman fitting on the fledge be-hind guides the horfe.

RELIGION.] This is a copious article, but I fhall confine myfelf to what is moft neceffary to be known. Before the re-formation introduced by Luther, the German bifhops were poffeffed (as indeed many of them are at this day) of prodigious power and revenues, and were the tyrants of the emperors as well as the people. Their ignorance was only equalled by their fuperftition. The Bohemians were the firft who had an idea of reformation, and made fo glorious a ftand for many years againft the errors of Rome, that they were indulged in the

liberty

liberty of taking the facrament in both kinds, and other freedoms not tolerated in the Romifh church. This was in a great .meafure owing to Wickliff, an Englifhman, who went much farther in reforming the real errors of popery than Luther himfelf. Wickliff was feconded by John Hufs, and Jerome of Prague, who, notwithftanding the emperor's fafe conduct, were infamoufly burnt at the council of Conftance.

The reformation introduced afterwards by Luther *, of which we have fpoke in the introduction, though it ftruck at the chief abufes in the church of Rome, was thought in fome points (particularly that of confubftantiation, by which the real body of Chrift, as well as the elements of bread and wine, is fuppofed to be taken in the facrament) to be imperfect. Calvinifm †, therefore, or the religion of Geneva (as now practifed in the church of Scotland) was introduced into Germany, and is now the religion of the king of Pruffia, the landgrave of Heffe, and fome other princes, who maintain a parity of orders in the church. Some go fo far as to fay that the numbers of proteftants and papifts in the empire are now almoft equal. Germany, particularly Bohemia, Moravia, and the Palatinate, is overrun with fectaries of all kinds ; and Jews abound in the empire. At prefent, the modes of worfhip and forms of church government are by the proteftant German princes confidered in a civil rather than a religious light. The proteftant clergy are learned and exemplary in their deportment, but the popifh ignorant and libertine.

ARCHBISHOPSEES AND BISHOPSEES.} Thefe are differently reprefented by authors, fome of whom reprefent Vienna as being a fuffragan to the archbifhopfee of Saltzburg ; and others as being an archbifhopric but depending immediately upon the pope. The others are the archbifhop of Mentz, who has under him twelve fuffragans, but one of them, the bifhop of Bamberg, is faid to be exempted from his jurifdiction ; —Triers has three fuffragans ; —Cologne has four ; —Magdeburg has five ; Saltzburg has nine, befides Vienna ; —and Bremen three.

At different periods fince the reformation it has been found expedient, to fatisfy the claims of temporal princes, to fecularize the following bifhopfees, Bremen, Verden, Magdeburg, Halberftadt, Minden, Ofnaburg, (which goes alternately to the houfes of Bavaria and Hanover, and is at prefent held by his Britannic

---

* Born in Saxony, in the year 1483, began to difpute the doctrines of the Romifh church 1517, and died 1546, in the 63d year of his age.

† John Calvin was born in the province of Picardy, in the north of France, anno 1506. Being obliged to fly from that kingdom, he fettled at Geneva in 1539, where he eftablifhed a new form of church difcipline, which was foon after embraced by feveral nations and ftates, who are now denominated Calvinifts, or Prefbyterians. He died at Geneva, in the year 1564 ; and his writings make nine volumes in folio.

Britannic majefty's fecond fon) and Lubec. Such of thofe fees as were archbifhoprics are now confidered as duchies, and the bifhoprics as principalities.

LANGUAGE.]   The Teutonic part of the German tongue is an original language, and has no relation to the Celtic.   It is called High Dutch, and is the mother tongue of all Germany; but varies fo much in its dialect, that the people of one province fcarcely underftand thofe of another.   Latin and French are the moft ufeful languages in Germany, when a traveller is ignorant of High Dutch.

The German Pater-Nofter is as follows : *Unfer Nater, de bu hift in himmel; geheiliget wer dein nahme : zukomm uns dein reich : dein wille gefchete auf erden, wie in himmel; unfer tæglich brod gib uns heut; und vergih uns unfer fchuld als wir vergehen unfern fcaldigern; und fuerro uns nicht in verfuchung fondern elæfe uns von vehel.* Amen.

LEARNING, LEARNED MEN, } No country has produced
    AND UNIVERSITIES. } a greater variety of authors than Germany, and there is no where a more general tafte for reading, efpecially in the proteftant countries.   Printing is encouraged to a fault; every man of letters is an author; they multiply books without number, thoufands of thefefes and difputations are annually publifhed; for no man can be a graduate in their univerfities, who has not publifhed one difputation at leaft.   In this country there are 36 univerfities, of which 17 are proteftant, 17 Roman-catholic, and two mixed; befides a vaft number of colleges, gymnafia, pedagogies, and Latin fchools.   There are alfo many academies and focieties for the promoting the ftudy of natural philofophy, the belles lettres, antiquities, &c. as the Imperial Leopoldine academy of the *naturæ curiofi*; the academy of fciences at Berlin, at Gottingen, at Erfurth, at Leipfic, at Duifburgh, to which we may add the Latin fociety at Gena.   Of the public libraries, the moft celebrated are thofe of Vienna, Wolfenbuttle, Hanover, Gottengen, Weimar, and the council library at Leipfic.   The Germans have written largely upon the Roman and Canon laws; Stahl, Van Swieten, Storck, and Hoffman, have contributed greatly to the improvement of phyfic; Ruvinus and Dillenius of botany; Heifter of anatomy and furgery; Newman, Zewmermann, Pott, and Margraff, of chymiftry. In philofophy, natural and moral, the reputation of Leibnitz, Wolfius, Puffendorf, Thomafius, Otto van Gueriche, and Kepler, is great.   Every prince, baron, and gentleman in Germany is a chymift or natural philofopher.   Germany has alfo produced good political writers, geographers, and hiftorians, of whom Bufhing is the moft voluminous : but they

seem

seem to have no great taste or capacity for works of wit and
entertainment, as poetry, plays, romances, and novels, or
what is called the belles lettres ; but they have had some good
critics and antiquarians. They have one great defect, however, in all their writings, namely, that they are extremely
prolix, dry, voluminous, and mechanical, and know little or
nothing of that valuable art in which some nations excel,
namely, of enlivening their performances, and mixing the
pleasant with the useful. With respect to the fine arts, the
Germans have acquitted themselves tolerably well. Germany
has produced some good painters, architects, sculptors, and
engravers. They even pretend to have been the first inventors
of engraving, etching, and metzotinto, as well as of gunpowder, guns and printing. For the improvement of some of
these arts academies have been established in some parts of
Germany ; at Vienna, in particular, and Berlin are academies
for painting, sculpture and architecture ; at Dresden and
Nurenberg are academies for painting ; and at Ausburgh is
the Imperial Francifcan academy of the fine arts. Germany
has likewise produced some excellent musicians ; Handel,
Bach, and Hasse, of whom Handel stands at the head ; and
it is acknowledged that he arrived at the sublime of music,
but he had not the smallest idea between music and sentimental
expreffion.

CITIES, TOWNS, FORTS, AND OTHER ⎫ This is a copious
   EDIFICES, PUBLIC AND PRIVATE ; ⎬ head in all coun-
   with occafional eftimates of RE- ⎪ tries, but more
   VENUES AND POPULATION. ⎭ particularly so in
Germany, on account of the numerous independent states it
contains. The reader therefore must be contented with the
mention of the most capital places and their peculiarities.

Though Berlin is accounted the capital of all his Pruffian
majefty's dominions, and exhibits perhaps the most illustrious
example of sudden improvement that this age can boast of ;
yet, during the late war, it was found a place of no strength,
and fell twice, almost without refiftance, into the hands of the
Auftrians, who, had it not been for the politenefs of their
generals, and their love of the fine arts, which always preferves
mankind from barbarity and inhumanity, would have levelled
it to the ground.

Berlin lies on the river Spree, and, besides a royal palace,
has many other superb palaces ; it contains fourteen Lutheran,
and eleven Calviniſt churches, besides a popish one. Its streets
and squares are spacious ; its manufacturers of all kinds are
numerous, and well provided : it abounds with theatres,
schools, libraries, and charitable foundations. The number

of

of its inhabitants, according to Busching, in 1755, was 126,661, including the garrison. In the same year, and according to the same author, there were no fewer than, 443 silk-looms, 149 of half-silks, 2858 looms for woollen stuffs, 453 for cotton, 248 for linen, 454 for lace-work, 39 frames for silk stockings, and 310 for worsted ones. They have here manufactures of tapestry, gold and silver lace, and mirrors.

The electorate of Saxony is by nature the richest country in Germany, if not in Europe : it contains 210 walled towns, 61 market towns, and about 3000 villages, according to the latest accounts of the Germans themselves (to which, however, we are not to give an implicit belief) and the revenue, estimating each rix-dollar at four shillings and sixpence, amounts to 1,350,000 l. This sum is so moderate, when compared to the richness of the soil, which, if we are to believe Dr. Busching, produces even diamonds, and almost all the precious stones to be found in the East-Indies and elsewhere, and the variety of splendid manufactures, that I am apt to believe the Saxon princes to have been the most moderate and patriotic of any in Germany.

We can say little more, than has been already said of all fine cities, of Dresden, the elector of Saxony's capital, that its fortifications, palaces, public buildings, churches, and charitable foundations ; and above all, its suburbs are magnificent beyond all expression; that it is beautifully situated on both sides the Elbe ; and that it is the school of Germany, for statuary, painting, enamelling, and carving ; not to mention its mirrors, and founderies for bells and cannon, and its foreign commerce carried on by means of the Elbe. The inhabitants of Dresden, by the latest accounts, amount to 110,000.

The city of Hanover, the capital of that electorate, stands on the river Leine, but is of no great consideration. It contains about 1,200 houses, among which there is an electoral palace. It carries on some manufactures ; and in its neighbourhood lies the palace and elegant gardens of Herenhausen. The dominions of the electorate of Hanover contain about 750,000 people, who live in 58 cities, and 60 market towns, besides villages. The city and suburbs of Bremen, belonging by purchase to the said elector, contains about 50,000 inhabitants, and has a considerable trade by the Weser. The other towns belonging to the said electorate have trade and manufactures ; but, in general, it must be remarked, that the electorate has suffered greatly by the accession of the Hanover family to the crown of Great-Britain. I shall here just mention,

E 4

on

on account of its relation to our royal family, the fecularized bifhopric of Ofnaburg, lying between the rivers Wefer and Ems. The chief city, Ofnaburg, has been long famous all over Europe for the manufacture known by the name of the duchy, and for the manufacture of the beft Weftphalia hams. The whole revenue of the bifhopric amounts to about 30,000 l.

Breflau, the capital of Silefia, which formerly belonged to the kingdom of Bohemia, lies on the river Oder, and is a fine city, where all fects of Chriftians and Jews are tolerated, but the magiftracy is Lutheran. Since Silefia fell under the Pruffian dominion, its trade is greatly improved, though very inconfiderable before. The manufactures of Silefia, which principally center at Breflau, are numerous. The revenue of the whole is by fome faid to bring his Pruffian majefty in near a million fterling; but this fum feems to be exaggerated, if, as other authors of good note write, it never brought into the houfe of Auftria above 500,000 l. yearly.

Vienna is the capital of the circle of Auftria, and being the refidence of the emperor, is fuppofed to be the capital of Germany. It is a noble and a ftrong city, and the princes of the houfe of Auftria have omitted nothing that could contribute to its grandeur and riches. The two Auftrias, and the hereditary dominions of that houfe, are by nature fo well furnifhed with all materials for the luxuries, the conveniencies, and the neceffaries of life, that foreign importations into this city are almoft totally prohibited. Vienna contains an excellent univerfity, a bank, which is in the management of her own magiftrates, and a court of commerce immediately fubject to the aulic council. Its religious buildings, with the walks and gardens, occupy a fixth part of the town; but the fuburbs are larger than the city. It would be endlefs to enumerate the many palaces, two of which are imperial, of this capital; its fquares, academies, and libraries; and, among others, the fine one of prince Eugene, with his and the imperial cabinets of curiofities. Among its rich convents is one for the Scotch nation, built in honour of their countryman St. Colman, the patron of Auftria; and one of the fix gates of this city is called the Scots gate, in remembrance of fome notable exploit performed there by the troops of that nation. The inhabitants, if we are to believe Dr. Bufching, are between 180,000 and 200,000; and the encouragement given them by their fovereigns, has rendered Vienna the rendezvous of all the nations round.

After all that has been faid of this magnificent city, the moft candid and fenfible of thofe who have vifited it, are far from being lavifh in its praife. The ftreets, excepting fome

in

in the fuburbs, are narrow and dirty ; the houfes and furniture of the citizens are greatly difproportioned to the magnificence of the palaces, fquares, and other public buildings ;
but above all, the exceffive impofts laid by the houfe of Auftria
upon every commodity in its dominions, muft always keep the
manufacturing part of their fubjects poor. His prefent imperial majefty feems to be fenfible of truths which were plain
to all the world but his predeceffors and their counfellors : he
examines things with his own eyes, and has defcended from
that haughtinefs of demeanour which rendered the imperial
court fo long difagreeable, and indeed ridiculous, to the reft
of Europe. ' In general, the condition of the Auftrian fubjects
has been greatly meliorated fince his acceffion to the imperial
throne ; but in this he acts agreeably to the fentiments of
his mother, who is the immediate poffeffor of thofe vaft dominions.

ANTIQUITIES AND CURIOSITIES }   I have, in defcribing
   NATURAL AND ARTIFICIAL. }   the mineral and other
fprings, anticipated great part of this article, which is of itfelf
very copious. Every court of Germany produces a cabinet of
curiofities, artificial and natural, antient and modern. The
tun at Heidelburg holds 800 hogfheads, and is generally full
of the beft Rhenifh wine, from which ftrangers are feldom
fuffered to retire fober. Vienna itfelf is a curiofity ; for here
you fee the greateft variety of inhabitants that is to be met
with any where, as Greeks, Tranfylvanians, Sclavonians,
Turks, Tartars, Hungarians, Croats, Germans, Poles, Spaniards, French, and Italians, in their proper habits. The
imperial library at Vienna, is a great literary rarity on account
of its ancient manufcripts. It contains upwards of 80,000
volumes, among which are many valuable manufcripts in
Hebrew, Syriac, Arabic, Turkifh, Armenian, Coptic, and
Chinefe ; but the antiquity of fome of them is queftionable,
particularly a New Teftament in Greek, faid to have been
written 1,500 years ago, in gold letters, upon purple. Here
are likewife many thoufand Greek, Roman, and Gothic coins
and medals ; with a vaft collection of other curiofities in art
and nature. The vaft Gothic palaces, cathedrals, caftles,
and above all, town-houfes, in Germany, are very curious :
they ftrike the beholder with an idea of rude magnificence ;
and fometimes they have an effect that is preferable even to
Greek architecture. The chief houfes in great cities and villages have the fame appearance, probably, as they had 400
years ago ; and their fortifications generally confift of a
brick-wall, trenches filled with water, and baftions or half-
moons.

Next

Next to the lakes and waters, the caves and rocks are the chief natural curiofities of Germany. Mention is made of a cave, near Blackenburg in Hartz-foreſt, of which none have yet found the end, though many have advanced into it for 20 miles ; but the moſt remarkable curiofity of that kind is near Hammelen, about 30 miles from Hanover, where at the mouth of a cave ſtands a monument which commemorates the loſs of 130 children, who were there ſwallowed up, in 1284. Though this fact is very ſtrongly atteſted, it has been diſputed by ſome critics. Frequent mention is made of two rocks near Blackenburg, exactly repreſenting two monks in their proper habits ; and of many ſtones which ſeem to be petrifactions of fiſhes, frogs, trees, and leaves.

COMMERCE AND MANUFACTURES.] Germany has vaſt advantages in point of commerce, from its fituation, in the heart of Europe, and perforated as it were with great rivers. Its native materials for commerce (befides the mines and mine-rals I have already mentioned) are hemp, hops, flax, aniſe, cummins, tobacco, ſaffron, madder, truffles, variety of ex-cellent roots and pot-herbs, and fine fruits, equal to thoſe of France and Italy. Germany exports to other countries corn, tobacco, horſes, lean cattle, butter, cheeſe, honey, wax, wines, linen, and woollen, yarn, ribbons, filk and cotton ſtuffs, toys, turnery wares in wood, metals, and ivory, goat-ſkins, wool, timber, both for ſhip-building and houſes, can-non, and bullets, bombs and bomb-ſhells, iron plates and ſtoves, tinned plates, ſteel work, copper, braſs-wire, porce-lain, the fineſt upon earth, earthen-ware, glaſſes, mirrors, hog's briſtles, mum, beer, tartar, ſmalts, zaffer, Pruffian blue, printer's ink, and many other things. Some think that the balance of trade between England and Germany is to the diſadvantage of the former ; but others are of a different opinion, as they cannot import coarſe woollen manufactures, and ſeveral other commodities, ſo cheap from any other coun-try.

The revocation of the edict of Nantes, by Lewis XIV. which obliged the French proteſtants to ſettle in different parts of Europe, was of infinite ſervice to the German manufactures. They now make velvets, filks, ſtuffs of all kinds, fine and coarſe ; linen and thread, and every thing neceſſary for wear, to great perfection. The porcelain of Meiſſen, in the electo-rate of Saxony, and its paintings, exceed that of all the world.

TRADING COMPANIES.] The Aſiatic company of Emb-den, eſtabliſhed by his preſent Pruffian majeſty, is, excluſive of the Hanſeatic league, the only commercial company in

Germany; but in the great cities very large extenfive partner-
fhips in trade fubfift.

CONSTITUTION AND GOVERNMENT.] Almoft every prince
in Germany (and there are about 300 of them) is arbitrary
with regard to the government of his own eftates, but the
whole of them form a great confederacy, governed by political
laws, at the head of which is the emperor, and whofe power
in the collective body or the diet, is not directorial but executive, and even that gives him vaft influence. The fupreme
power in Germany is in the diet, which is compofed of the
emperor, or in his abfence, of his commiffary, and of the three
colleges of the empire. The firft of thefe is the electoral college; the fecond is the college of princes; and the third, the
college of imperial towns.

The dignity of the empire, though elective, has for fome
centuries belonged to the houfe of Auftria, as being the moft
powerful of the German princes; but by French management
upon the death of Charles VI. grandfather, by the mother's
fide, to the prefent emperor, the elector of Bavaria was chofen
to that dignity, and died, as is fuppofed, of heart-break, after
a fhort uncomfortable reign. The power of the emperor is
regulated by the capitulation he figns at his election; and the
perfon, who in his life-time is chofen king of the Romans,
fucceeds without a new election to the empire. He can confer
titles and enfranchifements upon cities and towns, but as emperor he can levy no taxes, nor make war nor peace without
the confent of the diet. When that confent is obtained, every
prince muft contribute his quota of men and money, as valued
in the matriculation roll, though perhaps, as an elector or
prince, he may efpoufe a different fide from that of the diet.
This forms the intricacy of the German conftitution, for
George II. of England was obliged to furnifh his quota againft
the houfe of Auftria, and the king of Pruffia, while he was
fighting for them both. The emperor claims a precedency
for his ambaffadors in all chriftian courts.

The electors of the empire are nine in number. Each has
a particular office in the imperial court, and they have the fole
election of the emperor. They are in order,

Firft, The archbifhop of Mentz, who is high chancellor of
the empire when in Germany.

Second, The archbifhop of Treves, who is high chancellor
of the empire in France.

Third, The archbifhop of Cologne, who is the fame in
Italy.

The king, or rather elector of Bohemia, who is cup-
bearer.

The

· The elector of Bavaria, who is grand fewer, or officer who
serves out the feafts.

The elector of Saxony, who is great marfhal of the empire.

The elector of Brandenburg (now king of Pruffia) who is
great chamberlain.

The elector Palatine, who is great fteward; and,

The elector of Hanover, (king of Great-Britain) who
claims the part of arch-treafurer.

It is neceffary for the emperor before he calls a diet to have
the advice of thofe members ; and during the vacancy of the
imperial throne the electors of Saxony and Bavaria have jurifdiction, the former over the northern, and the latter over the
fouthern circles.

The ecclefiaftical princes are as abfolute as the temporal
ones in their feveral dominions. The chief of thefe, befides
the three ecclefiaftical electors already mentioned, are the
archbifhop of Saltzburg, the bifhops of Liege, Munfter,
Spire, Worms, Wirtfburg, Strafburg, Oinaburg, Bamberg,
and Paderborn. Befides thefe are many other ecclefiaftical
princes. Germany abounds with many abbots and abbefies,
whofe jurifdictions are likewife abfolute ; and fome of them
very confiderable, and all of them are chofen by their feveral
chapters. The chief of the fecular princes are the landgrave
of Heff, the dukes of Brunfwick Wolfenbuttel, Wirtemberg,
Mecklenburgh, Saxe-Gotha, the marquiffes of Baden and
Culmbach, with the princes of Naffau, Anhalt, Furftenburg,
and many others, who have all high titles, and are fovereigns
in their own dominions. The free cities are likewife fovereign ftates ; thofe which are imperial, or compofe a part of
the diet, bear the imperial eagle in their arms; thofe which
are Hanfe-towns, of which we have fpoken in the Introduction, have ftill great privileges and immunities, but they fubfift no longer as a political body.

The imperial chamber, and that of Vienna, which is better
known by the name of the Aulic-council, are the two fupreme
courts for determining the great caufes of the empire, arifing between its refpective members. The imperial council confifts of
50 judges or affeffors. The prefident and four of them are appointed by the emperor, and each of the electors chufe one, and
the other princes and ftates the reft. This court is at prefent held
at Wetzlar, but formerly it refided at Spire ; and caufes may
be brought before it by appeal. The aulic-council was originally no better than a revenue court of the dominions of the
houfe of Auftria. As that family's power encreafed, the jurifdiction of the aulic-council was extended ; and at laft, to the
great difguft of the princes of the empire, it ufurped upon the

powers

powers of the imperial chamber, and even of the diet. It confifts, of a prefident, a vice-chancellor, a vice-prefident, and a certain number of aulic-counfellors, of whom fix are proteftants, befides other officers, but the emperor in fact is mafter of the court.

Thefe courts follow the ancient laws of the empire for their guides, the golden bull, the pacification of Pafiau, and the civil law.

Befides thefe courts of juftice, each of the nine circles I have already mentioned has a director to take care of the peace and order of the circle. Thefe directors are commonly as follow. For Weftphalia, the bifhop of Munfter, or duke of Neuburg. For Lower Saxony, the elector of Hanover or Brandenburg. For Upper Saxony, the elector of Saxony. For the Lower Rhine, the archbifhop of Mentz. For the Upper Rhine, the elector Palatine or bifhop of Worms. For Franconia, the bifhop of Bamburg, or marquis of Culmbach. For Suabia, the duke of Wirtemberg, or bifhop of Conftance. For Bavaria, the elector of Bavaria, or archbifhop of Saltzburg; and for Auftria, the archduke of Auftria, his imperial majefty.

After, upon any great emergency, the votes of the diet are collected, and fentence pronounced, the emperor by his prero-gative commits the execution of it to a particular prince or princefs, whofe troops live at free quarter upon the eftates of the delinquent party, and he is obliged to make good all expences; upon the whole, the conftitution of the Germanic body is of itfelf a ftudy of no fmall difficulty. But however plaufibly invented the feveral checks upon the imperial power may be, it is certain that the houfe of Auftria has more than once endangered the liberties of the empire, and that they have been faved by France. At prefent a great power, the houfe of Brandenburg, has ftarted up to balance the Auftrian greatnefs; and there feems to be no great appearance of any internal commotions among the princes of the empire, a circumftance that is extremely favourable to the tranquillity of Europe, and the intereft of Great-Britain in particular. Before I clofe this head, it may be neceffary to inform the reader of the meaning of a term which has of late frequently appeared in the German hiftory, I mean that of the *Pragmatic Sanction*. This is no other than a provifion made by the emperor Charles VI. for preferving the indivifibility of the Auftrian dominions in the perfon of the next defcendant of the laft poffeffor, whether male or female. This provifion has been often difputed by other branches of the houfe of Auftria, who have been occafionally fupported by France from political views, though the

pragmatic

pragmatic fanction is ftrongly guarantied by almoft all the powers of Europe. The late emperor, elector of Bavaria, and the late king of Poland attempted to overthrow it, as being defcended from the daughters of the emperor Jofeph, elder brother to Charles VI. It has likewife been again and again oppofed by the court of Spain.

Few of the territories of the German princes are fo large as to be affigned to viceroys, to be opprefled and fleeced at pleafure; nor are they without redrefs when they fuffer any grievance; they may appeal to the general diet or great council of the empire for relief. Whereas in France the lives and fortunes of the fubject are entirely at the difpofal of the grand monarch. The fubjects of the petty princes in Germany are generally the moft unhappy; for thefe princes, affecting the grandeur and fplendor of the more powerful, in the number and appearance of their officers and domeftics, in their palaces, gardens, pictures, curiofities, guards, bands of mufic, tables, drefs, and furniture, are obliged to fupport all this vain pomp and parade at the expence of their vaffals and dependants. With refpect to the burghers and peafants of Germany, the former in many places enjoy great privileges; the latter alfo, in fome parts, for inftance, in Franconia, Swabia, and on the Rhine, are generally a free people, or perform only certain fervices to their fuperiors, and only pay taxes; whereas in the marquifate of Brandenburg, Pomerania, Lufatia, Moravia, Bohemia, Auftria, &c. they may juftly be denominated flaves, though in different degrees.

REVENUES.] The only revenue falling under this head is that of the emperor, who as fuch has an annual income of about 5 or 6000 pounds fterling, arifing from fome inconfiderable fiefs in the Black Foreft. The Auftrian revenues are immenfe, and are thought to amount to 7,000,000 fterling in Germany and Italy, a fum that goes far in thofe countries. The late king of Pruffia, whofe revenues were not near fo extenfive as thofe of his prefent majefty, though he maintained a large army, was fo good an œconomift that he left 7,000,000 fterling in his coffers; and fome have thought that Silefia alone brings half a million fterling every year to this king. To behold the magnificence of many of the German courts, a ftranger is apt to conceive very high ideas of the incomes of their princes, which is owing to the high price of money in that country, and confequently the low price of provifions and manufactures. In fact, though it is plain that fome princes have much larger revenues than others, yet we cannot fpeak with any tolerable precifion on a fubject of fuch variety and

and uncertainty, and which comprehends so many independent states.

MILITARY STRENGTH.] During the two last wars, very little regard was paid, in carrying them on, to the ancient German constitutions, the whole management being engrossed by the head of the house of Austria. The elector of Mentz keeps what is called a matriculation book or register, which among other letters contain the assessments of men and money, which every prince and state, who are members of the empire, is to advance when the army of the empire takes the field. The contributions in money are called Roman months, on account of the monthly assessments paid to the emperors when they visited Rome. Those assessments however are subject to great mutability. It is sufficient here to say, that upon a moderate computation the secular princes of the empire can bring to the field 379,000 men, and the ecclesiastical 74,500, in all 453,500; of those the emperor, as head of the house of Austria, is supposed to furnish 90,000.

The elector of Mentz may maintain	6000
The elector of Triers	6000
The elector of Cologne	6000
The bishop of Munster	8000
The bishop of Liege	8000
The archbishop of Saltzburg	8000
The bishop of Wurtzburg	2000
The bishop of Bamburg	5000
The bishop of Paderborn	3000
The bishop of Osnabrug	2500
The abbot of Fulda	6000
The other bishoprics of the empire	6000
The abbies and provostships of the empire	8000
Total of the ecclesiastical princes	74,500
The emperor, for Hungary	30000
—————For Bohemia, Silesia, and Moravia	30000
—————For Austria, and other dominions	30000
The king of Prussia	40000
The elector of Saxony	25000
The elector Palatine	15000
The duke of Wirtemburg	15000
The landgrave of Hesse Cassel	15000
The prince of Baden	10000
The elector of Hanover	30000
The duke of Holstein	12000
The duke of Mecklenburg	15000

The

The prince of Anhalt	—	—	6000
The prince of Lawenburg	—	—	6000
The elector of Bavaria	—	—	30000
The dukes of Saxony	—	—	10000
The prince of Naſſau	—	—	10000
The other princes and imperial towns	—	—	50000

The ſecular princes	—	—	379000
The eccleſiaſtical princes	—	—	74500

453,500

IMPERIAL, ROYAL, AND OTHER TITLES, ARMS, AND ORDERS.} The emperor of Germany pretends to be ſucceſſor to the emperors of Rome, and has long, on that account, been admitted to a tacit precedency on all public occaſions among the powers of Europe. Auſtria is but an archdukedom; nor has he, as the head of that houſe, a vote in the election of emperor, which is limited to Bohemia. Innumerable are the titles of principalities, dukedoms, baronies, and the like, with which he is veſted as archduke. The arms of the empire are a black eagle with two heads, hovering, with expanded wings, in a field of gold; and over the heads of the eagle is ſeen the imperial crown. It would be equally uſeleſs as difficult to enumerate all the different quarterings and armorial bearings of the archducal family. Every elector, and indeed every independent prince of any importance in Germany, claims a right of inſtituting orders; but the emperors pretend that they are not admiſſible unleſs confirmed by them. The emperors of Germany, as well as the kings of Spain, confer the order of the Golden Fleece, as deſcended from the houſe of Burgundy. The empreſs dowager Eleonora, in 1662 and 1666, created two orders of ladies, or female knights; and the preſent empreſs-queen inſtituted the order of St. Tereſa.

HISTORY.] The manners of the ancient Germans are deſcribed by the elegant and manly pencil of Tacitus, the Roman hiſtorian. They were a brave and independant race of men, and peculiarly diſtinguiſhed by their love of liberty and arms. They oppoſed the force of the Roman empire, not in its origin or in its decline, but after it had arrived at maturity, and ſtill continued in its full vigour. The country was divided into a number of principalities, independant of each other, though occaſionally connected by a military union for defending themſelves againſt ſuch enemies as threatened the liberty of them all. In this ſituation Germany remained, notwithſtanding the efforts of particular chieftains, or princes,

to

to reduce the reft into fubjection, until the beginning of the ninth century: then it was that Charlemaigne, one of thofe excentric and fuperior geniuffes who fometimes ftart up in a barbarous age, firft extended his military power, and afterwards his civil authority, over the whole of this empire. The pofterity of Charlemaigne inherited the empire of Germany until the year 880, at which time the different princes affuming their original independence, rejected the Carlovinian line, and placed Arnulph, king of Bavaria, on the throne. Since this time, Germany has ever been confidered as an elective monarchy. Princes of different families, according to the prevalence of their intereft and arms, have mounted the throne. Of thefe, the moft confiderable, until the Auftrian line acquired the imperial power, were the houfes of Saxony, Franconia, and Swabia. The reigns of thefe emperors contain nothing more remarkable than the contefts between them and the popes. From hence, in the beginning of the thirteenth century, arofe the factions of the Guelphs and Ghibelines, of which the former was attached to the popes, and the latter to the emperor; and both, by their virulence and inveteracy, tended to difquiet the empire for feveral ages. The emperors too were often at war with the infidels, and fometimes, as happens in all elective kingdoms, with one another about the fucceffion. But what more deferves the attention of a judicious reader than all thofe noify but uninterefting difputes, is the progrefs of government in Germany, which was in fome meafure oppofite to that of the other kingdoms of Europe. When the empire, raifed by Charlemaigne, fell afunder, all the different independent princes affumed the right of election; and thofe now diftinguifhed by the name of electors, had no peculiar or legal influence in appointing a fucceffor to the imperial throne: they were only the officers of the king's houfhold, his fecretary, his fteward, chaplain, marfhal, or mafter of his horfe, &c. By degrees, however, as they lived near the king's perfon, and had, like all the other princes, independant territories belonging to them, they encreafed their influence and authority; and in the reign of Otho III. 984, acquired the fole right of electing the emperor. Thus while in the other kingdoms of Europe, the dignity of the great lords, who were all originally allodial, or independant barons, was diminifhed by the power of the king, as in France, and by the influence of the people, as in Great Britain; in Germany, on the other hand, the power of the electors was raifed upon the ruins of the emperor's fupremacy, and of the peoples jurifdiction. In 1440, Frederic III. duke of Auftria, was elected emperor, and the imperial dignity continued in the male line of that family for three hundred years. His succeffor, Maximilian, married the heirefs of Charles, duke of Burgundy, whereby Burgundy, and the feventeen provinces of the Netherlands, were annex d to the houfe of Auftria. Charles V. grandfon of Maximilian, and heir to the kingdom of Spain, was elected emp or in the year 1519. Under him Mexico and Peru were conquered by the Spaniards, and in his reign happened the reformation of religion in feveral parts of Germany, which however was not confirmed by public authority till the year 1648, by the treaty of Weftphalia, and in the reign of Ferdinand III. The reign of Charles V. was continually difturbed by his wars with the German princes and French king, Francis I. Though fuccefsful in the beginning of his reign, his good fortune, towards the conclufion of it, began to forfake him ; which, with other reafons, occafioned his abdication of the crown.

His brother, Ferdinand I. who in 1558 fucceeded to the throne, proved a moderate prince with regard to religion. He had the addrefs to get his fon Maximilian declared king of the Romans in his own life time, and died in 1564. By his laft will he ordered, that if either his own male iffue, or that of his brother Charles, fhould fail, his Auftrian eftates fhould revert to his fecond daughter, Anne, wife to the elector of Bavaria, and her iffue. I mention this deftination, as it gave rife to the late oppofition made by the houfe of Bavaria to the pragmatic fanction, in favour of the emprefs-queen of Hungary, on the death of her father Charles VI. The reign of Maximilian II. was difturbed with internal commotions, and an invafion from the Turks; but he died in peace, in 1576. He was fucceeded by his fon Rodolph, who was involved in wars with the Hungarians, and in differences with his brother Matthias, to whom he ceded Hungary and Auftria in his life time. He was fucceeded in the empire by Matthias, under whom the reformers, who went under the names of Lutherans and Calvinifts, were fo much divided among themfelves, as to threaten the empire with a civil war. The ambition of Matthias, at laft, reconciled them ; but the Bohemians revolted, and threw the imperial commiffaries out of a window at Prague. This gave rife to a ruinous war which lafted thirty years. Matthias thought to have exterminated both parties, but they formed a confederacy, called the Evangelic League, which was counterbalanced by a catholic league.

Matthias dying in 1618, was fucceeded by his coufin, Ferdinand II. but the Bohemians offered their crown to Frederic the elector Palatine, the moft powerful proteftant prince in Germany, and fon-in-law to his Britannic majefty James I.

That

That prince was incautious enough to accept of the crown ; but he loſt it, by being entirely defeated by the duke of Bavaria and the imperial generals, at the battle of Prague, and he himſelf was deprived of his electorate, the beſt part of which was given to the duke of Bavaria. The proteſtant princes of Germany, however, had among them at this time many able commanders, who were at the head of armies, and continued the war with wonderful obſtinacy; among them were the margrave of Baden Durlach ; Chriſtian, duke of Brunſwic, and count Mansfeld : the laſt was one of the beſt generals of the age. Chriſtiern IV. king of Denmark, declared for them ; and Richelieu, the French miniſter, was not fond of ſeeing the houſe of Auſtria aggrandized. The emperor, on the other hand, had excellent generals ; and Chriſtiern, having put himſelf at the head of the evangelic league, was defeated by Tilly, an imperialiſt of great reputation in war. Ferdinand made ſo moderate a uſe of his advantages obtained over the proteſtants, that they formed a freſh confederacy at Leipſic, of which the celebrated Guſtavus Adolphus, king of Sweden, was the head. I have already deſcribed his amazing victories and progreſs, when he was killed at the battle of Lutzen, in 1632. But the proteſtant cauſe did not die with him. He had brought up a ſet of heroes, ſuch as the duke of Saxe Weimar, Torſtenſon, Bannier and others, who ſhook the Auſtrian power, till under the mediation of Sweden, a general peace was concluded among all the powers at war, at Munſter, in the year 1648 ; which forms the baſis of the preſent political ſyſtem of Europe.

Ferdinand II. was ſucceeded by his ſon Ferdinand III. who died in 1657, and was ſucceeded by the emperor Leopold, a ſevere, unamiable, and not very fortunate prince. He had two great powers to contend with, France on the one ſide, and the Turks on the other ; and was a loſer in his war with both. France took from him Alſace, and many other frontier places of the empire ; and the Turks would have taken Vienna, had not the ſiege been raiſed by John Sobieſki, king of Poland. Prince Eugene, of Savoy, was a young adventurer in arms about the year 1697 ; and being one of the imperial generals, gave the Turks the firſt checks they received in Hungary. The empire, however, could not have withſtood the power of France, had not the prince of Orange, afterwards king William III. of England, laid the foundation of the grand confederacy againſt the French power, the conſequences of which have been already deſcribed. The Hungarians, ſecretly encouraged by the French, and exaſperated by the

F 2   unſeel-

unfeeling tyranny of Leopold, were ftill in arms, under the protection of the Porte, when that prince died in 1705.

He was fucceeded by his fon Jofeph, who put the electors of Cologne and Bavaria to the ban of the empire ; but being very ill ferved by prince Lewis of Baden, general of the empire, the French partly recovered their affairs, notwithftanding their repeated defeats. The duke of Marlborough had not all the fuccefs he expected or deferved. Jofeph himfelf was fufpected of a defign to fubvert the Germanic liberties ; and it was plain by his conduct, that he expected England fhould take the labouring oar in the war, which was to be entirely carried on for his benefit. The Englifh were difgufted at his flownefs and felfifhnefs ; but he died in 1711, before he had reduced the Hungarians ; and leaving no male iffue, he was fucceeded in the empire by his brother, Charles VI. whom the allies were endeavouring to place on the throne of Spain, in oppofition to Philip, duke of Anjou, grandfon to Lewis XIV.

When the peace of Utrecht took place in 1713, Charles at firft made a fhew as if he would continue the war, but found himfelf unable, now that he was forfaken by the Englifh. He therefore was obliged to conclude a peace with France at Baden in 1714, that he might attend the progrefs of the Turks in Hungary, where they received a total defeat from prince Eugene, at the battle of Peterwaradin. They received another of equal importance from the fame general in 1717, before Belgrade, which fell into the hands of the imperialifts ; and next year the peace of Paffarowitz, between them and the Turks, was concluded. Charles employed every minute of his leifure in making arrangements for encreafing and preferving his hereditary dominions in Italy and the Mediterranean. Happily for him, the crown of Britain devolved to the houfe of Hanover, an event which gave him a very decifive weight in Europe, by the connections between George I. and II. in the empire. Charles was fenfible of this, and carried matters with fo high a hand, that about the years 1724 and 1725, a breach enfued between him and George I. and fo unfteady was the fyftem of affairs all over Europe at that time, that the capital powers often changed their old alliances, and concluded new ones contradictory to their intereft. Without entering into particulars, it is fufficient to obferve, that the fafety of Hanover, and its aggrandizement, was the main object of the Britifh court ; as that of the emperor was the eftablifhment of the pragmatic fanction, in favour of his daughter, the prefent emprefs queen, he having no male iffue. Mutual conceffions upon thofe great points, reftored a good underftanding between

George

George II. and the emperor Charles ; and the elector of Saxony being prevailed upon by the purport of gaining the throne of Poland, relinquifhed the great claims he had upon the Auftrian fucceffion.

The emperor, after this, had very bad fuccefs in a war he entered into with the Turks, which he had undertaken chiefly to indemnify himfelf for the great facrifices he had made in Italy to the princes of the houfe of Bourbon. Prince Eugene was then dead, and he had no general to fupply his place. The fyftem of France, however, under cardinal Fleury, happened at that time to be pacific, and fhe obtained for him, from the Turks, a better peace, than he had reafon to expect. Charles, to keep the German and other European powers eafy, had, before his death, given his eldeft daughter, the prefent emprefs-queen, in marriage to the duke of Lorrain, a prince who could bring no acceffion of power to the Auftrian family. Charles died in 1740.

He was no fooner in the grave, than all he had fo long laboured for muft have been overthrown, had it not been for the firmnefs of George II. The pragmatic fanction was attacked on all hands. The young king of Pruffia entered, and conquered with an irrefiftible army, Silefia, which he faid had been wrongfully difmembered from his family. The king of Spain and the elector of Bavaria fet up claims directly incompatible with the pragmatic fanction, and in this they were joined by France ; though all thofe powers had folemnly guarantied it. The imperial throne, after a confiderable vacancy, was filled up by the elector of Bavaria, who took the title of Charles VII. in January 1742. The French poured their armies into Bohemia, where they took Prague ; and the queen of Hungary, to take off the weight of Pruffia, was forced to cede to that prince the moft valuable part of the duchy of Silefia by a formal treaty.

Her youth, her beauty, and fufferings, and the noble fortitude with which fhe bore them, touched the hearts of the Hungarians, into whofe arms fhe threw herfelf and her little fon ; and though they had been always remarkable for their difaffection to the houfe of Auftria, they declared unanimoufly in her favour. Her generals drove the French out of Bohemia ; and George II. at the head of an Englifh and Hanoverian army, gained the battle of Dettingen, in 1743. Charles VII. was at this time miferable on the imperial throne, and would have given the queen of Hungary almoft her own terms ; but fhe haughtily and impoliticly rejected all accommodation, though advifed to it by his Britannic majefty, her beft, and indeed only friend. This obftinacy gave a colour for the king
of

of Pruffia to invade Bohemia, under pretence of fupporting the imperial dignity : but though he took Prague, and fubdued the greateft part of the kingdom, he was not fupported by the French ; upon which he abandoned all his conquefts, and retired to Silefia. This event confirmed the obftinacy of the queen of Hungary, who came to an accommodation with the emperor, that fhe might recover Silefia. Soon after, his imperial majefty, in the beginning of the year 1745, died ; and the duke of Lorrain, then grand duke of Tufcany, confort to her Hungarian majefty, after furmounting fome difficulties, was chofen emperor.

The bad fuccefs of the allies againft the French and Bavarians in the Low Countries, and the lofs of the battle of Fontenoy, retarded the operations of the emprefs-queen againft his Pruffian majefty. The latter beat the emperor's brother, prince Charles of Lorrain, who had before driven the Pruffians out of Bohemia ; and the conduct of the emprefs-queen was fuch, that his Britannic majefty thought proper to guarantee to him the poffeffion of Silefia, as ceded by treaty. Soon after, his Pruffian majefty pretended that he had difcovered a fecret convention which had been entered into between the emprefs-queen, the emprefs of Ruffia, and the king of Poland, as elector of Saxony, to ftrip him of his dominions, and to divide them among themfelves. Upon this his Pruffian majefty, all of a fudden, drove the king of Poland out of Saxony, defeated his troops, and took poffeffion of Drefden ; which he held till a treaty was made under the mediation of his Britannic majefty, by which the king of Pruffia acknowledged the duke of Lorrain, now great duke of Tufcany, for emperor. The war, however, continued in the Low Countries, not only to the difadvantage, but to the difcredit of the Auftrians and Dutch, till it was finifhed by the treaty of Aix-la-Chapelle, in April 1748. By that treaty, Silefia was once more guaranteed to the king of Pruffia. It was not long before that monarch's jealoufies were renewed and verified ; and the emprefs of Ruffia's views falling in with thofe of the emprefs-queen, and the king of Poland, who were unnaturally fupported by France in their new fchemes, a frefh war was kindled in the empire. The king of Pruffia declared againft the admiffion of the Ruffians into Germany, and his Britannic majefty againft that of the French. Upon thofe two principles all former differences between thefe monarchs were forgotten, and the Britifh parliament agreed to pay an annual fubfidy of 670,000 l. to his Pruffian majefty during the continuance of the war, the flames of which were now rekindled with more fury than ever.

His

His Pruffian majefty once more broke into Saxony, defeated the imperial general Brown at the battle of Lowofitz, forced the Saxons to lay down their arms, though almoft impregnably fortified at Pirna, and the elector of Saxony fled to his regal dominions in Poland. After this, his Pruffian majefty was put to the ban of the empire ; and the French poured, by one quarter, their armies, as the Ruffians did by another, into the empire. The conduct of his Pruffian majefty on this occafion is the moft amazing that is to be met with in hiftory. He broke once more into Bohemia with inconceivable rapidity, and defeated an army of near 100,000 Auftrians, under general Brown, who was killed, as the brave marfhal Schwerin was on the fide of the Pruffians. He then befieged Prague, and plied it with a moft tremendous artillery ; but juft as he was beginning to imagine that his troops were invincible, they were defeated at Collin, by the Auftrian general Daun, and obliged to raife the fiege, and to fall back upon Eifenach. The operations of the war now multiplied every day. The imperialifts, under count Daun, were formed into excellent troops : but they were beat at the battle of Liffa, and the Pruffians took Breflau, and obtained many other great advantages. The Ruffians, after entering Germany, gave a new turn to the afpect of the war ; and the cautious, yet enterprizing genius of count Daun, laid his Pruffian majefty under infinite difficulties, notwithftanding all his amazing victories. At firft he defeated the Ruffians at Zorndorff ; but an attack made upon his army, in the night time, by count Daun, at Hockkirchen, had almoft proved fatal to his affairs, though he retrieved them with admirable prefence of mind. He was obliged, however, to facrifice Saxony, for the fafety of Silefia ; and it has been obferved that few periods of hiftory afford fuch room for reflection as this campaign did ; fix fieges were raifed almoft at the fame time ; that of Colberg, by the Ruffians ; that of Leipfic, by the duke of Deux-Ponts, who commanded the army of the empire ; that of Drefden, by Daun ; thofe of Neifs, Cofel, and Torgau, by the Auftrians.

Brevity obliges me to omit many capital fcenes which paffed at the fame time in Germany, between the French, who were driven out of Hanover, and the Englifh, or their allies. The operations on both fides are of little importance to hiftory, becaufe nothing was done that was decifive, though extremely burdenfome and bloody to Great-Britain. It falls more within my plan to mention the ingratitude of the emprefs-queen to his Britannic majefty, and his allies and generals, who were threatened with the ban of the empire. The Ruffians had taken pof-

feffion

seffion of all the kingdom of Pruffia, and laid fiege to Colbe g, the only port of his Pruffian majefty in the Baltic. Till then, he had entertained too mean an opinion of the Ruffians, but he focn found them by far the moft formidable enemies he had, as they were advancing, under count Soltikoff, in a body of 100,000 men, to Silefia. In this diftrefs he acted with a courage and refolution that bordered upon defpair, but was, at laft, totally defeated by the Ruffians, with the lofs of 20,000 of his beft men, in a battle near Frankfort. He became now the tennis-ball of fortune. Succeeding defeats feemed to announce his ruin, and all avenues towards peace were fhut up. He had loft, fince the firft of October 1756, the great marfhal Keith, and 40 brave generals, befides thofe who were wounded and made prifoners. At Landfhut the imperial general, Laudohn, defeated his army under Fouquet, on which he had great dependence, and thereby opened to the Auftrians a ready gate into Silefia. None but his Pruffian majefty would have thought of continuing the war under fuch repeated loffes ; but every defeat he received feemed to give him frefh fpirits. It is not perhaps very eafy to account for the inactivity of his enemies after his defeat near Frankfort, but by the jealoufy which the imperial generals entertained of their Ruffian allies. They had taken Berlin, and laid the inhabitants under pecuniary contributions ; but towards the end of the campaign, he defeated the imperialifts in the battle of Torgau, in which count Daun was wounded. This was the beft fought action the king of Pruffia had ever been engaged in, but it coft him 10,000 of his beft troops, and was attended with no great confequences in his favour. New reinforcements which arrived every day from Ruffia, the taking of Colberg by the Ruffians, and of Schweidnitz by the Auftrian, was on the poin s of compleating his ruin, when his moft formidable enemy, the emprefs of Ruffia, died, January 5, 1762 ; George II. had died on the 25th of October, 1760.

The deaths of thofe illuftrious perfonages were followed by great confequences. The Britifh miniftry of George III. fought to finifh the war with honour, and the new emperor of Ruffia recalled his armies. His Pruffian majefty was, notwithftanding, fo very much reduced by his loffes, that the emprefs-queen, probably, would have compleated his deftruction, had it not been for the wife backwardnefs of the other German princes, not to annihilate the houfe of Brandenburg. At firft the emprefs-queen rejected all terms propofed to her, and ordered 30,000 men to be added to her armies. The vifible backwardnefs of her generals to execute her orders, and the fucceffes obtained by his Pruffian majefty, at laft prevailed

4   upon

upon her to agree to an armiftice, which was foon followed by the treaty of Hubertfburg, which fecured to his Pruffian majefty the poffeffion of Silefia. Upon the death of the emperor, her hufband, in 1765, her fon Jofeph, who had been crowned king of the Romans in 1764, fucceeded him in the empire. The imperial court has formed feveral arrangements of diftinct fovereignties in the Auftrian family out of their Italian dominions, and feem at prefent to cultivate a pacific fyftem both in the empire and all over Europe. His imperial majefty, though young, has difcovered great talents for government. He has paid a vifit, incognito, and with moderate attendance, to Rome, and the principal courts of Italy, and has had a perfonal interview with his Pruffian majefty ; all which circumftances indicate that he is determined to be his own mafter, and not to be impofed upon by his minifters *.

The KINGDOM of PRUSSIA, FORMERLY DUCAL PRUSSIA.

SITUATION, BOUNDARIES } THIS country is bounded
  AND EXTENT.   to the north by part of
Samogitia ; to the fouth, by Poland Proper and Mafovia ; to the eaft, by part of Lithuania ; and to the weft, by Polifh Pruffia and the Baltic. Its greateft length is about 160 miles, and breadth about 100.

NAME, AIR, SOIL, PRODUCE, } The name of Pruffia is
  AND RIVERS.   evidently derived from the
Boruffi, the antient inhabitants of the country. The air, upon the whole, is wholefome, and the foil fruitful in corn and other commodities, and affords plenty of pit-coal and fuel. Its animal productions are horfes, fheep, deer, and game ; bears, wolves, wild boars, and foxes. Its rivers and lakes are well ftored with fifhes ; and amber, which is thought to be formed of an oil coagulated with vitriol, is found on its coafts towards the Baltic. The woods furnifh the inhabitants with wax, honey, and pitch, befides quantities of pot-afhes. The rivers here fometimes do damage by inundations, and the principal are, the Viftula, the Pregel, the Meinel or Mammel, the Paffarge, and the Elbe.

---

* Maria Therefa, queen of Hungary and Bohemia, emprefs-dowager of Germany, was born in 1717. Her fon, Jofeph-Benedict-Auguftus, was crowned king of the Romans in 1764, fucceeded his father as emperor of Germany in 1765, married the fame year the princefs Jofephina-Maria, of Bavaria, who died in 1767. He had by his firft wife (the princefs of Parma) a daughter, Therefa-Elizabeth, born in 1762.

POPULATION, INHABITANTS, MAN-⎱   As Pruſſia, ſince
     NERS, CUSTOMS, AND DIVERSIONS. ⎰ the beginning of the
preſent century, has become a moſt reſpectable power upon
the continent of Europe, I ſhall, for the information of my
readers, deviate from my uſual plan, that I may bring before
their eyes the whole of his Pruſſian majeſty's territories, which
lie ſcattered in other diviſions of Germany, Poland, Swiſſerland, and the northern kingdoms, with their names; all
which they will find in the following table.

Proteſtants.	Countries Names	Square Miles.	Length.	Breadth.	Chief Cities.
Poland.	Pruſſia,	9,950	160	112	KONINGS. ⎰ 54-53 N. Lat. ⎱ 21-35 E. Lon.
Up. Saxony.	Brandenburg,	10,910	215	110	Berlin,
	Pomerania,	4,820	150	63	Camin,
	Swe. Pomerania,	2,991	90	48	Stetin,
Lo. Saxony.	Magdeburg,	1,535	63	50	Magdeburg,
	Halberſtat,	450	42	17	Halberſtat,
Sileſia.	Croſſen,	550	33	28	Croſſen,
Weſtphalia.	Minden,	595	42	26	Minden,
	Ravenſburg,	525	38	34	Ravenſburg,
	Lingen,	120	15	11	Lingen,
	Cleves,	630	43	21	Cleves,
	Meurs,	35	10	6	Meurs,
	Mark,	980	52	43	Ham,
Netherlands.	Gelder,	360	34	23	Gelders,
Switzerland.	Neufchatel,	320	32	20	Neufchatel.
	Total—	34,771			

I ſhall here confine myſelf to Pruſſia as a kingdom, becauſe
his Pruſſian majeſty's other dominions fall under the deſcription of the countries where they lie.

The inhabitants of this kingdom were, by Dr. Buſching,
computed to amount to 635,998 perſons capable of bearing
arms: and if ſo (for I greatly doubt their computation is
exaggerated) it muſt then be more populous than is generally
imagined. Since the year 1719, it is computed that about
34,000 coloniſts have removed thitherward from France,
Switzerland, and Germany; of which number, 17,000 were
Saltzburghers. Theſe emigrants have built 400 ſmall villages, 11 towns, 86 ſeats, and 50 new churches; and have
founded 1000 village ſchools, chiefly in that part of the country named Little Lithuania.

The manners of the inhabitants differ but little from thoſe
of the other inhabitants of Germany. The ſame may be ſaid
of their cuſtoms and diverſions.

RELIGION, SCHOOLS, ⎱ The religion of Pruffia is, thro'
AND ACADEMIES. ⎰ his prefent majefty's wifdom, very
tolerant. The eftablifhed religions are thofe of the Lutherans
and Calvinifts, but chiefly the former; but papifts, anabap-
tifts, and almoft all other fects, are here tolerated. The
country, as well as the towns, abounds in fchools. An univerfity was founded at Koningfberg in 1544, but we know of
no very remarkable learned men that it has produced.

CITIES.] The kingdom of Pruffia is divided into the German and Lithuanian departments; the former of which contains 280 parifhes, and the latter 105.

Koningfberg, the capital of the whole kingdom, feated on
the river Pregel, over which it has feven bridges, and is about
84 miles from Dantzic. According to Dr. Buiching, this
city is feven miles in circumference, and contains 3,800
houfes, and about 60,000 inhabitants. This computation, I
doubt, is a little exaggerated likewife, becaufe it fuppofes, at
an average, near fixteen perfons in every houfe. Koningfberg
has ever made a confiderable figure in commerce and fhipping;
its river being navigable for fhips; of which 493 foreign ones
arrived here in the year 1752, befides 298 coafters; and that
373 floats of timber were, in the compafs of that year, brought
down the Pregel. This city, befides its college or univerfity,
which contains 38 profeffors, boafts of magnificent palaces, a
town-houfe, and exchange; not to mention gardens and other
embellifhments. It has a good harbour and citadel, which is
called Fredericfburg, and is a regular fquare.

ANTIQUITIES AND CURIOSITIES, ⎱ See Germany.
NATURAL AND ARTIFICIAL. ⎰

COMMERCE AND MANUFACTURES.] The prefent king of
Pruffia, by the affiftance of an excellent police, has brought
the commerce and manufactures of this country to a very
flourifhing ftate, which is daily improving. The manufactures of Pruffia confift of glafs, iron-work, paper, gunpowder,
copper and brafs mills; manufactures of cloth, camblet, linen,
filk, ftockings, and other articles. The inhabitants export
variety of naval ftores, amber, linfeed, and hemp-feed, oat-
meal, fifh, mead, tallow, and caviar; and it is faid that 500
fhips are loaded every year with thofe commodities, chiefly
from Koningfberg.

CONSTITUTION AND GOVERNMENT.] His Pruffian ma-
jefty is abfolute through all his dominions, but is too wife to
opprefs his fubjects, though he avails himfelf to the full of his
power. The government of this kingdom is by a regency of
four chancellors of ftate, viz. 1. The great mafter; 2. The
great burgrave; 3. The great chancellor; and, 4. The
great

great marſhal. There are alſo ſome other councils, and 37 bailiwicks. The ſtates conſiſt, 1. Of councellors of ſtate; 2. Of deputies from the nobility; and, 3. From the commons. Beſides theſe inſtitutions, his majeſty has erected a board for commerce and navigation.

REVENUES.] His Pruſſian majeſty, by means of the happy ſituation of his country, its inland navigation, and his own excellent regulations, derives an amazing revenue from this country, which, about a century and a half ago, was the ſeat of boors and barbariſm. It is ſaid, that amber alone brings him in 26,000 dollars annually. His other revenues ariſe from his demeſnes, his duties of cuſtoms and tolls, and the ſubſidies yearly granted by the ſeveral ſtates; but the exact ſum is not known, though we may conclude that it is very conſiderable, from the immenſe charges of the late war.

MILITARY STRENGTH.] The regulations of this department, introduced by his majeſty, have a wonderful quick operation in forming his troops and recruiting his armies. Every regiment has a particular diſtrict aſſigned it, where the young men proper for bearing arms are regiſtered; and when occaſion offers, they join their regiment, and being incorporated with veterans, they ſoon become well diſciplined troops.

ARMS, AND ORDERS OF KNIGHTHOOD.] The royal arms of Pruſſia are argent, an eagle diſplayed ſable, crowned, or, for Pruſſia. Azure, the imperial ſceptre, or, for Courland. Argent, an eagle diſplayed, gules, with ſemicircular wreaths, for the marquiſate of Brandenburg. To theſe are added the reſpective arms of the ſeveral provinces ſubject to the Pruſſian crown.

There are two orders of knighthood; the firſt, that of the black eagle, inſtituted by Frederic I. on the day of his coronation at Koningſberg, with this motto, SUUM CUIQUE. The ſovereign is always grand maſter, and the number of knights, excluſive of the royal family, is limited to thirty.

Next to this is the order of Merit, inſtituted by his preſent majeſty; the motto is POUR LE MERITE.

HISTORY.] The ancient hiſtory of Pruſſia, like that of other kingdoms, is loſt in the clouds of fiction and romance. The inhabitants appear to have been a brave and warlike people, and refuſed to ſubmit to the neighbouring princes, who, on pretence of converting them to chriſtianity, wanted to ſubject them to ſlavery. They made a noble ſtand againſt the kings of Poland, one of whom, Boleſlaus IV. was by them defeated and killed in 1163. They continued independent and pagans till the time of the cruſades, when the German knights

knights of the Teutonic order, about the year 1230, undertook their converfion by the edge of the fword, but upon condition of having, as a reward, the property of the country,
when conquered. A long feries of wars followed, in which
the inhabitants of Pruffia were almoft extirpated by the religious knights, who in the thirteenth century, after committing the moft incredible barbarities, peopled the country with
Germans. After this vaft wafte of blood, in 1466, a peace
was concluded between the knights of the Teutonic order, and
Cafimir, king of Poland, by which it was agreed, that the
part now called Polifh Pruffia fhould continue a free province,
under the king's protection; and that the knights and the
grand mafter fhou'd poffefs the other part; but were to
acknowledge themfelves vaffals of Poland. This gave rife
to frefh wars, in which the knights endeavoured, but unfuc-
cefsfully, to throw off their vaffalage to Poland. In 1525,
Albert, margrave of Brandenburgh, and the laft grand mafter
of the Teutonic order, concluded a peace at Cracow, by
which the margrave was acknowledged duke of the eaft part of
Pruffia, (formerly called, for that reafon, Ducal Pruffia) but
to be held as a fief of Poland, and to defcend to his male heirs;
and upon failure of his male iffue, to his brothers and their
male heirs. Thus ended the fovereignty of the Teutonic
order in Pruffia, after it had fubfifted near 300 years. In
1657, the elector Frederic-William, of Brandenburgh, defervedly called the Great, had Ducal Pruffia confirmed to
him; and by the conventions of Welau and Bromberg, it was
freed, by Cafimir, king of Poland, from vaffalage; and he
and his defcendents were declared independent and fovereign
lords of this part of Pruffia.

As the proteftant religion had been introduced into this
country by the margrave Albert, and the electors of Brandenburgh were now of that perfuafion, the proteftant intereft
favoured them fo much, that Frederic, the fon of Frederic-
William the Great, was raifed to the dignity of king of
Pruffia, in a folemn affembly of the ftates of the empire, and
foon after acknowledged as fuch by all the powers of Chriftendom. His grandfon, the prefent king of Pruffia, in the me-
moirs of his family, gives us no high idea of this firft king's
talents for government, but expatiates on thofe of his own
father, Frederic-William, who fucceeded in 1713. He certainly was a prince of ftrong natural parts, and performed prodigious fervices to his country, but too often at the expence
of humanity, and the magnanimity which ought to adorn a
king. At his death, which happened in 1740, he is faid to
have left feven millions fterling in his treafury, which has
enabled

enabled his fon, by his wonderful victories, and the more
wonderful refources, by which he repaired his defeats, to become the admiration of the prefent age *.

The KINGDOM of BOHEMIA.

SITUATION AND EXTENT.

Length   300 ⎱ between ⎰ 48 and 52 north latitude.
Breadth , 250 ⎰   ⎱ 12 and 19 caft longitude.

BOUNDARIES.] **B**OUNDED by Saxony and Brandenburgh, on the north; by Poland and
Hungary, on the caft; by Auftria and Bavaria, on the fouth;
and by the palatinate of Bavaria, on the weft; comprehending, 1. Bohemia Proper; 2. Silefia; and, 3. Moravia.

Divifions.	Chief towns.
1. Bohemia Pro-per, W. moftly fubject to the Ho. of Auftria.	Prague, E. lon. 14-20. N. lat. 50. Koningfgratz, E. Glatz, E. fubject to the king of Pruffia. Egra, W.
2. Silefia, eaft, moftly fubject to the king of Pruffia.	Breflau, E. lon. 17. N. lat. 51-15. Glogaw, N. Croffen, N. Jagendorf, S. Tropaw, S. fubject to the houfe of Auftria. Tefchen, S. fubject to the houfe of Auftria.
3. Moravia, S. entirely fubject to the houfe of Auftria.	Olmutz, E. lon. 16-45. N. lat. 49-40. Brin, middle. Igla, S. W.

SOIL AND AIR.] The air of Bohemia is not thought fo
wholefome as that of the reft of Germany, though its foil and
produce are pretty much the fame.

MOUNTAINS.] Bohemia, though almoft furrounded with
mountains, contains none of note or diftinction.

METALS AND MINERALS.] This kingdom contains rich
mines of filver, quickfilver, copper, iron, lead, fulphur,
and faltpetre. Its chief manufactures are linen, copper, iron,
and glafs.

---

* Frederic III. king of Pruffia, and elector of Brandenburg, was born in 1712,
married in 1733 to Elizabeth-Chriftina, of Brunfwic-Wolfenbuttle, born in 1714,
by whom he has no iffue. The iffue of the late William-Auguftus, next brother to
the king, are, Frederic-William, prince royal of Pruffia, born in 1744, and
married in 1765 to the princefs Elizabeth-Ulrica, of Brunfwic. 2. Frederica-
Sophia-Wilhelmina, born in 1751, and married in 1767 to the prince of
Orange.

POPULATION, INHABITANTS, MANNERS, } We have no
    CUSTOMS AND DIVERSIONS. } certain ac-
count of the prefent population of Bohemia ; about 150
years ago, it was computed to contain 3,000,000 of inhabitants : they are thought at prefent not to be fo numerous. The
Bohemians, in their perfons, habits, and manners, refemble
the Germans. There is, among them, no middle ftate of
people ; for every lord is a fovereign, and every tenant a flave.
The lower ranks are accufed of being addicted to pilfering and
fuperftition. But though the Bohemians, at prefent, are not
remarkable either for arts or arms, yet they formerly diftinguifhed themfelves as the moft intrepid afferters of civil and
religious liberty in Europe; witnefs the early introduction of
the reformed religion into their country, when it was fcarcely
known in any other, the many glorious defeats they gave to
the Auftrian power, and their generous ftruggles for independen-
dency. Their virtues may be confidered as the caufes of their
decay ; as no means were left unemployed by their defpotic
mafters for breaking their fpirit : though it is certain, their
internal jealoufies and diffentions greatly contributed to their
fubjection. Their cuftoms and diverfions are the fame as in
Germany.

RELIGION.] Though popery is the eftablifhed religion,
of Bohemia, yet many of the Moravians have embraced a
vifionary unintelligible proteftantifm, if it deferves that name,
which they propagate, by their zealous miffionaries, through
all parts of the globe ; fome of whom have lately made pro-
felytes in Great-Britain : they have a meeting-houfe in London, and have obtained an act of parliament for a fettlement
in the plantations.

ARCHBISHOPRICS AND BISHOPRICS.] Prague is the only
Bohemian archbifhopric. The bifhoprics are Koningfgratz,
Breflau, and Olmutz.

LANGUAGE.] The proper language of the Bohemians is
a dialect of the Sclavonian, but they generally fpeak German
and High Dutch.

UNIVERSITY.] The only univerfity in Bohemia is that of
Prague.

CITIES AND TOWNS.] Prague, the capital of Bohemia, is
one of the fineft and moft magnificent cities in Europe, and
famous for its noble bridge. Its circumference is fo large,
that the grand Pruffian army, in its laft fiege, never could
completely inveft it. For this reafon it is able to make a vigorous defence in cafe of a regular fiege. The inhabitants,
however, are thought not to be proportioned to its capaciouf-
nefs, being thought not to exceed 70,000 Chriftians, and

4

about 13,000 Jews. It contains 92 churches and chapels, and 40 cloifters. It is a place of little or no trade, and therefore the middling inhabitants are not wealthy ; but the Jews are faid to c irry on a large commerce in jewels. Bohemia contains many other towns, fome of which are fortified, but they are remarkable neither for ftrength nor manufactures. Olmutz is the capital of Moravia : it is well fortified, and has manufactures of woollen, iron, glafs, paper, and gunpowder.

COMMERCE AND MANUFACTURES.] See Germany.

CONSTITUTION AND GOVERNMENT.] The forms, and only the forms, of the old Bohemian conftitution ftill fubfift ; but the government, under the emprefs-queen, is defpotic. Their ftates are compofed of the clergy, nobility, gentry, and reprefentatives of towns. Their fovereigns, of late, have not been fond of provoking them by ill ufage, and they have a general averfion towards the Auftrians. This kingdom is frequently defcribed as part of Germany, but with little reafon, for it is not in any of the nine circles, nor does it contribute any thing towards the forces or revenues of the empire, nor is it fubject to any of its laws. What gives fome colour to this miftake is, that the king of Bohemia is the firft fecular elector of the empire, and their kings have been elected emperors of Germany for many years.

REVENUES.] The revenues of Bohemia are whatever the fovereign is pleafed to exact from the ftates of the kingdom, when they are annually affembled at Prague. They may perhaps amount to 500,000 l. a year.

ARMS.] The arms of Bohemia are, argent, a lion gules, the tail moved, and paffed in faltier, crowned languid, and armed, or.

HISTORY.] The Bohemian nobility ufed to elect their own princes, though the emperors of Germany fometimes impofed a king upon them, and at length ufurped that throne themfelves. In 1414 John Hufs and Jerome of Prague, two of the firft reformers, were burnt at the council of Conftance, though the emperor of Germany had given them his protection. This occafioned an infurrection in Bohemia : the people of Prague threw the emperor's officers out of the windows of the council chambers ; and the famous Zifca affembling an army of 40,000 Bohemians, defeated the emperor's forces in feveral engagements, and drove the imperialifts out of the kingdom. The divifions of the Huffites among themfelves, enabled the emperors to keep poffeffion of Bohemia, though an attempt was made to throw off the imperial yoke, by electing a proteftant king in the perfon of the prince Palatine, fon-in-law to

James

James I. of England. The misfortunes of this prince are well known. He was driven from Bohemia by the emperor's generals, and being ftript of his other dominions, was forced to depend on the court of England for a fubfiftence; and the Bohemians, fince that time, have remained fubject to the houfe of Auftria.

HUNGARY.

SITUATION AND EXTENT.

	Miles.		Degrees.
Length	300	} between {	17 and 23 eaft longitude.
Breadth	200		45 and 49 north latitude.

BOUNDARIES.] THAT part of Hungary which belongs to the houfe of Auftria (for it formerly included Tranfylvania, Sclavonia, Croatia, Morlachia, Servia, Walachia, Temefwar, and other countries) is bounded by Poland, on the north; by Tranfylvania and Walachia, eaft; by Sclavonia, fouth; and by Auftria and Moravia, weft.

The general divifion of Hungary, is into Upper, by fome called Proper, and Lower Hungary; the former lying north, and the latter fouth of the Danube. Their chief towns being Prefburg and Buda.

AIR, SOIL, AND PRODUCE.] The air, and confequently the climate, of the fouthern parts of Hungary, is found to be unhealthful, owing to its numerous lakes, ftagnated waters, and marfhes; the northern parts being mountainous and barren, the air is fweet and wholefome. No country in the world can boaft a richer foil, than that plain which extends 300 miles from Prefburg to Belgrade, and produces corn, grafs, efculent plants, tobacco, faffron, afparagus, melons, hops, pulfe, millet, buck-wheat, delicious wine, fruits of various kinds, peaches, mulberry-trees, chefnuts, and wood: corn is in fuch plenty, that it fells for one fixth part of its price in England.

RIVERS.] Thefe are the Danube, Drave, Teyffe, Merifh, and the Temes.

WATER.] Hungary contains feveral lakes, particularly four among the Carpathian mountains of confiderable extent, and abounding with fifh. The Hungarian baths and mineral waters are efteemed the moft fovereign of any in Europe; but their magnificent buildings, raifed by the Turks when in pof-

VOL. II. G feffion

feſſion of the country, particularly thoſe of Buda, are ſuffered
to go to decay.

MOUNTAINS.] The Carpathian mountains, which divide
Hungary from Poland on the north, are the chief in Hungary,
though many detached mountains are found in the country.
Their tops are generally covered with wood, and on their
ſides grow the richeſt grapes in the world.

METALS AND MINERALS.] Hungary is remarkably well
ſtocked with both. It abounds not only with gold and ſilver
mines, but with plenty of excellent copper, vitriol, iron,
orpiment, quickſilver, cryſocolla, and terra ſigillata. Before
Hungary became the ſeat of deſtructive wars, between Turks
and Chriſtians, or fell under the power of the houſe of Auſtria,
thoſe mines were furniſhed with proper works and workmen,
and produced vaſt revenues to the native princes. The Hungarian gold and ſilver employed mint-houſes, not only in Hungary, but in Germany, and the continent of Europe; but all
thoſe mines are now greatly diminiſhed in their value, their
work being deſtroyed or demoliſhed, ſome of them however
ſtill ſubſiſt, to the great emolument of the natives.

VEGETABLE AND ANIMAL } Hungary is remarkable for
    PRODUCTIONS.   } a fine breed of horſes, gene-
rally mouſe coloured, and highly eſteemed by military officers,
ſo that great numbers of them are exported. There is a
remarkable breed of large rams in the neighbourhood of Prefburg. Its other vegetable and animal productions are in general the ſame with thoſe of Germany, and the neighbouring
countries. The Hungarian wines, however, particularly
Tockay, are preferable to thoſe of any other country, at leaſt
in Europe.

POPULATION, INHABITANTS, MAN- } It was late before
    NERS, CUSTOMS AND DIVERSIONS. } the northern bar-
barians drove the Romans out of Hungary, and ſome of the
deſcendants of their legionary forces, are ſtill to be diſtinguiſhed in the inland parts, by their ſpeaking Latin. Be that
as it will, before the Turks got poſſeſſion of Conſtantinople,
we have reaſon to think, that Hungary was one of the moſt
populous and powerful kingdoms in Europe; and if the houſe
of Auſtria ſhould give the proper encouragement to the inhabitants to repair their works, and clear their fens, it might
become ſo again in about a century hence. Both Hungaries
at preſent, excluſive of Tranſylvania, and Croatia, are thought
to contain about two millions and a half of inhabitants. The
Hungarians have manners peculiar to themſelves. They pique
themſelves on being deſcended from thoſe heroes, who formed
the bulwark of Chriſtendom againſt the infidels. In their

perfons they are well made. Their fur-caps, their clofe-bodied coats, girded by a fafh, and their cloak or mantle, which is fo contrived, as to buckle under one arm, fo that the right hand may be always at liberty, gives them an air of military dignity. The men fhave their beards, but preferve their whifkers on their upper lips. Their ufual arms are a broad fword, and a kind of pole-ax, befides their fire-arms. The ladies are reckoned handfomer than thofe of Auftria, and their fable drefs with fleeves ftrait to their arms, and their ftays faftened before with gold, pearl, or diamond little buttons, are well known to the French and Englifh ladies. Both men and women, in what they call the mine towns, wear fur and even fheep-fkin dreffes. The inns upon the roads are moft miferable hovels, and even thofe feldom to be met with. Their hogs, which yield the chief animal food for their peafants, and their poultry, live in the fame apartment with their owners. The gout, and the fever, owing to the unwholefomenefs of the air, are the predominant difeafes in Hungary. The natives in general are indolent, and leave trade and manufactures to the Greeks and other ftrangers, fettled in their country, the flatnefs of which renders travelling commodious, either by land or water. The diverfions of the inhabitants are of the warlike and athletic kind. They are in general a brave and magnanimous people. Their anceftors, even fince the beginning of the prefent century, were fo jealous of their liberties, that rather than be tyrannized over, by the houfe of Auftria, they often fubmitted to that of Othman; but their fidelity to the prefent emprefs-queen, notwithftanding the provocations they received from her houfe, will be always remembered to their honour.

RELIGION.] The eftablifhed religion of the Hungarians, is the Roman-catholic, though the major part of the inhabitants are proteftants or Greeks, and the prefent emprefs-queen, out of gratitude for their fervices, has reftored them to the full exercife of their civil and religious liberties.

ARCHBISHOPRICS AND BISHOPRICS.] The archbifhoprics are Prefburg, Gran and Colocza. The bifhoprics Great Waradin, Agria, Vefprin, Raab, and five churches.

LANGUAGE.] As the Hungarians are mixed with Germans, Sclavonians and Walachians, they have a variety of dialects, and one of them is faid to approach near the Hebrew. The better and the middlemoft rank fpeak German, and almoft all of them Latin, either pure or barbarous.

UNIVERSITIES.] In the univerfities (if they can be properly fo called) of Firnan, Buda, Raab, and Cafcham, are profeffors of the feveral arts and fciences, who are commonly Jefuits; fo that the Lutherans, and Calvinifts, who are more

numerous

numerous than the Roman-catholics in Hungary, go to German and other univerfities.

ANTIQUITIES AND CURIOSITIES, ⎱ The artificial curiofi-
   NATURAL AND ARTIFICIAL. ⎰   ties of this country,
confift of its bridges, baths and mines.   The bridge of Effek
built over the Danube, and Drave, is, properly fpeaking, a
continuation of bridges, five miles in length, fortified with
towers at certain diftances.   It was an important pafs during
the wars between the Turks and Hungarians.   A bridge of
boats runs over the Danube, half a mile long, between Buda
and Peft ; and about twenty Hungarian miles diftance from
Belgrade, is the remains of a bridge, erected by the Romans,
adjudged to be the moft magnificent of any in the world.   The
baths and mines here have nothing to diftinguifh them from
the like works in other countries.

One of the moft remarkable natural curiofities of Hungary,
is a cavern in a mountain near Szelitze ; the aperture of this
cavern, which fronts the fouth, is eighteen fathom high, and
eight broad ; its fubterraneous paffages confift entirely of folid
rock, ftretching away further fouth than has been yet difcovered ; as far as it is practicable to go, the height is found to
be 50 fathoms, and the breadth 26.   Many other wonderful
particulars are related of this cavern, which is an article in
natural philofophy.   Aftonifhing rocks are common in Hungary, and fome of its churches are of admirable architecture.

CITIES, TOWNS, FORTS, AND OTHER ⎱ Thefe are great-
   EDIFICES, PUBLIC AND PRIVATE. ⎰ ly decayed from
their antient magnificence, but many of the fortifications are
ftill very ftrong, and kept in good order.   Prefburg is fortified.
In it the Hungarian regalia are kept.   Buda, formerly the
capital of Hungary, retains little of its antient magnificence,
but its ftrength and fortifications, and the fame may be faid of
Peft, which lies on the oppofite fide of the Danube.   Raab is
likewife a ftrong city, as is Gran and Comorra.   Tockay has
been already mentioned for the excellency of its wines.

COMMERCE AND MANUFACTURES.] Having already mentioned the natural produce of the country, all I can add is,
that the chief manufactures and exports of the natives, confift
of metals, drugs and falt.

CONSTITUTION AND GOVERNMENT.] The Hungarians
diflike the term of queen, and call their prefent fovereign King
Terefa.   Their government preferves the remains of many
checks upon the regal power.   They have a diet or parliament,
a Hungary-office, which refembles our chancery, and which
refides at Vienna ; as the ftadtholder's council, which comes
pretty near the Britifh privy-council, but has a municipal
                             jurifdiction,

jurifdiction, does at Prefburg. Every royal town has its
fenate; and the Gefpan chafts refemble our juftices of the
peace. Befides this, they have an exchequer and nine chambers, and other fubordinate courts.

MILITARY STRENGTH.] The emprefs-queen can bring to the
field, at any time, 50,000 Hungarians in their own country,
but feldom draws out of it above 10,000; thefe are generally
light-horfe, and well known to modern times by the name of
huffars. They are not near fo large as the German horfe;
and therefore the huffars ftand upon their fhort ftirrups when
they ftrike. Their expedition and alertnefs has been found
fo ferviceable in war, that the greateft powers in Europe have
troops that go by the fame name. Their foot are called Hey-
dukes, and wear feathers in their caps, according to the number of enemies they pretend to have killed: both horfe and
foot are an excellent militia, very good at a perfuit, or ravaging and plundering a country, but not equal to regular
troops in a pitched battle.

COINS.] Hungary was formerly remarkable for its coinage,
and there are ftill extant in the cabinets of the curious, a complete feries of coins of their former kings. More Greek and
Roman medals have been difcovered in this country, than perhaps in any other in Europe.

ARMS.] The emprefs-queen, for armorial enfigns, bears
quarterly, barwife argent, and gules of eight pieces.

HISTORY.] The Huns, after fubduing this country, communicated their name to it, being then part of the ancient
Pannonia. Hungary was formerly an affemblage of different
ftates, and the firft who affumed the title of king, was Stephen, about the year 1000, when he embraced chriftianity.
About the year 1310, king Charles Robert afcended the
throne, and fubdued Bulgaria, Servia, Crontea, Dalmatia,
Sclavonia, and many other provinces; but many of thofe
conquefts were afterwards reduced by the Venetians, Turks,
and other powers. In the 15th century, Hunniades, who
was guardian to the infant king Ladiflaus, bravely repulfed
the Turks, who invaded Hungary; and upon the death of
Ladiflaus, the Hungarians in 1438, raifed Matthius Cor-
vinus, fon to Hunniades, to their throne. Lewis, king of
Hungary, in 1526, was killed in a battle, fighting againft
Solyman, emperor of the Turks. This battle had almoft
proved fatal to Hungary, but archduke Ferdinand, brother to
the emperor Charles V. having married the fifter of Lewis,
he claimed the title of Hungary, in which he fucceeded, with
fome difficulty, and that kingdom has ever fince belonged to
the houfe of Auftria, though by its conftitution its crown,

G 3   ought

ought to be elective. For the rest of the Hungarian history, see Germany.

TRANSYLVANIA, SCLAVONIA, and CROATIA.

I HAVE thrown those countries under one division, for several reasons, particularly because we have no precise, or authentic account of their extent and boundaries; and it is very difficult to fix what part of them belongs to the house of Austria, and what to the Turks, or other nations. The best account therefore I can give of them is as follows : Transylvania is generally reckoned to belong to Hungary, and is bounded on the north by the Carpathian mountains, which divide it from Poland; on the east by Moldavia and Walachia; on the south by Walachia; and on the west by Upper and Lower Hungary. It lies between 22 and 25 degrees of east longitude, and 45 and 48 of north latitude. Its length is extended about 180, and its breadth 120 miles; but surrounded on all sides by high mountains. Its produce, vegetables, and animals, are almost the same with those of Hungary. The air is wholesome and temperate; but their wine, though good, is not equal to the Hungarian. Its chief city is Hermanstat, and its interior government still partakes greatly of the ancient feudal system, being composed of many independent states and princes. They owe but a nominal subjection to the Austrians, who leave them in possession of all their privileges. Papists, Lutherans, Calvinists, Socinians, Arians, Greeks, Mahometans, and other sectaries, here enjoy their several religions. Transylvania is thought to add but little to the Austrian revenue, though it exports some metals and salt to Hungary. Hermanstat is a large, strong, and well-built city, as is Clausemburg and Wissemburg. All sorts of provisions here are very cheap, and excellent in their kinds. The seat of government is at Hermanstat, and the governor is assisted by a council made up of Roman-catholics, Calvinists, and Lutherans. The diet, or parliament, meets by summons, and receives the commands of the sovereign, to whom of late they appear to have been entirely devoted. They have a liberty of making remonstrances and representations in case of grievances.

Transylvania is part of the ancient Dacia, the inhabitants of which long employed the Roman arms, before they could be subdued. Their descendants retain the same military character. The population of the country is not ascertained, but if the Transylvanians can bring to the field, as has been asserted, afferted, 30,000 troops, the whole number of inhabitants muft be confiderable. At prefent its military force is reduced to fix regiments of 1,500 men each; but it is well known that, during the laft two wars, in which the houfe of Auftria was engaged, the Tranfylvanians did great fervices. Hermanftat is its only bifhopric, and the Tranfylvanians at prefent feem to trouble themfelves little, either about learning or religion, though the Roman-catholic is the eftablifhed church. The various revolutions in their government prove their impatience under flavery; and though the treaty of Carlowitz in 1699, gave the fovereignty of Tranfylvania to the houfe of Auftria, yet the natives enjoy what we may call a loyal ariftocracy, which their fovereigns do not think proper to invade.

Sclavonia lies between the 16th and 22d degrees of eaft longitude, and the 45th and 47th of north latitude. It is thought to be about 200 miles in length, and 60 in breadth, and is bounded by the Drave on the north, by the Danube on the eaft, by the Save on the fouth, and by Kiria in Auftria on the weft. The reafon why Hungary, Tranfylvania, Sclavonia, and the other nations, fubject to the houfe of Auftria in thofe parts, contain a furprizing variety of people, differing in name, language, and manners, is becaufe liberty here made its laft ftand againft the Roman arms, which by degrees forced the remains of the different nations they had conquered into thofe quarters. The thicknefs of the woods, the rapidity of rivers, and the ftrength of the country favoured their refiftance; and their defcendents, notwithftanding the power of the Turks, the Auftrians, the Hungarians, and the Poles, ftill retain the fame fpirit of independency. Without minding the arrangements made by the fovereigns of Europe, they are quiet under the government that leaves them moft at liberty. That they are generous, as well as brave, appears from their attachment to the houfe of Auftria, which till the laft two wars, never was fenfible of their value and valour; infomuch, that it is well known that they preferved the pragmatic fanction, and kept the imperial crown in that family. The Sclavonians formerly gave fo much work to the Roman arms, that it is thought the word Slave took its original from them, on account of the great numbers of them who were carried into bondage, fo late as the reign of Charlemaigne. Though Sclavonia yields neither in beauty nor fertility to Hungary and Tranfylvania, yet the ravages of war are ftill vifible in the face of the country, which lies in a great meafure unimproved. The Sclavonians, from their ignorance, perhaps, are zealous Roman-catholics, tho' Greeks and Jews are tolerated. Here we meet with two

G 4 bifhoprics,

bifhoprics, that of Rofega, which is the capital of the country, and Zagrab, which lies on the Drave ; but we know of
no univerfities.   The inhabitants are compofed of Servians,
Radzians, Croats, Walachians, Germans, Hungarians, and
a vaft number of other people, whofe names were never
known even to the Auftrians themfelves, but from the military mufter-rolls, when they poured their troops into the field
during the two laft wars.

Croatia lies between the 15th and 17th degrees of eaft longitude, and the 45th and 47th of north latitude. It is 80
miles in length, and 70 in breadth. The manners, government, religion, language, and cuftoms, of the Croats, are
fimilar to thofe of the Sclavonians and Tranfylvanians, who
are their neighbours. They are excellent irregular troops, and
as fuch are famed in modern hiftory, under the name of Pan-
dours, and various other defignations. The truth is, the houfe
of Auftria finds its intereft in fuffering them, and the neighbouring nations, to live in their own manner. Their towns
are blended with each other, there fcarcely being any diftinction of boundaries. Zagrab (which I have already mentioned)
for inftance, is thought to be the capital of Croatia. All the
fovereignty exercifed over them by the Auftrians, feems to
confift in the military arrangements for bringing them occafionally into the field.

As to the other Auftrian dominions, they are fo intermixed
with thofe of the Venetians, Turks, and other nations, that it
is impoffible to feparate them, and they fhall be mentioned
occafionally.

POLAND, including LITHUANIA.

SITUATION AND EXTENT.

Miles.		Degrees.
Length 700 }	between	{ 16 and 34 eaft longitude.
Breadth 680 }		{ 46 and 57 north latitude.

BOUNDARIES.] IT is very difficult, if not impoffible, to
afcertain with any precifion, the real
extent of the Polifh dominions, through the uncertain poffeffion of its extremities by the Turks, Tartars, Coffacs, and
other nations. It is bounded on the north by Livonia, Mufcovy, and the Baltic; on the eaft by Mufcovy, and Little
Tartary ; on the fouth by Turkey and Hungary ; and on the
weft by Germany.

DIVISIONS.] In a work like this, the reader cannot expect
to be entertained with a vaft variety of names that form the
divifions of this great country. They are not well known
even

even to the natives themselves, and a minute account of them can be of no use either to strangers or natives ; but the chief obstacle to such an undertaking, arises from the different claims of the great powers of the north. The geographers, for instance, have placed the kingdom of Prussia in Poland, tho' it is well known that his Prussian majesty is now the sole sovereign of that part of it called Ducal Prussia, as has been already mentioned. In like manner Courland is comprehended under Poland, though her Russian majesty has the entire disposal of that duchy. The best general division therefore of Poland is as follows.

Poland.		Square Miles.	Length.	Breadth	Chief Cities.	
Papists.	Lithuania,	64,800	333	310	Wilna	
	Podolia,	29,000	360	120	Caminieck	
	Volhinia,	25,000	305	150	Lucko	
	Red Russia,	25,200	232	185	Lemburg	
	Great Poland,	19,200	208	180	Gnefna	
	Little Poland,	18,000	230	130	Cracow	
	Polesia,	14,000	186	97	Breffici	
	Masovia,	8,400	152	90	WARSAW	E. lon. 21-5. N. lat. 52-15.
	Samogitia,	8,000	155	98	Rasiem	
	Prussia Royal,	6,400	118	104	Elbing	
	Polachia,	4,000	133	42	Bielh	
Protestants.	Courland, subject to Russia,	4,414	174	80	Mittaw.	
	Total—	226,414				

Dantzic, Thorn, and Elbing, in Prussia Royal, are free cities, under the protection of Poland.

NAME.] It is generally thought that Poland takes its name from Polu, or Pole, a Sclavonian word signifying a country fit for hunting, for which none was formerly more proper, on account of its plains, woods, wild beasts, and game of every kind.

CLIMATE.] The air of Poland is such as may be expected from so extensive but level a climate. In the north parts it is cold but healthy. The Carpathian mountains, which separate Poland from Hungary, are covered with everlasting snow, which has been known to fall in the midst of summer. Upon the whole, however, the climate of Poland is temperate, and far from being so unsettled, either in winter or summer, as might be supposed from so northerly a situation.

SOIL, PRODUCE AND WATERS.] Poland is in general a level country, and the soil is fertile in corn, as appears from the vast quantities that are sent from thence down the Vistula, to Dantzic, and are bought up by the Dutch, and other nations. The pastures of Poland, especially in Podolia, are rich beyond expression ; and it is said one can hardly see the

cattle

cattle that graze in the meadows. Here are mines of filver, copper, iron, falt and coals ; the interior parts of Poland
contain forefts, which furnifh timber in fo great quantities,
that it is employed in houfe-building, inftead of bricks, ftone,
and tiles. Various kinds of fruits and herbs, and fome grapes
are produced in Poland, and are excellent when they meet with
culture, but their wine feldom or never comes to perfection.
Poland produces various kinds of clays fit for pipes and earthen
ware. The water of many fprings is boiled into falt. The
virtues of a fpring, in the palatinate of Cracow, which en-
creafes and decreafes with the moon, are faid to be wonderful
for the prefervation of life, and it is reported, that the neighbouring inhabitants commonly live to 100, and fome of them
to 150 years of age. This fpring is inflammable, and by
applying a torch to it, it flames like the fubtleft fpirit of wine.
The flame however dances on the furface, without heating the
water, and if neglected to be extinguifhed, which it may eafily
be, it communicates itfelf by fubterraneous conduits, to the
roots of trees, in a neighbouring wood, which it confumes ;
and about 35 years ago, the flames are faid to have lafted for
three years, before they could be entirely extinguifhed.

RIVERS.] The chief rivers of Poland are, the Viftula or
Wevfel, the Neifter, Neiper or Borifthenes, the Bog, and
the Dwina.

LAKES.] The chief of the few lakes contained in Poland,
is Gopto, in the palatinate of Byzefty and Birals, or the
White Lake, and is faid to dye thofe who wafh in it of a
fwarthy complexion.

VEGETABLE AND ANIMAL ⎫ The vegetable productions
  PRODUCTIONS BY LAND ⎬ of Poland have been already
  AND WATER. ⎭ mentioned under the article
of SOIL, though fome are peculiar to itfelf, particularly a
kind of manna (if it can be called a vegetable) which in May
and June the inhabitants fweep into fieves with the dew, and
it ferves for food dreffed various ways.

The forefts of Warfovia or Mafovia, contain plenty of uri,
or buffaloes, whofe flefh the Poles powder, and efteem it an
excellent difh. Horfes, wolves, boars, elks, and deer, all of
them wild, are common in the Polifh forefts ; and there is a
fpecies of wild horfes and affes, that the nobility of the Ukrain,
as well as natives, are fond of. A kind of wolf, refembling a
hart, with fpots on his belly and legs, is found here, and
affords the beft furs in the country ; but the elk, which is
common in Poland, as well as in fome other northern countries, is a very extraordinary animal. The flefh of the Polifh
elk forms the moft delicious part of their greateft feafts. His
body

body is of the deer make, but much thicker and longer; the legs high, the feet broad and cloven, the horns large, rough, and broad, like a wild goat's.   Naturalists have observed, that upon diffecting an elk, there was found in its head some large flies, with its brains almost eaten away : and it is an observation, sufficiently attested, that in the large woods and wildernesses of the north, this poor animal is attacked, towards the winter chiefly, by a larger sort of flies, that, through its ears, attempt to take up their winter quarters in its head.   This persecution is thought to affect the elk with the falling-sickness, by which means it is taken, which would otherwise prove no easy matter.

Poland produces a creature called bohac : it resembles a guinea-pig, but they seem to be the beaver kid.   They are noted for digging holes in the ground, which they enter in October, and do not come out, except occasionally for food, till April : they have separate apartments for their provisions, lodgings, and their dead ; they live together by 10 or 12 in a herd.   We do not perceive that Poland contains any species of birds peculiar to itself; only we are told that the quails there have green legs, and that their flesh is reckoned to be unwholesome.   Poland contains no particular species of fish that we know of.

POPULATION, INHABITANTS, MANNERS, CUSTOMS, AND DIVERSIONS.   From what has been said of the extent of Poland, it is impossible to form an estimate of the numbers of its inhabitants : they undoubtedly, before the breaking out of the present war, were very numerous ; but they are so little known, even at present, that numbers of them, in remoter parts, continue still to be heathens, or have very imperfect notions of Christianity.   Some have supposed Poland and Lithuania to contain 15,000,000 of inhabitants, and to be at least as populous as France.   When we consider that the Poles have no colonies, and sometimes enjoy long tracts of peace, and that no fewer than 2,000,000 of Jews are said to inhabit their villages, exclusive of those who live in their cities and towns, perhaps this calculation is not exaggerated.   The Poles, in their persons, make a noble appearance ; their complexion is fair, and their shapes are well proportioned.   They are brave, honest, and hospitable ; and their women sprightly, yet modest, and submissive to their husbands.

The diversions of the Poles are warlike and manly ; vaulting, dancing, and riding the great horse, hunting, skating, bull and bear-baiting.   They usually travel on horseback : a Polish gentleman will not travel a stone's-throw without his

horse ;

horfe ; and they are fo hardy, that they will fleep upon the ground, without any bed or covering, in froft and fnow. The Poles never live above ftairs, and their apartments are not united ; the kitchen is on one fide, the ftable on another, the dwelling-houfe on the third, and the gate on the front. They content themfelves with a few fmall beds, and if any lodge at their houfes, they muft carry their bedding with them. When they fit down to dinner or fupper, they have their trumpets and other mufic playing, and a number of gentlemen to wait on them at table, all ferving with the moft profound refpect ; for the nobles who are poor frequently find themfelves under the neceffity of ferving them that are rich ; but their patron ufually treats them with civility, and permits the eldeft to eat with him at his table, with his cap off ; and every one of them has his peafant boy to wait on him, maintained by the mafter of the family. At an entertainment, the Poles lay neither knives, forks, nor fpoons, but every gueft brings them with him ; and they no fooner fit down to table, than all the doors are fhut, and not opened till the company return home. It is ufual for a nobleman to give his fervant part of his meat, which he eats as he ftands behind him, and to let him drink out of the fame cup with himfelf : but this is the lefs extraordinary, if it be confidered, that thefe fervants are efteemed his equal. Bumpers are much in fafhion, both here and in Ruffia ; nor will they eafily excufe any perfon from pledging them. It would exceed the bounds of this work to defcribe the grandeur and equipages of the Polifh nobility, and the reader may figure to himfelf an idea of all that is faftidious, ceremonious, expenfive, and fhewy in life, to have any conception of their way of living. They carry the pomp of their attendance, when they appear abroad, even to ridicule, for it is not unufual to fee the lady of a Polifh grandee, befides a coach and fix, with a great number of fervants, attended by an old gentleman-ufher, an old gentlewoman for her governante, and a dwarf of each fex to hold up her train ; and if it be night, her coach is furrounded by a great number of flambeaux. The figure of all their pomp, however, is proportioned to their eftates, but each perfon goes as far as his income can afford.

The Poles are divided into nobles, citizens, and peafants. Though Poland has its princes, counts, and barons, yet the whole body of the nobility are naturally on a level, except the difference that arifes from the public pofts they enjoy. Hence all who are of noble birth call one another brothers. They do not value titles of honour, but think a gentleman of Poland is the higheft appellation they can enjoy. They enjoy

many

many confiderable privileges, and indeed the boafted Polifh
liberty is properly limited to them alone, partly by the indulgence of former kings, but more generally from ancient
cuftom and prefcription. They have a power of life and
death over their tenants and vaffals ; pay no taxes ; are fubject to none but the king; may chufe whom they will for
their king, and lay him under what reftraints they pleafe by
the *pacta conventa* ; and none but they, and the burghers of
fome particular towns, can purchafe lands. In fhort, they
are almoft entirely independent, enjoying many other privileges entirely incompatible with a well regulated ftate; but if
they engage in trade, they forfeit their nobility. Thefe great
privileges make the Polifh gentry powerful ; many of them
have large territories, with a defpotic power, as we have faid,
over their tenants, whom they call their fubjects, and transfer
or affign over with the lands, cattle, and furniture. Some of
them have eftates of from five to thirty leagues in extent, and
are alfo hereditary fovereigns of cities, with which the king
has no concern. One of their nobles poffeffes above 4000
towns and villages. Some of them can raife 8 or 10,000 men.
The houfe of a nobleman is a fecure afylum for perfons who
have committed any crime ; for none muft prefume to take
them from thence by force. They have their horfe and foot
guards, which are upon duty day and night before their
palaces and in their anti-chambers, and march before them
when they go abroad. They make an extraordinary figure
when they come to the diet, fome of them having 5000 guards
and attendants ; and their debates in the fenate are often determined by the fword. When great men have fuits at law,
the diet, or rather tribunals, decide them ; yet the execution
of the fentence muft be left to the longeft fword ; for the
juftice of the kingdom is commonly too weak for the grandees.
Sometimes they raife 5 or 6000 men of a fide, plunder and
burn one another's cities, and befiege caftles and forts; for
they think it below them to fubmit to the fentence of judges,
without a field battle. As to the peafants, they are born
flaves, and have no notion of liberty. If one lord kills the
peafant of another, he is not capitally convicted, but only
obliged to make reparation, by another peafant equal in
value. A nobleman who is defirous of cultivating a piece of
land, builds a little wooden houfe, in which he fettles a peafant and his family, giving him a cow, two horfes, a certain
number of geefe, hens, &c. and as much corn as is fufficient
to maintain him the firft year, and to improve for his own
future fubfiftence and the advantage of his lord.

The

The peasants having no property, all their acquisitions serve only to enrich their master. They are indispensibly obliged to cultivate the earth ; they are incapable of entering upon any condition of life that might procure them freedom, without the permission of their lords ; and they are exposed to the dismal, and frequently fatal effects, of the caprice, cruelty, and barbarity of their tyrannical masters, who oppress them with impunity; and having the power of life and property in their hands, too often abuse it in the most gross and wanton manner, their wives and daughters being exposed to the most brutal treatment. One blessing, however, attends the wretched situation of the Polish peasants, which is their insensibility. Born slaves, and accustomed from their infancy to hardships and severe labour, they scarce entertain an idea of better circumstances and more liberty. They regard their masters as a superior order of beings, and hardly ever repine at their severe lot. Chearful and contented with their condition, they are ready upon every occasion to sacrifice themselves and their families for their master, especially if the latter takes care to feed them well. They think that a man can never be very wretched while he has any thing to eat. I have been the more circumstantial in describing the manners and present state of the Poles, as they bear a near resemblance, in many particulars, to those of our own country and Europe in general during the feudal ages.

DRESS.] The dress of the Poles is pretty singular. They cut the hair of their heads short, and shave their beards, leaving only large whiskers. They wear a vest which reaches down to the middle of the leg, and a kind of gown over it lined with fur and girded with a sash, but the sleeves sit as close to their arms as a waistcoat. Their breeches are wide, and make but one piece with their stockings. They wear a fur cap ; their shirts are without collar or wristbands, and they wear neither stock nor neckcloth. Instead of shoes, they wear Turkey leather boots, with thin soles, and deep iron heels bent like an half moon. They carry a pole-ax, and a sabre or cutlass, by their sides. When they appear on horseback, they wear over all a short cloak, which is commonly covered with furs both within and without. The people of the best quality wear sables, and others the skins of tygers, leopards, &c. Some of them have fifty suits of clothes, all as rich as possible, and which descend from father to son.

Were it not for our own partiality to short dresses, we must acknowledge that of the Poles to be picturesque and majestic. Charles II. of England, thought of introducing the Polish dress into his court, and, after his restoration, wore it for

two

two years, chiefly for the encouragement of Englifh broad-cloth, but difcontinued it through his connections with the French.

The habit of the women comes very near to that of the men; but fome people of fafhion, of both fexes, affect the French or Englifh modes. As to the peafants, in winter they wear a fheep's-fkin with the wool inwards, and in fummer a thick coarfe cloth; but as to linen, they wear none. Their boots are the rinds of trees wrapped about their legs, with the thicker parts to guard the foles of their feet. The women have a watchful eye over their daughters, and make them wear little bells before and behind, to give notice where they are, and what they are doing.

The inns of this country are long ftables built with boards and covered with ftraw, without furniture or windows; there is a chamber at one end, but none can lodge there, becaufe of flies and other vermin; fo that ftrangers generally chufe rather to lodge among the horfes. Travellers are obliged to carry provifions with them; and when foreigners want a fupply, they apply to the lord of the village, who forthwith provides them with neceffaries.

RELIGION.] No country has bred more deifts and free-thinkers in religious matters than Poland: the number of proteftants, confifting of Lutherans and Calvinifts, in their republic is very confiderable, and when thefe are joined to the Greek church, the whole are called Diffidents. At the fame time, the Polifh nobility, and the bulk of the nation, are tenacious of the Roman-catholic religion, even to enthufiafm, witnefs the prefent oppreffive war carried on in Poland. The treaty of Oliva, which was con-cluded in 1660, and tolerated the diffidents, was guaranteed by the principal powers in Europe, but has fince been fo far difregarded by the Poles, that about the year 1724, they made a public maffacre, under the fanction of law, of the prote-ftants at Thorn, for which no fatisfaction has been as yet obtained. The fame may be faid of the other numerous pro-vifions made for the protection of the proteftants, who were perfecuted, when Jews, Turks, and infidels of every kind, have been tolerated and encouraged. The monafteries in Po-land are by fome writers faid to be 576, and the nunneries 117, befides 246 feminaries or colleges, and 31 abbeys. The clergy are even poffeffed of two-thirds of the lands and revenues of the kingdom. The Polifh clergy, in general, are illiterate bigots, and the monks are the moft profligate of mankind. They are often feen drunk, and led from taverns, without apprehending any difgrace to their order, or dreading the cenfure of their fuperiors, who require equal indulgence.

After

After what has been said, the reader cannot be at a lofs to account for the vaft fway which the clergy at this time appear to have in Poland, in fpite of treaties and capitulations. Their difaffection to their king is, however, not to be imputed entirely to religion, but to the march of the Ruffians into the heart of the republic.

ARCHBISHOPRICS AND BISHOPRICS.] Poland contains two archbifhoprics; Guefna, and Lemburg. The archbifhop of Guefna, befides being primate, and during an interreign, prince-regent of the kingdom, is always a cardinal. The other bifhops, particularly Cracow, enjoy great privileges and immunities.

LANGUAGE.] The Polifh language is a dialect of Sclavonic, and is both harfh and unharmonious, on account of the vaft number of confonants it employs, fome of their words having no vowels at all. The Lithuanians and Livonians have a language full of corrupted Latin words; but the Ruffian and German tongues are underftood in the provinces bordering on thofe countries.

LEARNING AND LEARNED MEN.] Though Copernicus, the great reftorer of the true aftronomical fyftem, Vorftius, and fome other learned men, were natives of Poland, yet its foil is far from being favourable to learning. Latin is fpoken, tho' incorrectly, by the common people in fome provinces. But the contempt which the nobility, who place their chief importance in the privileges of their rank, have ever fhown for learning, the fervitude of the lower people, and the univerfal fuperftition among all ranks of men, thefe circumftances have wonderfully retarded, and notwithftanding the liberal efforts of his prefent majefty, ftill continue to retard the progrefs of letters in this kingdom.

UNIVERSITIES.] The univerfities of Poland are thofe of Cracow, Pofna or Pofen, and Wilna. The firft confifts of eleven colleges, and has the fupervirforfhip of 14 grammar-fchools difperfed through the city. That of Pofna is rather a jefuit's college than an univerfity. We know nothing particular of Wilna; and all of them, by this time, are probably ruined.

ANTIQUITIES AND CURIOSITIES,⎫ The frequent incur-
NATURAL AND ARTIFICIAL. ⎭ fions of the Tartars, and other barbarous nations, into Poland, probably forced the women fometimes to leave their children expofed in the woods, where we muft fuppofe they were nurfed by bears and other wild beafts, otherwife it is difficult to account for their fubfiftence. It is certain that fuch beings have been found in the woods both of Poland and Germany, divefted of all the properties

perties of humanity but the form. When taken, they generally went on all fours; but it is said, that some of them
have, by proper management, attained to the use of speech;
but this perhaps may be questioned.

The salt-mines of Poland consist of wonderful caverns several hundred yards deep, at the bottom of which are many
intricate windings and labyrinths. Out of these are dug four
different kinds of salts; one extremely hard, like chrystal;
another softer, but clearer; a third white, but brittle: these
are all brackish; but the fourth, somewhat fresher. These
four kinds are dug in different mines, near the city of Cracow; on one side of them is a stream of salt-water, and on
the other one of fresh. The revenue arising from those, and
other salt-mines, is very considerable, and form part of the
royal revenue; some having computed them at 40,000 l. sterling a year. Out of some mines at Itza, about 70 miles
north-east of Cracow, are dug several kinds of earth, which
are excellently adapted to the potters use, and supply all
Poland with earthen-ware. Under the mountains adjoining
to Kiow, in the deserts of Podolia, are several grottos, where
a great number of human bodies are preserved, though buried
a vast many years since, being neither so hard nor so black as
the Egyptian mummies. Among them are two princes, in
the habits they used to wear. It is thought that this preserving quality is owing to the nature of the soil, which is dry
and sandy. Poland can boast of few antiquities, as old Sar-
matia was never perfectly known to the Romans themselves.
Its artificial rarities are but few, the chief being the gold,
silver, and enamelled vessels, presented by the kings and pre-
lates of Poland, and preserved in the cathedral of Guesna.

CITIES, TOWNS, FORTS, AND OTHER EDIFICES, PUBLIC AND PRIVATE. } Warsaw lies on the Vistula, and almost in the
centre of Poland. It is
the royal residence; but though it contains many magnificent
palaces and other buildings, besides churches and convents, it
has little or no commerce. The same may be said of Cracow, which is the capital, (though that honour is disputed
by Warsaw) for we are told, that notwithstanding it lies in
the neighbourhood of the rich salt mines, and is said to contain fifty churches and convents, its commerce is inconsiderable.

Dantzic is the capital of Polish Prussia, and is famous in
history on many accounts, particularly that of its being formerly at the head of the Hanseatic association, commonly
called the Hanse-towns. It is situated on the Vistula, near
five miles from the Baltic, and is a large, beautiful, populous

city; its houfes generally are five ftories high ; and many of its ftreets are planted with chefnut-trees. It has a fine harbour, and is ftill a moft eminent commercial city, although it feems to be fomewhat paft its meridian glory, which was, probably about the time that the prefident de Thou wrote his much efteemed *Hiftoria fui Temporis*; wherein, under the year 1607, he fo highly celebrates its commerce and grandeur. It is a republic, with a fmall adjacent territory about forty miles round it, under the protection of the king and the republic of Poland. Its magiftracy, and the majority of its inhabitants, are Lutherans ; although the Romanifts and Calvinifts be equally tolerated in it. It is rich, and has 26 parifhes, with many convents and hofpitals. The elder inhabitants make her number amount to 200,000 ; but later computations fall very confiderably fhort of it ; as appears by its annual bill of mortality, exhibited by Dr. Bufching, who tells us, that in the year 1752, there died there but 1846 perfons. Its own fhipping is numerous, but the foreign fhips conftantly reforting to it are more fo, whereof 1014 arrived there in the year 1752 ; in which year alfo 1288 Polifh veffels came down the Viftula, chiefly laden with corn, for its matchlefs granaries ; from whence that grain is diftributed to many foreign nations ; Poland being juftly deemed the greateft magazine of corn in all Europe, and Dantzic the greateft port for diftributing it every where : befides which, Dantzic exports great quantities of naval ftores, and vaft variety of other articles. Dr. Bufching affirms, that it appears from ancient records, as early as the year 997, that Dantzic was a large commercial city, and not a village or inconfiderable town, as fome pretend.

The inhabitants of Dantzic have often changed their mafters, and have fometimes been under the protection of the Englifh and Dutch, but of late they have fhewed a great predilection for the kingdom and republic of Poland, as being lefs likely to rival them in their trade, or abridge them of their immunities, which reach even to the privilege of coining money. Though ftrongly fortified, and poffeffed of 150 large brafs cannon, it could not, through its fituation, ftand a regular fiege, being furrounded with eminences; and in 1734, the inhabitants difcovered a remarkable attachment and fidelity towards Staniflaus, king of Poland, not only when his enemies, the Ruffians, were at their gates, but even in poffeffion of the city.

The reafon why Dantzic, Thorn, and Elbing, enjoy privileges, both civil and religious, very different from thofe of the reft of Poland is, becaufe not being able to endure the

tyranny

tyranny of the Teutonic knights, they put themfelves under the protection of Poland; but referving to themfelves large and ample privileges, which they ftill enjoy.

COMMERCE AND MANUFACTURES.] Some linen and woollen cloths, and hard wares, are manufactured in the interior parts of Poland; but commerce is entirely confined to the city of Dantzic, and their other towns on the Viftula and the Baltic.

CONSTITUTION AND GOVERNMENT.] Whole volumes have been written upon this fubject, but it remains in a great meafure ftill unknown. The king is the head of the republic, and is elected by the nobility and clergy in the plains of War-faw. They elect him on horfeback; and in cafe there fhould be a refractory minority, the majority has no controul over them, but to cut them in pieces with their fabres. Imme-diately after his election, he figns the *pacta conventa* of the kingdom, by which he engages to introduce no foreigners into the army or government; fo that in fact he is no more than prefident of the fenate, which is compofed of the primate, the archbifhop of Lemburg, fifteen bifhops, and 130 laymen, confifting of the great officers of ftate, the palatines, and caftellans.

The diets of Poland are ordinary and extraordinary: the former meet once in two, and fometimes three years; the latter is fummoned by the king, upon critical emergencies; but one diffenting voice renders all their deliberations in-effectual.

The ftarofts properly are governors and judges in particular ftarofties or diftricts, though fome enjoy this title without any jurifdiction at all. The palatines and caftellans, befides being fenators, are lord-lieutenants and deputy-lieutenants in their refpective palatinates.

Previous to a general diet, either ordinary or extraordinary, which can fit but fix weeks, there are dietines, or provincial diets, held in different diftricts. The king fends them letters containing the heads of the bufinefs that is to be treated of in the general diet. The gentry of each palatinate may fit in the dietine, and chufe nuncios or deputies, to carry their refo-lutions to the grand diet. The great diet confifts of the king, fenators, and thofe deputies from provinces and towns, viz. 178 for Poland and Lithuania, and feventy for Pruffia; and it meets twice at Warfaw and once at Grodno, by turns, for the conveniency of the Lithuanians, who made it one of the articles of their union with Poland.

The king may nominate the great officers of ftate, but they are accountable only to the fenate; neither can he difplace

them

them when once appointed. When he is abfent from Poland, his place is fupplied by the archbifhop of Guefna, and if that fee is vacant, by the bifhop of Plofko.

The ten great officers of ftate in Poland, who are fenators, are, the two great marfhals, one of Poland, the other of Lithuania ; the chancellor of the kingdom, and the chancellor of the duchy ; the vice-chancellor of the kingdom, and the vice-chancellor of the duchy ; the treafurer of the kingdom, and the treafurer of the duchy ; the fub-marfhal, or marfhal of the court of the kingdom ; and the fub-marfhal, or marfhal of the court of the duchy.

Such are the outlines of this motley conftitution, which is new modelled with almoft every new king, according to the *paƐta conventa* which he is obliged to fign ; fo that nothing of it can be faid with certainty, and lefs at this time than ever ; there being now a total diffolution of all order in Poland. It muft, however, be acknowledged, that in the imperfeƐt fketch I have exhibited, we can difcern the great outlines of a noble and free government. The precautions taken to limit the king's power, and yet inveft him with an ample prerogative, are worthy of a wife people. The inftitutions of the diet and dietines are favourable to public liberty, as are many other provifions in the republic. It laboured, however, even in its beft ftate, under incurable diforders. The exercife of the *veto*, or the tribunitial negative, that is vefted in every member of a diet or dietine, muft always be deftruƐtive of order and government. It is founded, however, upon Gothic principles, and that unlimited jurifdiƐtion which the great lords, in former ages, ufed to enjoy all over Europe. The want of fubordination in the executive parts of the conftitution, and the rendering noblemen independent and unaccountable for their conduƐt, is a blemifh which perhaps may be impraƐticable to remove, as it can be done only by their own confent. After all, when we examine the beft accounts of the prefent conftitution of Poland, and compare them with the antient hiftory of Great Britain, and other European kingdoms, we may perceive a wonderful fimilarity between what thefe were formerly, and what Poland is at prefent. This naturally leads us to infer, that the government of Poland cannot be otherwife improved than by the introduƐtion of arts, manufaƐtures, and commerce, which would render the common people independent on the nobility, and prevent the latter from having it in their power to annoy their fovereign, and to maintain thofe unequal privileges which are fo hurtful to the community. If a nobleman of great abilities, and who happened to poffefs an extenfive territory within the kingdom,

should

should be elected fovereign, he might perhaps, by a proper ufe of the prerogatives of difpofing of all places of truft and profit, and of ennobling the plebeians, which are already vefted in the crown, eftablifh the fucceffion in his own family, and deliver the Poles from thofe perpetual convulfions which muft ever attend an elective kingdom.

REVENUES.] Though the king of Poland is ftinted in the political exercife of his prerogative, yet his revenue is fufficient to maintain him and his houfhold with great fplendor, as he pays no troops, or officers of ftate, nor even his body guards. The prefent king had 1,000,000 and half of florins fettled upon him by the commiffion of ftate ; and the income of his predeceffors generally amounted to 140,000 l. fterling. The public revenues arife chiefly from the crown-lands, the falt-mines in the palatinate of Cracow, antient tolls and cuftoms, particularly thofe of Elbing and Dantzic, the rents of Marienburg, Dirfhau, and Rogenhus, and of the government of Cracow and diftrict of Niepoliomicz.

MILITARY STRENGTH.] The innate pride of the Polifh nobility is fuch, that they always appear in the field on horfeback ; and it is faid that Poland can raife 100,000, and Lithuania 70,000 cavalry, and that with eafe ; but it muft be underftood that fervants are included. As to their infantry, they are generally hired from Germany, but are foon difmiffed, becaufe they muft be maintained by extraordinary taxes, of which the Polifh grandees are by no means fond. As to the ordinary army of the Poles, it confifts of 36,000 men, in Poland, and 12,000 in Lithuania, cantoned into crown-lands. The plofpolite confifts of all the nobility of the kingdom and their followers, excepting the chancellor, and the ftarofts of frontier places ; and they may be called by the king into the field upon extraordinary occafions, but he cannot keep them above fix weeks in arms, neither are they obliged to march above three leagues out of the kingdom.

The Polifh huffars are the fineft and moft fhewy body of cavalry in Europe ; next to them are the pancerns ; and both thofe bodies wear defenfive armour of coats of mail and iron caps. The reft of their cavalry are armed with mufkets and heavy fcimiters. After all that has been faid, the Polifh cavalry are extremely inefficient in the field, for though the men are brave, and their horfes excellent, they are ftrangers to all difcipline ; and when drawn out, notwithftanding all the authority their crown-general, their other officers, and even the king himfelf, have over them, they are oppreffive and deftructive to the court. It is certain, notwithftanding, that the Poles may be rendered excellent troops by difcipline, and that

on

on various occasions, particularly under John
made as great a figure in arms as any people
proved the bulwark of Christendom against t
did not suit the Saxon princes, who succeede
encourage a martial spirit in the Poles, whom
overawed with their electoral troops; nor ind
any reformation among them, either civil c
effects of which conduct has been since, and
felt in that devoted country.

ORDERS.] The order of the White Eag
by Augustus II. in the year 1705. Its ensign is
enamelled with red, and appendant to a blu
motto, *Pro fide, rege et lege.*

. HISTORY.] Poland, of old, was divided
states or principalities, each almost independ
though they generally had some prince who
over the rest. In the year 830, a peasant, c
elected to the sovereign throne. 'He lived to
years, and his reign was so long and auspicious,
Pole who has been since elected king is called
this period to the close of the 14th century, w
records of the history of Poland. Jagellon,
mounted the throne, was grand duke of Livon
but on his being elected king of Poland, he n
Christian, but was at pains to bring over hi
religion. He united his hereditary dominions
land, which gave such influence to his posterit
of the Poles, that the crown was preserve
until the male line extinguished in Sigismu
1552. At this time two powerful competitor:
crown of Poland. These were Henry, duke
ther to Charles IX. king of France, and
Austria. The French interest prevailed; bu
been four months on the throne of Poland,
died, and he returned privately into France,
he governed by the name of Henry III. Th
espoused Maximilian's interest, endeavoure
revive his pretensions; but the majority of
desirous to chuse a prince who might reside ar
choice of Stephen Batori, prince of Transy
the beginning of his reign, meeting with som
the Austrian faction, took the wisest method
self on the throne, by marrying Anne, the si
Augustus, and of the royal house of Jagello
duced a great change in the military affairs
establishing a new militia, composed of the C

and barbarous race of men, on whom he beftowed the Uckrain, or frontiers of his kingdom. Upon his death, in 1586, the Poles chofe Sigifmund, fon of John, king of Sweden, by Catharine, fifter of Sigifmund. II. for their king.

Sigifmund was crowned king of Sweden after his f ther's death, but being expelled, as we have already feen in the hiftory of Sweden, by the Swedes, a long war enfued between them and the Poles, but terminated in favour of the latter. Sigifmund being fecured in the throne of Poland, afpired to that of Ruffia as well as Sweden, but after long wars, he was defeated in both views. He was afterwards engaged in a variety of unfuccefsful wars with the Turks and the Swedes. At laft a truce was concluded under the mediation of France and England; but the Poles were forced to agree that the Swedes fhould keep Elbing, Memel, Branufberg and Pillan, together with all they had taken in Livonia. In the year 1632, Sigifmund died, and Uladiflaus his fon fucceeded. This prince was fuccefsful both againft the Turks and the Ruffians, and obliged the Swedes to reftore all the Polifh dominions they had taken in Pruffia. His reign, however, was unfortunate, by his being inftigated, through the avarice of his great men, to encroach upon the privileges of the Coffacs in the Ukraine. As the war which followed, was carried on againft the Coffacs upon ambitious and perfidious principles, the Coffacs, who are naturally a brave people, became defperate; and upon the fucceffion of John II. brother to Uladiflaus, the Coffac general Schmielinfki, defeated the Poles in two great battles, and at laft forced them to a difhonourable peace. It appears, that during the courfe of this war, the Polifh nobility behaved as the worft of ruffians, and their conduct was highly condemned by John; but his nobility difapproved of the peace he had concluded with them. While the jealoufy hereby occafioned continued, the Ruffians came to a rupture with the Poles; and being joined by many of the Coffacs, they, in the year 1654, took Smolenfko. This was followed with the taking of Wilna, and other places; and they committed moft horrid ravages in Lithuania. Next year, Charles X. of Sweden, after over-running the Great and Little Poland, fell into Polifh Pruffia, all the towns of which received him excepting Dantzic. The refiftance made by that city, gave the Poles time to reaffemble, and their king, John Cafimir, who had fled into Silefia, was joined by the Tartars, as well as Poles; fo that the Swedes, who were difperfed through the country, were every where cut in pieces. The Lithuanians, at the fame time, difowned the allegiance they had been forced to pay to Charles, who

returned

returned to Sweden, with no more than a handful of his army. It was during this expedition, that the Dutch and English protected Dantzic, the elector of Brandenburg acquired the sovereignty of the ducal Pruffia, which had submitted to Charles. Thus the latter loft Poland, of which he had made an almoft complete conqueft. The treaty of Oliva was begun after the Swedes had been driven out of Cracow and Thorn, by which Royal Pruffia was reftored to the Poles. They were, however, forced to quit all pretenfions to Livonia, and to cede Smolenfko, Kiow, and the duchy of Siveria, to the Ruffians.

During thofe tranfactions, the Polifh nobility grew very uneafy with their king. Some of them were diffatisfied with the conceffions he had made to the Coffacs, many of whom had thrown off the Polifh yoke ; others taxed him with want of capacity ; and fome, with an intention to rule by a mercenary army of Germans. Cafimir, who very poffibly had no fuch intentions, and was fond of retirement and ftudy, finding that cabals and factions encreafed every day, and that he himfelf might fall a facrifice to the public difcontent, abdicated his throne, and died abbot of St. Germains in France, employing the remainder of his days in Latin poetical compofitions, which are far from being defpicable.

The moft remote defcendents of the antient kings ending in John Cafimir, many foreign candidates prefented themfelves for the crown of Poland; but the Poles chofe for their king, a private gentleman of little intereft, and lefs capacity, one Michael Wiefnowifki, becaufe he was a Piaft. His reign was difgraceful to Poland. Large bodies of the Coffacs had put themfelves under the protection of the Turks, who conquered all the provinces of Podolia, and took Kaminieck, till then thought impregnable. The greateft part of Poland was then ravaged, and the Poles were obliged to pay an annual tribute to the fultan. Notwithstanding thofe difgraceful events, the credit of the Polifh arms was in fome meafure maintained by John Sobiefki, the crown general, a brave and an active commander, who had given the Turks feveral defeats. Michael dying in 1673, Sobiefki was chofen king ; and in 1676, he was fo fuccefsful againft the infidels, that he forced them to remit the tribute they had impofed upon Poland, but they kept poffeffion of Kaminieck. In 1683, Sobiefki, though he had not been well treated by the houfe of Auftria, was fo public fpirited, as to enter into the league that was formed for the defence of Chriftendom againft the infidels, and acquired immortal honour, by obliging the Turks to raife the fiege of Vienna, and making a terrible flaughter of
the

the enemy; for all which glorious fervices, and driving the
Turks out of Hungary, he was ungratefully requited by the
emperor Leopald.

Sobiefki returning to Poland, continued the war againſt
the Turks, but unfortunately quarrelled with the fenate,
who fufpected that he wanted to make the crown hereditary in
his family. He died, after a glorious reign, in 1696.

Poland fell into great diſtractions upon Sobiefki's death.
Many confederacies were formed, but all parties feemed inclined to exclude the Sobiefki family. In the mean while,
Poland was infulted by the Tartars, and her crown was in
a manner put up to fale. The prince of Conti, of the blood
royal of France, was the moſt liberal bidder; but while he
thought the election almoſt fure, he was difappointed by the
intrigues of the queen dowager, in favour of her younger fon
prince Alexander Sobiefki, for which ſhe was driven from
Warſaw to Dantzic. All of a fudden, Auguſtus, elector of
Saxony, ſtarted up as a candidate, and after a ſham election
being proclaimed by the biſhop of Cujavia, he took poffeffion
of Cracow, with a Saxon army, and actually was crowned in
that city, in 1697. The prince of Conti made feveral unfuccefsful efforts to re-eſtabliſh his intereſt, and pretended that
he had been actually chofen, but he was afterwards obliged to
return to France, and the other powers of Europe feemed to
acquiefce in the election of Auguſtus. The manner in which
he was driven from the throne, by Charles XII. of Sweden,
and afterwards reſtored by the czar, Peter the Great, has
been already related. It was not till the year 1712, that
Auguſtus was fully confirmed on the throne, which he held
upon precarious and difagreeable terms. The Poles were naturally attached to Staniſlaus, and were perpetually forming
confpiracies and plots againſt Auguſtus, who was obliged to
maintain his authority by means of his Saxon guards and regiments. In 1725, his natural fon prince Maurice, afterwards
the famous count Saxe, was chofen duke of Courland; but
Auguſtus was not able to maintain him in that dignity, againſt
the power of Ruffia, and the jealoufy of the Poles. Auguſtus
died, after an unquiet reign, in 1733, after he had done all
he could to infure the fucceffion of Poland to his fon Auguſtus II. (or, as he is called by fome III.) This occafioned a war, in which the French king maintained the intereſt
of his father-in-law Staniſlaus, who was actually re-elected to
the throne, by a confiderable party, of which the prince primate was the head. But Auguſtus, entering Poland with a
powerful army of Saxons and Ruffians, compelled his rival to
retreat into Dantzic, from whence he efcaped with great difficulty

ficulty into France. I have, in other parts of this work, mentioned the war between Auguftus II. as elector of Saxony, or rather as the ally of Ruffia and Auftria, and his prefent Pruffian majefty. It is fufficient to fay, that though Auguftus was a mild, moderate prince, and did every thing to fatisfy the Poles, he never could gain their hearts, and all he obtained from them was merely fhelter, when his Pruffian majefty drove him from his capital, and electorate. Auguftus died at Drefden, in 1763, upon which count Staniflaus Poniatowfki, rather on account of his perfonal merits, and the impatience of the Poles under the Saxon yoke, than any preeminence of birth or family, was unanimoufly chofen king of Poland, by the name of Staniflaus Auguftus. As he was eminently favoured by the Ruffians, the capitulation which he figned at the time of his election, and other acts of his government, were thought too favourable for the proteftants and the Greek diffidents, the latter of whom claim her imperial majefty of Ruffia, as their protector and patronefs. Her having an army lying, at that time, in Holland, gave a handle for many confederacies being formed by the catholics againft Poniatowfki. At firft they were crufhed with prodigious flaughter, and to the defolation of the country, by the Ruffians, the king not daring to truft even the Poles of his own party, for protection. The heads of the confederacy, at laft, moft unnaturally put themfelves under the protection of the grand fignior, who readily embraced their caufe, proclaimed war againft Ruffia, and invaded Poland with a powerful army, and it is at this time a theatre of as much mifery, blood, and devaftation, as perhaps ever was known in hiftory *.

SWITZERLAND.

SITUATION AND EXTENT.

	Miles.		Degrees.
Length	260	between	6 and 11 eaft longitude.
Breadth	100		45 and 48 north latitude.

BOUNDARIES.] IT is bounded by Alface and Suabia in Germany, on the north; by the lake of Conftance, Tirol, and Trent, on the eaft; by Italy, on the fouth; and by France, on the weft.

* Staniflaus Auguftus, (late count Poniatowfki) was born in 1732, and crowned king of Poland in 1764. This prince, while a private nobleman, refided fome time in London; and is a fellow of the Royal Society.

DIVISIONS.] Switzerland is divided into thirteen cantons, which ſtand in point of precedency as follows.: 1. Zurich; 2. Berne; 3. Lucern; 4. Wic;. 5. Switz; 6. Underwald; 7. Zug; 8. Glaris; 9. Baſil or Baſle; 10. Friburg; 11. Solothurn; 12. Schaffhauſen; 13. Appenzel.

The beſt account we have of the dimenſions, and principal towns of each canton, is as follows.

Countries Names.	Square Miles.	Length.	Breadth	Chief Cities.
Switzerland.				
Calviniſts. Berne	2,346	111	87	Berne
Zurich	728	34	33	Zurich
Schaffhauſen	140	23	9	Schaffhauſe
Baſil	240	21	18	BASIL { 47-40 N. Lat. 7-40 E. Lon.
Papiſts. Lucern	460	33	35	Lucern
Underwald	270	23	16	Stantz
Uri	612	48	21	Altorf
Suiſſe	250	27	13	Suiſſe
Friburg	370	24	21	Friburg
Zug	112	18	10	Zug
Solothurn	253	31	24	Solothurn
Calvin. and Papiſts. Appenzel	270	23	21	Apenzel
Glaris	257	24	18	Glaris
The ſubjects of the Switzers. Calviniſts and Papiſts, Baden				Baden
Bremgarten	216	26	12	Bremgarten
Mellingen				Mellingen
Rhintal	40	20	5	Rheineck
Turgow	119	18	11	Frowanfield
Lugano				Lugano
Locarno	850	52	30	Locarno
Mendris				Mendris
Magia				Magia
Total—	**7,533**			

Allies of the Switzers; the county of the Griſons, St. Gaul Repub. St. Gaul abbey, Tockenburg, Valais, Neufchatel, Mulhauſen, and Geneva, N. Lat. 46-20, E. Lon. 6.

SOIL, AIR, SEASONS AND WATER.] This being a mountainous country, lying upon the Alps, the froſts are conſequently bitter in winter, the hills being covered with ſnow, ſometimes all the year long. In ſummer the inequality of the ſoil renders the ſame province very unequal in its ſeaſons; on one ſide of thoſe mountains the inhabitants are often reaping, while they are ſowing on another. The vallies, however, are warm and fruitful, when well cultivated, as they generally are. The country is ſubject to rains and tempeſts, for which reaſon public granaries are every where erected to ſupply the failure of their crops. The water of Swiſſerland is generally excellent, and often deſcends from the mountains in large or ſmall cataracts, which have a pleaſing effect.

4

RIVERS AND LAKES.] The chief rivers are the Rhine, the Aar, the Rufs, the Jun, the Rhone, the Thur and the Oglios. The lakes are thofe of Geneva, Conftance, Thun, Lucern, Zurich, Neufchatel and Biende.

METALS AND MINERALS.] The mountains contain mines of iron, cryftal, virgin fulphur, and fprings of mineral waters.

VEGETABLE AND ANIMAL PRODUCTIONS.] Sheep and cattle are the chief animal productions of this country; corn and wood, and fome wine, with pot-herbs of almoft every kind, are likewife found here. The produce, however, of all thofe articles, are no more than fufficient for the inhabitants, who are too far removed from water-carriage to be profited by the ftately timber that grows in their woods. They have vaft plenty of game, fifh and fowl.

POPULATION, INHABITANTS, MAN- } According to the
NERS, CUSTOMS, AND DIVERSIONS. } beft accounts, the cantons of Switzerland contain about 2,000,000 of inhabitants, who are a brave, hardy, induftrious people, remarkable for their fidelity, and attachment to the caufe they undertake. Like the old Romans, they are equally inured to arms and agriculture. All the cantons are regimented in a manner, · that contributes equally to the fafety and profit of the inhabitants, who fupply foreign powers with excellent foldiers. They are fo jealous of their liberties, that they difcourage foreigners from fettling among them. Their nobility and gentry difdain the profeffion of trade and manufactures. It is faid, that in many places of Switzerland, the inhabitants, efpecially thofe towards France, begin to degenerate from the antient fimplicity of their manners and drefs. The cuftoms and diverfions are of the warlike and active kind, and the magiftrates of moft of the cantons, impofe fines upon plays, gaming, and even dancing, excepting at marriages.

RELIGION.] Though all the Swifs cantons form but one political republic, yet they are not united in religion, as the reader, in the table prefixed, may perceive. Thofe differences in religion formerly created many public commotions, which feem now to have fubfided. Zuing, commonly called Zuinglius, was the apoftle of proteftantifm in Switzerland. He was a moderate reformer, and differed from Luther, and Calvin, only in a few fpeculative points; fo that Calvinifm is faid to be the religion of the proteftant Swiffes.

LANGUAGE.] Several languages prevail in Switzerland; but the moft common is German. The Swiffes, who border upon France, fpeak a baftard French, as thofe near Italy do a corrupted Latin, or Italian.

Calvin, whose name is
so well known in all protestant countries, instituted laws for
the city of Geneva, which are held in high esteem by the most
learned of that country. The ingenious and eloquent Rousseau
too, whose works the present age have received with so much
approbation, is a citizen of Geneva. Rousseau has given a
force to the French language, which it was thought incapable of receiving. In England he is generally known as a
prose-writer only, but the French admire him as a poet. His
opera of the *Devin de Village* in particular is much esteemed ;
but in this he has acted with his usual consistency, in first
abusing the French music, and then composing an opera.

UNIVERSITIES.] The university of Basil contains a noble
library, some valuable manuscripts, and an excellent collection of medals. The other universities are those of Bern,
Lausanne and Zurich.

ANTIQUITIES AND CURIOSITIES, }   Every district of a
  NATURAL AND ARTIFICIAL.   }   canton in this mountainous country, presents the traveller with a natural curiosity ;
sometimes in the shape of wild but beautiful prospects, interspersed with lofty buildings, wonderful hermitages, especially
one two leagues from Friburg. This was formed by the hands
of a single hermit, who laboured on it for 25 years, and was
living in 1707. It is the greatest curiosity of the kind perhaps
in the world, as it contains a chapel, a parlour, 28 paces in
length, 12 in breadth, and 20 feet in height, a cabinet, a
kitchen, a cellar, and other apartments, with the altar, benches, flooring, cieling, all cut out of the rock. The mar-
casites, false diamonds, and other stones, found in those
mountains, are justly ranked among the natural curiosities of
the country. The ruins of Cæsar's wall, which extended
18 miles in length, from mount Jura, to the banks of lake
Leman, are still discernible. Many monuments of antiquity
have been discovered near the baths of Baden, which were
known to the Romans in the time of Tacitus. Switzerland
boasts of many noble religious buildings, particularly a college
of jesuits ; and many cabinets of valuable manuscripts, an-
tiques, and curiosities of all kinds.

CITIES.] Of these the most considerable is the city of Bern,
standing on the river Aar. This city and canton, it is said,
forms almost a third of the Helvetic confederacy, and can,
upon occasion, fit out 100,000 armed men. All the other
cities in Switzerland are excellently well provided in arsenals,
bridges, and public edifices. Basil is accounted by some the
capital of all Switzerland.

I shall here, to prevent a repetition, mention the city of
Geneva, which is an associate of Switzerland, and is under
the

the protection of the Helvetic body, but within itself is an independent state, and republic. The city is well built, and well fortified, contains 30,000 inhabitants, most of whom are Calvinists. It is situated upon the efflux of the Rhone, from the large fine lake of Geneva. It is celebrated for the learning of the professors of its university, and the good government of its colleges, the purity of its air, and the politeness of its inhabitants. By its situation, it is a thoroughfare from Germany, France, and Italy. It contains a number of fine manufactures and artists ; so that the protestants, especially such as are of a liberal turn, esteem it a most delightful place.

COMMERCE AND MANUFACTURES.] The productions of the loom, linen, dimity, lace, stockings, handkerchiefs, and gloves, are common in Switzerland, and the inhabitants are now beginning to fabricate, notwithstanding their sumptuary laws, silks, velvets, and woollen manufactures. Their great progress in those manufactures, and in agriculture, gives them a prospect of being able soon to make some exports.

CONSTITUTION AND GOVERNMENT.] These are very complicated heads, though belonging to the same body, being partly monarchical, partly aristocratical, and partly democratical. The bishop of Basil, and abbot of St. Gaul, are sovereigns. Every canton is absolute in its own jurisdiction, but those of Bern, Zurich, and Lucern, with other dependencies, are aristocratical ; those of Uri, Schwitz, Underwald, Zug, Glaris, and Appenzel, are democratical. But even those aristocracies, and democracies, differ in their particular modes of government. Perhaps in fact the democratical and popular part, as well as the aristocratical, are governed by their several leaders among the nobility, gentry, or eminent citizens.

The confederacy, considered as a republic, comprehends three divisions. The first, are the Swisses, properly so called. The second, are the Grisons, or the states, confederated with the Swisses, for their common protection. The third, are those prefectures, which, though subject to the other two, by purchase or otherwise, preserve each its own particular magistrates. Every canton forms within itself a little republic ; but when any controversy arises, that may affect the whole confederacy, it is referred to the general diet, which sits at Baden, where each canton having a vote, every question is decided by the majority. The general diet consists of two deputies from each canton, besides a deputy from the abbot of St. Gaul, and the cities of St. Gaul and Bienne.

REVENUES AND TAXES.] The variety of cantons that constitute the Swiss confederacy, renders it difficult to give a
precise

precife account of their revenues. Thofe of the canton of Bern, are faid to amount annually to 300,000 crowns, and thofe of Zurich to 150,000, the other cantons in proportion to their produce and manufactures. Whatever is faved, after defraying the neceffary expences of government, is laid up as a common ftock, and it has been faid, that the Swiffes are poffeffed of 500,000 l. fterling in the Englifh funds, befides thofe in other banks.

The revenues arife; 1. from the profits of the demefne lands; 2. the tenth of the produce of all the lands in the country; 3. cuftoms and duties on merchandize; 4. the revenues arifing from the fale of falt, and fome cafual taxes.

MILITARY STRENGTH.] The internal ftrength of the Swifs cantons confifts of 13,400 men, raifed according to the population and abilities of each. The œconomy and wifdom with which this force is raifed and employed, are truly admirable, as are the arrangements which are made by the general diet, for keeping up that great body of militia, from which foreign ftates and princes are fupplied, fo as to benefit the ftate, without any prejudice to its population.

HISTORY.] The prefent Swiffes and Grifons, as has been already mentioned, are the defcendents of the antient Helvetii, fubdued by Julius Cæfar. Their mountainous uninviting fituation, formed a better fecurity for their liberties, than their forts or armies, and the fame is their cafe at prefent. They continued long under little better than a nominal fubjection to the Burgundians and Germans, till about the year 1300, when the emperor Albert I. treated them with fo much rigour, that they petitioned him againft the cruelty of his governors. This ferved only to redouble the hardfhips of the people, and one of Albert's Auftrian governors Grifler, in the wantonnefs of tyranny, fet up a hat upon a pole, to which he ordered the natives to pay as much refpect as to himfelf. One William Tell, being obferved to pafs frequently without taking notice of the hat, and being an excellent markfman, the tyrant condemned him to be hanged, unlefs he cleft an apple upon his fon's head, at a certain diftance, with an arrow. Tell cleft the apple; and Grifler afking him the meaning of another arrow he faw ftuck in his belt, he bluntly anfwered, that it was intended to his [Grifler's] heart, if he had killed his fon. Tell was condemned to prifon upon this, but making his efcape, he watched his opportunity, and fhot the tyrant, and thereby laid the foundations of the Helvetic liberty.

Notwithftanding the above ftory, which might be true in the whole or part, it feems to be certain that the revolt of the Swiffes from the Auftrian tyranny had been planned among fome noble patriots for fome time before. Their meafures were

fo

fo juft, and their courage fo intrepid, that they foon found a union of feveral cantons, which daily encreafed, and repeatedly defeated the united powers of France and Germany; till by the treaty of Weftphalia in 1648, their confederacy was declared to be a free and independent ftate. With regard to the military character, and great actions of the Swiffes, I muft refer the reader to the hiftories of Europe.

S P A I N.

SITUATION AND EXTENT.

Miles.		Degrees.
Length near 700 }	between {	10 W. and 3 eaft longitude.
Breadth 500 }		36 and 44 north latitude.

BOUNDARIES. IT is bounded on the weft by Portugal and the Atlantic ocean; by the Mediterranean, on the eaft; by the Bay of Bifcay and the Pyrenean mountains, which feparate it from France, on the north; and by the ftrait of the fea of Gibraltar, on the fouth.

It is now divided into fourteen diftricts, befides iflands in the Mediterranean.

Spain.	Countries Names.	Square miles.	Length	Breadth	Chief cities.
	Caftile, New	27,840	220	180	MADRID { N. Lat. 40—30 / W. Lon. 4—15
Papifts.	Andalufia	16,500	273	135	Seville
	Caftile, Old	14,400	193	140	Burgos
	Arragon	13,818	190	105	Saragofa
	Eftremadura	12,600	180	123	Badajos
	Galicia	12,000	165	120	Compoftella
	Leon	11,200	167	96	Leon
	Catalonia	9000	172	110	Barcelona
	Granada	8100	200	45	Granada
	Valencia	6800	180	75	Valencia
	Bifcay and Ipufcoa	4760	140	55	Bilboa
	Afturia	4600	124	55	Oviedo
	Murcia	3600	87	65	Murcia
	Upper Navarre	3000	92	45	Pampelona
In the Mediterranean.	Majorca I.	1400	58	40	Majorca
	Yvica I.	625	37	25	Yvica
	Total—	150,263			

The town and fortrefs of Gibraltar, fubject to Great Britain.

ANCIENT NAMES AND DIVISIONS.] Spain formerly included Portugal, and was known to the ancients by the name of Iberia, and Hefperia, as well as Hifpania. It was, about

the

the time of the Punic wars, divided into Citerior and Ulterior; the Citerior, or hither part, contained the provinces
lying north of the river Ebro; and the Ulterior, which was
the largeft part, comprehending all that lay beyond that river.
Innumerable are the changes that it afterwards underwent;
but there is no country of whofe ancient hiftory, at leaft the
interior part of it, we know lefs of than that of Spain.

CLIMATE, SOIL, AND WATER.] Excepting during the
equinoxial rains, the air of Spain is dry and ferene, but exceffive hot in the fouthern provinces in June, July, and Auguft. The vaft mountains that run through Spain are, however, very beneficial to the inhabitants, by the refrefhing
breezes that come from them in the fouthernmoft parts; tho'
thofe towards the north and north-eaft, are in the winter very
cold, and in the night make a traveller fhiver.

So few writers have treated of the interior parts of Spain,
that the public knew little of them till within thefe fifty years.
The foil of Spain, it is well known, was formerly fruitful in
corn, but the natives now find a fcarcity of it, by their dif-
ufe of tillage, through their indolence; the caufes of which I
fhall explain afterwards. It produces, in many places almoft
fpontaneoufly, the richeft and moft delicious fruits that are to
be found in France and Italy, oranges, lemons, prunes,
citrons, almonds, raifins, and figs. Her wines, efpecially
her fack and fherry, are in high requeft among foreigners;
and Dr. Bufching fays, that the inhabitants of Malaga, and
the neighbouring country, export yearly wines and raifins to
the amount of 268,759 l. fterling. Spain indeed offers to
the traveller large tracts of unpromifing, becaufe uncultivated
ground; but no country perhaps maintains fuch a number of
inhabitants, who neither toil nor work for their food; fuch
are the generous qualities of its foil. Even fugar-canes thrive
in Spain; and it yields faffron, honey, and filk, in great
abundance. A late writer, Uftariz, a Spaniard himfelf, com-
putes the number of fhepherds in Spain to the amount of
40,000; and has given us a moft curious detail of their œconomy, their changes of pafture at certain times of the year,
and many other particulars unknown till lately to the public.
Thofe fheep-walks afford the fineft of wool, and are a treafure
in themfelves. Some of the mountains in Spain are cloathed
with rich trees, fruits, and herbage, to the tops; and Seville
oranges are noted all over the world. No country produces
a greater variety of aromatic herbs, which renders the tafte of
their kids and fheep fo exquifitely delicious. The kingdom
of Murcia abounds fo much with mulberry-trees, that the
product of its filk amounts to 200,000 l. a year. Upon the

VOL. II.   I   whole,

whole, few countries in the world owe more than Spain does to nature, and less to industry.

The waters (especially those that are medicinal) of Spain, are little known, but many salutiferous springs are found in Granada, Seville, and Cordoua. All over Spain the waters are found to have such healing qualities, that they are outdone by those of no country in Europe ; and the inclosing, and encouraging a resort to them, grow every day more and more in vogue, especially at Alhamar in Granada.

MOUNTAINS.] It is next to impossible to specify these, they are so numerous ; the chief are the Pyrenees, near 200 miles in length, which extend from the bay of Biscay to the Mediterranean, and divide Spain from France. Over these mountains there are only five narrow passages to France. The Cantabrian mountains (as they are called) are a kind of continuation of the Pyrenees, and reach to the Atlantic ocean, south of Cape Finisterre. No Englishman ought to be unacquainted with Mount Calpe, now called the Hill of Gibraltar, and in former times, one of the pillars of Hercules ; the other, Mount Abyla, lying opposite to it in Africa.

RIVERS AND LAKES.] These are the Douro, formerly Durius, which falls into the Atlantic ocean below Oporto in Portugal ; the Tajo, formerly celebrated by the name of the Tagus, which falls into the Atlantic ocean below Lisbon ; the Guadiana falls into the same ocean near Cape Finisterre ; as does the Guadalquivier, now Turio, at St. Lucar ; and the Ebro, the ancient Iberus, falls into the Mediterranean sea below Tortosa.

Several lakes in Spain, particularly that of Beneventa, abound with fishes, particularly excellent trout. The water of a lake near Antiquera is made into salt by the heat of the sun.

BAYS.] The chief bays are those of Biscay, Ferrol, Corunna (commonly called the Groyne) Vigo, Cadiz, Gibraltar, Carthagena, Alicant, Altea, Valentia, Rofer, and Majorca in that island. The harbour of Port-Mahon, in the island of Minorca, belongs to England. The strait of Gibraltar divides Europe from Africa.

METALS AND MINERALS.] Spain abounds in both, and in as great variety, and of the same kinds, as the other countries of Europe. Cornelian, agate, load-stones, jacinths, turquois-stones, quicksilver, copper, lead, sulphur. allum, calamine, chrystal, marbles of several kinds, with other stones ; and even diamonds, emeralds, and amethysts, are found here. The Spanish iron, next to that of Damascus, furnishes the best arms in the world ; and in former times, brought in a

vast

vaſt revenue to the crown; the art of working it being here in great perfection. Even to this day, Spaniſh gun-barrels, and ſwords of Toledo, are highly valued. Amongſt the ancients, Spain was celebrated for gold and ſilver mines; and ſilver was in ſuch plenty, that Strabo, who was contemporary with Auguſtus Cæſar, informs us, that when the Carthaginians took poſſeſſion of Spain, their domeſtic and agricultural utenſils were of that metal. Theſe mines have now diſappeared, but whether by their being exhauſted, or through the indolence of the inhabitants in not working them, we cannot ſay; though the latter cauſe ſeems to be the moſt probable.

ANIMAL PRODUCTIONS BY SEA AND LAND. The Spaniſh horſes, eſpecially thoſe of Andaluſia, are thought to be the handſomeſt of any in Europe, and at the ſame time very fleet and ſerviceable. The king does all he can to monopolize the fineſt breeds for his own ſtables and ſervice. Spain furniſhes likewiſe mules and black cattle; and their wild bulls have ſo much ferocity, that their bull-feaſts were the moſt magnificent ſpectacle the court of Spain could exhibit, nor are they now diſuſed. Wolves are the chief beaſts of prey that peſter Spain, which is well ſtored with all the game and wild fowl that are to be found in the neighbouring countries I have already deſcribed. The Spaniſh ſeas afford excellent fiſh of all kinds, eſpecially anchovies, which are here cured in great perfection.

POPULATION, INHABITANTS, MANNERS, CUSTOMS, DIVERSIONS, AND DRESS. Spain, formerly the moſt populous kingdom in Europe, is now but thinly inhabited. This is owing partly to the great drains of people ſent to America, and partly to the indolence of the natives, who are at no pains to raiſe food for their families. Another cauſe may be aſſigned, and that is, the vaſt numbers of eccleſiaſtics, of both ſexes, who lead a life of celibacy. Other writers have given ſeveral other cauſes, ſuch as their wars with the Moors and final expulſion of that people, but I apprehend that they are in a great meaſure removed by the regulations and checks upon the clergy that have been introduced by his preſent catholic majeſty. Be that as it will, ſome late writers have computed the inhabitants of Spain at 7,000,000 and a half; others ſay that they do not exceed 5,000,000. This calculation, I think, is under-rated, when we reflect on the numerous armies which Spain has raiſed and recruited ſince the beginning of this century.

The perſons of the Spaniards are generally tall, eſpecially the Caſtilians; their hair and complexions ſwarthy, but their countenances are very expreſſive. The court of Madrid has of late been at great pains to clear their upper lips of muſtachoes, and to introduce among them the French dreſs, inſtead of their black cloaks, their ſhort jerkin, ſtrait breeches, and long Toledo ſwords, which dreſs is now chiefly confined to the lower ranks. The Spaniards, before the acceſſion of the houſe of Bourbon to their throne, affected that antiquated dreſs in hatred and contempt of the French ; and the government, probably, will find ſome difficulty in aboliſhing it quite, as the ſame ſpirit is far from being extinguiſhed. An old Caſtilian, or Spaniard, who ſees none above him, thinks himſelf the moſt important being in nature ; and the ſame pride is commonly communicated to his deſcendents. This is the true reaſon why ſo many of them are ſo fond of removing to America, where they can retain all their native importance, without the danger of ſeeing a ſuperior.

Ridiculous, however, as this pride is, it is productive of the moſt exalted qualities. It inſpires the nation with generous, humane, and virtuous ſentiments ; it being ſeldom found that a Spaniſh nobleman, gentleman, or even trader, is guilty of a mean action. During the moſt embittered wars they have had with England for near 70 years paſt, we know of no inſtance of their taking advantage (as they might eaſily have done) of confiſcating the Britiſh property on board their galleons and Plate fleet, which was equally ſecure in time of war as peace. This is the more ſurprizing, as Philip V. was often needy, and his miniſters were far from being ſcrupulous of breaking their good faith with Great-Britain.

By the beſt and moſt credible accounts of the late war, it appears that the Spaniards in South America gave the moſt humane and noble relief to all Britiſh ſubjects who were in diſtreſs and fell into their hands, not only by ſupplying them with neceſſaries, but money ; and treating them in the moſt hoſpitable manner while they remained among them.

Having ſaid thus much, we are carefully to diſtinguiſh between the Spaniſh nobility, gentry, and traders, and their government, who are to be put on the ſame footing with the lower ranks of Spaniards, who are as mean and rapacious as thoſe of any other country. The kings of Spain of the houſe of Bourbon, have ſeldom ventured to employ native Spaniards of great families, as their miniſters. Theſe are generally French or Italians, but moſt commonly the latter, who riſe into power by the moſt infamous arts, and of late times from the moſt abject ſtations. Hence it is that the French kings of Spain, ſince their acceſſion to that monarchy, have been but very indifferently ſerved in the cabinet. Alberoni, who had the greateſt genius among them, embroiled his maſter with all

Europe,

Europe, till he was driven into exile and difgrace ; and Gri-maldi, the laft of their Italian minifters, hazarded a rebellion in the capital, by his oppreffive and unpopular meafures.

The common people who live on the coafts, partake of all the bad qualities that are to be found in other nations.   They are an affemblage of Jews, French, Ruffians, Irifh adven-turers, and Englifh fmugglers ; who being unable to live in their own country, mingle with the Spaniards.   In time of war, they follow privateering with great fuccefs; and when peace returns, they engage in all illicit practices, and often enter into the Irifh and Walloon guards in the Spanifh fervice.

The beauty of the Spanifh ladies reigns moftly in their novels and romances ; for though it muft be acknowledged that Spain produces as fine women as any country in the world, yet beauty is far from forming their general character. In their perfons, they are commonly fmall and flender ; but they are faid to employ vaft art in fupplying the defects of nature. If we are to hazard a conjecture, we might reafonably fuppofe that thofe artifices rather diminifh than encreafe their beauty, efpecially when they are turned of 25.   Their indif-criminate ufe of paint, not only upon their faces, but their necks, arms, and hands, undoubtedly disfigures their com-plexions, and fhrivels their fkin.   It is at the fame time uni-verfally allowed, that they have great wit and vivacity.

After all I have faid, it is more than probable that the vaft pains taken by the government of Spain, may at laft eradicate thofe cuftoms and habits among the Spaniards that feem fo ridiculous to foreigners.   They are univerfally known to have refined notions and excellent fenfe ; and this, if improved by ftudy and travelling, which they now ftand in great need of, would render them fuperior to the French themfelves.   Their flow deliberate manner of proceeding, either in council or war, has of late years worn off to fuch a degree, that during the two laft wars, they were found to be as quick both in refolving and executing, if not more fo, than their enemies. Their fecrecy, conftancy, and patience, have always been deemed exemplary ; and in feveral of their provinces, particu-larly Galicia, Granada, and Andalufia, the common people have, for fome time, affiduoufly applied themfelves to agricul-ture and labour.

Among the many good qualities poffeffed by the Spaniards, their fobriety in eating and drinking is remarkable.   They fre-quently breakfaft, as well as fup in bed ; their breakfaft is ufually chocolate, tea being very feldom drank.   Their dinner is generally beef, mutton, veal, pork, and bacon, greens, &c. all boiled together.   They live much upon garlic, chives,

salad,

falad, and radifhes; which, according to one of their pro-
verbs, are food for a gentleman. The men drink very little
wine ; and the women ufe water or chocolate. Both fexes
ufually fleep after dinner, and take the air in the cool of the
evenings. Dancing is fo much their favourite entertainment,
that you may fee a grandmother, mother, and daughter, all in
the fame country dance. Their theatrical exhibitions are
generally infipid and ridiculous bombaft. The prompter's
head appears through a trap door above the level of the ftage,
and he reads the play loud enough to be heard by the audience.
Gallantry is a ruling paffion in Spain. Jealoufy, fince the
acceffion of the houfe of Bourbon, has flept in peace. The
nightly mufical ferenades of miftreffes by their lovers are ftill
in ufe. The fights of the cavaliers, or bull-feafts, are almoft
peculiar to this country, and make a capital figure in painting
the genius and manners of the Spaniards. On thefe occafions,
young gentlemen have an opportunity of fhewing their courage
and activity before their miftreffes; and the valour of the
cavalier is proclaimed, honoured, and rewarded, according to
the number and fiercenefs of the bulls he has killed in thefe
encounters. Great pains are ufed in fettling the form and
weapons of the combat, fo as to give a relief to the gallantry
of the cavalier. The diverfion itfelf is undoubtedly of Moorifh
original, and was adopted by the Spaniards when upon good
terms with that nation, partly through complaifance, and
partly through rivalfhip.

RELIGION.] The horrors of the Romifh religion, the only
one tolerated in Spain, are now almoft extinguifhed there, by
moderating the penalties of the inquifition, a tribunal difgraceful to human nature; but though difufed, it is not abrogated;
only the ecclefiaftics and their officers can carry no fentence
into execution without the royal authority : It is ftill in force
againft the Moorifh and Jewifh pretended converts. The
Spaniards, however, embrace and practife the Roman-catholic
religion with all its abfurdities ; and in this they have been
fo fteady, that their king is diftinguifhed by the epithet of
Moft Catholic.

ARCHBISHOPRICS AND BISHOPRICS.] In Spain there are
eight archbifhoprics, and 46 bifhoprics. The archbifhop of
Toledo is ftiled the Primate of Spain ; he is great chancellor
of Caftile ; has a revenue of 100,000 l. fterling per annum.
The riches of the Spanifh churches and convents are the un-
varying objects of admiration to all travellers as well as natives ; but there is a famenefs in them all, excepting that they
differ in the degrees of treafure and jewels they contain.

LANGUAGE.] The ground-work of the Spaniſh language, like that of the Italian, is Latin ; and it might be called a baſtard Latin, were it not for the terminations, and the exotic words introduced into it by the Moors and Goths, eſpecially the former. It is at preſent a moſt majeſtic and expreſſive language ; and it is remarkable, that foreigners who underſtand it the beſt, prize it the moſt. It makes but a poor figure even in the beſt tranſlators ; and Cervantes ſpeaks as awkward Engliſh, as Shakeſpear does French. It may, however, be conſidered as a ſtandard tongue, having retained its purity for upwards of 200 years. Their Pater-noſter runs thus ; *Padro nueſtro, que eſtas en los cielos, ſanćtificade ſea tu nombre; venga tu regno ; hagaſe tu voluntad, aſſien la tierra como en el cielo ; da nos hoy nueſtro pan cotidiano ; y perdona nos nueſtras deudas aſſi como nos otros, perdonamos a nueſtros deudores ; y no nos metas en tentacion, mas libra nos de mal, porque tao es le regno ; y la potencia; y la gloria per los ſiglos.* Amen.

LEARNING AND LEARNED MEN.] Spain has not produced learned men in proportion to the excellent capacities of its natives. This defect may, in ſome meaſure, be owing to their indolence and bigotry, which does not ſuffer them to apply to the ſtudy of the polite arts. Several old fathers of the church were Spaniards ; and learning owes a great deal to Iſidore, biſhop of Seville, and cardinal Ximenes. Spain has likewiſe produced ſome excellent phyſicians. Calderoni and Lopez de Vega, have by ſome been put in competition with our Shakeſpear in the drama, where it muſt be owned they ſhew great genius. Such was the gloom of the Auſtrian government, that took place with the emperor Charles V. that the inimitable Cervantes, the author of Don Quixote, liſted in a ſtation little ſuperior to that of a common ſoldier, and died neglected, after fighting bravely for his country at the battle of Lepanto. His ſatire upon knight-errantry, in his adventures of Don Quixote, did as much ſervice to his country, by curing them of that ridiculous ſpirit, as it now does honour to his own memory. He is perhaps to be placed at the head of moral and humorous ſatiriſts.

Toſtatus, a divine, the moſt voluminous perhaps that ever wrote, was a Spaniard ; but his works have been long diſtinguiſhed only by their bulk. Herrera, and ſome other hiſtorians, particularly De Solis, have ſhewn great abilities in hiſtory, by inveſtigating the antiquities of America, and writing the hiſtory of its conqueſt by their countrymen. Spain has likewiſe produced many travellers and voyagers to both the Indies, who are equally amuſing and inſtructive. If it ſhould happen that the Spaniards could diſengage themſelves from

I 4   their

their abſtracted metaphyſical turn of thinking, they certainly
would make a capital figure in literature.

Some of the Spaniards have diſtinguiſhed themſelves in the
polite arts, particularly Murillo, in painting ; and not only
the cities, but the palaces, eſpecially .the Eſcurial, diſcover
many ſtriking ſpecimens of their abilities as ſculptors and
architects ; but neither their names nor works are much
known in other parts of Europe.

UNIVERSITIES.] In Spain are reckoned 22 univerſities,
ſome make them 24 ; as, Seville, Granada, Compoſtella,
Toledo, Valladolid, Salamanca, Alcala, Siguenza, Valencia,
Lerida, Hueſca, Saragoſa, Tortoſa, Oſſuna, Onata, Gandia,
Barcelona, Murcia, Taragona, Baeza, Avila, Oriuela,
Oviedo, and Palencia.

ANTIQUITIES AND CURIOSITIES ⎫   The former of theſe
   ARTIFICIAL AND NATURAL. ⎬ conſiſt chiefly of Roman and Mooriſh antiquities. Near Segovia, a grand aque-
duct, erected by Trajan, extends over a deep valley between
two hills, and is ſupported by a double row of 170 arches.
Other Roman aqueducts, theatres, and circi, are to be found
at Terragona, Toledo, and different parts of Spain. A ruinous watch-tower near Cadiz, is vulgarly, but erroneouſly,
thought to be one of the pillars of Hercules.

The Mooriſh antiquities, eſpecially the palace of Granada,
are magnificent and rich : the inſide is overlaid with jaſper
and porphyry, and the walls contain many Arabic inſcriptions ;
the whole is executed in what we improperly call the Gothic
taſte, but it is really Saracen, though the Goths of Spain
adopted it. Many other noble monuments, erected in the
Mooriſh times, remain in Spain, ſome of them in tolerable
preſervation, and others exhibiting ſuperb ruins.

Among the natural curioſities, the medicinal ſprings, and
ſome noiſy lakes, form a principal part, but we muſt not for-
get the river Guadiana, which, like the Mole in England,
runs under ground, and then is ſaid to emerge.

CHIEF CITIES.] Madrid, though unfortified, it being only
ſurrounded by a mud wall, is the capital of Spain, and contains about 300,000 inhabitants. All its grandeur, which the
Spaniards blazon with great pomp, does not prevent its being,
according to the beſt accounts, a dirty uncomfortable place to
live in, eſpecially for ſtrangers. It is ſurrounded with very
lofty mountains, whoſe ſummits are always covered with ſnow.
The houſes in Madrid are of brick ; and are laid out chiefly
for ſhew, conveniency being little conſidered ; thus you will
paſs through uſually two or three large apartments of no uſe,
in order to come at a ſmall room at the end where the family
ſit. The houſes in general look more like priſons, than the
                                                    habitations

habitations of people at their liberty ; the windows, beside
having a balcony, being grated with iron bars, particularly
the lower range ; and sometimes all the rest. Separate families
generally inhabit the same house, as in Paris and Edinburgh.
Foreigners are very much distressed for lodgings at Madrid,
as the Spaniards are not fond of taking strangers into their
houses, especially if they are not catholics. Its greatest excellency is the cheapness of its provisions, but neither tavern,
coffee-house, nor news paper, excepting the Madrid gazette,
are to be found in the whole city. The boasted royal palaces
round it are designed for hunting seats, or houses of retirement
for their kings. Some of them contain fine paintings and good
statues. The chief of those palaces, are the Buen Retiro,
Cusa de Campo, Aranjuez, and St. Ildefonso.

The pride of Spain, however, is the Escurial, and the
natives say, perhaps with justice, that the building of it cost
more than that of any palace in Europe. The description of
this palace forms a sizeable quarto volume, and it is said, that
Philip II. who was its founder, expended upon it 3,300,060 l.
sterling. The Spaniards say, that this building, besides its
palace, contains a church, a mausoleum, cloisters, a convent,
a college, and a library, besides large apartments for all kinds
of artists and mechanics, noble walks, with extensive parks
and gardens, beautified with fountains and costly ornaments.
The fathers that live in the convent are 200, and they have
an annual revenue of 12,000 l. The mausoleum, or burying-
place of the kings and queens of Spain, is called the Pantheon, because it is built upon the plan of that temple at
Rome, as the church to which it belongs is upon the model of
St. Peter's.

Allowing to the Spaniards their full estimate of the incredible sums bestowed on this palace, and on its furniture, statues,
paintings, columns, vases, and the like decorations, which
are most amazingly rich, and beautiful, yet we hazard nothing
in saying, that the fabric itself discovers a bad taste, upon the
whole. The conceit of building it in the form of a gridiron,
because St. Laurence, to whom it is dedicated, was broiled on
such a utensil, and multiplying the same figure through its
principal ornaments, could have been formed only in the brain
of a tasteless bigot, such as Philip II. who erected it to commemorate the victory he obtained over the French (but by
the assistance of the English forces) at St. Quintin, on St.
Laurence's day, in the year 1563. It has been enriched and
adorned by his successors, but its outside has a gloomy appearance, and the inside is composed of different structures, some
of which are master-pieces of architecture, but forming a disagreeable

greeable whole. It muft however be confeft, that the pictures and ftatues that have found admiffion here, are excellent in their kind, and fome of them not to be equalled even in Italy itfelf.

Cadiz is the great emporium of Spanifh commerce. It ftands on an ifland feparated from the continent of Andalufia, without the ftraits of Gibraltar, by a very narrow arm of the fea, over which a fortified bridge is thrown, and joins it to the main land. The entrance into the bay is about 500 fathoms wide, and guarded by two forts called the Puntals. The entrance has never been of late years attempted by the Englifh, in their wars with Spain, becaufe of the vaft intereft our merchants have in the treafures there, which they could not reclaim from the captors.

Seville is, next to Madrid, the largeft city in Spain, but is greatly decayed both in riches and population. Its manufacturers in wool and filk, which formerly amounted to 16,000, are now reduced to 400, and its great office of commerce to Spanifh America, is removed to Cadiz.

Barcelona, a large trading city containing 15,000 houfes, is fituated on the Mediterranean facing Minorca, and is faid to be the handfomeft place in Spain.

Notwithftanding the pride and oftentation of the Spaniards, their penury is eafily difcernible, but their wants are few, and their appetites eafily fatisfied. The inferior orders even in the greateft cities are miferably lodged, and thofe lodgings wretchedly furnifhed. The poorer forts, both men and women, wear neither fhoes nor ftockings. A traveller in Spain muft carry provifions and bedding with him, and if perchance he meets with the appearance of an inn, he muft even cook his victuals; it being beneath the dignity of a Spaniard, to perform thefe offices to ftrangers ; but lately fome tolerable inns have been opened by Irifh and Frenchmen in the cities, and upon the highways. The pride, indolence, and lazinefs of the Spaniards, are powerful inducements to their more induftrious neighbours the French, who are to be found in all parts of the kingdom; and here a wonderful contraft diftinguifhes the character of two neighbouring nations. The Spaniard feldom ftirs from home, or puts his hand to work of any kind. He fleeps, goes to mafs, takes his evening walk. While the induftrious Frenchman becomes a thorough domeftic ; he is butcher, cook, and taylor, all in the fame family ; he powders the hair, cuts the corn, wipes the fhoes, and after making himfelf ufeful in a thoufand different fhapes, he returns to his native country loaded with dollars, and laughs out the remainder of his days at the expence of his proud benefactor.

COMMERCE AND MANUFACTURES.] The Spaniards, unhappily for themselves, make gold and silver the chief branches both of their exports and imports. They import it from
America, from whence they export it to other countries of Europe. Cadiz is the chief emporium for this commerce. " Hither
(fays Mr. Anderfon, in his Hiftory of Commerce) other European nations fend their merchandize, to be fhipped off in
Spanifh bottoms for America, fheltered (or, as our old Englifh
phrafe has it, coloured) under the names of Spanifh factors.
Thofe foreign nations have here their agents and correfpon-
dents, and the confuls of thofe nations make a confiderable
figure. Cadiz has been faid to have the fineft ftorehoufes and
magazines for commerce of any city in Europe ; and to it the
flota and galleons regularly import the treafures of Spanifh
America. The proper Spanifh merchandize exported from
Cadiz to America are of no great value; but the duty on the
foreign merchandize fent thither would yield a great revenue,
(and confequently the profits of merchants and their agents
would fink) were it not for the many fraudulent practices for
eluding thofe duties."

The manufactures of Spain are chiefly of filk, wool, copper, and hard-ware. Great efforts have been made by the
government to prevent other European nations from reaping
the chief advantage of the American commerce ; but thefe
never can be fuccefsful, till a fpirit of induftry is awakened
among the natives, fo as to enable them to fupply their American poffeffions with their own commodities and merchandize.

Mean while, the good faith and facility with which the
Englifh, French, Dutch, and other nations, carry on this
contraband trade, render them greater gainers by it than the
Spaniards themfelves are, the clear profits feldom amounting to
lefs than 20 per cent. This evidently makes it an important
concern, that thofe immenfe riches fhould belong to the Spaniards rather than to any active European nation : but I
fhall have occafion to touch this fubject in the account of
America.

CONSTITUTION AND GOVERNMENT.] Spain, from being
the moft free, is now the moft defpotic kingdom in Europe.
The monarchy is hereditary, and females are capable of fucceffion. It has even been queftioned, whether his catholic
majefty may not bequeath his crown upon his demife, to any
branch of the royal family he pleafes. It is at leaft certain,
that the houfe of Bourbon mounted the throne of Spain, in
virtue of the laft will of Charles II.

The courts or parliaments of the kingdom, which formerly,
efpecially in Caftile, had greater power and privileges than

that of England, are now abolifhed, but fome faint remains of their conftitution, are ftill difcernible in the government, though all of them are.ineffectual, and under the controul of the king.

The privy-council, which is compofed of a number of noblemen or grandees, nominated by the king, fits only to prepare matters, and. to digeft papers for the cabinet-council or junta, which confifts of the firft fecretary of ftate, and three or four more named by the king, and in them refides the direction of all the executive part of government. The council of war takes cognizance of military affairs only. The council of Caftile is the higheft law tribunal of the kingdom. The feveral courts of the royal audiences, are thofe of Galicia, Seville, Majorca, the Canaries, Saragoffa, Valentia and Barcelona. Thefe judge primarily in all caufes within 15 miles of their refpective cities or capitals, and receive appeals from inferior jurifdictions. Befides thefe there are many fubordinate tribunals, for the police, the finances, and other branches of bufinefs.

The government of Spanifh America forms a fyftem of itfelf, and is delegated to viceroys, and other magiftrates, who are in their refpective diftricts almoft abfolute. A council for the Indies is eftablifhed in Old Spain, and confifts of a governor, four fecretaries, 22 councellors, befides officers. Their decifion is final in matters relating to America. The members are generally chofen from the viceroys and magiftrates, who have ferved in that country. The two great viceroyalties of Peru and Mexico are fo confiderable, that they are feldom trufted to one perfon for more than three years, but they are thought fufficient to make his fortune in that time.

The foreign poffeffions of the crown of Spain, befides thofe in America, are the towns of Ceuta, Oran, and Mafulquivir, on the coaft of Barbary in Africa; and the iflands of St. Lazaro, the Philippines and Ladrones, in Afia.

The chief iflands belonging to Spain in Europe, are thofe of Majorca, and Yvica, of which we have nothing particular to fay. Minorca is indeed a Spanifh ifland, but it was taken by the Englifh in 1708. The Spanifh inhabitants enjoy their religion, and particular privileges, to which they are entitled by treaties, and they are faid to amount to 27,000.

REVENUES.] The revenues arifing to the king from Old Spain, yearly amount to 5,000,000 fterling, though fome fay eight; and they form the fureft fupport of his government. His American income, it is true, is immenfe, but it is generally in a manner embezzled or anticipated before it arrives in

Old

Old Spain. The king has a fifth of all the filver mines that are worked, but little of it comes into his coffers. He falls upon means, however, in cafe of a war, or any public emergency, to fequefter into his own hands great part of the American treafures belonging to his fubjects, who never complain, becaufe they are always punctually repaid with intereft. The finances of his prefent catholic majefty are in excellent order, and on a better footing, both for himfelf and his people, than thofe of any of his predeceffors.

As to the taxes from whence the internal revenues arife, they are various, arbitrary, and fo much fuited to conveniency, that we cannot fix them at any certainty. They fall upon all kinds of goods, houfes, lands, timber, and provifions ; the clergy and military orders are likewife taxed.

MILITARY AND MARINE STRENGTH.] The land forces of the crown of Spain, in time of peace, are never fewer than 40,000 ; but in cafe of a war, they amount, without prejudice to the kingdom, to 96,000. The great dependence of the king, however, is upon his Walloon or foreign guards. His prefent catholic majefty has been at great care and expence to raife a powerful marine ; and his fleet in Europe and America at prefent exceeds 50 fhips of the line.

ROYAL ARMS, TITLES, NO- ⎫ Spain formerly compre-
    BILITY AND ORDERS.   ⎭ hended twelve kingdoms,
all which, with feveral others, were by name entered into the royal titles, fo that they amounted in all to about 32. This abfurd cuftom is ftill occafionally continued, but the king is now generally contented with the title of his Catholic majefty. The kings of Spain are inaugurated by the delivery of a fword without being crowned. Their fignature never mentions their name, but I THE KING. Their eldeft fon is called prince of Afturias, and their younger children of both fexes, are by way of diftinction called infants or infantas, that is children.

The armorial bearing of the kings of Spain, like their title, is loaded with the arms of all their kingdoms. It is now a fhield, divided into four quarters, of which the uppermoft on the right hand, and the loweft on the left contain a caftle, or, with three towers, for Caftile ; and in the uppermoft on the left, and the loweft on the right, are three lions gules for Leon ; with three lillies in the center for Anjou.

The general name for thofe Spanifh nobility and gentry, unmixed with the Moorifh blood, is Hidalgo. They are divided into princes, dukes, marquiffes, counts, vifcounts, and other inferior titles. Such as are created grandees, may ftand covered before the king, and are treated with princely diftinctions.

distinctions. A grandee cannot be apprehended without the king's order; and cardinals, archbishops, embassadors, knights of the golden fleece, and certain other great dignitaries, both in church and state, have the privilege, as well as the grandees, to appear covered before the king. The knights of the three military orders of St. James, Calatrava, and Alcantara, are esteemed noblemen; they were instituted in the long wars between the Christians and the Moors, as an encouragement to valour; and have large estates annexed to their respective orders, consisting chiefly of towers or territories recovered from the Moors. The order of the golden fleece is generally conferred on princes and sovereign dukes; but there are no commanderies or revenues annexed to it.

HISTORY.] See Portugal; the two kingdoms being formerly under one head *.

PORTUGAL.

SITUATION AND EXTENT.

	Miles.		Degrees.
Length	300 } between	{	37 and 42 north latitude.
Breadth	100 }	{	7 and 10 west longitude.

BOUNDARIES.] IT is bounded by Spain on the north and east, and on the south and west by the Atlantic ocean, being the most westerly kingdom on the continent of Europe.

ANTIENT NAMES AND } This kingdom was, in the time
DIVISIONS. } of the Romans, called Lusitania.
The etymology of the modern name is uncertain. It most probably is derived from some noted harbour or port, to which Gauls (for so strangers are called in the Celtic) resorted. By the form of the country it is naturally divided into three parts; the north, middle, and south provinces.

---

* Charles III. king of Spain, was born in 1716, succeeded to the throne in 1759; and has issue by his late queen,
   1. Maria-Josepha, born 1744.
   2. Maria-Louisa, born 1745, married 1765, to the archduke Leopold of Austria, great duke of Tuscany, and brother to the present emperor of Germany.
   3. Philip-Anthony, duke of Calabria, born 1747, declared uncapable of succeeding to the throne, on account of an invincible weakness of understanding.
   4. Charles-Anthony, prince of Asturias, born in 1748, married 1765 to Louisa-Maria-Theresa, princess of Parma.
   5. Ferdinand-Anthony, king of Naples, born in 1751, married 1768, to the archduchess Mary-Cardire-Louisa, sister to the emperor of Germany.
   6. Gabriel-Anthony, born in 1752, grand prior of the kingdom of Spain.
   7. Anthony-Pascal, born 1755.
   8. Francis-Xavier, born 1757.

Provinces.		Chief towns.
The North Division contains	Entre Minho Douro and Tralos Montes	Braga Oporto and Viana Miranda and Villa Real.
The Middle Division contains	Beira Eftremadura	Coimbra Guarda Caftel Rodrigo LISBON $\left\{\begin{array}{l}\text{38-42. N. lat.}\\\text{8-53. W. lon.}\end{array}\right.$ St. Ubes and Leira.
The South Division contains	Entre Tajo Guadiana Alentejo Algarva	Ebora, or Evara Portalegre, Elvas, Beia Lagos Faro, Tavira, and Silves.

SOIL, AIR, AND PRODUCTIONS.] The foil of Portugal is not in general equal to that of Spain for fertility, efpecially in corn, which they import from other countries. Their fruits are the fame as in Spain, but not fo high flavoured. The Portugueze wines, when old and genuine, are efteemed to be friendly to the human conftitution, and fafe to drink. Portugal contains mines, but they are not worked; variety of gems, marbles and millftones, and a fine mine of falt-petre, near Lifbon. Their cattle and poultry are but indifferent eating. The air, efpecially about Lifbon, is reckoned foft and beneficial to confumptive patients; it is not fo fearching as that of Spain, being refrefhed from the fea breezes.

MOUNTAINS.] The face of Portugal is mountainous, or rather rocky, for their mountains are generally barren: the chief are thofe which divide Algarve from Alentejo; thofe of Tralos Montes, and the rock of Lifbon, at the mouth of the Tajo.

WATER AND RIVERS.] Though every brook in Portugal is reckoned a river, yet the chief Portugueze rivers are mentioned in Spain, all of them falling into the Atlantic ocean. The Tagus, or Tajo, was celebrated for its golden fand. Portugal contains feveral roaring lakes and fprings, fome of them are abforbent even of the lighteft fubftances, fuch as wood, cork, and feathers; fome, particularly one about 45 miles from Lifbon, are medicinal and fanative; and fome hot baths are found in the little kingdom, or rather province of Algarve.

PROMONTORIES AND BAYS.] The promontories or capes of Portugal, are Cape Mondego, near the mouth of the river Mondego; Cape Roca, at the north entrance of the river Tajo; Cape Efpithel, at the fouth entrance of the river Tajo; and Cape St. Vincent, on the fouth-weft point of Algarve. The bays are thofe of Cadoan, or St. Ubes, fouth of Lifbon, and Lagos Bay in Algarve.

ANIMALS.] The sea-fish, on the coast of Portugal, are reckoned excellent ; on the land, the hogs and kids are tolerable eating. Their mules are sure and serviceable, both for draught and carriage ; and their horses, though slight, are lively.

POPULATION, INHABITANTS,⎱ According to the best
AND CUSTOMS. ⎰ calculation, Portugal contains near two million of inhabitants. By a survey made in the year 1732, there were in that kingdom, 3,344 parishes, and 1,742,230 lay persons (which is but 522 laity to each parish on a medium) besides about 300,000 ecclesiastics of both sexes.

The modern Portugueze retain nothing of that adventurous enterprizing spirit that rendered their forefathers so illustrious 300 years ago. They have, ever since the house of Braganza mounted the throne, degenerated in all their virtues, though some noble exceptions are still remaining among them, and no people are so little obliged as the Portugueze are to the reports of historians and travellers. Their degeneracy is evidently owing to the weakness of their monarchy, which renders them inactive, for fear of disobliging their powerful neighbours, and that inactivity has proved the source of pride, and other unmanly vices. Treachery has been laid to their charge, as well as ingratitude, and above all, an intemperate passion for revenge. They are, if possible, more superstitious, and, both in high and common life, affect more state than the Spaniards themselves. Among the lower people, thieving is commonly practised, and all ranks are accused of being unfair in their dealings, especially with strangers. It is hard, however, to say what alteration may be made in the character of the Portugueze, by the expulsion of the jesuits, and the diminution of the papal influence among them, but above all, by that spirit of independency, with regard to commercial affairs, upon Great Britain, which, not much to the honour of their gratitude, is now so much encouraged by their court and ministry.

The Portugueze are neither so tall, nor so well made as the Spaniards, whose habits and customs they imitate, only the Portugueze quality affect to be more gayly and richly dressed. The Portugueze ladies are thin and small of stature. Their complexion is olive, their eyes black and expressive, and their features generally regular. They are esteemed to be generous, moderate, and witty. They dress like the Spanish ladies, with much awkwardness and affected gravity, but in general more magnificent, and they are taught by their husbands to exact from their servants an homage, that in other countries is
paid

paid only to royal perfonages. The furniture of the houfes, efpecially of their grandees, is rich and fuperb to excefs; and they maintain an incredible number of domeftics, as they never difcharge any who furvive, after ferving their anceftors.

RELIGION.] The eftablifhed religion of Portugal is popery in the ftricteft fenfe. The Portugueze have a patriarch, but formerly he depended entirely upon the pope, unlefs when a quarrel fubfifted between the courts of Rome and Lifbon. The power of his holinefs in Portugal has been of late fo much curtailed, that it is difficult to defcribe the religious ftate of that country; all we know is, that the royal revenues are greatly encreafed at the expence of the religious inftitutions in the kingdom. The power of the inquifition is now taken out of the hands of ecclefiaftics, and converted to a ftate-trap for the benefit of the crown.

ARCHBISHOPRICS AND BISHOPRICS.] The archbifhoprics are thofe of Braga, Evora, and Lifbon. The firft of thefe has ten fuffragan bifhops; the fecond two; and the laft ten, including thofe of the Portugueze fettlements abroad. The patriarch of Lifbon is generally a cardinal, and a perfon of the higheft birth.

LANGUAGE.] The Portugueze language differs but little from that of Spain, and that provincially. Their Pater-nofter runs thus: *Padre noffo que eftas nos Ceos, fanctificado feio o tu nome; venha a nos ten reyno, feia feita a tua votade, affi nos ceos, commo na terra. O paonoffa de cadatia, dano lo oie n'eftodia. E perdoa nos feuhor, as noffas dividas, affi como nos perdoamos a os noffos devedores. E nao nos dexes cahir em tentatio, mas libra nos do mal.* Amen.

LEARNING AND LEARNED MEN.] Thefe are fo few, that they are mentioned with indignation, even by thofe of the Portugueze themfelves, who have the fmalleft tincture of literature. Some efforts, though very weak, have of late been made by the Portugueze, to draw their countrymen from this deplorable ftate of ignorance; but what their fuccefs may be, I fhall not pretend to fay. It is univerfally allowed that the defect is not owing to the want of genius, but of a proper education. The anceftors of the prefent Portugueze, were certainly poffeffed of more true knowledge, with regard to aftronomy, geography, and navigation, than all the world befides, about the middle of the 16th century, and for fome time after. Camoens, who himfelf was a great adventurer and voyager, was poffeffed of a true, but neglected poetical genius.

UNIVERSITIES.] Thefe are Lifbon, Evora and Coimbra; but that of Lifbon fcarcely deferves the name of an univerfity.

CURIOSITIES.] The lakes and fountains which have been already mentioned form the chief of thefe. The remains of fome caftles in the Moorifh tafte are ftill ftanding. The Roman bridge and aqueduct at Coimbra are almoft entire and defervedly admired. The walls of Santareen are faid to be of Roman work likewife. The church and monaftery near Lifbon, where the kings of Portugal are buried, are inexpreffibly magnificent, and feveral monafteries in Portugal are dug out of the hard rock. To thefe curiofities we may add, that his prefent moft faithful majefty is poffeffed of the largeft diamond, which was found in Brafil, that ever was perhaps feen in the world.

CHIEF CITIES.] The city of Oporto, confifting of about 50,000 inhabitants, carries on a great trade with England, efpecially for wines. Lifbon is the capital of Portugal, and is thought to contain 200,000 inhabitants. Great part of it was ruined by an earthquake, which alfo fet the remainder on fire, upon All-Saints-day, 1755. It ftill contains many magnificent palaces, churches, and public buildings. Its fituation (rifing from the Tagus in the form of a crefcent) renders its appearance at once delightful and fuperb, and it is defervedly accounted the greateft port in Europe, next to London and Amfterdam. The harbour is fpacious and fecure, and the city itfelf is guarded from any fudden attack towards the fea by forts, though they would make but a poor defence againft fhips of war.

COMMERCE AND MANUFACTURES.] Thefe, within thefe feven or eight years, have taken a furprizing turn in Portugal. The enterprizing minifter there, has projected many new companies and regulations, which have been again and again complained of, as unjuft and oppreffive to the privileges which the Britifh merchants formerly enjoyed by the moft folemn treaties.

The Portugueze exchange their wine, falt, and fruits, and moft of their own materials for foreign manufactures. They make a little linen, and fome coarfe filk, and woollen, with a variety of ftraw work, and are excellent in preferving and candying fruit. The commerce of Portugal, though feemingly extenfive, proves of little folid benefit to her, as the European nations, trading with her, engrofs all the productions of her colonies, as well as her own native commodities, as her gold, diamonds, pearls, fugars, cocoa-nuts, fine red wood, tobacco, hides, and the drugs of Brafil; her ivory, ebony, fpices, and drugs of Africa and Eaft-India; in exchange for the almoft numberlefs manufactures, and the vaft quantity of corn and falt-fifh, fupplied by thofe European nations, and by the Englifh North American colonies.

The

The Portugueze foreign fettlements are, however, not only of immenfe value, but vaftly improvable. They bring gold from their plantations on the eaft and weft coafts of Africa, and likewife flaves for manufacturing their fugars and tobacco in Brafil, and their fouth American fettlements.

What the value of thefe may be, is unknown perhaps to the Portugueze themfelves, but they certainly abound in all the precious ftones, and rich mines of gold and filver, and other commodities that are produced in the Spanifh dominions there. It is computed that the king's fifth of gold, fent from Brafil, amounts annually to 300,000 l. fterling, notwithftanding the vaft contraband trade. The little fhipping the Portugueze have, is chiefly employed in carrying on the flave trade, and a correfpondence with Goa, their chief fettlement in the Eaft-Indies, and their other poffeffions there.

CONSTITUTION AND GOVERNMENT.] The crown of Portugal is abfolute, but the nation ftill preferves an appearance of its ancient free conftitution, in the meeting of the cortes or ftates, confifting, like our parliaments, of clergy, nobility and commons. They pretend to a right of being confulted upon the impofition of new taxes, but the only real power they have is that their affent is neceffary in every new regulation, with regard to the fucceffion. In this they are indulged, to prevent all future difputes on that account. The fucceffion in Portugal may devolve to the female line.

All great preferments, both fpiritual and temporal, are difpofed of in the council of ftate, which is compofed of an equal number of the clergy and nobility, with the fecretary of ftate. A council of war regulates all military affairs, as the treafury courts do the finances. The council of the palace is the higheft tribunal that can receive appeals, but the Cafa da Supplicaçao is a tribunal, from which no appeal can be brought. The laws of Portugal are contained in three duodecimo volumes, and have the civil law for their foundation.

REVENUES AND TAXES.] The revenues of the crown amount to above 3,000,000 and a half fterling, annually. The cuftoms and duties on goods exported, and imported, are exceffive, and farmed out, but if the Portugueze miniftry fhould fucceed in all their ambitious projects, and in eftablifhing exclufive companies, to the prejudice of the Britifh trade, the inhabitants will be able to bear thefe taxes without murmuring. Foreign merchandize pays 23 per cent. on importation, and fifh from Newfoundland 25 per cent. Fifh taken in the neighbouring feas and rivers pay 27 per cent. and the tax upon lands and cattle that are fold is 10 per cent. The

K 2

king

king draws a confiderable revenue from the feveral orders of knighthood, of which he is grand mafter. The pope, in con- fideration of the large fums he draws out of Portugal, gives the king the money arifing from indulgencies and licences to eat flefh at times prohibited, &c. The king's revenue is now increafed by the fuppreffion of religious orders and inftitu- tions.

MILITARY AND MARINE STRENGTH.] The Portugueze government depends chiefly for protection on England, and therefore they have for many years fhamefully neglected both their army and fleet. Their troops in time of peace ought to amount to 14,000, but they are without difcipline or courage, and their regiments are thin. The prefent king, however, fince the late invafion of his dominions by the French and Spaniards, has employed Englifh and foreign officers, for dif- ciplining his troops, and repairing his fortifications. The marine of Portugal in 1754, confifted only of 12 fhips of war, who were employed as convoys and carriers, but were quite unprovided for action. The prefent king is preparing to put his fleet upon a more refpectable footing.

ROYAL TITLES AND ARMS.] The king's titles are, king of Portugal, and the Algarves, lord of Guinea, and of the navigation conqueft and commerce of Ethiopia, Arabia, Per- fia, and Brafil. The laft king was complimented by the pope, with the title of his moft Faithful majefty. That of his eldeft fon is prince of Brafil.

The arms of Portugal are, argent, five efcutcheons, azure, placed crofs-wife, each charged with as many befants as the firft, placed, falter-wife, and pointed fable, for Portugal. The fhield bordered, gules, charged with feven towers, or, three in chief, and two in each flanch. The creft is a crown, or, under the two flanches, and the bafe of the fhield appears at the end of it; two croffes, the firft flower-de-luce, vert, which is for the order of Avis, and the fecond petee, gules, for the order of Chrift; the motto is changeable, each king affuming a new one; but it is frequently thefe words, *Pro Rege et Grege*, viz. For the King and the People.

NOBILITY AND ORDERS.] The title and diftinctions of their nobility are pretty much the fame with thofe of Spain. Their orders of knighthood are four; 1. That of Chrift; 2. The order of James; 3. The order of Avis. All thofe orders have large commanderies, and revenues annexed to them. The order of Malta has likewife 23 commanderies in Portugal.

HISTORY OF SPAIN AND PORTUGAL.] Spain was proba- bly firft peopled from Gaul, to which it lies contiguous, or from

from Africa, from which it is only feparated by the narrow ftrait of Gibraltar. The Phenicians fent colonies thither, and built Cadiz and Malaga. Afterwards, upon the rife of Rome and Carthage, the poffeffion of this kingdom became an object of contention between thofe powerful republics; but at length the Roman arms prevailed, and Spain remained in their poffeffion until the fall of that empire, when it became a prey to the Goths.

Thefe, in their turn, were invaded by the Saracens, who, about the end of the 7th century, had poffeffed themfelves of the fineft kingdoms of Afia and Africa; and not content with the immenfe regions that formerly compofed great part of the Affyrian, Greek, and Roman empires, they crofs the Mediterranean, ravage Spain, and eftablifh themfelves in the foutherly provinces of that kingdom.

Don Pelago is mentioned as the firft Old Spanifh prince who diftinguifhed himfelf againft thefe infidels, (who were afterwards known by the name of Moors) and he took the title of king of Afturia about the year 720.

His fucceffes animated other Chriftian princes to take arms likewife, and the two kingdoms of Spain and Portugal for many ages were perpetually embroiled in bloody wars. In the mean while, every adventurer was entitled to the conquefts he made upon the Moors, till Spain at laft was divided into 12 or 14 kingdoms; and about the year 1095, Henry of Burgundy was declared, by the king of Leon, count of Portugal; but his fon, Alphonfo, threw off his dependence on Leon, and declared himfelf king. A feries of brave princes gave the Moors repeated overthrows in Spain, till about the year 1475, when all the kingdoms in Spain, Portugal excepted, were united by the marriage of Ferdinand, king of Arragon, and Ifabella, the heirefs, and afterwards queen, of Caftile, who took Granada, and expelled the Moors and Jews, to the number of 170,000 families, out of Spain. I fhall, in their proper places, mention the vaft acquifitions made at this time to Spain by the difcovery of America, and the firft expeditions of the Portuguefe to the Eaft-Indies, by the difcovery of the Cape of Good-Hope; but the fucceffes of both nations were attended with difagreeable confequences.

The expulfion of the Moors and Jews, in a manner depopulated Spain of artifts, labourers, and manufacturers; and the difcovery of America not only added to that calamity, but rendered the remaining Spaniards moft deplorably indolent. To complete their misfortunes, Ferdinand and Ifabella introduced the popifh inquifition, with all its horrors, into their

dominions,

dominions, as a safeguard against the return of the Moors and Jews.

Charles V. of the house of Austria, and emperor of Germany, succeeded to the throne of Spain, in right of his mother, who was the daughter of Ferdinand and Isabella. The extensive possessions of the house of Austria in Europe, Africa, and, above all, America, from whence he drew immense treasures, began to alarm the jealousy of neighbouring princes, but could not satisfy the ambition of Charles ; and we find him constantly engaged in foreign wars, or with his own protestant subjects, whom he in vain attempted to bring back to the catholic church. At last, after a long and turbulent reign, he came to a resolution that filled all Europe with astonishment, the withdrawing himself entirely from any concern in the affairs of this world, in order that he might spend the remainder of his days in retirement and solitude *.

Agreeable

* Charles, of all his vast possessions, reserved nothing for himself but an annual pension of 100,000 crowns; and chose for the place of his retreat, a vale in Spain, of no great extent, watered by a small brook, and surrounded by rising grounds, covered with lofty trees. He gave strict orders, that the stile of the building which he erected there, should be such as suited his present situation, rather than his former dignity. It consisted only of six rooms, four of them in the form of friars cells, with naked walls; and the other two, each twenty feet square, were hung with brown cloth, and furnished in the most simple manner : they were all level with the ground, with a door on one side into a garden, of which Charles himself had given the plan, and had filled it with various plants, which he proposed to cultivate with his own hands. After spending some time in the city of Ghent in Flanders, the place of his nativity, he set out for Zealand in Holland, where he prepared to embark for Spain, accompanied by his son, and a numerous retinue of princes and nobil ty; and taking an affectionate and last farewel of Philip and his attendants, he sat out, on the 17th of Sept. 1556, under convoy of a large fleet of Spanish, Flemish, and English ships. As soon as he landed in Spain, he fell prostrate on the ground ; and considering himself now as dead to the world, he kissed the earth, and said, " Naked came I out of my mother's womb, and naked I now return to thee, thou common mother of mankind." Some of the Spanish nobility paid their court to him as he passed along to the place of his retreat ; but they were so few in number, and their attendance was so negligent, that Charles observed it, and felt for the first time, that he was no longer a monarch. But he was more deeply affected with his son's ingratitude, who, forgetting already how much he owed to his father's bounty, obliged him to remain some weeks upon the road, before he paid him the first moiety of that small portion, which was all that he had reserved of so many kingdoms. At last the money was paid, and Charles having dismissed a great number of his domestics, whose attendance he thought would be superfluous, he entered into his humble retreat with twelve domestics only. Here he buried in solitude and silence, his grandeur, his ambition, together with all those vast projects which, during half a century, had alarmed and agitated Europe, filling every kingdom in it, by turns, with the terror of his arms, and the dread of being subjected to his power. Here he enjoyed, perhaps, more complete satisfaction than all his grandeur had ever yielded him. Far from taking any part in the political transactions of the princes of Europe, he restrained his curiosity even from any enquiry concerning them ; and he seemed to view the busy scene which he had abandoned, with all the contempt and indifference arising

from

Agreeable to this refolution, he refigned Spain and the Netherlands, with great formality, in the prefence of his principal nobility, to his fon Philip II. but could not prevail on the princes of Germany to elect him emperor, which they conferred on Ferdinand, Charles's brother, thereby dividing the dangerous power of the houfe of Auftria into two branches; Spain, with all its poffeffions in Africa and the new world, alfo the Netherlands, and fome Italian ftates, remained with the elder branch, whilft the empire, Hungary, and Bohemia fell to the lot of the younger, which they ftill poffefs.

Philip II. inherited all his father's vices, with few of his good qualities. He was auftere, haughty, immoderately ambitious, and through his whole life a cruel bigot in the caufe of popery. His marriage with queen Mary of England, an unfeeling bigot like himfelf, his unfuccefsful addreffes to her fifter Elizabeth, his refentment and unfuccefsful wars with that princefs, his tyranny in the Low-Countries, the revolt and lofs of the United Provinces, with other particulars of his reign, have been already mentioned.

In Portugal he was more fuccefsful. That kingdom, after being governed by a race of wife and brave princes, fell to Sebaftian about the year 1557. Sebaftian loft his life and a fine army, in a headftrong, unjuft, and ill-concerted expedition againft the Moors in Africa; and foon after, Philip united Portugal to his own dominions, though the Braganza family of Portugal pretended to a prior right. By this acquifition Spain became poffeffed of the Portugueze fettlements in India, fome of which fhe ftill holds.

The defcendents of Philip proved to be very weak princes; but Philip and his father had fo totally ruined the antient liberties of Spain, that they reigned almoft unmolefted in their own

K 4   dominions.

---

from his thorough experience of its vanity, as well as from the pleafing reflection of having difengaged himfelf from its cares.

New amufements and new objects now occupied his mind; fometimes he cultivated the plants in his garden with his own hands; fometimes he rode out to the neighbouring wood on a little horfe, the only one that he kept, attended by a fingle fervant on foot. When his infirmities confined him to his apartment, he either admitted a few gentlemen who refided in the neighbourhood, and entertained them familiarly at his table; or he employed himfelf in ftudying the principles and in forming curious works of mechanifm, of which he had always been remarkably fond. He was particularly curious with regard to the conftruction of clocks and watches; and having found, after repeated trials, that he could not bring any two of them to go exactly alike, he reflected, it is faid, with a mixture of furprize and regret on his own folly, in having beftowed fo much time and labour on the more vain attempt of bringing mankind to a precife uniformity of fentiment concerning the intricate and myfterious doctrines of religion. And here, after two years retirement, he was feized with a fever, which carried him off in the 59th year of his age.

dominions. Their viceroys, however, were at once fo tyrannical and infolent over the Portuguefe, that in the year 1640,
the nobility of that nation, by a well-conducted confpiracy,
expelled their tyrants, and placed the duke of Braganza, by
the title of John IV. upon their throne; and ever fince,
Portugal has bee ı a diftinct kingdom from Spain.

The kings of Spain, of the Auftrian line, failing in the perfon of Charles II. who left no iffue, Philip, duke of Anjou,
fecond fon to the Dauphin of France, and grandfon to Lewis
XIV. mounted that throne, by virtue of his predeceffor's will,
in the name of Philip V. anno 1701. After a long and bloody
ftruggle with the German branch of the houfe of Auftria, fupported by England, he was confirmed in his dignity, at the conclufion of the peace of Utrecht, 1713. And thus Lewis XIV.
thro' a mafterly train of politics, (for in his wars to fupport his
grandfon, as we have already obferved, he was almoft ruined)
accomplifhed his favourite project of transferring the kingdom
of Spain, with all its rich poffeffions in America and the
Eaft-Indies, from the houfe of Auftria to that of his own
family of Bourbon; an event which proved fatal to the commerce of Great Britain, efpecially in the American feas, where
a glaring partiality has been fhewn to the French nation ever
fince, and renders our being poffeffed of a port in the South-
Seas of equal importance to that of Gibraltar, at the entrance
of the Mediterranean, which ferves as a curb on the united
ftrength of France and Spain in Europe.

After a long and turbulent reign, which was difturbed by
the ambition of his wife, Elizabeth of Parma, Philip died in
1746, and was fucceeded by his fon, Ferdinand VI. who, in
1759, died without iffue, through melancholy for the lofs of his
wife. Ferdinand was fucceeded by his brother, Charles III.
the prefent king of Spain, fon to Philip V. by his wife, the
princefs of Parma.

The Portuguefe could not have fupported themfelves under
their revolt from Spain, had not the latter power been engaged
in wars with England and Holland; and upon the reftoration
of Charles II. of England, that prince having married a princefs of Portugal, prevailed with the crown of Spain, in 1668,
to give up all pretenfions to that kingdom. Alphonfo, fon to
John IV. was then king of Portugal. He had the misfortune
to difagree at once with his wife and his brother, Peter, and
they uniting their interefts, not only forced Alphonfo to
refign his crown, but obtained a difpenfation from the pope
for their marriage, which was actually confummated. They
had a daughter; but Peter, by a fecond marriage, had fons,
the eldeft of whom was John, his fucceffor, and father to his
prefent Portuguefe majefty. John, like his father, joined the
grand

grand confederacy formed by king William; but neither of them were of much service in humbling the power of France. On the contrary, they had almost ruined the allies, by occasioning the loss of the great battle of Almanza in 1707. John died in 1750, and was succeeded by his son, his present majesty. In 1760, the king was attacked by assassins, and narrowly escaped with his life in a solitary place near his country palace of Belim. The executions of nobility and others which followed, are shocking to humanity, especially as we know of no clear proof against the parties. From this conspiracy is dated the expulsion of the jesuits (who are supposed to have been at the bottom of the treason) from all parts of his most faithful majesty's dominions. The present king having no son, his eldest daughter was married, by dispensation from the pope, to don Pedro, her own uncle, to prevent the crown falling into a foreign family, and the next year, 1761, she was brought to bed of a son, called the prince of Beira.

In 1762, when war broke out between Spain and England, the Spaniards, and their allies the French, pretended to force his faithful majesty into their alliance, and to garrison his seatowns against the English with their troops. The king of Portugal rejected this proposal, and declared war against the Spaniards, who, without resistance, entered Portugal with a considerable army, while a body of French threatened it from another quarter. Some have doubted whether any of those courts were in earnest upon this occasion, and whether the whole of the pretended war was not concerted to force England into a peace with France and Spain, in consideration of Portugal's apparent danger. It is certain that both the French and Spaniards carried on the war in a very dilatory manner, and that had they been in earnest, they might have been masters of Lisbon long before the arrival of the English troops to the assistance of the Portuguese.

Be that as it will, a few English battalions put an effectual stop, by their courage and manœuvres, to the progress of the invasion. Portugal was saved, and a peace was concluded at Fontainbleau in 1763. Notwithstanding this eminent service performed by the English to the Portuguese, who had been often saved before in the like manner, the latter, ever since that period, cannot be said to have beheld their deliverers with a friendly eye. The most captious distinctions and frivolous pretences have been invented by the Portuguese ministers for cramping the English trade, and depriving them of their unquestionable privileges; not to mention that his most faithful majesty is said now to have become a party in the famous family compact of the house of Bourbon.

As

As to Spain, her king is fo warmly attached to that compact, that he even hazarded his American dominions to fupport it. War being declared between him and England, the
latter took from him the Havannah, in the ifland of Cuba,
and thereby rendered herfelf entirely miftrefs of the navigation
of the Spanifh plate fleets. Many circumftances concurred to
make a peace neceffary to England, and upon its conclufion,
the Havannah was reftored to Spain.

His prefent catholic majefty does all he can to oblige his
fubjects to defift from their antient drefs and manners, and
carried his endeavours fo far, that it occafioned fo dangerous
an infurrection at Madrid, as obliged him to part with his
minifter *.

I T A L Y.

SITUATION AND EXTENT.

	Miles.		Degrees.
Length	600 }	between	{ 38 and 47 north latitude.
Breadth	400 }		{ 7 and 19 eaft longitude.

THE form of Italy, however, renders it very difficult to
afcertain its extent and dimenfions ; for fome fay, that
according to the beft accounts it is, from the frontiers of Switzerland to the extremity of the kingdom of Naples, about 750
miles in length ; and from the frontiers of the duchy of Savoy,
to thofe of the dominions of the ftates of Venice, which is its
greateft breadth, about 400 miles, though in fome parts it is
fcarce 100.

BOUNDARIES.] Nature has fixed the boundaries of Italy ;
for towards the eaft it is bounded by the gulph of Venice,
or Adriatic fea ; on the fouth and weft by the Mediterranean
fea ; and on the north, by the lofty mountains of the Alps,
which divide it from France and Switzerland.

The whole of the Italian dominions, comprehending Corfica, Sardinia, the Venetian and other iflands, are divided and
exhibited in the following table.

---

* Jofeph, king of Portugal, was born in 1714; his queen, Mary-Anne-Victoria,
infanta of Spain, in 1716, and have iffue, befides three more daughters,
    Maria-Frances-Ifabella, princefs of Brazil, born in 1734, married, 1760, to her
uncle, Don Pedro, by whom fhe has iffue,
    1. Jofeph-Frances Xavier, prince of Beira, born in 1761.
    2. John-Maria-Jofepha.

	Countries Names.	Square Miles.	Length.	Breadth.	Chief Cities.
Italy.					
To the king of Sardinia	Piedmont	6619	140	98	Turin
	Savoy	3572	87	60	Chambery
	Montferrat	446	40	22	Cafal
	Alleffandrine	204	27	20	Alexandria
	Oneglia	132	24	7	Oneglia
	Sardinia I.	6600	135	57	Cagliara
To the king of Naples	Naples	22,000	275	120	Naples
	Sicily I.	9400	180	92	Palermo
To the emperor	Milan	5431	155	70	Milan
	Mantua	700	47	27	Mantua
	Mirandola	120	19	10	Mirandola
	Pope's dominions	14,348	235	143	ROME { N. Lat. 41-54. E. Lon. 12-45.
To their refpective princes	Tufcany	6640	115	94	Florence
	Maffa	82	16	11	Maffa
	Parma	1225	48	37	Parma
	Modena	1560	65	39	Modena
	Piombino	100	22	18	Piombino
	Monaco	24	12	4	Monaco
	Lucca	286	28	15	Lucca
Republics	St. Marino	8			St. Marino
	Genoa	2400	160	25	Genoa
To France	Corfica I.	2520	90	38	Baftia
To Venice	Venice	8434	175	95	Venice
	Iftria P.	1245	62	32	Capo d'Iftria
	Dalmatia P.	1400	135	20	Zara
	Ifles of Dalmatia	1364			
Iflands in the Venetian dominions	Cephalonia	428	40	18	Cephalonica
	Corfu, or Corcyra	194	31	10	Corfu
	Zant, or Zacynthus	120	23	12	Zant
	St. Maura	56	12	7	St. Maura
	Little Cephalonia	14	7	3	
	Ithaca olim				
	Total—	75,576			

SOIL AND AIR.] The happy foil of Italy produces the comforts and luxuries of life in great abundance ; each diftrict has its peculiar excellency and commodity; wines, the moft delicious fruits, and oil, are the moft general productions. As much corn grows here as ferves the inhabitants ; and was the ground duly cultivated, the Italians might export it to their neighbours. The Italian cheefes, particularly thofe called Parmefans, and their native filk, form a principal part of their commerce. There is here a great variety of air ; and fome parts of Italy bear melancholy proofs of the alterations that accidental caufes make on the face of nature ; for the Campagna di Roma, where the antient Romans enjoyed the moft falubrious air of any place perhaps on the globe, is now almoft peftilential through the decreafe of inhabitants, which has occafioned a ftagnation of waters, and putrid exhalations. The air of the northern parts, which lie among the Alps, or

in

in their neighbourhood, is keen and piercing, the ground being, in many places, covered with fnow in winter. The Appennines, which are a ridge of mountains that longitudinally almoft divide Italy, have great effects on its climate; the countries on the fouth being warm, thofe on the north mild and temperate. The fea-breezes refrefh the kingdom of Naples fo much, that no remarkable inconveniency of air is found there, notwithftanding its fouthern fituation. In general, the air of Italy may be faid to be dry and pure.

MOUNTAINS.] We have already mentioned the Alps and Appennines, which form the chief mountains of Italy. The famous volcano of Mount Vefuvius lies in the neighbourhood of Naples.

RIVERS AND LAKES.] The rivers of Italy are the Po, the Var, the Adige, the Trebia, the Arno, the Tiber, which runs through the city of Rome. The famous Rubicon forms the fouthern boundary between Italy and the antient Cifalpine Gaul.

The lakes of Italy are, the Maggiore, Lugano, Como, Ifco, and Garda, in the north; the Perugia or Thrafimene, Bracciano, Terni, and Celano, in the middle.

SEAS, GULPHS OR BAYS, CAPES, ⎫ Without a knowledge
PROMONTORIES, AND STRAITS. ⎭ of thefe, neither the antient Roman authors, nor the hiftory, nor geography of Italy, can be underftood. The feas of Italy are, the gulphs of Venice, or the Adriatic fea. The feas of Naples, Tufcany, and Genoa. The bays or harbours of Nice, Villa Franca, Oneglia, Final, Savona, Vado, Spezzia, Lucca, Pifa, Leghorn, Piombino, Civita Vecchia, Gaeta, Naples, Salerno, Policaftro, Rhegio, Quilace, Tarento, Manfredonia, Ravenna, Venice, Triefte, Iftria, and Fiume; Cape Spartavento del Alice, Otranto, and Ancona; and the ftrait of Maffina, between Italy and Sicily.

The gulphs and bays in the Italian iflands, are thofe of Fiorenzo, Baftia, Talada, Porto Novo, Cape Corfo, Bonifacio, and Ferro, in Corfica; and the ftrait of Bonifacio, between Corfica and Sardinia. The bays of Cagliari and Oriftagni; Cape de Sardis, Cavello, Monte Santo, and Polo, in Sardinia. The gulphs of Meffina, Melazzo, Palermo, Mazara, Syracufe, and Catania; cape Faro, Melazzo, Orlando, Gallo, Trapano, Paffaro, and Aleffia, in Sicily; and the bays of Porto Feraio, and Porto Longone, in the ifland of Ebba.

METALS AND MINERALS.] Many places of Italy abound in mineral fprings, fome hot, fome warm, and many of fulphureous, chalybeat, and medicinal qualities. Many of its
                                                                mountains

mountains abound in mines that produce great quantities of emeralds, jafper, agate, porphyry, lapis lazuli, and other valuable ſtones. Iron and copper mines are found in a few places ; and a mill for forging and fabricating theſe metals is erected near Tivoli, in Naples. Sardinia is ſaid to contain mines of gold, ſilver, lead, iron, ſulphur, and allum, tho' they are now neglected ; and curious chryſtals and coral are found on the coaſt of Corſica. Beautiful marble of all kinds is one of the chief productions of Italy.

VEGETABLE AND ANIMAL PRODUCTIONS, BY SEA AND LAND. } Beſides the rich vegetable productions mentioned under the article of ſoil, Italy produces citrons, and ſuch quantities of cheſnuts, cherries, plums, and other fruits, that they are of little value to the proprietors.

There is little difference between the animal productions of Italy, either by land or ſea, and thoſe of France and Germany already mentioned.

POPULATION, INHABITANTS, MANNERS, CUSTOMS, AND DIVERSIONS. } Authors are greatly divided on the head of Italian population. This may be owing, in a great meaſure, to the partiality which every Italian has for the honour of his own province. The number of the king of Sardinia's ſubjects in Italy is about 2,300,000. The city of Milan itſelf, by the beſt accounts, contains 300,000, and the duchy is proportionably populous. As to the other provinces of Italy, geographers and travellers have paid very little attention to the numbers of natives that live in the country, and inform us by conjecture only of thoſe who inhabit the great cities. Some doubts have ariſen whether Italy is as populous now as it was in the time of Pliny, when it contained 14,000,000 of inhabitants. I am apt to believe that the preſent inhabitants exceed that number. The Campagna di Roma, and ſome other of the moſt beautiful parts of Italy, are at preſent in a manner deſolate ; but we are to conſider that the modern Italians are in a great meaſure free from the unintermitting wars, not to mention the tranſmigration of colonies, which formerly, even down to the 16th century, depopulated their country. Add to this, that the princes and ſtates of Italy now encourage agriculture and manufactures of all kinds, which undoubtedly promotes population ; ſo that it may not perhaps be extravagant, if we aſſign to Italy 20,000,000 of inhabitants ; but ſome calculations greatly exceed that number. The Italians are generally well proportioned, and have ſuch meaning in their looks, that they have greatly aſſiſted the ideas of their painters. Their women are well ſhaped, and very amorous. The marriage ties, eſpecially

of

of the better fort, are of very little value in Italy. Every wife has her gallant or cicifbeo, with whom she keeps company, and fometimes cohabits, with very little ceremony, and no offence on either fide. This practice is chiefly remarkable at Venice. With regard to the modes of life, the beft quality of a modern Italian is fobriety, and contentment under the public government. With great taciturnity they difcover but little reflection. They are rather vindictive than brave, and more fuperftitious than devout. The middling ranks are attached to their native cuftoms, and feem to have no ideas of improvement. Their fondnefs for greens, fruits, and vegetables of all kinds, contributes to their contentment and fatisfaction ; and an Italian gentleman or peafant can be luxurious at a very fmall expence. Though perhaps all Italy does not contain five defcendents of the antient Romans, yet the prefent inhabitants fpeak of themfelves as fucceffors to the conquerors of the world, and look upon the reft of mankind with contempt.

The drefs of the Italians is little different from that of the neighbouring countries, and they affect a medium between the French volatility and the folemnity of the Spaniards. The Neapolitans are commonly dreft in black, in compliment to the Spaniards. It cannot be denied that the Italians excel in the fine arts : though they are as yet but defpicable proficients in the fciences. They cultivate and enjoy vocal mufic at a very dear rate, by emafculating their males when young, to which their mercenary parents agree without remorfe.

The Italians, the Venetians efpecially, have very little or no notion of the impropriety of many cuftoms that are confidered as criminal in other countries. Parents, rather than their fons fhould throw themfelves away by unfuitable marriage, or contract difeafes by promifcuous amours, hire miftreffes for them for a month or a year, or fome determined time ; and concubinage, in many places of Italy, is an avowed licenfed trade. The Italian courtezans or bona robas, as they are called, make a kind of profeffion in all their cities. Mafquerading and gaming, horfe-races without riders, and converfations or affemblies, are the chief diverfions of the Italians, excepting religious exhibitions, in which they are pompous beyond all other nations.

A modern writer, defcribing his journey through Italy, gives us a very unfavourable picture of the Italians and their manner of living. Give what fcope you pleafe to your fancy, fays he, you will never imagine half the difagreeablenefs that Italian beds, Italian cooks, and Italian naftinefs, offer to an Englifhman. At Turin, Milan, Venice, Rome, and perhaps
two

two or three other towns, you meet with good accommodations; but no words can exprefs the wretchednefs of the other inns. No other beds than thofe of ftraw, with a matrafs of ftraw, and next to that a dirty fheet, fprinkled with water, and confequently damp; for a covering, you have another fheet as coarfe as the firft, like one of our kitchen jack-towels, with a dirty coverlit. The bedftead confifts of four wooden forms or benches: an Englifh peer and peerefs muft lye in this manner, unlefs they carry an upholfterer's fhop with them. There are, by the bye, no fuch things as curtains; and in all their inns, the walls are bare, and the floor has never once been wafhed fince it was firft laid. One of the moft indelicate cuftoms here is, that men, and not women, make the ladies beds, and would do every office of a maid fervant, if fuffered. They never fcour their pewter; their knives are of the fame colour. In thefe inns they make you pay largely, and fend up ten times as much as you can eat. The foop, like wafh, with pieces of liver fwimming in it; a plate full of brains, fried in the fhape of fritters; a difh of livers and gizzards; a couple of fowls (always killed after your arrival) boiled to rags, without any the leaft kind of fauce or herbage; another fowl, juft killed, ftewed as they call it; then two more fowls, or a turkey roafted to rags. All over Italy, on the roads, the chickens and fowls are fo ftringy, you may divide the breaft into as many filaments as you can a halfpenny-worth of thread. Now and then we get a little piece of mutton or veal, and, generally fpeaking, it is the only eatable morfel that falls in our way. The bread all the way is exceeding bad, and the butter fo rancid, that it cannot be touched, or even borne within the reach of our fmell. But what is a greater evil to travellers than any of the above recited, are the infinite numbers of gnats, bugs, fleas, and lice, which infeft us by day and night.

RELIGION.] The religion of the Italians is Roman-catholic. The inquifition here is little more than a found; and perfons of all religions live unmolefted in Italy, provided no grofs infult is offered to their worfhip. In the introduction, we have given an account of the rife and eftablifhment of popery in Italy, from whence it fpread over all Europe; likewife of the caufes and fymptoms of its decline. The ecclefiaftical government of the papacy has employed many volumes in defcribing it. The cardinals, who are next in dignity to his holinefs, are feventy, but that number is feldom or never complete: they are appointed by the pope, who takes care to have a majority of Italian cardinals, that the chair may not be removed from Rome, as it was once to Avignon in France,

the

the then pope being a Frenchman.   In promoting foreign pre-
lates to the cardinalfhip, the pope regulates himfelf according
to the nomination of the princes who profefs that religion.
His chief minifter is the cardinal patron, generally his nephew,
or near relation, who improves the time of the pope's reign by
amaffing what he can.   When met in a confiftory, the cardinals pretend to controul the pope, in matters both fpiritual
and temporal, and have been fometimes known to prevail.
The reign of a pope is feldom of long duration, being generally
old men at the time of their election.   The conclave is a fcene
where the cardinals principally endeavour to difplay their parts,
and where many tranfactions pafs which hardly fhew their
infpiration from the Holy Ghoft.   During the election of a
pope in 1721, the animofities ran fo high, that they came to
blows with both their hands and feet, and threw the ink-
ftandifhes at each other.   We fhall here give an extract from
the creed of pope Pius IV. 1560, before his elevation to the
chair, which contains the principal points wherein the church
of Rome differs from the proteftant churches.   After declaring his belief in one God, and other heads wherein Chriftians in general are agreed, he proceeds as follows.

" I moft firmly admit and embrace the apoftolical and ecclefiaftical traditions, and all other conftitutions of the fame
church.

" I do admit the holy fcriptures in the fame fenfe that
holy mother church doth, whofe bufinefs it is to judge of the
true fenfe and interpretation of them; and I will interpret
them according to the unanimous confent of the fathers.

" I do profefs and believe that there are feven facraments of
the law, truly and properly fo called, inftituted by Jefus
Chrift our Lord, and neceffary to the falvation of mankind,
though not all of them to every one; namely, baptifm, confirmation, eucharift, penance, extreme unction, orders, and
marriage, and that they do confer grace; and that of thefe,
baptifm, confirmation, and orders, may not be repeated without facrilege.   I do alfo receive and admit the received and
approved rites of the catholic church in her folemn adminiftration of the abovefaid facraments.

" I do embrace and receive all and every thing that hath
been defined and declared by the holy council of Trent * concerning original fin and juftification.

'" I do

---

* A convocation of Roman-catholic divines, who affembled at Trent, by virtue
of a bull from the pope, anno 1546, to determine upon certain points of faith,
and to fupprefs what they were pleafed to term the Rifing Herefies in the church.

" I do alſo profeſs that in the maſs there is offered unto God a true, proper, and propitiatory ſacrifice for the quick and the dead, and that in the moſt holy ſacramènt of the euchariſt there is truly, really, and ſubſtantially, the body and blood, together with the ſoul and divinity of our Lord Jeſus Chriſt ; and that there is a converſion made of the whole ſubſtance of the bread into the body, and of the whole ſubſtance of the wine into the blood ; which converſion the catholic church calls Tranſubſtantiation.

" I confeſs that under one kind only, whole and intire, Chriſt and a true ſacrament is taken and received.

" I do firmly believe that there is a purgatory ; and that the ſouls kept priſoners there do receive help by the ſuffrages of the faithful.

" I do likewiſe believe that the ſaints reigning together with Chriſt are to be worſhipped and prayed unto ; and that they do offer prayers unto God for us, and that their relics are to be had in veneration.

" I do moſt firmly aſſert, that the images of Chriſt, of the bleſſed Virgin the mother of God, and of other ſaints, ought to be had and retained, and that due honour and veneration ought to be given unto them *.

" I do likewiſe affirm, that the power of indulgence was left by Chriſt to the church, and that the uſe of them is very beneficial to chriſtian people †.

" I

---

* An Engliſh Traveller ſpeaking of a religious proceſſion ſome years ago at Florence, in Italy, deſcribes it as follows. I had occaſion, ſays he, to ſee a proceſſion, where all the nobleſs of the city attended in their coaches. It was the anniverſary of a charitable inſtitution in favour of poor maidens, a certain number of whom are portioned every year. About two hundred of theſe virgins walked in proceſſion, two and two together. They were preceded and followed by an irregular mob of penitents, in ſack-cloth, with lighted tapers, and monks carrying crucifixes, bawling and bellowing the litanies : but the greateſt object was the figure of the Virgin Mary, as big as the life, ſtanding within a gilt frame, dreſſed in a gold ſtuff, with a large hoop, a great quantity of falſe jewels, her face painted and patched, and her hair frizzled and curled in the very extremity of the faſhion. Very little regard had been paid to the image of our Saviour on the croſs ; but when the Lady Mother appeared on the ſhoulders of three or four luſty friars, the whole populace fell upon their knees in the dirt.

† A long liſt of indulgences, or fees of the pope's chancery, may be ſeen in a book printed 150 years-ago, by authority of the then pope. It has been tranſlated into Engliſh, under the title of *Rome a great Cuſtom-houſe for Sin* ; from which we ſhall give a few extracts.

ABSOLUTIONS.

For him that ſtole holy or conſecrated things out of a holy place, 10 s. 6 d.
For him who lies with a woman in the church, 9 s.
For a layman for *murdering* a layman, 7 s. 6 d.
For him that *killeth* his father, mother, wife, or ſiſter, 10 s. 6 d.
For laying violent hands on a *clergyman*, ſo it be without effuſion of blood, 10 s. 6 d.

" I do acknowledge the holy, catholic, and apoſtolical Roman church, to be the mother and miſtreſs of all churches; and I do promiſe and ſwear true obedience to the biſhop of Rome, the ſucceſſor of St. Peter, the prince of the apoſtles, and vicar of Jeſus Chriſt.

" I do undoubtedly receive and profeſs all other things which have been delivered, defined, and declared by the ſacred canons and œcumenical councils, and eſpecially by the holy ſynod of Trent. And all other things contrary thereto, and all hereſies condemned, rejected, and anathematized by the church, I do likewiſe condemn, reject, and anathematize."

ARCHBISHOPRICS.] There are thirty-eight archbiſhoprics in Italy, but the ſuffragans annexed to them are too indefinite and arbitrary for the reader to depend upon, the pope creating or ſuppreſſing them as he pleaſes.

LANGUAGE.] The Italian language is remarkable for its ſmoothneſs, and the facility with which it enters into muſical compoſitions. The ground-work of it is Latin, and it is eaſily maſtered by a good claſſical ſcholar. Almoſt every ſtate in Italy has a different dialect; and the prodigious pains taken by the literary ſocieties there, may at laſt fix the Italian into a standard

---

For a prieſt that keeps a concubine; as alſo his diſpenſation for being irregular, 10s. 6d.
For him that lyeth with his *own mother, ſiſter*, or *godmother*, 7 s. 6 d.
For him that burns his neighbour's houſe, 12 s.
For him that forgeth the pope's hand, 1 l. 7 s.
For him that forgeth letters apoſtolical, 1 l. 7 s.
For him that takes two holy orders in one day, 2 l. 6 s.
For a king for going to the holy ſepulchre without licence, 7 l. 10 s.

DISPENSATIONS.

For a baſtard to enter all holy orders, 18 s.
For a man or woman that is found hanged, that they may have chriſtian burial, 1 l. 7 s. 6 d.

LICENCES.

For a layman to change his vow of going to Rome to viſit the apoſtolic churches, 18 s.
To eat fleſh and white meats in Lent, and other faſting days, 10 s. 6 d.
That a king or queen ſhall enjoy ſuch indulgences, as if they went to Rome, 15 l.
For a queen to adopt a child, 300 l.
To marry in times prohibited, 2 l. 5 s.
To eat fleſh in times prohibited, 1 l. 4 s.
Not to be tied to faſting days, 1 l. 4 s.
For a town to take out of a church them (murderers) that have taken ſanctuary therein, 4 l. 10 s.

FACULTIES.

To abſolve all delinquents, 3 l.
To diſpenſe with irregularities, 3 l.

ſtandard language. At preſent, the Tuſcan ſtile and writing is moſt in requeſt.

The Lord's Prayer runs thus : *Padro noſtro, che ſei ne cieli, ſia ſanctificato il tuo nome ; il tuo regno venga; la tua volunta ſia fatta, ſi come in cielo coſi anche in terra ; dacci hoggi il noſtro pane cotidiano ; cremitticii noſtri debiti, ſi come noi anchora remitticmo a noſtri debitori ; e non indurci in tentatione, ma liberaci dal maligno ; perchioche tuo è il regno, e la potenza, e la gloria in ſempiterno.* Amen.

LEARNING AND LEARNED MEN, PAINTERS, STATUARIES, ARCHITECTS, AND ARTISTS. In the introduction, we have particularized ſome of the great men which ancient Italy has produced. In modern times, that is, ſince the revival of learning, ſome Italians have ſhone in controverſial learning, but they are chiefly celebrated by bigots of their own perſuaſion. The mathematics and natural philoſophy owe much to Galileo, Torricelli, Malpighi, Borelli, and ſeveral other Italians. Strada is an excellent hiſtorian ; and the Hiſtory of the Council of Trent, by Fra. Paoli, is a ſtandard work. Guicciardin, Bentivolio, and Davila, have been much commended as hiſtorians by their ſeveral admirers. Machiavel is equally famous as an hiſtorian, and as a political writer. His comedies are excellent ; and the liberality of his ſentiments, for the age in which he lived, is amazing. The greateſt modern genius of Italy in poetry is Taſſo ; though ſome have preſumed to put Arioſto in competition with him. Sannazarius, Fracaſtorius, Bembo, Vida, and other natives of Italy, have diſtinguiſhed themſelves by the elegance, correctneſs, and ſpirit of their Latin poetry, many of their compoſitions not yielding to the Claſſics themſelves. Socinus, who has puzzled ſo many orthodox divines, was a native of Italy.

The Italian painters, ſculptors, architects, and muſicians, are unrivalled not only in their numbers, but their excellencies. The revival of learning, after the ſack of Conſtantinople by the Turks, revived taſte likewiſe, and gave mankind a reliſh for truth and beauty in deſign and colouring. Raphael, from his own ideas, aſſiſted by the ancients, ſtruck out a new creation with his pencil, and ſtill ſtands at the head of the painting art. Michael Angelo Buonaroti, united in his own perſon, painting, ſculpture, and architecture. The colouring of Titian has perhaps never yet been equalled. Bramante, Bernini, and many other Italians, carried ſculpture and architecture to an amazing height. Julio Romano, Coreggio, Caraccio, Veroneſe, and others, are, as painters, unequalled in their ſeveral manners. The ſame may be ſaid of Corelli, and other Italians, in muſic. At preſent, Italy cannot juſtly boaſt of any paramount genius in the fine arts.

UNIVERSITIES.] Thofe of Italy are, Rome, Venice, Florence, Mantua, Padua, Parma, Verona, Milan, Pavia, Bologna, Ferrara, Pifa, Naples, Salerno, and Perufia.

ANTIQUITIES AND CURIOSITIES, } Italy is the native
    NATURAL AND ARTIFICIAL.   } country of all that is
ftupendous, great, or beautiful, either in antient or modern times. A library might be filled by defcriptions and delineations of all that is rare and curious in the arts ; nor does the bounds of this work admit of mentioning even their general heads. All I can do is to give the reader the names of thofe objects that are moft diftinguifhed either for antiquity or excellence.

The amphitheatres claim the firft rank, as a fpecies of the moft ftriking magnificence; that which was erected by Vefpafian, and finifhed by Domitian, called the Colofeo, now ftands at Rome. The amphitheatre of Verona, erected by the conful Flaminius, is thought to be the moft entire of any in Italy. The ruins of other theatres and amphitheatres are vifible in other places. The triumphal arches of Vefpafian, Septimius Severus, and Conftantine the Great, are ftill ftanding, though decayed. The ruins of the baths, palaces, and temples, particularly that of the Pantheon, anfwer all the ideas we can form of the Roman grandeur. The pillars of Trajan and Antonine, the former 175 feet high, and the latter covered with inftructive fculptures, are ftill remaining. A traveller forgets the devaftations of the northern barbarians, when he fees the roftrated column erected by Duillius, in commemoration of the firft naval victory the Romans gained over the Carthaginians. The ftatue of the wolf giving fuck to Romulus and Remus, with vifible marks of the ftroke of lightning, mentioned by Cicero; the very original brafs plates containing the laws of the twelve tables ; and a thoufand other identical antiquities, fome of them tranfmitted unhurt to the prefent times ; not to mention medals and the infinite variety of feals and engraved ftones which abound in the cabinets of the curious. Many palaces, all over Italy, are furnifhed with bufts and ftatues fabricated in the times of the republic and the higher empire.

The Appian, Flaminian, and Æmilian roads, the firft 200 miles, the fecond 130, and the third 50 miles in length, are in many places ftill entire ; nor is the reader to expect any defcription of the magnificent ruins of villas, refervoirs, bridges, and the like, that prefent themfelves all over the country of Italy.

The fubterraneous conftructions of Italy are as ftupendous as thofe above ground, witnefs the cloacæ and catacombs, or

repofitories

repofitories for dead bodies, in the neighbourhood of Rome and Naples. It is not above 20 years fince a painter's apprentice difcovered the ancient city of Pæſtum or Poſidonia, in the kingdom of Naples, ſtill ſtanding ; for ſo indifferent are the country people of Italy about objects of antiquity, that it was a new difcovery to the learned. An inexhauſtible mine of curioſities are daily dug out of the ruins of Herculaneum, a city lying between Naples and Veſuvius, and ſunk in an earthquake 1700 years ago.

With regard to modern curioſities, they are as bewildering as the remains of antiquity. Rome itſelf contains 300 churches filled with all that is rare in architecture, painting, and ſculpture. Each city and town of Italy contains a proportionable number. The church of St. Peter, at Rome, is the moſt aſtoniſhing, bold, and regular fabric, that ever perhaps exiſted ; and when examined by the rules of art, it may be termed faultleſs. The houſe and chapel of Loretto is rich beyond imagination, notwithſtanding the ridiculous romance that compoſes its hiſtory.

The natural curioſities of Italy, though remarkable, are not ſo numerous as its artificial. Mount Veſuvius, near Naples, and Mount Ætna, in Sicily, are remarkable for emitting fire from their tops. Mount Ætna is 60 miles in circumference, and at the top there is a baſon of ſulphur ſix miles round, from whence ſometimes iſſue rivers of melted minerals that run down into the ſea. There is generally an earthquake before any great eruption. In 1693, the port town of Catania was overturned, and 18,000 people periſhed. Between the lakes Agnano and Puzzeli there is a valley called Solfatara, becauſe vaſt quantities of ſulphur are continually forced out of the clifts by ſubterranean fires. The grotto del Canæ is remarkable for its poiſonous ſteams, and is ſo called from their killing dogs that enter it, if forced to remain there. The poiſon of the tarantula, an inſect or ſpider, is well known to be removed only by muſic and dancing ; and ſcorpions, vipers, and ſerpents, are common in Apulia.

ARMS.] The chief armorial bearings in Italy, are as follow. The pope, as ſovereign prince over the land of the church, bears for his eſcutcheon, gules, conſiſting of a long headcape, or, ſurmounted with a croſs, pearled and garniſhed with three royal crowns, together with the two keys of St. Peter, placed in ſaltier. The arms of Tuſcany, or, five roundles, gules, two, two, and one, and one in chief, azure, charged with three flower-de-luces, or. Thoſe of Venice, azure, a lion winged, ſejant, or, holding under one of his paws, a book

covered,

covered, argent. Laftly, thofe of Genoa, argent, a crofs, gules, with a crown clofed for the ifland of Corfica ; and for fupporters, two griffins, or.

STATES OF ITALY, CONSTITU- ⎞　　Thus far I have been
　　TION, AND CHIEF CITIES.　⎰　enabled to treat of Italy
in general, but I am here conftrained to deviate from my ufual method. The Italian ftates are not like the republics of Holland, or Switzerland, or the empire of Germany, cemented by a political confederacy, to which every member is accountable ; for every Italian ftate has diftinct forms of government, trade, and interefts. I fhall be therefore obliged to take a feparate view of each, to affift the reader in forming an idea of the whole.

The duke of SAVOY, or as he is ufually ftiled, king of SARDINIA, taking his royal title from that ifland, is now a powerful prince in Italy, of which he is called the Janus, or keeper, againft the French. He has an order of knighthood which is called the Annunciade, inftituted by the firft duke of Savoy, to commemorate his brave defence of Rhodes againft the infidels.

His Sardinian majefty's capital, Turin, is ftrongly fortified, and one of the fineft cities in Europe ; but the country of Savoy is mountainous and barren, and its natives are forced to feek their bread all over the world. They are efteemed a fimble but very honeft people. The king is fo abfolute, that his revenues confift of what he pleafes to raife upon his fubjects. His ordinary income, befides his own family provinces, cannot be lefs than 500,000 l. fterling, out of which he maintains 15,000 men in time of peace. During a war, when affifted by foreign fubfidies, he can bring to the field 40,000 men. The aggrandizement of his prefent Sardinian majefty is chiefly owing to England, to whom, by his fituation and neighbourhood, he is a natural ally, for the prefervation of the balance of power in Europe.

The MILANESE, belonging to the houfe of Auftria, is a moft formidable ftate, and formerly gave law to all Italy, when under the government of its own dukes. The fertility and beauty of the country is almoft incredible. Milan, the capital, and its citadel, is very ftrong, and furnifhed with a magnificent cathedral in the Gothic tafte, which contains a very rich treafury, confifting chiefly of ecclefiaftical furniture, compofed of gold, filver, and precious ftones. The revenue of the duchy is above 300,000 l. annually, which is fuppofed to maintain an army of 30,000 men. The natives are fond of literary and political affemblies, where they hold forth

almoft

almoft on all fubjects. With all its natural and acquired advantages, the natives of Milan make but few exports, fo that its revenue, unlefs the court of Vienna fhould purfue fome other fyftem of improvement, cannot be much bettered.

The republic of GENOA is vaftly degenerated from its antient power and opulence, though the fpirit of trade ftill continues among its nobility and citizens. Genoa is a moft fuperb city. The inhabitants of diftinction drefs in black, in a plain, if not an uncouth manner, perhaps, to fave expences. Their chief manufactures are velvets, damafks, gold and filver tiffues, and paper. The city of Genoa contains about 150,000 inhabitants (but fome writers greatly diminifh that number) among whom are many rich trading individuals. Its maritime power is dwindled down to fix gallies, and about 600 foldiers. The chief fafety of this republic confifts in the jealoufy of other European powers, becaufe to any one of them it would be a moft valuable acquifition. The common people are wretched beyond expreffion, as is the foil of its territory. Near the fea fome parts are tolerably well cultivated. The government of Genoa is purely ariftocratical, being entirely vefted in the nobility.

VENICE is one of the moft celebrated republics in the world, on account both of its conftitution and former power. It is compofed of feveral fine provinces on the continent of Italy, fome iflands in the Adriatic and part of Dalmatia. The city of Venice is feated on 72 iflands at the bottom of the north end of the Adriatic fea, and is feparated from the continent by a marfhy lake of five Italian miles in breadth, too fhallow for large fhips to navigate, which forms its principal ftrength. Venice preferves the veftiges of its antient magnificence, but is in every refpect degenerated except in the paffion which its inhabitants ftill retain for mufic and mummery during their carnivals. They feem to have loft their antient tafte for painting and architecture, and to be returning to Gothicifm. They have however lately had fome fpirited differences with the court of Rome, and feem to be difpofed to throw off their obedience to its head. As to the conftitution of the republic, to which it is faid they owe their independency, we can write little with any precifion, becaufe it is kept a myftery to all but the members, and even of them (fuch are its intricacies and checks) few or none know it perfectly. All we know for certain is, that like Genoa, the government is ariftocratic, and that the nobility are divided into fix claffes, amounting in the whole to 2,500, each of whom, when twenty-five years of age, has a right to be a member of the council. Thefe

elect

elect a doge or chief magiſtrate, in a peculiar manner by ballot, which is managed by gold and ſilver balls. The doge is inveſted with great ſtate, and with emblems of ſupreme authority, but has very little power, and is ſhut up in the city as a priſoner. The government and laws are managed by five different councils of the nobles.

As every Venetian of a noble family is himſelf noble, great numbers of them go about the ſtreets begging, and generally preſent a ſilver or tin box, to ſtrangers, to receive their alms. All the orders are dreſt in black gowns, large wigs and caps, which they hold in their hands. The ceremony of the doge's marrying the Adriatic once a year, by dropping into it a ring, from his bucentaur or ſtate-barge, attended by thoſe of all the nobility, is the moſt ſuperb exhibition in Venice, but not comparable for magnificence to a lord mayor's ſhew. The inhabitants of Venice are ſaid to amount to 200,000. The grandeur and convenience of the city, particularly the public palaces, the treaſury, and the arſenal, are beyond expreſſion. Over the ſeveral canals of Venice, are laid near 500 bridges, the greateſt part of which are ſtone. The Venetians ſtill have ſome manufactures in ſcarlet cloth, gold and ſilver ſtuffs, and above all, fine looking-glaſſes, all which bring in a conſiderable revenue to the owners ; that of the ſtate annually is ſaid to amount to 8,000,000 of Italian ducats, each valued at twenty pence of our money. Out of this are defrayed the expences of the ſtate and the pay of the army, which in time of peace conſiſts of 16,000 regular troops, (always commanded by a foreign general,) and 10,000 militia. They keep up a ſmall fleet for curbing the inſolencies of the piratical ſtates of Barbary, and they have among them ſeveral orders of knighthood, the chief of which are thoſe of the Golden Star, ſo called from its badge, which is conferred only on the firſt quality, and the military order of St. Marc, the badge of which is a medal of that apoſtle.

In eccleſiaſtical matters the Venetians have two patriarchs ; the authority of one reaches over all the provinces, but neither of them have much power ; and both of them are choſen by the ſenate; and all religions, even the Mahometan and Pagan, excepting proteſtants, are here tolerated in the free exerciſe of their religion.

The Venetians live in the perpetual extremes of the moſt infamous debaucheries, or the moſt ridiculous devotion. Prieſts and nuns abandon themſelves to the former, during the carnival, which is chiefly held in St. Marc's place, where ſometimes 15,000 people aſſemble,

The

The principal city of Tuscany is Florence, which is now poſſeſſed by a younger branch of the houſe of Auſtria, after being long held by the illuſtrious houſe of Medicis, who made their capital the cabinet of all that is valuable, rich, and maſterly in architecture, literature and the arts, eſpecially thoſe of painting and ſculpture.   It is thought to contain above 70,000 inhabitants.   The beauties and riches of the grand duke's palaces, have been often deſcribed, but all deſcription falls ſhort of their contents, ſo that in every reſpect it is reckoned, after Rome, the ſecond city in Italy.   The celebrated Venus of Medici, which, take it all in all, is thought to be the ſtandard of taſte in female beauty and proportion, ſtands in a room called the Tribunal.   The inſcription on its baſe mentions its being made by Cleomenes, an Athenian, the ſon of Apollodorus.   It is of white marble, and ſurrounded by other maſter-pieces of ſculpture, ſome of which are ſaid to be the works of Praxiteles, and other Greek maſters.   Every corner of this beautiful city, which ſtands between mountains covered with olive trees, vineyards, and delightful villas, and divided by the Arno, is full of wonders in the arts of painting, ſtatuary, and architecture.   It is a place of ſome ſtrength, and contains an archbiſhop's ſee, and a univerſity.   The inhabitants boaſt of the improvements they have made in the Italian tongue, by means of their Academia della Cruſca, and ſeveral other academies are now eſtabliſhed at Florence.   Though the Florentines affect great ſtate, yet their nobility and gentry drive a retail trade in wine, which they ſell from their cellar windows, and ſometimes they even hang out a broken flaſk, as a ſign where it may be bought.   They deal, beſides wine and fruits, in gold and ſilver ſtuffs.   Since the acceſſion of the archduke Peter Leopald, brother to the preſent emperor, to this duchy, a great reformation has been introduced, both into the government, and manufactures, to the great benefit of the finances.   It is thought that the great duchy of Tuſcany could bring to the field, upon occaſion, 30,000 fighting men, and that its preſent revenues are above 500,000 l. a year.   The other principal towns of Tuſcany, are Piſa, Leghorn, and Sienna; the firſt and laſt are much decayed.

The inhabitants of Lucca, which is a ſmall free commonwealth, lying on the Tuſcan ſea, in a moſt delightful plain, are the moſt induſtrious of all the Italians.   They have improved their country into a beautiful garden, ſo that though they do not exceed 120,000, their annual revenue amounts to 80,000 l. ſterling.   Their capital is Lucca, which contains about 40,000 inhabitants, who deal in mercery goods, wines,

and

and fruits, especially olives. This republic is under the protection of the house of Austria.

The republic of St. MARINO is here mentioned as a geographical curiosity. Its territories consist of a high, craggy mountain, with a few eminences at the bottom, and the inhabitants boast of having preserved their liberties, as a republic, for 1300 years. It is under the protection of the pope, and the inoffensive manners of the inhabitants, who are not above 5000 in all, with the small value of their territory, have preserved its constitution.

The duchy and city of PARMA, together with the duchies of Placentia and Guastalla, now form one of the most flourishing states in Italy of its extent. The soil of Parma and Placentia are fertile, and produce the richest fruits and pasturages, and contain considerable manufactures of silk. It is the seat of a bishop's see, and an university; and some of its magnificent churches are painted by the famous Coreggio. The present duke of Parma, is a prince of the house of Bourbon, and son to Don Philip the king of Spain's younger brother. This country was lately the seat of a bloody war between the Austrians, Spaniards, and Neapolitans. The cities of Parma and Placentia are enriched with magnificent buildings, but his catholic majesty, on his accession to the throne of Naples, is said to have carried with him thither, the most remarkable pictures, and moveable curiosities. The duke's court is thought to be the politest of any in Italy, and it is said that his revenues exceed 100,000 l. sterling a year, a sum which I am apt to think is exaggerated. The city of Parma is said to contain 50,000 inhabitants.

MANTUA, formerly a rich duchy, bringing to its own dukes 500,000 crowns a year, is now much decayed. The government of it is annexed to that of the Milanese, in possession of the house of Austria. The capital is one of the strongest fortresses in Europe, and contains about 16,000 inhabitants, who boast that Virgil was a native of their country.

The duchy of MODENA (formerly Mutina) is still governed by its own duke, the head of the house of Este, from whom the family of Brunswick descended. The duke is absolute within his own dominions, which are fruitful. The duke is under the protection of the house of Austria, and is a vassal of the empire. His dominions, however, are far from being flourishing, though very improveable, they having been alternately wasted by the late belligerent powers in Italy.

The

The ECCLESIASTICAL STATE, which contains Rome, formerly the capital of the world, lies about the middle of Italy. The bad effects of Popish tyranny, superstition, and oppression, are here seen in the highest perfection. Those spots, which, under the masters of the world, were formed into so many terrestrial paradises, surrounding their magnificent villas, and enriched with all the luxuries that art and nature could produce, are now converted into noxious pestilential marshes and quagmires; and the Campagna di Roma, that formerly contained a million of inhabitants, affords at present a miserable subsistence to about five hundred. Notwithstanding this, the pope is a considerable temporal prince, and some suppose that his annual revenue amounts to above a million sterling, tho' some authors calculate them to be much higher. When we speak comparatively, the sum of a million sterling is too high a revenue to arise from his territorial possessions; his accidental income, which formerly far exceeded that sum, is now diminished by the suppression of the order of the Jesuits, from whom he drew vast supplies, and the measures taken by the popish powers, for preventing the great ecclesiastical issues of money to Rome. According to the best and latest accounts, the taxes upon the provisions and lodgings, furnished to foreigners, who spend immense sums in visiting his dominions, form now the greatest part of his accidental revenues. From what has happened, within these 20 years past, there is reason to believe that the pope's territories will be reduced to the limits, which the houses of Austria, and Bourbon, shall please to describe. Some late popes have aimed at the improvement of their territories, but their labours have had no great effect. The discouragement of industry and agriculture, seems to be interwoven in the constitution of the papal government, which is vested in proud lazy ecclesiastics. Their indolence, and the fanaticism of their worship, infect their inferiors, who prefer begging, and imposing upon strangers, to industry and agriculture, especially as they must hold their properties, by the precarious tenure of the will of their superiors. In short, the inhabitants of many parts of the ecclesiastical state must perish through their sloth, did not the fertility of their soil spontaneously afford them subsistence. I am here, however, to make one general remark on Italy, which is, that the poverty and sloth of the lower ranks, do not take their rise from their natural dispositions.

This observation is not confined to the papal dominions. The Italian princes affected to be the patrons of all the curious and costly arts, and each vied with the other to make his court the repository of taste and magnificence. This passion
disabled

difabled them from laying out money upon works of public
utility, or from encouraging the induftry, or relieving the
wants of their fubjects, and its miferable effects are feen in
many parts of Italy.   The fplendour and furniture of churches
in the papal dominions, are inexpreffible, and partly account
for the mifery of the fubjects.   This cenfure, however,
admits of exceptions, even in a manner at the gates of Rome.

Modern Rome contains, within its circuit, a vaft number
of gardens and vineyards.   I have already touched upon its
curiofities and antiquities.   It ftands upon the Tyber, an
inconfiderable river, when compared to the Thames, and
navigated by fmall boats, barges and lighters.   The caftle of
St. Angelo, though its chief fortrefs, would be found to be
a place of fmall ftrength, were it regularly befieged.   The
city ftanding upon the ruins of antient Rome lies much higher,
fo that it is difficult to diftinguifh the feven hills on which
it was originally built.   When we confider Rome, as it now
ftands, there is the ftrongeft reafon to believe that it exceeds
antient Rome itfelf, in the magnificence of its ftructures ;
nothing in the old city, when miftrefs of the would, could
come in competition with St. Peter's church, and perhaps
many other churches in Rome, exceed in beauty of architecture, and value of materials, utenfils and furniture, her antient
temples, though it muft be acknowledged that the Pantheon
muft have been an amazing ftructure.   The inhabitants of
Rome in 1714, amounted to 143,000.   If we confider that
the fpirit of travelling is much encreafed fince that time, we
cannot reafonably fuppofe them to be diminifhed at prefent.

There is nothing very particular in the pope's temporal
government at Rome.   Like other princes, he has his guards,
or fbirri, who take care of the peace of the city, under proper
magiftrates, both ecclefiaftical and civil.   The Campagna di
Roma, which contains Rome, is under the infpection of his
holinefs.   In the other provinces he governs by legates and
vice legates.   He monopolizes all the corn in his territories,
and has always a fufficient number of troops on foot, under
proper officers, to keep the provinces in awe.   The prefent
pope, who has taken the name of Clement XIV. has wifely
difclaimed all intention of oppofing any arms to the neighbouring princes, but thofe of prayers and fupplications.

I have under the head of religion mentioned the ecclefiaftical
government of the papacy.

As to the rota, and other fubordinate chambers of this
complicated jurifdiction, they are too numerous to be even
named, and do not fall properly under my plan.   Under
a government fo conftituted, it cannot be fuppofed that the
                                                        com-

commercial exports of the ecclefiaftical ftate are of much value.

Next to Rome, Bologna, the capital of the Bolognefe, is the moft confiderable city in the ecclefiaftical ftate, and an exception to the indolence of its other inhabitants. The government is under a legate a latere, who is always a cardinal, and changed every three years. The people here live more fociably and comfortably, than the other fubjects of the pope; and perhaps their diftance from Rome, which is 165 miles north-weft, has contributed to their eafe. The reft of the ecclefiaftical ftate contains many towns celebrated in antient hiftory, and even now exhibiting the moft ftriking veftiges of their flourifhing ftate about the beginning of the 16th century; but they are at prefent little better than defolate, though here and there, a luxurious magnificent church and convent may be found, which is fupported by the toil and fweat of the neighbouring peafants.

The grandeur of FERRARA, RAVENNA, RIMINI, URBINO, (the native city of the celebrated painter Raphael) ANCONA, and many other ftates, and cities, illuftrious in former times, are now to be feen only in their ruins, and antient hiftory. LO-RETTO, on the other hand, an obfcure fpot never thought or heard of, in times of antiquity, is now the admiration of the world, for the riches it contains, and the prodigious refort to it of pilgrims, and other devotees, from a notion induftrioufly propagated by the Romifh clergy, that the houfe, in which the Virgin Mary is faid to have dwelt at Nazareth, was carried thither through the air by angels, attended with many other miraculous circumftances, fuch as that all the trees, on the arrival of the facred manfion, bowed with the profoundeft reverence; and great care is taken to prevent any bits of the materials of this houfe, from being carried to other places, and expofed as relicks to the prejudice of Loretto. The image of the Virgin Mary, and of the divine infant, are of cedar, placed in a fmall apartment, feparated from the others by a filver balluftrade, which has a gate of the fame metal. It is impoffible to defcribe the gold chains, the rings, and jewels, emeralds, pearls, and rubies, wherewith this image is loaded, and the angels of folid gold, who are here placed on every fide, are equally enriched with the moft precious diamonds. To the fuperftition of Roman-catholic princes, Loretto is indebted for this mafs of treafure. It has been matter of furprize, that no attempt has yet been made by the Turks upon Loretto, efpecially as it is badly fortified, and ftands near the fea.

The

The king of NAPLES and SICILY, or, as he is more properly called, the King of the Two Sicilies, (the name of Sicily
being common to both) is possessed of the largest dominions of
any prince in Italy, as they comprehend the ancient countries
of Samnium Campania, Apulia, Magna Grecia, and the island
of Sicily. They are bounded on all sides by the Mediterranean
and the Adriatic, except on the north east, where Naples terminates on the ecclesiastical state. The air is hot, and its soil
fruitful of every thing produced in Italy. The wines called
Vino Greco, and Lachrymæ Christi, are excellent. The city
of Naples its capital, which is extremely superb, and adorned
with all the profusion of art and riches, and its neighbourhood,
would be one of the most delightful places in Europe to live
in, were it not for their vicinity to the volcano of Vesuvius,
which sometimes threaten the city with destruction, and the
soil being pestered with insects and reptiles, some of which are
venomous.

Though above two-thirds of the property of the kingdom
are in the hands of the ecclesiastics, the protestants live here
with great freedom ; and though his Neapolitan majesty presents to his holiness every year, a palfrey, as an acknowledg-
ment that his kingdom is a fief of the pontificate, yet no in-
quisition is established in Naples. The present revenues of
that king, amount to above 750,000 l. sterling a year, but it
is more than probable that, by the new established police pursued by the princes of the house of Bourbon, of abridging the
influence and revenues of the clergy, his Neapolitan majesty's
annual income will considerably exceed a million sterling. He
has a numerous but poor nobility, consisting of princes,
dukes, marquisses, and other high-sounding titles ; and his
capital, by far the most populous in Italy, contains, at least,
300,000 inhabitants. Through every spot of this kingdom
the traveller may be said to tread on Classic ground, and no
country presents the eye with more beautiful prospects.

The island of SICILY, once the granary of the world for
corn, still continues to supply Naples, and other parts, with
that commodity, but its cultivation, and consequently fertility, is greatly diminished. Its vegetable, mineral, and animal productions, are pretty much the same with those of
Italy. Palermo, its capital, is said to contain 120,000 inhabitants, and both that city and Messina, carry on a brisk
trade.

The island of SARDINIA, which gives a royal title to the duke
of Savoy, lies about 150 miles west of Leghorn. Its capital,
Cagliari, is an university, an archbishopric, and the seat of the
viceroy.

viceroy. It is thought that his Sardinian majefty's revenues, from this ifland, does not exceed 5000 l. fterling a year, though it yields plenty of corn and wine, and has a coral fifhery. Its air is bad from its marfhes and moraffes. It was formerly annexed to the crown of Spain, but at the peace of Utrecht it was given to the emperor, and in 1719 to the houfe of Savoy.

The ifland of CORSICA lies oppofite the Genöefe continent, between the gulph of Genoa and the ifland of Sardinia, and is heft known by the noble ftand which the inhabitants have made of late under general Paoli, for their liberty, againft their Genoefe tyrants, and afterwards the French arms, than from any advantages they enjoy, from nature or fituation. Though mountainous and woody, it produces corn, wine, figs, almonds, chefnuts, olives, and other fruits. It has alfo fome cattle and horfes, and is plentifully fupplied, both by the fea and rivers, with fifh. The inhabitants are faid to amount to 120,000. Baftia, the capital, is a place of fome ftrength, but other towns of the ifland, that were in poffeffion of the malecontents, appear to have been but poorly fortified.

CAPEA, ISCHIA, and other iflands, on the coafts of Naples and Italy, have nothing to diftinguifh them, but the ruins of their antiquities, and their being now beautiful fummer retreats for their owners.

I fhall here mention the ifle of MALTA, though it is not properly ranked with the Italian iflands. It was formerly called Melita, and is fituated in 15 deg. E. long. and 45 deg. N. lat. 60 miles fouth of cape Paffaro in Sicily, and is of an oval figure, 20 miles long, and 12 broad. Its air is clear, but exceffively hot ; the whole ifland feems to be a white rock covered with a thin furface of earth, which is however amazingly productive of excellent fruit and vegetables, and garden ftuff of all kinds. This ifland, or rather rock, was given to the knights of St. John of Jerufalem in 1530, by the emperor Charles V. when the Turks drove them out of Rhodes, and they are now known by the diftinction of the knights of Malta. They are under vows of celibacy and chaftity, but they keep the former much better than the latter. They have confiderable poffeffions in the Roman-catholic countries on the continent, and are under the government of a grand-mafter, who is elected for life. They are confidered as the bulwark of Chriftendom againft the Turks on that fide. They wear croffes of a particular form, and they never have degene-

Fated

rated from the military glory of their predeceffors. They are generally of noble families, and are ranked according to their nations. Not only their chief town Valetta, or Malta, and its harbour, but their whole ifland is fo well fortified, as to be deemed impregnable by the infidels.

HISTORY.] Italy was probably firft peopled from Greece, as we have mentioned in the Introduction, to which we refer the reader, for the antient hiftory of this country, which, for many ages, gave law to the then known world under the Romans. The fucceffors of Charlemagne claimed, and for fome time poffeffed the fovereignty of Italy, but their civil wars at home, foon gave an opportunity to their governors, to either affume or purchafe the fovereignty of the feveral ftates over which they prefided.

Savoy and Piedmont, in time, fell to the lot of the courts of Maurienne, the anceftors of his prefent Sardinian majefty, whofe father (as I have already obferved) became king of Sardinia, in virtue of the quadruple alliance concluded in 1718 *.

The Milanefe, the faireft portion in Italy, went thro' feveral hands; the Vifcontis were fucceeded by the Galeazzos, and the Sfo:zas, but fell at laft into the hands of the emperor Charles V. about the year 1525, who gave it to his fon Philip II. king of Spain. It remained with that crown till the French were driven out of Italy, in 1706, by the imperialifts. They were difpoffeffed of it in 1743; but by the emperor's ceffion of Naples and Sicily, to the prefent king of Spain, it returned to the houfe of Auftria, who governs it by a viceroy.

The duchy of Mantua was formerly governed by the family of Gonzaga, who adhering to France, the territory was forfeited, as a fief of the empire, to the houfe of Auftria, which now poffeffes it, the laft duke dying without male iffue; but Guaftella was feparated from it in 1748, and made part of the duchy of Parma.

The firft duke of Parma was natural fon to pope Paul III. the duchy having been annexed to the holy fee in 1545, by pope Julius II. The defcendants of the houfe of Farnefe terminated in the late queen dowager of Spain, whofe fon, his prefent catholic majefty, obtained that duchy, and his nephew now holds it with the duchy of Placentia.

---

* Charles Emanuel III. king of Sardinia, was born in 1701, and afcended the throne in 1730. He hath iffue,
1. Victor-Ame-Maria, duke of Savoy, born in 1726; and married in 1750, to Maria-Antonietta, of Spain, born in 1729.
2. Benedict-Maurice, duke de Chablais, born 1741: and four daughters.

The Venetians were formerly the moſt formidable maritime power in Europe. In 1194, they conquered Conſtantinople itſelf, and held it for ſome time, together with great part of the continent of Europe and Aſia. They were more than once brought to the brink of deſtruction, by the confederacies formed againſt them, among the other powers of Europe, eſpecially by the league of Cambray, in 1509, but were as often ſaved by the diſunion of the confederates. The diſcovery of a paſſage to India, by the cape of Good Hope, gave the firſt blow to their greatneſs, as it loſt them the Indian trade. By degrees the Turks took from them their moſt valuable poſſeſſions, on the continent, and ſo late as the year 1715, they loſt the Morea.

The Genoeſe, for ſome time, diſputed the empire of the Mediterranean ſea, with the Venetians, but were ſeldom or never able to maintain their own independency by land, being generally protected, and ſometimes ſubjected by the French and imperialiſts. Their doge or firſt magiſtrate is crowned king of Corſica, though it does not clearly appear by what title, and that iſland is now ceded to the French by the Genoeſe. The ſucceſsful effort they made in driving the victorious Auſtrians out of their capital, during the war which was terminated by the peace of Aix-la-Chapelle in 1748, has few parallels in hiſtory, and ſerves to ſhew the effects of deſpair under oppreſſion. At preſent they are poſſeſſed of revenue, barely ſufficient to preſerve the appearance of a ſovereign ſtate.

The great duchy of Tuſcany belonged to the emperors of Germany, who governed it by deputies, to the year 1240, when the famous diſtinctions of the Gwelphs, who were the partizans of the pope, and the Gibellines, who were in the emperor's intereſt, took place. The popes then perſuaded the imperial governors in Tuſcany, to put themſelves under the protection of the church, but the Florentines, in a ſhort time, formed themſelves into a free common-wealth, and bravely defended their liberties againſt both parties by turns. Faction at laſt ſhook their freedom, and the family of Medici, long before they were declared either princes or dukes, in fact governed Florence, though the rights and privileges of the people ſeemed ſtill to exiſt. The Medici, particularly Coſmo, who was deſervedly called the Father of his Country, being in the ſecret, ſhared with the Venetians in the immenſe profits of the Eaſt-India trade, before the diſcoveries made by the Portugueze. His revenue, in ready money, which exceeded that of any ſovereign prince in Europe,

enabled his fuccessors to rife to fovereign power, and pope Pius
V; gave one of his defcendents Cofmo (the great patron of the
arts) the title of great duke of Tufcany in 1570, which continued in his family to the death of Gaston de Medicis in 1737,
without iffue. The great duchy was then claimed by the emperor
Charles VI. as a fief of the empire, and given to his fon-in-law,
the duke of Lorrain, and late emperor, in lieu of the duchy
of Lorrain, which was ceded to France by treaty. Leopold,
his fecond fon, brother to the prefent emperor, is now grand
duke, and Tufcany affumes a new face. Leghorn, which belongs to him, carries on a great trade, and feveral fhips of
very confiderable force are now ftationed on the Tufcan coafts
to prevent the depredation of the infidels.

No country has undergone greater viciffitudes of government
than Naples or Sicily, chiefly owing to the inconftancy of the
natives, which feems to be incorporated with their air. Chriftians and Saracens by turns conquered it. The Normans
under Tancred drove out the Saracens, and by their connections with the Greeks eftablifhed there, while the reft of
Europe was plunged in monkifh ignorance, a moft refpectable
monarchy flourifhing in arts and arms. About the year 1166,
the popes being then all powerful in Europe, their intrigues
broke into the fucceffion of Tancred's line, and Naples and
Sicily at laft came into the poffeffion of the French ; and the
houfe of Anjou, with fome interruptions, and tragical revolutions, held it till the Spaniards drove them out in 1504, and
it was then annexed to the crown of Spain.

The government of the Spaniards was fo oppreffive, that it
gave rife to the famous revolt, headed by Maffaniello, a young
fifherman, without fhoes or ftockings. His fuccefs was fo
furprizing, that he obliged the haughty Spaniards to abolifh
the oppreffive taxes, and to confirm the liberties of the people.
Before thefe could be re-eftablifhed perfectly, he turned de-
lirious, through his continual agitations of body and mind,
and he was put to death at the head of his own mob. Naples
and Sicily continued with the Spaniards till the year 1706,
when the archduke Charles, afterwards emperor, took poffeffion of the kingdom. By virtue of various treaties, which had
introduced Don Carlos, the king of Spain's fon, to the poffeffion of Parma and Placentia, a new war broke out in 1733,
between the houfes of Auftria and Bourbon, about the poffeffion of Naples, and Don Carlos was received into the capital,
where he was proclaimed king of both Sicilies ; this was followed by a very bloody campaign, but the farther effufion of
blood was ftopt by a peace between France and the emperor,

2   to

to which the courts of Madrid and Naples at firſt demurred, but afterwards acceded in 1736, and Don Carlos remained king of Naples.

Upon his acceſſion to the crown of Spain in 1759, it being found, by the inſpection of phyſicians, and other trials, that his eldeſt ſon was by nature incapacitated for reigning, he reſigned the crown of Naples to his third ſon; Ferdinand IV. who lately married an archducheſs of Auſtria *.

The hiſtory of the Papacy is connected with that of Chri-ſtendom itſelf. The moſt ſolid foundations for its temporal power were laid by the famous Matilda, counteſs of Tuſcany, and heireſs to the greateſt part of Italy, who bequeathed a large portion of her dominions to the famous pope Gregory VII. (who, before his acceſſion in 1073, was ſo well known by the name of Hildebrand.) It is not to be expected, that I am here to enter into a detail of the ignorance of the laity, and the other cauſes that operated to the aggrandizement of the papacy, previous to the reformation. Even ſince that æra the ſtate of Europe has been ſuch, that the popes have had more than once great weight in its public affairs, chiefly through the weakneſs and bigotry of temporal princes, who ſeem now to be recovering from their religious deluſions.

The papal power is evidently now at a low ebb. The order of Jeſuits, who are not improperly called its Janiſſaries, has been exterminated out of France, Spain, Naples, and Portugal; and is but juſt tolerated in other popiſh countries. The pope himſelf is treated by Roman-catholic princes, with very little more ceremony than is due to him as biſhop of Rome, and poſſeſſed of a temporal principality. This humiliation, it is reaſonable to believe, will terminate in a total ſeparation from the holy ſee of all its foreign emoluments, which even, ſince the beginning of the preſent century, were immenſe, and to the reducing his holineſs to the exer-ciſe of his eccleſiaſtical functions as firſt biſhop of Chri-ſtendom †.

---

* Ferdinand IV. king of the Two Sicilies, third ſon of the preſent king of Spain, was born in 1751, and married 1768, to the archducheſs Maria-Caroline-Louiſa, ſiſter to the emperor of Germany, born in 1752.

† Francis Laurentius Ganganelli, was elected pope in 1769, and took upon him the name of Clement XIV.

TURKEY.

The Grand Signior's Dominions are divided into

    1. TURKEY in EUROPE.
    2. TURKEY in ASIA.
    3. TURKEY in AFRICA.

TURKEY in EUROPE.

SITUATION AND EXTENT.

	Miles.		Degrees.
Length	1000 }	between {	17 and 40 east longitude.
Breadth	900 }		36 and 49 north latitude.

BOUNDARIES.] BOUNDED by Ruſſia, Poland, and Sclavonia, on the north; by Circaſſia, the Black Sea, the Propontis, Helleſpont, and Archipelago, on the eaſt; by the Mediterranean, on the ſouth; by the ſame ſea, and the Venetian and Auſtrian territories on the weſt.

Diviſions.	Subdiviſions.	Chief towns.
On the north coaſt of the Black Sea are the provinces of — —	Crim and Little Tartary, the ancient Taurica Cherſoneſe	Precop Brachiſeria Kaffa
	Budziac Tartary —	Oczakow.
North of the Danube are the provinces of —	Beſſarabia —	Bender Belgorod
	Moldavia, olim Dacia — —	Jazy Chotzim Falczin
	Wallachia, another part of the ancient Dacia —	Tergoviſc.
South of the Danube are	Bulgaria, the eaſt part of the ancient Myſia ——	Widin Nicopoli Siliſtria Scopia
	Servia, the weſt part of Myſia	Belgrade Semendria Niſſa
	Boſnia, part of the antient Illyricum	Seraio.

Divisions.	Subdivisions.	Chief towns.
On the Bosphorus and Hellespont ———	Romania, olim Thrace ——	Constantinople, N.L.41-E.L.29 Adrianople
South of mount Rhodope or Argentum, the north Part of the ancient Greece — —	Macedonia —	Strymon Contessa
	Theffaly, now Janua	Salonichi
	Achaia and Bœotia, now Livadia	Athens Thebes Lepanto.
On the Adriatic sea or Gulph of Venice, the ancient Illyricum —	Epirus ———	Chimæra Butrinto
	Albanea — —	Durazzo Dulcigno
	Dalmatia —	Drino Narenza
	Ragusa republic	Ragusa.
In the Morea, the ancient Peloponnesus, being the south division of Greece, are ———	Corinthia ——	Corinth
	Argos ——	Argos Napoli de Romania
	Sparta ——	Lacedæmon, now Mifitra, on the river Eurotus
	Olympia, where the Games were held	Olympia, or Longinica, on the river Alpheus
	Arcadia ———	Modon Coron
	Elis ———	Patras Elis, or Belvidere, on the river Peneus.

SOIL, AIR, SEASONS AND WATER.] Nature has lavished upon the inhabitants of Turkey, all her blessings in those four particulars. The soil, though unimproved, is luxuriant beyond description. The air is salubrious, and friendly to the imagination, unless when it is corrupted from the neighbouring countries, or through the indolence and uncleannefs of the Turkish manner of living. The seasons are here regu-

lar]

lar, and pleafant, and have been celebrated from the remoteſt times of antiquity. The Turks are invited to frequent bathings, by the purity and wholeſomeneſs of the water all over their dominions.

MOUNTAINS.] Theſe are the moſt celebrated of any in the world, and at the ſame time often the moſt fruitful. Mount Athos lies on a peninſula, running into the Egean ſea ; the mounts Pindus and Olympus, celebrated in Grecian fables, ſeparate Theſſaly from Epirus. Parnaſſus, ſo famous for being conſecrated to the Muſes, is well known. Mount Haenus is likewiſe often mentioned by the poets ; but moſt of the other mountains have changed their names, witneſs the mountains Suha, Witoſka, Staras, Plamina, and many others. Even the moſt celebrated mountains above mentioned, have had modern names impoſed upon them, by the Barbarians in their neighbourhood.

SEAS.] The Euxine or Black Sea ; the Palus Maeotis, or Sea of Aſaph ; the ſea of Marmora, which ſeparates Europe from Aſia ; the Archipelago ; the Ionian ſea, and the Levant, are ſo many evidences that Turkey in Europe, particularly that part of it where Conſtantinople ſtands, of all other countries had the beſt claim to be miſtreſs of the world.

STRAITS.] Thoſe of the Helleſpont and Boſphorus, are joined to the ſea Marmora, and are remarkable in modern as well as antient hiſtory.

RIVERS.] The Danube, the Save, the Neiſter, the Neiper, and the Don, are the beſt known rivers in this country, though many others have been celebrated by poets and hiſtorians.

LAKES.] Theſe are not extremely remarkable, nor are they mentioned with any great applauſe, either by the antients or moderns. The Lago di Sentari lies in Albania. It communicates with the Lago di Plave, and the Lago di Holti. The Stymphalus, ſo famous for its harpies, and ravenous birds, lies in the Morea ; and Peneus, from its qualities, is thought to be the lake from which the Styx, conceived by the antients to be the paſſage into hell, iſſues.

METALS AND MINERALS.] Turkey in Europe contains a variety of all ſorts of mines, and its marbles are eſteemed the fineſt in the world.

VEGETABLES AND PRODUCTIONS.] Theſe are excellent all over the European Turkey, eſpecially when aſſiſted by the ſmalleſt degree of induſtry. Beſides pot and garden herbs of almoſt every kind, this country produces in great abundance and perfection, oranges, lemons, citrons, pomegranates, grapes of an uncommon ſweetneſs, excellent figs, almonds, olives
and

and cotton. Befides thefe, many drugs, not common in other parts of Europe, are produced here.

· ANIMALS.] The Theffalian, or Turkifh horfes, are excellent both for their beauty and fervice. The black cattle are large, efpecially in Greece. The goats are a moft valuable part of the animal creation to the inhabitants, for the nutrition they afford, both of milk and flefh. The large eagles which abound in the neighbourhood of Babadagi, furnifh the beft feathers for arrows for the Turkifh and Tartan archers, and they fell at an uncommon price. Partridges are very plentiful in Greece, as are all other kinds of fowls and quadrupedes, all over Turkey in Europe, but the Turks and Mahometans in general, are not very fond of animal food.

ANTIQUITIES AND CURIOSITIES } Almoft every fpot of NATURAL AND ARTIFICIAL. ſ ground, every river, and every fountain in Greece, prefents the traveller with the ruins of a celebrated antiquity. On the Ifthmus of Corinth, the ruins of Neptune's temple, and the theatre, where the Ifthmean games were celebrated, are ftill vifible. Athens, which contains at prefent above 10,000 inhabitants, is a fruitful fource of the moft magnificent and celebrated antiquities in the world, and to particularize them would be endlefs. I cannot, however, omit mentioning the temple of Minerva, thought by fome to be the fineft extant. The temple of the eight winds, and the lantern of Demofthenes, are ftill entire. The remains of the temple of the oracle of Apollo, are ftill vifible at Caftri, on the fouth fide of mount Parnaffus, and the marble fteps that defcend to a pleafant running water, fuppofed to be the renowned Caftalian fpring, with the niches for ftatues in the rock, are ftill difcernible. The famous cave of Trophonius is ftill a natural curiofity in Livadiæ, the old Bœotia.

CITIES.] Conftantinople, the capital of this great empire, is fituated on the European fide of the Bofphorus. It was built upon the ruins of the ancient Byzantium, by the Roman emperor Conftantine the Great, as a more inviting fituation than Rome, for the feat of empire. It became afterwards the capital of the Greek empire, and having efcaped the deftructive rage of the barbarous nations, it was the greateft as well as the moft beautiful city in Europe, and the only one during the Gothic ages, in which there remained any image of the antient elegance in manners and arts. While it remained in the poffeffion of the Greek emperors, it was the only mart in Europe, for the commodities of the Eaft-Indies. It derived great advantages from its being the rendezvous of the crufaders, and being then in the meridian of its glory, the Euro-

peau

pean writers, in the ages of the crufades, fpeak of it with
aftonifhment. " O what a vaft city is Conftantinople, (exclaims one when he firft beheld it) and how beautiful! how
many monafteries are there in it, and how many palaces built
with wonderful art ! how many manufactures are there in the
city amazing to behold ! It would be aftonifhing to relate how
it abounds with all good things, with gold, filver, and ftuffs
of various kinds ; for every hour fhips arrive in the port with
all things neceffary for the ufe of man." Conftantinople is
at this day one of the fineft cities in the world by its fituation
and its port. It is frequently called the Port, by way of
eminence. The profpect from it is noble. It abounds with
antiquities. The mofque of St. Sophia, once a Chriftian
church, is thought in fome refpects to exceed in grandeur and
architecture St. Peter's at Rome. The city itfelf is built in a
triangular form, with the Seraglio ftanding on a point of one
of the angles, from whence there is a profpect of the delightful coaft of the Leffer Afia, which is not to be equalled. Both
the magnitude and population of Conftantinople have been
greatly exaggerated by credulous travellers. The beft authors
think that it does not contain above 800,000 inhabitants,
three-fourths of whom are faid to be Greeks and Armenians,
and the reft are Jews and Turks. Others fuppofe the inhabitants not to exceed 600,000.

As to the population, manners, religion, government,
revenues, learning, military ftrength, commerce, and manufactures of the Turks, thefe feveral heads depending on the
fame principles all over the empire, fhall be mentioned under
Turkey in Afia.

ISLANDS belonging to TURKEY in EUROPE, being Part of Antient GREECE.

I Shall mention thofe iflands chiefly for the ufe of fuch
readers as are converfant with antient hiftory, of which
they make fo diftinguifhed a part.

NEGROPONT, the antient Eubœa, ftretches from the
fouth-eaft to the north-weft, and on the eaftern coaft of Achaia
or Livadia. It is 90 miles long, and 25 broad. Here the
Turkifh gallies lie. The tides on its coafts are irregular ; and
the ifland itfelf abounds in corn, wine, and fruit.

LEMNOS, lies on the north part of the Egean fea or
Archipelago, and is almoft a fquare of 25 miles in length and
breadth. Though it produces corn and wine, yet its principal
riches arife from its mineral earth, fometimes called terra Lemna

or

or *figillata*, becaufe it is fealed up by the Turks, who receive therefrom a confiderable revenue.

TENEDOS, is remarkable only for its lying oppofite to old Troy, and its being mentioned by Virgil as the place to which the Greeks retired and left the Trojans in a fatal fecurity.

SCYROS, is about 60 miles in circumference, and is remarkable chiefly for the remains of antiquity which it contains.

LESBOS, or MYTELINE, is about 60 miles long, and is famous for the number of philofophers and poets it produced. The inhabitants were formerly noted for their prodigality.

SCIO, or CHIOS, lies about 80 miles weft of Smyrna, and is about 100 miles in circumference. This ifland, though rocky and mountainous, produces excellent wine, but no corn. It is inhabited by 100,000 Greeks, 10,000 Turks, and above 3,000 Latins. The inhabitants have manufactures of filk, velvet, gold and filver ftuffs. The ifland likewife produces oil and filk, and the lentifk-tree, or maftic, from which the government draws its chief revenue. The women of this, and almoft all the other Greek iflands, have in all ages been celebrated for their beauty, and their perfons have been the moft perfect models of fymmetry to painters and ftatuaries. They are not, however, renowned for their modefty or virtue; and even the Greek nuns are faid to be lavifh of their favours. Among the poets and hiftorians faid to be born here, the inhabitants reckon Homer, and fhew a little fquare houfe, which they call Homer's School. The Greeks pay a capitation tax for the exercife of their religion and laws; the rate of the higheft rank is 10 crowns a-head, the fecond three, and the meaneft two and a half, yearly.

SAMOS, lies oppofite to Ephefus, on the coaft of the Leffer Afia, about feven miles from the continent. It is 30 miles long and 15 broad. This ifland gave birth to Pythagoras, and is inhabited by Greek Chriftians, who are well treated by the Turks, their mafters. The mufcadine Samian wine is in high requeft; and the ifland, befides, produces wool, which they fell to the French; oil, pomegranates, and filk. This ifland is fuppofed to have been the native country of Juno; and fome travellers think that the ruins of her temple, and of the antient city Samos, are the fineft remains of antiquity in the Levant.

To the fouth of Samos lies PATMOS, about 20 miles in circumference, but fo barren and dreary, that it may be called

a rock

a rock rather than an island. It has, however, a convenient haven; and the few Greek monks who are upon the island, shew a cave where St. John is supposed to have written the 'Apocalypse.

The CYCLADES islands lie like a circle round Delos, the chief of them, which lies south of the islands Mycone and Tirse, and almost midway between the continents of Asia and Europe. Though Delos is not above six miles in circumference, it is one of the most celebrated of all the Grecian islands, as being the birth-place of Apollo and Diana, the magnificent ruins of whose temples are still visible. This island is almost destitute of inhabitants.

PAROS, lies between the islands of Luxia and Melos. Like all the other Greek islands, it contains the most striking and magnificent ruins of antiquity; but is chiefly renowned for the beauty and whiteness of its marble.

CERIGO, or CYTHEREA, lies south-east of the Morea, and is about 50 miles in circumference, but rocky and mountainous, and chiefly remarkable for being the favourite residence of Venus.

SANTORIN, is one of the most southermost islands in the Archipelago, and was formerly called Calista, and afterwards Thera. Though seemingly covered with pumice-stones, yet, through the industry of the inhabitants, who are about 10,000, it produces barley and wine, with some wheat. One third of the people are of the Latin church, and subject to a popish bishop. Near this island another arose of the same name, from the bottom of the sea, in 1707. At the time of its birth, there was an earthquake, attended with most dreadful lightnings and thunders and boilings of the sea for several days, so that when it arose out of the sea it was a mere volcano, but the burnings soon ceased. It is about 200 feet above the sea, and at the time of its first emerging it was about a mile broad and five miles in circumference, but it has since encreased. Several other islands of the Archipelago appear to have had the like original, but the sea in their neighbourhood is so deep as not to be fathomed.

The famous island of RHODES is situated in the 28th degree of east longitude, and 36 deg. 20 minutes north latitude, about 20 miles south-west of the continent of Lesser Asia, being about 50 miles long, and 25 broad. This island abounds in wine, and many of the necessaries of life, but the inhabitants import their corn from the neighbouring country. The colossus of brass, which anciently stood at the mouth of its harbour, and was 50 fathom wide, was deservedly accounted one of the wonders of the world: one foot being placed on each side of the harbour, ships passed between its legs; and it held in one hand a light-house for the direction of mariners. The face of the colossus represented the sun, to whom this image was dedicated; and its height was about 135 feet. The inhabitants of this island were formerly masters of the sea; and the Rhodian law was the directory of the Romans in maritime affairs. The knights of St. John of Jerusalem, after losing Palestine, took this island from the Turks in 1308, but lost it to them in 1522, and afterwards retired to Malta.

CANDIA, the ancient Crete, is still renowned for its hundred cities, for its being the birth-place of Jupiter, the seat of legislature to all Greece, and many other historical and political distinctions. It lies between 35 and 36 degrees of north latitude, being 200 miles long and sixty broad, almost equally distant from Europe, Asia, and Africa. The famous Mount Ida stands in the middle of the island, and is no better than a barren rock; and Lethe, the river of oblivion, is a torpid stream. Some of the vallies of this island produce wine, fruits, and corn; all of them remarkably excellent in their kinds. The siege of Candia, the capital of the island, in modern times, was far more wonderful and bloody than that of Troy. The Turks invested it in the beginning of the year 1645, and its Venetian garrison, after bravely defending itself till the latter end of September 1669, made, at last, an honourable capitulation. The siege cost the Turks 180,000 men, and the Venetians 80,000.

CYPRUS, lies in the Levant sea, about 30 miles distant from the coasts of Syria and Palestine. It is 150 miles long, and 70 broad, and lies at almost an equal distance from Europe and Africa. It was formerly famous for the worship of Venus, the Cyprian goddess; and during the time of the Crusades, was a rich flourishing kingdom, inhabited by Christians. Its wine, especially that which grows at the bottom of the celebrated Mount Olympus, is the most palatable and richest of all that grows in the Greek islands. Nicosia is the capital, and the see of a Greek archbishop. Famagusta, its ancient capital, has a good harbour; and the natural produce of the island is so rich, that many European nations find their account in keeping consuls residing upon it; but the oppressions of the Turks have depopulated and impoverished it to a surprizing degree, though the revenue they get from it does not exceed 1250 l. a year. Its female inhabitants do not degenerate

nerate from their anceftors as devotees to Venus ; and Paphos, the antient feat of pleafure and corruption, is one of the divifions of the ifland.   Richard I. king of England, fubdued Cyprus, on account of its king's treachery ; and its royal title was transferred to Guy Lufignan, king of Jerufalem, from whence it paffed to the Venetians, who ftill hold that empty honour.

The iflands in the Ionian fea are, S A P I E N Z A, S T I-V A L I, Z A N T E, C E P H A L O N I A, S A N T A M A U R A, C O R F U, and others of fmaller note, particularly I S O L A D E L   C O M P A R E, which would not deferve mention, had it not been the ancient Ithaca, the birth-place and kingdom of Ulyffes.

Thofe iflands in general are fruitful.   Zante, belonging to the Venetians, has a populous capital of the fame name, and is a place of confiderable trade, efpecially in fruits.   Corfu, which is the capital of that ifland, is a place of great ftrength, and belongs likewife to the Venetians, who concern themfelves very little about the welfare or government of thofe and other iflands, fo that the inhabitants, who are generally Greeks, bear a very indifferent character.

A S I A.

AS Afia exceeds Europe and Africa in the extent of its territories, it is alfo fuperior to them in the ferenity of its air, the fertility of its foil, the delicioufnefs of its fruits, the fragrancy and balfamic qualities of its plants, fpices, and gums ; the falubrity of its drugs ; the quantity, variety, beauty, and value of its gems ; the richnefs of its metals, and the finenefs of its filks and cottons.   It was in Afia, according to the facred records, that the Allwife Creator planted the garden of Eden, in which he formed the firft man and firft woman, from whom the race of mankind was to fpring. Afia became again the nurfery of the world after the deluge, whence the defcendants of Noah difperfed their various colonies into all the other parts of the globe.   It was in Afia that God placed his once favourite people, the Hebrews, whom he enlightned by revelations delivered by the prophets, and to whom he gave the oracles of truth.   It was here that the great and merciful work of our redemption was accomplifhed by his divine Son ; and it was from hence that the light of
his

his glorious gofpel was carried with amazing rapidity into all the known nations by his difciples and followers. Here the firft Chriftian churches were founded, and the Chriftian faith miraculoufly propagated and watered with the blood of innumerable martyrs. It was in Afia that the firft edifices were reared, and the firft empires founded, while the other parts of the globe were inhabited only by wild animals. On all thefe accounts, this quarter claims a fuperiority over the reft ; but it muft be owned, that a great change hath happened in that part of it called Turkey, which hath loft much of its antient fplendor, and from the moft populous and beft cultivated fpot in Afia, is become a wild uncultivated defert. The other parts of Afia continue much in their former condition, the foil being as remarkable for its fertility, as moft of the inhabitants for their indolence, effeminacy, and luxury. This effeminacy is chiefly owing to the warmth of the climate, though in fome meafure heightened by cuftom and education ; and the fymptoms of it are more or lefs vifible, as the feveral nations are feated nearer or farther from the north. Hence the Tartars, who live near the fame latitudes with us, are as brave, hardy, ftrong, and vigorous, as any European nation. What is wanting in the robuft frame of their bodies among the Chinefe, Mogul-Indians, and all the inhabitants of the more fouthern regions, is in a great meafure made up to them by the vivacity of their minds, and ingenuity in various kinds of workmanfhip, which our moft fkilful mechanics have in vain endeavoured to imitate.

This vaft extent of territory was fucceffively governed in antient times by the Affyrians, the Medes, the Perfians, and the Greeks ; but the immenfe regions of India and China were little known to Alexander or the conquerors of the antient world. Upon the decline of thofe empires, great part of Afia fubmitted to the Roman arms ; and afterwards, in the middle ages, the fucceffors of Mahomet, or, as they were ufually called, Saracens, founded in Afia, in Africa, and in Europe, a more extenfive empire than that of Cyrus, Alexander, or even the Roman when in its height of power. The Saracen greatnefs ended with the death of Tamerlane ; and the Turks, conquerors on every fide, took poffeffion of the middle regions of Afia, which they ftill enjoy. Befides the countries poffeffed by the Turks and Ruffians, Afia contains at prefent three powerful empires, the Chinefe, the Mogul, and the Perfian, upon which the leffer kingdoms and fovereignties of Afia generally depend. The prevailing form of government in this divifion of the globe is abfolute monarchy. If any of them can be faid to enjoy fome fhare of liberty, it

is

is the wandering tribes, as the Tartars and Arabs. Many of the Afiatic nations, when the Dutch firft came among them, could not conceive how it was poffible for any people to live under any other form of government than that of a defpotic monarchy. Turkey, Arabia, Perfia, part of Tartary, and part of India, profefs Mahometifm. The Perfian and Indian Mahometans are of the fect of Hali, and the others of that of Omar ; but both own Mahomet for their law-giver, and the Koran for their rule of faith and life. In the other parts of Tartary, India, China, Japan, and the Afiatic iflands, they are generally heathens and idolaters. Jews are to be found every where in Afia. Chriftianity, though planted here with wonderful rapidity by the apoftles and primitive fathers, fuffered an almoft total eclipfe by the conquefts of the Saracens, and afterwards of the Turks. Incredible indeed have been the hazards, perils, and fufferings of popifh mif-fionaries, to propagate their doctrines in the moft diftant regions, and among the groffeft idolaters ; but their labours have hitherto failed of fuccefs, owing, in a great meafure, to the avarice and profligacy of the Europeans, who refort thi-ther in fearch of wealth and dominion.

The principal languages fpoken in Afia are, the modern Greek, the Turkifh, the Ruffian, the Tartarian, the Perfian, the Arabic, the Malayan, the Chinefe, and the Japanefe. The European languages are alfo fpoken upon the coafts of India and China.

The continent of Afia is fituated between 25 and 180 degrees of eaft longitude, and between the equator and 80 degrees of north latitude. It is about 4740 miles in length, from the Dardanels on the weft, to the eaftern fhore of Tar-tary ; and about 4380 miles in breadth, from the n..t fouthern part of Malacca, to the moft northern cape of Nova Zembla. It is bounded by the Frozen Ocean on the north ; on the weft it is feparated from Africa by the Red Sea, and from Europe by the Levant or Mediterranean, the Archipe-lago, the Hellefpont, the fea of Marmora, the Bofphorus, the Black Sea, the river Don, and a line drawn from it to the river Tobol, and from thence to the river Oby, which falls into the Frozen Ocean. On the eaft, it is bounded by the Pacific Ocean, or South-Sea, which feparates it from America ; and on the fouth, by the Indian Ocean ; fo that it is almoft furrounded by the fea. The principal regions which divide this country are as follow.

Nations.	Length.	Breadth.	Chief cities.	Dift. & bearing from London.	Diff. of time from London.	Religions.
Ruffian Chinefe Mogulean Independant	The bounds of thefe parts are unlimited, each power pufhing on his conquefts as far as he can.		Tobolfkoi Chynian Tibet Samercand	2160 N. E. 4480 N. E. 3780 E. 2800 E.	4 10 bef. 8 4 bef. 5 40 bef. 4 36 bef.	Chrift. & Pag. Pagans Pagans Pagans
China	1440	1000	Pekin	4320 S. E.	7 24 bef.	Pagans
Moguls	2000	1500	Delly	3720 S. E.	5 16 bef.	Mah. & Pag.
India	2000	1000	Siam or Pegu	5040 S. E.	6 44 bef.	Pagans
Perfia	1300	1100	Ifpahan	2460 S. E.	3 20 bef.	Mahometans
Part of Arabia	1300	1200	Mecca	2640 S. E.	2 52 bef.	Mahometans
Syria	270	160	Aleppo	1860 S. E.	2 10 bef.	Chrift. & Mah.
Holy Land	210	90	Jerufalem	1920 S. E.	2 24 bef.	Chrift. & Mah.
Natolia	750	308	Burfa or Smyrna	1440 S. E.	1 48 bef.	Mahometans
Diarbick or Mefopotamia	560	310	Bagdad	2160 S. E.	2 56 bef.	Mahometans, with fome few Chriftians
Turcomania	360	300	Erzerum	1860 S. E.	2 44 bef.	
Georgia	* * *	* * *	Teflis	1920 E.	3 10 bef.	

All the iflands of Afia (except Cyprus, already defcribed, in the Levant, belonging to the Turks) lie in the Pacific or Eaftern Ocean, and the Indian Seas, of wnich the principal, where the Europeans trade or have fettlements, are

Iflands.	Towns.	Trade with or belong to.
The Japanefe ifles	Jeddo	Dutch
The Ladrones	Guam	Spain
Formofa	Tai-ouan-fou	China
The Philippines	Manilla	Spain
The Molucca, or Clove ifles,	Victoria Fort	Dutch
The Banda, or Nutmeg ifles,	Lantor	Dutch
Amboyna ⎰ furrounding the ⎱	Amboyna	Dutch
Celebes ⎰ Molucca and ⎱	Macaffar	Dutch
Gilolo, &c. ⎰ Banda ifles ⎰	Gilolo	Dutch
⎰ Borneo	Borneo, Caytongee	All nations
The Sunda ifles ⎰ Sumatra	Achen, Bencoolen	Englifh and Dutch
⎰ Java, &c.	Batavia, Bantam	Dutch
The Andaman and Nicobar ifles	Andaman, Nicobar	All nations
Ceylon	Candy	Dutch
The Maldives	Caridon	All nations
Bombay	Bombay	Englifh
The Kurile ifles, and thofe in the fea of Kamptfchatza, lately difcovered by the Ruffians,		Ruffia.

TURKEY IN ASIA.

SITUATION AND EXTENT.

Miles. : Degrees.

Length 1000 ⎱ between ⎰ 27 and 46 eaft longitude.
Breadth 800 ⎰ ⎱ 28 and 45 north latitude.

BOUNDARIES.] BOUNDED by the Black Sea and Circaffia, on the north; by Perfia, on the eaft; by Arabia and the Levant Sea, on the fouth; and

by

by the Archipelago, the Hellefpont, and Propontis, which feparate it from Europe, on the weft.

Divifions.	Subdivifions.	Chief towns.
The eaftern provinces are	1. Eyraco Arabic or Chaldea ——	Boffora and Bagdat.
	2. Diarbec or Mefo-potamia ——	Diarbec, Orfa, and Moufoul.
	3. Curdiftan or Affy-ria —— ——	Nineveh and Betlis.
	4. Turcomania or Ar-menia —— ——	Erzerum and Van.
	5. Georgia, including Mengrelia and Ima-retta, and part of Circaffia —— ——	Amarchia and Gonie.
Natolia, or the Leffer Afia, on the weft,	1. Natolia Proper ——	Burfa, Nici, Smyrna, and Ephefus.
	2. Amafia ——	Amafia, Trapezond, and Sinope.
	3. Aladulia ——	Ajazzo and Marat.
	4. Caramania ——	Satalia and Teraffo.
Eaft of the Le-vant Sea,	Syria, with Paleftine, or the Holy Land	Aleppo, Antioch, Da-mafcus, Tyre, Sidon, Tripoli, Scanderoon, and Jerufalem.

MOUNTAINS.] Thefe are famous in facred as well as prophane writings. The moft remarkable are, Olympus; Taurus and Anti-taurus; Caucafus and Arrarat; Lebanon; and Hermon.

RIVERS.] The fame may be obferved of the rivers, which are the Euphrates; Tigris; Orantes; Meander; Sarabat; Kara; and, Jordan.

AIR AND CLIMATE.] Though both are delightful in the utmoft degree, and naturally falubrious to the human confti-tution, yet fuch is the equality with which the Author of nature has difpenfed his benefits, that Turkey, both in Eu-rope and Afia, is often vifited by the plague; a frightful fcourge of mankind, wherever it takes place, but here doubly deftruÖtive, from the native indolence of the Turks, and their fuperftitious belief in predeftination, which prevents them from ufing precaution to defend themfelves againft this calamity.

SOIL AND PRODUCE.] As this country contains the moft fertile provinces of Afia, I need fcarcely inform the reader that it produces all the luxuries of life in the utmoft abun-dance,

dance, notwithftanding the indolence of its owners. Raw filk, corn, wine, oil, honey, fruit of every fpecies, coffee, myrrh, frankincenfe, and odoriferous plants and drugs, are natives here almoft without culture, which is practifed chiefly by Greek and Armenian Chriftians. The olives, citrons, lemons, oranges, figs, and dates, produced in thofe provinces, are highly delicious, and in fuch plenty, that they coft the inhabitants a mere trifle, and it is faid, in fome places nothing. Their afparagus is often as large as a man's leg, and their grapes far exceed thofe of other countries in largenefs. In fhort, nature has brought all her productions here to the higheft perfection.

ANIMAL PRODUCTIONS } The fame may be faid of their BY SEA AND LAND. } animals. The breed of the Turkifh and Arabian horfes, the latter efpecially, are valuable beyond any in the world, and have confiderably improved that of the Englifh. We know of no quadrupeds that are peculiar to thofe countries, but they contain all that are neceffary for the ufe of mankind. Camels are here in much requeft, from their ftrength, their agility, and, above all, their moderation in eating and drinking, which is greater than that of any other known animal. Their numerous herds of goats furnifh the materials for their camblets. Their kids and fheep are exquifite eating, and are faid to furpafs, in flavour and tafte, thofe of Europe; but their other butchers meat, beef particularly, is not fo fine.

As to birds, they have wild fowl in vaft perfection; their oftriches are well known by their tallnefs, ftupidity, and heavinefs. The Roman epicures prized no fifh except lampreys, mullets, and oyfters, but thofe that were found in Afia.

METALS AND MINERALS.] This country contains all the metals that are to be found in the richeft kingdoms and provinces of Europe; and its medicinal fprings and baths exceed thofe of any in the known world.

OF THE TURKS IN EUROPE AND ASIA.

POPULATION, INHABITANTS, } MANNERS, CUSTOMS AND } DIVERSIONS. } THE population of this great country is by no means equal either to its extent or fertility, nor have the beft geographers been able to afcertain it, becaufe of the uncertainty of its limits. It certainly is not fo great as it was before the Chriftian æra, or even under the Roman emperors; owing to various caufes, and above all, to the tyranny under which the natives live, and their polygamy, which is undoubtedly an enemy to population, as may be evinced from many reasons, and particularly because the Greeks and Armenians, among whom it is not practised, are incomparably more prolific than the Turks, notwithstanding the rigid subjection in which they are kept by the latter. The plague is another cause of depopulation. The Turkish emperor, however, has more subjects than any two European princes.

As to the inhabitants, they are generally well made and robust men: when young their complexions are fair, and their faces handsome ; their hair and eyes are black or dark brown. The women, when young, are commonly handsome, but they generally look old at thirty. In their demeanour, the Turks are rather hypochondriac, grave, sedate, and passive ; but when agitated by passion, furious, raging, ungovernable; big with dissimulation, jealous, suspicious, and vindictive beyond conception : in matters of religion, tenacious, superstitious, and morose. Though uncapable of much benevolence, or even humanity with regard to Jews, Christians, or any who differ from them in religious matters, they are not devoid of social affections for those of their own religion. But interest is their supreme good, and when that comes in competition, all ties of religion, consanguinity, or friendship, are speedily dissolved. The morals of the Asiatic Turks are far preferable to those of the European. They are hospitable to strangers ; and the vices of avarice and inhumanity reign chiefly among their great men. They are likewise said to be charitable to one another, and punctual in their dealings. Their charity and public spirit is most conspicuous in their building caravan-seras or places of entertainment on roads that are destitute of accommodations, for the refreshment of poor pilgrims or travellers. With the same laudable view, they search out the best springs, and dig wells, which in those countries is a luxury to weary travellers. The Turks sit crofs-legged upon mats, not only at their meals but in company. Their ideas, except what they acquire from opium, are simple and confined, seldom reaching without the walls of their own houses, where they sit conversing with their women, drinking coffee, smoaking tobacco, or chewing opium. They have little curiosity to be informed of the state of their own, or any other country. If a visier, bashaw, or other officer, is turned out, or strangled, they say no more on the occasion, than that there will be a new visier or governor, seldom enquiring into the reason of the disgrace of the former minister. They are perfect strangers to wit and agreeable conversation. They have few printed books, and seldom read any other than the Alcoran, and the

comments

comments upon it.   Nothing is negociated in Turkey without
prefents ; and here juftice may be bought and fold.

The Turks dine about eleven o'clock in the forenoon, and
they fup at five in the winter and fix in the fummer, and this
is their principal meal.   Among the great people, their difhes
are ferved up one by one ; but they have neither knife nor
fork, and they are not permitted by their religion to ufe gold
or filver fpoons.   Their victuals are always high feafoned.
Rice is the common food of the lower fort, fometimes it is
boiled up with gravy ; but their chief difh is pilau, which is
mutton and fowl boiled to rags, and the rice being boiled
quite dry, the foup is high feafoned, and poured upon it.
They drink water, fherbet, and coffee; and the only debauch
they know is in opium, which gives them fenfations refembling
thofe of intoxication.   Guefts of high rank fometimes have
their beards perfumed by a female flave of the family.   They
are temperate and fober from a principle of their religion,
which forbids them the ufe of wine ; though in private many
of them indulge themfelves in the ufe of ftrong liquors.
Their common falutation is by an inclination of the head,
and laying their right hand on their breaft.   They fleep, in
linen waiftcoats and drawers, upon mattreffes, and cover
themfelves with a quilt.   Few or none of the confiderable
inhabitants of this vaft empire have any notion of walking or
riding either for health or diverfion.   The moft religious
among them find, however, fufficient exercife when they
conform themfelves to the frequent oblations, prayers, and
rites prefcribed them by Mahomet.

Their active diverfions confift in fhooting at a mark, or
tilting it with darts, at which they are very expert.   Some of
their great men are fond of hunting, and take the field with
numerous equipages, which are joined by their inferiors ; but
this is often done for political purpofes, that they may know
the ftrength of their dependants.   Within doors, the chefs
or draught-board are their ufual amufements ; and if they play
at chance games, they never bet money, that being prohibited
by the Alcoran.

Dress.]   The men fhave their heads, leaving a lock on
the crown, and wear their beards long.   They cover their
heads with a turban, and never put it off but when they fleep.
Their fhirts are without collar or wriftband, and over them
they throw a long veft, which they tie with a fafh, and over
the veft they wear a loofe gown fomewhat fhorter.   Their
breeches, or drawers, are of a piece with their ftockings ;
and inftead of fhoes they wear flippers, which they put off

when they enter a temple or houfe. They fuffer no Chriftians, or other people, to wear white turbans. The drefs
of the women differs little from that of the men, only they
wear ftiffened caps upon their heads with horns fomething like
a mitre, and wear their hair down. When they appear
abroad they are fo muffled up as not to be known by their
neareft relations. Such of the women as are virtuous make
no ufe of paint to heighten their beauty, or to difguife their
complexion, but they often tinge their hands and feet with
henna, which gives them a deep yellow. The men make ufe
of the fame expedient to colour their beards.

MARRIAGES.] Marriages in this country are chiefly negociated by the ladies. When the terms are agreed upon, the
bridegroom pays down a fum of money, a licence is taken
out from the cade, or proper magiftrate, and the parties are
married. The bargain is celebrated, as in other nations, with
mirth and jollity, and the money is generally employed in
furnifhing the houfe of the young couple. A man may marry
as many women as he can maintain, but under the reftriction
of a cenforial power, to prevent too great a plurality of wives.
Befides their wives, the wealthy Turks keep a kind of Seraglio
of women ; but all thefe indulgencies are fometimes infuffi-
cient to gratify their unnatural defires.

FUNERALS.] The burials of the Turks are decent. The
corpfe is attended by the relations, chanting paffages from the
Koran ; and after being depofited in a mofque (for fo they
call their temples) they are buried in a field, by the iman or
prieft, who pronounces a funeral fermon at the time of the
interment. The male relations exprefs their forrow by alms
and prayers ; the women, by decking the tomb on certain
days with flowers and green leaves ; and in mourning for a
hufband, they wear a particular head-drefs, and leave off all
finery for twelve months.

RELIGION.] The eftablifhed religion is that of the Mahometan, fo called from Mahomet, the author of it ; fome account of which the reader will find in the following hiftory of
Arabia, the native country of that impoftor. The Turks
profefs that of the fe07 of Omar ; but thefe are fplit into as
many fectaries as their neighbours the Chriftians. There is
no ordination among their clergy, any perfon may be a prieft
that pleafes to take the habit and perform the functions of his
order, and may lay down his office when he pleafes. Their
chief prieft or mufti feems to have great power in the ftate.

ECCLESIASTICAL INSTITUTIONS } The Turkifh govern-
        OF CHRISTIANS.   } ment having formed
thefe into part of its finances, they are tolerated where they
                                                          are

are moſt profitable; but the hardſhips impoſed upon the Greek church are ſuch, as muſt always diſpoſe that people to favour any revolution of government. Jeruſalem, Alexandria, and Antioch, are patriarchates; and their heads are indulged, according as they pay for their privilege, with a civil as well as an eccleſiaſtical authority over their votaries. The ſame may be ſaid of the Neſtorian and Armenian patriarchs; and every great city that can pay for the privilege has its archbiſhop or biſhop.

LANGUAGE.] The radical languages of this empire are the Sclavonian, which ſeems to have been the mother tongue of the antient Turks; the Greek modernized, but ſtill bearing a relation to the old language; the Arabic, and the Syriac, a dialect of which is ſtill ſpoken. A ſpecimen of the modern Greek follows in their Paternoſter:

Pater hemas, opios iſo ees tos ouranous: hagia ſthito to onoma ſou: na erti he baſilia ſou: to thelema ſou na genetez itzon en te ge, os is ton ouranon: to ptſomi hemas doze hemas ſemoren: kæ ſi choraſe hemos ta crimata bemon itzone, kæ hemas ſichoraſomen ekinous opou: mas adikounkæ men ternes hemais is to piraſmo, alla ſoſon hemas apo to kaxo. Amen.

LEARNING AND LEARNED MEN.] I know of none among the Turks, who profeſs a ſovereign contempt for our learning. Greece, which was the native country of genius, arts, and ſciences, produces at preſent, beſides Turks, numerous bands of Chriſtian biſhops, prieſts, and monks, who in general are as ignorant as the Turks themſelves, and are divided into various abſurd ſects of what they call Chriſtianity.

ANTIQUITIES AND CURIOSITIES, NATURAL AND ARTIFICIAL.] Theſe are ſo various, that they have furniſhed matter for many voluminous publications, and others are appearing every day. Thoſe countries contained all that was rich and magnificent in architecture, and ſculpture, and neither the barbarity of the Turks, nor the depredations they have ſuffered from the Europeans, ſeem to have diminiſhed their number. They are more or leſs perfect, according to the air, ſoil, or climate, in which they ſtand, and all of them bear deplorable marks of neglect. Many of the fineſt temples are converted into Turkiſh moſques, or Greek churches, and are more disfigured than thoſe which remain in ruins. Amidſt ſuch a plenitude of curioſities, all that can be done here is to ſelect ſome of the moſt ſtriking; and I ſhall begin with Balbec and Palmyra, which form the pride of all antiquity.

Balbec is ſituated on a riſing plain, between Tripoli in Syria and Damaſcus, and is the Heliopolis of Cælo Syria. Its

remains

remains of antiquity difplay, according to the beft judges, the boldeft plan that ever was attempted in architecture. The portico of the temple of Heliopolis is inexpreffibly fuperb, though disfigured by two Turkifh towers. The hexagonal court behind it, is now known only by the magnificence of its ruins. Their walls were adorned with Corinthian pilafters and ftatues, and it opens into a quadrangular court of the fame tafte and grandeur. The great temple to which this leads, is now fo ruined, that it is known only by an entablature, fupported by nine lofty columns, each confifting of three pieces joined together, by iron pins, without cement. Some of thofe pins are a foot long, and a foot in diameter, and the fordid Turks are daily at work to deftroy the columns, for the fake of the iron. A fmall temple is ftill ftanding, with a pedeftal of eight columns in front, and fifteen in flank, and every where richly ornamented with figures in alto relief, expreffing the heads of gods, heroes, and emperors, and part of the antient mythology. To the weft of this temple is another, of a circular form, of the Corinthian and Ionic order, but disfigured with Turkifh mofques and houfes. The other parts of this antient city are proportionably beautiful and ftupendous.

Various have been the conjectures concerning the founders of thofe immenfe buildings. The inhabitants of Afia afcribe them to Solomon, but fome make them fo modern, as the time of Antoninus Pius. Perhaps they are of different æras, and though that prince, and his fucceffors, may have rebuilt fome part of them, yet the boldnefs of their architecture, the beauty of their ornaments, and the ftupendous execution of the whole, feem to fix their foundation to a period before the Chriftian æra, but without mounting to the times of the Jews, or the Phenicians, who probably knew little of the Greek ftile, in building and ornamenting. Balbec is at prefent a little city, encompaffed with a wall. The inhabitants, who are about 5000 in number, live in or near the circular temple, in houfes built out of the antient ruins. A freeftone quarry, in the neighbourhood, furnifhed the ftones for the body of the temple, and one of the ftones, not quite detached from the bottom of the quarry, is 70 feet long, 14 broad, and 14 feet five inches deep, and reduced to our meafure is 1135 tons. A coarfe white marble quarry, at a greater diftance, furnifhed the ornamental parts.

Palmyra, or as it was called by the antients, Tadmor in the Defart, is fituated in the wilds of Arabia Petræa, about 33 deg. N. lat. and 200 miles to the fouth-eaft of Aleppo. It is approached through a narrow plain lined as it were with

4

the

the remains of antiquity, and opening all at once, the eye is prefented with the moft ftriking objects that are to be found in the world. The temple of the Sun lies in ruins, but the accefs to it is through a vaft number of beautiful Corinthian columns of white marble, the grandeur and beauty of which can only be known by the plates of it, which have been drawn, and publifhed by Mr. Wood, who, with his friends, paid it a vifit fome years ago, purpofely to preferve fome remembrance of fuch a curiofity. As thofe drawings or copies from them are now common, we muft refer the reader to them, efpecially as he can form no very adequate ideas of the ruins, from the printed relation. Superb arches, amazing columns, a colonade extending 4000 feet in length, terminated by a noble maufoleum, temples, fine porticos, periftyles, intercolumniations, and entablatures, all of them in the higheft ftile, and finifhed with the moft beautiful materials, appear on all hands, but fo difperfed and disjointed, that it is impoffible from them to form an idea of the whole when perfect. Thofe ftriking ruins are contrafted by the miferable huts of the wild Arabs, who refide in or near them.

Nothing but ocular proof could convince any man, that fo fuperb a city, formerly 10 miles in circumference, could exift in the midft of tracts of barren uninhabitable fands. Nothing however is more certain, than that Palmyra was formerly the capital of a great kingdom; that it was the pride as well as the emporium of the eaftern world, and that its merchants dealt with the Romans, and the weftern nations, for the merchandizes and luxuries of India and Arabia. Its prefent altered fituation, therefore, can be accounted for only by natural caufes, which have turned the moft fertile tracts into barren defarts. The Afiatics think that Palmyra, as well as Balbec, owes its original to Solomon, and in this they receive fome countenance from facred hiftory. In profane hiftory it is not mentioned before the time of Marc Anthony, and its moft fuperb buildings, are thought to be of the lower empire, about the time of Gallienus.

Odenathus, the laft king of Palmyra, was highly careffed by that emperor, and even declared Auguftus. His widow Zenobia reigned in great glory for fome time, and Longinus, the celebrated critic, was her fecretary. Not being able to brook the Roman tyranny, fhe declared war againft the emperor Aurelian, who took her prifoner, led her in triumph to Rome, and butchered her principal nobility, and among others, the excellent Longinus. He afterwards deftroyed her city, and maffacred its inhabitants, but expended large fums out of Zenobia's treafures in repairing the temple of the Sun,

N 4   the

the majeftic ruins of which have been mentioned. This, it muft be acknowledged, is but a very lame account of that celebrated city; nor do any of the Palmyrene infcriptions reach above the Chriftian æra, though there can be no doubt that the city itfelf is of much higher antiquity. The emperor Juftinian made fome efforts to reftore it to its antient fplendor, but without effect, for it dwindled by degrees to its prefent wretched ftate. It has been obferved very juftly, that its architecture, and the proportions of its columns, are by no means equal in purity to thofe of Balbec.

Nothing can be more futile, than the boafted antiquities fhewn by the Greek and Armenian priefts in and near Jerufalem, which is well known to have been fo often razed to the ground, and rebuilt anew, that no fcene of our Saviour's life and fufferings, can be afcertained, and yet thofe ecclefiaftics fubfift by their forgeries, and pretending to guide travellers to every fpot mentioned in the Old and New Teftament. They are, it is true, under fevere contributions to the Turks, but the trade ftill goes on though much diminifhed in its profits. The church of the Holy Sepulchre, as it is called, faid to be built by Helena, mother to Conftantine the Great, is ftill ftanding, and of tolerable good architecture, but its different divifions, and the difpofitions made round it, are chiefly calculated to fupport the forgeries of its keepers. Other churches, built by the fame lady, are found in Paleftine; but the country is fo altered in its appearance and qualities, that it is one of the moft defpicable of any in Afia, and it is in vain for a modern traveller to attempt to trace in it any veftiges of the kingdom of David and Solomon.

Mecca and Medina are curiofities only through the fuperftition of the Mahometans. Their buildings are mean, when compared to European houfes or churches; and even the temple of Mecca, in point of architecture, makes but a forry appearance, though erected on the fpot where the great prophet is faid to have been born. The fame may be faid of the mofque at Medina, where that impoftor was buried; fo that the vaft fums fpent yearly by Mahometan pilgrims, in vifiting thofe places, are undoubtedly converted to temporal ufes. I fhall not amufe the reader with any accounts of the fpot which faid to have formed Paradife, and to have been fituated between the rivers Euphrates and Tigris, where there are fome which undoubtedly deferve that name. The different ruins, them inexpreffibly magnificent, that are to be found in immenfe regions, cannot be appropriated with any certainty original founders; fo great is the ignorance in have been buried for thefe thoufand years paft. It to pronounce whether the ftile of their buildings

are

are Greek, Roman, or Saracen, but all other information muft come from their infcriptions.

The neighbourhood of Smyrna (now called Ifmir) contains many valuable antiquities, but it cannot be imagined that a learned man could devote his whole life to explain them. The fame may be, faid of Aleppo, and a number of other places celebrated in antiquity, and now known only by geographical obfervations. The feat of old Troy cannot be diftinguifhed by the fmalleft veftige, and is known only by its lying oppo-fite to the ifle of Tenedos, and the name of a brook, which the poets magnified into a wonderful river. A temple of marble built in honour of Auguftus Cæfar, at Milaffo in Caria, and a few ftructures of the fame kind, in the neigh-bourhood, are among the antiquities that are ftill entire. Three theatres of white marble, and a noble circus near Laodicea, have fuffered very little from time or barbarifm, and fome travellers think that they difcern the ruins of the celebrated temple of Diana, near Ephefus.

PROVINCES, CHIEF CITIES, MOSQUES, AND OTHER BUILDINGS.
} Thefe are very numerous, and at the fame time very infignificant, becaufe they have little or no trade, and are greatly decayed from their antient grandeur. Scanderoon ftands upon the fite of Old Alexandria, but it is now almoft depopulated. Superb re-mains of antiquity are found in its neighbourhood. Aleppo, however, preferves a refpectable rank among the cities of the Afiatic Turkey. It is ftill the capital of Syria, and is fuperior in its buildings and conveniencies to moft of the Turkifh cities. Its houfes, as ufual in the Eaft, confift of a large court, with a dead wall to the ftreet, an arcade or piazza running round it, paved with marble, and an elegant foun-tain of the fame in the middle. Aleppo, and its fuburbs, are feven miles in compafs, and contain 235,000 inhabitants, of whom 30,000 are Chriftians, and 5000 are Jews. It is fur-nifhed with moft of the conveniencies of life, excepting good water, within the walls, and even that is fupplied by an aque-duct, faid to have been erected by the emprefs Helena. Their gardens are pleafant, being laid out in vineyards, olive, fig, and piftachio trees, but the country round is rough and bar-ren. Foreign merchants are numerous here, and tranfact their bufinefs in caravanferas, or large fquare buildings, con-taining their ware-houfes, lodging-rooms, and compting-houfes. This city abounds in neat, and fome of them m g-nificent mofques, public bagnios, which are very refrefhing, and bazars, or market-places, which are formed into long, narrow, covered ftreets, with little fhops, as in other parts of the

the Eaſt. Their coffee is excellent, and conſidered by the Turks as a high luxury, and their ſweetmeats and fruits are delicious. European merchants live here in greater ſplendor and ſafety than in any other city of the Turkiſh empire, which is owing to particular capitulations with the Porte. The Engliſh, French, and Dutch, have conſuls, who are much reſpected, and appear abroad, the Engliſh eſpecially, with marks of diſtinction.

The heat of the country makes it convenient for the inhabitants to ſleep in the open air, here and over all Arabia, and many other parts of the Eaſt; for which reaſon their houſes are flat on the top. This practice accounts for the early acquaintance thoſe nations had with aſtronomy, and the motions of the heavenly bodies, and explains ſome parts of the holy ſcripture. As the Turks are very uniform in their way of living, this account of Aleppo may give the reader an idea of the other Turkiſh cities.

Bagdat, built upon the Tygris, is the capital of the ancient Chaldea, and was once the metropolis of the califate, under the Saracens, the moſt powerful monarchy in the earth.

Bagdat retains but few marks of its ancient grandeur. It is rudely fortified, but the conveniency of its ſituation renders it one of the ſeats of the Turkiſh government, and has ſtill a conſiderable trade, being annually viſited by the Smyrna, Aleppo, and weſtern caravans.

Antient Aſſyria is now called the Turkiſh Curdiſtan, tho' part of it is ſubject to the Perſians. The capital is Curdiſtan; the ancient Niniveh being now a heap of ruins. Curdiſtan is ſaid to be for the moſt part cut out of a mountain, and is the reſidence of a viceroy, or beglerbeg. Orfa, formerly Edeſſa, is the capital of the fine province of Meſopotamia. It is now a mean place, and chiefly ſupported by a manufacture of Turkey leather.

Georgia, or Gurgiſtan, though ſubject to the Turks, is chiefly peopled by Chriſtians, a brave, warlike race of men, and now at war with the Mahometans. Their capital, Teflis, is a handſome city, and makes a fine appearance, its inhabitants being about 30,000. The Georgians in general are by ſome travellers ſaid to be the handſomeſt people in the world; and ſome think that they early received the practice of inoculation for the ſmall-pox. They make no ſcruple of ſelling and drinking wines in their capital, and other towns; and their valour has procured them many diſtinguiſhing liberties and privileges.

The ancient cities of Damaſcus, Tyre, and Sidon, ſtill retain part of their former trade. Damaſcus is called Sham,

and

and the approach to it by the river is inexpreffibly beautiful.
It contains a fine mofque, which was formerly a Chriftian
church.   It ftill is famous for its fteel works, fuch as fword
blades, knives, and the like; the excellent temper of which
is faid to be owing to a quality in the water.   The inhabitants ftill manufacture thofe beautiful filks, called Damafks
from their city, and carry on a confiderable traffic in raw and
worked filk; rofe-water, extracted from the famous damafk
rofes, fruits and wine.   The neighbourhood of this city is
ftill beautiful, efpecially to the Turks, who delight in verdure and gardens.   Sidon, which likewife lies within the antient Phenicia, has ftill fome trade, and a tolerable harbour.
Tyre, now called Sur, about 20 miles diftant from Sidon, fo
famous formerly for its rich dye, is now only inhabited by a
few miferable fifhermen, who live in the ruins of its ancient
grandeur.

Natolia, or Afia Minor, comprehending the antient provinces of Lydia, Pamphylia, Pifidia, Lycoania, Cilicia, Cap-
padocia, and Pontus, or Amafia; all of them territories celebrated in the Greek and Roman hiftory, are now, through
the Turkifh indolence and tyranny, either forfaken, or a
theatre of ruins.   The fites of antient cities are ftill difcernible, and fo luxurious is nature in thofe countries, that
in many places fhe triumphs over her forlorn condition.   The
felfifh Turks cultivate no more land than maintain themfelves,
and their gardens and fummer-houfes fill up the circuit of
their moft flourifhing cities.   The moft judicious travellers,
upon an attentive furvey of thofe countries, fully vindicate all
that has been faid by facred and profane writers of their
beauty, ftrength, fertility, and population.   Even Paleftine
and Judæa, the moft defpicable at prefent of all thofe countries, lies buried within the luxuries of its own foil.   The
Turks feem particularly fond of reprefenting it in the moft
dreadful colours, and have formed a thoufand falfehoods concerning it, which being artfully propagated by fome among
ourfelves, have impofed upon weak Chriftians *.   Whether
thofe

* The late reverend Dr. Shaw, profeffor of Greek at Oxford, who feems to have
examined that country with an uncommon degree of accuracy, and was qualified by
the foundeft philofophy, to make the moft juft obfervations, fays, that was the
Holy Land as well cultivated as in former times, it would be more fertile than the
very beft parts of Syria and Phœnicia, becaufe the foil is generally much richer,
and, every thing confidered, yields larger crops.   Therefore the barrennefs, fays
he, of which fome authors complain, does not proceed from the natural unfruit-
fulnefs of the country, but from the want of inhabitants, the indolence which
prevails among the few who poffefs it, and the perpetual difcords and depredations
of the petty princes who fhare this fine country.

those countries could ever be restored to their ancient grandeur, trade, and population, may be a question with some; but I apprehend that it would now be impossible (let the Turkish government be ever so beneficent) to divert commerce (without which, all attempts of that kind must be feeble) from its European channels. There can, however, be no question, that a government less brutal and bigotted than that of the Turks, might make the natives a powerful as well as a happy people within themselves. The misfortune is, that the Greeks, Armenians, and other sects of Christians there, partake but too much of the Turkish stupidity. Tho' they are not suffered to wear white turbans, or to ride on horseback, and are subjected to a thousand indignities and miseries, and are even, in many places, far more numerous than their oppressors, yet so abject is their spirit, that they make no efforts for their own deliverance, and they are contented under all their mortifications. If they are less indolent than their oppressors, it is because they must otherwise starve; and they dare not enjoy even the property they acquire, lest it should be discovered to their tyrants, who would consider it as their own.

COMMERCE AND MANUFACTURES.] These objects are little attended to in the Turkish dominions. The nature of their government destroys that happy security which is the mother of arts, industry, and commerce; and such is the debasement of the human mind when borne down by tyranny and oppression, that all the great advantages of commerce which nature has as it were thrown under the feet of the inhabitants by their situation, are here totally neglected. The advantages of Tyre, Sidon, Alexandria, and all those countries which carried on the commerce of the ancient world, are overlooked. They command the navigation of the Red Sea, which opens a communication to the southern ocean, and presents them with all the riches of the Indies. Whoever looks on a map of Turkey, must admire the situation of their capital, upon a narrow strait that separates Europe from Asia, and communicates on the south with the Mediterranean sea, thereby opening a passage to all the European nations as well as the coast of Africa. The same strait, communicating northwards with the Black Sea, opens a passage, by means of the

Danube

Indeed the inhabitants can have but little inclination to cultivate the earth. " In Palestine, says Mr. Wood, we have often seen the husbandman sowing, " accompanied by an armed friend, to prevent his being robbed of the seed." And, after all, whoever sows is uncertain whether he shall ever reap the harvest.

Danube and other great rivers, into the interior parts of Germany, Poland, and Ruffia.

In this extenfive empire, where all the commodities necef-fary for the largeft plan of induftry and commerce are produced, the Turks content themfelves with manufacturing cottons, carpets, leather, and foap. The moft valuable of their com-modities, fuch as filk, a variety of drugs, and dying ftuffs, they generally export without giving them much additional value from their own labour. The internal commerce of the empire is extremely fmall, and managed entirely by Jews and Armenians. In their traffic with Europe the Turks are altogether paffive. The Englifh, French, Dutch, and other Europeans, refort hither with their commodities, and bring back thofe of Turkey in the fame bottoms. They fel-dom attempt any diftant voyages, and are poffeffed only of a few coafting veffels in the Afiatic Turkey; their chief royal navy lying on the fide of Europe. The inattention of the Turks to objects of commerce is perhaps the beft fecurity to their government. The balance of power eftablifhed among the princes of Europe, and their jealoufies of one another, fecures to the infidels the poffeffion of countries, which in the hands of the Ruffians, or any active ftate, might endanger the commerce of their neighbours, efpecially their trade with India.

CONSTITUTION AND GOVERNMENT.] The Turkifh go-vernment is commonly exhibited as a picture of all that is fhocking and unnatural in arbitrary power. But from the late accounts of Sir James Potter, who refided at the Porte, in quality of ambaffador from his Britannic majefty, it appears that the rigours of that defpotic government are confiderably moderated by the power of religion. For though in this em-pire there is no hereditary fucceffion to property, the rights of individuals may be rendered fixed and fecure, by being annexed to the church, which is done at an inconfiderable expence. Even Jews and Chriftians may in this manner fecure the enjoyment of their lands to the lateft pofterity ; and fo facred and inviolable has this law been held, that there is no inftance of an attempt on the fide of the prince to trefpafs or reverfe it. Neither does the obfervance of this inftitution altogether de-pend on the fuperftition of the fultan ; he knows that any attempt to violate it, would fhake the foundations of his throne, which is folely fupported by the laws of religion. Were he to trefpafs thefe laws, he becomes an infidel, and ceafes to be the lawful fovereign. The fame obfervation ex-tends to all the rules laid down in the Koran, which was defigned by Mahomet, both as a political code, and as a religious

gious fyftem. The laws there enacted, having all the force of religious prejudices to fupport them, are inviolable; and by them the civil rights of the Mahometans are regulated. Even the comments on this book, which explain the law where it is obfcure, or extend and compleat what Mahomet had left imperfect, are conceived to be of equal validity with the firft inftitution of the prophet; and no member of the fociety, however powerful, can tranfgrefs them without cenfure, or violate them without punifhment.

The Afiatic Turks, or rather fubjects of the Turkifh empire, who hold their poffeffions by a kind of military tenure, on condition of their ferving in the field with a particular number of men, think themfelves, while they perform that agreement, almoft independent of his majefty, who feldom calls for the head of the eftate of a fubject, who is not an immediate fervant of the court. The moft unhappy fubjects of the Turkifh government, are thofe who approach the higheft dignities of ftate, and whofe fortunes are conftantly expofed to fudden alterations, and depend on the breath of their mafter. There is a gradation of great officers in Turkey, of whom the vizir, or prime minifter; the chiaya, fecond in power to the vizir; the reis effendi, or fecretary of ftate, are the moft confiderable. Thefe, as well as the mufti, or high prieft, the bafhaws, or governors of provinces, the civil judges, and many others, are commonly raifed by their application and affiduity, from the meaneft ftations in life, and are often the children of Tartar, or Chriftian flaves taken in war. Tutored in the fchool of adverfity, and arriving at pre-eminence through a thoufand difficulties and dangers, thefe men are generally as diftinguifhed for abilities, as deficient in virtue. They poffefs all the diffimulation, intrigue, and corruption, which often accompanies ambition in a humble rank, and they have a farther reafon for plundering the people, becaufe they are uncertain how long they may poffefs the dignities to which they are arrived. The adminiftration of juftice, therefore, is extremely corrupt over the whole empire; but this proceeds from the manners of the judges, and not from the laws of the kingdom, which are founded on very equitable principles.

REVENUES.] The riches drawn from the various provinces of this empire muft be immenfe. The revenues arife from the cuftoms, and a variety of taxes which fall chiefly on the Chriftians, and other fubjects, not of the Mahometan religion. Another branch of the revenue arifes from the annual tribute paid by the Tartars, and other nations bordering upon Turkey, but governed by their own princes and laws.

All

All thefe, however, are trifling, when compared with the vaft fums extorted from the governors of provinces, and officers of ftate, under the name of prefents. Thefe harpies, to indemnify themfelves, as we have already obferved, exercife every fpecies of oppreffion that their avarice can fuggeft, till becoming wealthy from the vitals of the countries they are fent to govern, their riches frequently give rife to a pretended fufpicion of difloyalty or mifconduct, and the whole fortune of the offender devolves to the crown. The devoted victim is feldom acquainted with the nature of the offence, or the names of his accufers; but, without giving him the leaft opportunity of making a defence, an officer is difpatched, with an imperial decree, to take off his head. The unhappy baffa receives it with the higheft refpect, putting it on his head, and after he has read it, fays, *the will of God and the emperor be done*, or fome fuch expreffion, teftifying his entire refignation to the will of his prince. Then he takes the filken cord, which the officer has ready in his bofom, and having tied it about his own neck, and faid a fhort prayer, the officer's fervants throw him on the floor, and, drawing the cord ftrait, foon difpatch him; after which his head is cut off, and carried to court.

FORCES.] The militia of the Turkifh empire is of two forts; the firft have certain lands appointed for their maintenance, and the other is paid out of the treafury. Thofe that have certain lands, amount to about 268,000 troopers, effective men. Befides thefe, there are alfo certain auxiliary forces raifed by the tributary countries of this empire; as the Tartars, Walachians, Moldavians, and Georgians, who are commanded by their refpective princes. The Kan of the Crim Tartars is obliged to furnifh 100,000 men, and to ferve in perfon, when the grand fignior takes the field. In every war, befides the above forces, there are great numbers of volunteers, who live at their own charge, in expectation of fucceeding the officers. Thefe adventurers do not only promife themfelves an eftate if they furvive, but are taught, that if they die in a war againft the Chriftans, they fhall go immediately to paradife. The forces, which receive their pay, from the treafury, are called the Spahis, or horfe-guards, and are in number about 12,000; and the janizaries, or footguards, who are efteemed the beft foldiers in the Turkifh armies, and on them they principally depend in an engagement. Thefe amount to about 25,000 men, who are quartered in and near Conftantinople. They frequently grow mutinous, and have proceeded fo far fometimes as to depofe the fultan. They are educated in the feraglio, and trained

up-

up to the exercife of arms from their infancy ; and there are
not lefs than 100,000 foot foldiers, fcattered over every province of the empire, who procure themfelves to be regiftered
in this body, to enjoy the privileges of janizaries, which are
very great, being fubject to no jurifdiction, but that of their
aga, or chief commander.

ARMS AND TITLES.] The emperor's titles are fwelled
with all the pomp of eaftern magnificence. He is ftiled by
his fubjects, *the Shadow of God, a God on Earth, Brother
to the Sun and Moon, difpofer of all earthly Crowns, &c.* The
grand fignior's arms are, vert, a crefcent argent, crefted with
a turbant, charged with three black plumes of heron's quills,
with this motto, *Donec totum impleat orbem.*

COURT AND SERAGLIO.] Great care is taken in the education of the youths, who are defigned for the ftate, the army,
or the navy ; but they are feldom preferred till they are about
40 years of age, and they rife by their merit. They are generally the children of Chriftian parents, either taken in war,
purchafed, or prefents from the viceroys and governors of diftant provinces, the moft beautiful, well made, and fprightly
children, that can be met with, and are always reviewed and
approved of by the fignior, before they are fent to the colleges,
or feminaries, where they are educated for employments, according to their genius or abilities.

The ladies of the feraglio, are a collection of beautiful
young women, chiefly fent as prefents from the provinces,
and the Greek iflands, moft of them the children of Chriftian parents. On their admiffion they are committed to the
care of old ladies, taught mufic, dancing, and other accom-
plifhments, and furnifhed with the richeft clothes and ornaments. Thefe ladies are fcarce ever fuffered to go abroad,
except when the grand fignior removes from one place to another, when a troop of black eunuchs conveys them to the
boats, which are inclofed with lattices; and, when they go
by land, they are put into clofe chariots, and fignals are made
at certain diftances, to give notice that none approach the
roads, through which they march. Among the emperor's
attendants are a number of mutes, who act and converfe by
figns with great quicknefs, and fome dwarfs who are exhibited
for the diverfion of his majefty.

ORIGIN AND PROGRESS OF THE TURKS.] It has been the
fate of the more fouthern and fertile parts of Afia, at different
periods, to be conquered by that warlike and hardy race of
men, who inhabit the vaft country, known to the antients
by the name of Scythia, and among the moderns by that of
Tartary. One tribe of thefe people, called Turks or Turco-
mans,

mans, which name fignifies Wanderers, extended its conquefts under various leaders, and during feveral centuries,
from the fhore of the Cafpian, to the ftraits of the Darda-
nelles. Being long refident, in the capacity of body guards,
about the courts of the Saracens, they embraced the doctrine
of Mahomet, and acted for a long time, as mercenaries in the
armies of contending princes. Their chief refidence was in
the neighbourhood of mount Caucafus, from whence they
removed to Armenia Major, and after being employed as
mercenaries by the fultans of Perfia, they feized that kingdom,
and fpread their ravages over all the neighbouring countries.
Bound by their religion to make converts to Mahometanifm,
they never were without a pretence for invading and ravaging
the dominions of the Greek emperors, and were fometimes
commanded by very able generals. Upon the declenfion of
the califate or empire of the Saracens, they made themfelves
mafters of Paleftine; and the vifiting the Holy City of Jerufalem, being then part of the Chriftian exercifes, in which
they had been tolerated by the Saracens, the Turks laid the
European pilgrims under fuch heavy contributions, and exercifed fuch horrible cruelties upon the Chriftian inhabitants of
the country, as gave rife to the famous Crufades, which we
have mentioned more fully in the Introduction.

It unfortunately happened, that the Greek emperors were
generally more jealous of the progrefs of the Chriftians than
the Turks; and though after oceans of blood were fpilt, a
Chriftian kingdom was erected at Jerufalem under Godfrey
of Bouillon, neither he nor his fucceffors were poffeffed of any
real power for maintaining it. The Turks, about the year
1347, had extended their dominions on every fide, and poffeffed themfelves under Othman, of fome of the fineft provinces in Afia, of Nice, and Prufa in Bithynia, which Othman made his capital, and, as it were, firft embodied them
into a nation; hence they took the name of Othmans from
that leader, the appellation of Turks, as it fignifies in the
original, wanderers, or banifhed men, being confidered by
them as a term of reproach. Othman was fucceeded by a
race of the moft warlike princes that are mentioned in hiftory.
About the year 1357, they paffed the Hellefpont, and got a
footing in Europe, and Amurath fettled the feat of his empire
at Adrianople. Such were their conquefts, that Bajazet I, after
defeating the Greek emperor Sigifmund, laid fiege to Conftantinople, in hopes of fubjecting all the Greek empire.
His greatnefs and infolence provoked Tarmerlane, who was
juft then returned from his eaftern conquefts, to declare war
againft him. A decifive battle was fought between thofe

rival conquerors, in the plain where Pompey defeated Mithridates, in which Bajazet's army was cut in pieces, and he himself taken prisoner. The successors of Tamerlane, by declaring war against one another, left the Turks more powerful than ever; and though their career was checked by the valour of the Venetians and Hungarians, they gradually reduced the dominions of the Greek emperors; and, after a long siege, Mahomet II. took Constantinople in 1453. Thus, after an existence of ten centuries, from its first commencement under Constantine the Great, ended the Greek empire; an event which had been long foreseen, and was owing to many causes; the chief was the total degeneracy of the Greek emperors themselves, their courts and families; the dislike their subjects had to the popes, and the western church, one of their patriarchs declaring publickly to a Romish legate, " that he would rather see a turban, than the pope's tiara, " upon the great altar of Constantinople." But as the Turks, when they extended their conquests, did not exterminate, but reduced the nations to subjection, the remains of the antient Greeks still exist, as we have already observed, particularly in Constantinople, and the neighbouring islands, where, though under grievous oppressions, they profess Christianity under their own patriarchs. It is said that the modern Greeks, though pining under the tyrannical yoke of the Turkish government, still preserve somewhat of the exterior appearance, though nothing of the internal principles which distinguished their ancestors.

The conquest of Constantinople was followed by the submission of all Greece; and from this time the Turks have been looked upon as an European power.

Mahomet died in 1481, and was succeeded by Bajazet II. who carried on war against the Hungarians and Venetians, as well as the Persians and Egyptians. Bajazet falling ill of the gout, became indolent, was harrassed by family differences, and at last, by order of his second son, Selim, he was poisoned by a Jew physician.

Selim afterwards ordered his elder brother, Achmet, to be strangled, with many other princes of the Othman race. He defeated the Persians and the prince of Mount Taurus; but being unable to penetrate into Persia, he turned his arms against Egypt, which, after many bloody battles, he annexed to his own dominions, as he did Aleppo, Antioch, Tripoli, Damascus, Gaza, and many other towns.

He was succeeded, in 1520, by his son, Soliman the magnificent; who taking advantage of the differences which prevailed among the Christian powers, took Rhodes, and drove
the

the knights from that ifland to Malta, which was given them by the emperor Charles V. The reign of Soliman, after this, was a continual war with the Chriftian powers, and generally fuccefsful, both by fea and lahd; but he mifcarried in an attempt he made to take the ifle of Malta. This Soliman is looked upon as the greateft prince that ever filled the throne of Othman.

He was fuccecded, in 1566, by his fon, Selim II. In his reign, the Turkifh marine received an irrecoverable blow from the Chriftians, in the battle of Lepanto. This defeat might have proved fatal to the Turkifh power, had the blow been purfued by the Chriftians, efpecially the Spaniards. Selim, however, took Cyprus from the Venetians, and Tunis, in Africa, from the Moors. He was fucceeded, in 1575, by his fon, Amurath III. who forced the Perfians to cede Tauris, Teflis, and many other cities, to the Turks. He likewife took the important fortrefs of Raab, in Hungary; and in 1593, he was fucceeded by Mahomet III. The memory of this prince is diftinguifhed, by his ordering nineteen of his brothers to be ftrangled, and ten of his father's concubines, who were fuppofed to be pregnant, to be thrown into the fea. He was often unfuccefsful in his wars with the Chriftians; and died of the plague in 1604. Though his fucceffor, Achmet, was beaten by the Perfians, yet he forced the Auftrians to a treaty in 1606, and to confent that he fhould keep what he was poffeffed of in Hungary. Ofman, a prince of great fpirit, but no more than fixteen years of age, being unfuccefsful againft the Poles, he was put to death by the janifaries, whofe power he intended to have reduced. Morad IV. fucceeded in 1623, and took Bagdat from the Perfians. His brother, Ibrahim, fucceeded him in 1640; a worthlefs, inactive prince, and ftrangled by the janifaries in 1648. His fucceffor, Mahomet IV. was excellently well ferved by his grand vizir, Cuperli. He took Candy from the Venetians, after it had been befieged for thirty years. This conqueft coft the Venetians, and their allies, 80,000 men, and the Turks, it is faid, 180,000. A bloody war fucceeded between the imperialifts and the Turks, in which the latter were fo fuccefsful, that they laid fiege to Vienna, but were forced (as has been already mentioned) to raife it with great lofs, by John Sobiefki, king of Poland, and other Chriftian generals. Mahomet was, in 1687, fhut up in prifon by his fubjects, and fucceeded by his brother, Soliman II.

The Turks continued unfuccefsful in their wars during this reign, and that of his brother and fucceffor, Achmet II. but Muftapha II. who mounted the throne in 1694, headed his

armies in perfon, and after fome brifk campaigns, he was defeated by prince Eugene; and the peace of Carlowitz, between
the imperialifts and Turks, was concluded in 1699. Soon after,
Muftapha was depofed, his mufti was beheaded, and his brother, Achmet III. mounted the throne. He was the prince
who gave fhelter, at Bender, to Charles XII. of Sweden;
and ended a war with the Ruffians by a glorious peace concluded at Pruth. He had afterwards a war with the Venetians, which alarmed all the Chriftian powers. The fcene of
action was tranflated to Hungary, where the imperial general,
prince Eugene, gave fo many repeated defeats to the infidels,
that they were forced to conclude a difgraceful peace, at Paffarowitz, in 1718. An unfortunate war with the Perfians,
under Kouli Khan, fucceeding, the populace demanded the
heads of the vizir, the chief admiral, and the fecretary, which
were accordingly ftruck off; but Achmet was depofed, and
Mahomet V. advanced to the throne. He was unfuccefsful
in his wars with Kouli Khan, and at laft obliged to recognize
that ufurper as fophi of Perfia. He was, after that, engaged
in a war with the imperialifts and Ruffians; againft the former he was victorious, but the fucceffes of the latter, which
threatened Conftantinople itfelf, forced him to agree to a
hafty treaty with the emperor, and after that to another with
the Ruffians, which was greatly to his difadvantage. Mahomet died in 1754. He was fucceeded by his brother, Ofman
III. who died in 1757, and was fucceeded by his brother,
Muftapha III. born in 1723, who is now reigning, and engaged in (1771) a hitherto unfuccefsful war with the Ruffians.
 The perfeverance of the Turks, fupplied by their numerous
Afiatic armies, and their implicit fubmiffion to their officers,
rather than any excellency in military difcipline or courage in
war, have been the great fprings of thofe fucceffes which render their empire at prefent fo formidable. The extenfion, as
well as duration of their empire, may indeed be in fome meafure owing to the military inftitution of the janifaries, a corps
originally compofed of the children of fuch Chriftian parents
as could not pay their taxes. Thefe being collected together,
were formed to the exercife of arms under the eyes of their
officers in the Seraglio. They were generally in number
about 40,000; and fo excellent was their difcipline, that they
were deemed to be invincible: and they ftill conftitute the
flower of the Turkifh armies. After all, we muft confider
the political ftate of Europe, and the jealoufies that fubfift
among its princes, as the fureft bafis of this empire, and the
principal reafon why the fineft provinces in the world are fuffered to remain in the poffeffion of thefe haughty infidels.

4

TARTARY in ASIA.

SITUATION AND EXTENT.

Miles.		Degrees.
Length 4000 } between {		50 and 150 eaſt longitude.
Breadth 2400 } between {		30 and 72 north latitude.

BOUNDARIES.] IT would be deceiving the reader to defire him to depend upon any accounts given us by geographers, of the extent, limits, and ſituation of thoſe vaſt regions. Even the empreſs of Ruſſia and her miniſtry are ignorant of her preciſe limits with the Chineſe, the Perſians, and other nations. Tartary, taken in its fulleſt extent, is bounded by the Frozen Ocean, on the north; by the Pacific Ocean, on the eaſt; by China, India, Perſia, and the Caſpian Sea, on the ſouth; and by Muſcovy, on the weſt.

Grand diviſions.	Subdiviſions.	Chief towns.
North-eaſt diviſion	{ Kamtſchatka Tartars { Jakutſkoi Tartars	{ Kamtſchatka { Jakutſkoi
South-eaſt diviſion	{ Bratſki — — { Thibet and Mongul { Tartars ———	{ Bratſki { Poion { Kudak
North-weſt diviſion	{ Samoieda — — { Oſtiack — —	{ Mangaſia { Kortſkoi
South-weſt diviſion	{ Circaſſian and Aſtracan { Tartary — —	{ Terki { Aſtracan
Middle diviſion	{ Siberia — — { Kalmuc and Uſbec { Tartary — —	{ Tobolſki { Bokharia { Samarcand.

MOUNTAINS.] The principal mountains are thoſe of Caucaſus, in Circaſſia.

SEAS.] Theſe are the Frozen Ocean, the Pacific Ocean, and the Caſpian Sea.

RIVERS.] The rivers are, the Wolga, which runs a courſe of two thouſand miles; the Obey, which divides Aſia from Europe; the Tabol, Irtis, Geneſa or Jenſka; the Lena, and the Argun, which divides the Ruſſian and Chineſe empires.

AIR, CLIMATE, SOIL, } The air of this country is very
AND PRODUCE. } different, by reaſon of its vaſt extent from north to ſouth; the northern parts reaching beyond the arctic polar circle, and the ſouthern being in the ſame latitudes with Spain, France, Italy, and part of Turkey. Nova Zembla and Ruſſian Lapland are moſt uncomfortable

O 3

regions;

regions ; the earth, which is covered with fnow nine months in the year, being extremely barren, and every where incumbered with unwholefome marfhes, uninhabited mountains, and impenetrable thickneffes. Though Siberia is as it were another name for a country of horror, yet we are told that the air in the fouthern parts is tolerably mild, the foil furnifhed with good water, and cultivated with fome fuccefs. The beft accounts we have of its interior appearance, is from the ingenious French gentlemen who were fent thither to make aftronomical obfervations ; they all agree in reprefenting it as a difmal region, and almoft uninhabited. Aftracan, and the fouthern parts of Tartary, are extremely fertile, owing more to nature than induftry. The parts that are cultivated produce excellent fruits of almoft all the kinds known in Europe, efpecially grapes, which are reckoned the largeft and fineft in the world. Their fummers are very dry; and from the end of July to the beginning of October, the air is peftered and the foil fometimes ruined by incredible quantities of locufts. Mr. Bell, who travelled with the Ruffian ambaffador to China, reprefents fome parts of Tartary as defirable and fertile countries, the grafs growing fpontaneoufly to an amazing height.

METALS AND MINERALS.] It is faid that Siberia contains mines of gold, filver, copper, iron, jafper, lapis lazuli, and loadftones ; a fort of large teeth found here, creates fome difpute among the naturalifts, whether they belong to elephants, or are a marine production ; their appearance is certainly whimfical and curious when polifhed with art and fkill.

ANIMALS.] Thefe are camels, dromedaries, bears, wolves, and all the other land and amphibious animals that are common in the north parts of Europe. Their horfes are of a good fize for the faddle, and very hardy ; as they run wild till they are five or fix years old, they are generally headftrong. Near Aftracan there is a bird called by the Ruffians baba, of a grey colour, and fomething larger than a fwan ; he has a broad bill, under which hangs a bag that may contain a quart or more ; he wades near the edge of the river, and on feeing a fhoal of fry or fmall fifhes, fpreads his wings and drives them to a fhallow, where he gobbles as many of them as he can into his bag, and then going afhore, eats them or carries them to the young. Some travellers take this bird to be the pelican.

POPULATION, INHABITANTS, MANNERS, ⎫ We can form
    CUSTOMS, DIVERSIONS, AND DRESS. ⎭ no probable guefs as to the number of inhabitants in Tartary, but from many circumftances we may conclude that they are not pro-
portioned

portioned to the extent of their country. They are in general strong made, stout men; their faces broad, their noses flattish, their eyes small and black, but very quick; their beards are scarcely visible, as they continually thin them by pulling up the hairs by the roots. The beauty of the Circassian women is a kind of staple commodity in that country; for parents there make no scruple of selling their daughters to recruit the seraglios of the great men of Turkey and Persia. They are purchased, when young, by merchants, and taught such accomplishments as suit their capacities, to render them more valuable against the day of sale. The Tartars are in general a wandering sort of people; in their perigrinations they set out in the spring, their number in one body being frequently 10,000, preceded by their flocks and herds. When they come to an inviting spot, they live upon it till all its grass and verdure is eaten up. They have little money, except what they get from their neighbours the Russians, Persians, or Turks, in exchange for cattle; with this they purchase cloth, silks, stuffs, and other apparel for their women. They have few mechanics, except those who make arms. They avoid all labour as the greatest slavery, their only employment is tending their flocks, hunting, and managing their horses. If they are angry with a person, they wish he may live in one fixed place, and work like a Russian. Among themselves they are very hospitable, and wonderfully so to the strangers and travellers who confidentially put themselves under their protection. They are naturally of an easy chearful temper, always disposed to laughter, and seldom depressed by care or melancholy. There is a strong resemblance between the northern Tartars and some nations of Canada in North America, particularly when any of their people are infirm through great age, or seized with distempers reckoned incurable, they make a small hut for the patient near some river, in which they leave him with some provisions, and seldom or never return to visit him. On such occasions they say they do their parents a good office, in sending them to a better world. Notwithstanding this behaviour, many nations of the Tartars, especially towards the south, are tractable, humane, and are susceptible of pious and virtuous sentiments. Their affection for their fathers, and their submission to their authority, cannot be exceeded; and this noble quality of filial love has distinguished them in all ages. History tells us, that Darius, king of Persia, having invaded them with all the forces of his empire, and the Scythians retiring by little and little, Darius sent an ambassador to demand where it was they proposed to conclude their retreat, and when they intended to

begin

begin fighting. They returned for anfwer, with a fpirit fo peculiar to that people, " That they had no cities nor culti- vated fields, for the defence of which they fhould give him battle; but when once he was come to the place of their fathers monuments, he fhould then underftand in what man- ner the Scythians ufed to fight."

The Tartars are inured to horfemanfhip from their infancy; they feldom appear on foot. They are dextrous in fhooting at a mark, infomuch that a Tartar, while at full gallop, will cleft a pole with an arrow, though at a confiderable diftance. The drefs of the men is very fimple and fit for action; it generally confifts of a fhort jacket, with narrow fleeves made of deers fkin, having the fur outward; trowfers and hofe of the fame kind of fkin, both of one piece, and light to the limbs. The Tartars live in huts half funk under ground; they have a fire in the middle, with a hole in the top to let out the fmoak, and benches round the fire to fit or lie upon. This feems to be the common method of living among all the northern nations, from Lapland eaftward, to the Japanefe ocean. In the extreme northern provinces, during the winter, every family burrows itfelf as it were under-ground; and we are told, that fo fociable are they in their difpofitions, that they make fubterraneous communications with each other, fo that they may be faid to live in an invifible city. The Tar- tars are immoderately fond of horfe-flefh, efpecially if it be young, and a little tainted, which makes their cabins ex- tremely naufeous. Though horfe-flefh be preferred raw by fome northern tribes, the general way of eating it is after it has been fmoaked and dried. The Tartars purchafe their wives with cattle. In their marriages they are not very deli- cate. Little or no difference is made between the child of a concubine or flave, and that of the wife; but among the heads of tribes, the wife's fon is always preferred to the fucceffion. After a wife is turned of forty, fhe is employed in menial duties as another fervant, and as fuch muft attend the young wives who fucceed to their places; nor is it uncommon in fome of the more barbarous tribes for a father to marry his own daughter.

RELIGION.] The religion of the Tartars fomewhat refem- bles their civil government, and is commonly accommodated to that of their neighbours, for it partakes of the Mahometan, the Gentoo, the Greek, and even the popifh religions. Some of them are the grofieft idolators, and worfhip little rude images drefied up in rags. Each has his own deity, with whom they make very free when matters do not go according to their own mind. The religion and government of the kingdom

of

of Tibet, a large tract of Tartary, bordering upon China, form the moſt extraordinary article that is to be found in the hiſtory of mankind. The Tibettians are governed by a living, eating, and drinking god, whom they believe to be omnipotent, and whom they call the Grand Lama, or Dalay Lama. He reſides in a pagoda or temple, upon the mountain Putali, in a croſs-legged poſture, but without ſpeaking or moving, otherwiſe than by ſometimes lifting his hand in approbation of a favourite worſhipper. Not only the Tibettians, but the neighbouring princes and people flock in incredible numbers, with rich preſents, to pay him their adorations; and he generally appea s to be a healthy, ruddy-faced young man, about twenty-ſeven years of age. This being appoints. deputies under him, the chief of whom is called the Tipa, who takes care of all the temporal affairs of the kingdom, and has a number of ſubſtituted lamas. Theſe are properly the king and the governors of Tibet, both civil and military; it being below the dignity of the grand lama to ſuperintend any temporal concerns.

As to the grand lama, he is himſelf the moſt miſerable wretch in the empire. He is purchaſed, when young, from a healthy peaſant, and privately brought up by the lamas to the buſineſs of his function, which is to move by clock-work, and to be carried in ſtate to the place of his impriſonment, where he remains till next day, when the farce of his enthronement is repeated. When he falls ill, or becomes too old to act his part, he is diſpatched by his miniſters, who produce another, as like him as they can find, in his room; and when any alteration is obſerved, they always give ſatisfactory reaſons why the dalay lama has changed his appearance. He is never ſuffered to touch any of the fine fruits or viands that are brought to his ſhrine, all which are devoured by his miniſters, who take care to diet him in his priſon. Such are the general outlines of this pretended theocracy, in which all travellers are agreed, however they may differ among themſelves as to modes and circumſtances.

LEARNING.] The reader may be ſurprized to find this article among a nation of Tartars, yet nothing is more certain than that under Zingis Khan, and Tamerlane, and their early deſcendants, Aſtracan and the neighbouring countries were the ſeats of learning and politeneſs, as well as empire and magnificence. Modern luxury, be it ever ſo ſplendid, falls ſhort of that of thoſe princes; and ſome remains of their taſte in architecture are ſtill extant, but in ſpots ſo deſolate, that they are almoſt inacceſſible. The cultivation of learning was the firſt care of the prince, and generally committed to the

care

care of his own relations or principal grandees. They wrote in the Perfian and Arabic tongues; and their hiftories, many of which are ftill extant in manufcript, carry with them the ftrongeft marks of authenticity.

CURIOSITIES.] Thefe are comprehended in the remains of the buildings, left by the abovementioned great conquerors, and their fucceffors; they are, however, but little known to Europeans, though many of them are faid to have been dif- covered by the wandering Tartars in the internal parts of the country. Some gold and filver coins of the fame princes have likewife been found, with feveral manufcripts neatly written, which have been carried to Peterfburg. In 1720, fays Mr. Voltaire, in his Hiftory of Peter the Great, there was found in Calmuc Tartary, a fubterraneous houfe of ftone, fome urns, lamps, and earrings, an equeftrian ftatue, an oriental prince with a diadem on his head, two women feated on thrones, and a roll of manufcripts, which was fent by Peter the Great to the Academy of Infcriptions at Paris, and pro- ved to be in the language of Tibet.

CITIES AND TOWNS.] Of thefe we know little but the names, and that they are no better than fixed herds. They may be faid to be places of abode rather than towns or cities, for we do not find that they are under any regular govern- ment, or that they can make a defence againft an enemy. The few places, however, that are mentioned in the preced- ing divifions of this country, merit notice. Tobolfki and Aftracan are confiderable cities, the firft containing 15,000, and the latter 70,000 inhabitants. Forts, villages, and towns have lately been erected in different parts of Siberia, for civi- lizing the inhabitants, and rendering them obedient to the Ruf- fian government. But I apprehend it will require a confiderable time before any fixed plan of government can be formed in this country.

COMMERCE AND MANUFACTURES.] This head makes no figure in the hiftory of Tartary, their chief traffic confift- ing in cattle, fkins, beavers, rhubarb, mufk, and fifh. The Aftracans, notwithftanding their interruptions by the wild Tartars, carry on a confiderable traffic into Perfia, to which they export red leather, woollen and linen cloth, and fome European manufactures.

HISTORY.] Though it is certain that Tartary, formerly known by the name of Scythia, peopled the northern parts of Europe, and furnifhed thofe amazing numbers who, un- der various names, deftroyed the Roman empire, yet it is now but very thinly inhabited; and thofe fine provinces, where learning and the arts refided, are now fcenes of horror
and

and barbarity. This muſt have been owing to the dreadful maſſacres made among the nations by the two abovementioned conquerors and their deſcendants; for nothing is more common in their hiſtories than their putting to the ſword three or four hundred thouſand people in a few days.

The country of Uſbec Tartary was once the ſeat of a more powerful empire than that of Rome or Greece. It was not only the native country, but the favourite reſidence of Zingis Khan and Tamerlane, who enriched it with the ſpoils of India and the eaſtern world. It is ſo difficult to diſcover any remains of magnificence here, that ſome authors have abſurdly queſtioned the veracity of the hiſtorians of theſe great conquerors, though it be better eſtabliſhed than that of the Greek or Roman writers. The ſame may be ſaid of Tamerlane, whoſe memory has been more permanent than that of Zingis Khan, and whoſe deſcent is claimed not only by all the Khans and petty princes of Tartary, but by the emperor of Indoſtan himſelf. The capital of this country is Bokharia, which was known to the antients by the name of Bucharia, and it is ſituated in the latitude of 39 degrees 15 minutes, and 13 miles diſtant from the once famous city of Samarcand, the birthplace of Tamerlane the Great.

The preſent inhabitants of this immenſe common compoſe innumerable tribes, who range at pleaſure with their flocks and their herds, in the old patriarchal manner. Their tribes are commanded by ſeparate Khans or leaders, who, upon particular emergencies, elect a great Khan, who claims a paramount power, over ſtrangers as well as natives, and who can bring into the field from 20 to 100,000 horſemen. Their chief reſidence is a kind of military ſtation, which is moved and ſhifted according to the chance of war and other occaſions. They are bounded on every ſide by the Ruſſian, the Chineſe, the Mogul, the Perſian, or the Turkiſh empires; each of whom are puſhing on their conqueſts in this extenſive, and in ſome places fertile country. The Khans pay a tribute, or acknowledgement of their dependency, upon one or other of their powerful neighbours, who treat them with caution and lenity; as the friendſhip of theſe barbarians is of the utmoſt conſequence to the powers with whom they are allied. Some tribes, however, affect independency, and when united they form a powerful body, and of late have been very formidable to their neighbours, particularly to the Chineſe, as we ſhall mention in our account of that empire.

The method of carrying on war, by waſting the country, is very antient among the Tartars, and practiſed by all of them from the Danube eaſtward. This circumſtance renders

5   them

them a dreadful enemy to regular troops, who muft thereby be deprived of all fubfiftence; while the Tartars, having always many fpare horfes to kill and eat, are at no lofs for provifions.

The Empire of CHINA.

SITUATION AND EXTENT.

	Miles.		Degrees.
Length	1450	between	20 and 42 north latitude.
Breadth	1260		98 and 123 eaft longitude.

BOUNDARIES.] IT is bounded by the Chinefe Tartary, on the north; by the Pacific ocean, which divides it from North America, on the eaft; by the Chinefian fea, fouth; and by Tonquin, and the Tartarian countries of Tibet and Ruffia, on the weft.

DIVISIONS.] The great divifion of this empire, according to the authors of the Univerfal Hiftory, is into fifteen provinces (exclufive of that of Lyau-tong, which is fituate without the great wall, though under the fame dominion); each of which might, for their largenefs, fertility, populoufnefs, and opulence, pafs for fo many diftinct kingdoms.

But it is neceffary to inform the reader, that the informations contained in Du Halde's voluminous account of China, are drawn from the papers of Jefuits, and other religious fent thither by the pope, but whofe miffions have been at an end for above half a century. Some of thofe fathers were men of penetration and judgment, and had great opportunities of being informed about a century ago; but even their accounts of this empire are juftly to be fufpected. They had powerful enemies at the court of Rome, where they maintained their footing, only by magnifying their own labours and fucceffes, as well as the importance of the Chinefe empire.

NAME.] It is probably owing to a Chinefe word, fignifying Middle, from a notion the natives had that their country lay in the middle of the world.

MOUNTAINS.] China, excepting to the north, is a plain country, and contains no remarkable mountains.

RIVERS AND WATER.] The chief are the Yamour, and the Argun, which are the boundary between the Ruffian and Chinefe Tartary; the Crocceus, or Whambo, or the Yellow River; the Kiam, or the Blue River, and the Tay. Common water in China, is very indifferent, and is in fome places boiled to make it fit for ufe.

BAYS.] The chief are thofe of Nanking and Canton.

CANALS.] Thefe are fufficient to entitle the antient Chinefe to the charaĉter of being the wifeft and moft induftrious people in the world. The commodioufnefs and length of their canals are incredible. The chief of them are lined with hewn ftone on the fides, and they are fo deep, that they carry large veffels, and fometimes they extend above 1000 miles in length. Thofe veffels are fitted up for all the conveniencies of life, and it has been thought by fome that in China the water contains as many inhabitants as the land. They are furnifhed with ftone quays, and fometimes with bridges of an amazing conftruĉtion. The navigation is flow, and the veffels fometimes drawn by men. No precautions are wanting, that could be formed by art or perfeverance for the fafety of the paffengers in cafe a canal is croffed by a rapid river, or expofed to torrents from the mountains. Thofe canals, and the variety that is feen upon their borders, renders China the moft delightful to the eye of any country in the world, as well as fertile, in places that are not fo by nature.

FORESTS.] Such is the induftry of the Chinefe, that they are not encumbered with forefts or wood, though no country is better fitted for producing timber of all kinds. They fuffer, however, none to grow but for ornament and ufe, or on the fides of mountains, from whence the trees, when cut down, can be conveyed to any place by water.

AIR, SOIL, AND PRODUCE.] The air, of this empire is according to the fituation of the places. Towards the north it is fharp, in the middle mild, and in the fouth hot. The foil is either by nature or art fruitful of every thing than can minifter to the neceffities, conveniencies, or luxuries of life. The culture of the cotton, and the rice fields, from which the bulk of the inhabitants are cloathed and fed, is ingenious almoft beyond defcription. The rare trees, and aromatic produĉtions, either ornamental or medicinal, that abound in other parts of the world, are to be found in China, and fome are peculiar to itfelf; but even a catalogue of them would form a little volume. Some, however, muft be mentioned.

The tallow tree has a fhort trunk, a fmooth bark, crooked branches, red leaves, fhaped like a heart, and is about the height of a common cherry-tree. The fruit it produces has all the qualities of our tallow, and when manufaĉtured with oil, ferve the natives as candles, but they fmell ftrong, nor is their light clear. Of the other trees, peculiar to China, are fome which yield a kind of flour; fome partake of the nature of pepper. The gum of fome are poifonous, but afford the fineft varnifh in the world. After all that can be faid of thofe,

thofe, and many other beautiful and ufeful trees, the Chinefe, notwithftanding their induftry, are fo wedded to their antient cuftoms, that they are very little, if at all, meliorated by cultivation. The fame may be faid of their richeft fruits, which, in general, are far from being fo delicious as thofe of Europe, and indeed of America. This is owing to the Chinefe never practifing grafting, or inoculation of trees, and knowing nothing of experimental gardening.

It would be unpardonable here not to mention the raw-filk, which fo much abounds in China, and above all, the tea plant or fhrub. It is planted in rows, and pruned to prevent its luxuriancy. Notwithftanding our long intercourfe with China, writers are ftill divided about the different fpecies and culture of this plant. It is generally thought that the green and bohea grows on the fame fhrub, but that the latter admits of fome kind of preparation, which takes away its raking qualities, and gives it a deeper colour. The other kinds, which go by the names of imperial, congo, finglo, and the like, are occafioned probably by the nature of the foils, and from the provinces in which they grow. The culture of this plant feems to be very fimple, and it is certain, that fome kinds are of a much higher and delicious flavour than others. It is thought that the fineft, which is called the Flower of the tea, is imported over land to Ruffia; but we know of little difference in their effects on the human body. The greateft is between the bohea and the green.

I am apt to think that the Portugueze had the ufe of tea long before the Englifh, and that it was introduced among the latter, before the reftoration, as mention of it is made in the firft act of parliament, that fettled the excife on the king for life in 1660. Catharine of Lifbon, wife to Charles II. rendered the ufe of it common at his court. The ginfeng, fo famous among the Chinefe, as the univerfal remedy, and monopolized even by their emperors, is now found to be but a common root, and is difcovered in the Britifh America. When brought to Europe, it is little diftinguifhed for its healing qualities, and this inftance alone ought to teach us with what caution the former accounts of China are to be read. The ginfeng, however, is a native of the Chinefe Tartary.

METALS AND MINERALS.] China (if we are to believe naturalifts) produces all metals and minerals that are known in the world. White copper is peculiar to itfelf, but we know of no extraordinary quality it poffeffes. One of the fundamental maxims of the Chinefe government is that of not introducing a fuperabundancy of gold and filver, for fear of hurting induftry.

induſtry. Their gold mines, therefore, are but ſlightly worked, and the currency of that metal is ſupplied by the grains
the people pick up in the ſand of rivers and mountains. The
ſilver ſpecie is furniſhed from the mines of Honan.

POPULATION AND INHABITANTS.] The number of Chi-
neſe, by the beſt accounts, does not fall ſhort of fifty millions ;
a number diſproportioned to what we are told of the vaſt population of particular cities and provinces. Moſt of thoſe accounts are exaggerated, and perſons, who viſit China without
any view of becoming authors, are greatly diſappointed in
their mighty expectations. The Chineſe, in their perſons,
are middle-ſized, their faces broad, their eyes black and
ſmall, their noſes rather ſhort. The Chineſe have particular
ideas of beauty. They pluck up the hairs of the lower part
of their faces, by the roots, with tweezers, leaving a few
ſtraggling ones by way of beard. Their Tartar princes compel them to cut off the hair of their heads, and like Mahometans, to wear only a lock on the crown. Their complexions towards the north is fair, towards the ſouth ſwarthy,
and the fatter a man is, they think him the handſomer. Men
of quality, and learning, who are not much expoſed to the
ſun, are delicately complexioned, and they who are bred to
letters, let the nails of their fingers grow to an enormous
length, to ſhew that they are not employed in manual
labour.

The women have little eyes, plump, roſy lips, black hair,
regular features, and a delicate though florid complexion.
The ſmallneſs of their feet is reckoned a principal part of
their beauty, and no ſwathing is omitted, when they are
young, to give them that accompliſhment, ſo that when they
grow up, they may be ſaid to totter rather than to walk.
This fanciful piece of beauty was probably invented by the
antient Chineſe, to palliate their jealouſy.

To enter into all the ſtarch ridiculous formalities of the
Chineſe, eſpecially their men of quality, when paying or
receiving viſits, would give my reader little information, and
leſs amuſement, and very probably come too late, as the manners of the Chineſe, ſince they fell under the power of the
Tartars, are greatly altered, and daily vary. It is ſufficient
to obſerve, that the legiſlators of China, looking upon ſub-
miſſion and ſubordination as the corner-ſtones of all ſociety,
deviſed thoſe outward marks of reſpect, ridiculous as they
appear to us, as the teſt of duty and reſpect from inferiors to
ſuperiors, and their capital maxim was, that the man who
was deficient in civility, was void of good ſenſe.

By

By the lateſt and beſt accounts, the Chineſe in general are the moſt diſhoneſt, low, thieving ſet in the world, and they employ their natural quickneſs only to improve the arts of cheating the nations they deal with, eſpecially the Europeans, whom they cheat with great eaſe, particularly the Engliſh, but they obſerve that none but a Chineſe can cheat a Chineſe. They are fond of law diſputes beyond any people in the world. Their hypocriſy is without bounds, and the men of property among them, practiſe the moſt avowed bribery, and the loweſt meanneſſes to obtain preferment.

Dress.] This varies according to the degrees of men among them. The men wear caps on their heads of the faſhion of a bell, thoſe of quality are ornamented with jewels. The reſt of their dreſs is eaſy and looſe, conſiſting of a veſt and a ſaſh, a coat or gown thrown over them, ſilk boots quilted with cotton, and a pair of drawers. The ladies towards the ſouth wear nothing on their head. Sometimes their hair is drawn up in a net, and ſometimes it is diſhevelled. Their dreſs differs but little from that of the men, only their gown or upper garment has very large open ſleeves. The dreſs, both of men and women, varies however according to the temperature of the climate.

Marriages.] The parties never ſee each other in China till the bargain is concluded by the parents, and that is generally when the parties are perfect children. Next to being barren, the greateſt ſcandal is to bring females into the world; and if a woman of a poor family happens to have three or four girls, ſucceſſively, ſhe will expoſe or ſtrangle them, which is the principal reaſon of ſo many children being found in the ſtreets and highways.

Funerals.] People of note cauſe their coffins to be made, and their tombs to be built in their life-time. No perſons are buried within the walls of a city, nor is a dead corpſe ſuffered to be brought into a town, if a perſon died in the country. Every Chineſe keeps in his houſe a table, upon which are written the names of his father, grandfather, and great grandfather; before which they frequently burn incenſe, and proſtrate themſelves; and when the father of a family dies, the name of the great grandfather is taken away, and that of the deceaſed is added.

Language.] The Chineſe language conſiſts of a very few words, or rather ſyllables, which admit of ſo many variations, and ſo much modified by ſounds and action, that it is generally thought no ſtranger can attain it, ſo as to ſpeak it.

Genius and learning.] The genius of the Chineſe is peculiar to themſelves. They have no conception of what is beautiful in writing, regular in architecture, or natural in
painting

painting, and yet in their gardening, and planning their grounds, they hit upon the true fublime and beautiful. The learning of the Chinefe has been difplayed in feveral fpecimens publifhed by Du Halde, as well as of poetry, but they contain no more than a fet of maxims and precepts, accommodated to public and private life, without any thing argumentative or defcriptive. They perform all the operations of arithmetic with prodigious quicknefs, but differently from the Europeans. Till the latter came among them, they were ignorant of mathematical learning, and all its depending arts. They had no apparatus for aftronomical obfervations; and metaphyfical learning, if it exifted among them, was only known to their philofophers; but even the arts introduced by the Jefuits, were of very fhort duration among them, and lafted very little longer than the reign of Cang-hi, who was contemporary with our Charles II. nor is it very probable they ever will be revived. It has been generally faid, that they underftood printing before the Europeans; but that can be only applied to block printing, for the fufile and moveable types were undoubtedly Dutch or German inventions. The Chinefe, however, had almanacs, which were ftamped from plates or blocks, many hundred years before printing was difcovered in Europe. The invention of gunpowder is juftly claimed by the Chinefe, who made ufe of it againft Zingis Khan and Tamerlane. They feem to have known nothing of fmall fire-arms, and to have been acquainted only with the cannon, which they call the fire-pan. Their induftry in their manufactures of ftuffs, porcelane, japanning, and the like fedentary trades is amazing, and can be equalled only by their labours in the field, in making canals, levelling mountains, raifing gardens, and navigating their junks and boats.

ANTIQUITIES AND CURIOSITIES.] Few natural curiofities prefent themfelves in China, that have not been comprehended under preceding articles. Some volcanos, rivers and lakes of particular qualities, are to be found in different parts of the empire. The volcano of Linefung is faid fometimes to make fo furious a difcharge of fire and afhes, as to occafion a tempeft in the air, and fome of their lakes are faid to petrify fifhes when put into them. The artificial curiofities of China are ftupendous. The great wall, feparating China from Tartary, to prevent the incurfions of the Tartars, is fuppofed to extend 1500 miles. It is carried over mountains and valleys, and reaches from the province of Xenfi to the Kang fea, between the provinces of Pekin and Lænotum. It is in moft places built of brick and mortar, which is fo well tempered, that though it has ftood for 1800 years, it is but little decayed.

The beginning of this wall is a large bulwark of ſtone raiſed in the ſea, in the province of Petcheli, to the eaſt of Pekin, and almoſt in the ſame latitude; it is built like the walls of the capital city of the empire, but much wider, being terraſſed and caſed with bricks, and is from twenty to twenty-five feet high. P. Regis, and the other gentleman, who took a map of theſe provinces, often ſtretched a line on the top, to meaſure the baſis of triangles, and to take diſtant points with an inſtrument. They always found it paved wide enough for five or ſix horſemen to travel abreaſt with eaſe. Mention has been already made of the prodigious canals and roads, that are cut through this empire.

The artificial mountains preſent on their tops temples, monaſteries, and other edifices, fabricated by hands. Some part, however, of what we are told concerning the cavities in theſe mountains, ſeems to be fabulous. The Chineſe bridges cannot be ſufficiently admired. They are built ſometimes upon barges ſtrongly chained together, yet ſo as to be parted, and to let the veſſels paſs that ſail up and down the river. Some of them run from mountain to mountain, and conſiſt only of one arch; that over the river Saffrany is 400 cubits long, and 500 high, though a ſingle arch, and joins two mountains, and ſome in the interior parts of the empire, are ſaid to be ſtill more ſtupendous. The triumphal arches of this country form the next ſpecies of artificial curioſities. Though they are not built in the Greek or Roman ſtile of architecture, yet they are ſuperb and beautiful, and erected to the memories of their great men, with vaſt labour and ex-pence. They are ſaid in the whole to be eleven hundred, two hundred of which are particularly magnificent. Their ſepulchral monuments, make likewiſe a great figure. Their towers, the models of which are now ſo common in Europe under the name of pagodas, are vaſt embelliſhments to the face of their country. They ſeem to be conſtructed by a regular order, and all of them are finiſhed with exquiſite carvings and gildings, and other ornaments; that at Nanking, which is 200 feet high, and 40 in diameter, is the moſt ad-mired. It is called the Porcelane Tower, becauſe it is lined with Chineſe tiles. Their temples are chiefly remarkable for the diſagreeable taſte in which they are built, for their capaciouſneſs, their whimſical ornaments, and the uglineſs of the idols they contain. The Chineſe are remarkably fond of bells, which gave name to one of their principal feſtivals. A bell of Pekin weighs 120,000 pound, but its ſound is ſaid to be diſagreeable. The laſt curioſity I ſhall mention, is their fire-works, which in China exceed thoſe of all other nations.

In

In ſhort, every province of China is a ſcene of curioſities·
Their buildings, excepting as mentioned, their pagodas,
being confined to no order, and ſuſceptible of all kinds of
ornaments, have a wild variety, and a pleaſing elegance not
void of magnificence, that it is agreeable to the eye, and the
imagination, and preſents a diverſity of objects not to be found
in European architecture.

CHIEF CITIES.] Little can be ſaid of theſe more than that
ſome of them are immenſe, and there is great reaſon to believe
their population is much exaggerated. The empire is ſaid to
contain 4400 walled cities ; the chief of which are Pekin,
Nankin, and Canton. The former is the reſidence of the
preſent royal family, and is moderately reckoned to contain
two million of inhabitants, but Nanking is ſaid to exceed it
both in extent and population. The walls of Pekin are 50
cubits high, and are defended by towers, at a bow-ſhot diſtance from each other, with redoubts at every gate. It is
divided into two parts like London and Weſtminſter, the
Chineſe and the Tartar. The imperial palace, which is no
other than an amazing aſſemblage of neat beautiful buildings,
but without order or regularity, ſtands in the latter.

TRADE AND MANUFACTURES.] China is ſo happily ſituated, and produces ſuch a variety of materials for manufactures,
that it may be ſaid to be the native land of induſtry; but it is an
induſtry without taſte or elegance, though carried on with vaſt
art and neatneſs. They make paper of the bark of bamboo,
and other trees, as well as of cotton, but not comparable for
records, or printing, to the European. Their ink, for the
uſe of drawing, is well known in England, and is ſaid to be
made of oil and lamp-black. I have already mentioned the
antiquity of their printing, which they ſtill do by cutting
their characters on blocks of wood. The manufacture of
that earthen ware, generally known by the name of China,
was long a ſecret in Europe, and brought immenſe ſums to
that country. The antients knew and eſteemed it highly
under the name of Porcelain, but it was of a much better
fabric than the modern. Though the Chineſe affect to keep
that manufacture ſtill a ſecret, yet it is well known that the
principal material is a prepared pulverized earth, and that
ſeveral European countries far exceed the Chineſe in manufacturing this commodity. The Chineſe ſilks are generally plain
and flowered gawſes, and they are ſaid to have been originally
fabricated in that country, where the art of rearing ſilk-worms
was firſt diſcovered. They manufacture ſilks likewiſe of a
more durable kind, and their cotton, and other cloths, are famous for furniſhing a light warm wear.

Their

Their trade, it is well known, is open to all the European nations, with whom they deal for ready money; for such is the pride and avarice of the Chinese, that they think no manufactures equal to their own. But it is certain, that since the discovery of the porcelane manufactures, and the vast improvements the Europeans have made in the weaving branches, the Chinese commerce has been on the decline.

CONSTITUTION AND GOVERNMENT.] This was a most instructive entertaining article, before the conquest of China by the Tartars, for though their princes retain many fundamental maxims of the old China, they have obliged the inhabitants to deviate from the ancient discipline in many respects. Perhaps their acquaintance with the Europeans may have contributed to their degeneracy. The original plan of the Chinese government was patriarchal, almost in the strictest sense of the word. Duty and obedience to the father of each family was recommended and enforced in the most rigorous manner, but at the same time, the emperor was considered as the father of the whole. His mandarines, or great officers of state, were looked upon as his substitutes, and the degrees of submission which were due from the inferior ranks to the superior, were settled and observed with the most scrupulous precision, and in a manner that to us seems highly ridiculous. This simple claim of obedience required great address and knowledge of human nature, to render it effectual; and the Chinese legislators, Confucius particularly, appear to have been men of wonderful abilities. They enveloped their dictates in a number of mystical appearances, so as to strike the people with awe and veneration. The mandarines had modes of speaking and writing, different from those of other subjects, and the people were taught to believe that their princes partook of divinity, so that they were seldom seen, and more seldom approached.

Though this system preserved the public tranquillity, for an incredible number of years, yet it had a fundamental effect that often convulsed, and at last proved fatal to the state, because the same attention was not paid to the military as the civil duties. The Chinese had passions like other men, and sometimes a weak or wicked administration, drove them into arms, and a revolution easily succeeded, which they justified by saying, that their sovereign had ceased to be their father. During those commotions, one of the parties naturally invited their neighbours the Tartars to their assistance, and it was thus those barbarians, who had great sagacity, became acquainted with the weak side of their constitution, and they availed themselves accordingly, by invading and conquering the empire.

Besides

Besides the great doctrine of patriarchal obedience, the Chinese had sumptuary laws, and regulations for the expences of all degrees of subjects, which were very useful in preserving the public tranquillity, and preventing the effects of ambition. By their institutions likewise the mandarines might remonstrate to the emperor, but in the most submissive manner, upon the errors of his government, and when he was a virtuous prince, this freedom was often attended with the most salutary effects. No country in the world is so well provided with magistrates for the discharge of justice, both in civil and criminal matters, as China, but they are often ineffectual through want of public virtue in the execution. The emperor is stiled Holy son of Heaven, Sole Governor of the Earth, Great Father of his People.

RELIGION.] This article is nearly connected with the preceding. Though the ancient Chinese worshipped idols, and seemed to admit of a particular providence, yet their philosophers and legislators were atheists or materialists, and indulged the people in the worship of sensible objects, only to make them more submissive to government. The Jesuits long imposed upon the public of Europe, on this head, and suffered their proselytes to worship Tien, pretending, that it was no other than the name of God, but a strict scrutiny being made by the court of Rome, it was found to signify universal matter. The truth is, Confucius, and the Chinese legislators, introduced a most excellent system of morals among the people, and endeavoured to supply the belief of a future state, by prescribing to them the worship of inferior deities. Their morality approximates to that of Christianity, but as we know little of their religion, but through the Jesuits, we cannot adopt for truth the numerous instances, which they tell us of the conformity of the Chinese with the Christian religion. Those fathers, it must be owned, were men of great abilities, and made a wonderful progress above a century ago in their conversions; but they mistook the true character of the emperor who was their patron, for he no sooner found that they were in fact aspiring to the civil direction of the government, than he expelled them, levelled their churches with the ground, and prohibited the exercise of their religion; since which time Christianity has made no figure in China.

REVENUES.] These are said by some, to amount to twenty millions sterling a year; but this cannot be meant in money, which does not at all abound in China. The taxes collected for the use of the government in rice, and other commodities,

are

are certainly very great, and very possibly amount to that sum.

MILITARY AND MARINE STRENGTH.] China is, at this time, a far more powerful empire, than it was before its conquest by the eastern Tartars in 1644. This is owing to the consummate policy of Chun-tchi, the first Tartarian emperor of China, who obliged his hereditary subjects to conform themselves to the Chinese manners and policy, and the Chinese to wear the Tartar dress and arms. The two nations were thereby incorporated. The Chinese were appointed to all the civil offices of the empire. The emperor made Pekin the seat of his government, and the Tartars quietly submitted to a change of their country and condition which was so much in their favour.

This security, however, of the Chinese from the Tartars, takes from them all military objects ; the Tartar power alone being formidable to that empire. The only danger that threatens it at present, is the disuse of arms. The Chinese land army is said to consist of five millions of men, but in these are comprehended all who are employed in the collection of the revenue, and the preservation of the canals, the great roads and the public peace. The imperial guards amount to about 30,000. As to the marine force, it is composed chiefly of the junks, we have already mentioned, and other small ships, that trade coast-ways, or to the neighbouring countries, or to prevent sudden descents.

HISTORY.] The Chinese pretend as a nation to an antiquity beyond all measure of credibility, but though their pretensions have been repeatedly confuted by learned men, they certainly have evidences of a much higher antiquity, than any people on earth (the Jews perhaps excepted) can produce. Their exactness in astronomical observations, rude as they were in that science, before their commerce with the Europeans ; their immemorial use of printing ; their peaceable patriarchal scheme of government, and several other incidental advantages contributed to this priority. A succession of excellent princes, and a duration of domestic tranquillity united legislation with philosophy, and produced their Fo-hi, whose history however is wrapped up in mysteries, their Li-Laokum, and above all their Confucius, at once the Solon and the Socrates of China. After all, the internal revolutions of the empire, though rare, produced the most dreadful effects, in proportion as its constitution was pacific, and they were attended with the most bloody exterminations in some provinces ; so that though the Chinese empire is hereditary, the imperial succession was more than once broken into.

Neither

Neither the great Zinghis Khan, nor Tamerlane, though they often defeated the Chinefe, could fubdue their empire, and neither of them could keep the conquefts they made there. The celebrated wall, proved but a feeble barrier againft the arms of thofe famous Tartars. After their invafions were over, the Chinefe went to war with the Manchew Tartars, while an indolent worthlefs emperor Tfong-tching, was upon the throne. In the mean while a bold rebel, named Li-cong-tfe, in the province of Se-tchuen, dethroned the emperor, who hanged himfelf, as did moft of his courtiers and women. Ou-fan-quey, the Chinefe general, on the frontiers of Tartary, refufed to recognize the ufurper, and made a peace with Tfongate, the Manchew prince, who drove the ufurper from the throne, and took poffeffion of it himfelf, about the year 1644. The Tartar maintained himfelf in his authority, and as has been already mentioned, wifely incorporated his hereditary fubjects with the Chinefe, fo that in effect Tartary became an acquifition to China. He was fucceeded by a prince of great natural and acquired abilities, who was the patron of the jefuits, but knew how to check them when he found them intermeddling with the affairs of his government.

About the year 1661, the Chinefe, under this Tartar family, drove the Dutch out of the ifland of Formofa, which the latter had taken from the Portuguefe. Though the intercourfe between Europe and China has been greatly improved fince that time, yet we know very little of the internal events of China, excepting thofe that affect our trade, which is now at a low pafs in that country, owing to the vaft diftance and uncertainty of the voyage, the native chicanery of the Chinefe themfelves, and the Europeans having fupplied themfelves either at home or from other countries with many of their commodities.

INDIA IN GENERAL.

SITUATION AND BOUNDARIES.] THIS vaft country is fituated between the 66th and 109th deg. of eaft longitude, and between 1 and 40 of north latitude. It is bounded on the north by the countries of Ufbec Tartary and Tibet; on the fouth, by the Indian Ocean; on the eaft, by China and the Chinefe fea; and on the weft, by Perfia and the Indian fea.

DIVISIONS.] I fhall divide, as others have done, India at large into three great parts; firft, the Peninfula of India beyond the Ganges, called the Further Peninfula; fecond, the

main

main land, or the Mogul's empire; thirdly, the Peninfula within or on this fide the Ganges : all of them vaft populous and extended empires. But it is neceffary, in order to fave many repetitions, to premife an account of fome particulars that are in common to thofe numerous nations, which fhall be extracted from the moft enlightened of our modern writers who have vifited the country in the fervice of the Eaft India company.

POPULATION, INHABITANTS, } Mr. Orme, an excellent
RELIGION AND GOVERNMENT. } and an authentic hiftorian, comprehends the two latter divifions under the title of Indo-ftan. The Mahometans (fays he) who are called Moors, of Indoftan, are computed to be about ten millions, and the Indians about an hundred millions. Above half the empire is fubject to rajahs, or kings, who derive their defcent from the old princes of India, and exercife all rights of fovereignty, only paying a tribute to the great mogul, and obferving the treaties by which their anceftors recognized his fuperiority. In other refpects, the government of Indoftan is full of wife checks upon the overgrowing greatnefs of any fubject; but (as all precautions of that kind depend upon the adminiftration) the indolence and barbarity of the moguls or emperors, and their great viceroys, have rendered them fruitlefs.

The original inhabitants of India are called Gentoos, or, as others call them, Hindoos. They pretend that Brumma, who was their legiflator both in politics and religion, was inferior only to God, and that he exifted many thoufand years before our account of the creation. This Brumma, probably, was fome great and good genius, whofe beneficence, like that of the pagan legiflators, led his people and their pofterity to pay him divine honours. The bramins (for fo the Gentoo priefts are called) pretend that he bequeathed to them a book called the Vidam, containing his doctrines and inftitutions; and that though the original is loft, they are ftill poffeffed of a commentary upon it, called the Shahftah, which is wrote in the Sanfcrit language, now a dead language, and known only to the bramins who ftudy it. The foundation of Brumma's doctrine confifted in the belief of a fupreme Being, who has created a regular gradation of beings, fome fuperior, and fome inferior to man : in the immortality of the foul, and a future ftate of rewards and punifhments, which is to confift of a tranfmigration into different bodies, according to the lives they have led in their pre-exiftent ftate. From this it appears more than probable that the Pythagorean metempfichofis took its rife in India.

The

The neceffity of inculcating this fublime, but otherwife complicated doctrine, into the lower ranks, induced the bramins, who are by no means unanimous in their doctrines, to have recourfe to fenfible reprefentations of the Deity and his attributes; fo that the original doctrines of Brumma have degenerated to rank ridiculous idolatry, in the worfhip of the moft hideous figures, either delineated or carved; and the belief of an omnipotent Being is now almoft loft among the Gentoos.

Thofe Indians are particularly diftinguifhed from the reft of mankind by their divifion into tribes, the four principal of which are the bramins, foldiers, labourers, and mechanics. Thefe are again fubdivided into a multiplicity of inferior diftinctions. The bramins have an intire power, which they ufe commonly to very bad purpofes, over the minds of the people; though fome of them are fuperftitious, moral, and innocent. They are all of them fuch bigots, that excepting the Hallachores, who are the refufe and outcafts of the other tribes, and difowned and detefted by them all, Mr. Scrafton doubts (whatever the Roman-catholics may pretend) whether there ever was an inftance of any other of the Gentoos being converted by the miffionaries. In fhort, the bramins in general are a defigning degenerate fet of men; but Mr. Scrafton, who gives us that picture of them, acknowledges that, amidft all their errors, they agree in thofe truths which form the harmony of the univerfe, that there is *one fupreme God, and that he is beft pleafed by charity and good works.*

The foldiers are commonly called Rajah-poots, or perfons defcended from rajahs, and refide chiefly in the northern provinces, and are generally more fair-complexioned than the people of the fouthern provinces, who are quite black. Thefe rajah-poots are a robuft, brave, faithful people, and enter into the fervice of thofe who will pay them; but when their leader falls in battle, they think that their engagements to him are finifhed, and they run off the field without any ftain upon their reputation.

The labourers are the farmers and all who are concerned in the cultivation of lands.

The mechanics are merchants, bankers, traders of all kinds, and are divided into many fubordinations.

Thofe different tribes (fays Mr. Scrafton) are forbid to intermarry, to cohabit, to eat with each other, or even to drink out of the fame veffel with one of another tribe; and every deviation in thefe points, fubjects them to be rejected by their tribe, renders them for ever polluted, and they are thenceforward obliged to herd with the Hallachores. This divifion
is

is attended with infinite inconveniencies, for excepting the rajah-poots, no Gentoo thinks of defending himfelf in cafe of invafions, which, when made from the fea, have been generally fuccefsful. The fame divifion, however, has, notwithftanding all the convulfions of their government, and all their oppreffions under the Mahometans, preferved their manufactures among them, which, while the fon can follow no other trade than that of his father, can never be loft but by exterminating the people.

Different kinds of food are affigned to different tribes. The bramins touch nothing that has life; the foldiers are permitted to eat venifon, mutton, and fifh; the labourers and merchants live differently, according to their fex and profeffions, fome of them being allowed to eat fifh, but none of them animal food.

The practice of women burning themfelves, upon the death of their hufbands, is now faid to be difufed all over Indoftan; and the Gentoos in general chufe death by famine rather than pollute themfelves by eating a forbidden food. This picture of the Gentoos feems to be drawn before our wars with the French in that country; for if we are to believe fome travellers, they begin now to relax in the practice of their religious duties. The Gentoos are as careful of the cultivation of their lands, and their public works and conveniencies, as the Chinefe; and there fcarcely is an inftance of a robbery in all Indoftan, though the diamond merchants travel without defenfive weapons.

The temples or pagodas of the Gentoos, are ftupendous, but difguftful ftone buildings, erected in every capital, and under the tuition of the bramins. If the bramins are mafters of any uncommon art or fcience, they turn it to the purpofes of profit from their ignorant votaries. Mr. Scrafton fays, that they know how to calculate eclipfes; and that judicial aftrology is fo prevalent among them, that half the year is taken up with unlucky days; the head aftrologer being always confulted in their councils. The Mahometans likewife encourage thofe fuperftitions, and look upon all the fruits of the Gentoo induftry as belonging to themfelves. Though the Gentoos are entirely paffive under all their oppreffions, and by their ftate of exiftence, the practice of their religion, and the fcantinefs of their food, have nothing of that refentment in their nature that animates the reft of mankind; yet they are fufceptible of avarice, and fometimes bury their money, and rather than difcover it put themfelves to death by poifon or otherwife. This practice, which it feems is not uncommon,

accounts

accounts for the vaſt ſcarcity of ſilver that till of late prevailed in Indoſtan.

The reaſons abovementioned account likewiſe for their being
free of all thoſe paſſions, particularly that of love, and ſen-
ſations that render the reſt of mankind either happy or miſerable. Their perpetual uſe of rice, their chief food, gives
them but little nouriſhment; and their marrying early, the
males before fourteen, and their women at ten or eleven years
of age, keeps them low and feeble in their perſons. A man
is in the decline of life at thirty, and the beauty of the women is on decay at eighteen : at twenty-five they have all the
marks of old age. We are not therefore to wonder at their
being ſoon ſtrangers to all perſonal exertion and vigour of
mind; and it is with them a frequent ſaying, that it is better
to ſit than to walk, to lie down than to ſit, to ſleep than to
wake, and death is the beſt of all.

The Mahometans, who, in Indoſtan, are called Moors,
are of Perſian, Turkiſh, Arabic, and other extractions. They
early began, in the reigns of the califs of Bagdat, to invade
Indoſtan. They penetrated as far as Delhi, which they
made their capital. They ſettled colonies in ſeveral places,
whoſe deſcendants are called Pytans; but their empire was
overthrown by Tamerlane, who founded the Mogul government, which ſtill ſubſiſts. Thoſe princes being ſtrict Mahometans, received under their protection all who profeſſed the
ſame religion, and who being a brave active people, counterbalanced the numbers of the natives. They are ſaid to have
introduced the diviſion of provinces, over which they appointed ſoubahs; and thoſe provinces, each of which might
be ſtiled an empire, were ſubdivided into nabobſhips, each
nabob being immediately accountable to his ſoubah, who in
proceſs of time became almoſt independent on the emperor,
or, as he is called, the great mogul, upon their paying him
an annual tribute. The vaſt reſort of Perſian and Tartar
tribes have likewiſe ſtrengthened the Mahometan government;
but it is obſervable, that in two or three generations, the progeny of all thoſe adventurers, who though they bring nothing
with them but their horſes and their ſwords, degenerate into
all eaſtern indolence and ſenſuality.

Of all thoſe tribes, the Marattas at preſent make the greateſt
figure. They are a kind of mercenaries, who live on the
mountains between Indoſtan and Perſia. They commonly
ſerve on horſeback, and when well commanded, they have
been known to give law even to the court of Delhi. Though
they are originally Gentoos, yet they are of bold active ſpirits,
and pay no great reſpect to the principles of their religion.

Mr.

Mr. Scrafton fays, that the Mahometans or Moors are of fo deteftable a character, that he never knew above two or three exceptions, and thofe were among the Tartar and Perfian officers of the army. They are void of every principle even of their own religion ; and if they have a virtue, it is an appearance of hofpitality, but it is an appearance only ; for while they are drinking with, and embracing a friend, they will ftab him to the heart.

The people of Indoftan are governed by no written laws, and their courts of juftice are directed by precedents. The Mahometan inftitutes prevail only in their great towns and their neighbourhood. The empire is hereditary, and the emperor is heir only to his own officers. All lands go in the hereditary line, and continue in that ftate even down to the fubtenants, while the lord can pay his taxes, and the latter their rent, both which are immutably fixed in the public books of each diftrict. The imperial demefne lands are thofe of the great rajah families, which fell to Tamerlane and his fucceffors. Certain portions of them are called jaghire lands, and are beftowed by the crown on the great lords or omrahs, and upon their death revert to the emperor ; but the rights of the fubtenants, even of thofe lands, are indefeafible.

Such are the outlines of the government by which this great empire long fubfifted, without almoft the femblance of virtue among its great officers either civil or military. It was fhaken, however, after the invafion of Mahomet Shah, which was attended by fo great a diminution of the imperial authority, that the foubahs and nabobs became abfolute in their own governments. Though they could not alter the fundamental laws of property, yet they invented new taxes, which beggared the people, to pay their own armies and fupport their power ; fo that many of the people, a few years ago, after being unmercifully plundered by collectors and taxmafters, were left to perifh through want. To fum up the mifery of the inhabitants, thofe foubahs and nabobs, and other Mahometan governors, employ the bramins and the Gentoos themfelves as the minifters of their rapacioufnefs and cruelties. Upon the whole, ever fince the invafion of Kouli Kan, Indoftan, from being the beft regulated government in the world, is become a fcene of mere anarchy or ftratocracy ; every great man protects himfelf in his tyranny by his foldiers, whofe pay far exceeds the natural riches of his government. As private affaffinations and other murders are here committed with impunity, the people, who know they can be in no worfe eftate, concern themfelves very little in the revolutions of government. To the above caufes are owing the prefent
fucceffes

fucceffes of the Englifh in Indoftan ; and it is their intereft to bring, as foon as poffible, that government back to its firft principles under the family of Tamerlane. The reader, from this reprefentation, may perceive likewife, that all that the Englifh have acquired in point of territory, has been gained from ufurpers and robbers; and their poffeffion of it being guarantied by the prefent lawful emperor, is founded upon the laws and conftitutions of that country.

It may be here proper juft to obferve, that the complexion of the Gentoos is black, their hair long, and the features of both fexes regular. At court, however, the great families are ambitious of intermarrying with Perfians and Tartars, on account of the fairnefs of their complexion, refembling that of their conqueror Tamerlane and his great generals.

The PENINSULA of INDIA beyond the GANGES, called the FARTHER PENINSULA.

SITUATION AND EXTENT.

	Miles.		Degrees.
Length	2000 }	between {	1 and 30 north latitude.
Breadth	1000 }	{	92 and 109 eaft longitude.

BOUNDARIES.] THIS peninfula is bounded by Tibet and China, on the north ; by China and the Chinefe Sea, on the eaft; by the fame fea and the ftraits of Malacca, on the fouth ; and by the bay of Bengal and the Hither India, on the weft.

Grand divifions.	Subdivifions.	Chief towns.
On the north-weft	Acham — — Ava —— — Aracan — —	Chamdara Ava Aracan.
On the fouth-weft	Pegu — — Martaban —— Siam, — — Malacca ——	Pegu, E. lon. 97. N. lat. 17-30. Martaban Siam, E. lon. 100-55. N. lat. 14-18. Malacca, E. lon. 102-10. N. lat. 2-12.
On the north-eaft	Tonquin —— Laos — ——	Cachao, or Keccio, E. lon. 105. N. lat. 21-30. Lanchang.
On the fouth-eaft	Cochin China — Cambodia — Chiàmpa ——	Thoanoa Cambodia Padram.

NAME.] The name of India is taken from the river Indus, which of all others was beft known to the Perfians. The whole of this peninfula was unknown to the ancients, and is partly fo to the moderns.

AIR AND CLIMATE.] This country is fo little known, that authors differ concerning its air, fome preferring that of the fouthern, and fome that of the northern parts. It is gene-rally agreed, that the air of the former is hot and dry, but in fome places moift, and confequently unhealthy. The cli-mate is fubject to hurricanes, lightnings, and inundations, fo that the people build their houfes upon high pillars to defend them from floods; and they have no other idea of feafons, but wet and dry. Eafterly and wefterly monfoons (which is an Indian word) prevail in this country.

MOUNTAINS.] Thefe run from north to fouth almoft the whole length of the country; but the lands near the fea are low, and annually overflowed in the rainy feafon.

RIVERS.] The chief are Domea, Mecon, Menan, and Ava.

BAYS AND STRAITS.] The bays of Bengal, Siam, and Cochin-China. The ftraits of Malacca and Sincapora. The promontories of Siam, Romana, and Banfac.

SOIL AND PRODUCT OF THE ⎱   The foil of this peninfula
    DIFFERENT NATIONS. ⎰ is fruitful in general, and produces all the delicious fruits that are found in other coun-tries, as well as roots and vegetables. It abounds likewife in filks, elephants, and quadrupeds, both domeftic and wild, that are common in the fouthern kingdoms of Afia. The natives drive a great trade in gold, diamonds, rubies, topazes, amethyfts, and other precious ftones. Tonquin produces little or no corn or wine, but is the moft healthful country of all the peninfula. In fome places, efpecially to-wards the north, the inhabitants have fwellings in their throats, owing to the badnefs of their water.

INHABITANTS, CUSTOMS, ⎱   The Tonquinefe are excel-
    AND DIVERSIONS. ⎰   lent mechanics and fair tra-ders; but greatly oppreffed by their king and great lords. His majefty engroffes the trade, and his factors fell by retale to the Dutch and other nations. The Tonquinefe are fond of lacquer houfes, which are unwholefome and poifonous. The people in the fouth are a favage race, and go almoft naked, with large filver and gold ear-rings, and coral, amber, or fhell bracelets. In Tonquin and Cochin-China, the two fexes are fcarcely diftinguifhable by their drefs, which refem-bles that of the Perfians. The people of quality are fond of Englifh broad-cloth, red or green, and others wear a dark
coloured

coloured cotton cloth. In Azem, which is thought one of the beſt countries in Aſia, the inhabitants prefer dogs fleſh to all other animal food. The people of that kingdom pay no taxes, becauſe the king is ſole proprietor of all the gold and ſilver and other metals found in his kingdom. They live, however, eaſily and comfortably. Almoſt every houſe-keeper has an elephant for the conveniency of his wives and women, polygamy being practiſed all over India.

It is unqueſtionable that thoſe Indians, as well as the Chineſe, had the uſe of gunpowder before it was known in Europe, and the invention is generally aſcribed to the Azemeſe. The inhabitants of the ſouthern diviſion of this peninſula go under the name of Malayans, from the neighbouring country of Malacca.

Though the religious ſuperſtitions that prevail in this peninſula are as groſs as thoſe deſcribed under the article of Tibet, and the civil government of the two countries in many particulars reſemble each other, yet the people believe in a future ſtate; and when their kings are interred, a number of animals are buried with them, and ſuch veſſels of gold and ſilver as they think can be of uſe to them in their future life. The people in this peninſula, are commonly very fond of ſhew, and often make an appearance beyond their circumſtances. They are delicate in no part of their dreſs but in their hair, which they buckle up in a very agreeable manner. In their food they are loathſome, for beſides dogs, they eat rats, mice, ſerpents, and ſtinking fiſh. The people of Arraken are equally indelicate in their amours, for they hire Dutch and other foreigners to conſummate the nuptials with their virgins, and value their women moſt when in a ſtate of pregnancy. Their treatment of the ſick is ridiculous beyond belief; and in many places, when a patient is judged to be incurable, he is expoſed on the bank of ſome river, where he is either drowned or devoured by birds or beaſts of prey.

The diverſions common in this country are fiſhing and hunting, the celebration of feſtivals, and their acting comedies by torch-light from evening to morning.

LANGUAGE.] The language of the court of Delhi is Perſian, but in this peninſula it is chiefly Malayan, as we have already obſerved, interſperſed with other dialects.

LEARNING AND LEARNED MEN.] It is more than probable that the Egyptians, the nation from which the Greeks and Romans drew the fine arts, owed them to the bramins, and the Gentoos, who are ſometimes called Banians. The names, however, of the legiſlators and bramins, or whoever their learned men were who ſpread their knowledge among the

Eaſt-

Eaſt-Indians, have either periſhed or are obſcured by impenetrable clouds of allegory. Some late Engliſh authors, who were well acquainted with the affairs of Indoſtan, have aſſured us that that empire ſtill contains men of the moſt unſpotted lives and profound knowledge of all the original bramin theology, morality, and civil conſtitutions. Such men are hard to be diſcovered, but when acceſſible, they are modeſt and communicative in all branches of their learning, but thoſe in which they are enjoined an inviolable ſecrecy; and we have ſome well atteſted inſtances where they have ſuffered death rather than betray their ſecrets, which are hereditary in their families. Others, from the profligate ſelfiſh characters of the common bramins, think that all this ſanctity and learning is mere pretext and grimace. I have already mentioned their underſtanding aſtronomy ſo far as to calculate eclipſes.

MANUFACTURES AND COMMERCE.] Theſe vary in the different countries of this peninſula, but the chief branches have been already mentioned. The inhabitants, in ſome parts, are obliged to manufacture their ſalt out of aſhes. In all handicraft trades that they underſtand, the people are more induſtrious and better workmen than the Europeans; and in weaving, ſewing, embroidering, and ſome other manufactures, it is ſaid that the Indians do as much work with their feet as their hands. Their painting, though they are ignorant of drawing, is amazingly vivid in its colours. The fineneſs of their linen, and their fillagree work in gold and ſilver, are beyond any thing of thoſe kinds to be found in other parts of the world. The commerce of India, in ſhort, is courted by all trading nations in the world, and probably has been ſo from the earlieſt ages: it was not unknown even in Solomon's time; and the Greeks and Romans drew from thence their higheſt materials of luxury. The greateſt ſhare of it, through events foreign to this part of our work, is now centered in England, though that of the Dutch is ſtill very conſiderable; that of the French has been for ſome time on the decline; nor is that of the Swedes and Danes entirely diſcontinued.

CONSTITUTION, GOVERNMENT, RARITIES, AND CITIES.] This article is ſo extenſive, that it requires a ſlight review of the kingdoms that form this peninſula. In Azem, I have already obſerved, the king is proprietor of all the gold and ſilver: he pays little or nothing to the great mogul. We know little or nothing of the kingdom of Tipra, but that it was antiently ſubject to the kings of Arrakan; and that they ſend to the Chineſe gold and ſilk, for which they receive ſilver in return. Arrakan lies to the ſouth of Tipra, and is governed by 12 princes, ſubject to the chief king,

king, who refides in his capital. His palace is very large, and contains, as we are told, feven idols caft in gold of two inches thick, each of a man's height, and covered over with diamonds and other precious ftones. Pegu is about 350 Englifh miles in length, and almoft the fame in breadth. It is uncertain whether is it not at prefent fubject to the king or emperor of Ava. The riches of the king (whoever he is) are almoft incredible; fome of his idols, as big as life, being of maffy gold and filver. His revenues arife from the rents of lands, of which he is fole proprietor, and from duties on merchandife; fo that fome think him to be the richeft monarch in the world, excepting the Chinefe emperor. He can bring a million, and on occafion, a million and a half of foldiers to the field, well cloathed and armed; and he is faid to be mafter of 800 trained elephants, each with a caftle on his back holding four foldiers. The conftitution of his empire is of the feudal kind, for he affigns lands and towns to his nobles upon military tenures. Macao is the great mart of trade in Pegu.

We know little of the kingdom of Ava; we are not even fure to whom it belongs. It is faid, the honours the king affumes are next to divine. His fubjects trade chiefly in mufk and jewels, rubies and faphires. In other particulars, the inhabitants refemble thofe of Pegu. In thofe kingdoms, and indeed in the greateft part of this peninfula, the doctrines of the Lama or Dairo, the living god, already defcribed, equally prevail as thofe of the bramins. Whether the former is not a corruption of the latter, and both of them of ill underftood Chriftianity and Judaifm, is an enquiry fcarcely worth purfuing. The principles of the Lama are beft calculated for rendering the king a mere cypher in his government, which is entirely vefted in his priefts and minifters.

The kingdom of Laos or Lahos, formerly included that of Jangoma or Jangomay, but we know few particulars of it that can be depended upon. It is faid to be immenfely populous, to abound in all the rich commodities as well as the grofs fuperftitions of the eaft, and to be divided into a number of petty kingdoms, all of them holding of one fovereign, who, like his oriental brethren, is abfolutely defpotic, and lives in inexpreffible pomp and magnificence; but being of the Lama religion, is the flave of his priefts and minifters.

The kingdom of Siam has been often defcribed by miffionaries and pretended travellers, in the moft romantic terms, and therefore we can pay little other credit to their accounts, further than that it a rich and flourifhing kingdom, and that it approaches in its government, policy, the quick-

nefs and acutenefs of its inhabitants, very near to the Chi‑
nefe. The kingdom of Siam is furrounded by high mountains, which, on the eaft fide, feparate it from the kingdoms
of Camboja and Laos; on the weft, from Pegu; and on the
north, from Ava, or, more properly, from Jangoma, which
is fubject to Ava; on the fouth it is wafhed by the river Siam,
and has the peninfula of Malacca, the north-weft part whereof
is under its dominion. The extent of the country, however,
is very uncertain, and it is but indifferently peopled. The
inhabitants, of both fexes, are more modeft than any found
in the reft of this peninfula. Great care is taken of the education of their children. Their marriages are fimple, and
performed by their talapoins or priefts, fprinkling holy water
upon the couple, and repeating fome prayers. We are told
that gold is fo abundant in this country, that their moft ponderous images are made of it, and that it is feen in vaft quantities on the outfide of the king's palace. Thofe relations are
found by modern travellers to be the fictions of French and
other miffionaries; for though the country has mines of gold,
their ornaments are either exceffive thin plates of that metal, or
a very bright lacker that cover wooden or other materials. The
government here is exceffively defpotic; even fervants muft
appear before their mafters in a kneeling pofture; and the
mandarines are proftrated before the king. Siam, the capital,
is reprefented as a large city, but fcarcely a fixth part of it is
inhabited; and the palace is about a mile and a half in circuit.
Bankok, which ftands about 18 leagues to the fouth of Siam,
and 12 miles from the fea, is the only place towards the coaft
that is fortified with walls, batteries, and brafs cannon; and
the Dutch have a factory at Ligor, which ftands on the eaft
fide of the peninfula of Malacca, but belonging to Siam.

The peninfula of Malacca is a large country, and contains
feveral kingdoms or provinces. The Dutch, however, are
faid to be the real mafters and fovereigns of the whole peninfula, being in poffeffion of the capital (Malacca.) The
inhabitants differ but little from brutes in their manner
of living; and yet the Malayan language is reckoned the
pureft of any fpoken in all the Indies. We are told by
the lateft travellers, that its chief produce is tin, pepper,
elephants teeth, canes, and gums. Some miffionaries pretend that it is the Golden Cherfonefus or Peninfula of the
antients, and that the inhabitants ufed to meafure their riches
by bars of gold. The truth is, that the excellent fituation of
this country admits of a trade with India; fo that when it was
firft difcovered by the Portuguefe, who were afterwards expelled
by the Dutch, Malacca was the richeft city in the eaft, next
to

to Goa and Ormus, being the key of the China, the Japan, the Moluccas, and the Sunda trade. The country, however, at prefent, is chiefly valuable for its trade with the Chinefe. This degeneracy of the Malayans, who were formerly an induftrious ingenious people, is eafily accounted for, by the tyranny of the Dutch, whofe intereft it is that they fhould never recover from their prefent ftate of ignorance and flavery.

The Englifh carry on a fmuggling kind of trade in their country fhips, from the coaft of Coromandel and the bay of Bengal, to Malacca. This commerce is connived at by the Dutch governor and council among them, who little regard the orders of their fuperiors, provided they can enrich themfelves.

Cambodia, or Camboja, is a country little known to the Europeans; but according to the beft information, its greateft length, from north to fouth, is about 520 Englifh miles; and its greateft breadth, from weft to eaft, about 398 miles. This kingdom has a fpacious river running through it, the banks of which are the only habitable parts of the nation, on account of its fultry air, and the peftiferous gnats, ferpents, and other animals bred in the woods. Its foil, commodities, trade, animals, and products by fea and land, are much the fame with the other kingdoms of this vaft peninfula. The betel, a creeping plant of a particular flavour, and, as they fay, an excellent remedy for all thofe difeafes that are common to the inhabitants of the Eaft-Indies, is the higheft luxury of the Cambodians, from the king to the peafant, but is very unpalatable and difagreeable to the Europeans. The fame barbarous magnificence, defpotifm of their king, and ignorance of the people, prevail here as throughout the reft of the peninfula. Between Cambodia and Cochin-China lies the little kingdom of Chiampa, the inhabitants of which trade with the Chinefe, and feem therefore to be fomewhat more civilized than their neighbours.

Cochin-China, or the weftern China, is fituated under the torrid zone, and extends, according to fome authors, about 500 miles in length; but it is much lefs extenfive in its breadth from eaft to weft. Laos, Cambodia, and Chiampa, as well as fome other fmaller kingdoms, are faid to be tributary to Cochin-China, fome particulars of which I have mentioned in the general view of this peninfula. The manners and religion of the people feem to be originally Chinefe, and they are much given to trade. Their king is faid to be immenfely rich, and his kingdom enjoys all the advantages of commerce that are found in the other parts of the Eaft-Indies; but at the fame time we are told, that this mighty prince, as

well

well as the king of Tonquin, are subject to the Chinese emperor. It is reasonable to suppose, that all those rich countries were peopled from China, or at least, that they had, some time or other, been governed by one head, till the mother empire became so large, that it might be convenient to parcel it out, reserving to itself a kind of feudal superiority over them all.

Tonquin has been already mentioned, and I can add little to what has been said, unless I was to adopt the fictions of the popish missionaries. The government of this kingdom, however, is particular. The Tonquinese had revolted from the Chinese, which was attended by a civil war. A compromise at last took place between the chief of the revolt and the representative of the antient kings, by which the former was to have all the executive powers of the government, under the name of the Chouah; but that the Bua, or real king, should retain the royal titles, and be permitted some inconsiderable civil prerogatives within his palace, from which neither he nor any of his family can stir without the permission of the chouah. This history seems to be of the lama extraction, or at least copied from that worship.

The chouah resides generally in the capital Cachao, which is situated near the center of the kingdom. The bua's palace is a vast structure, and has a fine arsenal. The English have a very flourishing house on the north side of their city, conveniently fitted up with storehouses and office-houses, a noble dining-room, and handsome apartments for the merchants factors, and officers of the company.

The above is the imperfect account I am enabled, without departing from the rules of probability, to give of this vast peninsula. Its rarities, consisting of houses overlaid with gold, and solid idols of the same metal, adorned with an infinite number of precious stones and jewels, are mentioned by many travellers; but it is difficult to give them credit, when we consider the undisciplined weakness of the inhabitants, their superstition, indolence, ignorance, and native timidity; which must render them a prey not only to European adventurers, but to the Tartar conquerors of China. To this we may add, the universally admitted passion of those people for ostentation, and the many discoveries that have been made by candid travellers, of their displaying plated or gilded furniture and ornaments, at which they are wonderfully expert, for those of massy gold.

The possession of rubies, and other precious stones of an extraordinary size, and even of white or party-coloured elephants, convey among those credulous people a pre-eminence

of

of rank and royalty, and has fometimes occafioned bloody
wars. After all, it muft be acknowledged that however dark
the accounts we have of thofe kingdoms may be, yet there is
fufficient evidence to prove that they are immenfely rich in all
the treafures of nature ; but that thofe advantages are attended
with many natural calamities, fuch as floods, volcanos, earthquakes, tempefts, and above all, rapacious and poifonous
animals, which render the poffeffion of life, even for an hour,
precarious and uncertain.

INDIA within the GANGES, or the Empire of the GREAT MOGUL.

SITUATION AND EXTENT; including the peninfula weft of the Ganges.

	Miles.		Degrees.
Length	2000	between	7 and 40 north latitude.
Breadth	1500		66 and 92 eaft longitude.

BOUNDARIES.] THIS empire is bounded by Ufbec
Tartary and Tibet, on the north ;
by Tibet and the Bay of Bengal, on the eaft ; by the Indian
Ocean, on the fouth ; by the fame and Perfia, on the weft.
The main land being the Mogul empire, or Indoftan properly
fo called,

Grand divifions.	Provinces.	Chief towns.
The north-eaft divifion of India, containing the provinces of Bengal, on the mouths of the Ganges, and thofe of the mountains of Naugracut	Bengal Proper	Calcutta Fort William Huegly — } Englifh Dacca — Malda, Eng. and Dutch Chatigan Caffumbazar
	Naugracut — Jefuat — — Patna — — Necbal — — Gore — — Rotas — —	Naugracut Rajapour Patna Necbal Gore Rotas
The north-weft divifion on the frontiers of Perfia, and on the river of Indus	Soret — — Jeffelmere —— Tata, or Sinda Bucknor —— Multan —— Haican — — Cabul — —	Jaganal Jaffelmere Tata Bucknor Multan Haican Cabul

Q 3

The

Grand divisions.	Provinces.	Chief towns.
The middle division	Candish ——	Medipour
	Berar ——	Berar
	Chitor ——	Chitor
	Ratipor ——	Ratipor
	Narvar ——	Narvar
	Gualeor ——	Gualeor
	Agra — —	Agra
	Delly — —	DELLY, E. lon. 79. N. lat. 28.
	Lahor, or Pencah	Lahor
	Hendowns —	Hendowns
	Caffimere ——	Caffimere
	Jengapour ——	Jengapour
	Afmer, or Bando	Afmer.

AIR AND SEASONS.] The winds in this climate generally blow for fix months from the fouth, and fix from the north. April, May, and the beginning of June, are exceffively hot, but refrefhed by fea breezes: and in fome dry feafons, the hurricanes, which tear up the fands and let them fall in dry fhowers, are exceffively difagreeable. The Englifh, and confequently the Europeans in general, who arrive at Indoftan, are commonly feized with fome illnefs, fuch as flux or fever, in their different appearances; but when properly treated, efpecially if the patients are abftemious, they recover, and afterwards prove healthy.

MOUNTAINS.] The moft remarkable mountains are thofe of Caucafus and Naugracut, which divide India from Perfia, Ufbec Tartary, and Tibet, and are inhabited by Marattas, Afghans or Patans, and other people more warlike than the Gentoos. As to the mountains of Balagate, which run almoft the whole length of India from north to fouth, they are fo high that they ftop the weftern monfoon, the rains beginning fooner on the Malabar coaft than they do on the coaft of Coromandel.

RIVERS.] Thefe are the Indus and the Ganges, both of them known to the antients, and held in the higheft efteem, and even veneration, by the modern inhabitants. Befides thofe rivers, many others water this country.

SEAS, BAYS AND CAPES.] Thefe are the Indian ocean; the bay of Bengal; the gulph of Cambaya; the ftraits of Ramanakoel; cape Comorin and Diu.

INHABITANTS.] I have already made a general review of this great empire, and I have only to add to what I have faid of their religion and fects, that the fakirs are a kind of Mahometan mendicants or beggars, who travel about practifing the greateft aufterities, but many of them are impoftors. Their number is faid to be 800,000. Another fet of mendicants are
the

the joghis, who are idolaters, and are suppofed to be twelve millions in number, but all of them vagabonds, and lazy impoftors, who live by amufing the credulous Gentoos with foolifh fictions. The Banians, who are fo called from their affected innocence of life, ferve as brokers, and profefs the Gentoo religion, or fomewhat like it.

The Perfees, or Parfes, of Indoftan, are originally the Gaurs, defcribed in Perfia, but are a moft induftrious people, particularly in weaving, and architecture of every kind. They pretend to be poffeffed of the works of Zoroafter, whom they call by various names, and which fome Europeans think contain many particulars that would throw lights upon the antient hiftory both facred and profane. This opinion is countenanced by the few parcels of thofe books that have been publifhed; but fome are of opinion that the whole is a modern impofture, founded upon facred, traditional, and profane hiftories and religions.

The nobility and people of rank delight in hunting with the bow as well as the gun, and often train the leopards to the fports of the field. They affect fhady walks and cool fountains, like other people in hot countries. They are fond of tumblers, mountebanks, and jugglers; of barbarous mufic, both in wind and ftring inftruments, and play at cards in their private parties. Their houfes make no appearance, and thofe of the commonalty are poor and mean, and generally thatched, which renders them fubject to fire; but the manufacturers chufe to work in the open air; and the infides of houfes belonging to principal perfons are commonly neat, commodious, and pleafant, nay many of them magnificent.

COMMERCE OF INDOSTAN.] I have already mentioned this article, as well as the manufactures of India; but the Mahometan merchants here carry on a trade that has not been defcribed, I mean that with Mecca, in Arabia, from the weftern parts of this empire, up the Red-Sea. This trade is carried on in a particular fpecies of veffels called junks, the largeft of which, we are told, befides the cargoes, will carry 1700 Mahometan pilgrims to vifit the tomb of their prophet. At Mecca they meet with Abyffinian, Egyptian, and other traders, to whom they difpofe of their cargoes for gold and filver; fo that a Mahometan junk returning from this voyage is often worth 200,000 l.

PROVINCES, CITIES, AND OTHER ⎫ Thefe are pretty
BUILDINGS, PUBLIC AND PRIVATE. ⎰ uncertain, efpecially fince the late revolutions of the empire.

Guzarat is a maritime province on the gulph of Cambaya, and one of the fineft in India, but inhabited by a fierce rapa-

Q 4   cious

cious people. It is said to contain 35 cities. Amed-Abad is the capital of the province, where there is an English factory, and is said, in wealth, to vie with the richest towns in Europe. About 43 French leagues distant lies Surat, where the English have a flourishing factory. It was taken by them in the late war, but it is uncertain whether it is still in their possession.

The province of Agra is the largest in all Indostan, containing 40 large towns and 340 villages. Agra is the greatest city, and its castle the largest fortification in all the Indies. The Dutch have a factory there, but the English have none.

The city of Dehli, which is the capital of that province, is likewise the capital of Indostan. It is described as being a fine city, and containing the imperial palace, which is adorned with the usual magnificence of the East. Its stables formerly contained 12,000 horses, brought from Arabia, Persia, and Tartary; and 500 elephants. When the forage is burnt up by the heats of the season, as is often the case, these horses are said to be fed in the morning with bread, butter, and sugar, and in the evening with rice-milk properly prepared.

Tatta, the capital of Sinda, is a large city; and it is said that a plague which happened in 1699 carried off above 80,000 of its manufacturers in silk and cotton. It is still famous for the manufacture of palanquins, which are a kind of canopied couches, on which the great men all over India, Europeans as well as natives, repose when they appear abroad. They are carried by four men, who will trot along, morning and evening, 40 miles a day; 10 being usually hired, who carry the palanquin by turns, four at a time. Though a palanquin is dear at first cost, yet the porters may be hired for nine or ten shillings a month each, out of which they maintain themselves. The Indus, at Tatta, is about a mile broad, and famous for its fine carp.

Though the province of Multan is not very fruitful, yet it yields excellent iron and canes; and the inhabitants, by their situation, are enabled to deal with the Persians and Tartars yearly for above 60,000 horses.

The province of Caffimere, being surrounded with mountains, is difficult of access, but when entered, it appears to be the paradise of the Indies. It is said to contain 100,000 villages, to be stored with cattle and game, without any beasts of prey. The capital (Caffimere) stands by a large lake; and both sexes, the women especially, are almost as fair as the Europeans, and are said to be witty, dexterous, and ingenious.

The province and city of Lahor formerly made a great figure in the Indian history, and is still one of the largeft and fineft provinces in the Indies, producing the beft fugars of any in Indoftan. Its capital was once about nine miles long, but is now much decayed. We know little of the provinces of Ayud, Varad, Bekar, and Hallabas, that is not in common with the other provinces of Indoftan, excepting that they are inhabited by a hardy race of men, who feem never to have been conquered, and though they fubmit to the moguls, live in an eafy, independent ftate. In fome of thofe provinces many of the European fruits, plants, and flowers, thrive as in their native foil.

Bengal, of all the Indian provinces, is perhaps the moft interefting to an Englifh reader. It is efteemed to be the ftorehoufe of the Eaft-Indies. Its fertility exceeds that of Egypt after being overflowed by the Nile; and the produce of its foil confifts of rice, fugar-canes, corn, fefamum, fmall mulberry, and other trees. Its callicoes, filks, falt-petre, lakka, opium, wax, and civet, go all over the world; and provifions here are in vaft plenty, and incredibly cheap, efpecially pullets, ducks, and geefe. The country is interfeded by canals cut out of the Ganges for the benefit of commerce; and extends near 100 leagues on both fides the Ganges, being full of cities, towns, villages and caftles.

In Bengal, the worfhip of the Gentoos is praftifed in its greateft purity; and their facred river (Ganges) is in a manner lined with their magnificent pagods or temples. The women, notwithftanding their religion, are faid by fome to be lafcivious and enticing.

The principal Englifh faftory in Bengal is at Calcutta, and is called Fort William; it is fituated on the river Hughly, the moft wefterly branch of the Ganges. The fort itfelf is faid to be irregular, and untenable againft difciplined troops; but the fervants of the company have provided themfelves with an excellent houfe, and moft convenient apartments for their own accommodation. As the town itfelf may be now faid to be in poffeffion of the company, an Englifh civil government, by a mayor and aldermen, has been introduced into it. It does not, however, feem to give general fatisfaction, on account of the vaft influence which the company has always over the magiftrates, and many complaints from private perfons have lately reached England.

In 1756, the Indian nabob, or viceroy, quarrelled with the company, and invefted Calcutta with a large body of black troops. The governor, and fome of the principal perfons of the place, threw themfelves, with their chief effects, on board the ships in the river ; they who remained, for some hours, bravely defended the place ; but their ammunition being expended, they surrendered upon terms. The soubah, a capricious, unfeeling tyrant, instead of observing the capitulation, forced Mr. Holwell, the governor's chief servant, and 145 British subjects, into a little but secure prison, called the Black-hole, a place about eighteen feet square, and shut up from almost all communication of free air. Their miseries during the night were inexpressible, and before morning no more than twenty-three were found alive, the rest dying of suffocation, which was generally attended with a horrible phrensy. Among those saved was Mr. Holwell himself, who has written a most affecting account of the catastrophe. The insensible tyrant returned to his capital, after plundering the place, imagining he had routed the English out of his dominions ; but the seasonable arrival of admiral Watson and colonel (now lord) Clive, put them once more, with some difficulty, in possession of the place ; and the war was concluded by the glorious battle of Plassey, gained by the colonel, and the death of the tyrant Suraja Dowla, in whose place Mhir Jaffeir was advanced to the soubahship.

The capital of Bengal, where the nabob keeps his court, is Patna or Maksudabad ; and Bannares, lying in the same province, is the Gentoo university, and celebrated for its sanctity.

Chandenagore, is the principal place possessed by the French in Bengal : it lies higher up the river than Calcutta. But though strongly fortified, furnished with a garrison of 500 Europeans, and 1200 Indians, and defended by 123 pieces of cannon and three mortars, it was taken in the late war by the English admirals Watson and Pocock, and colonel Clive. Hugley, which lies fifty miles to the north of Calcutta, upon the Ganges, is a place of prodigious trade for the richest of all Indian commodities. The Dutch have here a well fortified factory. The search for diamonds is carried on by about 10,000 people from Saumelpour, which lies thirty leagues to the north of Hugley, for about fifty miles farther. Dakka is said to be the largest city of Bengal, and the tide comes up to its walls. It contains an English and a Dutch factory. The other chief towns are Cassumbazar, Chinchura, Barnagur, and Maldo ; besides a number of other places of less note, but all of them rich in the Indian manufactures.

We know little concerning the province of Malva, which lies to the west of Bengal, but that it is as fertile as the other provinces, and that its chief city is Ratispor. The province of Kandish includes that of Berar and part of Orixa, and its capital is Brampur, so that it is of prodigious extent, and carries

carries on a vaſt trade in chintzes, callicoes, and embroidered
ſtuffs.

The above are the provinces belonging to the mogul's empire to the north of what is properly called the peninſula within
the Ganges. Thoſe that lie to the ſouthward fall into the
deſcription of the peninſula itſelf.

HISTORY.] It is not at all to the credit of our Eaſt-India
company's ſervants, that notwithſtanding their long reſidence
in Indoſtan, they differ in their accounts of the revolutions
of that country. All we know for certain is, that Tamerlane
made a deep impreſſion upon this country, and that the preſent emperor pretends to reign in his right. The hiſtory of
his immediate deſcendents has been variouſly repreſented, but
all agree in the main that they were magnificent and deſpotic
princes, that they committed their provinces, as has been already obſerved, to rapacious governors, or to their own ſons,
by which their empire was often miſerably torn in pieces. At
length, towards the middle of the laſt century, the famous
Aurengzebe, in the year 1667, though the youngeſt among
many ſons of the reigning emperor, after defeating or murdering all his brethren, mounted the throne of Indoſtan, and
may be conſidered as the real founder and legiſlator of the
empire. He was a great and a politic prince, and the firſt
who extended his dominion, though it was little better than
nominal, over the peninſula within the Ganges, which is
at preſent ſo well known to the Engliſh. He lived ſo late as
the year 1707, and it is ſaid that ſome of his great officers of
ſtate were alive in the year 1750. From what has been
already ſaid of this empire, Aurengzebe ſeems to have left too
much power to the governors of his diſtant provinces, and to
have been at no pains in preventing the effects of that dreadful
deſpotiſm, which while in his hands preſerved the tranquillity
of his empire, but when it deſcended to his weak indolent
ſucceſſors, occaſioned its overthrow.

In 1713, four of his grandſons diſputed the empire, which,
after a bloody ſtruggle, fell to the eldeſt, Mauzo'din, who
took the name of Jehandar Shah. This prince was a ſlave
to his pleaſures, and was governed by his miſtreſs ſo abſolutely,
that his great omrahs conſpired againſt him, and raiſed to the
throne one of his nephews, who ſtruck off his uncle's head.
The new emperor, whoſe name was Furrukhſir, was governed
and at laſt enſlaved by two brothers of the name of Seyd, who
abuſed his power ſo groſsly, that being afraid to puniſh them
publicly, he ordered them both to be privately aſſaſſinated.
They diſcovered his intention, and dethroned the emperor,
in whoſe place they raiſed a grandſon of Aurengzebe, by his
daughter,

daughter, a youth of seventeen years of age, after imprisoning and strangling Furrukhsir. The young emperor proved disagreeable to the brothers, and being soon poisoned, they raised to the throne his elder brother, who took the title of Shah Jehan. The rajahs of Indostan, whose ancestors had entered into stipulations, or what may be called *pacta·conventa*, when they admitted the Mogul family, took the field against the two brothers, but the latter were victorious, and Shah Jehan was put in tranquil possession of the empire, but died in 1719. He was succeeded by another prince of the Mogul race, who took the name of Mohammed Shah, and entered into private measures with his great rajahs for destroying the Seyds, who were declared enemies to Nizam al Muluck, one of Aurengzebe's favourite generals. Nizam, it is said, was privately encouraged by the emperor to declare himself against the brothers, and to proclaim himself soubah of Decan, which belonged to one of the Seyds, who was assassinated by the emperor's order, who immediately advanced to Delhi to destroy the other brother; but he no sooner understood what had happened, than he proclaimed the sultan Ibrahim, another of the Mogul princes, emperor. A battle ensued in 1720, in which the emperor was victorious, and is said to have used his conquest with great moderation, for he remitted Ibrahim to the prison from whence he had been taken; and Seyd, being likewise a prisoner, was condemned to perpetual confinement, but the emperor took possession of his vast riches. Seyd did not long survive his confinement; and upon his death, the emperor abandoned himself to the same course of pleasures that had been so fatal to his predecessors. As to Nizam, he became now the great imperial general, and was often employed against the Marattas, whom he defeated, when they had almost made themselves masters of Agra and Dehli. He was confirmed in his soubahship, and was considered as the first subject in the empire. Authors, however, are divided as to his motives for inviting Nadir Shah, otherwise Kouli Khan, the Persian monarch, to invade Indostan. It is thought that he had intelligence of a strong party formed against him at court; but the truth perhaps is, that Nizam did not think that Nadir Shah could have success, and at first wanted to make himself useful by opposing him. The success of Nadir Shah is well known, and the immense treasure which he carried from Indostan in 1739. Besides those treasures, he obliged the Mogul to surrender to him all the lands to the west of the rivers Attock and Synd, comprehending the provinces of Peyshor, Kabul, and Gagna, with many other

rich

rich and populous principalities, the whole of them almoſt equal in value to the crown of Perſia itſelf.

This invaſion coſt the Gentoos 200,000 lives. As to the plunder made by Nadir Shah, ſome accounts, and thoſe too ſtrongly authenticated, make it amount to the incredible ſum of two hundred and thirty-one millions ſterling,' as mentioned by the London Gazette of thoſe times. The moſt moderate ſay that Nadir's own ſhare amounted to conſiderably above ſeventy millions. Be that as it will, the invaſion of Nadir Shah may be conſidered as putting a period to the greatneſs of the Mogul empire in the houſe of Tamerlane. The hiſtory of it, ſince that time, is leſs known than that of Tamerlane itſelf. According to the beſt accounts, upon the retreat of Nadir Shah, who left the emperor in poſſeſſion of his dignity, the Patans invaded his dominions; and ſo treacherous were the emperor's generals and miniſtry, that none of them would head an army againſt them, till the emperor's ſon, a youth of eighteen years of age, bravely undertook the command, puniſh- ed the conſpiracy that had been formed againſt his father, and completely defeated the invaders. During this campaign, the emperor was ſtrangled by his vizier: but by a courſe of well- acted diſſimulation, the young emperor, who was called Amet Shah, found means to put the conſpirators to death, but ſoon after was driven from his throne by a freſh invaſion of the Patans and Marattas. Some pretend that one Allum Geer was firſt proclaimed emperor, and then murdered by the ſame vizier, who raiſed another prince to the throne. Whether this Allum Geer is the ſame with Amet Shah is uncertain, as are the intermediate revolutions that followed. At preſent, the imperial dignity of Indoſtan is veſted in Shah Zadah, who is univerſally acknowledged to be the true heir of the Tamerlane race; but his power is feeble, and he depends upon the pro- tection of the Engliſh, whoſe intereſt it is to ſupport him, as his authority is the beſt legal guarantee.

As to the government and conſtitution of Indoſtan, we muſt refer to what we have already obſerved. The emperor of Indoſtan, or great Mogul (ſo called from being deſcended from Tamerlane the Mongul or Mogul Tartar) on his ad- vancement to the throne, aſſumes ſome grand title; as, *The Conqueror of the World*; *the Ornament of the Throne, &c.* but he is never crowned.

The PENINSULA within the GANGES.

Grand divisions.	Provinces.	Chief towns.
The south-east coast of India, situate on the bay of Bengal, usually called the coast of Coromandel	Madura ——	Madura
	Tanjour ——	Tanjour
	Eaft fide of Bif-nagar, or Car-nate ——	Trincombar, Danes Negapatan, Dutch Bifnagar Portanova, Dutch Fort St. David, Englifh Pondicherry, } French Conymere, } Coblon Sadrafapatan, Dutch St. Thomas, Portuguefe Fort St. George, or Madrafs, E. lon. 80-32. N. lat. 13-11. Englifh. Pellicate, Dutch
	Golconda ——	Golconda Gani, or Coulor, diamond mines Muffulapatan, Englifh and Dutch Vizacapatan, Englifh Bimlipatan, Dutch
	Orixa ——	Orixa Ballafore, Englifh
The south-west coast of India, usually called the coast of Malabar	Weft fide of Bef-nagar, or Car-nate ——	Tegapatan, Dutch Angengo, Englifh Cochin, Dutch Callicut, } Englifh Tillicherry, } Canannore, Dutch Monguelore, } Dutch and Baffilore } Portuguefe Raalconda, diamond mines.
	Decan, or Vifia-pour ——	Cawar, Englifh Goa, Portuguefe Rajapore, French Dabal, Englifh Dundee, } Portuguefe Shoule, } Bombay, ifle and town, Eng-lifh, 19-18 N. lat. 73-6 E. lon. Baffaim, } Portuguefe Salfette, }

Grand divifions.	Provinces.	Chief towns.
The fouth-weft coaft of India, ufually called the coaft of Malabar	Cambaya, or Guzarat	Damon, Portuguefe Surat, E. lon. 72-25. N. lat. 21-10 Swalley Barak, Englifh and Dutch Amedabat Cambaya Dieu, Portuguefe.

CLIMATE, SEASONS, AND PRODUCE.] The chain of mountains already mentioned, running from north to fouth, renders it winter on one fide of this peninfula, while it is fummer on the other. About the end of June, a fouth-weft wind begins to blow from the fea, on the coaft of Malabar, which, with continual rains, laft four months, during which time all is ferene upon the coaft of Coromandel (the weftern and eaftern coafts being fo denominated.) Towards the end of October, the rainy feafon, and the change of the monfoon begins on the Coromandel coaft, which being deftitute of good harbours, renders it extremely dangerous for fhips to remain there, during that time, and to this is owing the periodical returns of the Englifh fhipping to Bombay, upon the Malabar coaft. The air is naturally hot in this peninfula, but is refrefhed by breezes, the wind altering every twelve hours; that is, from midnight to noon it blows off the land, when it is intolerably hot, and during the other twelve hours from the fea, which laft proves a great refrefhment to the inhabitants of the coaft. The produce of the foil is the fame with that of the other part of the Eaft-Indies. The like may be faid of their quadrupeds, fifh, fowl, and noxious creatures and infects.

INHABITANTS.] The inhabitants of this part are more black in complexion, than thofe of the other peninfula of India, though lying nearer to the equator, which makes fome fufpect them to be the defcendents of an ancient colony from Ethiopia. The greateft part of them have but a faint notion at prefent, of any allegiance they owe to the emperor of Indoftan, whofe tribute from thence has been ever fince the invafion of Shah Nadir, intercepted by their foubahs and nabobs, who now exercife an independent power in the government, though even Suraja Dowla was glad to receive a deputation from the emperor, now reigning, or his father; but befides thofe foubahs, and other imperial viceroys, many eftates in this peninfula belong to rajahs or lords, who are the defcendents of their old princes, and look upon themfelves as being independent on the mogul, and his authority.

PROVINCES, CITIES, AND OTHER BUILD- } From what
   INGS, PUBLIC AND PRIVATE. } has been said
above, this peninsula is rather to be divided into great governments, or foubahships, than into provinces. One foubah
often engroffes feveral provinces, and fixes the feat of his government, according to his own conveniency. I fhall fpeak of
thofe provinces, as belonging to the Malabar or Coromandel
coaft, the two great objects of Englifh commerce in that country; and firft, of the eaftern, or Coromandel coaft.

Madura begins at Cape Comorin, the fouthermoft point of
the peninfula. It is about the bignefs of the kingdom of
Portugal, and is faid to be governed by a fovereign king, who
has under him feventy tributary princes, each of them independent in his own dominions, but paying him a tax. The
chief value of this kingdom feems to confift of a pearl fifhery
upon its coaft. Tanjour is a little kingdom, lying to the
eaft of Madura. The foil is fertile, and its prince, rich.
Within it lies the Danifh Eaft-India settlement of Tranquebar,
and the Dutch fortrefs of Negapatan, and the capital city is
Tanjour.

The Carnatic, as it is now called, is well known to the
Englifh. It is bounded on the eaft by the bay of Bengal, on
the north by the river Chriftina, which divides it from Golkonda; on the weft by Vifapur, or Vifiapur, and, on the
fouth, by the kingdoms of Meffaur and Tanjour; being in
length, from fouth to north, about 345 miles, and 276 in
breadth from eaft to weft. The capital of the Carnatic is
Bifnagar, and the country in general is efteemed healthful,
fertile, and populous. Within this country, upon the Coromandel coaft, lies fort St. David's, belonging to the Englifh,
with a diftrict round it. The fort is ftrong, and of great importance to our trade. Five leagues to the north, lies Pondicherry, once the emporium of the French in the Eaft-Indies,
but now demolifhed by the Englifh, who took it in the late
war. It was reftored by the peace of Fontainbleau, in 1763.

Fort St. George, better known by the name of Madrafs,
is the capital of the Englifh Eaft-India company's dominions
in the Eaft-Indies, and is diftant eaftward from London, about
4800 miles. Great complaints have been made of the fituation of this fort. No pains have been fpared by the company,
in rendering it impregnable to any force that can be brought
againft it by the natives. It protects two towns, called, from
the complexions of their feveral inhabitants, the White and
the Black. The White Town is fortified, and contains an
Englifh corporation of a mayor and aldermen. Nothing has
been omitted to mend the natural badnefs of its fituation,
which

which feems originally to be owing to the neighbourhood of the diamond mines, which are but a week's journey diftant. Thofe mines are under the tuition of a mogul officer, who lets them out by admeafurement, and enclofing the contents by pallifadoes, all diamonds above a certain weight belong to the emperor. The diftrict belonging to Madrafs, is of little value for its product, and muft import its own provifions. 80,000 inhabitants of various nations, are faid to be dependent upon Madrafs; but its fafety confifts in the fuperiority of the Englifh by fea. It carries on a confiderable trade with China, Perfia, and Mocha.

The reader needs not be informed of the immenfe fortunes acquired by the Englifh, upon this coaft, within thefe twenty years. The governor of Madrafs has a council to affift him, and when he goes abroad, appears in vaft fplendor. The differences that now rage among the directors and proprietors of the company in England, prevent my faying any thing concerning the police of this government. The company has received all the encouragement and affiftance the Englifh parliament can give them, even to the introducing of martial law into their poffeffions. There feems, however, to be fome fundamental errors in their conftitution. The directors confider the riches acquired by their governors and other fervants, as being plundered from the company, and of late they have fent out fuperintendents to controul their governors and overgrown fervants, but with what fuccefs time muft demonftrate. As this is a fubject of the greateft importance, that ever perhaps occurred in the geography of a commercial country, the reader will indulge me in one or two reflections, as I am not to refume the fubject.

The Englifh Eaft-India company, through the diftractions of the Mogul empire, the fupport of our government, and the undaunted but fortunate fuccefles of their military officers, have acquired fo amazing a property in this peninfula, and in Indoftan, that it is fuperior to the revenues of many crowned heads, and fome of their own fervants pretend, that when all their expences are paid, their clear revenue amounts to near two millions fterling, out of which they are to pay 400,000 l. annually, to the government, while they are fuffered to enjoy their revenues. How that revenue is collected, or from whence it arifes, is beft known to the company, part of it however has been granted in property, and part of it is fecured on mortgages, for difcharging their expences in fupporting the interefts of their friends, the emperor, and the refpective foubahs and nabobs they have affifted.

Be that as it may, this company exercises at present many rights appropriated to sovereignty, such as those of holding forts, coining money, and the like. Those powers are undoubtedly incompatible with the principles of a commercial limited company, and it became the dignity of the English government, to send out an officer of their own, (as they have done in the person of Sir John Lindsay) to take such measures with the Eastern princes and potentates, as may render the acquisitions of the company permanent and national.

Without entering into any disputes agitated of late between the directors and the government, the possibility of such a permanency and even extending our influence in India, is pretty evident. From what has been already said, the Gentoos are entirely passive in all the revolutions of their government. The Moors, or Mahometans, ignorant and treacherous as they are, appear to have no violent attachments to any religious principle, and are abject enough to live under any form of government, that their emperor shall prescribe; nor are they at present, when the English are his friends, in any condition to dispute their joint wills. These considerations manifest the wisdom of not driving them into desperate measures, and thereby effecting a union of their forces, which must prove fatal to the British interest there; and in any event must render it precarious, unless supported in the name, and by the authority of the British empire.

Polikar, lying to the north of Madrass, belongs to the Dutch. We know little of the kingdom and capital of Ikkari. The celebrated Heyder Ally, with whom the company has lately made a peace, is said to be a native of the kingdom of Mesur, which lies to the south-west of the Carnatic; and the Christians of the apostle St. Thomas, live at the foot of the mountains Gatti, that separate Messar from Malabar. I have already mentioned the kingdom of Golkonda, which besides its diamonds, is famous for the cheapness of its provisions, and for making white wine of grapes that are ripe in January. Golkonda is said to be subject to a prince, who, though tributary to the Mogul, is immensely rich, and can raise 100,000 men. The capital of his dominions is called Bagnagar, but the kingdom takes its name from the city of Golkonda. East-south-east of Golkonda, lies Masulipatan, where the English and Dutch have factories. The English have also factories at Ganjam, and Vizigapatam, on this coast; and the Dutch at Narsipore. The province of Orixa, from whence the English company draw great part of their revenues, lies to the north of Golkonda, extending in length

2   from

from east to west, about 550 miles, and in breadth about 240. It is governed likewife by a tributary prince. In this province stands the idolatry temple of Jagaryunt, which they fay is attended by 500 priests. The idol is an irregular pyramidal black stone, of about 4 or 500 weight, with two rich diamonds near the top, to reprefent eyes, and the nofe and mouth painted with vermillion.

The country of Dekan comprehends feveral large provinces, and fome kingdoms, particularly thofe of Baglana, Balagate, Telenga, and the kingdom of Vifiapur. The truth is, the names, dependencies, and governments of thofe provinces, are extremely unfettled; they having been reduced by Aurengzebe, or his father, and fubject to almost annual revolutions and alterations. Modern geographers are not agreed upon their fituation and extent, but we are told, that the principal towns are Aureng-abad, and Dolt-abad, or Dowlet-abad; and that the latter is the strongest place in all Indostan. Near it lies the famous pagods of Elora, in a plain about two leagues fquare. The tombs, chapels, temples, pillars, and many thoufand figures that furround it, are faid to be cut out of the natural rock, and to furpafs all the other efforts of human art. Telenga lies on the east of Golkonda, and its capital Beder, contains a garrifon of 3000 men. The inhabitants of this province fpeak a language peculiar to themfelves.

Baglana lies to the west of Telenga, and forms the smallest province of the empire; its capital is Mouler. The Portugueze territory begins here at the port of Daman, twenty-one leagues fouth of Surat, and extends almost twenty leagues to the north of Goa.

Vifiapur is a large kingdom tributary to the Mogul, but its particular extent is uncertain. The western part is called Konkan, which is intermingled with the Portugueze poffeffions. The king of Vifiapur is faid to have a yearly revenue of fix millions sterling, and to bring to the field 150,000 foldiers. His capital is of the fame name, and his country very fruitful. The principal places on this coast are, Daman, Baffaim Trapor, or Tarapor, Chawl, Dandi-Rajahpur, Dabul-Rajupur, Ghiria; and Vingurla. The Portugueze have loft feveral valuable poffeffions on this coast, and thofe which remain are on the decline.

Among the iflands lying upon the fame coast is that of Bombay, belonging to the English East-India company. Its harbour can conveniently hold 1000 fhips at anchor. The ifland itfelf is about feven miles in length, and twenty in circumference, but its fituation and harbour are its chief re-

R 2

commendations,

commendations, being deftitute of almoft all the conveniencies
of life. The town is about a mile long, and poorly built,
and the climate was fatal to Englifh conftitutions, till experience, caution and temperance, taught them prefervatives
againft its unwholefomenefs. The beft water there is preferved
in tanks, which receive it in the rainy feafons. The fort is a
regular quadrangle, and well built of ftone. Many black
merchants refide here. This ifland was part of the portion
paid with the infanta of Portugal, to Charles II. who gave
it to the Eaft-India company, and the ifland is ftill divided
into three Roman-catholic parifhes, inhabited by Portugueze,
and what are called popifh Meftizos and Canarins, the former
being a mixed breed of the natives and Portugueze, and the
other the aborigines of the country. The Englifh have fallen
upon methods to render this ifland and town, under all their
difadvantages, a fafe, if not an agreeable refidence. The
reader need fcarcely be informed, that the governor and council
of Bombay, have lucrative pofts as well as the officers under
them. The troops on the ifland, are commanded by Englifh
officers, and the natives, when formed into regular companies,
and difciplined, are here, and all over the Eaft-Indies, called
Seapoys. The inhabitants of the ifland amount to near 60,000
of different nations ; each of whom enjoys the practice of his
religion unmolefted.

Near Bombay are feveral other iflands, one of which, called
Elephanta, contains the moft inexplicable antiquity, perhaps
in the world. A figure of an elephant of the natural fize
cut coarfely in ftone, prefents itfelf on the landing place,
near the bottom of a mountain. An eafy flope then leads to
a ftupendous temple, hewn out of the folid rock, eighty or
ninety feet long, and forty broad. The roof, which is cut
flat, is fupported by regular rows of pillars, about ten feet
high, with capitals, refembling round cufhions, as if preffed
by the weight of the incumbent mountain. At the farther
end, are three gigantic figures, which have been multiplied
by the blind zeal of the Portugueze. Befides the temple,
are various images, and groupes on each hand cut in the
ftone ; one of the latter bearing a rude refemblance of the
judgment of Solomon ; befides a colonnade, with a door of
regular architecture ; but the whole bears no manner of refemblance to any of the Gentoo works.

The ifland and city of Goa, the capital of the Portugueze
fettlements in the Eaft-Indies, lies about thirty miles fouth
of Vingurla. The ifland is about twenty-feven miles in compafs. It has one of the fineft and beft fortified ports in the
Indies. This was formerly a moft fuperb fettlement, and

was

was furpaffed either in bulk or beauty by few of the European cities. It is faid that the revenues of the Jefuits upon this ifland, equalled thofe of the crown of Portugal. Goa, as well as the reft of the Portugueze poffeffions on this coaft, are under a viceroy, who ftill keeps up the remains of the antient fplendor of the government. The rich peninfula of Salzete, is dependant on Goa. Sunda lies fouth of the Portugueze territories, and is governed by a rajah, tributary to the mogul. The Englifh factory of Corwar, is one of the moft pleafant and healthful of any upon the Malabar coaft. Kanora lies about forty miles to the fouth of Goa, and reaches to Calicut. Its foil is famous for producing rice, that fupplies many parts of Europe, and fome of the Indies. The Kanorines are faid generally to be governed by a lady, whofe fon has the title of rajah, and her fubjects are accounted the braveft and moft civilized of any in that peninfula, and remarkably given to commerce.

Though Malabar gives name to the whole fouth-weft coaft of the peninfula, yet it is confined at prefent to the country fo called, lying on the weft of cape Comorin, and called the Dominions of the Samorin. The Malabar language, however, is common in the Carnatic, and the country itfelf is rich and fertile, but peftered with green adders, whofe poifon is incurable. It was formerly a large kingdom of itfelf. The moft remarkable places in Malabar are Kannamore, containing a Dutch factory and fort; Tillicheri, where the Englifh have a fmall fettlement, keeping a conftant garrifon of thirty or forty foldiers. Calicut, where the French and Portugueze have fmall factories, befides various other diftinct territories and cities. Cape Comorin, which is the foutthermoft part of this peninfula, though not above three leagues in extent, is famous for uniting in the fame garden, the two feafons of the year ; the trees being loaded with bloffoms and fruit on the one fide, while on the other fide they are ftripped of all their leaves. This furprizing phenomenon is owing to the ridge of mountains fo often mentioned, which traverfe the whole peninfula from fouth to north. On the oppofite fides of the Cape, the winds are conftantly at variance ; blowing from the weft on the weft fide, and from the eaft on the eaftern fide.

Before I take my leave of India, it may be proper to obferve, that in the little diftrict of Cochin within Malabar, are to be found fome thoufands of Jews, who pretend to be of the tribe of Manaffeh, and to have records engraved on copper plates in Hebrew characters. They are faid to be fo poor, that many of them embrace the Gentoo religion. The like dif-

coveries

coveries of the Jews and their records have been made in China, and other places of Afia, which have occafioned various fpeculations among the learned.

P E R S I A.

SITUATION AND EXTENT.

Miles.		Degrees.
Length 1300	} between {	44 and 70 eaft longitude.
Breadth 1100		25 and 44 north latitude.

BOUNDARIES.] MODERN Perfia is bounded by the mountains of Ararat, or Daghiftan, which divide it from Circaffian Tartary, on the north-weft; by the Cafpian fea, which divides it from Ruffia, on the north; by the river Oxus, which divides it from Ufbec Tartary, on the north-eaft; by India on the eaft, and by the Indian ocean, and the gulphs of Perfia and Ormus, on the fouth; and by Arabia and Turkey on the weft.

Modern Perfia comprehends the ancient Hyrcania, Bactria, Sufiana, Parthia, Media, and part of Affyria, Iberia, and Colchis. The modern divifions of Perfia are extremely uncertain, and of little importance to the reader.

NAME.] Perfia, according to the poets, derived its name from Perfius, the fon of Jupiter and Danae. Lefs fabulous authors, fuppofe it derived from Paras, which fignifies a horfeman, the Perfians or Parthians, being always celebrated for their fkill in horfemanfhip.

AIR.] In fo extenfive an empire this is very different. Thofe parts which border upon Caucafus and Daghiftan, and the mountains near the Cafpian fea, are cold, as lying in the neighbourhood of thofe mountains which are commonly covered with fnow. The air in the midland provinces of Perfia is ferene, pure, and exhilarating, but in the fouthern provinces it is hot, and fometimes communicates noxious blafts to the midland parts, which are fo often mortal, that the inhabitants fortify their heads with very thick turbans.

SOIL AND PRODUCTIONS.] Thofe vary like the air. The foil is far from being luxuriant towards Tartary, and the Cafpian fea, but with cultivation it might produce abundance of corn and fruits. South of mount Taurus, the fertility of the country in corn, fruits, wine, and the other luxuries of life, are equalled by few countries. It produces wine and oil in plenty, fenna, rhubarb, and the fineft of drugs. The fruits are

are delicious, especially their dates, oranges, pistachio-nuts, melons, cucumbers, and garden stuff, not to mention vast quantities of excellent silk; and the gulph of Bastora, formerly furnished great part of Europe and Asia with very fine pearls. Some parts near Ispahan especially produce almost all the flowers that are valued in Europe; and from some of them, the roses especially, they extract waters of a salubrious and odorific kind, which form a gainful commodity in trade. In short, the fruits, vegetables, and flowers of Persia, are of a most exalted flavour; and had the natives the art of horticulture, to as great perfection as some nations in Europe, by transplanting, engrafting, and other meliorations, they would add greatly to the natural riches of the country. The Persian assa foetida flows from a plant called Hiltot, and turns into a gum. Some of it is white, and some black; but the former is so much valued, that the natives make very rich sauces of it, and sometimes eat it as a rarity.

MOUNTAINS.] These are Caucasus and Ararat, which are called the mountains of Daghistan; and the vast collection of mountains called Taurus, and their divisions run through the middle of the country from Natolia to India.

RIVERS.] It has been observed, that no country, of so great an extent, has so few navigable rivers as Persia. The most considerable are those of the Kur, anciently Cyrus; and Aras, anciently Araxes, which rise in or near the mountains of Ararat, and joining their streams, fall into the Caspian sea. Some small rivulets falling from the mountains, water the country, but their streams are so inconsiderable, that few or none of them can be navigated even by boats. The Oxus can scarcely be called a Persian river, though it divides Persia from Uibec Tartary. Persia has the river Indus on the east, and the Euphrates and Tigris on the west.

WATER.] The scarcity of rivers in Persia, is joined to a scarcity of water; but the defect, where it prevails, is admirably well supplied by means of reservoirs, aqueducts, canals, and other ingenious methods.

METALS AND MINERALS.] Persia contains mines of iron, copper, lead, and above all, turquoise stones, which are found in Chorasan. Sulphur, salt-petre, and antimony, are found in the mountains. Quarries of red, white, and black marble, have been discovered near Tauris, and natural salt in the province of Carkmenia.

POPULATION, INHABITANTS, MANNERS, CUSTOMS, AND DIVERSIONS.] It is impossible to speak with any certainty concerning the population of a country so little known as that of Persia. If we are to judge by by the vaft armies in modern as well as in ancient times, raifed there, the numbers it contains muft be very great. The Perfians of both fexes are generally handfome, the men being fond of Georgian and Circaffian women. Their complexions towards the fouth, are fomewhat fwarthy. The men fhave their heads, but the young men fuffer a lock of hair to grow on each fide, and the beard of their chin to reach up to their temples; but religious people wear long beards. Men of rank and quality wear very magnificent turbans, many of them coft twenty-five pounds, and few under nine or ten. They have a maxim to keep their heads very warm, fo that they never pull off their caps or their turbans out of refpect, even to the king. Their drefs is very fimple. Next to their fkin they wear callico fhirts, over them a veft, which reaches below the knee, girt with a fafh, and over that a loofe garment fomewhat fhorter. The materials of their cloaths, however, are commonly very expenfive, confifting of the richeft furs, filks, muflin, cottons, and the like valuable ftuffs, richly embroidered with gold and filver. They wear a kind of loofe boots on their legs, and flippers on their feet. They are fond of riding, and very expenfive in their equipages. They wear at all times a dagger in their fafh, and linen trowzers. The collars of their fhirts and cloaths are open, fo that their drefs upon the whole is far better adapted for the purpofes both of health and activity, than the long flowing robes of the Turks.

The drefs of the women is not much different; their wear, as well as that of the men, is very coftly, and they are at great pains to heighten their beauty by art, colours, and wafhes.

The Perfians accuftom themfelves to frequent wafhings and ablutions, which are the more neceffary, as they feldom change their linen. In the morning early they drink coffee, about eleven go to dinner, upon fruits, fweetmeats, and milk. Their chief meal is at night, when they fup upon pilau, already defcribed. They are temperate, but ufe opium, though not in fuch abundance as the Turks, nor are they very delicate in their entertainments of eating and drinking. They are great mafters of ceremony towards their fuperiors, and fo polite, that they accommodate Europeans who vifit them with ftools, that they may not be forced to fit crofs-legged. They are fo immoderately fond of tobacco, which they fmoke through a tube fixed in water, fo as to be cool in the mouth, that when it has been prohibited by their princes, they have been known to leave their country, rather than be debarred from that enjoyment. The Perfians are naturally fond of poetry, moral fentences, and hyperbole. Their long wars, and their national revolutions, have mingled
the

the native Perfians with barbarous nations, and are faid to have taught them diffimulation; but they are ftill pleafing and plaufible in their behaviour, and in all ages they have been remarkable for hofpitality.

· The Perfians write like the Hebrews, from the right to the left, and are neat in their feals and materials for writing, and are wonderfully expeditious in the art. The number of people employed on their manufcripts (for no printing is allowed there) is incredible. Their great foible feems to be oftentation in their equipages and dreffes; nor are they lefs jealous of their women than the Turks, and other eaftern nations. They are fond of mufic, and take a pleafure in converfing in large companies; but their chief diverfions are thofe of the field, hunting, hawking, horfemanfhip, and the exercife of arms, in all which they are very dexterous. They excel, as their anceftors the Parthians did, in archery. They are fond of rope-dancers, jugglers, and fighting of wild beafts, and privately play at games of chance.

Men may marry for life, or for any determined time, in Perfia, as well as through all Tartary; and travellers or merchants, who intend to ftay fome time in any city, commonly apply to the cadee, or judge, for a wife during the time he propofes to ftay. The cadee, for a ftated gratuity, produces a number of girls, whom he declares to be honeft, and free from difeafes, and he becomes furety for them. A gentleman who lately attended the Ruffian embaffy to Perfia declares, that amongft thoufands, there has not been one inftance of their difhonefty, during the time agreed upon.

RELIGION.] The Perfians are Mahometans of the fect of Ali, for which reafon the Turks, who follow the fucceffion of Omar and Abu Bekr, call them heretics. Their religion is, if poffible, in fome things more fantaftical and fenfual than that of the Turks, but in many points it is mingled with fome bramin fuperftitions. When they are taxed by the Chriftians with drinking ftrong liquors, as many of them do, they anfwer very fenfibly, " You Chriftians whore and get drunk, though " you know you are committing fins, which is the very cafe " with us." To enumerate their fuperftitions, fafts, and ceremonies, would require a volume, which, when read, could communicate neither inftruction nor entertainment. Having mentioned the bramins, the comparifon between them and the Perfian guebres or gaurs, who pretend to be the difciples and fucceffors of the antient magi, the followers of Zoroafter, may be highly worth a learned difquifition: that both of them held originally pure and fimple ideas of a fupreme Being, may be eafily proved, but the Indian bramins and

parfes

parfes accufe the gaurs, who ftill worfhip the fire, of having fenfualized thofe ideas, and of introducing an evil principle into the government of the world. A combuftible ground, about ten miles diftant from Baku, a city in the north of Perfia, is the fcene of the guebres devotions. It muft be admitted, that this ground is impregnated with very furprifing inflammatory qualities, and contains feveral old little temples, in one of which the guebres pretend to preferve the facred flame of the univerfal fire, which rifes from the end, and a large hollow cane ftuck into the ground, refembling a lamp burning, with very pure fpirits. The Mahometans are the declared enemies of the gaurs, who were banifhed ou of Perfia, by Shah Abbas. Their fect, however, is faid to be numerous, though tolerated in very few places.

The long wars between the Perfians and the Romans, feem early to have driven the antient Chriftians into Perfia, and the neighbouring countries. Even to this day, many fects are found, that evidently have Chriftianity for the ground-work of their religion. Some of them called fouffees, who are a kind of quietifts, facrifice their paffions to God, and profefs the moral duties. The Sabean Chriftians have, in their religion, a mixture of Judaifm and Mahometanifm, and are numerous towards the Perfian Gulph. I have already mentioned the Armenian and Georgian Chriftians, who are very numerous in Perfia.

I have been the more explicit on the head of religion, as the prefent race of Perfians are faid to be very cool in the doctrines of Mahomet, owing chiefly to their ignorance of all religion, and their late wars with the Turks. It has therefore been thought by fome writers, that great advantages, in point of commerce, may be derived from this indifference in matters of religion, if the natives fhould be properly fupported by the Chriftian powers.

LANGUAGE.] It has been difputed among the learned, whether the Arabs had not their language from the Perfians; but this chiefly refts on the great intermixture of Arabic words in the Perfian language, and the decifion feems to be in favour of the Arabs. The common people, efpecially towards the fouthern coafts of the Cafpian fea, fpeak Turkifh, and the Arabic probably was introduced into Perfia, under the califate, when learning flourifhed in thofe countries. The learned Perfians have generally written in the Arabic, and people of quality among them have adopted it as the modifh language, as we do the French. The pure Perfic is faid to be fpoken in the fouthern parts, on the coaft of the Perfian gulph, and in Ifpahan, but many of the provinces fpeak a barbarous mixture

ture of the Turkiſh, Ruſſian, and other languages. Their Pater-Noſter is of the following tenour : *Ei Padere ma kih der oſmoni ; pak baſched mâm tu; bayayed padſchahi tu ; ſehwad ihwâaſte tu henzjunáaukih der oſmon niz derzemin ; béh mâra jmrouz nân kefâf rouz mara ; wadargudſar mara konâhan ma zjunankihma niz mig ſarim ormân mara ; wador ozmajiſch minedâzzmara ; likin chalâs kun mara ez eſcherir.* Amen.

LEARNING AND LEARNED MEN.] The Perſians, in antient times, were famous for both, and their poets renowned all over the eaſt. At preſent their learning is merely mechanical, nor do they even underſtand the Koran, which they read in Arabic. Their boaſted ſkill in aſtronomy is now reduced to a mere ſmattering in that ſcience, and terminates in judicial aſtrology ; ſo that no people in the world are more ſuperſtitious than the Perſians. The learned profeſſion in greateſt eſteem among them is that of medicine, which is at perpetual variance with aſtrology, becauſe every doſe muſt be adminiſtered in the lucky hour fixed by the aſtrologer, which often defeats the ends of the preſcription. It is ſaid, however, that the Perſian phyſicians are acute and ſagacious. Their drugs are excellent, and they are no ſtrangers to the practices of Galen and Avicenna. Add to this, that the plague is but little known in this country, as equally rare are many other diſeaſes that are fatal in other places, ſuch as the gout, the ſtone, the head-ach, the tooth-ach, the ſmall-pox, conſumptions, and apoplexies. The Perſian practice of phyſic is therefore pretty much circumſcribed, ſo that they are very ignorant in ſurgery, which is exerciſed by barbers, whoſe chief knowledge of it is in letting blood, for they truſt the healing of green wounds to the excellency of the air, and the good habit of the patient's body.

ANTIQUITIES AND CURIOSITIES, NATURAL AND ARTIFICIAL.} The monuments of antiquity in Perſia, are more celebrated for their magnificence and expence, than their beauty or taſte. No more than nineteen columns which formerly belonged to the famous palace of Perſepolis, are now remaining. Each is about fifteen feet high, and compoſed of excellent Parian marble. The ruins of other antient buildings are found in many parts of Perſia, but void of that elegance and beauty, that is diſplayed in the Greek architecture. The tombs of the kings of Perſia are ſtupendous works, being cut out of a rock, and highly ornamented with ſculptures. The chief of the modern edifices is a pillar to be ſeen at Iſpahan, ſixty feet high, conſiſting of the ſkulls of beaſts, erected by Shah Abbas, after the ſuppreſſion of a rebellion. Abbas had vowed to erect ſuch a column of human ſkulls, but upon the

submiſſion

submiffion of the rebels, he performed his vow by fubftituting
thofe of brutes, each of the rebels furnifhing one.

The baths near Gombroon, work fuch cures, that they are
efteemed among the natural curiofities of Perfia. The fprings
of the famous Naphtha, near Baku, are mentioned often in
natural hiftory for their furprizing qualities ; but the chief of
the natural curiofities in this country, is the burning phæ-
nomenon, and its inflammatory neighbourhood, already mentioned under the article of Religion.

HOUSES, CITIES, AND } The houfes of men of quality
   PUBLIC EDIFICES. } in Perfia, are in the fame tafte
with thofe of the Afiatic Turks already defcribed. They are
feldom above one ftory high, built of bricks, with flat roofs
for walking on, and thick walls. The hall is arched, the
doors are clumfey and narrow, and the rooms have no communication but with the hall ; the kitchens and office-houfes
being built apart. Few of them have chimnies, but a round
hole in the middle of the room. Their furniture chiefly
confifts of carpets, and their beds are two thick cotton quilts,
which ferve them likewife as coverlits, with carpets under them.

Ifpahan or Spahawn, the capital of Perfia, is feated on a fine
plain, within a mile of the river Zenderhend, which fupplies
it with water. It is faid to be twelve miles in circumference.
The ftreets are narrow and crooked, and the chief amufement
of the inhabitants is on the flat roofs of their houfes, where
they fpend their fummer evenings, and different families
affociate together. The royal fquare is a third of a mile in
length, and about half as much in breadth, and we are told,
that the royal palace, with the buildings and gardens belonging to it, is three miles in circumference. There are in Ifpahan 160 mofques, 1800 caravanferas, 260 public baths, a
prodigious number of fine fquares, ftreets, and palaces, in
which are canals, and trees planted to fhade and better accommodate the people. This capital is faid formerly to have contained 650,000 inhabitants; but was often depopulated by
Kouli Khan during his wars, fo that we may eafily fuppofe,
that it has loft great part of its antient magnificence. In 1744,
when Mr. Hanway was there, it was thought that not above
5000 of its houfes were inhabited.

Schiras lies about 200 miles to the fouth of Aftracan. It is
an open town, but its neighbourhood is inexpreffibly rich and
beautiful, being laid out for many miles in gardens, the
flowers, fruits, and wines of which are incomparable. The
vines of Schiras are reckoned the beft of any in Perfia. This
town is the capital of Fars, the antient Perfia, and contains a
kind of a college for the ftudy of eaftern learning. It contains
an uncommon number of mofques, is adorned by many noble
buildings,

buildings, but its ftreets are narrow and inconvenient, and not above 4000 of its houfes are inhabited.

The cities of Ormus and Gombroon, on the narrow part of the Perfian Gulph, were formerly places of great commerce and importance. The Englifh, and other Europeans, have factories at Gombroon, where they trade with the Perfians, Arabians, Banyans, Armenians, Turks, and Tartars, who come hither with the caravans which fet out from various inland cities of Afia, under the convoy of guards.

MOSQUES AND BAGNIOS.] I thought proper to place them here under a general head, as their form of building is pretty much the fame all over the Mahometan countries.

Mofques are religious buildings, fquare, and generally of ftone; before the chief gate there is a fquare court, paved with white marble, and low galleries round it, whofe roof is fupported by marble pillars. Thofe galleries ferve for places of ablution before the Mahometans go into the mofque. About every mofque there are fix high towers, called minarets, each of which has three little open galleries, one above another. Thefe towers, as well as the mofques, are covered with lead, and adorned with gilding and other ornaments; and from thence, inftead of a bell, the people are called to prayer by certain officers appointed for that purpofe. No woman is allowed to enter the mofque, nor can a man with his fhoes or ftockings on. Near moft mofques is a place of entertainment for ftrangers during three days, and the tomb of the founder, with conveniencies for reading the Koran, and praying for the fouls of the deceafed.

The bagnios in the Mahometan countries are wonderfully well conftructed for the purpofe of bathing. Sometimes they are fquare, but oftener circular, built of white well polifhed ftone or marble. Each bagnio contains three rooms; the firft for dreffing and undreffing; the fecond contains the water, and the third the bath; all of them paved with black and white marble. The operation of the bath is very curious, but wholefome; though to thofe not accuftomed to it, it is painful. The waiter rubs the patient with great vigour, then handles and ftretches his limbs as if he was diflocating every bone in the body; all which exercifes are, in thofe inert warm countries, very conducive to health. In public bagnios, the men bathe from morning to four in the afternoon, when all male attendants being removed, the ladies fucceed, and when coming out of the bath difplay their fineft cloaths.

I might here attempt to defcribe the eaftern feraglios or harams, the womens apartments; but from the moft credible accounts, they are contrived according to the tafte and conveniency of the owner, and divided into a certain number of

apartments,

apartments, which are feldom or never entered by ftrangers ;
and there is no country where women are fo ftrictly guarded
and confined as among the great men in Perfia.

MANUFACTURES AND COMMERCE.] The Perfians equal,
if not exceed, all the manufacturers in the world in filk, woollen, mohair, carpets, and leather. Their works in thefe,
join fancy, tafte and elegance, to richnefs, neatnefs, and
fhew, and yet they are ignorant of painting, and their drawings are very rude. Their dying excels that of Europe.
Their filver and gold laces, and threads, are admirable for
preferving their luftre. Their embroideries and horfe furniture
are not to be equalled, nor are they ignorant of the pottery,
and window glafs manufactures. On the other hand, their
carpenters are very indifferent artifts, which is faid to be owing to the fcarcity of timber all over Perfia. Their jewellers and goldfmiths are clumfey workmen, and they are
ignorant of lock-making, and the manufacture of looking-
glaffes. Upon the whole, they lie under inexpreffible difadvantages from the form of their government, which renders
them flaves to their kings, who often engrofs either their labour or their profits.

The trade of the Perfians, who have little or no fhipping
of their own, is carried on in foreign bottoms. That between
the Englifh and other nations, by the gulph of Ormus at
Gombroon, was the moft gainful they had, but the perpetual
wars they have been engaged in, have ruined their commerce.
The great fcheme of the Englifh in trading with the Perfians
through Ruffia, promifed vaft advantages to both nations, but
it has hitherto anfwered the expectations of neither. Perhaps
the court of Peterfburgh is not fond of fuffering the Englifh
to eftablifh themfelves upon the Cafpian fea, the navigation
of which is now poffeffed by the Ruffians; but nothing can be
faid with certainty on that head, till the government of Perfia
is in a more fettled condition than it is at prefent.

CONSTITUTION AND GOVERNMENT.] Both thefe are extremely precarious, as refting in the breaft of a defpotic and
often capricious monarch. The Perfians however had fome
fundamental rules of government. They excluded from their
throne females, but not their male progeny. Blindnefs likewife was a difqualification for the royal fucceffion. In other
refpects the king's will was a law for the people. The inftances that have been given of the cruelties and inhumanities
practifed by the Mahometan kings of Perfia, are almoft incredible, efpecially during the two laft centuries. The reafon
given to the Chriftian ambaffadors, by Shah Abbas, the greateft and moft polite among them, was, that the Perfians were
fuch

fuch brutes, and fo infenfible by nature, that they could not be governed, without the exercife of exemplary cruelties. The favourites of the prince, female, as well as male, are his only counfellors, and the fmalleft difobedience to their will, is attended with immediate death. The Perfians have no degrees of nobility, fo that the refpect due to every man, on account of his high ftation, expires with himfelf. The king has been known to prefer a younger fon to his throne, by putting out the eyes of the elder brother.

REVENUES.] The crown claims one-third of the cattle, corn and fruits of his fubjects, and likewife a third of filk and cotton. No rank, or condition of Perfians, is exempted from fevere taxations and fervices. The governors of provinces have particular lands affigned to them for maintaining their retinues and troops, and the crown lands defray the expences of the court, king's houfhold, and great officers of ftate; after faying thus much, the reader cannot doubt that the revenues of the Perfian kings, or as they are called Sophis, were prodigious, but nothing can be faid with any certainty in the prefent diftracted ftate of that country. Even the water that is let into fields and gardens is fubject to a tax, and foreigners, who are not Mahometans, pay each a ducat a head.

MILITARY STRENGTH.] This confifted formerly of cavalry, and it is now thought to exceed that of the Turks. Since the beginning of this century, however, their kings have raifed bodies of infantry. The regular troops of both brought to the field, even under Kouli Khan, did not exceed 60,000; but according to the modern hiftories of Perfia, they are eafily recruited in cafe of a defeat. The Perfians have few fortified towns; nor had they any fhips of war, until Kouli Khan built a royal navy, but fince his death we hear no more of their fleet.

ARMS AND TITLES.] The arms of the Perfian monarch are a lion couchant looking at the rifing fun. His title is Shah, or the Difpofer of Kingdoms. Shah or Khan, and Sultan, which he affumes likewife, are Tartar titles. To acts of ftate the Perfian monarch does not fubfcribe his name, but the grant runs in this manner, viz. This act is given by him whom the univerfe obeys.

HISTORY.] All ancient hiftorians mention the Perfian monarchs and their grandeur, and no empire has undergone a greater variety of governments. It is here fufficient to fay, that the Perfian empire fucceeded the Affyrian or Babylonian, and that Cyrus laid its foundation about 556 years before Chrift; and reftored the Ifraelites, who had been captive at

Babylon,

Babylon, to liberty. It ended in the perfon of Darius, who was conquered by Alexander 329 years before Chrift. When Alexander's empire was divided among his great general officers, their pofterity were conquered by the Romans. Thefe laft, however, never fully fubdued Perfia, and the natives had princes of their own, who more than once defeated the Roman legions. The fucceffors of thofe princes furvived the Roman empire itfelf, but were fubdued by the famous Tamerlane, whofe pofterity were fupplanted by a doctor of law, the anceftor of the Sophi family, and pretended to be defcended from Mahomet himfelf. His fucceffors, though fome of them were valiant and politic, proved in general to be a difgrace to humanity, by their cruelty, ignorance, and indolence, which brought them into fuch difrepute with their fubjects, barbarous as they were, that Haffein, a prince of the Sophi race, who fucceeded in 1694, was murdered by Mahmud, fon and fucceffor to the famous Miriweis; as Mahmud himfelf was by Efref, one of his general officers, who ufurped the throne. Prince Tahmas, the reprefentative of the Sophi family, had efcaped from the rebels, and affembling an army, took into his fervice Nadir Shah, who defeated and killed Efref, and re-annexed to the Perfian monarchy all the places difmembered from it by the Turks and Tartars during the late rebellions. At laft the fecret ambition of Nadir broke out, and after affuming the name of Tahmas Kouli Khan, and pretending that his fervices were not fufficiently rewarded, he rebelled againft his fovereign, made him a prifoner, and, it is fuppofed, put him to death.

This ufurper afterwards mounted the throne, under the title of Shah Nadir. The hiftory of his expedition into Indoftan, and the amazing booty he made there, has been treated of in the defcription of that country. It has been remarked, that he brought back an inconfiderable part of his booty from India, lofing great part of it upon his return by the Marattas and accidents. He next conquered Ufbec Tartary; but was not fo fuccefsful againft the Dagheftan Tartars, whofe country he found to be inacceffible. He beat the Turks in feveral engagements, but was unable to take Bagdad. The great principle of his government was to ftrike terror into all his fubjects by the moft cruel executions. His conduct became fo intolerable, that it was thought his brain was touched; and he was affaffinated in his own tent, partly in felf-defence, by his chief officers and his relations, in the year 1747. Many pretenders, upon his death, ftarted up; but the fortunate candidate was Kerim Khan, who was crowned at Tauris in 1763, and, according to the lateft accounts, ftill keeps poffeffion of the throne.

ARABIA.

SITUATION AND EXTENT.

	Miles.		Degrees.
Length	1300	between	35 and 60 eaſt longitude.
Breadth	1200		12 and 30 north latitude.

BOUNDARIES.] BOUNDED by Turkey, on the north ; by the gulphs of Perſia or Baſſora, and Ormus, which ſeparate it from Perſia, on the eaſt; by the Indian Ocean, ſouth; and the Red Sea, which divides it from Africa, on the weſt.

Diviſions.	Subdiviſions.	Chief towns.
1. Arabia Petræa, N. W.	— — —	SUEZ, E. lon. 33-27. N. lat. 29-50.
2. Arabia Deſerta, in the middle.	Haggiaz or Mecca Tehama — —	MECCA, E. lon. 43-40. N. lat. 21-20. Siden Medina Dhafar
3. Arabia Felix, S. E.	Mocho — — Hadramut — — Caſſeen — — Segur — — — Oman or Muſcat— Jamama — — Bahara — —	MOCHO, E. lon. 44-4. N. lat. 13-45. Sibit Hadramut Caſſeen Segur Muſcat Jamama Elcalf.

NAME.] It is remarkable that this country has always preſerved its antient name. The word *Arab*, it is generally ſaid, ſignifies a robber, or freebooter. The word *Saracen*, by which one tribe is called, is ſaid to ſignify both a thief and an inhabitant of the Deſert. Theſe names juſtly belong to the Arabians, for they ſeldom let any merchandize paſs thro' the country without extorting ſomething from the owners, if they do not rob them.

MOUNTAINS.] The mountains of Sinai and Horeb, lying in Arabia Petræa, eaſt of the Red-Sea, and thoſe called Gabel el Ared, in Arabia Felix, are the moſt noted.

RIVERS, SEAS, GULPHS, AND CAPES.] There are few fountains, ſprings, or rivers in this country, except the Euphrates, which waſhes the north-eaſt limits of it. It is almoſt ſurrounded with ſeas ; as the Indian Ocean, the Red-Sea, the gulphs of Perſia and Ormus. The chief capes or promontories are thoſe of Roſalgate and Muſledon.

VOL. II.   S

CLIMATE, AIR, SOIL, and PRODUCE.] As a confiderable
part of this country lies under the Torrid Zone, and the
Tropic of Cancer paffes over Arabia Felix, the air is exceffive dry and hot, and the country is fubject to hot poifonous
winds, like thofe on the oppofite fhores of Perfia, which often
prove fatal, efpecially to ftrangers. The foil, in fome parts,
is nothing more than immenfe fands, which, when agitated
by the winds, roll like the troubled ocean, and fometimes
form mountains, by which whole caravans have been buried
or loft. In thefe deferts, the caravans, having no tracks, are
guided, as at fea, by a compafs, or by the ftars, for they
travel chiefly in the night. Here, fays Dr. Shaw, are no
paftures clothed with flocks, nor vallies ftanding thick with
corn; here are no vineyards or olive-yards; but the whole is a
lonefome defolate wildernefs, no other ways diverfified than
by plains covered with fand, and mountains that are made up
of naked rocks and precipices. Neither is this country ever,
unlefs fometimes at the equinoxes, refrefhed with rain; and
the intenfenefs of the cold in the night is almoft equal to that
of the heat in the day-time. The fouthern part of Arabia,
defervedly called the Happy, is bleffed with an excellent foil,
and, in general, is very fertile. There the cultivated lands,
which are chiefly about the towns near the fea coaft, produce
balm of Gilead, manna, myrrh, caffia, aloes, frankincenfe,
fpikenard, and other valuable gums; cinnamon, pepper,
cardamum, oranges, lemons, pomegranates, figs, and other
fruits; honey and wax in plenty, with a fmall quantity of
corn and wine. But this country is moft famous for its coffee
and its dates, which laft are found fcarce any where in fuch
perfection as here and in Perfia. There are few trees fit for
timber in Arabia, and little wood of any kind.

ANIMALS.] The moft ufeful animals in Arabia are camels
and dromedaries; they are amazingly fitted by providence for
traverfing the dry and parched deferts of this country, for
they are fo formed, that they can throw up the liquor from
their ftomach into their throat, by which means they can
travel fix or eight days without water. The camels ufually
carry 800 weight upon their backs, which is not taken off
during the whole journey, for they naturally kneel down to
reft, and in due time rife with their load. The dromedary is
a fmall camel that will travel many miles a day. It is an obfervation among the Arabs, that wherever there are trees, the
water is not far off; and when they draw near a pool, their
camels will fmell it at a diftance, and fet up their great trot
till they come to it. The Arabian horfes are well known
in Europe, and have contributed to improve the breed of
thofe

thofe in England. They are only fit for the faddle, and are admired for their make as much as for their fwiftnefs and high mettle.

INHABITANTS, MANNERS, } The Arabians, like moft of
  CUSTOMS, AND DRESS. } the nations of Afia, are of a middle ftature, thin, and of a fwarthy complexion, with black hair and black eyes. They are fwift of foot, excellent horfe-men, and are faid to be a brave people, expert at the bow and lance, and, fince they became acquainted with fire-arms, good markfmen. The inhabitants of the inland country live in tents, and remove from place to place with their flocks and herds, as they have ever done fince they became a nation.

The Arabians in general are fuch thieves by nature, that travellers and pilgrims, who are led thither from all nations thro' motives of devotion or curiofity, are ftruck with terror on their approaches towards the Deferts. Thofe robbers, headed by a captain, traverfe the country in confiderable troops on horfe-back, affault and plunder the caravans ; and we are told, that ·fo late as the year 1750, a body of 50,000 Arabians attacked a caravan of merchants and pilgrims returning from Mecca, killed about 60,000 perfons, and plundered it of every thing valuable, though efcorted by a Turkifh army. On the fea coaft they are mere pirates, and make prize of every veffel they can mafter of whatever nation.

The habit of the roving Arabs is a kind of blue fhirt, tied about them with a white fafh or girdle; and fome of them have a veft of furs or fheep-fkins over it ; they alfo wear drawers, and fometimes flippers, but no ftockings; and have a cap or turban on their head. Many of them go almoft naked ; but, as in the eaftern countries, the women are fo wrapped up, that nothing can be difcerned but their eyes. Like other Mahometans, the Arabs eat all manner of flefh, except that of hogs; and prefer the flefh of camels, as we prefer venifon, to other meat. They take care to drain the blood from the flefh, as the Jews do, and like them refufe fuch fifh as have no fcales. Coffee and tea, water, and fher-bet made of oranges water and fugar, is their ufual drink ; they have no ftrong liquors.

RELIGION.] Of this the reader will find an account in the following hiftory of Mahomet their countryman. Many of the wild Arabs are ftill pagans, but the people in general profefs Mahometanifm.

LEARNING AND LANGUAGE.] Though the Arabians in former ages were famous for their learning and fkill in all the liberal arts, there is fcarce a country at prefent where the people are fo univerfally ignorant. The vulgar language

ufed

ufed in the three Arabias is the Arabefk, or corrupt Arabian, which is likewife fpoken, with fome variation of dialect, over great part of the Eaft, from Egypt to the court of the great mogul. The pure old grammatical Arabic, which is faid to be a dialect of the Hebrew, and by the people of the Eaft accounted the richeft, moft energic and copious language in the world, is taught in their fchools, as Greek and Latin is amongft Europeans, and ufed by Mahometans in their worfhip; for as the Koran was written in this language, they will not fuffer it to be read in any other: they look upon it to have been the language of Paradife, and think no man can be mafter of it without a miracle, as confifting of feveral millions of words. The books which treat of it fay, they have no fewer than a thoufand terms to exprefs the word *camel*, and five hundred for that of a *lion*. The Pater-nofter in the Arabic is as follows.

Abuna elladhi fi-ffamwat; jetkaddas efmâc; tati malacutac: taouri mafchiatac, cama fi-ffama; kedhalec ala lardh aating chobzena kefatna iaum beiaum; wagfor lena donubena, wachataina, cama nogfor nachna lemen aca doina; walâ tadalhchalna fihajarib; laken mejjina me nnefcherir. Amen.

CHIEF CITIES, CURIOSITIES, } What is called the Defert
      AND ARTS.   } of Sinai, is a beautiful plain near nine miles long and above three in breadth; it lies open to the north-eaft, but to the fouthward is clofed by fome of the lower eminences of Mount Sinai; and other parts of that mountain make fuch encroachments upon the plain as to divide it in two, each fo capacious as to be fufficient to receive the whole camp of the Ifraelites.

From Mount Sinai may be feen Mount Horeb, where Mofes kept the flocks of Jethro, his father-in-law, when he faw the burning bufh. On thofe mountains are many chapels and cells, poffeffed by the Greek and Latin monks, who, like the religious at Jerufalem, pretend to fhew the very fpot where every miracle or tranfaction recorded in fcripture happened.

The chief cities in Arabia are Mocho, Aden, Mufchat and Suez, where moft of the trade of this country is carried on; but thofe of Mecca, which is the capital of all Arabia, and Medina, deferve particular notice. At Mecca, the birthplace of Mahomet, is a mofque fo glorious that it is generally counted the moft magnificent of any temple in the Turkifh dominions: its lofty roof being raifed in fafhion of a dome, and covered with gold, with two beautiful towers at the end, of extraordinary height and architecture, make a delightful appearance, and are confpicuous at a great diftance. The
                                   mofque

mofque hath a hundred gates, with a window over each; and the whole building within is decorated with the fineft gildings and tapeftry. The number of pilgrims who yearly vifit this place is almoft incredible, every muffulman being obliged by his religion to come hither once in his life time, or fend a deputy.

At Medina, about fifty miles from the Red-Sea, the city to which Mahomet fled when he was driven out of Mecca, and the place where he was buried, is a ftately mofque, fupported by 400 pillars, and furnifhed with 300 filver lamps, which are continually burning. It is called the Moft Holy by the Turks, becaufe in it is placed the coffin of their prophet Mahomet, covered with cloth of gold, under a canopy of filver tiffue, which the bafhaw of Egypt, by order of the grand fignior, renews every year. The camel which carries it derives a fort of fanctity from it, and is never to be ufed in any drudgery afterwards. Over the foot of the coffin is a rich golden crefcent, fo curioufly wrought, and adorned with precious ftones, that it is efteemed a mafter-piece of great value. Thither the pilgrims refort, as to Mecca, but not in fuch numbers.

GOVERNMENT.] The inland country of Arabia is under the government of many petty princes, who are ftiled xerifs and imans, both of them including the offices of king and prieft, in the fame manner as the califs of the Saracens, the fucceffors of Mahomet. Thefe monarchs appear to be abfolute, both in fpirituals and temporals; the fucceffion is hereditary, and they have no other laws than thofe found in the Koran and the comments upon it. The northern Arabs owe fubjection to the Turks, and are governed by bafhaws refiding among them; but it is certain they receive large gratuities from the grand fignior for protecting the pilgrims that pafs through their country from the robberies of their countrymen. The Arabians have no ftanding regular militia, but the kings command both the perfons and the purfes of their fubjects as the neceffity of affairs require.

HISTORY.] The hiftory of this country in fome meafure differs from that of all others: for as the flavery and fubjection of other nations make a great part of their hiftory, that of the Arabs is intirely compofed of their conquefts or independence. The Arabs are defcended of Ifmael, of whofe pofterity it was foretold, that they fhould be invincible, "have their hands againft every man, and every man's hands againft theirs." They are at prefent, and have remained from the remoteft ages, during the various conquefts of the Greeks, Romans, and Tartars, a convincing proof of the divinity of this prediction.

Toward

Toward the north, and the sea-coasts of Arabia, indeed the inhabitants are kept in awe by the Turks; but the wandering tribes in the southern and inland parts, acknowledge themselves for subjects of no foreign power, and do not fail to harrass and annoy all strangers who come into their country. The conquests of the Arabs make as wonderful a part of their history, as the independence and freedom which they have ever continued to enjoy. These, as well as their religion, began with one man, whose character forms a very singular phenomenon in the history of mankind. This was the famous Mahomet, a native of Mecca, a city of that division of Arabia, which, for the luxuriancy of its soil, and happy temperature of its climate, has ever been esteemed the loveliest and sweetest region of the world, and is distinguished by the epithet of Happy. He was born in the sixth century, in the reign of Justinian XI. emperor of Constantinople. Though descended of mean parentage, illiterate and poor, Mahomet was endowed with a subtile genius, like those of the same country, and possessed an enterprize and ambition peculiar to himself, and much beyond his condition. He had been employed, in the early part of his life, by an uncle, Abuteleb, as a factor, and had occasion, in this capacity, to travel into Syria, Palestine, and Egypt. He was afterwards taken into the service of a rich merchant, upon whose death he married his widow, Cadiga, and by her means came to be possessed of great wealth and of a numerous family. During his peregrinations into Egypt and the East, he had observed the vast variety of sects in religion, whose hatred against each other was strong and inveterate, while at the same time there were many particulars in which the greater part of them were agreed. He carefully laid hold of these particulars, by means of which, and by addressing himself to the love of power, riches, and pleasure, passions universal among men, he expected to raise a new system of religion, more general than any which hitherto had been established. In this design he was assisted by a Sergian monk, whose libertine disposition had made him forsake his cloister and profession, and engage in the service of Cadiga, with whom he remained as a domestic when Mahomet was taken to her bed. This monk was perfectly qualified, by his great learning, for supplying the defects which his master, for want of a liberal education, laboured under, and which, in all probability, must have obstructed the execution of his design. It was necessary, however, that the religion they proposed to establish should have a divine sanction; and for this purpose Mahomet turned a calamity, with which he was afflicted, to his advantage. He was often subject to fits of the epilepsy, a

disease

difeafe which thofe whom it afflicts are defirous to conceal ; Mahomet gave out therefore that thefe fits were trances, into which he was miraculoufly thrown by God Almighty, and during which he was inftructed in his will, which he was commanded to publifh to the world. By this ftrange ftory, and by leading a retired, abftemious, and auftere life, he eafily acquired a character for fuperior fanctity among his acquaintance and neighbours. When he thought himfelf fufficiently fortified by the numbers and enthufiafm of his followers, he boldly declared himfelf a prophet, fent by God into the world, not only to teach his will, but to compel mankind to obey it. As we have already mentioned, he did not lay the foundation of his fyftem fo narrow as only to comprehend the natives of his own country. His mind, though rude and enthufiaftic, was enlarged by travelling into diftant lands, whofe manners and religion he had made a peculiar ftudy. He propofed that the fyftem he eftablifhed fhould extend over all the neighbouring nations, to whofe doctrines and prejudices he had taken care to adapt it. The eaftern countries were at this time ftrongly infected with the herefy of Arius, who allowed the prophetic office, but denied the divinity of Jefus Chrift. Egypt and Arabia were filled with Jews, who had fled into thefe corners of the world from the perfecution of the emperor Adrian, who threatened the total extinction of that people. The other inhabitants of thefe countries were pagans. Thefe, however, had little attachment to their decayed and derided idolatry ; and like men whofe religious principle is weak, had given themfelves over to pleafure and fenfuality, or to the acquifition of riches, in order to be the better able to indulge in the gratification of fenfe, which, together with the doctrine of predeftination, compofed the fole principles of their religion and philofophy. Mahomet's fyftem was exactly fuited to thefe three kinds of men. To gratify the two former, he declared that there was one God, who created the world and governed all things in it ; that he had fent various prophets into the world to teach his will to mankind, among whom Mofes and Jefus Chrift were the moft eminent ; but the endeavours of thefe had proved ineffectual, and God had therefore now fent his laft and greateft prophet, with a commiffion more ample than what Mofes or Chrift had been entrufted with. He had commanded him not only to publifh his laws, but to fubdue thofe who were unwilling to believe or obey them ; and for this end to eftablifh a kingdom upon earth which fhould propagate the divine law throughout the world ; that God had defigned utter ruin and deftruction to thofe who fhould refufe to fubmit to him ; but to his faith-

ful

ful followers, had given the spoils and possessions of all the
earth, as a reward in this life, and had provided for them
hereafter a paradise of all sensual enjoyments, especially those
of love; that the pleasures of such as died in propagating the
faith, would be peculiarly intense, and vastly transcend those
of the rest. These, together with the prohibition of drinking
strong liquors (a restraint not very severe in warm climates)
and the doctrine of predestination, were the capital articles of
Mahomet's creed. They were no sooner published, than a
vast many of his countrymen embraced them with implicit
faith. They were written by the priest we formerly mentioned, and compose a book called the Koran, or Alkoran, by
way of eminence, as we say the Bible, which means The
Book. The person of Mahomet, however, was familiar to
the inhabitants of Mecca; so that the greater part of them
were sufficiently convinced of the deceit. The more enlightened and leading men entered into a design to cut him
off; but Mahomet getting notice of their intention, fled from
his native city to Medina Talmachi, or the city of the Prophet. The fame of his miracles and doctrine was, according
to custom, greatest at a distance, and the inhabitants of Medina received him with open arms. From this flight, which
happened in the 622d year of Christ, the forty-fourth year of
Mahomet's age, and the tenth of his ministry, his followers,
the Mahometans, compute their time, and the æra is called in
Arabic, Hegira, i. e. the Flight.

Mahomet, by the assistance of the inhabitants of Medina,
and of others whom his insinuation and address daily attached
to him, brought over all his countrymen to a belief, or at
least to an acquiescence in his doctrines. The speedy propa-
gation of his system among the Arabians was a new argument
in its behalf among the inhabitants of Egypt and the East,
who were previously disposed to it. Arians, Jews, and Gen-
tiles, all forsook their ancient faith, and became Mahometans.
In a word, the contagion spread over Arabia, Syria, Egypt,
and Persia; and Mahomet, from a deceitful hypocrite, became
the most powerful monarch in his time. He died in 629,
leaving two branches of his race, both esteemed divine among
their subjects. These were the caliphs of Persia and of Egypt,
under the last of which Arabia was included. The former of
these turned their arms to the East, and made conquests of
many countries. The caliphs of Egypt and Arabia directed
their ravages towards Europe, and under the name of Saracens
or Moors (which they obtained because they entered Europe
from Mauritania, in Africa, the country of the Moors) reduced
most

moſt of Spain, France, Italy, and the iſlands in the Mediterranean.

In this manner did the ſucceſſors of that impoſtor ſpread their religion and conqueſts over the greateſt part of Aſia, Africa, and Europe; and they ſtill give law to a very conſiderable part of mankind.

The INDIAN and ORIENTAL ISLANDS are,

THE JAPAN ISLANDS, which together form what has been called the empire of Japan, and are governed by a moſt deſpotic prince, who is ſometimes called emperor and ſometimes king. They are ſituated about 150 miles eaſt of China, and extend from the 30th to the 41ſt degree of north latitude, and from the 130th to the 147th of eaſt longitude. The chief town is Jeddo, in the 141ſt degree of eaſt longitude, and the 36th of north latitude. The ſoil and productions of the country are pretty much the ſame with thoſe of China; and the inhabitants are famous for their lacquer ware, known by the name of Japan. The iſlands themſelves are very inacceſſible, through their high rocks and tempeſtuous ſeas; they are ſubject to earthquakes, and have ſome volcanos. I have already mentioned the circumſtance of the Dutch expelling the Portugueſe from this gainful trade. The Japaneſe themſelves are the groſſeſt of all idolators, and ſo irreconcileable to Chriſtianity, that it is commonly ſaid the Dutch, who are the only European people with whom they now trade, pretend themſelves to be no Chriſtians, and humour the Japaneſe in the moſt abſurd ſuperſtitions. Notwithſtanding all this compliance, the natives are very ſhy and rigorous in all their dealings with the Dutch, and Nanghazal, in the iſland of Ximo, is the only place where they are ſuffered to trade. Authors pretend to give us very particular accounts of the inhabitants, cuſtoms, and manners of thoſe iſlanders, their ſoil, commodities, and trade; but their information conveys little inſtruction, and the whole ſubſiſts on a precarious foundation. All we know for certain is, that notwithſtanding their ſuperſtition and ignorance, the natives are a moſt induſtrious penetrating people; that they excel the Chineſe themſelves in the manufactures that are common to both countries, and at leaſt equal them in huſbandry and the arts of life.

The LADRONE ISLANDS, of which the chief town is ſaid to be Guam, eaſt longitude 140, north latitude 14;
they

they are about twelve in number. The people took their name from their pilfering qualities. We know nothing of them worth a particular mention, excepting that lord Anson landed upon one of them (Tinian) where he found great refreshment for himself and his crew.

FORMOSA is likewise an oriental island. It is situated to the east of China, near the province of Fo-kien, and is divided into two parts by a chain of mountains, which runs through the middle, beginning at the south coast, and ending at the north. This is a very fine island, and abounds with all the necessaries of life. That part of the island which lies to the west of the mountains belongs to the Chinese, who consider the inhabitants of its eastern part as savages, though they are said to be a very inoffensive people. The inhabitants of the cultivated parts are the same with the Chinese already described. The Chinese have likewise made themselves masters of several other islands in these seas, of which we scarcely know the names ; that of Ainan, is between sixty and seventy leagues long, and between fifty and sixty in breadth, and but twelve miles from the province of Canton. The original inhabitants are a shy, cowardly people, and live in the most unwholesome part of the island, the coast and cultivated parts, which are very valuable, being possessed by the Chinese.

The PHILIPPINES, of which there are 1100 in number, lying in the Chinese sea, (part of the Pacific Ocean) 300 miles south-east of China, of which Manilla or Luconia, the chief, is 400 miles long and 200 broad. The inhabitants consist of Chinese, Ethiopians, Malays, Spaniards, Portuguese, Pintudos, or painted people, and Mestes, a mixture of all these. The property of the islands belong to the king of Spain, they having been discovered by Magellan, and afterwards conquered by the Spaniards in the reign of Philip II. from whom they take their name. Their situation is such, between the eastern and western continents, that the inhabitants trade with Mexico and Peru, as well as all the islands and places of the East-Indies. Two ships from Acapulco, in Mexico, carry on this commerce for the Spaniards, who make 400 per cent. profit. The country is fruitful in all the necessaries of life, and beautiful to the eye. Venison of all kinds, buffaloes, hogs, sheep, goats, and a particular large species of monkeys, are found here in great plenty. The nest of the bird saligan affords that dissolving jelly which is so voluptuous a rarity at European tables. Many European fruits and flowers thrive surprizingly in those islands. If a sprig of an orange or lemon tree is planted there, it becomes within the year a
fruit-

fruit-bearing tree; so that the verdure and luxuriancy of the soil is almost incredible. The tree amet supplies the natives with water; and there is also a kind of cane, which if cut yields fair water enough for a draught, of which there is plenty in the mountains, where water is most wanted.

. The city of Manilla contains about 3000 inhabitants; its port is Cavite, lying at the distance of three leagues, and defended by the castle of St. Philip. In the year 1762, Manilla was reduced by the English under general Draper and admiral Cornish, who took it by storm, and humanely suffered the archbishop, who was the Spanish viceroy at the same time, to ransom the place for about a million sterling. The bargain, however, was ungenerously disowned by him and the court of Spain, so that great part of the ransom is still unpaid. The Spanish government is settled there, but the Indian inhabitants pay a capitation tax. The other islands, particularly Mindanao, the largest next to Manilla, are governed by petty princes of their own, whom they call sultans. The sultan of Mindanao is a Mahometan.

Upon the whole, though these islands are enriched with all the profusion of nature, yet they are subject to most dreadful earthquakes, thunder, rains, and lightning; and the soil is pestered with many noxious and venemous creatures, and even herbs and flowers, whose poisons kill almost instantaneously. Some of their mountains are volcanos.

The MOLUCCAS, commonly called the SPICE or CLOVE ISLANDS. These are not out of sight of each other, and lie all within the compass of twenty-five leagues to the south of the Philippines, in 125 degrees of east longitude, and between one degree south, and two north latitude. They are in number five, viz. Bachian, Machian, Motyr, Ternate, and Tydore. Those islands produce neither corn nor rice, so that the inhabitants live upon a bread made of sagoe. Their chief produce consists of cloves, mace, and nutmegs, in vast quantities, which are monopolized by the Dutch with so much jealousy, that they destroy the plants lest the natives should sell the supernumerary spices to other nations. Those islands, after being subject to various powers, are now governed by three kings, subordinate to the Dutch. The latter, however, if at war with England, might be easily dispossessed, and their possession of them at this time is precarious, when they differ with those princes. Ternate is the largest of those islands, though no more than thirty miles in circumference. The Dutch have here a fort called Victoria, and another, called Fort Orange, in Machiam.

The

The BANDA, or NUTMEG ISLANDS, are fituated between 127 and 128 degrees eaft longitude, and between four and five fouth latitude, comprehending the iflands of Lantor, the chief town of which is Lantor, Poleron, Rofing- ing, Pooloway, and Gonapi.   The chief forts belonging to the Dutch on thofe iflands, are thofe of Revenge and Naffau. The nutmeg, covered with the mace, grows on thofe iflands only, and they are entirely fubject to the Dutch.   In feveral iflands that lie near Banda and Amboyna, the nutmeg and clove would grow, becaufe, as naturalifts tell us, birds, efpe- cially doves and pigeons, fwallow the nutmeg and clove whole, and void them in the fame ftate ; which is one of the reafons why the Dutch declare war againft both birds and their wild plantations.   The great nutmeg harveft is in June and Auguft.

AMBOYNA. This ifland, taken in a large fenfe, is one, and the moft confiderable, of the Moluccas, which, in fact, it commands.   It is fituated in the Archipelago of St. Lazarus, between the third and fourth degree of fouth lati- tude, and 120 leagues to the eaftward of Batavia.   Amboyna is about feventy miles in circumference, and defended by a Dutch garrifon of 7 or 800 men, befides fmall forts, who protect their clove plantations.   It is well known that when the Portuguefe were driven off this ifland, the trade of it was carried on by the Englifh and Dutch ; and the barbarities of the latter in firft torturing and then murdering the Englifh, and thereby engroffing the whole trade, and that of Banda, can never be forgotten, for it muft be tranfmitted as a memo- rial of Dutch infamy to all pofterity.   This tragical event happened in 1622, and is ftill unrevenged.

The ifland of CELEBES, or MACASSAR, is fitu- ated under the equator, between the ifland of Borneo and the Spice Iflands, at the diftance of 160 leagues from Batavia, and is 500 miles long, and 200 broad. This ifland, notwithftand- ing its heat, is rendered habitable by breezes from the north, and periodical rains.   Its chief product is pepper and opium ; and the natives are expert in the ftudy of poifons, with a variety of which nature has furnifhed them.   The Dutch have a fortification on this ifland, but the internal part of it is governed by three kings, the chief of whom refides in the town of Macaffar.   In this, and indeed in almoft all the Orien- tal iflands, the inhabitants live in houfes built on large pofts, which are acceffible only by ladders, which they pull up in the night-time, for their fecurity againft venemous animals.   They are faid to be hofpitable and faithful, if not provoked.   They
carry

carry on a large trade with the Chinese; and if their chiefs were not perpetually at war with each other, they might easily drive the Dutch from their island. Their port of Jampoden is the most capacious of any in that part of the world.

The Dutch have likewise fortified GILOLO and CERAM, two other spice islands lying under the equator, and will sink any ships that attempt to traffic in those seas.

The SUNDA ISLANDS. These are situated in the Indian Ocean, between 93 and 120 degrees of east longitude, and between eight degrees north and eight degrees south latitude, comprehending the islands of Borneo, Sumatra, Java, Bally, Lamboe, Banca, &c. The three first, from their great extent and importance, require to be separately described.

BORNEO is said to be 800 miles long and 700 broad, and is therefore thought to be the largest island in the world. The inland part of the country is marshy and unhealthy, and the inhabitants live in towns built upon floats in the middle of the rivers. The soil produces rice, cotton, canes, pepper, camphire, the tropical fruits, gold, and excellent diamonds. The famous ourang-outang, one of which was dissected by Dr. Tyson at Oxford, is a native of this country, and is thought of all irrational beings, to resemble a man the most. The original inhabitants are said to live in the mountains, and make use of poisoned darts, but the sea coast is governed by Mahometan princes; the chief port of the island is Benjar-Masseen, and carries on a commerce with all trading nations.

SUMATRA has Malacca on the north, Borneo on the east, and Java on the south-east, from which it is divided by the straits of Sunda; it is divided into two equal parts by the equator, extending five degrees, and upwards, north-west of it, and five on the south-east; and is 1000 miles long, and 100 broad. This island produces so much gold, that it is thought to be the Ophir mentioned in the scriptures; but its chief trade with the Europeans lies in pepper. The English East-India company have two settlements here, Bencoolen and Fort-Marlborough, from whence they bring their chief cargoes of pepper. The king of Achen is the chief of the Mahometan princes who possess the sea coasts. The interior parts are governed by pagan princes; and the natural products of Sumatra are pretty much the same with those of the adjacent islands.

The greatest part of JAVA belongs to the Dutch, who have here erected a kind of commercial monarchy, the capital of which is Batavia, a noble and populous city, lying in the
latitude

latitude of fix degrees fouth, at the mouth of the river Jucata, and furnifhed with one of the fineft harbours in the world. The town itfelf is built in the manner of thofe in Holland, and is about a league and a half in circumference, with five gates, and furrounded by regular fortifications ; but its fub-urbs are faid to be ten times more populous than itfelf. The government here is a mixture of Eaftern magnificence and European police, and held by the Dutch governor-general of the Indies. When he appears abroad, he is attended by his guards and officers, and with a fplendor fuperior to that of any European potentate, excepting upon folemn occa-fions. The city is as beautiful as it is ftrong, and its fine canals, bridges, and avenues, render it a moft agreeable refi-dence. The defcription of it, its government, and public edi-fices, have employed whole volumes. The citadel, where the governor has his palace, commands the town and the fuburbs, which are inhabited by natives of almoft every nation in the world ; the Chinefe refiding in this ifland being computed at 100,coo ; but about 30,000 of that nation were barbaroufly maffacred, without the fmalleft offence that ever was proved upon them, in 1740. This maffacre was too unprovoked and deteftable to be defended even by the Dutch, who, when the governor arrived in Europe, fent him back to be tried at Ba-tavia ; but he never has been heard of fince. A Dutch gar-rifon of three thoufand men conftantly refides at Batavia, and about 15,000 troops are quartered in the ifland and the neigh-bourhood of the cit . Their government is admirably well calculated to prevent the independency either of the civil or military power; and England itfelf would find it difficult to fhake that republican empire.

The ANDAMAN and NICOBAR iflands. Thefe iflands lie at the entrance of the bay of Bengal, and furnifh provi-fions, confifting of tropical fruits and other neceffaries, for the fhips that touch there. They are otherwife too inconfi-derable to be mentioned. They are inhabited by a harmlefs, inoffenfive, but idolatrous people.

CEYLON. This ifland, tho' not the largeft, is thought to be by nature the richeft and fineft ifland in the world. It is fituated in the Indian Ocean, near cape Comorin, the fouthern extremity of the Hither Peninfula of India, being feparated from the coaft of Coromandel by a narrow ftrait, and is 250 miles long and 200 broad. The natives call it, with fome fhew of reafon, the terreftrial paradife; and it produces, befides excellent fruits of all kinds, long pepper, fine cotton, ivory, filk, tobacco, ebony, mufk, cryftal, falt-petre, fulphur, lead, iron, fteel, copper, befides

fides cinnamon, gold, and filver, and all kinds of precious ftones, except diamonds. All kinds of fowls and fifh abound here. Every part of the ifland is well wooded and watered, and befides fome curious animals peculiar to itfelf, it has plenty of cows, buffaloes, goats, hogs, deer, hares, dogs, and other quadrupeds. The Ceylon elephant is preferred to all others, efpecially if fpotted; but feveral noxious animals, fuch as ferpents and ants, are likewife found here. The chief commodity of the ifland, however, is its cinnamon, which is by far the beft in all Afia. Though its trees grow in great profufion, yet the beft is found in the neighbourhood of Columbo, the chief fettlement of the Dutch, and Negambo. The middle of the country is mountainous and woody, fo that the rich and beautiful vallies are left in the poffeffion of the Dutch, who have in a manner fhut up the king in his capital city, Candy, which ftands on a mountain in the middle of the ifland, fo that he has fcarcely any communication with other nations, or any property in the riches of his own dominions. The defcendants of the ancient inhabitants are called Cinglaffes, who, though idolators, value themfelves upon maintaining their ancient laws and cuftoms. They are in general a fober inoffenfive people, and are mingled with Moors, Malabars, Portuguefe, and Dutch.

It may be here proper to obferve, that the cinnamon-tree, which is a native of this ifland, has two, if not three barks, which form the true cinnamon; the trees of a middling growth and age afford the beft; and the body of the tree, which when ftripped is white, ferves for building and other ufes. In 1656, the Dutch were invited by the natives of this delicious ifland, to defend them againft the Portuguefe, whom they expelled, and have monopolized it ever fince to themfelves.

The MALDIVES. Thefe are a vaft clufter of fmall iflands or little rocks juft above the water, lying between the equator and eight degrees north latitude, near Cape Comorin. They are chiefly reforted to by the Dutch, who drive on a profitable trade with the natives for couries, a kind of fmall fhells, which go, or rather formerly went for money upon the coafts of Guinea and other parts of Africa. The cocoa of the Maldives is an excellent commodity in a medicinal capacity: " of this tree (fays a well-informed author) they build veffels " of twenty or thirty tons; their hulls, mafts, fails, rigging, " anchors, cables, provifions, and firing, are all from this " ufeful tree."

The other iflands in Afia, are thofe of KAMTSCHATKA, and the KURILE ISLES in the eaftern or Pacific ocean, many of them lately difcovered by the Ruffians, and but little known. We have already mentioned BOMBAY on the Malabar coaft, in fpeaking of India.

With regard to the language of all the Oriental iflands, nothing certain can be faid. Each ifland has a particular tongue; but the Malayan, Chinefe, Portuguefe, Dutch and Indian words are fo frequent among them, that it is difficult for an European, who is not very expert in thofe matters, to know the radical language. The fame may be almoft faid of their religion, for though its original is certainly Pagan, yet it is intermixed with many Mahometan, Jewifh, Chriftian, and other foreign fuperftitions.

AFRICA.

AFRICA, the third grand divifion of the globe, is generally reprefented as bearing fome refemblance to the
form of a pyramid, the bafe being the northern part of it,
which runs along the fhores of the Mediterranean, and the point
or top of the pyramid, the cape of Good-Hope. Africa is a
peninfula of a prodigious extent, joined to Afia only by a
neck of land, about fixty miles over, between the Red-Sea
and the Mediterranean, ufually called the Ifthmus of Suez,
and its utmoft length from north to fouth, from cape Bona in
the Mediterranean, in 37 deg. N. to the cape of Good-Hope
in 34-7 fouth lat. is 4300 miles ; and the broadeft part from
cape Verd in 17-20 deg. to cape Guarda-fui near the ftraits
of Babel-Mandel in 51-20 E. lon. is 3500 miles from eaft
to weft. It is bounded on the north by the Mediterranean
fea, which feparates it from Europe; on the eaft by the Ifthmus
of Suez, the Red-Sea, and the Indian ocean, which divides
it from Afia ; on the fouth by the fouthern ocean ; and on
the weft by the great Atlantic ocean, which feparates it from
America. As the equator divides this extenfive country almoft in the middle, and the far greateft part of it is within
the tropics, the heat is in many places almoft infupportable to
an European ; it being there greatly increafed by the rays
of the fun from vaft deferts of burning fands. The coafts,
however, and banks of rivers, fuch as the Nile, are generally
fertile ; and moft parts of this region are inhabited, though
it is far from being fo populous as Europe or Afia. From
what has been faid, the reader cannot expect to find here a
variety of climates. In many parts of Africa, fnow feldom
falls in the plains : and it is generally never found, but on
the tops of the higheft mountains. The natives, in thefe
fcorching regions, would as foon expect that marble fhould
melt, and flow in liquid ftreams, as that water by freezing
fhould lofe its fluidity, be arrefted by the cold, and ceafing
to flow become like the folid rock.

The moft confiderable rivers in Africa, are the Niger, which
falls into the Atlantic or weftern ocean at Senegal, after a
courfe of 2800 miles. It increafes and decreafes as the Nile,
fertilifes the country, and has grains of gold in many parts of
it. The Gambia and Senegal are only branches of this river.
The Nile, which dividing Egypt into two parts, difcharges
itfelf into the Mediterranean, after a prodigious courfe from
its fource in Abyffinia. The moft confiderable mountains in
Africa, are the Atlas, a ridge extending from the weftern ocean,
to which it gives the name of Atlantic ocean, as far as Egypt

and had its name from a king of Mauritania, a great lover of aftronomy, who ufed to obferve the ftars from its fummit, on which account the poets reprefent him as bearing the heavens on his fhoulders. The mountains of the Moon, extending themfelves between Abyffinia and Monopotapa, and are ftill higher than thofe of Atlas. Thofe of Sierra Leona, or the mountains of the Lions, which divide Nigritia from Guinea, and extend as far as Ethiopia. Thefe were ftiled by the antients, the Mountains of God, on account of their being fubject to thunder and lightning. The pike of Teneriffe, which the Dutch make their firft meridian, is faid to be three miles high in the form of a fugar-loaf, and is fituated on an ifland of the fame name near the coaft. The moft noted capes, or promontories, in this country, are Cape Verd, fo called, becaufe the land is always covered with green trees, and moffy ground. It is the moft wefterly point of the continent of Africa. The cape of Good Hope, fo denominated by the Portuguefe, when they firft went round it in 1498, and difcover d the paffage to Afia. It is the fouth extremity of Africa, the country of the Hottentots ; and at prefent in the poffeffion of the Dutch, and the general rendezvous of fhips of every nation, who trade to India, being about half way from Europe. There is but one ftreight in Africa, which is called Babel Mandel, and joins the Red-Sea with the Indian ocean.

The fituation of Africa for commerce is extremely favourable, ftanding as it were in the centre of the globe, and having thereby a much nearer communication with Europe, Afia, and America, than any of the other quarters has with the reft. That it abounds with gold, we have not only the teftimony of the Portuguefe, the Dutch, the Englifh, and the French, who have fettlements on the coaft of Africa, but that of the moft authentic hiftorians. It is however the misfortune of Africa, which, though it has 10,000 miles of fea coaft, with noble, large, deep rivers, penetrating into the very centre of the country, it fhould have no navigation, nor receive any benefit from them ; that it fhould be inhabited by an innumerable people, ignorant of commerce, and of each other. At the mouths of thefe rivers are the moft excellent harbours, deep, fafe, calm and fheltered from the wind, and capable of being made perfectly fecure by fortifications; but quite deftitute of fhipping, trade, and merchants, even where there is plenty of merchandize. In fhort, Africa, though a full quarter of the globe, ftored with an inexhauftible treafure, and capable, under proper improvements, of producing fo many things delightful, as well as convenient, within itfelf, feems to be almoft entirely neglected, not only by the natives, who

are

are quite unfollicitous of reaping the benefits which nature has provided for them, but alfo by the more civilized Europeans, who are fettled in it, particularly the Portugueze.

Africa once contained feveral kingdoms and ftates, eminent for the liberal arts, for wealth and power, and the moft extenfive commerce. The kingdoms of Egypt and Ethiopia, in particular, were much celebrated ; and the rich and powerful ftate of Carthage, that once formidable rival to Rome itfelf, extended her commerce to every part of the then known world ; even the Britifh fhores were vifited by her fleets, till Juba, who was king of Mauritania, but tributary to the republic of Carthage, unhappily called in the Romans, who, with the affiftance of the Mauritanians, fubdued Carthage, and by degrees, all the neighbouring kingdoms and ftates. After this the natives, conftantly plundered, and confequently impoverifhed, by the governors fent from Rome, neglected their trade, and cultivated no more of their lands than might ferve for their fubfiftence. Upon the decline of the Roman empire, in the fifth century, the north of Africa was over-run by the Vandals, who contributed ftill more to the deftruction of arts and fciences ; and, to add to this country's calamity, the Saracens made a fudden conqueft of all the coafts of Egypt and Barbary, in the feventh century. Thefe were fucceeded by the Turks, and both being of the Mahometan religion, whofe profeffors carried defolation with them, wherever they came, the ruin of that once flourifhing part of the world, was thereby compleated.

The inhabitants of this continent, with refpect to religion, may be divided into three forts ; namely, Pagans, Mahometans, and Chriftians. The firft are the moft numerous, poffeffing the greateft part of the country, from the tropic of Cancer, to the cape of Good-Hope, and thefe are generally black. The Mahometans, who are of a tawny complexion, poffefs Egypt, and almoft all the northern fhores of Africa, or what is called the Barbary coaft. The people of Abyffinia, or the Upper Ethiopia, are denominated Chriftians, but retain many Pagan and Jewifh rites. There are alfo fome Jews, on the north of Africa, who manage all the little trade that part of the country is poffeffed of.

There are fcarce any two nations, or indeed any two of the learned that agree in the modern divifions of Africa; and for this very reafon, that fcarce any traveller has penetrated into the heart of the country, and confequently we muft acknowledge our ignorance of the bounds, and even the names of feveral of the inland nations, which may be ftill reckoned among the unknown, and undifcovered parts of the world, but according to the beft accounts and conjectures, Africa may be divided according to the following table.

Nations.	Length.	Breadth.	Chief cities.	Dist. & bearing from London.	Diff. of time from London	Religions.
Morocco	500	480	Fez	1080 S.	0 24 aft.	Mahometans
Algiers	480	100	Algiers	920 S.	0 13 bef.	Mahometans
Tunis	220	170	Tunis	990 S. E.	0 39 bef.	Mahometans
Tripoli	700	240	Tripoli	1260 S. E.	0 56 bef.	Mahometans
Barca	400	300	Tolemeta	1440 S. E.	1 26 bef.	Mahometans
Egypt	600	250	Grand Cairo	1920 S. E.	2 21 bef.	Mahometans
Bilidulgerid	2500	350	Dara	1565 S.	0 32 aft.	Pagans
Zaara	2400	660	Tegella	1840 S.	0 24 aft.	Pagans
Negroland	2200	840	Madinga	2500 S.	0 38 aft.	Pagans
Guinea	1800	360	Benin	2700 S.	0 20 bef.	Pagans
Nubia	940	600	Nubia	2418 S. E.	2 12 bef.	Mah. & Pag.
Abyssinia	900	800	Gondar	2880 S. E.	2 20 bef.	Christians
Abex	540	130	Doncala	3580 S. E.	2 36 bef.	Christ. & Pag.
The Middle Parts, called Lower Ethiopia, are very little known to the Europeans.						
Loango	410	300	Loango	3300 S.	0 44 bef.	Christ. & Pag.
Congo	540	420	St. Salvador	3480 S.	1 0 bef.	Christ. & Pag.
Angola	360	250	Loando	3750 S.	0 58 bef.	Christ. & Pag.
Benguela	430	180	Beneguela	3900 S.	0 58 bef.	Pagans
Matanan	450	240	No Towns	* * *	* * *	Pagans
Ajan	900	300	Brava	3702 S. E.	2 40 bef.	Pagans
Zanguebar	1400	350	Melinda or Mozambique	4440 S. E.	2 38 bef.	Pagans
Monomotapa	960	660	Monomotapa	4500 S.	1 18 bef.	Pagans
Monemugi	900	660	Chicova	4260 S.	1 44 bef.	Pagans
Sofola	480	300	Sofola	4600 S. E.	2 18 bef.	Pagans
Terra de Nat.	600	350	No Towns	* * *	* * *	Pagans
Caffaria or Hottentots	780	660	Cape of Good Hope	5200 S.	1 4 bef.	Most stupid Pagans

Left margin brackets: Barbary. / Up. Ethiopia. / Lower Guinea.

The principal islands of Africa lie in the Indian seas and Atlantic ocean; of which the following belong to, or trade with the Europeans, and serve to refresh their shipping to and from India.

Islands.	Towns.	Trade with or belong to
Babelmandel, at the entrance of the Red Sea	Babelmandel	All nations
Zocotra, in the Indian Ocean	Calanfia	Ditto
The Comora Isles, ditto	Joanna	Ditto
Madagascar, ditto	St. Austin	Ditto
Mauritius, ditto	Mauritius	French
Bourbon, ditto	Bourbon	Ditto
St. Helena, in the Atlantic Ocean	St. Helena	English
Ascension, ditto		Uninhabited
St. Mathew, ditto		Ditto
St. Thomas, Anabon, Princes-Island, Fernandopo	ditto St. Thomas, Anabon	Portugueze
Cape Verd Islands, ditto	St. Domingo	Ditto
Goree, ditto	Fort St. Michael	French
Canaries, ditto	Palma, St. Christophers	Spanish
Madeiras, ditto	Santa Cruz, Funchal	Portugueze
The Azores, or Western Isles, lie nearly at an equal distance from Europe, Asia, and Africa	ditto Angra	Ditto

Having given the reader fome idea of Africa, in general, with the principal kingdoms, and their fuppofed dimenfions, we fhall now confider it under three grand divifions: firft, Egypt; fecondly, the ftates of Barbary, ftretching along the coaft of the Mediterranean, from Egypt in the eaft, to the Atlantic Ocean, weft; and, laftly, that part of Africa between the tropic of Cancer, and the cape of Good Hope; the laft of thefe divifions, indeed, is vaftly greater than the other two; but the nations, which it contains, are fo little known, and fo barbarous, and like all barbarous nations, fo fimilar in moft refpects to one another, that they may, without impropriety, be thrown under one general head.

E G Y P T.

SITUATION AND EXTENT.

	Miles.	Degrees.
Length	600 } between	{ 20 and 32 north latitude.
Breadth	250 }	{ 28 and 36 eaft longitude.

BOUNDARIES.] IT is bounded by the Mediterranean fea, north; by the Red fea, eaft; by Abyffinia, or the Upper Ethiopia, on the fouth; and by the defart of Barca, and the unknown parts of Africa, weft,

Divifions.	Subdivifions.	Chief towns,
Northern divifion contains	{ Lower Egypt	{ GRAND CAIRO, E. lon. 32, N. lat. 30. Bulac Alexandria Rofetto Damietta
Southern divifion contains	{ Upper Egypt	{ Sayd or Thebes Coffiar

AIR.] In April and May the air is hot, and often infectious; the inhabitants are blinded with drifts of fand. Thofe evils are remedied by the rifing and overflowing of the Nile.

SOIL AND PRODUCE.] Whoever is in the leaft acquainted with literature, knows that the vaft fertility of Egypt is not owing to rain, (little falling in that country) but to the annual overflowing of the Nile. It begins to rife when the fun is vertical in Ethiopia, and the annual rains fall there, viz. the latter end of May to September, and fometimes October. At the height of its flood in the Lower Egypt, nothing is to be feen in the plains, but the tops of forefts and fruit-trees, their

towns

towns and villages being built upon eminences either natural
or artificial. When the river is at its proper height, the inhabitants celebrate a kind of a jubilee, with all sorts of festi-
vities. The banks or mounds which confine it, are cut by
the Turkish basha, attended by his grandees; but according to captain Norden, who was present on the occasion,
the spectacle is not very magnificent. When the banks
are cut, the water is let into what they call the Chalis,
or grand canal, which runs through Cairo, from whence it is
distributed into cuts, for supplying their fields and gardens.
This being done, and the waters beginning to retire, such is
the fertility of the soil, that the labouring husbandman is next
to nothing. He throws his wheat and barley into the ground
in October and May. He turns his cattle out to graze in
November, and in about six weeks, nothing can be more
charming than the prospect, which the face of the country
presents, in rising corn, vegetables, and verdure of every sort.
Oranges, lemons, and fruits, perfume the air. The culture
of pulse, melons, sugar canes, and other plants, which require moisture, is supplied by small but regular cuts from
cisterns and reservoirs. Dates, plantanes, grapes, figs, and
palm-trees, from which wine is made, are here plentiful.
March and April are the harvest months, and they produce
three crops; one of lettuces and cucumbers, (the latter being
the chief food of the inhabitants) one of corn, and one of
melons. The Egyptian pasturage is equally prolific, most of
the quadrupeds producing two at a time, and the sheep four
lambs a year.

ANIMALS.] Egypt abounds in black cattle, and it is said
that the inhabitants employ every day 200,000 oxen, in raising
water for their grounds. They have a fine large breed of
asses, upon which the Christians ride, those people not being
suffered by the Turks to ride on any other beast. The Egyptian horses are very fine; they never trot, but walk well, and
gallop with great speed, turn short, stop in a moment, and are
extremely tractable. The hippopotamus, or river horse, an amphibious animal, resembling an ox, in its hinder parts, with the
head like a horse, is common in Upper Egypt. Tygers,
hyenas, camels, antelopes, apes, with the head like a dog,
and the rat, called Ichneumon, are natives of Egypt. The
camelion, a little animal something resembling a lizard, that
changes colour, as you stand to look upon him, is found here
as well as in other countries. The crocodile was formerly
thought peculiar to this country; but there does not seem to
be any material difference between it, and the alligators of
India and America. They are both amphibious animals, in
the form of a lizard, and grow till they are about twenty feet

in length, and have four short legs, with large feet armed
with claws, and their backs are covered with a kind of impenetrable scales, like armour. The crocodile waits for his
prey in the sedge, and other cover, on the sides of rivers, and
pretty much resembling the trunk of an old tree, sometimes
surprizes the unwary traveller with his fore paws, or beats
him down with his tail.

This country produces likewise great numbers of eagles,
hawks, pelicans, and water-fowls of all kinds. The ibis, a
creature (according to Mr. Norden) somewhat resembling a
duck, was deified by the antient Egyptians for its destroying
serpents, and pestiferous insects. They were thought to be
peculiar to Egypt, but a species of them is said to have been
lately discovered in other parts of Africa. Ostriches are common here, and are so strong, that the Arabs sometimes ride
upon their backs.

POPULATION, MANNERS, CUS-
TOMS, AND DIVERSIONS. As the population of
Egypt is almost confined
to the banks of the Nile, and the rest of the country inhabited
by Arabs, and other nations, we can say little upon this head,
with precision. It seems however to be certain, that Egypt
is at present not near so populous as formerly, and that its
depopulation is owing to the inhabitants being slaves to the
Turks. They are, however, still very numerous, but the
populousness of Cairo, as if it contained two millions, is a
mere fiction.

The descendents of the original Egyptians, are an ill-looked
slovenly people, immersed in indolence, and are distinguished
by the name of Coptis; in their complexions they are rather
sun-burnt than swarthy, or black. Their ancestors were once
Christians, and in general they still pretend to be of that religion. Mahometanism is the prevailing worship among the
natives. Those who inhabit the villages and fields, at any
considerable distance from the Nile, I have already mentioned
to consist of Arabs or their descendents, who are of a deep
swarthy complexion, and they are represented by the best
authorities, as retaining the patriarchal tending their flocks
and many of them without any fixed place of abode. The
Turks, who reside in Egypt, retain all their Ottoman pride
and insolence, and the Turkish habit, to distinguish themselve
from the Arabs and Coptis, who dress very plain, their chie
finery being an upper garment of white linen, and linen
drawers, but their ordinary dress is of blue linen, with
long cloath coat, either over or under it. The Christians and
Arabs of the meaner kind, content themselves with a linen o
woollen wrapper, which they fold, blanket-like, round thei
body

body. The Jews wear blue leather flippers, the other natives of the country wear red, and the foreign Chriftians yellow. The drefs of the women is tawdry and unbecoming, but their cloaths are filk, when they can afford it, and fuch of them as are not expofed to the fun, have delicate complexions and features. The Coptis are generally excellent accomptants, and many of them live by teaching the other natives to read and write. Their exercifes and diverfions are much the fame as thofe made ufe of in Perfia, and other Afiatic dominions. All Egypt is over-run with jugglers, fortune-tellers, mountebanks, and travelling flight-of-hand men.

RELIGION.] To what I have already faid concerning the religion of Egypt, it is proper to add, that the bulk of the Mahometans are enthufiafts, and have among them their fantos or fellows who pretend to a fuperior degree of holinefs, and without any ceremony intrude into the beft houfes, where it would be dangerous to turn them out. The Egyptian Turks mind religious affairs very little, and it would be hard to fay what fpecies of Chriftianity is profefied by the Chriftian Cops, which are here numerous, but they profefs themfelves to be of the Greek church, and enemies to that of Rome. In religious, and indeed many civil matters, they are under the jurifdiction of the patriarch of Alexandria, who by the dint of money generally purchafes a protection at the Ottoman court.

LANGUAGE.] The Coptic is the moft antient language of Egypt. This was fucceeded by the Greek, about the time of Alexander the Great; and that by the Arabic, upon the commencement of the califate, when the Arabs difpoffeffed the Greeks of Egypt. The Arabic, or Arabefque, as it is called, is ftill the current language, but the Coptic and modern Greek continue to be fpoken.

LEARNING AND LEARNED MEN.] Though it is paft difpute that the Greeks derived all their knowledge from the antient Egyptians, yet fcarce a veftige of it remains among their defcendents. This is owing to the bigotry and ignorance of their Mahometan mafters, but here it is proper to make one obfervation which is of general ufe. The califs or Saracens who fubdued Egypt, were of three kinds. The firft, who were the immediate fucceffors of Mahomet, made war from confcience and principle upon all kind of literature excepting the Alcoran; and hence it was that when they took poffeffion of Alexandria, which contained the moft magnificent library the world ever beheld, its valuable manufcripts were applied for fome months in cooking their victuals, and warming their baths. The fame fate attended upon the other magnificent Egyptian libraries. The califs of the fecond race, were men

of

of tafte and learning, but of a peculiar ftrain. They bought up all the manufcripts that furvived the general conflagration relating to aftronomy, medicine, and fome ufelefs parts of philofophy, but they had no tafte for the Greek arts of architecture, fculpture, painting, or poetry, and learning was confined to their own courts and colleges, without ever finding its way back to Egypt. The lower race of califs, efpecially thofe who called themfelves califs of Egypt, difgraced human nature; and the Turks have rivetted the chains of barbarous ignorance which they impofed.

All the learning therefore poffeffed by the modern Egyptians confifts in arithmetical calculations for the difpatch of bufinefs, the jargon of aftrology, a few noftrums in medicine, and fome knowledge of Arabefque or the Mahometan religion.

CURIOSITIES AND ANTIQUITIES.] Egypt abounds more with thofe than perhaps any other part of the world. Its pyramids have been often defcribed. Their antiquity is beyond the refearches of hiftory itfelf, and their original ufes are ftill unknown. The bafis of the largeft, covers eleven acres of ground, and its perpendicular height is 500 feet, but if meafured obliquely to the terminating point 700 feet. It contains a room thirty-four feet long, and feventeen broad, in which is a marble cheft, but without either cover or contents, fuppofed to have been defigned for the tomb of the founder. In fhort, the pyramids of Egypt are the moft ftupendous, and, to appearance, the moft ufelefs ftructures that ever were raifed by the hands of men.

The mummy pits, fo called for their containing the mummies or embalmed bodies of the antient Egyptians, are fubterraneous vaults of a prodigious extent; but the art of preparing the mummies is now loft. It is faid that fome of the bodies thus embalmed, are perfect and diftinct at this day, though buried 3000 years ago. The labyrinth is a curiofity thought to be more wonderful than the pyramids themfelves. It is partly under ground, and cut out of a marble rock, confifting of twelve palaces, and 1000 houfes, the intricacies of which occafion its name. The lake Mæris was dug by order of an Egyptian king, to correct the irregularities of the Nile, and to communicate with that river, by canals and ditches which ftill fubfift, and are evidences of the utility, as well as grandeur of the work. Wonderful grottos and excavations, moftly artificial, abound in Egypt. The whole country towards Grand Cairo, is a continued fcene of antiquities, of which the oldeft are the moft ftupendous, but the more modern the moft beautiful. Cleopatra's needle, and its fculptures, are admirable. Pompey's pillar is a fine regular column of the

Corinthian

Corinthian order, the fhaft of which is one ftone, being eighty-eight feet, nine inches in height, or ten diameters of the column, the who'e height is 114 feet, including the capital and the pedeftal. The Sphynx, as it is called, is no more than the head and part of the fhoulders of a woman hewn out of the rock, and about thirty feet high, near one of the pyramids.

The papyrus is one of the natural curiofities of Egypt, and ferved the antients to write upon, but we know not the manner of preparing it. The pith of it is a nourifhing food. The manner of hatching chickens in ovens, is common in Egypt, and now.practifed in fome parts of Europe. The conftruction of the oven is very curious.

CITIES, TOWNS, AND} Even a flight review of thefe
  PUBLIC EDIFICES. } would amount to a large volume.
In many places, not only temples, but the walls of cities, built before the time of Alexander the Great, are ftill entire, and many of their ornaments, particularly the colours of their paintings, are as frefh and vivid, as when firft laid on.

Alexandria, which lies on the Levant coaft, was once the emporium of all the world, and by means of the Red-Sea, furnifhed Europe, and great part of Afia, with the riches of India. It owes its name to its founder, Alexander the Great. It ftands forty miles weft from the Nile, and a hundred and twenty north-weft of Cairo. It rofe upon the ruins of Tyre and Carthage, and is famous for the light-houfe erected on the oppofite ifland of Pharos, for the direction of mariners, defervedly efteemed one of the wonders of the world. All the other parts of the city were magnificent in proportion, as appears from their ruins, particularly the cifterns and aqueducts. Many of the materials of the old city, however, have been employed in building Nero Alexandria, which at prefent is a very ordinary feaport, known by the name of Scandercon. Notwithftanding the poverty, ignorance, and indolence of the inhabitants, their mofques, bagnios, and the like buildings, erected within thefe ruins, preferve an inexpreffible air of majefty. Some think that Old Alexandria was built from the materials of the antient Memphis.

Rofetta, or Rafchid, ftands twenty-five miles to the north-weft of Alexandria, and is recommended for its beautiful fituation, and delightful profpects, which command the fine country, or ifland of Delta, formed by the Nile, near its mouth. It is likewife a place of great trade.

Cairo, the prefent capital of Egypt, is a large and populous, but a difagreeable refidence, on account of its peftilential air, and its narrow ftreets. It is divided into two towns, the old,

and the new, and defended by an old caftle, the works of
which are faid to be three miles in circumference. The well
called Jofeph's well, is a curious piece of mechanifm, about
300 feet deep. The memory of that patriarch is ftill revered
in Egypt, where they fhew granaries, and many other works
of public utility, that go under his name. They are certainly
of vaft antiquity, but it is very queftionable whether they
were erected by him. One of his granaries is fhewn in Old
Cairo, but captain Norden fufpects it is a Saracen work, nor
does he give us any high idea of the buildings of the city
itfelf. On the bank of the Nile, facing Cairo, lies the village
of Gize, which is thought to be the antient Memphis. The
Chriftians of Cairo practife a holy cheat, during the Eafter
holidays, by pretending that the limbs and bodies of the dead
arife from their graves, to which they return peaceably. The
ftreets of Cairo are peftered with the jugglers and fortune-tellers already mentioned. One of their favourite exhibitions is
their dancing camels, which, when young, they place upon
a large heated floor : the intenfe heat makes the poor creatures
caper, and being plied all the time with the found of drums,
the noife of that inftrument fets them a dancing all their lives
after.

The other towns of note in Egypt are Damietta, fuppofed
to be the antient Pelufium ; Bulac ; Seyd, on the weft bank
of the Nile, 200 miles fouth of Cairo, faid to be the antient
Egyptian Thebes, and by the few who have vifited it, it is
reported to be the moft capital antique curiofity that is now
extant. The general practice of ftrangers, who vifit thofe
places, is to hire a janifary, whofe authority commonly protects them from the infults of the other natives. Suez, formerly a place of great trade, is now a fmall city, and gives
name to the ifthmus, that joins Africa with Afia. The children of Ifrael are fuppofed to have marched near this city,
when they left Egypt, in their way towards the Red-Sea.
The above is all the account my bounds will admit of the
topography of this country, where almoft every object and
village prefents fome amazing piece of antiquity. The difficulties in vifiting it are great ; fo that the accounts we can
depend upon, are but few, nor do they always agree together.

MANUFACTURES AND COMMERCE.] Modern geographers
mention little of Egyptian manufactures at this time, but
captain Norden, who travelled to that country, at the expence
of his prefent Danifh majefty's grandfather, about the year
1737, has been pretty explicit on the fubject of commerce,
and from him we learn that the Egyptians export prodigious

quantities of unmanufactured as well as prepared flax, thread, cotton, and leather of all forts, callicoes, yellow wax, fal armoniac, faffron, fugar, fenna, caffia. They trade with the Arabs, for coffee, drugs, fpices, callicoes, and other merchandizes, which are landed at Suez, from whence they fend them to Europe. Several European ftates have confuls refident in Egypt, but the cuftoms of the Turkifh government are managed by Jews. A number of Englifh veffels arrive yearly at Alexandria, fome of which are laden on account of the owners, but moft of them are hired and employed as carriers to the Jews, Armenians, and Mahometan traders. Captain Norden feems to think that the Englifh conful and merchants make no great figure at Alexandria, but that they are in much lefs danger, and lefs troubled than the French.

CONSTITUTION AND GOVERNMENT.] Thefe feem to be but little known to modern times. It is certain that Egypt is fubject to the Turks, and that even the meaneft janifary is refpected by the natives. A viceroy is fent to Egypt, under the title of the pafha or bafhaw of Cairo, and is one of the greateft officers of the Ottoman empire ; but as the interior parts of Egypt are almoft inacceffible to ftrangers, we know little of their government and laws. It is generally agreed, that the pafha is very careful how he provokes the little princes, or rather heads of clans, who have parcelled out Egypt among themfelves, and whom he governs chiefly by playing one againft another. He has however a large regular army, and a militia, which ferve as nurferies from whence the Ottoman troops are recruited. The keeping up this army employs his chief attention. It has fometimes happened, that thofe pafhas have employed their arms againft their mafters ; and they are fometimes difplaced by the Porte, upon complaints from thofe petty princes. Thofe circumftances may account for the reafon why Egypt is not over-loaded with taxes. Captain Norden and Dr. Pocock have given us the beft, and indeed a very unfavourable account of thofe petty princes, who are called the Schechs of the Bedouins, or wandering Arabs, who are fometimes too powerful to receive laws from the Turkifh government.

A certain number of beys or begs, are appointed over the provinces of Egypt, under the pafha. Though thefe beys are defigned to be checks upon him, yet they often affume independent powers, and many of them have confiderable revenues.

REVENUES.] Thefe are very inconfiderable, when compared to the natural riches of the country, and the defpotifm of its government. Some fay that they amount to a million fterling, but that two-thirds of the whole is fpent in the country.

MILITARY STRENGTH.] Authors are greatly divided on this article. Captain Norden tells us, that it is divided into two corps of janisaries, and assafs are the chief, the former amounting to about six or eight thousand, and the latter to between three and four thousand. The other troops are of little account. After all, it does not at all appear, that the pasha ever ventures to employ those troops against the Arab or Egyptian princes I have already mentioned, and who have separate armies of their own; so that, in fact, their dependance upon the Porte, is little more than nominal, and amounts at most to feudal services.

HISTORY.] It is generally agreed, that the princes of the line of the Pharaohs, sat on the throne of Egypt, in an uninterrupted succession, till Cambyses II. king of Persia, conquered the Egyptians 520 years before the birth of Christ; and that in the reign of these princes, those wonderful structures the pyramids were raised, which cannot be viewed without astonishment. Egypt continued a part of the Persian empire, till Alexander the Great vanquished Darius, when it fell under the dominion of that prince, who soon after built the celebrated city of Alexandria. The conquests of Alexander, who died in the prime of life, being seized upon by his generals, the province of Egypt fell to the share of Ptolemy, by some supposed to have been a half-brother of Alexander, when it again became an independent kingdom, about 300 years before Christ. His successors, who sometimes extended their dominion over great part of Syria, ever after retained the name of Ptolemies, and in that line Egypt continued between two and three hundred years, till the famous Cleopatra, the wife and sister of Ptolemy Dionysius, the last king, ascended the throne. After the death of Cleopatra, who had been mistress successively to Julius Cæsar and Mark Anthony, Egypt became a Roman province, and thus remained till the reign of Omar, the second calif of the successors of Mahomet, who expelled the Romans, after it had been in their hands 700 years. The famous library of Alexandria, said to consist of 700,000 volumes, was collected by Ptolemy Philadelphus, son of the first Ptolemy; and the same prince caused the Old Testament to be translated into Greek, but whether by seventy-two interpreters, and in the manner commonly related, is justly questioned; this translation is known by the name of the Septuagint, and is often quoted by commentators. About the time of the crusades, between the year 1150, and 1190, Egypt was governed by Noreddin, whose son, the famous Saladin, was so dreadful to those Christian adventurers, and retook from them Jerusalem. He instituted the military corps
of

of Mamalukes, who, about the year 1242, advanced one of their own officers to the throne, and ever after chose their prince out of their own body. Egypt, for some time, made a figure under those illustrious usurpers, and made a noble stand against the prevailing power of the Turks, under Selim, who, about the year 1517, after giving the Mamalukes several bloody defeats, reduced Egypt to its present state of subjection.

While Selim was settling the government of Egypt, great numbers of the antient inhabitants withdrew into the desarts and plains, under one Zingancus, from whence they attacked the cities and villages of the Nile, and plundered whatever fell in their way. Selim and his officers perceiving that it would be a matter of great difficulty to extirpate those marauders, left them at liberty to quit the country, which they did in great numbers, and their posterity is known all over Europe and Asia, by the name of Gipsies. Though I shall not warrant the truth of this account, yet it seems to be countenanced from the roving dispositions, and the peculiar manners, features, and complexion of those swarthy begging itinerants. Of late, however, many of them have incorporated with, and adopted the manners of the people among whom they reside.

THE STATES OF BARBARY.

UNDER this head I shall rank the countries of, 1. Morocco and Fez, 2. Algiers, 3. Tunis, 4. Tripoli and Barca.

The empire of Morocco, including Fez, is bounded on the north by the Mediterranean sea; on the south, by Tafilet; and on the east, by Segelmessa and the kingdom of Algiers; being 500 miles in length, and 480 in breadth.

Fez, which is now united to Morocco, is about 125 miles in length, and much the same in breadth. It lies between the kingdom of Algiers to the east, and Morocco on the south, and is surrounded in other parts by the sea.

Algiers, formerly a kingdom, is bounded on the east by the kingdom of Tunis, on the north by the Mediterranean, on the south by Mount Atlas, and on the west by the kingdoms of Morocco and Tafilet. According to Dr. Shaw, who resided twelve years at Algiers in quality of chaplain to the British factory, and has corrected many errors of ancient and modern geographers respecting the states of Barbary, this country extends in length 480 miles along the coast of the Mediterranean, and is between 40 and 100 miles in breadth.

Tunis

Tunis is bounded by the Mediterranean on the north and east; by the kingdom of Algiers on the west; and by Tripoli, with part of Biledulgerid, on the south; being 220 miles in length from north to south, and 170 in breadth from east to west.

Tripoli, including Barca, is bounded on the north by the Mediterranean sea; on the south by the country of the Beriberies; on the west by the kingdom of Tunis, Biledulgerid, and a territory of the Gadamis; and on the east by Egypt; extending about 1100 miles along the sea-coast; and the breadth is from 1 to 300 miles.

Each capital bears the name of the state or kingdom to which it belongs.

This being premised, I shall consider the Barbary states as forming (which they really do) a great political confederacy, however independent each may be as to the exercise of its internal policy; nor is there a greater difference than happens in different provinces of the same kingdom, in the customs and manners of the inhabitants.

AIR AND SEASONS.] The air of Morocco is mild, as is that of Algiers, and indeed all the other states, excepting in the months of July and August.

SOIL, VEGETABLE AND ANIMAL ⎱ Those states, under
   PRODUCTIONS, BY SEA AND LAND. ⎰ the Roman empire, were justly denominated the garden of the world, and to have a residence there was considered as the highest stage of luxury. The produce of their soil formed those magazines, which furnished all Italy, and great part of the Roman empire, with corn, wine, and oil. Though the lands are now uncultivated, through the oppression and barbarity of their constitution, yet they are still fertile, not only in the above-mentioned commodities, but in dates, figs, raisins, almonds, apples, pears, cherries, plums, citrons, lemons, oranges, pomegranates, with plenty of roots and herbs in their kitchen-gardens. Excellent hemp and flax grow on their plains; and by the report of Europeans, who have lived there for some time, the country abounds with all that can add to the pleasures of life; for their great people find means to evade the sobriety prescribed by the Mahometan law, and make free with excellent wines, and spirits of their own growth and manufacture. Algiers produces salt-petre, and great quantities of excellent salt, and lead and iron have been found in several places of Barbary.

Neither the elephant nor the rhinoceros are to be found in the states of Barbary, but their deserts abound with lions, tigers, leopards, hyænas, and monstrous serpents. The Barbary horses were formerly very valuable, and thought equal to the Arabian.

bian. Though their breed are now said to be decayed, yet
some very fine ones have been lately imported into England.
Camels and dromedaries, asses, mules, and kumrahs, a most
serviceable creature, begot by an ass upon a cow, are their
beasts of burden. Their cows are but small, and barren of
milk. Their sheep yield but indifferent fleeces, but are very
large, as are their goats. Bears, porcupines, foxes, apes, hares,
rabbits, ferrets, weafels, moles, cameleons, and all kinds of
reptiles are found here. Besides vermin, says Dr. Shaw, (speaking of his travels thro' Barbary) the apprehensions we were
under in some parts at least of this country, of being bitten
or stung by the scorpion, the viper, or the venomous-spider,
rarely failed to interrupt our repose; a refreshment so very
grateful, and so highly necessary to a weary traveller. Partridges and quails, eagles, hawks, and all kind of wild fowl,
are found on this coast; and of the smaller birds, the capfa-
sparrow is remarkable for its beauty, and the sweetness of
its note, which is thought to exceed that of any other bird,
but it cannot live out of its own climate. The seas and bays of
Barbary abound with the finest and most delicious fish of every
kind, and were preferred by the ancients to those of Europe.

POPULATION, INHABITANTS, MAN-⎫ Morocco was cer-
  NERS, CUSTOMS,' AND DIVERSIONS. ⎰ tainly formerly far
more populous than it is now, if, as travellers say, its capital
contained 100,000 houses, whereas at present, it is thought
not to contain above 25,000 inhabitants, nor can we think
that the other parts of the country are more populous, if it is
true, that their king or emperor has 80,000 horse and foot, of
foreign negroes, in his armies.

The city of Algiers is said to contain 100,000 Mahometans,
15,000 Jews, and 2000 Christian slaves; but no estimate can
be formed as to the populousness of its territory. Some travellers report, that it is inhabited by a friendly hospitable people, who are very different in their manners and character
from those of the metropolis.

Tunis is the most polished republic of all the Barbary states.
The capital contains 10,000 families, and above 3000 tradef-
mens shops, and its suburbs confist of 1000 houses. The
Tunifines are indeed exceptions to the other states of Barbary;
for even the most civilized of the European governments,
might improve from their manners. Their distinctions are
well kept up, and proper respect is paid to the military, mercantile, and learned professions. They cultivate friendship
with the European states; arts and manufactures have been
lately introduced among them, and the inhabitants are said at
present to be well acquainted with the various labours of the
loom.

loom. The Tunisine women are excessively handsome in
their persons, and though the men are sun-burnt, the complexion of the ladies is very delicate, nor are they less neat
and elegant in their dress; but they improve the beauty of
their eyes by art, particularly the powder of lead ore, the
same pigment, according to the opinion of the learned Dr.
Shaw, that Jezebel made use of when she is said (2 Kings chap.
ix. verse 30.) to have painted her face, the words of the original being, that she set off her eyes with the powder of lead-
ore. The gentlemen in general are sober, orderly, and clean
in their persons, their behaviour genteel and complaisant, and
a wonderful regularity reigns through all the streets and city.

Tripoli was once the richest, most populous, and opulent of
all the states on the coast; but it is now much reduced, and
the inhabitants, who are said to amount to between 4 and
500,000, have all the vices of the Algerines.

Their manners are pretty much of a piece with those of the
Egyptians already described. The subjects of the Barbary
states, however, in general subsisting by piracy, are allowed to
be bold intrepid mariners, and will fight desperately when
they meet with a prize at sea. They are notwithstanding far
inferior to the English, and other European states, both in the
construction and management of their vessels. They are, if
we except the Tunisines, void of all arts and literature. The
misery and poverty of the inhabitants of Morocco, who are not
immediately in the emperor's service, are beyond all description; but those who inhabit the inland parts of the country,
are a hospitable inoffensive people, and indeed it is a general
observation, that the more distant the inhabitants of those
states are from the seats of their government, their manners
are the more pure. Notwithstanding their poverty, they have
a liveliness about them, especially those who are of Arabic de-
scent, that gives them an air of contentment, and having
nothing to lose, they are peaceable among themselves. The
Moors are supposed to be the original inhabitants, but are now
blended with the Arabs, and both are cruelly oppressed by a
handful of insolent domineering Turks, the refuse of the
streets of Constantinople.

DRESS.] The dress of these people is a linen shirt, over
which they tie a silk or cloth vestment with a sash, and over
that a loose coat. Their drawers are made of linen. The
arms and legs of the wearer are bare, but they have slippers
on their feet; and persons of condition sometimes wear buskins.
They never move their turbans, but pull off their slippers
when they attend religious duties, or the person of their sovereign. They are fond of striped and fancied silks. The dress

of

of the women is not very different from that of the men, but
their drawers are longer, and they wear a fort of a cawl on their
heads inftead of a turban.   The chief furniture of their houfes
confifts of carpets and mattreffes, on which they fit and lie.
In eating, their flovenlinefs is fhocking.   They are prohibited
gold and filver veffels; and their meat, which they fwallow
by handfuls, is boiled or roafted to rags.   Adultery in the
women is punifhed with death; but though the men are
indulged with a plurality of wives and concubines, they commit the moft unnatural crimes with impunity.

RELIGION.]   The inhabitants of thofe ftates are Mahometans : but many fubjects of Morocco follow the tenets of
one Hamed, a modern fectarift, and an enemy to the antient
doctrine of the califs.   All of them are very fond of ideots,
and in fome cafes their protection fcreens offenders from punifhment, for the moft notorious crimes.   In the main, however, the Moors of Barbary, as the inhabitants of thofe ftates are
now promifcuoufly called, have adopted the very worft parts of
the Mahometan religion, and feem to have retained only as much
of it as authorizes them to commit the moft horrible villanies.

LANGUAGE.]   As the ftates of Barbary poffefs thofe countries that formerly went by the name of Mauritania and
Numidia, the antient African language is ftill fpoken in fome
of the inland countries, and even by fome inhabitants of the
city of Morocco.   In the fea port towns, and maritime countries, a baftard kind of Arabic is fpoken, and fea-faring
people are no ftrangers to that medley of living and dead languages, that is fo well known in all the ports of the Mediterranean, by the name of Lingua Franca.

ANTIQUITIES AND CURIOSITIES, ⎰   This article is well
    NATURAL AND ARTIFICIAL. ⎱   worth the ftudy of an
antiquary, but the fubjects of it are difficult of accefs.   The
reader can fcarcely doubt that the countries which contained
Carthage, and the pride of the Phenician, Greek, and Roman
works, is replete with the moft curious remains of antiquity,
but they lie fcattered amidft ignorant, barbarous inhabitants.
Some remains of the Mauritanian and Numidian greatnefs are
ftill to be met with, and many ruins which bear evidences of
their antient grandeur and populoufnefs.   Thefe point out the
old Julia Cæfarea of the Romans, which was little inferior in
magnificence to Carthage itfelf.   A few of the aqueducts of
Carthage are faid to be ftill remaining, but no veftige of its
walls.   The fame is the fate of Utica, and many other renowned cities of antiquity; and fo over-run is the country
with barbarifm, that their very fcites are not known, even by
their ruins, amphitheatres, and other public buildings which
                                                    remain

remain ftill in tolerable prefervation. Befides thofe of claffical antiquity, many Saracen monuments of the moft ftupendous magnificence are likewife found in this vaft tract; thefe were erected under the califs of Bagdat, and the antient kings of the country before it was fubdued by the Turks, or reduced to its prefent form of government. Their walls form the principal fortifications in the country, both inland and maritime. We know of few or no natural curiofities belonging to this country, excepting its falt-pits, which in fome places take up an area of fix miles. Dr. Shaw mentions fprings found here that are fo hot as to boil a large piece of mutton very tender in a quarter of an hour.

Before I clofe this article it may be proper to obferve, that this country has been but little vifited by the curious, if we except Dr. Shaw; but it certainly deferves a more accurate inveftigation.

CITIES AND PUBLIC BUILDINGS.] Mention has already been made of Morocco, the capital of that kingdom, but now almoft in ruins, the court having removed to Mequinez, a city of Fez. Incredible things are recorded of the magnificent palaces in both cities, but by the beft accounts, the common people live in a dirty flovenly manner.

The city of Algiers, is not above a mile and a half in circuit, though, as I have already obferved, it is computed to contain near 120,000 inhabitants, 15,000 houfes, and 107 mofques. Their public baths are large, and handfomely paved with marble. The profpect of the country and fea from Algiers is very beautiful; but the city, though for feveral ages it has braved the greateft powers in Chriftendom, could make but a faint defence againft a regular fiege; and it is faid that three Englifh fifty-gun fhips might batter it about the ears of its inhabitants from the harbour.

The kingdom of Tunis, which is naturally the fineft of all thefe ftates, contains the remains of many noble cities, fome of them ftill in good condition. The town itfelf has fortifications, and is about three miles in circumference. The houfes are not magnificent, but neat and commodious; as is the public exchange for merchants and their goods; but, like Algiers, it is diftreffed for want of frefh water.

The city of Tripoli confifts of an old and new town, the latter being the moft flourifhing; but never can make any confiderable figure, on account of the inconveniencies attending its fituation, particularly the want of fweet water. The city of Oran, lying upon this coaft, is about a mile in circumference, and is fortified both by art and nature. It was a place of confiderable trade, and the object of many bloody

U 2

difputes between the Spaniards and the Moors. Conftantina was the antient Cirta, and one of the ftrongeft cities of Numidia, being inacceffible on all fides, excepting the fouth-weft.

Befides the above towns and cities, many other, formerly · of great renown, lie fcattered up and down this immenfe tract of country. I cannot, however, leave it without mentioning the city of Fez, at prefent the capital of that kingdom: fome fay that it contains near 300,000 inhabitants, befides merchants and foreigners. Its mofques amount to 500, one of them magnificent beyond defcription, and about a mile and a half in circumference. Mequinez is efteemed the great emporium of all Barbary. Sallee lies in the fame kingdom, and was formerly famous for the piracies of its inhabitants. Tangier, fituated about two miles within the ftraits of Gibraltar, was given by the crown of Portugal as part of the dowry of queen Catharine, confort of Charles II. of England. It was intended to be to the Englifh what Gibraltar is now; and it muft have been a moft noble acquifition, had not the mifunderftandings between the king and his parliament obliged him to blow up its fortifications and demolifh its harbour; fo that from being one of the fineft cities in Africa, it is now little better than a fifhing town. Ceuta, upon the fame ftrait, almoft oppofite to Gibraltar, is ftill in the hands of the Spaniards, but often, if not always befieged or blocked up by the Moors. Tetuan, which lies within twenty miles of Ceuta, is now but an ordinary town, containing about 800 houfes; but the inhabitants are faid to be rich, extremely complaifant, and they live in an elegant manner.

The provinces of Suz, Tafilet, and Gefula, form no part of the ftates of Barbary, though the king of Morocco pretends to be their fovereign; nor do they contain any thing that is particularly curious.

MANUFACTURES AND COMMERCE.] The lower fubjects of thofe ftates, know very few imaginary wants, and depend partly upon their piracies, to be fupplied with neceffary utenfils and manufactures, fo that their exports confift chiefly of leather, fine mats, embroidered handkerchiefs, fword knots and carpets, which are cheaper and fofter than thofe of Turkey, though not fo good in other refpects. As they leave almoft all their commercial affairs to the Jews and Chriftians fettled among them, the latter have eftablifhed filk and linen works, which fupply the higher ranks of their own fubjects. They have no fhips that, properly fpeaking, are employed in commerce; fo that the French and Englifh carry on the greateft part of their trade. Their exports, befides thofe

2   already

already mentioned, confift in elephants teeth, oftrich feathers, copper, tin, wool, hides, honey, wax, dates, raifins, olives, almonds, gum arabic, and fandrac.   The inhabitants of Morocco are likewife faid to carry on a confiderable trade by caravans to Mecca, Medina, and fome inland parts of Africa, from whence they bring back vaft numbers of negroes, who ferve in their armies, and are flaves in their houfes and fields.

In return for their exports, the Europeans furnifh them with timber, artillery of all kinds, gunpowder, and whatever they want, either in their public or private capacities, the particulars of which are too many to fpecify.   The duties paid by the Englifh in the ports of Morocco, are but half thofe paid by other Europeans.   It is a general obfervation that no nation is fond of trading with thefe ftates, not only on account of their capricious defpotifm, but the villainy of their individuals, both natives and Jews, who take all opportunities of cheating, and when detected, are feldom punifhed.

It has often been thought furprizing, that the Chriftian powers fhould fuffer their marine to be infulted by thofe barbarians, who take the fhips of all nations with whom they are at peace, or rather, who do not pay them a fubfidy either in money or commodities.   We cannot account for this forbearance otherwife, than by fuppofing, firft, that a breach with them might provoke the Porte, who pretends to be their lord paramount; fecondly, that no Chriftian power would be fond of feeing Algiers, and the reft of that coaft, in poffeffion of another; and, thirdly, that nothing could be got by a bombardment of any of their towns, as the inhabitants would inftantly carry their effects into their defarts and mountains, fo that the benefit, refulting from the conqueft, muft be tedious and precarious.

CONSTITUTION AND GOVERNMENT.]   In Morocco, government cannot be faid to exift.   The emperors have for fome ages been parties, judges, and even executioners, with their own hands, in all criminal matters, nor is their brutality more incredible than the fubmiffion with which their fubjects bear it.   In abfence of the emperor, every military officer has the power of life and death in his hand, and it is feldom that they mind the form of a judicial proceeding. Some veftiges, however, of the califate government ftill continue, for in places where no military officer refides, the mufti or high prieft is the fountain of all juftice, and under him the cadis, or civil officers, who act as our juftices of the peace. Though the emperor of Morocco is not immediately fubject to the Porte, yet he acknowledges the grand fignior to be his

U 3   fuperior,

superior, and he pays him a diftant allegiance as the chief reprefentative of Mahomet. What I have faid of Morocco is applicable to Fez, both kingdoms being now under one emperor.

Though Algiers, Tunis, and Tripoli, have each of them a Turkifh pafha or dey, who governs in the name of the grand fignior, yet very little regard is paid by his ferocious fubjects, to his authority. He cannot even be faid to be nominated by the Porte. When a vacancy of the government happens, which it commonly does by murder, every foldier in the army has a vote in chufing the fucceeding dey; and though the election is often attended with blood-fhed, yet it is no fooner fixed than he is chearfully recognized and obeyed. It is true, he muft be confirmed by the Porte, but that is feldom refufed, as the divan is no ftranger to the difpofitions of the people. The power of the dey is defpotic, and the income of the dey of Algiers, amounts to about 150,000 l, a year, without greatly oppreffing the fubjects, who are very tenacious of their property. Thefe deys pay flight annual tributes to the Porte. When the grand fignior is at war with a Chriftian power, he requires their affiftance, as he does that of the king of Morocco, but he is obeyed only as they think proper. Subordinate to the deys are officers, both military and civil; and in all matters of importance, the dey is expected to take the advice of a common council, which confifts of thirty pafhas. Thefe pafhas feldom fail of forming parties, among the foldiers, againft the reigning dey, whom they make no fcruple of affaffinating, even in council, and the ftrongeft candidate then fills his place. Sometimes he is depofed; fometimes, though but very feldom, he refigns his authority to fave his life, and it is feldom he dies a natural death upon the throne. The authority of the dey is unlimited, but an unfuccefsful expedition, or too pacific a conduct feldom fails to put an end to his life and government.

REVENUES.] I have already mentioned thofe of Algiers, but they are now faid to be exceeded by Tunis. They confift of a certain proportion of the prizes taken from Chriftians, a fmall capitation tax, and the cuftoms paid by the Englifh, French, and other nations, who are fuffered to trade with thofe ftates. As to the king of Morocco, we can form no idea of his revenues, becaufe none of his fubjects can be faid to poffefs any property. From the manner of his living, his attendance and appearance, we may conclude he does not abound in riches. The ranfoms of Chriftian flaves are his perquifites. He fometimes fhares in the veffels of the other ftates, which entitles him to part of their prizes. He claims a
tenth

tenth of the goods of his Mahometan fubjects, and fix crowns
a year from every Jew merchant. He has likewife confiderable
profits in the Negroland, and other caravans, efpecially the
flave trade towards the fouth. It is thought that the whole of
his ordinary revenue in money, does not exceed 165,000 l.
a year.

MILITARY STRENGTH } By the beft accounts we have
 AT SEA AND LAND. } received, the king of Morocco
can bring to the field 100,000 men; but the ftrength of his
army confifts of cavalry mounted by his negro flaves. Thofe
wretches are brought young to Morocco, know no other ftate
but fervitude, and no other mafter but that king, and prove
the firmeft fupport of his tyranny. About the year 1727, all
the naval force of Morocco confifted only of three fmall fhips,
which lay at Sallee, and being full of men, fometimes brought
in prizes. The Algerines maintain about 6500 foot, confifting of Turks, and cologlies, or the fons of foldiers. Part
of them ferve as marines on board their veffels. About 1000
of them do garrifon duty, and part are employed in fomenting
differences among the neighbouring Arab princes. Befides
thefe, the dey can bring 2000 Moorifh horfe to the field, but
as they are enemies to the Turks, they are little trufted. Thofe
troops are under excellent difcipline, and the deys of all the other
Barbary ftates, keep up a force in proportion to their abilities,
fo that a few years ago, they refufed to fend any tribute to
the Turkifh emperor, who feems to be fatisfied with the fha-
dow of obedience which they pay him.

It is very remarkable, that though the Carthaginians, who
inhabited this very country of Barbary, had greater fleets,
and a more extenfive commerce than any other nation, or than
all the people upon the face of the earth, when that ftate
flourifhed, the prefent inhabitants have fcarce any merchant
fhips belonging to them, nor indeed any other than what
Sallee, Algiers, Tunis, and Tripoli fit out for piracy; which
are but few and fmall, and fome years ago did not exceed fix
fhips from thirty-fix to fifty guns. The admiral's fhip belongs
to the government, the other captains are appointed by private
owners, but fubject to military law. With fuch a contemptible fleet, thefe infidels not only harrafs the nations of Europe, but oblige them to pay a kind of tribute by way of
prefents.

HISTORY.] There perhaps is no problem in hiftory fo unaccountable as the decadence of the fplendor, power, and
glory of the ftates of Barbary, which, when Rome was
miftrefs of the world, formed the faireft jewels in the imperial
diadem, It was not till the feventh century that, after thefe

ftates

states had been by turns in poffeffion of the Vandals and the Greek emperors, the califs or Saracens of Bagdat conquered them, and from thence became mafters of almoft all Spain, from whence their pofterity was totally driven about the year 1492, when the exiles fettled among their friends and country-men on the Barbary coaft. This naturally begot a perpetual war between them and the Spaniards, who preffed them fo hard, that they called to their affiftance the two famous bro-thers Barbaroffa, who were admirals of the Turkifh fleet, and who after breaking the Spanifh yoke, impofed upon the inha-bitants of all thofe ftates (excepting Morocco) their own. Some attempts were made by the emperor Charles V. to reduce Algiers and Tunis, but they were unfuccefsful; and, as we have already obferved, the inhabitants have in fact fhaken off the Turkifh yoke likewife.

The emperors or kings of Morocco, are the fucceffors of thofe fovereigns of that country who were called xeriffs, and whofe powers refembled that of the califat of the Saracens. They have been in general a fet of bloody tyrants, though they have had among them fome able princes, particularly Muley Moluc, who defeated and killed don Sebaftian, king of Portugal. They have lived in almoft a continued ftate of warfare with the kings of Spain and other Chriftian princes ever fince; nor does the crown of Great-Britain fometimes difdain, as in the year 1769, to purchafe their friendfhip with prefents *.

Of AFRICA, from the Tropic of Cancer to the Cape of Good-Hope. *See the Table and Map.*

THIS immenfe territory is, comparatively fpeaking, very little known; there is no traveller that has penetrated into the interior parts, fo that we are ignorant not only of the bounds but even of the names of feveral inland countries. In many material circumftances, the inhabitants of this exten-five continent agree with each other. If we except the people of Abyffinia, who are tawny, and profefs a mixture of Chri-ftianity, Judaifm and Paganifm, they are all of a black com-plexion: in their religion, except on the fea coafts, which have been vifited and fettled by ftrangers, they are pagans: and

---

* The inhabitants of the Barbary coaft have been long known by the name of Moors, becaufe the Saracens firft entered Europe from Mauritania in Africa, the country of the Moors.

and the form of government is every where monarchical. Few princes, however, possess a very extensive jurisdiction; for as the natives of this part of Africa are grosly ignorant in all the arts of utility or refinement, they are little acquainted with one another; and generally united in small societies, each governed by its own prince. In Abyssinia indeed, as well as in Congo, Loango, and Angola, we are told of powerful monarchs; but on examination, it is found that the authority of these princes stands on a precarious footing, each tribe or separate body of their subjects being under the influence of a petty chieftain of their own, to whose commands, however contrary to those of the negascha negascht, or king of kings, they are always ready to submit. This indeed must always be the case among rude nations, where the art of governing, like all others, is in a very simple and imperfect state. In the succession to the throne, force generally prevails over right; and an uncle, a brother, or other collateral relation, is on this account commonly preferred to the descendants, whether male or female.

The fertility of a country so prodigiously extensive, might be supposed more various than we find it is; in fact, there is no medium in this part of Africa with regard to the advantages of soil; it is either perfectly barren, or extremely fertile: this arises from the intense heat of the sun, which, where it meets with sufficient moisture, produces the utmost luxuriancy; and in those countries where there are few rivers, reduces the surface of the earth to a barren sand. Of this sort are the countries of Anian and Zaara, which, for want of water, and consequently of all other necessaries, are reduced to perfect deserts, as the name of the latter denotes. In those countries, on the other hand, where there is plenty of water, and particularly where the rivers overflow the land part of the year, as in Abyssinia, the productions of nature, both of the animal and vegetable kinds, are found in the highest perfection and greatest abundance. The countries of Mandingo, Ethiopia, Congo, Angola, Batua, Truticui, Monomotapa, Cafati, and Mehenemugi, are extremely rich in gold and silver. The baser metals likewise are found in these and many other parts of Africa. But the persons of the natives make the most considerable article in the produce and traffic of this miserable quarter of the globe. On the Guinea or western coast, the English trade to James Fort, and other settlements near the river Gambia, where they exchange their woollen and linen manufactures, their hard ware and spirituous liquors, for the persons of the natives. Among the Negroes, a man's wealth consists in the number of his family, whom he sells like so

many

many cattle, and often at an inferior price. Gold and ivory, next to the flave trade, form the principal branches of African commerce. Thefe are carried on from the fame coaft where the Dutch and French, as well as Englifh, have their fettlements for this purpofe. The Portuguefe are in poffeffion of the eaft and weft coaft of Africa, from the Tropic of Capricorn to the Equator; which immenfe tract they became mafters of by their fucceffive attempts and happy difcovery and navigation of the Cape of Good Hope. From the coaft of Zanguebar, on the eaftern fide, they trade not only for the articles abovementioned, but likewife for feveral others, as fenna, aloes, civet, ambergris, and frankincenfe. The Dutch have fettlements towards the fouthern parts of the continent, in the country called Caffraria, or the land of the Hottentots, where their fhips bound for India ufually put in, and trade with the natives for their cattle, in exchange for which they give them fpirituous liquors.

HISTORY.] The hiftory of this continent is little known, and probably affords no materials which deferve to render it more fo. We know from the antients, who failed a confiderable way round the coafts, that the inhabitants were in the fame rude fituation near 2000 years ago in which they are in at prefent, that is, they had nothing of humanity about them but the form. This may either be accounted for by fuppofing that nature has placed fome infuperable barrier between the natives of this divifion of Africa and the inhabitants of Europe, or that the former, being fo long accuftomed to a favage manner of life, and degenerating from one age to another, at length became altogether incapable of making any progrefs in civility or fcience. It is very certain that all the attempts of the Europeans, particularly of the Dutch at the Cape of Good Hope, have been hitherto ineffectual for making the leaft impreffion on thefe favage mortals, or giving them the leaft inclination or even idea of the European manner of life.

AFRICAN ISLANDS.

OF the African iflands, fome lie in the Eaftern or Indian Ocean, and fome in the Weftern or Atlantic. We fhall begin with thofe in the Indian Ocean, the chief of which are Zocotra, Babelmandel, Madagafcar, the Comora Iflands, Bourbon, and Mauritius. *See the Map.*

ZOCOTRA. This ifland is fituated in eaft lon. 53, north lat. 12, thirty leagues eaft of Cape Gardefoi, on the continent of Africa; it is eighty miles long and fifty-four broad, and has

has two good harbours, where the European fhips ufed formerly to put in when they loft their paffage to India. It is a populous plentiful country, yielding moft of the fruits and plants that are ufually found within the tropics, together with frankincenfe, gum-tragacanth, and aloes. The inhabitants are Mahometans, of Arab extraction, and are under the government of a prince who is probably tributary to the Porte.

BABELMANDEL. The ifland of Babelmandel gives name to the ftraits at the entrance of the Red-Sea, where it is fituated in eaft lon. 44-30, north lat. 12, about four miles both from the Arabian and Abyffinian fhores. The Abyffinians or Ethiopians, and the Arabians, formerly contended with great fury for the poffeffion of this ifland, as it commands the entrance into the South-Sea, and preferves a communication with the ocean. This ftrait was formerly the only paffage through which the commodities of India found their way to Europe; but fince the difcovery of the Cape of Good Hope the trade by the Red-Sea is of little importance. The ifland is of little value, being a barren fandy fpot of earth not five miles round.

COMORA. Thefe iflands are fituated between 41 and 46 eaft lon. and between 10 and 14 fouth lat. at an equal diftance from Madagafcar and the continent of Africa. Joanna, the chief, is about 30 miles long and 15 broad, and affords plenty of provifions, and fuch fruits as are produced between the tropics. Eaft-India fhips, bound to Bombay, ufually touch here for refrefhments. The inhabitants are Negroes of the Mahometan perfuafion, and entertain our feamen with great humanity.

MADAGASCAR. This is the largeft of the African iflands, and is fituated between 43 and 51 deg. eaft lon. and between 10 and 26 fouth lat. 300 miles fouth-eaft of the continent of Africa; it being near 1000 miles in length from north to fouth; and generally between 2 and 300 miles broad. The fea rolls with great rapidity, and is exceeding rough between this ifland and the continent of the Cape of Good Hope, forming a channel or paffage, through which all European fhips, in their voyage to and from India, generally fail, unlefs prevented by ftorms.

Madagafcar is a pleafant, defirable, and fertile country, abounding in fugar, honey, vines, fruit trees, vegetables, valuable gums, corn, cattle, fowls, precious ftones, iron, fome filver, copper, fteel, and tin. It affords an agreeable variety of hills, vallies, woods, and champaign; watered with

I   numerous

numerous rivers, and well ſtored with fiſh. The air is generally temperate, and ſaid to be very healthy, though in a hot
climate. The inhabitants are of different complexions and
religions; ſome white, ſome Negroes, ſome Mahometans,
ſome pagans. The whites and thoſe of a tawny complexion
who inhabit the coaſts, are deſcended from the Arabs, as is
evident from their language, and their religious rites; but
here are no moſques, temples, nor any ſtated worſhip, except
that they offer ſacrifice of beaſts on particular occaſions; as
when ſick, when they plant yams, or rice, when they hold
their aſſemblies, circumciſe their children, declare war, enter
into new built houſes, or bury their dead. Many of them
obſerve the Jew ſabbath, and give ſome account of the ſacred
hiſtory, the creation and fall of man, as alſo of Noah, Abra-
ham, Moſes, and David; from whence it is conjectured they
are deſcended of Jews who formerly ſettled here, though none
knows how or when. This iſland was diſcovered by the
Portugueſe, and the French took poſſeſſion of it in 1642;
but the people diſliking their government, they were driven
out in 1651; ſince which the natives have had the ſole
poſſeſſion of the iſland, under a number of petty princes, who
make war upon one another for ſlaves and plunder. It is
thought the French will again attempt to eſtabliſh themſelves
here, if the other maritime powers do not interfere.

MAURITIUS. Maurice, or Mauritius, was ſo called by
the Dutch, who firſt touched here in 1598, in honour of
prince Maurice their ſtadtholder. It is ſituated in eaſt lon.
56, ſouth lat. 20. about 400 miles eaſt of Madagaſcar. It is
of an oval form, about 150 miles in circumference, with a
fine harbour, capable of holding fifty large ſhips, ſecure againſt
any wind that blows, and 100 fathoms deep at the entrance.
The climate is extremely healthy and pleaſant. The mountains, of which there are many, and ſome ſo high that their
tops are covered with ſnow, produce the beſt ebony in the
world, beſides various other kinds of valuable wood, two of
which greatly reſemble ebony in quality; one red, the other
yellow as wax. The iſland is watered with ſeveral pleaſant
rivers well ſtocked with fiſh; and though the ſoil is none of
the moſt fruitful, yields plenty of tobacco, rice, fruit, and
feeds a great number of cattle, deer, goats, and ſheep. It
was formerly ſubject to the Dutch, but is now in the poſſeſſion of the French.

BOURBON. The Iſle of Bourbon is ſituated in eaſt lon.
54, ſouth lat. 21, about 300 miles eaſt of Madagaſcar, and is
about 90 miles round. There are many good roads for ſhipping

ping round Bourbon, particularly on the north and south fides; but hardly a fingle harbour where fhips can ride fecure againft thofe hurricanes which blow during the monfoons. Indeed the coaft is fo furrounded with blind rocks, funk a few feet below the water, that coafting along fhore is at all times dangerous. On the fouthern extremity is a volcano, which continually throws out flames, fmoke, and fulphur, wi h a hideous roaring noife, terrible in the night to mariners. The climate here, though extremely hot, is healthy, being refrefhed with cooling gales, that blow morning and evening from the fea and land : fometimes, however, terrible hurricanes fhake the whole ifland almoft to its foundation ; but generally without any other bad confequence than frightening the inhabitants. The ifland abounds in brooks and fprings, and in fruits, grafs, and cattle, with excellent tobacco (which the French have planted there) aloes, white pepper, ebony, palm, and other kinds of wood, and fruit trees. Many of the trees yield odoriferous gums and raifins, particularly benzoin of an excellent fort and in great plenty. The rivers are well ftocked with fifh, the coaft with land and fea tortoifes, and every part of the country with horned cattle, as well as hogs and goats. Ambergris, coral, and the moft beautiful fhells, are found upon the fhore. The woods are full of turtle doves, paroquets, pigeons, and a great variety of other birds, beautiful to the eye and pleafant to the palate. The French firft fettled here in the year 1672, after they were drove from the ifland of Madagafcar. They have now fome confiderable towns in the ifland, with a governor ; and here their Eaft-India fhips touch and take in refrefhments.

There are a great many more fmall iflands about Madagafcar, and on the eaftern coaft of Africa, laid down in maps, but no where defcribed.

Leaving therefore the eaftern world and the Indies, we now turn round the Cape of Good-Hope, which opens to our view the Atlantic, an immenfe ocean, lying between the two grand divifions of the globe, having Europe, Afia, and Africa, or the old world, on the eaft; and America, or the new world, on the weft ; towards which divifion we now fteer our courfe, touching in our way at the following iflands upon the African coaft, that have not yet been defcribed, viz. St. Helena, Afcenfion, St. Matthew, St. Thomas, &c. Goree, Cape Verd, the Canary and Madeira iflands. *See the Map.*

ST. HELENA. The firft ifland on this fide the Cape is St. Helena, fituated in weft lon. 6-4, fouth lat. 16, being 1200 miles weft of the continent of Africa, and 1800 eaft of
South

South America. The island is a rock about 21 miles in circumference, very high and very steep, and only accessible at the landing-place, in a small valley at the east side of it, which is defended by batteries of guns planted level with the water; and as the waves are perpetually dashing on the shore, it is generally difficult landing even here. There is no other anchorage about the island but at Chapel Vally Bay; and as the wind always blows from the south-east, if a ship overshoots the island ever so little, she cannot recover it again. The English plantations here afford potatoes and yams, with figs, plantains, bananas, grapes, kidney-beans, and Indian corn; of the last, however, most part is destroyed by the rats, which harbour in the rocks, and cannot be destroyed; so that the flour they use is almost wholly imported from England; and in times of scarcity they generally eat yams and potatoes instead of bread. Though the island appears on every side a hard barren rock, yet it is agreeably diversified with hills and plains, adorned with plantations of fruit-trees and garden-stuff. They have great plenty of hogs, bullocks, poultry, ducks, geese, and turkeys, with which they supply the sailors, taking in exchange shirts, drawers, or any light cloths, pieces of callico, silks, muslins, arrack, sugar, &c.

St. Helena is said to have been first discovered by the Portuguese on the festival of the empress, Helena, mother of the emperor Constantine the Great, whose name it still bears. It does not appear that the Portuguese ever planted a colony here: and the English East-India company took possession of it in 1600, and held it without interruption till the year 1673, when the Dutch took it by surprize. However, the English, under the command of captain Munden, recovered it again within the space of a year, and at the same time took three Dutch East-India ships that lay in the road. There are about 200 families in the island, most of them descended from English parents. The East-India ships take in water and fresh provisions here, in their way home; but the island is so small, and the wind so much against them outward bound, that they very seldom see it then.

The company's affairs are here managed by a governor, deputy-governor, and store-keeper, who have standing salaries allowed by the company, besides a public table well furnished, to which all commanders, masters of ships, and principal passengers are welcome.

ASCENSION. This island is situated under the 7th degree south lat. 600 miles north-west of St. Helena: it received its name from its being discovered by the Portuguese on Ascension-day;

fion-day; and is a mountainous barren ifland, about 20 mile round, and uninhabited; but has a fafe convenient harbour where the Eaft-India fhips generally touch to furnifh themfelves with turtles or tortoifes, which are very plentiful here, and vaftly large, fome of them weighing above an hundred pounds each. The failors going afhore in the night time, frequently turn two or three hundred of them on their backs before morning; and are fometimes fo cruel, as to turn many more than they ufe, leaving them to die on the fhore.

Sт. MATTHEW. This is a fmall ifland, lying in 6-1 weft lon. and 1-30 fouth lat. 300 miles to the north-eaft of Afcenfion, and was alfo difcovered by the Portuguefe, who planted and kept poffeffion of it for fome time; but afterwards deferting it, this ifland now remains uninhabited, having little to invite other nations to fettle there except a fmall lake of frefh water.

The four following iflands, viz. Sт. THOMAS, ANABOA, PRINCES ISLAND, and FERNANDO PO, are fituated in the gulph of Guinea, between Congo and Benin; all of them were difcovered by the Portuguefe, and are ftill in the poffeffion of that nation, and furnifh fhipping with frefh water and provifions as they pafs by.

CAPE VERD ISLANDS. Thefe iflands are fo called from a cape of that name on the African coaft, near the river Gambia, over againft which they lie, at the diftance of 300 miles, between 23 and 26 deg. weft lon. and 14 and 18 deg. north lat. They were difcovered in the year 1460, by the Portuguefe, and are about 20 in number; but fome of them, being only barren uninhabited rocks, are not worth notice. St. Jago, Bravo, Fago, Mayo, Bonavifta, Sal, St. Nicholas, St. Lucia, St. Vincent, Santa Cruz, and St. Antonio, are the moft confiderable, and are fubject to the Portuguefe. The air, generally fpeaking, is very hot, and in fome of them very unwholefome. They are inhabited by Europeans, or the defcendants of Europeans, and Negroes.

Sт. JAGO, where the Portuguefe viceroy refides, is the moft fruitful, beft inhabited, and largeft of them all, being 150 miles in circumference; yet it is mountainous, and has much barren land in it. Its produce is fugar, cotton, fome wine, Indian corn, cocoa-nuts, oranges, and other tropical fruits; plenty of roots, garden-ftuffs, and they have plenty of hogs and poultry, and fome of the prettieft green monkies, with black faces, that are to be met with any where. Baya, fituated on the eaft fide, has a good port, and is feldom with-

out

out ſhips, thoſe outward bound to Guinea or the Eaſt-Indies, from England, Holland, and France, often touching here for water and refreſhments.

In the iſland of Mayo or May, immenſe quantities of ſalt is made by the heat of the ſun from the ſea water, which, at ſpring tides, is received into a ſort of pan, formed by a ſand-bank, which runs along the coaſt for two or three miles. Here the Engliſh drive a conſiderable trade for ſalt, and have commonly a man of war to guard the veſſels that come to load with it, which in ſome years amount to a hundred or more. The ſalt coſts nothing, except for raking it together, wheel-ing it out of the pond, and carrying it on aſſes to the boats, which is done at a very cheap rate. Several of our ſhips come hither for a freight of aſſes, which they carry to Barbadoes and other Britiſh plantations. The inhabitants of this iſland, even the governor and prieſts, are all Negroes, and ſpeak the Portugueſe language. The Negro governor expects a ſmall preſent from every commander that loads ſalt, and is pleaſed to be invited aboard their ſhips. The ſea water is ſo exceſſive clear on this coaſt, that an Engliſh ſailor who dropped his watch, perceived it at the bottom, though many fathoms deep, and had it brought up by one of the natives, who are in gene-ral expert at diving.

The iſland of Fogo is remarkable for being a volcano, continually ſending up ſulphureous exhalations; and ſome-times the flame breaks out like Ætna, in a terrible manner, throwing out pumice ſtones that annoy all the adjacent parts.

GOREE is ſituated within cannon-ſhot of Cape Verd, N. lat. 14-43, W. lon. 17-20. and was ſo called by the Dutch from an iſland and town of the ſame name in Holland. It is a ſmall ſpot not exceeding two miles in circumference, but its impor-tance ariſes from its ſituation for trade ſo near Cape Verd, and has been therefore a bone of contention between European nations. It was firſt poſſeſſed by the Dutch, from whom in 1663 it was taken by the Engliſh, but in 1665 it was retaken by the Dutch, and in 1677 ſubdued by the French, in whoſe poſſeſſion it remained till the year 1759, when the Britiſh arms were every where triumphant, and it was reduced by com-modore Keppel, but reſtored to the French at the treaty of peace in 1763.

CANARIES. The Canaries, antiently called the Fortu-nate Iſlands, are ſeven in number, and ſituated between 12 and 19 deg. weſt lon. and between 27 and 29 deg. north lat. about 150 miles ſouth-weſt of Morocco. Their particular names are, Palma, Hiero, Gomera, Teneriffe, Grand Canaria, Fuertu-

Fuertuventura, and Langarote. Thefe iflands enjoy a pure temperate air, and abound in the moſt delicious fruits, eſpecially grapes, which produce thofe rich wines that obtain the name of the Canary, whereof the greateſt part is exported to England, which in time of peace is computed at ten thouſand hogſheads annually. The Canaries abound with thofe little beautiful birds that bear their name, and are now ſo common and ſo much admired in Europe; but their wild notes in their native land far excel thofe in a cage or foreign clime.

Grand Canary, which communicates its name to the whole, is about 150 miles in circumference, and ſo extremely fertile, as to produce two harveſts in the year. Teneriffe, the largeſt of thefe iflands next to that of the Grand Canary, is about 120 miles round; a fertile country, abounding in corn, wine, and oil; though it is pretty much encumbered with mountains, particularly the Peak, of which Capt. Glafs obferves, that in coming in with this ifland, in clear weather, the Peak may be eafily difcerned at 120 miles diſtance, and in failing from it at 150. The Peak is an afcent in the form of a fugarloaf, about fifteen miles in circumference, and according to the account of Sprat, bifhop of Rochefter, publiſhed in the Philofophical Tranfactions, near three miles perpendicular. This mountain is a volcano, and fometimes throws out fuch quantities of fulphur and melted ore, as to convert the richeſt lands into barren deferts. Thefe iflands were firſt difcovered and planted by the Carthaginians; but the Romans deſtroying that ſtate, put a ſtop to the navigation on the weſt coaſt of Africa, and the Canaries lay concealed from the reſt of the world, until they were again difcovered by the Spaniards in the year 1405, to whom they ſtill belong. It is remarkable, that though the natives refembled the Africans in their ſtature and complexion when the Spaniards firſt came among them, their language was different from that fpoken on the continent; they retained none of their cuſtoms, were maſters of no fcience, and did not know there was any country in the world befides their own.

MADEIRAS. The three iflands called the Madeiras, are fituated, according to the author of Anfon's voyage, in a fine climate in 32-27 north lat. and from 18-30 to 19-30 weſt lon. about 100 miles north of the Canaries, and as many weſt of Sallee, in Morocco. The largeſt, from which the reſt derive the general name of Madeiras, or rather Mattera, on account of its being formerly almoſt covered with wood, is about 75 miles long, 60 broad, and 180 in circumference. It is compofed of one continued hill, of a confiderable height, ex

tending from east to west ; the declivity of which, on the
south side, is cultivated and interspersed with vineyards ; and
in the midst of this slope the merchants have fixed their country seats, which form a very agreeable prospect.   There is
but one considerable town in the whole island, which is named
Fonchial, seated on the south part of the island, at the bottom of a large bay ; towards the sea, it is defended by a high
wall, with a battery of cannon, and is the only place where
it is possible for a boat to land, and even here the beach is
covered with large stones, and a violent surf continually beats
upon it.

    Though this island seems to have been known to the an-
tients, yet it lay concealed for many generations, and was at
length discovered by the Portuguese in 1519 : but others assert
that it was first discovered by an Englishman, in the ʼyear
1344.   Be that as it will, the Portuguese took possession of it,
and are still almost the only people who inhabit it.   The Portuguese, at their first landing, finding it little better than a
thick forest, rendered the ground capable of cultivation by
setting fire to this wood ; and it is now very fertile, producing
in great abundance the richest wine, sugar, the most delicate
fruits, especially oranges, lemons, and pomegranates ; together with corn, honey, and wax : it abounds also with boars
and other wild beasts, and with all sorts of fowls, besides
numerous groves of cedar trees, and those that yield dragons
blood, mastic, and other gums.   The inhabitants of this isle
make the best sweet-meats in the world, and succeed wonderfully in preserving citrons and oranges, and in making marma-
lade and perfumed pastes, which exceed those of Genoa.   The
sugar they make is extremel beautiful, and smells naturally
of violets.   This indeed is said to be the first place in the west,
where that manufacture was set on foot, and from thence was
carried to the Brazils in America.   The Portuguese not finding it so profitable as at first, have pulled up the greatest part
of their sugar canes, and planted vineyards in their stead,
which produce several sorts of excellent wine, particularly
that which bears the name of the island, malmsey, and tent ;
of all which the inhabitants make and sell prodigious quan-
tities.ʼ No less than 20,000 hogsheads of Madeira, it is said,
are yearly exported, the greatest part to the West-Indies, especially to Barbadoes, the Madeira wine not only enduring a
hot climate better than any other, but even being improved
when exposed to the sun in barrels after the bung is taken out,
It is said no venomous animal can live here.   Of the two
other islands, one is called Port Santo, which lies at a small
distance from Madeira, is about eight miles in compass, and
                                                    extremely

extremely fertile.   It has very good harbours, where ſhips may ride with ſafety againſt all winds, except the ſouth-weſt; and is frequented by Indiamen outward and homeward bound. The other iſland is an inconſiderable barren rock.

AZORES.   Leaving the Madeiras, with which we cloſe the account of Africa, we continue our courſe weſtward through this immenſe ocean, which brings us to the Azores, or, as they are called, the Weſtern Iſlands, that are ſituated between 25 and 32 deg. weſt lon. and between 37 and 40 north lat. 900 miles weſt of Portugal, and as many eaſt of Newfoundland, lying almoſt in the mid-way between Europe and America.   They are nine in number, and are named Santa Maria, St. Miguel or St. Michael, Tercera, St. George, Gracioſa, Fayal, Pico, Flores, and Corvo.   They were diſcovered by the Portugueſe, to whom they ſtill belong, and were called in general the Azores, from the great number of hawks and falcons found among them.   All theſe iſlands enjoy a very clear and ſerene ſky, with a ſalubrious air; but are expoſed to violent earthquakes, from which they have frequently ſuffered; and alſo by the inundations of ſurrounding waves. They are, however, extremely fertile in corn, wine, and a variety of fruits, alſo cattle, fowl, and fiſh.

It is remarkable that no poiſonous or noxious animal breeds on the Azores, and if carried thither will expire in a few hours.

St. Michael, which is the largeſt, being near 100 miles in circumference, and containing 50,000 inhabitants, was twice invaded and plundered by the Engliſh in the reign of queen Elizabeth.   Tercera is the moſt important of theſe iſlands, on account of its harbour, which is ſpacious, and has good anchorage, but is expoſed to the ſouth-eaſt winds.   Its capital town, Angra, contains a cathedral and five churches, and is the reſidence of the governor of theſe iſlands, as well as the biſhop.

AMERICA.

WE are now to treat of a country of vast extent and fertility, and which, though little cultivated by the hand of art, owes in many respects more to that of nature than any other division of the globe. The particular circumstances of this country require that we should in some measure vary our plan, and, before describing its present state, afford such information with regard to its discovery, as is most necessary for satisfying our readers.

Towards the close of the 15th century, Venice and Genoa were the only powers in Europe who owed their support to commerce. An interference of interests inspired a mutual rivalship; but in traffic Venice was much superior. She engrossed the whole commerce of India, then, and indeed always, the most valuable in the world, but hitherto intirely carried on through the inland parts of Asia, or by the way of Egypt and the Red-Sea. In this state of affairs, Columbus, a native of Genoa, whose knowledge of the true figure of the earth, however attained, was much superior to the general notions of the age in which he lived, conceived a project of sailing to the Indies by a bold and unknown rout, and of opening to his country a new source of opulence and power. But this proposal of sailing westward to the Indies was rejected by the Genoese as chimerical, and the principles on which it was founded were condemned as absurd. Stung with disappointment and indignation, Columbus retired from his country, laid his scheme before the court of France, where his reception was still more mortifying, and where, according to the practice of that people, he was laughed at and ridiculed. Henry VII. of England was his next resort; but the cautious politics of that prince were the most opposite imaginable to a great but uncertain design. In Portugal, where the spirit of adventure and discovery about this time began to operate, he had reason to expect better success. But the Portuguese contented themselves with creeping along the coast of Africa, and discovering one cape after another; they had no notion of venturing boldly into the open sea, and of risking the whole at once. Such repeated disappointments would have broken the spirit of any man but Columbus. The expedition required expence, and he had nothing to defray it. His mind, however, still remained firm; he became the more enamoured of his design the more difficulty he found in accomplishing it, and he was inspired with that noble enthusiasm which always animates an

adventrous

adventrous and original genius. Spain was now his only refource, and there, after eight years attendance, he fucceeded through the intereft of a woman. This was the celebrated queen Ifabella, who raifed money upon her jewels to defray the expence of his expedition and to do honour to her fex. Columbus now fet fail, anno 1492, with a fleet of three fhips, upon the moft adventrous attempt ever undertaken by man, and in the fate of which the inhabitants of two worlds were interefted. In this voyage he had a thoufand difficulties to contend with ; the moft ftriking was the variation of the compafs, then firft obferved, and which feemed to threaten that the laws of nature were altered on an unknown ocean, and the only guide he had left was ready to forfake him. His failors, always difcontented, now broke out into open mutiny, threatening to throw him overboard, and infifted on their return. But the firmnefs of the commander, and much more the difcovery of land, after a voyage of 33 days, put an end to the commotion. Columbus firft landed on one of the Bahama iflands, but there, to his furprize and forrow, difcovered, from the poverty of the inhabitants, that thefe could not be the Indies he was in queft of. In fteering fouthward, however, he found the ifland called Hifpaniola, abounding in all the neceflaries of life, inhabited by a humane and hofpitable people, and what was of ftill greater confequence, as it infured his favourable reception at home, promifing, from fome famples he received, confiderable quantities of gold. This ifland therefore he propofed to make the centre of his difcoveries : and having left upon it a few of his companions, as the ground-work of a colony, returned to Spain to procure the neceffary reinforcements.

The court was then at Barcelona; Columbus travelled thither from Seville, amidft the acclamations of the people, attended by fome of the inhabitants, the gold, the arms, utenfils, and ornaments of the country he had difcovered. This entry into Barcelona was a fpecies of triumph more glorious than that of conquerors, more uncommon, and more innocent. In this voyage he had acquired a general knowledge of all the iflands in that great fea which divides north and fouth America; but he had no idea that there was an ocean between him and China. Thus were the Weft-Indies difcovered by feeking a paffage to the Eaft ; and even after the difcovery, ftill conceived to be a part of the eaftern hemifphere. The prefent fuccefs of Columbus, his former difappointments, and the glory attending fo unexpected a difcovery, rendered the court of Spain as eager to forward his defigns now, as it had been dilatory before. A fleet of feventeen fail was imme-

diately

diately prepared ; all the neceffaries for conqueft or difcovery
were embarked ; and 1500 men, among whom were feveral
of high rank and fortune, prepared to accompany Columbus,
now appointed governor with the moft ample authority. It is
impoffible to determine whether the genius of this great man
in firft conceiving the idea of thefe difcoveries, or his fagacity
in the execution of the plan he had conceived, moft deferve
our admiration. Inftead of hurrying from fea to fea, and
from one ifland to another, which, confidering the ordinary
motives to action among mankind, was naturally to be expected, Columbus, with fuch a field before him, unable to
turn on either hand without finding new objects of his curiofity
and his pride, determined rather to turn to the advantage of
the court of Spain the difcoveries he had already made, than
to acquire for himfelf the unavailing applaufe of vifiting a
number of unknown countries, from which he reaped no other
benefit but the pleafure of feeing them. With this view he
made for Hifpaniola, where he eftablifhed a colony, and erected
forts in the moft advantageous grounds for fecuring the dependence of the natives. Having fpent a confiderable time in
this employment, and laboured for the eftablifhing of this
colony with as much zeal and affiduity as if his views had extended no farther, he next proceeded to afcertain the importance of his other difcoveries, and to examine what advantages
were moft likely to be derived from them. He had already
touched at Cuba, which, from fome fpecimens, feemed a rich
difcovery ; but whether it was an ifland, or a part of fome
great continent, he was altogether uncertain. To afcertain
this point was the prefent object of his attention. In coafting
along the fouthern fhore of Cuba, Columbus was entangled
in a multitude of iflands, of which he reckoned 160 in one
day. Thefe iflands, which were well inhabited, and abounding in all the neceffaries of life, gave him an opportunity of
reflecting on this fertility of nature where the world expected
nothing but the barren ocean ; he called them *Jardin de la
reina*, or the Queen's Garden, in gratitude to his royal bene-
factrefs, who was always uppermoft in his memory. In the
fame voyage Jamaica was difcovered. But to fo many difficulties was Columbus expofed, on an unknown fea, among
rocks, fhelves, and lands, that he returned to Hifpaniola,
without learning any thing more certain with regard to Cuba,
the main object of this enterprize.

By the firft fuccefs of this great man, the public diffidence
was turned into admiration ; but by a continuance of the fame
fuccefs, their admiration degenerated into envy. His enemies
in Spain fet every fpring in motion againft him ; and there is
no

no difficulty in finding fpecious grounds of accufation againft fuch as are employed in the execution of an extenfive and complicated plan. An officer was difpatched from Spain, fitted by his character to act the part of a fpy and informer, and whofe prefence plainly demonftrated to Columbus the neceffity of returning into Europe, for obviating the objections or calumny of his enemies.

It was not without great difficulty that he was enabled to fet out on a third expedition, ftill more famous than any he had hitherto undertaken. He defigned to ftand to the fouthward from the Canaries until he came under the equinoctial line, and then to proceed directly weftward, that he might difcover what opening that might afford to India, or what new iflands, or what continent might reward his labour. In this navigation, after being long buried in a thick fog, and fuffering numberlefs inconveniencies from the exceffive heats and rains between the tropics, they were at length favoured by a fmart gale, and went before it feventeen days to the weftward. At the end of this time, a feaman faw land, which was an ifland on the coaft of Guiana, now called Trinidad. Having paffed this ifland, and two others which lie in the mouth of the great river Oronoco, the admiral was furprized with an appearance he had never feen before; this was the frightful tumult of the waves, occafioned by a conflict betwixt the tide of the fea and the rapid current of the immenfe river Oronoco. But failing forward, he plainly difcovered that they were in frefh water; and judging rightly that it was improbable any ifland fhould fupply fo vaft a river, he began to fufpect he had difcovered the continent; but when he left the river, and found that the land continued on to the weftward for a great way, he was convinced of it. Satisfied with this difcovery, he yielded to the uneafinefs and diftreffes of his crew, and bore away for Hifpaniola. In the courfe of this difcovery, Columbus landed at feveral places, where in a friendly manner he traded with the inhabitants, and found gold and pearl in tolerable plenty.

About this time the fpirit of difcovery fpread itfelf widely, and many adventurers all over Europe wifhed to acquire the reputation of Columbus, without poffeffing his abilities. The Portuguefe difcovered Brazil, which makes at prefent the moft valuable part of their poffeffions: Cabot, a native of Briftol, difcovered the north-eaft coafts, which now compofe the Britifh empire in North-America; and Americus Vefpufius, a merchant of Florence, failed to the fouthern continent of America, and, being a man of addrefs, had the honour of giving his name to half the globe. But no one is now impofed

on

on by the name; all the world knows that Columbus was the first difcoverer. The being deprived of the honour of giving name to the new world, was one of the fmalleft mortifications to which this great man was compelled to fubmit. For fuch were the clamours of his enemies, and the ingratitude of the court of Spain, that after difcovering the continent, and making fettlements in the iflands of America, he was treated like a traitor, and carried over to Europe in irons. He enjoyed, however, the glory of rendering the one half of the world known to the other; a glory fo much the more precious, as it was untainted by cruelty or plunder, which disfigured all the exploits of thofe who came after him, and accomplifhed the execution of his plan. He died at Valladolid, in 1506. The fucceeding governors of Cuba and Hifpaniola, endeavoured to purchafe the fame advantages by the blood of the natives, which Columbus had obtained by his good fenfe and humanity. Thefe iflands contained mines of gold. The Indians only knew where they were placed; and the extreme avarice of the Spaniards, too furious to work by the gentle means of perfuafion, hurried them to acts of the moft fhocking violence and cruelty againft thofe unhappy men, who, they believed, concealed from them part of their treafure. The flaughter once begun, they fet no bounds to their fury; in a few years they depopulated Hifpaniola, which contained three millions of inhabitants; and Cuba, that had above 600,000. Bartholomew de la Cafas, a witnefs of thofe barbarous depopulations, fays that the Spaniards went out with their dogs to hunt after men. The unhappy favages, almoft naked and unarmed, were purfued like deer into the thick of the forefts, devoured by dogs, killed with gun-fhot, or furprized and burnt in their habitations.

The Spaniards had hitherto only vifited the continent: from what they faw with their eyes, or learned by report, they conjectured that this part of the new world would afford a ftill more valuable conqueft. Fernando Cortez is difpatched from Cuba with 600 men, 18 horfes, and a fmall number of field pieces. With this inconfiderable force, he propofes to fubdue the moft powerful ftate on the continent of America: this was the empire of Mexico; rich, powerful, and inhabited by millions of Indians, paffionately fond of war, and then headed by Montezuma, whofe fame in arms ftruck terror into the neighbouring nations, and extended over one half the globe. Never hiftory, to be true, was more improbable and romantic than that of this war. The empire of Mexico had fubfifted for ages: its inhabitants were not rude and barbarous; every thing announced a polifhed and intelligent people. They knew,

knew, like the Egyptians of old, whofe wifdom is ftill admired in this particular, that the year confifted nearly of 365 days. Their fuperiority in military affairs was the object of admiration and terror over all the continent; and their government, founded on the fure bafis of laws combined with religion, feemed to bid defiance to time itfelf. Mexico, the capital of the empire, fituated in the middle of a fpacious lake, was the nobleft monument of American induftry: it communicated with the continent by immenfe caufeways, which were carried through the lake. The city was admired for its buildings, all of ftone, its fquares and market places, the fhops which glittered with gold and filver, and the fumptuous palaces of Montezuma, fome erected on columns of jafper, and containing whatever was moft rare, curious, or ufeful. But all the grandeur of this empire could not defend it againft the Spaniards. Cortez, in his march, met with feeble oppofition from the nations along the coaft of Mexico, who were terrified at their firft appearance: the warlike animals, on which the Spanifh officers were mounted, the artificial thunder which iffued from their hands, the wooden caftles which had wafted them over the ocean, ftruck a panic into the natives, from which they did not recover until it was too late. Wherever the Spaniards marched they fpared no age or fex, nothing facred or prophane. At laft, the inhabitants of Tlafca, and fome other ftates on the coaft, defpairing of being able to oppofe them, enter into their alliance, and join armies with thofe terrible, and, as they believed, invincible conquerors. Cortez, thus reinforced, marched onward to Mexico; and in his progrefs difcovers a volcano of fulphur and faltpetre, whence he could fupply himfelf with powder. Montezuma heard of his progrefs, without daring to oppofe it. This fovereign commanded 30 vaffals of whom each could appear at the head of 100,000 combatants, armed with bows and arrows, and yet he dares not refift a handful of Spaniards aided by a few Americans whofe allegiance would be fhaken by the firft reverfe of fortune. Such was the difference between the inhabitants of the two worlds, and the fame of the Spanifh victories, which always marched before them.

By fending a rich prefent of gold, which only whetted the Spanifh avarice, Montezuma haftened the approach of the enemy. No oppofition is made to their entry into his capital. A palace is fet apart for Cortez and his companions, who are already treated as the mafters of the new world. He had good reafon, however, to diftruft the affected politenefs of this emperor, under which he fufpected fome plot for his deftruction was concealed; but he had no pretence for violence;

Montezuma

Montezuma loaded him with kindness, and with gold in greater quantities than he demanded, and his palace was surrounded with artillery, the most frightful of all engines to the Americans. At last a circumstance fell out which afforded Cortez a pretext for beginning hostilities. In order to secure a communication by sea to receive the necessary reinforcements, he had erected a fort, and left a small garrison behind him at Vera Cruz, which has since become an emporium of commerce between Europe and America. He understood that the Americans in the neighbourhood had attacked this garrison in his absence, and that a Spaniard was killed in the action, that Montezuma himself was privy to this violence, and had issued orders that the head of the slain Spaniard should be carried through his provinces, to destroy a belief, which then prevailed among them, that the Europeans were immortal. Upon receiving this intelligence, Cortez went in person to the emperor, attended by a few of his most experienced officers. Montezuma pleaded innocence, in which Cortez seemed extremely ready to believe him, though at the same time he alleged that the Spaniards in general would never be persuaded of it unless he returned along with them to their residence, which would remove all jealousy between the two nations. The success of this interview shewed the superiority of the European address. A powerful monarch, in the middle of his own palace, and surrounded by his guards, gave himself up a prisoner, to be disposed of according to the inclination of a few gentlemen who came to demand him. Cortez had now got into his hands an engine by which every thing might be accomplished. The Americans had the highest respect, or rather a superstitious veneration for their emperor. Cortez therefore, by keeping him in his power, allowing him to enjoy every mark of royalty but his freedom, and at the same time, from a thorough knowledge of his character, being able to flatter all his tastes and passions, maintained the easy sovereignty of Mexico, by governing its prince. Did the Mexicans, grown familiar with the Spaniards, begin to abate of their respect? Montezuma was the first to teach them more politeness. Was there a tumult, excited through the cruelty or avarice of the Spaniards? Montezuma ascended the battlements of his prison, and harangued his Mexicans into order and submission. This farce continued a long while: but on one of these occasions, when Montezuma was shamefully disgracing his character by justifying the enemies of his country, a stone, from an unknown hand, struck him on the temple, which in a few days occasioned his death. The Mexicans, now delivered from this emperor, who co-operated so strongly

with

with the Spaniards, elect a new prince, the famous Gatimozin, who from the beginning difcovered an implacable ani-
mofity againft the Spanifh name. Under his ' conduct the
unhappy Mexicans rufhed againft thofe very men, whom a
little before they had offered to worfhip. The Spaniards,
however, by the dexterous management of Cortez, were too
firmly eftablifhed to be expelled from Mexico. The immenfe
tribute which the grandees of this country had agreed to pay
to the crown of Spain, amounted to 600,000 marks of pure
gold, befides an amazing quantity of precious ftones, a fifth
part of which was diftributed among the foldiers, ftimulated
their avarice and their courage, and made them willing to
perifh rather than part with fo precious a booty. The Mexicans, however, made no fmall efforts for independence ; but
all their valour, and defpair itfelf, gave way before what they
called the Spanifh thunder. Gatimozin and the emprefs were
taken prifoners. This was the prince who, when he lay
ftretched on burning coals, by order of one of the receivers of
the king of Spain's exchequer, who inflicted the torture to
make him difcover into what part of the lake he had thrown
his riches, faid to his high prieft, condemned to the fame
punifhment, and making hideous cries, " Do you take me to
" lay on a bed of rofes ?" The high prieft remained filent,
and died in an act of obedience to his fovereign. Cortez, by
getting a fecond emperor into his hands, made a complete
conqueft of Mexico ; with which the Caftiile D'Or, Darien,
and other provinces, fell into the hands of the Spaniards.

While Cortez, and his foldiers, were employed in reducing
Mexico, they got intelligence of another great empire, fituated
towards the equinoctial line, and the tropic of Capricorn,
which was faid to abound in gold and filver, and precious
ftones, and to be governed by a prince more magnificent than
Montezuma. This was the empire of Peru, which extended
in length near thirty degrees, and was the only other country
in America, which deferved the name of a civilized kingdom.
Whether it happened, that the Spanifh government had not
received certain intelligence concerning Peru, or that, being
engaged in a multiplicity of other concerns, they did not chufe
to adventure on new enterprizes ; certain it is, that this extenfive country, more important than Mexico itfelf, was
reduced by the endeavours, and at the expence, of three private perfons. The names of thefe were, Francis Pizarro,
Almagro, and Lucques, a prieft, and a man of confiderable
fortune. The two former were natives of Panama, men of
doubtful birth, and of low education. Pizarro, the foul of
the enterprize, could neither read nor write. They failed over
into

into Spain, and without difficulty, obtained a grant of what they fhould conquer. Pizarro then fet out for the conqueft of Peru, with 250 foot, 60 horfe, and 12 fmall pieces of cannon, drawn by flaves from the conquered countries. If we reflect that the Peruvians naturally entertained the fame prejudices with the Mexicans, in favour of the Spanifh nation, and were befide, of a character ftill more foft and unwarlike, it need not furprize us, after what has been faid of the conqueft of Mexico, that with this inconfiderable force, Pizarro fhould make a deep impreffion on the Peruvian empire. There were particular circumftances likewife which confpired to affift him, and which, as they difcover fomewhat of the hiftory, religion, and ftate of the human mind · in this immenfe continent, it may not be improper to relate.

Mango Capac was the founder of the Peruvian empire. He was one of thofe uncommon men who, calm and difpaffionate themfelves, can obferve the paffions of their fellow creatures, and turn them to their own profit or glory. He obferved that the people of Peru were naturally fuperftitious, and had a particular veneration for the fun. He pretended therefore to be defcended from that luminary, whofe worfhip he was fent to eftablifh, and whofe authority he was entitled to bear. By this ftory, romantic as it appears, he eafily deceived a credulous people, and brought a large extent of territory under his jurifdiction; a larger he ftill fubdued by his arms; but both the force, and the deceit, he employed for the moft laudable purpofes. He united and civilized the diftreffed and barbarous people; he bent them to laws and arts; he foftened them by the inftitutions of a benevolent religion; in fhort, there was no part of America, where agriculture and the arts were fo affiduoufly cultivated, and where the people were of fo mild and ingenuous manners. A race of princes fucceeded Mango, diftinguifhed by the title of Yncas, and revered by the people as defcendants of their great God the Sun. The twelfth of thefe was now on the throne, and named Atabalipa. His father, Guaiana Capac, had conquered the province of Quito, which now makes a part of Spanifh Peru. To fecure himfelf in the poffeffion, he had married the daughter of the natural prince of that country, and of this marriage was fprung Atabalipa. His elder brother, named Huefcar, of a different mother, had claimed the fucceffion to the whole of his father's dominions, not excepting Quito, which devolved on the younger by a double connection. A civil war had been kindled on this account, which after various turns of fortune, and greatly weakening the kingdom, ended in favour of Atabalipa, who detained Huefcar, as a

prifoner,

prifoner, in the tower of Cufco, the capital of the Peruvian empire. In this feeble, and disjointed ftate, was the kingdom of Peru, when Pizarro made his arrival. The ominous predictions of religion too, as in moft other cafes, joined their force to human calamities. Prophecies were recorded, dreams were recollected, which foretold the fubjection of the empire, by unknown perfons, whofe defcription exactly correfponded to the appearance of the Spaniards. In thefe circumftances, Atabalipa, inftead of oppofing the Spaniards, fet himfelf to procure their favour. Pizarro, however, whofe temper partook of the meannefs of his education, had no conception of dealing gently with thofe he called Barbarians, but who, however, though lefs acquainted with the cruel art of deftroying their fellow creatures, were more civilized than himfelf. While he was engaged in conference therefore with Atabalipa, his men, as they had been previoufly inftructed, furioufly attacked the guards of that prince, and having butchered 5000 of them, as they were prefling forward, without regard to their particular fafety, to defend the facred perfon of their monarch, feized Atabalipa himfelf, whom they carried off to the Spanifh quarters. Pizarro, with the fovereign in his hands, might already be deemed the mafter of Peru; for the inhabitants of this country were as ftrongly attached to their emperor, as the Mexicans themfelves. Atabalipa was not long in their hands before he began to treat of his ranfom. On this occafion the antient ornaments, amaffed by a long line of magnificent kings, the hallowed treafures of the moft magnificent temples, were brought out to fave him, who was the fupport of the kingdom, and of the religion. While Pizarro was ingaged in this negotiation, by which he propofed, without releafing the emperor, to get into his poffeffion an immenfe quantity of his beloved gold, the arrival of Almagro caufed fome embarraffment in his affairs. The friendfhip, or rather the external fhew of friendfhip between thefe men, was folely founded on the principle of avarice, and a bold enterprizing fpirit, to which nothing appeared too dangerous, that might gratify their ruling paffion. When their interefts therefore happened to interfere, it was not to be thought that any meafures could be kept between them. Pizarro expected to enjoy the moft confiderable fhare of the treafure, arifing from the emperor's ranfom, becaufe he had the chief hand in acquiring it. Almagro infifted on being upon an equal footing; and at length, left the common caufe might fuffer by any rupture between them, this difpofition was agreed to. The ranfom is paid in without delay, a fum exceeding their conception, but not capable to gratify their avarice.

avarice. It exceeded 1,500,000 l. sterling, and considering
the value of money at that time, was prodigious : on the
dividend, after deducting a fifth for the king of Spain, and
the shares of the chief commanders and officers, each private
soldier had above 2000 l. English money. With such fortunes
it was not to be expected that a mercenary army would
incline to be subjected to the rigours of military discipline.
They insisted on being disbanded, that they might enjoy the
fruits of their labour in quiet. Pizarro complied with this
demand, sensible that avarice would still detain a number in
his army, and that those who returned with such magnificent
fortunes, would induce new adventurers to pursue the same
plan for acquiring gold. These wise reflections were abun-
dantly verified ; it was impossible to send out better recruiting
officers, than those who had themselves so much profited by
the field ; new soldiers constantly arrived, and the American
armies never wanted reinforcements.

This immense ransom was only a farther reason for detain-
ing Atabalipa in confinement, until they discovered whether
he had another treasure to gratify their avarice. But whether
they believed he had no more to give, and were unwilling to
employ their troops in guarding a prince, from whom they
expected no farther advantage, or that Pizarro had conceived
an aversion against the Peruvian emperor, on account of some
instances of craft and policy, which he observed in his character, and which he conceived might prove dangerous to his
affairs, it is certain, that by his command Atabalipa was put
to death. To justify this cruel proceeding, a sham charge
was exhibited against the unhappy prince, in which he was
accused of idolatry, of having many concubines, and other
circumstances of equal impertinence. The only just ground
of accusation against him was, that his brother Huescar had
been put to death by his command ; and even this was considerably palliated, because Huescar had been plotting his destruction, that he might establish himself on the throne. Upon
the death of the Ynca, a number of candidates appeared for
the throne. The principal nobility set up the full brother of
Huescar ; Pizarro set up a son of Atabalipa ; and two generals
of the Peruvians endeavoured to establish themselves by the
assistance of the army. These distractions, which in another
empire would have been extremely hurtful, and even here at
another time, were at present rather advantageous to the Peruvian affairs. The candidates fought against one another,
their battles accustomed the harmless people to blood ; and such
is the preference of a spirit of any kind raised in a nation to a
total lethargy, that in the course of those quarrels among

4

them-

themselves, the inhabitants of Peru assumed some courage against the Spaniards, whom they regarded as the ultimate cause of all their calamities. The losses which the Spaniards met with in these quarrels, though inconsiderable in themselves, were rendered dangerous, by lessening the opinion of their invincibility, which they were careful to preserve among the inhabitants of the new world. This consideration engaged Pizarro to conclude a truce; and this interval he employed in laying the foundations of the famous city Lima, and in settling the Spaniards in the country. But as soon as a favourable opportunity offered, he renewed the war against the Indians, and after many difficulties made himself master of Cusco, the capital of the empire. While he was engaged in these conquests, new grants and supplies arrived from Spain. Pizarro obtained 200 leagues along the sea-coast, to the southward of what had been before granted, and Almagro 200 leagues to the southward of Pizarro's government. This division occasioned a warm dispute between them, each reckoning Cusco within his own district. But the dexterity of Pizarro brought about a reconciliation. He persuaded his rival, that the country which really belonged to him, lay to the southward of Cusco, and that it was no way inferior in riches, and might be as easily conquered as Peru. He offered him his assistance in the expedition, the success of which he did not even call in question.

Almagro, that he might have the honour of subduing a kingdom for himself, listened to his advice; and joining as many of Pizarro's troops to his own, as he judged necessary, penetrated, with great danger and difficulty, into Chili; losing many of his men as he passed over mountains of an immense height, and always covered with snow. He reduced, however, a very considerable part of this country. But the Peruvians were now become too much acquainted with war, not to take advantage of the division of the Spanish troops. They made an effort for regaining their capital, in which, Pizarro being indisposed, and Almagro removed at a great distance, they were well nigh successful. The latter, however, no sooner got notice of the siege of Cusco, than, relinquishing all views of distant conquests, he returned, to secure the grand object of their former labours. He raised the siege with infinite slaughter of the assailants; but having obtained possession of this city, he was unwilling to give it up to Pizarro, who now approached with an army, and knew of no other enemy but the Peruvians. This dispute occasioned a long and bloody struggle between them, in which the turns of fortune were various, and the resentment fierce on both sides, because

the

the fate of the vanquifhed was certain death. This **was the**
lot of Almagro, who, in an advanced age, fell a victim to the
fecurity of a rival, in whofe dangers and triumphs he had
long fhared, and with whom, from the beginning of the
enterprize, he had been intimately connected. During the
courfe of this civil war, many Peruvians ferved in the Spanifh
armies, and learned, from the practice of Chriftians, to
butcher one another. That blinded nation, however, at
length opened their eyes, and took a very remarkable refolution. They faw the ferocity of the Europeans, their unex-
tinguifhable refentment and avarice, and they conjectured that
thefe paffions would never permit their contefts to fubfide.
Let us retire, faid they, from among them, let us fly to our
mountains; they will fpeedily deftroy one another, and then
we may return in peace to our former habitations. This
refolution was inftantly put in practice; the Peruvians difperfed, and left the Spaniards in their capital. Had the force
on each fide been exactly equal, this fingular policy of the
natives of Peru, might have been attended with fuccefs. But
the victory of Pizarro put an end to Almagro's life, and the
hopes of the Peruvians, who have never fince ventured to
make head againft the Spaniards.

Pizarro, now fole mafter of the field, and of the richeft
empire in the world, was ftill urged on by his ambition, to
undertake new enterprizes. The fouthern countries of America, into which he had fome time before difpatched Almagro,
offered the richeft conqueft. Towards this quarter the mountain of Potofi, compofed of entire filver, had been difcovered,
the fhell of which only remains at prefent. He therefore followed the tract of Almagro into Chili, and reduced another
part of that country. Orellana, one of his commanders, paffed
the Andes, and failed down to the mouth of the river of
Amazons: an immenfe navigation, which difcovered a rich
and delightful country, but as it is moftly flat, and therefore
not abounding in minerals, the Spaniards then, and ever fince,
neglected it. Pizarro meeting with repeated fuccefs, and
having no fuperior to controul, nor rival to keep him within
bounds, now gave loofe reins to the natural ferocity of his
temper, and behaved with the bafeft tyranny and cruelty
againft all who had not concurred in his defigns. This conduct raifed a confpiracy againft him, to which he fell a facrifice in his own palace, and in the city of Lima, which he
himfelf had founded. The partifans of old Almagro, declared
his fon of the fame name their viceroy. But the greater part
of the nation, though extremely well fatisfied with the fate of
Pizarro, did not concur with this declaration. Theywaited
the

the orders of Charles V. then king of Spain, who fent over
Vaca di Caftro to be their governor. Th's man, by his in-
tegrity and wifdom, was admirably well fitted to heal the
wounds of the colony, and to place every thing on the moft
advantageous footing, both for it and for the mother country.
By his prudent management the mines of la Plata and Potofi,
which were formerly a matter of private plunder, became an
object of public utility to the court of Spain. The part'es
were filenced or crufhed ; young Almagro, who would hear-
ken to no terms of accommodation, was put to death ; and a
tranquillity, fince the arrival of the Spaniards unknown, was
reftored to Peru. It feems, however, that De Caftro had
not been fufficiently fkilled, in gaining the favour of the Spanifh miniftry, by proper bribes or promifes, which a miniftry
would always expect from the governor of fo rich a country.
By their advice, a council was fent over to controul de Caftro,
and the colony was again unfettled. The parties but juft extinguifhed, began to blaze anew ; and Gonzalo, the brother
of the famous Pizarro, fet himfelf at the head of his brother's
partifans, with whom many new male-contents had united.
It was now no longer a difpute between governors, about the
bounds of their jurifdiction. Gonzalo Pizarro only paid a
nominal fubmiffion to the king. He ftrengthened daily, and
even went fo far as to behead a governor, who was fent over to
curb him. He gained the confidence of the admiral of the
Spanifh fleet in the South Seas, by whofe means he propofed
to hinder the landing of any troops from Spain, and he had a
view of uniting the inhabitants of Mexico in his revolt.

Such was the fituation of affairs, when the court of Spain,
fenfible of their miftake in not fending into America, men
whofe character and virtue only, and not importunity and
cabal, pleaded in their behalf, difpatched with unlimited
powers, Peter de la Gafga, a man differing only from Caftro,
by being of a more mild and infinuating behaviour, but with
the fame love of juftice, the fame greatnefs of foul, and the
fame difinterefted fpirit. All thofe who had not joined in
Pizarro's revolt, flocked under his ftandard ; many of his
friends, charmed with the behaviour of Gafga, forfook their
old connections : the admiral was gained over by infinuation
to return to his duty ; and Pizarro himfelf was offered a full
indemnity, provided he fhould return to the allegiance of the
Spanifh crown. But fo intoxicating are the ideas of royalty,
that Pizarro was inclined to run every hazard, rather than
fubmit to an officer of Spain. With thofe of his partifans
therefore, who ftill continued to adhere to his intereft, he
determined to venture a battle, in which he was conquered and

taken prifoner. His execution followed foon after; and thus the brother of him, who conquered Peru for the crown of Spain, fell a facrifice to the fecurity of the Spanifh dominion over that country.

The conqueft of the great empires of Mexico and Peru, is the only part of the American hiftory, which deferves to be treated under the prefent head. What relates to the reduction of the other parts of the continent, or of the iflands, if it contains either inftruction or entertainment, fhall be handled under thefe particular countries. We now proceed to treat of the manners, government, religion, and whatever compofes the character of the natives of America; and as thefe are extremely fimilar all over this part of the globe, we fhall fpeak of them in general, in order to fave continual repetitions, noticing at the fame time, when we enter upon the defcription of the particular countries, whatever is peculiar or remarkable in the inhabitants of each.

On the original Inhabitants of AMERICA.

THE difcovery of America has not only opened a new fource of wealth to the bufy and commercial part of Europe, but an extenfive field of fpeculation to the philofo-pher, who would trace the character of man under various degrees of refinement, and obferve the movements of the human heart, or the operations of the human underftanding, when untutored by fcience, and untainted with corruption. So ftriking feemed the difparity between the inhabitants of Europe, and the natives of America, that fome fpeculative men have ventured to affirm, that it is impoffible they fhould be of the fame fpecies, or derived from one common fource. This conclufion, however, is extremely ill founded. The characters of mankind may be infinitely varied according to the different degrees of improvement at which they are arrived, the manner in which they acquire the neceffaries of life, the force of cuftom and habit, and a multiplicity of other circum-ftances too particular to be mentioned, and too various to be reduced under any general head. But the great outlines of humanity are to be difcovered among them all, notwithftand-ing the various fhades which characterife nations, and diftin-guifh them from each other.

When the thirft of gold carried the inhabitants of Europe beyond the Atlantic, they found the inhabitants of the new world immerfed in what they reckoned barbarity, but which, however, was a ftate of honeft independence, and noble fim-plicity.

plicity. Except the inhabitants of the great empires of Peru and Mexico, who, comparatively fpeaking, were refined nations, the natives of America were unacquainted with almoft every European art; even agriculture itfelf, the moft ufeful of them all, was hardly known, or cultivated very fparingly. The only method on which they depended for acquiring the neceffaries of life, was by hunting the wild animals, which their mountains and forefts fupplied in great abundance. This exercife, which among them is a moft ferious occupation, gives a ftrength and agility to their limbs, unknown among other nations. The fame caufe perhaps renders their bodies in general, where the rays of the fun are not too violent, uncommonly ftraight and well proportioned. Their mufcles are firm and ftrong; their bodies and heads flattifh, which is the effect of art; their features are regular, but their countenances fierce, their hair long, black, lank, and as ftrong as that of a horfe. The colour of their fkin is a reddifh brown, admired among them, and heightened by the conftant ufe of bears fat and paint. The character of the Indians is altogether founded upon their circumftances and way of life. A people who are conftantly employed in procuring the means of a precarious fubfiftence, who live by hunting the wild animals, and who are generally engaged in war with their neighbours, cannot be fuppofed to enjoy much gaiety of temper, or a high flow of fpirits. The Indians therefore are in general grave even to fadnefs; they have nothing of that giddy vivacity peculiar to fome nations of Europe, and they defpife it. Their behaviour to thofe about them is regular, modeft, and refpectful. Ignorant of the arts of amufement, of which that of faying trifles agreeably is one of the moft confiderable, they never fpeak but when they have fomething important to obferve; and all their actions, words, and even looks, are attended with fome meaning. This is extremely natural to men who are almoft continually engaged in purfuit, which to them are of the higheft importance. Their fubfiftence depends entirely on what they procure with their hands, and their lives, their honour, and every thing dear to them, may be loft by the fmalleft inattention to the defigns of their enemies. As they have no particular object to attach them to one place rather than another, they fly wherever they expect to find the neceffaries of life in greateft abundance. Cities, which are the effects of agriculture and arts, they have none. The different tribes or nations are for the fame reafon extremely fmall, when compared with civilifed focieties, in which induftry, arts, agriculture, and commerce, have united a vaft number of individuals, whom a complicated

luxury

luxury renders useful to one another. These small tribes live
at an immense distance; they are separated by a desart frontier, and hid in the bosom of impenetrable and almost bound-
less forests.

There is established in each society a certain species of government, which over the whole continent of America prevails
with exceeding little variation; because over the whole of this
continent the manners and way of life are nearly similar and
uniform. Without arts, riches, or luxury, the great instru-
ments of subjection in polished societies, an American has no
method by which he can render himself considerable among his
companions, but by a superiority in personal qualities of body
or mind. But as nature has not been very lavish in her personal distinctions, where all enjoy the same education, all are
pretty much equal, and will desire to remain so. Liberty
therefore is the prevailing passion of the Americans, and their
government, under the influence of this sentiment, is better
secured than by the wisest political regulations. They are
very far, however, from despising all sort of authority; they
are attentive to the voice of wisdom, which experience has
conferred on the aged, and they enlist under the banners of
the chief, in whose valour and military address they have
learned to repose their confidence. In every society therefore
there is to be considered the power of the chief and of the
elders; and according as the government inclines more to the
one or to the other, it may be regarded as monarchical, or as a
species of aristocracy. Among those tribes which are most
engaged in war, the power of the chief is naturally predominant, because the idea of having a military leader, was the
first source of his superiority, and the continual exigencies of
the state requiring such a leader, will continue to support and
even to enhance it. His power, however, is rather persuasive
than coercive; he is reverenced as a father, rather than feared
as a monarch. He has no guards, no prisons, no officers of
justice, and one act of ill-judged violence would pull him from
the throne. The elders, in the other form of government,
which may be considered as an aristocracy, have no more
power. In some tribes indeed there are a kind of hereditary
nobility, whose influence being constantly augmented by time,
is more considerable. But this source of power, which depends chiefly on the imagination, by which we annex, to the
merit of our contemporaries, that of their fore-fathers, is too
refined to be very common among the natives of America.
In most countries therefore, age alone is sufficient for acquiring
respect, influence, and authority. It is age which teaches
experience, and experience is the only source of knowledge
among

among a barbarous people. Among those persons business is conducted with the utmost simplicity, and which may recal to those who are acquainted with antiquity a picture of the most early ages. The heads of families meet together in a house or cabin, appointed for the purpose. Here the business is discussed, and here those of the nation, distinguished for their eloquence or wisdom, have an opportunity of displaying those talents. Their orators, like those of Homer, express themselves in a bold figurative stile, stronger than refined, or rather softened nations can well bear, and with gestures equally violent, but often extremely natural and expressive. When the business is over, and they happen to be well provided in food, they appoint a feast upon the occasion, of which almost the whole nation partakes. The feast is accompanied with a song, in which the real, or fabulous exploits of their forefathers are celebrated. They have dances too, though like those of the Greeks and Romans, chiefly of the military kind, and their music and dancing accompanies every feast.

It often happens, that those different tribes or nations, scattered as they are at an immense distance from one another, meet in their excursions after prey. If there subsists no animosity between them, which seldom is the case, they behave in the most friendly and courteous manner. But if they happen to be in a state of war, or if there has been no previous intercourse between them, all who are not friends, are deemed enemies, they fight with the most savage fury.

War, if we except hunting, is the only employment of the men ; as to every other concern, and even the little agriculture they enjoy, it is left to the women. Their most common motive for entering into war, when it does not arise from an accidental rencounter or interference, is either to revenge themselves for the death of some lost friends, or to acquire prisoners, who may assist them in their hunting, and whom they adopt into their society. These wars are either undertaken by some private adventurers, or at the instance of the whole community. In the latter case, all the young men, who are disposed to go out to battle, for no one is compelled contrary to his inclination, give a bit of wood to the chief, as a token of their design to accompany him. For every thing among these people is transacted with a great deal of ceremony and many forms. The chief, who is to conduct them, fasts several days, during which he converses with no one, and is particularly careful to observe his dreams, which the presumption natural to savages, generally renders as favourable as he could desire. A variety of other superstitions and ceremonies are observed. One of the most hideous is setting the war kettle

on the fire, as an emblem that they are going out to devour
their enemies, which among fome nations muft formerly have
been the cafe, fince they ftill continue to exprefs it in clear
terms, and ufe an emblem fignificant of the ancient ufage.
Then they difpatch a porcelane, or large fhell to their allies,
inviting them to come along, and drink the blood of their
enemies. For with the Americans, as with the Greeks of old,

     " A generous friendfhip no cold medium knows,
     " But with one love, with one refentment glows."

They think that thofe in their alliance muft not only adopt
their enmities, but have their refentment wound up to the
fame pitch with themfelves. And indeed no people carry
their friendfhips, or their refentment, fo far as they do; and
this is what fhould be expected from their peculiar circumftances; that principle in human nature, which is the fpring
of the focial affections, acts with fo much the greater force,
the more it is reftrained. The Americans, who live in fmall
focieties, who fee few objects and few perfons, become wonderfully attached to thefe objects and perfons, and cannot be
deprived of them, without feeling themfelves miferable. Their
ideas are too confined, their breafts are too narrow to entertain the fentiments of general benevolence, or even of ordinary humanity. But this very circumftance, while it makes
them cruel and favage to an incredible degree, towards thofe
with whom they are at war, adds a new force to their particular friendfhips, and to the common tie which unites the
members of the fame tribe, or of thofe different tribes which
are in alliance with one another. Without attending to this
reflection, fome facts we are going to relate, would excite
our wonder without informing our reafon, and we fhould be
bewildered in a number of particulars feemingly oppofite to
one another, without being fenfible of the general caufe from
which they proceed.

Having finifhed all the ceremonies previous to the war, they
iffue forth with their faces blackened with charcoal, intermixed with ftreaks of vermillion, which give them a moft
horrid appearance. Then they exchange their cloaths with
their friends, and difpofe of all their finery to the women,
who accompany them to a confiderable diftance to receive
thofe laft tokens of eternal friendfhip.

The great qualities in an Indian war are vigilance and attention, to give and to avoid a furprize; and indeed in thefe
they are fuperior to all nations in the world. Accuftomed to
continual wandering in the forefts, having their perceptions
                                fharpened

sharpened by keen necessity, and living in every respect according to nature, their external senses have a degree of acute-
ness which at first view appears incredible.   They can trace
out their enemies, at an immense distance, by the smoak of
their fires, which they smell, and by the tracks of their feet
on the ground, imperceptible to an European eye, but which
they can count and distinguish with the utmost facility.   They
even distinguish the different nations with whom they are acquainted, and can determine the precise time when they passed,
where an European could not, with all his glasses, distinguish
footsteps at all.   These circumstances, however, are of small
importance, because their enemies are no less acquainted with
them.   When they go out, therefore, they take care to avoid
making use of any thing by which they might run the danger
of a discovery.   They light no fire to warm themselves, or
to prepare their victuals : they lie close to the ground all day,
and travel only in the night ; and marching along in files, he
that closes the rear, diligently covers with leaves the tracks
of his own feet, and of theirs who preceded him.   When
they halt to refresh themselves, scouts are sent out to recon-
noitre the country, and beat up every place, where they suspect an enemy may lie concealed.   In this manner they enter
unawares the villages of their foes, and while the flower of
the nation are engaged in hunting, massacre all the children,
women, and helpless old men, or make prisoners of as many
as they can manage, or have strength enough to be useful to
their nation.   But when the enemy is apprised of their design,
and coming on in arms against them, they throw themselves
flat on the ground among the withered herbs and leaves, which
their faces are painted to resemble.   Then they allow a part
to pass unmolested, when all at once, with a tremendous
shout, rising up from their ambush, they pour a storm of musket bullets on their foes.   The party attacked, returns the
same cry.   Every one shelters himself with a tree, and returns
the fire of the adverse party, as soon as they raise themselves
from the ground to give a second fire.   Thus does the battle
continue until the one party is so much weakened, as to be
uncapable of farther resistance.   But if the force on each side
continues nearly equal, the fierce spirits of the savages, inflamed by the loss of their friends, can no longer be restrained.
They abandon this distant war, they rush upon one another with
clubs and hatchets in their hands, magnifying their own courage, and insulting their enemies with the bitterest reproaches.
A cruel combat ensues, death appears in a thousand hideous
forms which would congeal the blood of civilized nations to
behold, but which rouse the fury of savages.   They trample,

they

they infult over the dead bodies, tearing the fcalp from the
head, wallowing in their blood like wild beafts, and fometimes
devouring their flefh. The flan e rages on till it meets with no
refiftance, then the prifoners are fecured, thofe unhappy men,
whofe fate is a thoufand times more dreadful than theirs who
have died in the field. The conquerors fet up a hideous
howling to lament the friends they have loft. They approach
in a melancholy and fevere gloom to their own village, a mef-
fenger is fent to announce their arrival, and the women with
frightful fhrieks come out to mourn their dead brothers, or
their hufbands. When they are arrived, the chief relates in
a low voice to the elders a circumftantial account of every particular of the expedition. The orator proclaims aloud this
account to the people, and as he mentions the names of thofe
who have fallen, the fhrieks of the women are redoubled.
The men too join in thefe cries, according as each is moft
connected with the deceafed, by blood or friendfhip. The
laft ceremony is the proclamation of the victory ; each individual then forgets his private misfortunes, and joins in the
triumph of his nation ; all tears are wiped from their eyes, and
by an unaccountable tranfition, they pafs in a moment from
the bitternefs of forrow, to an extravagance of joy. But the
treatment of the prifoners, whofe fate all this time remains
undecided, is what chiefly characterifes the favages.

We have already mentioned the ftrength of their affections
or refentments. United as they are in fmall focieties, connected within themfelves by the firmeft ties, their friendly
affections, which glow with the moft intenfe warmth within
the walls of their own village, feldom extend beyond them.
They feel nothing for the enemies of their nation ; and their
refentment is eafily extended from the individual, who has
injured them, to all others of the fame tribe. The prifoners,
who have themfelves the fame feelings, know the intentions
of their conquerors, and are prepared for them. The perfon,
who has taken the captive, attends him to the cottage, where,
according to the diftribution made by the elders, he is to be
delivered to fupply the lofs of a citizen. If thofe who receive
him have their family weakened by war or other accidents,
they adopt the captive into the family, of which he becomes a
member. But if they have no occafion for him, or their refentment for the lofs of their friends be too high to endure
the fight of any connected with thofe who were concerned in
it, they fentence him to death. All thofe who have met with
the fame fevere fentence being collected, the whole nation is
affembled at the execution, as for fome great folemnity. A
fcaffold is erected, and the prifoners are tied to the ftake,
                                                      where

where they commence their death-fong, and prepare for the enfuing fcene of cruelty with the moft undaunted courage. Their enemies, on the other fide, are determined to put it to the proof, by the moft refined and exquifite tortures. They begin at the extremity of his body, and gradually approach the more vital parts. One plucks out his nails by the roots, one by one; another takes a finger into his mouth, and tears off the flefh with his teeth; a third thrufts the finger, mangled as it is, into the bowl of a pipe made red hot, which he fmoaks like tobacco; then they pound his toes and fingers to pieces between two ftones; they pull off the flefh from the teeth, and cut circles about his joints, and gafhes in the flefhy parts of his limbs, which they fear immediately with red hot irons, cutting, burning, and pinching them alternately; they pull off this flefh, thus mangled and roafted, bit by bit, devouring it with greedinefs, and fmearing their faces with the blood in an enthufiafm of horror and fury. When they have thus torn off the flefh, they twift the bare nerves and tendons about an iron, tearing and fnapping them, whilft others are employed in pulling and extending the limbs in every way that can increafe the torment. This continues often five or fix hours, and fometimes, fuch is the ftrength of the favages, days together. Then they frequently unbind him, to give a breathing to their fury, to think what new torments they fhall inflict, and to refrefh the ftrength of the fufferer, who, wearied out with fuch a variety of unheard of torments, often falls into fo profound a fleep, that they are obliged to apply the fire to awake him and renew his fufferings. He is again faftened to the ftake, and again they renew their cruelty; they ftick him all over with fmall matches of wood, that eafily takes fire but burns flowly; they continually run fharp reeds into every part of his body; they drag out his teeth with pincers, and thruft out his eyes; and laftly, after having burned his flefh from the bones with flow fires; after having fo mangled the body that it is all but one wound; after having mutilated his face in fuch a manner as to carry nothing human in it; after having peeled the fkin from the head, and poured a heap of red hot coals or boiling water on the naked fkull, they once more unbind the wretch, who, blind, and ftaggering with pain and weaknefs, affaulted and pelted upon every fide with clubs and ftones, now up, now down, falling into their fires at every ftep, runs hither and thither, until one of the chiefs, whether out of compaffion, or weary of cruelty, puts an end to his life with a club or a dagger. The body is then put into the kettle, and this barbarous employment is fucceeded by a feaft as barbarous.

The

The women, forgetting the human as well as the female nature, and transformed into something worse than furies, act their parts, and even outdo the men in this scene of horror, while the principal persons of the country sit round the stake, smoaking and looking on without the least emotion. What is most extraordinary, the sufferer himself, in the little intervals of his torments, smoaks too, appears unconcerned, and converses with his torturers about indifferent matters. Indeed, during the whole time of his execution, there seems a contest between him and them which shall exceed, they in inflicting the most horrid pains, or he in enduring them, with a firmness and constancy almost above human : not a groan, not a sigh, not a distortion of countenance escapes him ; he possesses his mind entirely in the midst of his torments ; he recounts his own exploits ; he informs them what cruelties he has inflicted upon their countrymen, and threatens them with the revenge that will attend his death ; and, though his reproaches exasperate them to a perfect madness of rage and fury, he continues his insults even of their ignorance of the art of tormenting, pointing out himself more exquisite methods, and more sensible parts of the body to be afflicted. The women have this part of courage as well as the men ; and it is as rare for any Indian to behave otherwise, as it would be for any European to suffer as an Indian. Such is the wonderful power of an early institution, and a ferocious thirst of glory. *I am brave and intrepid,* exclaims the savage in the face of his tormentors, *I do not fear death, nor any kind of tortures; those who fear them are cowards; they are less than women; life is nothing to those that have courage : may my enemies be confounded with despair and rage; Oh! that I could devour them, and drink their blood to the last drop.*

I do not dwell upon these circumstances of cruelty, which so degrade human nature, out of choice ; but, as all who mention the customs of this people have insisted upon their behaviour in this respect very particularly, and as it seems necessary to give a true idea of their character, I did not chuse to omit it. And what is still more important, it serves to shew in the strongest light, to what an inconceivable degree of barbarity, to what a pitch the passions of men may be carried, when untamed by the refinements of polished society, when let loose from the government of reason, and uninfluenced by the dictates of Christianity ; a religion that teaches compassion to our enemies, which is neither known nor practised in other institutions ; and it will make us more sensible than some appear to be, of the value of commerce, the arts of a civilized life, and the light of literature ; which, if they have abated the force of some of the natural virtues, by the luxury which attends them, have taken out likewife the fting of our natural vices, and foftened the ferocity of the human race.

Nothing in the hiftory of mankind, as I have already obfer-ved, forms a ftronger contraft than this cruelty of the favages towards thofe with whom they are at war, and the warmth of their affection towards their friends, who confift of all thofe who live in the fame village, or are in alliance with it : among thefe all things are common; and this, though it may in part arife from their not poffeffing very diftinct notions of feparate property, is chiefly to be attributed to the ftrength of their attachment; becaufe in every thing elfe, with their lives as well as their fortunes, they are ready to ferve their friends. Their houfes, their provifion, even their young women, are not enough to oblige a gueft. Has any one of thefe fucceeded ill in his hunting? Has his harveft failed? or is his houfe burned? He feels no other effect of his misfortune, than that it gives him an opportunity to experience the benevolence and regard of his fellow citizens; but to the enemies of his coun-try, or to thofe who have privately offended, the American is implacable. He conceals his fentiments, he appears recon-ciled, until by fome treachery or furprize he has an opportu-nity of executing an horrible revenge. No length of time is fufficient to allay his refentment; no diftance of place great enough to protect the object; he croffes the fteepeft mountains, he pierces the moft impracticable forefts, and traverfes the moft hideous bogs and deferts for feveral hundreds of miles; bearing the inclemency of the feafons, the fatigue of the expe-dition, the extremes of hunger and thirft, with patience and chearfulnefs, in hopes of furprifing his enemy, on whom he exercifes the moft fhocking barbarities, even to the eating of his flefh. To fuch extremes do the Indians pufh their friend-fhip or their enmity; and fuch indeed in general is the cha-racter of all ftrong and uncultivated minds.

But what we have faid refpecting the Indians would be a faint picture, did we omit obferving the force of their friend-fhip, which principally appears by the treatment of their dead. When any one of the fociety is cut off, he is lamented by the whole: on this occafion a thoufand ceremonies are practifed, denoting the moft lively forrow. Of thefe, the moft remark-able, as it difcovers both the height and continuance of their grief, is what they call the feaft of the dead, or the feaft of fouls. The day of this ceremony is appointed by public order, and nothing is omitted that it may be celebrated with the utmoft pomp and magnificence. The neighbouring tribes are invited to be prefent, and to join in the folemnity. At this time all who have died fince the laft folemn occafion, (which is renewed every ten years among fome tribes, and

every

every eight among others) are taken out of their graves : thofe
who have been interred at the greateft diftance from the villages are diligently fought for, and brought to this great rendezvous of carcaffes.

It is not difficult to conceive the horror of this general difin-
terment. I cannot defcribe it in a more lively manner than it
is done by Lafitau, to whom we are indebted for the moft authentic account of thofe nations.

Without queftion, fays he, the opening of thefe tombs
difplays one of the moft ftriking fcenes that can be conceived ;
this humbling portrait of human mifery, in fo many images
of death, wherein fhe feems to take a pleafure to paint herfelf
in a thoufand various fhapes of horror, in the feveral carcafes,
according to the degree in which corruption has prevailed
over them, or the manner in which it has attacked them.
Some appear dry and withered ; others have a fort of parchment
upon their bones ; fome look as if they were baked and fmoaked, without any appearance of rottennefs ; fome are juft
turning towards the point of putrefaction ; whilft others are
all fwarming with worms, and drowned in corruption. I
know not which ought to ftrike us moft, the horror of fo
fhocking a fight, or the tender piety and affection of thefe
poor people towards their departed friends ; for nothing deferves our admiration more than that eager diligence and attention with which they difcharge this melancholy duty of their
tendernefs ; gathering up carefully even the fmalleft bones ;
handling the carcaffes, difguftful as they are, with every
thing loathfome, cleanfing them from the worms, and carrying them upon their fhoulders through tirefome journeys of
feveral days, without being difcouraged from the offenfivenefs
of the fmell, and without fuffering any other emotions to
arife than thofe of regret, for having loft perfons who were
fo dear to them in their lives, and fo lamented in their death.

They bring them into their cottages, where they prepare a
feaft in honour of the dead, during which their great actions
are celebrated, and all the tender intercourfes which took
place between them and their friends are pioufly called to
mind. The ftrangers, who have come fometimes many hundred miles to be prefent on the occafion, join in the tender
condolance ; and the women, by frightful fhrieks, demonftrate
that they are pierced with the fharpeft forrow. Then the
dead bodies are carried from the cabins for the general reinter-
ment. A great pit is dug in the ground, and thither, at a
certain time, each perfon attended by his family and friends,
marches in folemn filence, bearing the dead body of a fon, a
father, or a brother. When they are all convened, the dead
bodies, or the duft of thofe which were quite corrupted, are
depofited

depofited in the pit : then the torrent of grief breaks out anew. Whatever they poffefs moft valuable is interred with the dead. The ftrangers are not wanting in their generofity, and confer thofe prefents which they have brought along with them for the purpofe. Then all prefent go down into the pit, and every one takes a little of the earth, which they afterwards preferve with the moft religious care. The bodies, ranged in order, are covered with intire new furs, and over thefe with bark, on which they throw ftones, wood, and earth. Then taking their laft farewell, they return each to his own cabin.

We have mentioned that in this ceremony the favages offer, as prefents to the dead, whatever they value moft highly. This cuftom, which is univerfal among them, arifes from a rude notion of the immortality of the foul. They believe this doctrine moft firmly, and it is the principal tenet of their religion. When the foul is feparated from the body of their friends, they conceive that it ftill continues to hover around it, and to require and take delight in the fame things with which it formerly was pleafed. After a certain time, however, it forfakes this dreary manfion, and departs far weftward into the land of fpirits. They have even gone fo far as to make a diftinction between the inhabitants of the other world ; fome, they imagine, particularly thofe who in their life-time have been fortunate in war, poffefs a high degree of happinefs, have a place for hunting and fifhing, which never fails, and enjoy all fenfual delights, without labouring hard in order to procure them. The fouls of thofe, on the contrary, who happen to be conquered or flain in war, are extremely miferable after death. A future ftate therefore is not at all confidered among the favages as a place of retribution, as the reward of humble virtue, or as the punifhment of profperous vice. They rather judge of our happinefs in the next world by what we have enjoyed in the prefent.

Their tafte for war, which forms the chief ingredient in their character, gives a ftrong bias to their religion. Arefkoui, or the god of battle, is revered as the great god of the Indians. Him they invoke before they go into the field, and according as his difpofition is more or lefs favourable to them, they conclude they will be more or lefs fuccefsful. Some nations worfhip the fun and moon ; among others there are a number of traditions, relative to the creation of the world, and the hiftory of the gods : traditions which refemble the Grecian fables, but which are ftill more abfurd and inconfiftent. But religion is not the prevailing character of the Indians ; and except when they have fome immediate occafion for the affiftance of their gods, they pay them no fort of worfhip. Like all rude nations, however, they are ftrongly addicted to fuperftition.

They

They believe in the exiſtence of a number of good and bad genii or ſpirits, who interfere in the affairs of mortals, and produce all our happineſs or miſery. It is from the evil genii, in particular, that our diſeaſes proceed; and it is to the good genii we are indebted for a cure. The miniſters of the genii are the jugglers, who are alſo the only phyſicians among the ſavages. Theſe jugglers are ſuppoſed to be inſpired by the good genii, moſt commonly in their dreams, with the knowledge of future events; they are called in to the aſſiſtance of the ſick, and are ſuppoſed to be informed by the genii whether they will get over the diſeaſe, and in what way they muſt be treated. But theſe ſpirits are extremely ſimple in their ſyſtem of phyſic, and, in almoſt every diſeaſe, direct the juggler to the ſame remedy. The patient is incloſed in a narrow cabin, in the midſt of which is a ſtone red hot; on this they throw water, until he is well ſoaked with the warm vapour and his own ſweat. Then they hurry him from the bagnio, and plunge him ſuddenly into the next river. This coarſe method, which coſts many their lives, often performs very extraordinary cures. The jugglers have likewiſe the uſe of ſome ſpecifics of wonderful efficacy; and all the ſavages are dextrous in curing wounds by the application of herbs. But the power of theſe remedies is always attributed to the magical ceremonies with which they are adminiſtered.

A general Deſcription of AMERICA.

THIS great weſtern continent, frequently denominated the new world, extends from the 80 deg. north, to the 56 deg. ſouth lat; and where its breadth is known, from the 35 to the 136 deg. of weſt lon. from London, ſtretching between 8 and 9000 miles in length, and in its greateſt breadth 3690. It ſees both hemiſpheres, has two ſummers, and a double winter, and enjoys all the variety of climates which the earth affords. It is waſhed by the two great oceans. To the eaſtward it has the Atlantic, which divides it from Europe and Africa. To the weſt it has the Pacific, or great South-Sea, by which it is ſeparated from Aſia. By theſe ſeas it may, and does, carry on a direct commerce with the other three parts of the world. It is compoſed of two great continents, one on the north, the other upon the ſouth, which are joined by the kingdom of Mexico, which forms a ſort of Iſthmus 1500 miles long, and in one part at Darien, ſo extremely narrow, as to make the communication between the two oceans by no means difficult, being only 60 miles over. In the great gulph, which is formed between the Iſthmus, and

the northern and fouthern continents, lie an infinite multitude
of iflands, many of them large, moft of them fertile, and
denominated the Weft-Indies, in contradiftinction to the
countries and iflands of Afia, beyond the cape of Good-Hope,
which are called the Eaft-Indies.

Before we begin to treat of feparate countries in their order,
we muft according to juft method take notice of thofe mountains and rivers, which difdain, as it were, to be confined
within the limits of particular provinces, and extend over a
great part of the continent. For though America in general
be not a mountainous country, it has the greateft mountains
in the world. In fouth America the Andes, or Cordilleras,
run from north to fouth along the coaft of the Pacific ocean.
They exceed in length any chain of mountains in the other
parts of the globe; extending from the Ifthmus of Darien, to
the ftreights of Magellan, they divide the whole fouthern parts
of America, and run a length of 4300 miles. Their height
is as remarkable as their length, for though in part within
the torrid zone, they are conftantly covered with fnow. In
North America, which is chiefly compofed of gentle afcents,
or level plains, we know of no confiderable mountains, except
thofe towards the pole, and that long ridge which lies on the
back of our fettlements, feparating our colonies from Canada
and Louifiana, which we call the Apalachian, or Alegeny
mountains; if that may be confidered as a mountain, which
upon one fide is extremely lofty, but upon the other is nearly
on a level with the reft of the country.

America is, without queftion, that part of the globe which
is beft watered; and that not only for the fupport of life, and
all the purpofes of fertility, but for the convenience of trade,
and the intercourfe of each part with the others. In North
America, fuch is the wifdom and goodnefs of the Creator of
the univerfe, thofe vaft tracts of country, fituated beyond the
Apalachian mountains, at an immenfe and unknown diftance
from the ocean, are watered by inland feas, called the Lakes
of Canada, which not only communicate with each other,
but give rife to feveral great rivers, particularly the Miffifippi,
running from north to fouth till it falls into the gulph of
Mexico, after a courfe, including its turnings, of 4500 miles,
and receiving in its progrefs the vaft tribute of the Illinois, the
Mifaures, the Ohio, and other great rivers fcarcely inferior
to the Rhine, or the Danube; and on the north, the river
St. Laurence, running a contrary courfe from the Miffifippi,
till it empties itfelf into the ocean near Newfoundland; all of
them being almoft navigable to their heads, lay open the inmoft
receffes of this great continent, and afford fuch an inlet for
commerce, as muft produce the greateft advantages, whenever
                                                            the

the country adjacent fhall come to be fully inhabited, and by an induftrious and civilized people. The eaftern fide of North America, which makes a part of the Britifh empire, befides the noble rivers Hudfon, Delaware, Sufquehana, and Potowmack, fupplies feveral others of great depth, length, and commodious navigation : hence many parts of our fettlements are fo advantageoufly interfected with navigable rivers and creeks, that our planters, without exaggeration, may be faid to have each a harbour at his door.

South America is, if poffible, in this refpect even more fortunate. It fupplies much the two largeft rivers in the world, the river of Amazones, and the Rio de la Plata, or Plate River. The firft rifing in Peru, not far from the South Sea, paffes from weft to eaft, and falls into the ocean between Brazil and Guiana, after a courfe of more than 3000 miles, in which it receives a prodigious number of great and navigable rivers. The Rio de la Plata, rifes in the heart of the country, and having its ftrength gradually augmented, by an acceffion of many powerful ftreams, difcharges itfelf with fuch vehemence into the fea, as to make its tafte frefh for many leagues from land. Befides thefe there are other rivers in South America, of which the Oronoquo is the moft confiderable.

A country of fuch vaft extent on each fide of the equator, muft neceffarily have a variety of foils as well as climates. It is a treafury of nature, producing moft of the metals, minerals, plants, fruits, trees, and wood, to be met with in the other parts of the world, and many of them in greater quantities and high perfection. The gold and filver of America has fupplied Europe with fuch immenfe quantities of thofe valuable metals, that they are become vaftly more common ; fo that the gold and filver of Europe now bears little proportion to the high price fet upon them before the difcovery of America.

This country alfo produces diamonds, pearls, emeralds, amethyfts, and other valuable ftones, which by being brought into Europe, have contributed likewife to lower their value. To thefe, which are chiefly the production of Spanifh America, may be added a great number of other commodities, which, though of lefs price, are of much greater ufe, and many of them make the ornament and wealth of the Britifh empire in this part of the world. Of thefe are the plentiful fupplies of cochineal, indigo, anatto, logwood, brazil, fuftic, pimento, lignum vitæ, rice, ginger, cocoa, or the chocolate nut, fugar, cotton, tobacco, banillas, red-wood, the balfams of Tolu, Peru, and China, that valuable article in medicine the Jefuit's bark, mechoacan, faffafras, farfaparilla, caffia, tamarinds, hides,

hides, furs, ambergris, and a great variety of woods, roots, and plants, to which, before the difcovery of America, we were either entire ftrangers, or forced to buy at an extravagant rate from Afia and Africa, through the lands of the Venetians and Genoefe, who then engroffed the trade of the eaftern world.

This continent has alfo a variety of excellent fruits, which here grow wild to great perfection ; as pine-apples, pomegranates, citrons, lemons, oranges, malicatons, cherries, pears, apples, figs, grapes, great numbers of culinary, medicinal, and other herbs, roots and plants ; and fo fertile is the foil, that many exotic productions are nourifhed in as great perfection, as in their native ground.

Though the Indians ftill live in the quiet poffeffion of many large tracts, America fo far as known, is chiefly claimed, and divided into colonies, by three European nations, the Spaniards, Englifh, and Portuguefe. The Spaniards, who, as they firft difcovered it, have the largeft and richeft portion, extending from New Mexico and Louifiana, in North America, to the ftreights of Magellan in the fouth fea, excepting the large province of Brazil, which belongs to Portugal ; for though the French and Dutch have fome forts upon Surinam and Guiana, they fcarcely deferve to be confidered as proprietors of any part of the fouthern continent.

Next to Spain, the moft confiderable proprietor of America is Great Britain, who derives her claim to North America, from the firft difcovery of that continent, by Sebaftian Cabot, in the name of Henry VII. anno 1497, about fix years after the difcovery of South America by Columbus, in the name of the king of Spain. This country was in general called Newfoundland, a name which is now appropriated folely to an ifland upon its coaft. It was a long time before we made any attempt to fettle this country. Sir Walter Raleigh, an uncommon genius, and a brave commander, firft fhewed the way by planting a colony in the fouthern part, which he called Virginia, in honour of his miftrefs queen Elizabeth.

The French indeed, from this period until the conclufion of the late war, laid a claim to, and actually poffeffed Canada and Louifiana, comprehending all that extenfive inland country, reaching from Hudfon's Bay on the north, to Mexico and the gulph of the fame name on the fouth ; regions which all Europe could not people in the courfe of many ages : but no territory however extenfive, no empire however boundlefs, could gratify the ambition of that afpiring nation; hence, under the moft folemn treaties, they continued in a ftate of hoftility, making gradual advances upon the back of our fet-

tlements, and rendering their acquisitions more secure and
permanent by a chain of forts, well supplied with all the
implements of war. At the same time they laboured incessantly to gain-the friendship of the Indians, whom they not
only trained to the use of arms, but infused into these savages
the most unfavourable notion of the English, and the strength
of their nation. The British colonies thus hemmed in, and
confined to a slip of land along the sea coast, by an ambitious
and powerful nation, the rivals and the natural enemies of
Great Britain, began to take the alarm. The British empire
in America, yet in its infancy, was threatened with a total
dissolution. The colonies, in their distress, called out aloud
to the mother country. The bulwarks, and the thunder of
England, were sent to their relief, accompanied with powerful armies, well appointed, and commanded by a set of heroes,
the Scipios of the present age. A long war succeeded, which
ended gloriously for Great Britain; for after oceans of blood
were spilt, and every inch of ground bravely disputed, the
French were not only driven from Canada, and its dependancies, but obliged to relinquish all that part of Louisiana,
lying on the east side of the Missisippi.

Thus at an immense expence, and with the loss of many
brave men, our colonies were preserved, secured, and extended
so far, as to render it difficult to ascertain the precise bounds
of our empire in North America, to the northern and
western sides; for to the northward, it should seem that we
might extend our claims quite to the pole itself, nor does any
nation seem inclined to dispute the property of this northern-most country with us. If we should choose to take our stand
upon the northern extremity, and look towards the south, we
have a territory extending in that aspect, from the pole to
Cape Florida in the gulph of Mexico, N. lat. 25, and consequently near 4000 miles long in a direct line; which is the
more valuable, as it includes the most temperate climates of
this new world, and such as are best suited to British constitutions. But to the westward, our boundaries reach to
nations unknown even to the native Indians of Canada. If
we might hazard a conjecture, it is nearly equal to the extent
of all Europe. This vast empire is all the way washed by the
Atlantic ocean on the east, and on the south by the gulph of
Mexico. We have already taken notice of the river St. Lawrence, the Missisippi, the lakes of Canada, and other great
bodies of water, which fertilize and enrich its northern and
western boundaries, as well as the interior parts.

In describing the situation, extent, and boundaries of the
numerous colonies which now compose this great empire, we
have totally rejected the accounts given us by partial French
                                                    writers,

writers, as well as thofe of Salmon and other Englifh geographers, if men deferve that name, who have wandered fo widely from the truth, and who feem either unacquainted with the fubjeƈt, or have been at no pains to confult the lateft and moft authentic materials. This we thought neceffary to premife, that the reader may be prepared for the following table, which he will find to differ widely from any book of geography hitherto publifhed, being compofed from the lateft treaties and the beft maps and drawings in confequence of thefe treaties, and the fureft guides in giving the geography of thefe important provinces.

The multitude of iflands, which lie between the two continents of North and South America, are divided amongft the Spaniards, Englifh, and French. The Dutch indeed poffefs three or four fmall iflands, which in any other hands would be of no confequence : and the Danes have one or two, but they hardly deferve to be named among the proprietors of America. We fhall now proceed to the particular provinces, beginning, according to our method, with the north ; but as Labrador or New Britain, and the countries round Hudfon's Bay, with thofe vaft regions towards the pole, are little known, we can only include within the following table, the colonies that have been formed into regular governments, which bring us to the 50th degree north lat. viz.

The grand Divifions of NORTH AMERICA.

Colonies.	Length	Breadt.	Chief Towns.	Dift. & bearing from London.	Belongs to
Province of Quebec	800	200	Quebec		Great Britain
New Scotland	350	250	Hallifax		Ditto
New England	550	200	Bofton	2760 W.	Ditto
New York	300	150	New York		Ditto
New Jerfey	160	60	Perth Amboy		Ditto
Penfylvania	300	240	Philadelphia		Ditto
Maryland	140	135	Anapolis		Ditto
Virginia	750	240	Williamfburg		Ditto
No. Carolina So. Carolina Georgia	700	380	Wilmington Charles-town Savannah		Ditto Ditto Ditto
Eaft Florida Weft Florida	500	440	St. Auguftin Penfacola		Ditto Ditto
Louifiana	Bounds undeter.		New Orleans	4080 S. W.	Spain
New Mexico & California	2000	1600	St. Fee St. Juan	4320 S. W.	Ditto Ditto
Mexico or New Spain	2000	600	Mexico	4900 S. W.	Ditto

The

The principal ISLANDS in North America belonging to Europeans are,

	ISLANDS.	Length.	Breadt.	Chief Towns.	Belongs to
In the Gulph of St. Lawr.	Newfoundland	350	200	Placentia	Great Britain
	Cape Breton	110	80	Louisburg	Ditto
	St. John's	60	30	Charlotte Town	Ditto
In the Atlantic.	The Bermudas isles	20,000 acres		St. George	Ditto
	The Bahama ditto			Naſſau	Ditto
West-India iſlands, lying in the Atlantic between North and South America.	Jamaica	140	60	Kingſton	Ditto
	Barbadoes	21	14	Bridgetown	Ditto
	St. Chriſtopher's	20	7	Baſſe-terre	Ditto
	Antigua	20	20	St. John's	Ditto
	Nevis and Montſerrat	each of theſe is 18 circum		Charles-Town Plymouth	Ditto Ditto
	Barbuda	20	12		Ditto
	Anguilla	30	10		Ditto
	Dominica	28	13		Ditto
	St. Vincent	24	18		Ditto
	Granada	30	15	Lewis	Ditto
	Tobago	32	9		Ditto
	Cuba	700	70	Havannah	Spain
	Hiſpaniola	450	150	St. Domingo	Ditto & France
	Porto Rico	100	40	Porto Rico	Spain
	Trinidad	90	60		Ditto
	Margaritta	40	24		Ditto
	Martinico	60	30	St. Peter's	France
	Guadalupe	45	38	Baſſ-terre	Ditto
	St. Lucia	23	12		Ditto
	St. Bartholomew, Defeada, and Maragalante	very ſmall			Ditto Ditto Ditto
	St. Fuſtatia	29	circum.	The Bay	Dutch
	Curaſſou	30	10		Ditto
	St. Thomas	15	circum.		Denmark
	St. Croix	30	10	Baſſe End	Ditto

Grand Diviſions of SOUTH AMERICA.

Nations.	Length	Breadt.	Chief Cities.	Diſt. & bearing from London.	Belongs to
Terra Firma	1400	700	Panama	4650 S. W.	Spain
Peru	1800	500	Lima	5520 S. W.	Spain
Amazonia, a very large country, but little known to the Europeans, 1200 L. 960 B.					
Guiana	780	480	Surinam or Cayenne	3840 S. W.	Dutch & French
Braſil	2500	700	St. Salvador	6000 S. W.	Portugal
Paraguay or Laplata	1500	1000	Buenos Ayres	6040 S. W.	Spain & Jeſuits
Chili	1200	500	St. Jago	6600 S. W.	Spain
Terra Magellanica, or Patagonia.	The Spaniards took poſſeſſion of it, but did not think it worth while to ſettle there. 700 L. 300 B.				

BRITISH AMERICA.

NEW BRITAIN.

NEW BRITAIN, or the country lying round Hudson's bay, and commonly called the country of the
Eſquimaux, comprehending Labrador, now North and South
Wales, is bounded by unknown lands, and frozen ſeas, about
the pole, on the north; by the Atlantic ocean on the eaſt;
by the bay and river of St. Lawrence and Canada, on the
ſouth; and by unknown lands on the weſt.

MOUNTAINS.] The tremendous high mountains in this
country towards the north, their being covered with eternal
ſnow, and the winds blowing from thence three quarters of
the year, occaſions a degree of cold in the winter, over all this
country, which is not experienced in any other part of the
world in the ſame latitude.

RIVERS, BAYS, STRAITS,} Theſe are numerous in this
 AND CAPES. country, and take their names
generally from the Engliſh navigators and commanders, by
whom they were firſt diſcovered; the principal bay is that of
Hudſon, and the principal ſtraits are thoſe of Hudſon, Davies,
and Belleiſle.

SOIL AND PRODUCE.] This country is extremely barren;
to the northward of Hudſon's Bay, even the hardy pine-tree is
ſeen no longer, and the cold womb of the earth is incapable of
any better production than ſome miſerable ſhrubs. Every
kind of European ſeed, which we have committed to the
earth, in this inhoſpitable climate, has hitherto periſhed;
but, in all probability, we have not tried the ſeed of corn from
the northern parts of Sweden and Norway; in ſuch caſes, the
place from whence the ſeed comes is of great moment. All
this ſeverity, and long continuance of winter, and the bar-
renneſs of the earth which comes from thence, is experienced
in the latitude of fifty-one; in the temperate latitude of
Cambridge.

ANIMALS.] Theſe are the mooſe deer, ſtags, rein deer,
bears, tygers, buffaloes, wolves, foxes, beavers, otters,
lynxes, martins, ſquirrels, ermins, wild cats, and hares. Of
the feathered kind, they have geeſe, buſtards, ducks, partridges, and all manner of wild fowls. Of fiſh, there are
whales, morſes, ſeals, cod-fiſh, and a white fiſh, preferable
to herrings; and in their rivers and freſh waters, pike, perch,
carp, and trout. There have been taken at Port Nelſon, in
one ſeaſon, ninety thouſand partridges, which are here as large
as hens, and twenty-five thouſand hares.

All

All the animals of thefe countries, are cloathed with a clofe, foft, warm fur. In fummer there is here, as in other places, a variety in the colours of the feveral animals; when that feafon is over, which holds only for three months, they all affume the livery of winter, and every fort of beafts, and moft of their fowls, are of the colour of the fnow; every thing animate and inanimate is white. This is a furprizing phenomenon. But what is yet more furprizing, and what is indeed one of the moft ftriking things, that draw the moft inattentive to an admiration of the wifdom and goodnefs of Providence, is, that the dogs and cats from England, that have been carried into Hudfon's Bay, on the approach of winter, have entirely changed their appearance, and acquired a much longer, fofter, and thicker coat of hair, than they had originally.

Before we advance further in the defcription of America, it may be proper to obferve in general, that all the quadrupedes of this new world, are lefs than thofe of the old; even fuch as are carried from hence to breed there, are often found to degenerate, but are never feen to improve. If with refpect to fize, we fhould compare the animals of the new and the old world, we fhall find the one bear no manner of proportion to the other. The Afiatic elephant, for inftance, often grows to above fifteen feet high, while the tapurette, which is the largeft native of America, is not bigger than a calf of a year old. The lama, which fome alfo call the American camel, is ftill lefs. Their beafts of prey are quite divefted of that courage, which is fo often fatal to man in Africa or Afia. They have no lions, nor, properly fpeaking, either leopard or tiger. Travellers, however, have affixed thofe names to fuch ravenous animals, as are there found moft to refemble thofe of the antient continent. The congar, the taquar, and the taquaretti among them, are defpicable in comparifon of the tiger, the leopard, and the panther of Afia. The tyger of Bengal has been known to meafure fix feet in length, without including the tail, while the congar, or American tyger, as fome affect to call it, feldom exceeds three. All the animals therefore in the fouthern parts of America, are different from thofe in the fouthern parts of the ancient continent; nor does there appear to be any common to both, but thofe, which being able to bear the colds of the north, have travelled from one continent to the other. Thus the bear, the wolf, the rain-deer, the ftag, and the beaver, are known as well by the inhabitants of New Britain and Canada, as Ruffia; while the lion, the leopard, and the tyger, which are natives of the fouth with us, are utterly unknown in fouthern America.

But

But if the quadrupedes of America be fmaller than thofe of the ancient continent, they are in much greater abundance; for it is a rule that obtains through nature, and evidently points out the wifdom of the author of it, that the fmalleft animals multiply in the greateft proportion. The goat, imported from Europe to fouthern America, in a few generations becomes much lefs, but then it alfo becomes more prolific, and inftead of one kid at a time, or two at the moft, generally produces five, fix, and fometimes more. The wifdom of Providence in making formidable animals unprolific is obvious; had the elephant, the rhinoceros, and the lion, the fame degree of fecundity with the rabbit, or the rat, all the arts of man would foon be unequal to the conteft, and we fhould foon perceive them become the tyrants of thofe who call themfelves the mafters of the creation.

PERSONS AND HABITS.] The men of this country fhew great ingenuity in their manner of kindling a fire, in cloathing themfelves, and in preferving their eyes from the ill effects of that glaring white which every where furrounds them, for the greateft part of the year; in other refpects they are very favage. In their fhapes and faces they do not refemble the Americans who live to the fouthward; they are much more like the Laplanders and Samoeids of Europe already defcribed, from whom they are probably defcended. The other Americans feem to be of a Tartar original.

DISCOVERY AND COMMERCE.] The knowledge of thefe northern feas and countries, was owing to a project ftarted in England for the difcovery of a north-weft paffage to China, and the Eaft Indies, as early as the year 1576. Since then it has been frequently dropped, and as often revived, but never yet compleated. Forbifher only difcovered the main of New Britain, or Terra de Labrador, and thofe ftraits to which he has given his name. In 1585, John David failed from Portfmouth, and viewed that and the more northerly coafts, but he feems never to have entered the bay. Hudfon made three voyages on the fame adventure, the firft in 1607, the fecond in 1608, and his third and laft in 1610. This bold and judicious navigator entered the ftraits that lead into this new Mediterranean, the bay known by his name, coafted a great part of it, and penetrated to eighty degrees and a half into the heart of the frozen zone. His ardour for the difcovery not being abated by the difficulties he ftruggled with in this empire of winter, and world of froft and fnow, he ftaid here until the enfuing fpring, and prepared in the beginning of 1611 to purfue his difcoveries; but his crew, who fuffered equal hardfhips, without the fame fpirit to fupport them, mutinied,

feized

feized upon him, and feven of thofe who were moft faithful
to him, and committed them to the fury of the icy feas, in an
open boat. Hudfon and his companions were either fwal-
lowed up by the waves, or, gaining the inhofpitable coaft,
were deftroyed by the favages ; but the fhip, and the reft of
the men returned home.

The laft attempt towards a difcovery was made in 1746 by
captain Ellis, who wintered as far north as 57 degrees and a
half; but though the adventurers failed in the original purpofe,
for which they navigated this bay, their project, even in its
failure, has been of great advantage to this country. The
vaft countries which furround Hudfon's Bay, as we have
already obferved, abound with animals, whofe fur and fkins
are excellent. In 1670, a charter was granted to a company,
which does not confift of above nine or ten perfons, for the
exclufive trade to this bay, and they have acted under it ever
fince with great benefit to the private men, who compofe the
company, though comparatively with little advantage to Great
Britain. The fur and peltry trade might be carried on to a
much greater extent, were it not entirely in the hands of this
exclufive company, whofe intereft, not to fay iniquitous fpirit
has been the fubject of long and juft complaint. The company employ four fhips, and 130 feamen. They have four
forts, viz. Churchill, Nelfon, New Severn, and Albany,
which ftand on the weft fide of the bay, and are garrifoned
by 186 men. They export commodities to the value of
16,000 l. and bring home returns to the value of 29,340 l.
which yield to the revenue 3,734 l. This includes the fifhery
in Hudfon's Bay. This commerce, fmall as it is, affords immenfe profits to the company, and even fome advantages to
Great Britain in general ; for the commodities we exchange
with the Indians for their fkins and furs, are all manufactured
in Britain ; and as the Indians are not very nice in their
choice, fuch things are fent, of which we have the greateft
plenty, and which in the mercantile phrafe, are drugs with
us. Though the workmanfhip too happen to be in many
refpects fo deficient, that no civilized people would take it
off our hands, it may be admired among the Indians. On
the other hand, the fkins and furs we bring from Hudfon's
Bay, enter largely into our manufactures, and afford us materials for trading with many nations of Europe, to great advantage. Thefe circumftances tend to prove inconteftibly the
immenfe benefit, that would redound to Great Britain, by
throwing open the trade to Hudfon's Bay, fince even in its
prefent reftrained ftate it is fo advantageous. This company,
it is probable, do not find their trade fo advantageous now,

as

as it was before we got poffeffion of Canada. The only attempt made to trade with Labrador, has been directed towards
the fifhery. Great Britain has no fettlement here, though the
annual produce of the fifhery, amounting to upward of
49,000 l. and the natural advantages of the country fhould
encourage us to fet about this defign.

CANADA, or the PROVINCE OF QUEBEC.

SITUATION AND EXTENT.

Miles.		Degrees.
Length 800	} between	{ 61 and 81 weft longitude.
Breadth 200		{ 45 and 52 north latitude.

BOUNDARIES.] THE French comprehended under the
name of Canada, a very large terri-
tory, taking into their claim part of New Scotland, New
England, and New York, on the eaft ; and, to the weft,
extending it as far as the Pacific Ocean. That part, however, which they have been able to cultivate, and which bore
the face of a colony, lay chiefly upon the banks of the river
St. Lawrence, and the numerous fmall rivers falling into that
ftream. This being reduced by the Britifh arms in the late
war, is now formed into a Britifh colony, called the Province
of Quebec. *See the Royal Proclamation.*

AIR AND CLIMATE.] The climate of this extenfive province is not very different from the colonies mentioned above,
but as it is much further from the fea, and more northerly
than a great part of thefe provinces, it has a much feverer
winter, though the air is generally clear ; but like moft of
thofe American tracts, that do not lie too far to the northward,
the fummers are very hot and exceeding pleafant.

SOIL AND PRODUCE.] Though the climate be cold, and
the winter long and tedious, the foil is in general very good,
and in many parts both pleafant and fertile, producing wheat,
barley, rye, with many other forts of grains, fruits and vegetables ; tobacco, in particular, thrives well, and is much
cultivated. The ifle of Orleans near Quebec, and the lands
upon the river St. Laurence, and other rivers are remarkable
for the richnefs of their foil. The meadow grounds in Canada, which are well watered, yield excellent grafs, and breed
vaft numbers of great and fmall cattle. As we are now entering upon the cultivated provinces of Britifh America, and as
Canada, ftretching a confiderable way upon the back of our
other fettlements, contains almoft all the different fpecies of

wood

wood, and animals, that are found in thefe colonies, we fhall, to avoid repetitions, fpeak of them here at fome length.

TIMBER AND PLANTS.] The uncultivated parts of North America, contain the greateft forefts in the world. They are a continued wood not planted by the hands of men, and in all appearance as old as the world itfelf. Nothing is more magnificent to the fight ; the trees lofe themfelves in the clouds ; and there is fuch a prodigious variety of fpecies, that even among thofe perfons who have taken moft pains to know them, there is not one perhaps that knows half the number. The province we are defcribing, produces amongft others, two forts of pines, the white and the red ; four forts of firs ; two forts of cedar and oak, the white and the red ; the male and female maple ; three forts of afh-trees, the free, the mungrel, and the baftard ; three forts of walnut-trees, the hard, the foft, and the fmooth ; vaft numbers of beech-trees, and white wood ; white and red elms, and poplars. The Indians hollow the red elms into canoes, fome of which, made out of one piece, will contain 20 perfons, others are made of the bark, the different pieces of which they few together with the inner rind, and daub over the feams with pitch, or rather a bituminous matter refembling pitch, to prevent their leaking ; and the ribs of thefe canoes are made of boughs of trees. About November the bears and wild cats take up their habitation in the hollow elms, and remain there till April. Here are alfo found cherry-trees, plum-trees, the vinegar-tree, the fruit of which, infufed in water, produces vinegar ; an aquatic plant, called Alaco, the fruit of which may be made into a confection ; the white thorn ; the cotton-tree, on the top of which grow feveral tufts of flowers, which, when fhaken in the morning, before the dew falls off, produce honey, that may be boiled up into fugar, the feed being a pod, containing a very fine kind of cotton ; the fun-plant, which refembles a marigld, and grows to the height of feven or eight feet ; Turky corn ; French beans ; gourds, melons, capillaire ; and the hop-plant.

METALS AND MINERALS.] Near Quebec is a fine lead mine, and in fome of the mountains, we are told, filver has been found, though we have not heard any great advantage made of it as yet. This country alfo abounds with coals.

RIVERS.] The rivers branching through this country are very numerous, and many of them large, bold and deep. The principal are, the Outtauais, St. John's, Seguinay, Defprairies, and Trois Rivieres, but they are all fwallowed up by the river St. Laurence. This river iffues from the lake Ontario, and taking its courfe north-eaft, wafhes Montreal, where it

receives

receives the Outtauáis, and forms many fertile iflands. It continues the fame courfe, and meets the tide upwards of 400 miles from the fea, where it is navigable for large veffels, and below Quebec, 320 miles from the fea, it becomes broad, and fo deep that fhips of the line contributed, in the laft war, to reduce that capital. After receiving in its progrefs innumerable ftreams, this great river falls into the ocean at cape Rofieres, where it is 90 miles broad, and where the cold is intenfe, and the fea boifterous. In its progrefs it forms a variety of bays, harbours, and iflands, many of them fruitful, and extremely pleafant.

LAKES.] The great river St. Laurence, is that only upon which the French (now fubjeɛ̃s of Great-Britain) have fettlements of any note; but if we look forward into futurity, it is nothing improbable that Canada, and thofe vaft regions to the weft, will be enabled of themfelves to carry on a confiderable trade upon the great lakes of frefh water, which thefe countries environ. Here are five lakes, the fmalleft of which is a piece of fweet water, greater than any in the other parts of the world; this is the lake Ontario, which is not lefs than 200 leagues in circumference; Erie, or Ofwego, longer, but not fo broad, is about the fame extent. That of the Huron fpreads greatly in width, and is in circumference not lefs than 300, as is that of Michigan, though like lake Erie, it is rather long and comparatively narrow. But the lake Superior, which contains feveral large iflands, is 500 leagues in the circuit. All of thefe are navigable by any veffels, and they all communicate with one another, except that the paffage between Erie and Ontario, is interrupted by a ftupendous fall or cataract, which is called the falls of Niagara. The water here is about half a mile wide, where the rock croffes it, not in a direct line, but in the form of a half moon. When it comes to the perpendicular fall, which is 150 feet, no words can exprefs the confternation of travellers at feeing fo great a body of water falling, or rather violently thrown, from fo great an height, upon the rocks below; from which it again rebounds to a very great height, appearing white as fnow, being all converted into foam, through thofe violent agitations. The noife of this fall is often heard at the diftance of 15 miles, and fometimes much farther. The vapour arifing from the fall may fometimes be feen at a great diftance, appearing like a cloud, or pillar of fmoak, and in the appearance of a rainbow, whenever the fun, and the pofition of the traveller, favours. Many beafts and fowls here lofe their lives, by attempting to fwim, or crofs the ftream in the rapids above the fall, and are found dafhed in pieces below, and fometimes the Indians,

through

through carelessnefs or drunkennefs, have met with the fame fate; and perhaps no place in the world is frequented by fuch a number of eagles as are invited hither by the carnage of deer, elks, bears, &c. on which they feed. The river St. Laurence, as we have already obferved, is the outlet of thefe lakes; by this they difcharge themfelves into the ocean. The French have built forts at the feveral ftraits, by which thefe lakes communicate with each other, as well as where the laft of them communicates with the river. By thefe they effectually fecured to themfelves the trade of the lakes, and an influence upon all the nations of America which lay near them.

ANIMALS.] Thefe make the moft curious, and hitherto the moft interefting part of the natural hiftory of Canada. It is to the fpoils of thefe that we owe the materials of many of our manufactures, and moft of the commerce as yet carried on between us and the country we have been defcribing. The animals that find fhelter and nourifhment in the immenfe forefts of Canada, and which indeed traverfe the uncultivated parts of all this continent, are ftags, elks, deer, bears, foxes, martens, wild cats, ferrets, wefels, fquirrels of a large fize and greyifh hue, hares, and rabbits. The fouthern parts in particular breed great numbers of wild bulls, deer of a fmall fize, divers forts of roebucks, goats, wolves, &c. The marfhes, lakes, and pools, which in this country are very numerous, fwarm with otters, beavers or caftors, of which the white are highly valued, being fcarce, as well as the right black kind. The American beaver, though refembling the creature known in Europe by that name, has many particulars which render it the moft curious animal we are acquainted with. It is near four feet in length, and weighs fixty or feventy pounds; they live from fifteen to twenty years, and the females generally bring forth four young ones at a time. It is an amphibious quadruped, that continues not long at a time in the water, but yet cannot live without frequently bathing in it. The favages, who waged a continual war with this animal, believed it to be a rational creature, that it lived in fociety, and was governed by a leader, refembling their own fachem or prince. It muft indeed be allowed, that the curious accounts given of this animal by ingenious travellers, the manner in which it contrives its habitation, provides food to ferve during the winter, and always in proportion to the continuance and feverity of it, are fufficient to fhew the near approaches of inftinct to reafon, and even in fome inftances the fuperiority of the former. Their colours are different; black, brown, white, yellow, and ftraw-colour; but it is obferved, that the lighter their colour, the lefs quantity of

fur

fur they are cloathed with, and live in warmer climates. The furs of the beaver are of two kinds, the dry and the green; the dry fur is the fkin before it is applied to any ufe; the green are the furs that are worn, after being fewed to one another, by the Indians, who befmear them with unctuous fubftances, which not only render them more pliable, but give the fine down that is manufactured into hats, that oily quality which renders it proper to be worked up with the dry fur. Both the Dutch and Englifh have of late found the fecret of making excellent cloths, gloves, and ftockings, as well as hats, from the beaver fur. Befides the fur, this ufeful animal produces the true caftoreum, which is contained in bags in the lower part of the belly, different from the tefticles: the value of this drug is well known. The flefh of the beaver is a moft delicious food, but when boiled it has a difagreeable relifh.

The mufk rat is a diminutive kind of beaver, (weighing about five or fix pounds) which it refembles in every thing but its tail; and it affords a very ftrong mufk.

The elk is of the fize of a horfe or mule. Many extraordinary medicinal qualities, particularly for curing the falling-ficknefs, are afcribed to the hoof of the left foot of this animal. Its flefh is very agreeable and nourifhing, and its colour a mixture of light-grey and dark-red. They love the cold countries; and when the winter affords them no grafs, they gnaw the bark of trees. It is dangerous to approach very near this animal when he is hunted, as he fometimes fprings furioufly on his purfuers, and tramples them to pieces. To prevent this, the hunter throws his clothes to him, and while the deluded animal fpends his fury on thefe, he takes proper meafures to difpatch him.

. There is a carnivorous animal here, called the carcajou, of the feline or cat kind, with a tail fo long, that Charlevoix fays he twifted it feveral times round his body. Its body is about two feet in length, from the end of the fnout to the tail. It is faid, that this animal, winding himfelf about a tree, will dart from thence upon the elk, twift his ftrong tail round his body, and cut his throat in a moment.

The buffaloe, a kind of wild ox, has much the fame appearance with thofe of Europe: his body is covered with a black wool, which is highly efteemed. The flefh of the female is very good; and the buffaloe hides are as foft and pliable as chamoes leather, but fo very ftrong, that the bucklers which the Indians make ufe of are hardly penetrable by a mufket ball. The Canadian roebuck is a domeftic animal, but differs in no other refpect from thofe of Europe. Wolves are fcarce in Canada, but they afford the fineft furs in all the country:

I   their

their flesh is white, and good to eat; and they purfue their prey to the tops of the talleft trees. The black foxes are greatly efteemed, and very fcarce; but thofe of other colours are more common: and fome on the Upper Miffifippi are of a filver colour, and very beautiful. They live upon water-fowls, which they decoy within their clutches by a thoufand antic tricks, and then fpring upon, and devour them. The Canadian poll-cat has a moft beautiful white fur, except the tip of his tail, which is as black as jet. Nature has given this animal no defence but its urine, the fmell of which is naufeous and intolerable; this, when attacked, it fprinkles plentifully on its tail, and throws it on the affailant. The Canadian wood-rat is of a beautiful filver colour with a bufhy tail, and twice as big as the European: the female carries under her belly a bag, which fhe opens and fhuts at pleafure; and in that fhe places her young when purfued. Here are three forts of fquirrels; that called the flying-fquirrel will leap forty paces and more, from one tree to another. This little animal is eafily tamed, and is very lively, except when afleep, which is often the cafe; and he puts up wherever he can find a place, in one's fleeve, pocket, or muff; he firft pitches on his mafter, whom he will diftinguifh among 20 perfons. The Canadian porcupine is lefs than a middling dog; when roafted, he eats full as well as a fucking pig. The hares and rabbits differ little from thofe in Europe, only they turn grey in winter. There are two forts of bears here, one of a reddifh, and the other of a black colour; but the former is the moft dangerous. The bear is not naturally fierce, unlefs when wounded, or oppreffed with hunger. They run themfelves very poor in the month of July, when it is fomewhat dangerous to meet them, and they are faid to fupport themfelves during the winter, when the fnow lies from four to fix feet deep, by fucking their paws. Scarce any thing among the Indians is undertaken with greater folemnity than hunting the bear; and an alliance with a noted bear-hunter, who has killed feveral in one day, is more eagerly fought after than that of one who has rendered himfelf famous in war. The reafon is, becaufe the chace fupplies the family with both food and raiment.

Of the feathered creation, they have eagles, falcons, gofhawks, tercols, partridges, grey, red, and black, with long tails, which they fpread out as a fan, and make a very beautiful appearance; woodcocks are fcarce in Canada, but fnipes, and other water-game, are plentiful. A Canadian raven is faid by fome writers to eat as well as a pullet, and an owl better. Here are black-birds, fwallows, and larks; no

lefs

lefs than twenty-two different fpecies of ducks, and a great number of fwans, turkeys, geefe, buftards, teal, water-hens, cranes, and other large water-fowl; but always at a diftance from houfes. The Canadian woodpecker is a beautiful bird. Thrufhes and goldfinches are found here; but the chief Canadian bird of melody is the white-bird, which is a kind of ortelan, very fhewy, and remarkable for announcing the return of fpring. The fly-bird is thought to be the moft beautiful of any in nature; with all his plumage, he is no bigger than a cock-chafer, and he makes a noife with his wings like the humming of a large fly.

Among the reptiles of this country, the rattle-fnake only deferves attention. Some of thefe are as big as a man's leg, and they are long in proportion. What is moft remarkable in this animal is the tail, which is fcaly like a coat of mail, and on which it is faid there grows every year one ring, or row of fcales; fo that they know its age by its tail, as we do that of a horfe by his teeth. In moving, it makes a rattling noife, from which it has its name. The bite of this ferpent is mortal, if a remedy is not applied immediately. In all places where this dangerous reptile is bred, there grows a plant which is called rattle-fnake herb, the root of which (fuch is the goodnefs of Providence) is a certain antidote againft the venom of this ferpent, and that with the moft fimple preparation, for it requires only to be pounded or chewed, and applied like a plaifter to the wound. The rattle-fnake feldom bites paffengers, unlefs it is provoked, and never darts itfelf at any perfon without firft rattling three times with its tail. When purfued, if it has but a little time to recover, it folds itfelf round, with the head in the middle, and then darts itfelf with great fury and violence againft its purfuers: neverthelefs, the favages chace it, and find its flefh very good, and being alfo of medicinal quality it is ufed by the American apothecaries in particular cafes.

Some writers are of opinion that the fifheries in Canada, if properly improved, would be more likely to enrich that country than even the fur trade. The river St. Lawrence contains perhaps the greateft variety of any in the world, and thefe in the greateft plenty and of the beft forts.

Befides a great variety of other fifh in the rivers and lakes, are fea-wolves, fea-cows, porpoifes, the lencornet, the goberque, the fea-plaife, falmon, trout, turtle, lobfters, the chaourafou, fturgeon, the achigau, the gilthead, tunny, fhad, lamprey, fmelts, conger-eels, mackarel, foals, herrings, anchovies, and pilchards. The fea-wolf, fo called from its howling, is an amphibious creature; the largeft are faid to

weigh

weigh two thousand pounds; their flesh is good eating; but the profit of it lies in the oil, which is proper for burning, and currying of leather; their skins make excellent coverings for trunks, and though not so fine as Morocco leather, they preserve their freshness better, and are less liable to cracks. The shoes and boots made of those skins let in no water, and, when properly tanned, make excellent and lasting covers for seats. The Canadian sea-cow is larger than the sea-wolf, but resembles it in figure: it has two teeth of the thickness and length of a man's arm, that, when grown, look like horns, and are very fine ivory as well as its other teeth. Some of the porpoises of the river St. Lawrence are said to yield a hogshead of oil; and of their skins waistcoats are made, which are excessive strong, and musket proof. The lencronet is a kind of kuttle-fish, quite round, or rather oval: there are three sorts of them, which differ only in size; some being as large as a hogshead, and others but a foot long; they catch only the last, and that with a torch: they are excellent eating. The goberque has the taste and smell of a small cod. The sea-plaise is good eating; they are taken with long poles armed with iron hooks. The chaourasou is an armed fish, about five feet long, and as thick as a man's thigh, resembling a pike; but is covered with scales that are proof against a dagger: its colour is a silver grey; and there grows under his mouth a long bony substance, ragged at the edges. One may readily conceive, that an animal so well fortified is a ravager among the inhabitants of the water; but we have few instances of fish making prey of the feathered creation, which this fish does, however, with much art. He conceals himself among the canes and reeds, in such a manner that nothing is to be seen besides his weapon, which he holds raised perpendicularly, above the surface of the water: the fowls, which come to take rest, imagining the weapon to be only a withered reed, perch upon it, but they are no sooner alighted, than the fish opens his throat, and makes such a sudden motion to seize his prey, that it seldom escapes him. This fish is an inhabitant of the lakes. The sturgeon is both a fresh and salt-water fish, taken on the coasts of Canada and the lakes, from eight to twelve feet long, and proportionably thick. There is a small kind of sturgeon, the flesh of which is very tender and delicate. The achigau, and the gilthead, are fish peculiar to the river St. Lawrence. Some of the rivers breed a kind of crocodile, that differs but little from those of the Nile.

INHABITANTS AND PRINCIPAL TOWNS.] Before the late war, the banks of the river St. Lawrence, above Quebec, were vastly populous, but we cannot precisely determine the number

number of French and Englifh fettled in this province, who are undoubtedly upon the encreafe. The different tribes of Indians in Canada are almoft innumerable ; but thefe people are obferved to decreafe in population where the Europeans are moft numerous, owing chiefly to the immoderate ufe of fpirituous liquors, of which they are exceffively fond. But as liberty is the ruling paffion of the Indians, we may naturally fuppofe that as the Europeans advance, the former will retreat to more diftant regions.

Quebec, the capital, not only of this province, but of all Canada, is fituated at the confluence of the rivers St. Lawrence and St. Charles, or the little river, about 320 miles from the fea. It is built on a rock, partly of marble and partly of flate. The town is divided into an upper and a lower ; the houfes in both are of ftone, and built in a tolerable manner. The fortifications are ftrong, though not regular. The town is covered with a regular and beautiful citadel, in which the governor refides. The number of inhabitants are computed at 12 or 15,000. The river, which from the fea hither is four or five leagues broad, narrows all of a fudden to about a mile wide. The haven, which lies oppofite the town, is fafe and commodious, and about five fathom deep. The harbour is flanked by two baftions, that are raifed 25 feet from the ground, which is about the height of the tides at the time of the equinox.

From Quebec to Montreal, which is about 170 miles, in failing up the river St. Lawrence, the eye is entertained with beautiful landfcapes, the banks being in many places very bold and fteep, and fhaded with lofty trees. The farms lie pretty clofe all the way ; feveral gentlemens houfes, neatly built, fhew themfelves at intervals, and there is all the appearance of a flourifhing colony ; but there are few towns or villages. It is pretty much like the well fettled parts of Virginia and Maryland, where the planters are wholly within themfelves. Many beautiful iflands are interfperfed in the channel of the river, which have an agreeable effect upon the eye. After paffing the Richlieu iflands, the air becomes fo mild and temperate, that the traveller thinks himfelf tranfported to another climate ; but this is to be underftood in the fummer months.

The town called Trois Rivieres, or the Three Rivers, is about half way between Quebec and Montreal, and has its name from three rivers which join their currents here, and fall into the St. Lawrence. It is much reforted to by feveral nations of Indians, who by means of thefe rivers, refort hither and trade with the inhabitants in various kinds of furs and skins. The country here is pleasant, and fertile in corn, fruit, &c. and great numbers of handsome houses stand on both sides the rivers.

Montreal stands on an island in the river St. Lawrence, which is ten leagues in length and four in breadth, at the foot of a mountain which gives name to it, about half a league from the south shore. While the French had possession of Canada, both the city and island of Montreal belonged to private proprietors, who had improved them so well, that the whole island was become a most delightful spot, and produced every thing that could administer to the conveniences of life. The city forms an oblong square, divided by regular and well formed streets; and when it fell into the hands of the English, the houses were built in a very handsome manner, and every house might be seen at one view from the harbour, or from the southernmost side of the river, as the hill on the side of which the town stands, falls gradually to the water. This place is surrounded by a wall and a dry ditch, and its fortifications have been much improved by the English. Montreal is nearly as large as Quebec; but since it fell into the hands of the English it hath suffered much by fires.

GOVERNMENT.] Before the late war, the French lived in affluence, being free from all taxes, and having full liberty to hunt, fish, fell timber, and to sow and plant as much land as they could cultivate. By the capitulation granted to the French, when this country was reduced, both individuals and communities are entitled to all their former rights and privileges. The Roman-catholic is still to continue their established religion; but the king of Great-Britain succeeds to all the power and prerogatives of which the French king was possessed. Canada is now divided into three governments, viz. Quebec, Montreal, and Trois Rivieres.

TRADE AND COMMERCE.] By expelling the French from the back of our settlements, we secured them from the danger of being molested or attacked by an active and formidable enemy, and enabled our people to attend, with proper spirit and industry, to agriculture, and the improvement of that country. While the important conquest of Canada removed a rival power from that part of North America, it put us in the sole possession of the fur and peltry trade, the use and importance of which is well known to the manufacturers of Great-Britain, and enables us to extend the scale of a general commerce.

The nature of the climate, severely cold in winter, and the people manufacturing nothing, shews what Canada principally wants from Europe; wine, or rather rum, cloths, chiefly coarse, coarfe, linen, and wrought iron. The Indian trade requires rum, tobacco, a fort of duffil blankets, guns, powder, balls, and flints, kettles, hatchets, toys, and trinkets of all kinds.

While this country was poffeffed by the French, the Indians fupplied them with peltry; and the French had traders, who, in the manner of the original inhabitants, traverfed the vaft lakes and rivers in canoes, with incredible induftry and patience, carrying their goods into the remoteft parts of America, and amongft nations entirely unknown to us. Thefe again brought the market home to them, as the Indians were thereby habituated to trade with them. For this purpofe, people from all parts, even from the diftance of 1000 miles, came to the French fair at Montreal, which began in June, and fometimes lafted three months. On this occafion, many folemnities were obferved, guards were placed, and the governor affifted, to preferve order, in fuch a concourfe, and fo great a variety of favage nations. But fometimes great diforder and tumults happened; and the Indians, being fo fond of brandy, frequently gave for a dram all they were poffeffed of. It is remarkable, that many of thefe nations, actually paffed by our fettlement of Albany in New York, and travelled 200 miles further to Montreal, though they might have purchafed the goods cheaper at the former. So much did the French exceed us in the arts of winning the affections of thefe favages!

Since we became poffeffed of Canada, our trade with that country employs 34 fhips, and 400 feamen. Their exports, at an average of three years, in fkins, furs, ginfeng, fnake-root, cappillaire and wheat, amount to 105,500 l. Their imports from Great-Britain, in a variety of articles, are computed at nearly the fame fum. It is unneceffary to make any remarks on the value and importance of this trade, which not only fupplies us with unmanufactured materials, indifpenfibly neceffary in many articles of our commerce, but alfo takes in exchange, the manufactures of our own country, or the production of our other fettlements in the Eaft and Weft Indies.

But with all our attention to the trade and peopling of Canada, it will be impoffible to overcome certain inconveniences, proceeding from natural caufes; I mean the feverity of the winter, which is fo exceffive from December to April, that the greateft rivers are frozen over, and the fnow lies commonly from four to fix feet deep on the ground, even in thofe parts of the country, which lie three degrees fouth of London, and in the temperate latitude of Paris. Another inconvenience arifes from the falls in the river St. Lawrence, below Montreal, which prevents fea veffels from penetrating to that emporium of inland commerce. Our communication therefore

with

with Canada, and the immenfe regions beyond it, will always be interrupted during the winter-feafon, until roads are formed, that can be travelled with fafety from the Indians. For it may here be obferved, that thefe favage people often commence hoftilities againft us, without any previous notice; and frequently, without any provocation, they commit the moft horrid ravages for a long time with impunity. But when at laft their barbarities have roufed the ftrength of our people, they are not afhamed to beg a peace; they know we always grant it readily; they promife it fhall endure as long as the fun and moon; and then all is quiet till fome incident, too often co-operating with ill ufage received from our traders, gives them a frefh opportunity of renewing their cruelties.

HISTORY.]   See the general account of America.

NEW SCOTLAND.

SITUATION AND EXTENT.

	Miles.		Degrees.
Length	350	} between {	43 and 49 north latitude.
Breadth	250		60 and 67 weft longitude.

BOUNDARIES.]   BOUNDED by the river St. Lawrence on the north; by the gulph of St. Lawrence, and the Atlantic ocean, eaft; by the fame ocean, fouth; and by Canada and New-England, weft.

RIVERS.]   The river of St. Lawrence forms the northern boundary. The rivers Rifgouche and Nipifiguit run from weft to eaft, and fall into the bay of St. Lawrence. The rivers of St. John, Paffamagnadi, Penobfcot, and St. Croix, which run from north to fouth, fall into Fundy bay, or the fea a little to the eaftward of it.

SEAS, BAYS AND CAPES.]   The feas adjoining to it are, the Atlantic ocean, Fundy bay, and the gulph of St. Lawrence. The leffer bays are, Chenigto and Green bay upon the Ifthmus, which joins the north part of Nova Scotia to the fouth; and the bay of Chaleurs on the north-eaft; the bay of Chedibucto on the fouth-eaft: the bay of the iflands, the ports of Bart, Chebucto, Profper, St. Margaret, La Heve, port Maltois, port Ryfignol, port Vert and port Joly, on the fouth; port La Tour, on the fouth-eaft; port St. Mary, Annapolis, and Minas on the fouth fide of Fundy bay.

The chief capes are, cape Portage, Ecoumenac, Tourmentin, cape Port and Epis, on the eaft. Cape Fogeri, and cape Canceau, on the fouth-eaft. Cape Blanco, cape Vert,
cape

cape Theodore, cape Dore, cape La Heve, and cape Negro, on the fouth. Cape Sable, and cape Fourche, on the fouth-weſt.

LAKES.] The lakes are very numerous, but have not yet received particular names.

CLIMATE.] The climate of this country, though within the Temperate Zone, has been found rather unfavourable to European conſtitutions. They are wrapt up in the gloom of a fog during great part of the year, and for four or five months it is intenſely cold. But though the cold in winter and the heat in ſummer are great, they come on gradually, ſo as to prepare the body for enduring both.

SOIL AND PRODUCE.] From ſuch an unfavourable climate little can be expected. New Scotland is almoſt a continued foreſt; and agriculture, tho' attempted by the Engliſh ſettlers, has hitherto made little progreſs. In moſt parts, the ſoil is thin and barren, the corn it produces of a ſhrivelled kind like rye, and the graſs intermixed with a cold ſpungy moſs. However, it is not uniformly bad; there are tracts in the peninſula to the fouthward, which do not yield to the beſt land in New England; and, in general, the ſoil is adapted to the produce of hemp and flax. The timber is extremely proper for ſhip-building, and produces pitch and tar.

ANIMALS.] This country is not deficient in the animal productions of the neighbouring provinces, particularly deer, beaver and otters. Wild fowl, and all manner of game, and many kinds of European fowls and quadrupedes have, from time to time, been brought into it, and thrive well. At the cloſe of March, the fiſh begin to ſpawn, when they enter the rivers in ſuch ſhoals, as are incredible. Herrings come up in April, and the ſturgeon and ſalmon in May. But the moſt valuable appendage of New Scotland, is the cape Sable coaſt, along which is one continued range of cod-fiſhing banks, and excellent harbours.

HISTORY, SETTLEMENT, CHIEF ⎱ Notwithſtanding the
    TOWNS AND COMMERCE. ⎰ forbidding appearance
of this country, it was here that ſome of the firſt European ſettlements were made. The firſt grant of lands in it were given by James I. to his ſecretary Sir William Alexander, from whom it had the name of Nova Scotia, or New Scotland. Since then it has frequently changed hands, from one private proprietor to another, and from the French to the Engliſh nation backward and forward. It was not confirmed to the Engliſh, till the peace of Utrecht, and their deſign in acquiring it, does not ſeem to have ſo much ariſen from any proſpect of direct profit to be obtained by it, as from an apprehenſion that the French, by poſſeſſing

          this

this province, might have had it in their power to annoy our other settlements, Upon this principle, 3000 families were transported in 1749, at the charge of the government, into this country. The town they erected is called Hallifax, from the earl of that name, to whose wisdom and care we owe this settlement, The town of Hallifax stands upon Chebucto bay, very commodiously situated for the fishery, and has a communication with most parts of the province, either by land carriage, the sea, or navigable rivers, with a fine harbour, where a small squadron of ships of war lies during the winter, and in summer puts to sea, under the command of a commodore, for the protection of the fishery, and to see that the articles of the late peace, relating thereto, are duly observed by the French. The town has an intrenchment, and is strengthened with forts of timber. Three regiments of men are stationed in it, to protect the inhabitants from the Indians, whose resentment, however excited or fomented, has been found implacable against the English. The number of inhabitants is said to be 15 or 16,000, who live very comfortably by the trade they carry on in furs and naval stores, by their fisheries, and its being the residence of the governor, and the garrison already mentioned. The other towns of less note are Anapolis, which stands on the east side of the bay of Fundy, and though but a small wretched place, was formerly the capital of the province. It has one of the finest harbours in America, capable of containing a thousand vessels at anchor, in the utmost security. This place is also protected by a fort and garrison. St John's is a new settlement at the mouth of the river of that name, that falls into the bay of Fundy on the west side.

The exports from Great Britain to this country, consist chiefly of woollen and linen cloth, and other necessaries for wear, of fishing tackle, and rigging for ships. The amount of our exports, at an average of three years, is about 26,500 l. The only articles we can get in exchange, are timber, and the produce of the fishery, which, at a like average, amounts to 38,000 l. But, as we have already observed, the negative advantage of this colony, by which our enemies, while it remains in our hands, are prevented from doing harm to our other settlements, have principally engaged the British ministry to expend such sums, and to take such pains in supporting it.

NEW ENGLAND.

SITUATION AND EXTENT.

Miles.		Degrees.
Length 550	} between {	41 and 49 north latitude.
Breadth 200		67 and 74 weft longitude.

BOUNDARIES.] **B**OUNDED on the north-eaft by New-Scotland; on the weft, by Canada; on the fouth by New York; and on the eaft by the Atlantic.

Divifions.	Provinces.	Chief towns.
The north divifion, or government	} New Hampfhire — }	} { Portfmouth.
The middle divifion	} Maffachufet's Colony }	} { BOSTON, N. Lat. 42-20. W. Lon.71.
The fouth divifion	Rhode Ifland, &c.	Newport.
The weft divifion	} Connecticut ———— }	} { New London. Hertford.

RIVERS.] Their rivers are, 1. Connecticut; 2. Thames; 3. Patuxent; 4. Merimac; 5. Pifcataway; 6. Saco; 7. Cafco; 8. Kinebeque; and, 9. Penobfcot, or Pentagonet.

BAYS AND CAPES.] The moft remarkable bays and harbours are thofe formed by Plymouth, Rhode-Ifland, and Providence plantations; Monument-Bay; Weft-Harbour, formed by the bending of Cape-Cod; Bofton-Harbour; Pifcataway, and Cafco-Bay.

The chief capes are, Cape-Cod, Marble-Head, Cape-Anne, Cape-Netic, Cape-Porpus, Cape-Elizabeth, and Cape-Small-Point.

AIR AND CLIMATE.] New England, though fituated almoft ten degrees nearer the fun than the mother country, has an earlier winter, which continues longer, and is more fevere than with us. The fummer again is extremely hot, and much beyond any thing known in Europe, in the fame latitude. The clear and ferene temperature of the fky, however, makes amends for the extremity of heat and cold, and renders the climate of this country fo healthy, that it is reported to agree better with Britifh conftitutions, than any other of the American provinces. The winds are very boifterous in the winter feafon, and naturalifts afcribe the early approach, the length and feverity of the winter, to the large frefh water lakes lying to the north-weft of New England, which being froze over feveral months, occafion thofe piercing winds, which prove fo fatal to mariners on this coaft.

A a 4

The

The fun rifes at Bofton, on the longeft day, at 26 minutes after four in the morning, and fets at 34 minutes after feven in the evening; and on their fhorteft day, it rifes at 35 minutes after feven in the morning, and fets at 27 minutes after four in the afternoon: thus their longeft day is about fifteen hours, and the fhorteft about nine.

SOIL AND PRODUCE.] We have already obferved, that the lands lying on the eastern fhore of America, are low, and in fome parts fwampy, but further back they rife into hills. In New England, towards the north-eaft, the lands become rocky and mountainous. The foil here is various, but beft as you approach the fouthward. Round Maffachufet's bay the foil is black, and rich as in any part of England; and here the firft planters found the grafs above a yard high. The uplands are lefs fruitful, being for the moft part a mixture of fand and gravel, inclining to clay. The low grounds abound in meadows and pafture land. The European grains have not been cultivated here with much fuccefs; the wheat is fubject to be blafted; the barley is an hungry grain, and the oats are lean and chaffy. But the Indian corn flourifhes in high perfection, and makes the general food of the lower fort of people. They likewife malt and brew it into a beer, which is not contemptible. However, the common table drink is cyder and fpruce beer: the latter is made of the tops of the fpruce fir, with the addition of a fmall quantity of molaffes. They likewife raife in New England a large quantity of hemp and flax. The fruits of Old England come to great perfection here, particularly peaches and apples. Seven or eight hundred fine peaches may be found on one tree, and a fingle apple-tree has produced feven barrels of cyder in one feafon.

But New England is chiefly diftinguifhed for the variety and value of its timber, as oak, afh, pine, fir, cedar, elm, cyprefs, beech, walnut, chefnut, hazel, faffafras, famach, and other woods ufed in dying or tanning leather, carpenters work, and fhip building. The oaks here are faid to be inferior to thofe of England; but the firs are of an amazing bulk, and furnifh the royal navy of England with mafts and yards. They draw from their trees confiderable quantities of pitch, tar, rofin, turpentine, gums, and balm; and the foil produces hemp and flax. A fhip may here be built and rigged out with the produce of their foreft, and indeed fhip-building forms a confiderable branch of their trade.

METALS.] Rich iron mines, of a moft excellent kind and temper, have been difcovered in New England, and, if improved, in a fhort time they may fupply Great Britain, without having recourfe to Sweden, and other European nations

for

for that commodity; especially as the parliament, to encourage the undertaking, allows both pig and bar iron to be imported duty free.

ANIMALS.] The animals of this country furnish many articles of New England commerce. All kinds of European cattle thrive here, and multiply exceedingly; the horses of New England are hardy, mettlesome, and serviceable, but smaller than ours, though larger than the Welsh. They have few sheep; and the wool, though of a staple sufficiently long, is not near so fine as that of England. Here are also elks, deer, hares, rabbits, squirrels, beavers, otters, monkies, minks, martens, racoons, sabbs, bears, wolves, which are only a kind of wild dogs, foxes, ounces, and a variety of other tame and wild quadrupedes, some of which are imported into Great Britain as foreign curiosities. But one of the most singular animals, of this and the neighbouring countries, is the mose or moose deer, of which there are two sorts; the common light grey moose, which resembles the ordinary deer; these herd sometimes thirty together; and the large black moose, whose body is about the size of a bull; his neck resembles a stag's, and his flesh is extremely grateful. The horns, when full grown, are about four or five feet from the head to the tip, and have shoots or branches to each horn, which generally spread about six feet. When this animal goes through a thicket, or under the boughs of a tree, he lays his horns back on his neck, to place them out of his way; and these prodigious horns are shed every year. This animal does not spring or rise in going, like a deer; but a large one, in his common walk, has been seen to step over a gate five feet high. When unharboured, he will run a course of twenty or thirty miles before he takes to a bay; but when chafed, he generally takes to the water.

There is hardly any where greater plenty of fowls, as turkeys, geese, partridges, ducks, widgeons, dappers, swans, heathcocks, herons, storks, blackbirds, all sorts of barn-door fowl, vast flights of pigeons, which come and go at certain seasons of the year, cormorants, ravens, crows, &c. The reptiles are, rattle-snakes, frogs, and toads, which swarm in the uncleared parts of these countries, where, with the owls, they make a most hideous noise in the summer evenings.

The seas round New England, as well as its rivers, abound with fish, and even whales of several kinds, such as the whale-bone whale, the spermaceti-whale, which yields ambergris, the fin-backed whale, the scrag whale, and the bunch whale, of which they take great numbers, and send besides some ships every year to fish for whales in Greenland. A terrible creature, called the whale-killer, from 20 to 30 feet

long,

long, with ftrong teeth and jaws, perfecutes the whale in
thefe feas; but, afraid of his monftrous ftrength, they feldom
attack a full grown whale, or indeed a young one, but in
companies of ten or twelve. At the mouth of the river Penobfcot, there is a mackarel fifhery; they likewife fifh for cod in
winter, which they dry in the froft.

POPULATION, INHABITANTS, AND } There is not one
    FACE OF THE COUNTRY. } of our fettlements
which can be compared, in the abundance of people, the
number of confiderable and trading towns, and the manufactures that are carried on in them, to New-England. The
moft populous and flourifhing parts of the mother country,
hardly make a better appearance, than the cultivated parts of
this province, which reach about 60 miles back. There are
here many gentlemen of confiderable landed eftates, but the
greateft part of the people is compofed of a fubftantial yeo-
manry, who cultivate their own freeholds, without a dependance upon any but Providence, and their own induftry.
Thefe freeholds generally pafs to their children in the way of
gavelkind : which keeps them from being almoft ever able to
emerge-out of their original happy mediocrity. In no part of
the world are the ordinary fort fo independant, or poffefs more
of the conveniences of life; they are ufed from their infancy,
to the exercife of arms; and they have a militia, which for a
militia is by no means contemptible. The population of the
four provinces, of which New-England is comprized, is proportioned by Douglafs, who feems to be well informed in this
point, as follows,

Maffachufet's bay	———	200,000
Connecticut	———	100,000
Rhode ifland	———	30,000
New Hampfhire	———	24,000

But the number fince his time is fo greatly increafed, that
according to the lateft calculation, the four provinces contain
600,000 fouls, including a fmall number of Negroes and
Indians.

RELIGION.] The church of England, in this part of America, is far from being in a flourifhing condition; in feveral
places, the number of auditors do not amount to twelve perfons. In the year 1768, the four provinces contained upwards
of 700 religious affemblies; of which 36 only obferved the
forms of the church of England. Every particular fociety
among them, is independant of all other ecclefiaftical jurifdiction; nor does there lie any appeal from their punifhments or
cenfures. The minifters of Bofton depend entirely on the
generofity

generofity of their hearers for fupport; a voluntary contribu-
tion being made for them, by the congregation, every time
divine fervice is celebrated. It is not long fince they fuffered
any member of the church of England to have a fhare in the
magiftracy, or to be elected a member of the Commons, or
Houfe of Reprefentatives. Their laws againft quakers feem
to have been very fevere. To bring one in was a forfeiture of
100 l. to conceal one 40 s. an hour; to go to a quaker's meeting 10 s. to preach there 5 s. If a quaker was not an inhabitant, he was fubject to banifhment, and if he returned,
death; but thefe and fome other ecclefiaftical laws equally
abfurd, are now either repealed, or greatly mitigated.

CHIEF TOWNS.] Bofton, the capital of New-England,
and of all the Britifh empire in America, ftands on a peninfula
at the bottom of Maffachufet's bay, about nine miles from its
mouth. At the entrance of this bay are feveral rocks, which
appear above water, and upwards of a dozen fmall iflands,
fome of which are inhabited. There is but one fafe channel
to approach the harbour, and that fo narrow, that two fhips
can fcarcely fail through abreaft, but within the harbour there
is room for 500 fail to lie at anchor, in a good depth of water.
On one of the iflands of the bay, ftands Fort William, the
moft regular fortrefs in the Britifh plantations. This caftle
is defended by 100 guns, twenty of which lie on a platform
level with the water, fo that it is fcarce poffible for an enemy
to pafs the caftle. To prevent furprize, they have a guard
placed on one of the rocks, at two leagues diftance, from
whence they make fignals to the caftle, when any fhips come
near it. There is alfo a battery of guns at each end of the
town. At the bottom of the bay is a noble pier, near 2000
feet in length; along which, on the north fide, extends a row
of warehoufes for the merchants, and to this pier fhips of the
greateft burthen may come and unload, without the help of
boats. The greateft part of the town lies round the harbour,
in the fhape of a half moon; the country beyond it rifing
gradually, and affording a delightful profpect from the fea.
The head of the pier joins the principal ftreet of the town,
which is, like moft of the others, fpacious and well built.
Bofton contains at prefent about 18,000 inhabitants; 50 years
ago they were more numerous. The furprifing increafe of
Newbury port, Salem, Marblehead, Cape Ann, Plymouth,
Dartmouth, and the ifland of Nantucket, hath checked the
growth and trade of the capital. The trade of Bofton is,
however, fo very confiderable, that in the year 1768, 1200
fail entered or cleared at the Cuftom-houfe there.

Cambridge,

Cambridge, in the same province, four miles from Boston, has an university, containing two spacious colleges, called by the names of Harvard college, and Stoughton Hall, with a well furnished library. It consists of a president, five fellows, a treasurer, three professors, four tutors, and a librarian. The college charter was first granted in 1650, and renewed in 1692, and is held under the colony seal.

The other towns in New-England, the chief of which have already been mentioned, are generally neat, well built, and commodiously situated upon fine rivers, with capacious harbours.

COMMERCE AND MANUFACTURES.] The trade of New-England is great, as it supplies a large quantity of goods from within itself; but it is yet greater, as the people of this country are in a manner the carriers for all the colonies of North America, and the West Indies, and even for some parts of Europe. The commodities which the country yields, are principally, pig and bar iron, which is imported to Great Britain duty-free; also masts and yards, pitch, tar, and turpentine, for which they contract largely with the royal navy; pot and pearl ashes, staves, lumber, boards; all sorts of provisions, which they send to the French and Dutch sugar islands, and to Barbadoes, and the other British isles, as grain, biscuit, meal, beef, pork, butter, cheese, apples, cyder, onions, mackarel, and cod fish dried. They likewise send thither cattle, horses, planks, hoops, shingles, pipe staves, oil, tallow, turpentine, bark, calf skins and tobacco. Their peltry trade is not very considerable. They have a most valuable fishery upon their coasts, in mackarel and cod, which employs vast numbers of their people, with the produce of which they trade to Spain, Italy, the Mediterranean, and West-Indies, to a considerable amount. Their whale fishery has been already mentioned. The arts most necessary to subsistence are those, which the inhabitants of New-England have been at pains to cultivate. They manufacture coarse linen and woollen cloth for their own use; hats are made here, which in a clandestine way, find a good vent in all the other colonies. Sugar baking, distilling, paper making, and salt works, are upon the improving hand. The business of ship-building is one of the most considerable, which Boston, or the other sea port towns in New-England carry on. Ships are sometimes built here upon commission; but frequently, the merchants of New-England have them constructed upon their own account; and loading them with the produce of the colony, naval stores, fish, and fish oil principally, they send them out upon a trading voyage to Spain, Portugal, or the Mediterranean; where,

where, having difpofed of their cargo, they make what advantage they can by freight, until fuch time as they can fell the veffel herfelf to advantage, which they feldom fail to do in a reafonable time.

It was computed, that before the late unhappy differences arofe, the amount of Englifh manufactures, and India goods fent into this colony from Great Britain, was not lefs at an average of three years, than 395,000 l. Our imports from the fame were calculated at 370,500 l.

HISTORY AND GOVERNMENT.] New-England is at prefent divided into the four provinces of New-Hampfhire, Maffachufet's, Rhode Ifland, and Connecticut. As early as 1606, king James I. had by letters patent erected two companies, with a power to fend colonies into thofe parts, then comprehended under the general name of Virginia, as all the north eaft coaft of America was fome time called. No fettlements, however, were made in New-England, by virtue of this authority. The companies contented themfelves with fending out a fhip or two, to trade with the Indians for their furs, and to fifh upon their coaft. This continued to be the only fort of correfpondence between Great Britain and this part of America, till the year 1621. By this time the religious diffentions, by which England was torn to pieces, had become warm and furious. Laud perfecuted all forts of non-conformifts with an unrelenting feverity. Thofe men, on the other hand, were ready to fubmit to all the rigour of perfecution, rather than depart from their favourite tenets, and conform to the ceremonies of the church of England, which they confidered as abufes of the moft dangerous tendency. There was no part of the world into which they would not fly, rather than be compelled to adopt the practices which prevailed in their native country, and as they imagined endangered the eternal falvation of all who adhered to them. America opened an extenfive field. There they might tranfport themfelves, and eftablifh whatever fort of religious policy they were inclined to. The defign, befides, had fomething in it noble, and admirably fuited to the enterprifing fpirit of innovators in religion. With this view, having purchafed the territory, which was within the jurifdiction of the Plymouth company, and having obtained from the king the privilege of fettling it in whatever way they had a mind, 150 perfons embarked for New-England, and built a city, which, becaufe they had failed from Plymouth, they called by that name. Notwithftanding the feverity of the climate, the unwholefomenefs of the air, and the difeafes to which, after a long fea voyage, and in a country, which was new to them, they were expofed;

poſed ; notwithſtanding the want of all ſort of conveniences, and even of many of the neceſſaries of life, thoſe who had conſtitutions fit to endure ſuch hardſhips, not diſpirited or broken by the death of their companions, and ſupported by the vigour then peculiar to Engliſhmen, and the ſatisfaction of finding themſelves beyond the reach of the ſpiritual arm, ſet themſelves to cultivate this ungrateful country, and to take the beſt ſteps for the advancement of their infant colony. New adventurers, encouraged by their example, and finding themſelves for the ſame reaſons, uneaſy at home, paſſed over into this land of religious and civil liberty. By the cloſe of the year 1630, they had built four towns, Salem, Dorcheſter, Charles Town, and Boſton, which has ſince become the capital of New-England. But as neceſſity is the natural ſource of that active and frugal induſtry, which produces every thing great among mankind, ſo an uninterrupted flow of proſperity and ſucceſs, occaſions thoſe diſſentions, which are the bane of human affairs, and often ſubvert the beſt founded eſtabliſhments.

The inhabitants of New-England, who had fled from perſecution, became in a ſhort time ſtrongly tainted with this illiberal vice, and were eager to introduce an uniformity in religion, among all who entered their territories. The minds of men were not in this age ſuperior to many prejudices ; they had not that open and generous way of thinking, which at preſent diſtinguiſhes the natives of Great Britain ; and the doctrine of univerſal toleration, which, to the honour of the firſt ſettlers in America, began to appear among them, had few abetters, and many opponents. In all perſuaſions the bigots are perſecutors ; the men of a cool and reaſonable piety are favourers of toleration ; becauſe the former ſort of men, not taking the pains to be acquainted with the grounds of their adverſaries tenets, conceive them to be ſo abſurd and monſtrous, that no man of ſenſe can give into them in good earneſt. For which reaſon they are convinced, that ſome oblique bad motive induces them to pretend to the belief of ſuch doctrines, and to the maintaining of them with obſtinacy. This is a very general principle in all religious differences, and it is the corner ſtone of all perſecution. It was not the general idea of the age, that men might live comfortably together in the ſame ſociety, without maintaining the ſame religious opinions, and wherever theſe were at variance, the members of different ſects kept at a diſtance from each other, and eſtabliſhed ſeparate governments. Hence ſeveral ſlips, torn from the original government of New-England, by religious violence, planted themſelves in a new ſoil, and ſpread

over

over the country. Such was that of New-Hampſhire, which
continues to this day a ſeparate juriſdiction; ſuch too was
that of Rhode Iſland, whoſe inhabitants were driven out from
the Maſſachuſet colony (for that is the name by which the
government firſt erected in New-England was diſtinguiſhed)
for ſupporting the freedom of religious ſentiment, and maintaining that the civil magiſtrate had no right over the ſpecula-
tive opinions of mankind. Theſe liberal men founded a city,
called Providence, which they governed by their own principles; and ſuch is the connection between juſtneſs of ſentiment,
and external proſperity, that the government of Rhode Iſland,
though ſmall, is extremely populous and flouriſhing. Another
colony driven out by the ſame perſecuting ſpirit, ſettled on
the river Connecticut, and received frequent reinforcements
from England, of ſuch as were diſſatisfied either with the
religious or civil government of that country.

America indeed was now become the main reſource of all
diſcontented and enterprizing ſpirits, and ſuch were the numbers which embarked for it from England, that in 1637 a
proclamation was publiſhed, prohibiting any perſon from
ſailing thither, without an expreſs licenſe from the government. For want of this licenſe, it is ſaid, that Oliver Cromwell, Mr. Hampden, and others of that party, were detained
from going into New-England, after being a-ſhipboard for
that purpoſe.

Theſe four provinces, though always confederates for their
mutual defence, were at firſt, and ſtill continue under ſeparate
juriſdictions. They were all of them by their charters originally free, and in a great meaſure independant of Great Britain. The inhabitants had the choice of their own magiſtrates,
the governor, the council, the aſſembly, and the power of
making ſuch laws, as they thought proper, without ſending
them to Great Britain, for the approbation of the crown.
Their laws, however, were not to be oppoſite to thoſe of
Great Britain. Toward the latter end of the reign of Charles
II. the Maſſachuſet's colony was accuſed of violating their
charter, and by a judgment in the King's-Bench of England,
was deprived of it. From that time to the Revolution, they
remained without any charter. Soon after that period, they
received a new one, which, though very favourable, was
much inferior to the extenſive privilege of the former. The
appointment of a governor, lieutenant-governor, ſecretary,
and all the officers of the admiralty, is veſted in the crown;
the power of the militia is wholly in the hands of the governor,
as captain-general; all judges, juſtices, and ſheriffs, to whom
the execution of the law is entruſted, are nominated by the
governor.

governor, with the advice of the council; the governor has
a negative on the choice of counsellors, peremptory, and unlimited; and he is not obliged to give a reason for what he does
in this particular, or restrained to any number; authentic
copies of the several acts passed by this colony, as well as
others, are to be transmitted to the court of England, for the
royal approbation; but if the laws of this colony are not
repealed within three years after they are presented, they are
not repealable by the crown after that time; that no laws,
ordinances, election of magistrates, or acts of government
whatsoever, are valid, without the governor's consent in writing; and appeals for sums above 300l. are admitted to the
king and council. Notwithstanding these restraints, the
people have still a great share of power in this colony; for
they not only choose the assembly, but this assembly, with
the governor's concurrence, choose the council, resembling
our house of lords, and the governor depends upon the assembly for his annual support; which has sometimes tempted the
governor of this province to give up the prerogative of the
crown, and the interests of Great Britain.

To the Massachuset's government is united the antient colony of Plymouth, and the territory called Main.

By the laws of this province no person can be arrested, if
there are any means of satisfaction; nor imprisoned, unless
there be a concealment of effects. Adultery is death to both
parties.

New-Hampshire is still more under the influence of Great
Britain. The council itself is appointed by the crown, and
in other respects it agrees with the former.

The colonies of Connecticut and Rhode Island, have preserved their antient charters, and enjoy the same privileges
which the Massachusets did formerly.

There were originally three sorts of governments established
by the English on the continent of America, viz. royal
governments, charter governments, and proprietary governments.

A royal government is properly so called, because the colony is immediately dependent on the crown; and the king
remains sovereign of the colony; he appoints the governor,
council, and officers of state, and the people only elect the
representatives, as in England; such are the governments of
Canada, Nova Scotia, Virginia, New-Hampshire, New-
York, New-Jersey, and both Carolinas, Georgia, East and
West-Florida, the West-India islands, and that of St. John's.

A charter government is so called, because the company,
incorporated by the king's charter, were in a manner vested

with

with fovereign authority, to eftablifh what fort of government they thought fit; and thefe charter governments have generally transferred their authority to the people; for in fuch governments, or rather corporations, the freemen do not only choofe their reprefentatives, but annually choofe their governor, council and magiftrates, and make laws, without the concurrence, and even without the knowledge of the king; and are under no other reftraint than this, that they enact no laws contrary to the laws of England; if they do, their charters are liable to be forfeited. Such, as we have already obferved, are the governments of Rhode Ifland, and Connecticut, in New-England, and fuch was that of the Maffachufet's formerly, but it appears now to be a mixture of both. Such likewife was the two Carolinas.

The third kind of government is the proprietary, properly fo called, becaufe the proprietor is invefted with fovereign authority: he appoints the governor, council, and magiftrates, and the reprefentatives are fummoned in his name, and by their advice he enacts laws, without the concurrence of the crown; but, by a late ftatute, the proprietor muft have the king's confent in the appointing a governor, when he does not refide in the plantation in perfon, and of a deputy governor, when he does. And all the governors of the plantations are liable to be called to an account for their adminiftration, by the court of King's Bench. The only proprietary governments now remaining, are thofe of Penfylvania and Maryland.

NEW YORK.

SITUATION AND EXTENT.

	Miles.		Degrees.
Length	300	between	40 and 46 north latitude.
Breadth	150		72 and 76 weft longitude.

BOUNDARIES.] NEW YORK is bounded on the fouth and fouth-weft, by Hudfon's and Delaware rivers, which divide it from New Jerfey and Penfylvania; on the eaft and north-eaft, by New England and the Atlantic Ocean; and on the north-weft, by Canada.

This province, including the Ifland of New York, Long-Ifland, and Statin-Ifland, is divided into the ten following counties:

Counties.	Chief Towns.
New York — — }	NEW YORK { 40-40 N. lat. 74-00 W. lon.
Albany — — —	Albany
Ulfter — — — } Duchefs — — }	None
Orange — — —	Orange
Weft-Chefter — —	Weft-Chefter
King's — — —	None
Queen's — — —	Jamaica
Suffolk — — —	Southampton
Richmond — — —	Richmond.

RIVERS.] The principal of thefe are Hudfon's and the Mohawk ; the former abounds with excellent harbours, and is well ftored with great variety of fifh : on this the cities of New York and Albany are fituated. On the Mohawk is a large cataract, called the Cohoes, the water of which is faid to fall 70 feet perpendicular, where the river is a quarter of a mile in breadth.

CAPES.] Thefe are Cape May, on the eaft entrance of Delaware river ; Sandy-Hook, near the entrance of Raritan river ; and Montock Point, at the eaft end of Long-Ifland.

CLIMATE, SOIL, AND PRODUCE.] This province, lying to the fouth of New England, enjoys a more happy tempe-rature of climate. The air is very healthy, and agrees well with all conftitutions. The face of the country, refembling that of our other colonies in America, is low, flat, and marfhy towards the fea. As you recede from the coaft, the eye is entertained with the gradual fwelling of hills, which become large in proportion as you advance into the country. The foil is extremely fertile, producing wheat, rye, Indian corn, oats, barley, flax, and fruits in great abundance and perfection. The timber is much the fame with that of New England. A great deal of iron is found here.

HISTORY AND GOVERNMENT.] The Swedes and Dutch were the firft Europeans who formed fettlements on this part of the American coaft. The tract claimed by the two nations, extended from the 38th to the 41ft degree of latitude, and was called the New Netherlands. It continued in their hands till the time of Charles II. who obtained it from them by right of conqueft in 664, and it was confirmed to the Eng-lifh by the treaty of Breda, 1667. The New Netherlands were not long in our poffeffion, before they were divided into different provinces. New York took that name from the king's brother, James, duke of York, to whom the king

granted

granted it, with full powers of government, by letters patent, dated March 20, 1664. On James's acceſſion to the throne, the right to New York became veſted in the crown, ſince which time it has been a royal government. The king appoints the governor and council; and the people, once in ſeven years, elect their repreſentatives to ſerve in general aſſembly. Theſe three branches of the legiſlature (anſwering to thoſe of Great Britain) have power to make any laws not repugnant to thoſe of England; but, in order to their being valid, the royal aſſent to them muſt firſt be obtained.

CITIES, POPULATION, COMMERCE, RELIGION AND LEARNING. The city of New York ſtands on the ſouth-weſt end of York-Iſland, which is twelve miles long, and near three in breadth, extremely well ſituated for trade, at the mouth of Hudſon's river, where it is three miles broad, and proves a noble conveyance from Albany and many other inland towns towards Canada and the lakes. This city is in length above a mile, and its mean breadth a quarter of a mile. The city and harbour are defended by a fort and battery: in the front is a ſpacious manſion houſe for the uſe of the governor. Many of the houſes are very elegant; and the city, though irregularly built, affords a fine proſpect. The greateſt part of the inhabitants, who are computed at 12 or 15,000, are deſcended from the Dutch families who remained here after the ſurrender of the New Netherlands to the Engliſh, and the whole province is ſuppoſed to contain between 80 and 100,000. The better ſort are rich and hoſpitable, the lower ranks are eaſy in their circumſtances; and both are endowed with a generous and liberal turn of mind, which renders their ſociety and converſation more agreeable than in moſt countries either of Europe or America.

The commerce of this province does not materially differ from that of New England. The commodities in which they trade are wheat, flour, barley, oats, beef, and other kinds of animal food. Their markets are the ſame with thoſe which the New Englanders uſe; and they have a ſhare in the logwood trade, and that which is carried on with the Spaniſh and French plantations. They take almoſt the ſame ſort of commodities from England with the inhabitants of Boſton. At an average of three years, their exports are ſaid to amount to 526,000 l. and their imports from Great Britain to 531,000 l.

All religious denominations, except Jews and Papiſts, enjoy equal privileges here, as there is no eſtabliſhed church, unleſs the eighth article of the capitulation, made on the ſurrender of the place (" The Dutch ſhall enjoy the liberty of their con-" ſciences in divine worſhip and church diſcipline") may be termed an eſtabliſhment. Judaiſm is tolerated, but popery is not. The inhabitants of the province conſiſt chiefly of Dutch, Engliſh, and Scots preſbyterians, German Calviniſts, Lutherans, quakers, baptiſts, &c. who have their reſpective houſes of worſhip. The Dutch preſbyterians being in ſubordination to the Claſſis of Amſterdam, ſend all their youth, who are intended for the miniſtry, to Holland for ordination, as the epiſcopalians do theirs to England. The Engliſh preſbyterians are on the model of the church of Scotland *.

A college was erected in New York, by act of parliament, about the year 1755; but as the aſſembly was at that time divided into parties, it was formed on a contracted plan, and has for that reaſon never met with the encouragement which might naturally be expected for a public ſeminary in ſo populous a city. It contains at preſent about twenty ſtudents.

NEW JERSEY.

SITUATION AND EXTENT.

	Miles.		Degrees.
Length	160	} between {	39 and 43 north latitude.
Breadth	60		74 and 76 weſt longitude.

BOUNDARIES. NEW JERSEY is bounded on the weſt and ſouth-weſt, by Delaware river and Bay; on the ſouth-eaſt and eaſt, by the Atlantic Ocean; and by the Sound, which ſeparates Staten Iſland from the continent, and Hudſon's river, on the north.

Diviſions.	Counties.	Chief Towns.	
Eaſt Diviſion contains	Middleſex	Perth-Amboy and New-Brunſwick	
	Monmouth	None	
	Eſſex	Elizabeth and Newark	
	Somerſet	None	
	Bergen	Bergen.	
Weſt diviſion contains	Burlington	BURLINGTON	{ 40-8 N. lat. { 75-0 W. lon.
	Glouceſter	Glouceſter	
	Salem	Salem	
	Cumberland	Hopewell	
	Cape May	None	
	Hunterdon	Trenton	
	Morris	Morris	
	Suſſex	None.	

* In the year 1770, the number of places for public worſhip in the city of New York ſtood as follows;

Dutch preſbyterians	—	3	Baptiſts	—	—	1	
Engliſh ditto	—	—	2	Moravians	—	—	1
Scotch ditto	—	—	1	German Calviniſts	—	—	2
Epiſcopalians	—	—	3	—— Lutherans	—	—	1
French refugees	—	—	1	Methodiſts	---	---	1
Quakers	—	—	1	Jews	---	---	---	1

RIVERS.] Thefe are Delaware, Raritan, and Paffaick, on the latter of which is a remarkable cataract; the height of the rock from which the water falls is faid to be about 70 feet perpendicular, and the river there 80 yards broad.

CLIMATE, SOIL, AND PRODUCE.] The climate is much the fame with that of New York; the foil is various, at leaft one fourth part of the province is barren fandy land, producing pines and cedars; the other parts in general are good, and produce wheat, barley, rye, Indian corn, &c. in great perfection.

HISTORY, GOVERNMENT, POPULA- ⎫ New Jerfey is part
TION, CHIEF TOWNS, COMMERCE, ⎬ of that vaft tract
RELIGION, AND LEARNING. ⎭ of land, which we
have obferved was given by king Charles II. to his brother, James duke of York: he fold it, for a valuable confideration, to lord Berkley and Sir George Carteret, (from whom it received its prefent name, becaufe Sir George had, as the family ftill have, eftates in the ifland of Jerfey) and they again to others, who in the year 1702 made a furrender of the powers of government to queen Anne, which fhe accepted: fince that time it has been a royal government. By an account publifhed in 1765, the number of inhabitants appears to have been about 100,000. Perth-Amboy and Burlington are the feats of government; the governor generally refides in the latter, which is pleafantly fituated on the fine river Delaware, within 20 miles of Philadelphia. The former is as good a port as moft on the continent; and the harbour is fafe, and capacious enough to contain many large fhips. This province has no foreign trade worth mentioning, owing to its vicinity to the large trading cities of New York and Philadelphia, by which it is fupplied with merchandizes of all kinds, and makes returns to them in lumber, wheat, flour, &c. In Bergen county is a very valuable copper mine.

RELIGION AND LEARNING.] The ftate of religion here may be feen by the following lift of the houfes for public worfhip throughout the province, which was made in 1765 by a member of the council for the province *.

Learning has of late been greatly encouraged in this province. A college was eftablifhed at the town of Princeton, by governor Belcher in 1746, and has a power of conferring

---

* Englifh and Scotch prefbyterians	57	Moravians	—	—	—	1
Quakers — — —	39	Separatifts	—	—	—	1
Dutch prefbyterians — —	22	Rogereens	—	—	—	1
Epifcopalians — —	22					
Baptifts — — —	22			In all	172
Lutherans — — —	7					

B b 3

degrees

degrees as Oxford or Cambridge. There are generally
between 80 and 100 ftudents here, who come from all parts
of the continent, fome even from the extremities of it.

PENSYLVANIA.

SITUATION AND EXTENT.

Miles.		Degrees.
Length 300	between	74 and 81 W. longitude.
Breadth 240		39 and 44 N. latitude.

BOUNDARIES.] BOUNDED by the country of the
Iroquois, or five nations, on the north ;
by Delaware river, which divides it from the Jerfeys, on the
caſt ; and by Maryland, on the fouth and weſt, and contains
the following counties.

Counties.	Chief Towns.	
Philadelphia	PHILADELPHIA,	N. lat. 40. W. lon. 75-20.
Cheſter	Cheſter	
Bucks	Newtown	
Berks	Reading	
Northampton	Eaſton	
Lancaſter	Lancaſter	
York	York	
Cumberland	Carliſle	

Befides the above, there are the three following

Counties,		Chief Towns.
Newcaſtle		Newcaſtle
Kent and	on Delaware	Dover
Suffex		Lewes,

which form in fome meafure a diſtinct government, having an
affembly of their own, though the fame governor with the
province of Penfylvania.

RIVERS.] The rivers are Delaware, which is navigable
for veffels of one fort or other, more than 200 miles above
Philadelphia. Sufquehanna, and Schuylkill, are alfo navigable
a confiderable way up the country. Thefe rivers, with the
numerous bays and creeks, in Delaware bay, capable of
containing the largeft fleets, render this province admirably
fuited to carry on an inland and foreign trade.

CLIMATE, AIR, SOIL, AND FACE OF THE COUNTRY.} The face of the country,
air, foil, and produce, do
not materially differ from that of New-York. If there be
any difference, it is in favour of this province. The air is
fweet

sweet and clear. The winters continue from December till
March, and are so extremely cold and severe, that the river
Delaware, though very broad, is often frozen over.   The
months of July, August, and September, are almost intolerably hot,   but the   country is refreshed by frequent cold
breezes.   It may be remarked in general, that in all parts of
our plantations from New-York to the southern extremity, the
woods are full of wild vines of three or four species, all different from those we have in Europe.   But, whether from
some fault in their nature, or in the climate, or the soil where
they grow, or what is much more probable, from a fault in
the planters, they have yet produced no wine that deserves to
be mentioned, though the Indians from them make a sort of
wine, with which they regale themselves.   It may also be
observed of the timber of these colonies, that towards the
south it is not so good for shipping, as that of the more northern provinces.   The further southward you go, the timber
becomes less compact, and rives easily ; which property, as it
renders it less serviceable for ships, makes it more useful for
staves.

HISTORY, GOVERNMENT, SET- ⎫   This country, under
  TLEMENT, POPULATION, CHIEF ⎬   the name of the New
  TOWNS, AND COMMERCE.   ⎭   Netherlands, was originally possessed by the Dutch and Swedes.   When these
nations, however, were expelled from New-York, by the
English, admiral Pen, who, in conjunction with Venables,
had conquered the island of Jamaica, being well with Charles
II. obtained a promise of a grant of this country from that
monarch.   Upon the admiral's death, his son, the celebrated
quaker, availed himself of this promise, and after much court
follicitation, obtained the performance of it.   Though as an
author and a divine, Mr. Pen be little known, but to those
of his own persuasion, his reputation in a character no less
respectable, is universal among all civilized nations.   The
circumstances of the times engaged vast numbers to follow
him into his new settlement, to avoid the persecutions, to
which the quakers, like other sectaries, were then exposed,
but it was to his own wisdom and ability, that they are indebted for that charter of privileges, which has put this colony
on so respectable a footing.   Civil and religious liberty in the
utmost latitude, was laid down by that great man, as the
great and only foundation of all his institutions.   Christians
of all denominations might not only live unmolested, but
have a share in the government of the colony *.   No laws

B b 4   can

_____

* At present the church of England is but barely tolerated here.

can be made but by the confent of the inhabitants. Even matters of benevolence, to which the laws of few nations have extended, were by Pen fubjected to regulations. The affairs of widows and orphans were to be inquired into by a court conftituted for that purpofe. The caufes between man and man were not to be fubjected to the delay and chicanery of the law, but decided by wife and honeft arbitrators. His benevolence and generofity extended alfo to the Indian nations: inftead of immediately taking advantage of his patent, he pur- chafed of thefe people the lands he had obtained by his grant, judging that the original property, and eldeft right, was vefted in them. William Pen, in fhort, had he been a native of Greece, would have had his ftatue placed next to that of Solon and Lycurgus. His laws, founded on the folid bafis of equity, ftill maintain their force; and as a proof of their effects, it is only neceffary to mention that land is now granted at twelve pounds an hundred acres, with a quit-rent of four fhillings referved, whereas the terms on which it was formerly granted where at twenty pound the thoufand acres, with one fhilling quit-rent for every hundred. Near Philadelphia, land rents at twenty fhillings the acre, and even at feveral miles diftance from that city, fells at twenty years purchafe.

In fome years, more people have tranfported themfelves into Penfylvania, than into all the other fettlements together. In fhort, this province has increafed fo greatly from the time of its firft eftablifhment, that the number of inhabitants in the whole province, is computed at 350,000. Upon the principal rivers fettlements are made, and the country cultivated 150 miles above Philadelphia. The people are hardy, induftrious, and moft of them fubftantial, though but few of the landed people can be confidered as rich; but they are all well lodged, well fed, and, for their condition, well clad; and this at the more eafy rate, as the inferior people manufacture moft of their own wear, both linens and woollens.

This province contains many very confiderable towns, fuch as German town, Chefter, Oxford, Radnor, all which, in any other colony, would deferve being taken notice of more particularly. But here the city of Philadelphia, containing upwards of 30,000 inhabitants, beautiful beyond any city of America, and in regularity unequalled by any in Europe, totally eclipfes the reft, and deferves all our attention. It was built after the plan of the famous Pen, the founder and legifla- tor of this colony. It is fituated 100 miles from the fea, be- tween two navigable rivers, the Delaware, where it is above a mile in breadth on the north, and the Schuylkill, on the fouth, which it unites as it were, by running in a line of two

miles

miles between them. The whole town, when the original plan can be fully executed, is in this manner; every quarter of the city forms a fquare of eight acres, and almoft in the center of it, is a fquare of ten acres, furrounded by the town-houfe, and other public buildings. The High Street is 100 feet wide, and runs the whole breadth of the town : parallel to it run nineteen other ftreets, which are croffed by eight more at right angles, all of them 30 feet wide, and communicating with canals, from the two rivers, which add not only to the beauty, but to the wholefomenefs of the city. According to the original plan, every man in poffeffion of 1000 acres in the province, had his houfe either in one of the fronts, facing the rivers, or in the High Street, running from the middle of one front, to the middle of the other. Every owner of 5000 acres, befides the above-mentioned privilege, was entitled to have an acre of ground in the front of his houfe, and all others might have half an acre for gardens and court yards. The proprietor's feat, which is the ufual place of the governor's refidence, and is about a mile above the town, is the firft private building both for magnificence and fituation in all Britifh America. The barracks for the king's troops, the market and other public buildings, are proportionably grand. The quays are fpacious and fine, the principal quay is 200 feet wide, and to this a veffel of 500 tuns may lay her broadfide, though above 100 miles from the fea.

There are in this city a great number of very wealthy merchants; which is no way furprizing, when we confider the great trade which it carries on with the Englifh, Spanifh, French and Dutch colonies in America; with the Azores, the Canaries, and the Madeira iflands; with Great Britain and Ireland; with Spain, Portugal and Holland. Befides the Indian trade, and the quantity of grain, provifions, and all kinds of the produce of this province, which is brought down the rivers upon which this city is fo commodioufly fituated, the Germans, who are fettled in the interior parts of this province, employ feveral hundred waggons, drawn each by four horfes, in bringing the product of their farms to this market. In the year 1749, 303 veffels entered inwards at this port, and 291 cleared outwards.

The commodities exported from Great Britain into Penfylvania, at an average of three years, amount to the value of 611,000 l. Thofe exported to Great Britain and other markets, befides timber, fhips built for fale, copper ore, and iron in pigs and bars, confift of grain, flour, and many forts of
animal

animal food ; and at an average of three years, are calculated
at 705,500 l.

There is a flourishing academy established at Philadelphia,
which has been greatly encouraged by contributions from
England, and Scotland, and which bids fair to become a
bright seminary of learning.

MARYLAND.

SITUATION AND EXTENT.

	Miles.		Degrees.

Length 140 } between { 75 and 80 W. longitude.
Breadth 135 } 37 and 40 N. latitude.

BOUNDARIES.] BOUNDED by Penfylvania, on the
north ; by another part of Penfylvania,
and the Atlantic ocean, on the eaft ; by Virginia, on the
fouth ; and by the Apalachian mountains, on the weft.

Maryland is divided into two parts by the bay of Chefapeak,
viz. 1. The eaftern ; and 2. The weftern divifion.

Divifions.	Counties.	Chief Towns.
The eaft divifion contains the counties of	Worcefter	Princefs Anne
	Somerfet	Snow Hill
	Dorfet	Dorfet, or Dorchefter
	Talbot	Oxford
	Cecil	
	Queen Anne's	Queen's Town
	Kent	Chefter.
The weft divifion contains	St. Mary's county	St. Mary's
	Charles county	Briftol
	Prince George county	Mafterkout
	Calvert county	Abington
	Arundel county	ANNAPOLIS, W.lon. 76-50. N. lat. 39.
	Baltimore county	Baltimore.
	Frederic county	

RIVERS.] This country is indented with a vaft number of
navigable creeks and rivers. The chief are Patowmac, Poco-
moac, Patuxent, Cheptonk, Severn and Saffafras.

FACE OF THE COUNTRY, } In thefe particulars this pro-
AIR, SOIL AND PRODUCE. } vince has nothing particular
by which it may be diftinguifhed from thofe already defcribed.
The hills in the inland country are of fo eafy afcent, that
they rather feem an artificial than a natural production. The
vaft number of rivers diffufes fertility through the foil, which
is admirably adapted to the rearing of tobacco, which is the
ftaple

ſtaple commodity of that country, hemp, Indian corn and grain, which they now begin to cultivate in preference to tobacco.

COMMERCE.] The commerce of Maryland depends on the ſame principles with that of Virginia, and is ſo cloſely connected with it, that any ſeparation of them would rather confuſe than edify. It will be conſidered therefore under that head.

HISTORY AND GOVERNMENT.] It ſeems as if all the provinces of North America were planted from motives of religion. Maryland, like thoſe we have formerly deſcribed, owes its ſettlement to religious conſiderations. As they however were peopled by proteſtants, and even ſectaries, Maryland was originally planted by Roman-catholics. This ſect, towards the cloſe of Charles I.'s reign, was the object of great hatred with the bulk of the Engliſh nation; the laws in force againſt the Roman-catholics, were executed with the utmoſt ſeverity. This in part aroſe from an opinion, perhaps not without ſome foundation, that the court was too favourably diſpoſed towards this form of religion. It is certain, that many marks of favour were conferred on Roman-catholics. Lord Baltimore was one of the moſt eminent, one in greateſt favour with the court, and on that account moſt odious to the generality of Engliſhmen. This nobleman, in 1632, obtained a grant from Charles of that country, which formerly was conſidered as a part of Virginia, but was now called Maryland, in honour of queen Henrietta Mary, daughter to Henry IV. and ſpouſe to king Charles. The year following about 200 popiſh families, ſome of conſiderable diſtinction, embarked with lord Baltimore, to enter into poſſeſſion of this new territory. Theſe ſettlers, who had that liberality and good breeding, which diſtinguiſhes gentlemen of every religion, bought their lands at an eaſy price from the native Indians; they even lived with them for ſome time in the ſame city; and the ſame harmony continued to ſubſiſt between the two nations, until the Indians were impoſed on by the malicious inſinuations of ſome planters in Virginia, who envied the proſperity of this popiſh colony, and inflamed the Indians againſt them by ill-grounded reports, but ſuch as were ſufficient to ſtir up the reſentment of men naturally jealous, and who from experience had reaſon to be ſo. The colony, however, was not wanting to its own ſafety on this occaſion. Though they continued their friendly intercourſe with the natives, they took care to erect a fort, and to uſe every other precaution for their defence againſt ſudden hoſtilities; the defeat of this attempt gave a new ſpring to the activity of this plantation: which was likewiſe receiving frequent reinforcements from England of thoſe who found

themſelves

themselves in danger by the approaching revolution. But during the protectorship of Cromwell, every thing was overturned in Maryland. Baltimore was ungenerously deprived of his rights, and a new governor, appointed by the protector, substituted in his room. At the restoration, however, the property of this province reverted to its natural possessor. Baltimore was reinstated in his rights, and fully discovered how well he deserved to be so. He established a perfect toleration in all religious matters: the colony encreased and flourished, and dissenters of all denominations, allured by the prospect of gain, flocked into Maryland. The tyrannical government of James II. which without discernment of friends or enemies, but with the fury of a mad-dog, snapped at every thing before it, again deprived this noble family of their possession, acquired by royal bounty, and improved by much care and expence. At the revolution, however, lord Baltimore was again restored to all the profits of the government, though not to the right of governing, which could not consistently be conferred on a Roman-catholic. But since the family have changed their religion, they have obtained the power as well as the interest. At present but a small part of it belongs to that family. The government of this country exactly resembles that in Virginia, except that the governor is appointed by the proprietors, and only confirmed by the crown. The customs too are reserved to the crown, and the officers belonging to them are independent of the government of the province. So far is Maryland from being at present a popish government, that the protestants, by far more numerous, have excluded them from all offices of trust and power. They have even adopted the penal laws of England against them. The church of England is by law established here, and the clergy are paid in tobacco : a tax for this purpose is annually levied, and every male white person above the age of 16 is obliged to pay 40 lb. of tobacco (or if he raises no tobacco, he must take an oath that he does not, and pay the value in cash;) dissenting clergy are not exempted.

VIRGINIA.

SITUATION AND EXTENT.

	Miles.		Degrees.
Length	750	between	75 and 90 W. longitude.
Breadth	240		36 and 40 N. latitude.

BOUNDARIES.] BOUNDED by the river Patowmac, which divides it from Maryland, on the north-east; by the Atlantic ocean, on the east; by Carolina, on the south; and by the river Mississippi, on the west.

It may be divided into four parts, viz. The north : The middle : The fouth : And, the eaftern divifion.

Divifions.	Counties.	Parifhes.
The north divi-fion contains	1. Northumberland ———	Wincomoca
	2. Lancashire ———	Chrift-Church
	3. Weftmoreland ———	
	4. Richmond ———	
	5. Stafford ———	St. Paul's.
The middle divifion contains	6. Effex — ———	Farnham
	7. Middlefex ———	Chrift-Church
	8. Gloucefter ———	Abingdon
	9. King and Queen county	Stratton
	10. King William county	St. John's
	11. New Kent ———	St. Peter's
	12. Elizabeth county ——	Elizabeth
	13. Warwick county ——	Denby
	14. York county ———	York
	15. Princefs Anne county	Lynhaven.
The fouth divi-fion contains	16. Norfolk county ———	Elizabeth
	17. Nanfamund county —	Chutakuk
	18. Ifle of Wight county	Newport
	19. Surry county	Southwark
	20. Prince George county	Wyanoke
	21. Charles county ———	Weftover
	22. Henrico county ———	Briftol
	23. James county ———	James Town
		WILLIAMS-BURG, 37-15
		N. 76-50 W.
The eaftern divifion between Chefapeak bay and the ocean	24. Acomac county ———	Acomac.

CAPES, BAYS AND RIVERS.] In failing to Virginia or Maryland, you pafs a ftreight between two points of land, called the Capes of Virginia, which opens a paffage into the bay of Chefapeak, one of the largeft and fafeft in the whole world ; for it enters the country near 300 miles from the fouth to the north, is about 18 miles broad for a confiderable way, and feven where it is narroweft, the waters in moft places being nine fathoms deep. This bay, through its whole extent, receives a vaft number of navigable rivers from the fides of both Maryland and Virginia. From the latter, befides others of lefs note, it receives James River, York River, the Rappahannock, and the Patowmac ; thefe are not only navigable for large fhips into the heart of the country, but have fo many creeks, and receive fuch a number of fmaller navigable rivers, that Virginia is without all manner of doubt the country of the world of the moſt convenient navigation. It has been obſerved, and the obſervation is not exaggerated, that every planter has a river at his door. ·

FACE OF THE COUNTRY.] The whole face of this country is ſo extremely low towards the ſea, that you are very near the ſhore, before you can diſcover land from the maſt-head. The lofty trees, which cover the ſoil, gradually riſe as it were from the ocean, and afford an enchanting proſpect. You travel 100 miles into the country, without meeting with a hill, which is nothing uncommon on this extenſive coaſt of North America.

AIR AND CLIMATE.] In ſummer the heats here are exceſ-ſive, tho' not without refreſhing breezes from the ſea. The weather is changeable, and the changes ſudden and violent. Their winter froſts come on with the leaſt warning. To a warm day, there ſometimes ſucceeds ſuch an intenſe cold in the evening as to freeze over the largeſt rivers.

The air and ſeaſons here depend very much upon the wind, as to heat and cold, dryneſs and moiſture. In winter they have a fine clear air, and dry, which renders it very pleaſant. Their ſpring is about a month earlier than in England; in April they have frequent rains; in May and June, the heat increaſes; and the ſummer is much like ours, being refreſhed with gentle breezes from the ſea, that riſe about nine o'clock, and decreaſe and increaſe as the ſun riſes or falls. In July and Auguſt theſe breezes ceaſe, and the air becomes ſtagnant, and violently hot; in September the weather generally changes, when they have heavy and frequent rains, which occaſion all the train of diſeaſes incident to a moiſt climate, particularly agues, and intermitting fevers. They have frequent thunder and lightning, but it rarely does any miſchief.

SOIL AND PRODUCE.] Towards the ſea-ſhore, and the banks of the rivers, the ſoil of Virginia conſiſts of a dark rich mould, which, without manure, returns plentifully whatever is committed to it. At a diſtance from the water there is a lightneſs and ſandineſs in the ſoil, which however is of a generous nature, and helped by a kindly ſun, yields corn and tobacco extremely well.

From what has been ſaid of the ſoil and climate, it is eaſy to infer the variety and perfection of the vegetable productions of this country. The foreſts are covered with all ſorts of lofty trees; and no underwood or bruſhes grow beneath; ſo that people travel with eaſe through the foreſts on horſeback, under a fine ſhade, to defend them from the ſun; the plains are enamelled with flowers and flowering ſhrubs of the richeſt colours, and moſt fragrant ſcent. Silk grows ſpontaneous in

many

many places, the fibres of which are as ftrong as hemp. Medicinal herbs and roots, particularly the fnake root, and the ginfeng of the Chinefe, are here in great plenty. There is no fort of grain but might be cultivated to advantage. The inhabitants however are fo engroffed with the culture of the tobacco plant, that they think, if corn fufficient for their fupport can be reared, they do enough in this way. But flax and hemp are produced not only for their own confumption, but for export, though not in fuch quantities as they might be expected from the nature of the foil, admirably fitted for producing this commodity.

Animals.] We fhall here obferve, that there were neither horfes, cows, fheep, nor hogs in America, before they were carried thither by the Europeans; but now they are multiplied fo extremely that many of them, particularly in Virginia, and the fouthern colonies, run wild. Beef and pork is fold here from one penny to twopence a pound; their fatteft pullets at fixpence a-piece; chickens, at three or four fhillings a dozen; geefe, at ten pence; and turkeys, at eighteen pence a-piece. But fifh, and wild fowl, are ftill cheaper in the feafon, and deer are fold from five to ten fhillings a-piece. This eftimate may ferve for the other American colonies, where provifions are equally plentiful and cheap, and in fome ftill lower. Befides the animals tranfported from Europe, thofe natural to the country are deer, of which there are great numbers, a fort of panther or tyger, bears, wolves, foxes, and racoons. Here is likewife that fingular animal, called the Opoffum, which feems to be the wood-rat mentioned by Charlevoix, in his hiftory of Canada. It is about the fize of a cat, and befides the belly common to it with other animals, it has another peculiar to itfelf, and which hangs beneath the former. This belly has a large aperture, towards the hinder legs, which difcovers a large number of teats on the ufual part of the common belly. Upon thefe, when the female of this creature conceives, the young are formed, and there they hang like fruit upon the ftalk, until they grow in bulk and weight to their appointed fize; then they drop off, and are received into the falfe belly, from which they go out at pleafure, and in which they take refuge when any danger threatens them. In Virginia there are all forts of tame and wild fowl. They have the nightingale, called from the country, whofe plumage is crimfon and blue; the mocking bird, thought to excel all others in his own note, and including that of every one; the humming bird, the fmalleft of all the winged creation, and by far the moft beautiful, all arrayed in fcarlet, green and gold. It fips the dew from the flowers,

which

which is all its nourishment, and is too delicate to be brought
alive into England.

HISTORY, GOVERNMENT, POPULA- } This is the first
   TION, TOWNS, AND COMMERCE. } country which the
English planted in America. We derived our right, not only
to this, but to all our other settlements, as has been already
observed, from the discovery of Sebastian Cabot, who, in
1497, first made the northern continent of America, in the
service of Henry VII. of England. No attempts, however,
were made to settle it, till the reign of queen Elizabeth. It
was then that Sir Walter Raleigh, the most extraordinary genius of the age in which he lived, perhaps in any age, applied
to court, and got together a company which was composed of
several persons of distinction and several eminent merchants,
who agreed to open a trade and settle a colony in that part of
the world, which, in honour of queen Elizabeth, he called
Virginia. Towards the close of the sixteenth century, several
attempts were made for settling this colony before any proved
successful. The three first companies who sailed into Virginia perished through hunger and diseases, or were cut off by
the Indians. The fourth was reduced almost to the same situation ; and, being dwindled to a feeble remainder, had set sail
for England, in despair of living in such an uncultivated
country, inhabited by such hostile and warlike savages. But
in the mouth of Chesapeak bay, they were met by lord Dela-
war, with a squadron loaded with provisions, and with every
thing necessary for their relief and defence. At his persuasion
they returned : by his advice, his prudence, and winning behaviour, the government of the colony was settled within
itself, and put on a respectable footing with regard to its enemies. This nobleman, who had accepted the government of
the unpromising province of Virginia from the noblest motives,
was compelled, by the decayed state of his health, to return
into England. He left behind him, however, his son, as deputy ; with Sir Thomas Gates, Sir George Summers, the
honourable George Piercy, and Mr. Newport, for his council.
By them, James-Town, the first town built by the English
in the new world, was erected. The colony continued to
flourish, and the true sources of its wealth began to be discovered and improved. The first settlers, like those of Maryland, were generally persons of consideration and distinction.
It remained a steady ally to the royal party during the troubles
of Great Britain. Many of the Cavaliers, in danger at
home, took refuge here ; and under the government of Sir
William Berkley, held out for the crown, until the parliament, rather by stratagem than force, reduced them. After
         the

the Reſtoration, there is nothing very intereſting in the hiſtory of this province. Soon after this time, a young gentleman, named Bacon, a lawyer, availing himſelf of ſome diſcontents in the colony, on account of reſtraints on trade, became very popular, and ſet every thing in confuſion. His natural death, however, reſtored peace and unanimity; and the inhabitants of Virginia ceaſed to deſtroy themſelves.

The government of this province was not at firſt adapted to the principles of the Engliſh conſtitution, and to the enjoyment of that liberty to which a ſubject of Great-Britain thinks himſelf entitled in every part of the globe. It was governed by a governor and council, appointed by the king of Great-Britain. As the inhabitants encreaſed, the inconveniency of this form became more grievous; and a new branch was added to the conſtitution, by which the people, who had formerly no conſideration, were allowed to elect their repreſentatives from each county, into which this country is divided, with privileges reſembling thoſe of the repreſentatives of the commons of England. Thus two houſes, the upper and lower houſe of aſſembly, were formed. The upper houſe, which was before called the council, remained on its former footing; its members are appointed, during pleaſure, by the crown; they are ſtiled Honourable, and anſwer in ſome meaſure to the houſe of peers in the Britiſh conſtitution. The lower houſe is the guardian of the peoples liberties. And thus, with a governor repreſenting the king, an upper and lower houſe of aſſembly, this government bears a ſtriking reſemblance to our own. When any bill has paſſed the two houſes, it comes before the governor, who gives his aſſent or negative as he thinks proper. It now acquires the force of a law, until it be tranſmitted to England, and his majeſty's pleaſure known on that ſubject. The upper houſe of aſſembly acts not only as a part of the legiſlature, but alſo as a privy-council to the governor, without whoſe concurrence he can do nothing of moment: it ſometimes acts as a court of Chancery.

The number of white people in Virginia, which is daily encreaſing, is ſuppoſed to amount to above 100,000. The negroes, of whom ſome thouſands are annually imported into Virginia and Maryland, are at leaſt as many; they thrive too much better here than in the Weſt Indies. The inhabitants of Virginia are a chearful, hoſpitable, and in general a genteel ſort of people: ſome of them are accuſed of vanity and oſtentation; which accuſation is not without ſome ground. Here are only two towns that deſerve that name; the largeſt of which, and the capital of the province, is Williamſburg, containing about fixty houfes, and fome fpacious public buildings.

In the following account of the commerce of Virginia, is alfo included that of Maryland. Thefe provinces are fuppofed to export, of tobacco alone, to the annual value of 768,000 l. into Great-Britain. This, at eight pounds per hogfhead, makes the number of hogfheads amount to 96,000. Of thefe, it is computed that about 13,500 hogfheads are confumed at home, the duty on which, at 26 l. 1 s. per hogfhead, comes to 351,675 l. the remaining 82,500 hogfheads are exported by our merchants to the other countries of Europe, and their value returned to Great-Britain. The advantages of this trade appear by the bare mention of it. It may not be improper to add, that this fingle branch employs 330 fail of fhips, and 7960 feamen. Not only our wealth therefore, but the very finews of our national ftrength are powerfully braced by it. The other commodities of thefe colonies, of which naval ftores, wheat, Indian corn, iron in pigs and bars, are the moft confiderable, make the whole exportation, at an average of three years, amount to 1,040,000 l. The exports of Great-Britain, the fame as to our other colonies, at a like average, come to 865,000 l.

Though an intire toleration be allowed to all religions in this country, there are few diffenters from the church of England. The bifhop of London fends over a fuperintendant to infpect the character of the clergy; who live comfortably here, (a prieft to each parifh) with about 100 l. per annum, paid in tobacco.

Here is alfo a college, founded by king William, called William and Mary college, who gave 2000 l. towards it, and 20,000 acres of land, with power to purchafe and hold lands to the value of 2000 l. a year, and a duty of one penny per pound on all tobacco exported to the other plantations. There is a prefident, fix profeffors, and other officers, who are named by the governors or vifitors. The honourable Mr. Boyle made a very large donation to the college for the education of Indian children.

NORTH and SOUTH CAROLINA, with GEORGIA.

SITUATION AND EXTENT.

	Miles.		Degrees.
Length	700	between	76 and 91 weft longitude.
Breadth	380		30 and 37 north latitude.

BOUNDARIES.] **B**OUNDED by Virginia, on the north ; by the Atlantic ocean, on the eaſt ; by the river St. John, which ſeparates Georgia from Florida, on the ſouth ; and by the Miſſiſippi, on the weſt.

Diviſions.	Counties.	Towns.
North Carolina con-tains the counties of ———	Albemarle ——— Bath county, and Clarendon in part	Divided into pariſhes, but have no towns.
The middle diviſion, or South Carolina, contains the counties of ———	Clarendon in part Craven county — Berkley county — Colleton county — Granville county —	St. James Chriſt-Church CHARLES-TOWN, W. lon. 79-15. N. lat. 32-45. Port-Royal.
The ſouth-diviſion contains only	Georgia ———	Savannah Frederica Puriſburgh.

RIVERS.] Theſe are the Roanoke, or Albemarle river ; Pamtico ; Neus ; Cape Fear, or Clarendon river ; Pedee ; Santee ; Savannah ; Alatamaha, or George river, and St. Mary's, which divides Georgia from Florida : all which rivers riſe in the Apalachian mountains, and running eaſt, fall into the Atlantic Ocean. The back parts are watered by the Cherokees, Yaſous, Mobile, Apalachicola, the Pearl river, and many other noble ſtreams which fall into the Miſſiſippi or the gulph of Mexico.

SEAS, BAYS, AND CAPES.] The only ſea bordering on this country is that of the Atlantic ocean ; which is ſo ſhallow near the coaſt, that a ſhip of any great burden cannot approach it, except in ſome few places. There has not yet been found one good harbour in North Carolina ; the beſt are thoſe of Roanoke, at the mouth of Albemarle river, and Pamtico. In South Carolina, there are the harbours of Winyaw, or George-Town, Charles-Town, and Port-Royal. In Georgia, the mouths of the rivers Savannah and Alatamaha form good harbours.

The moſt remarkable promontories are, Cape Hatteras, in 35 deg. odd minutes north lat. Cape Fear to the ſouth of it, and Cape Cartaret ſtill further ſouth.

CLIMATE AND AIR.] There is not any conſiderable dif-ference between the climate of theſe countries. In general it agrees with that of Virginia ; but, where they differ, it is much to the advantage of Carolina. The ſummers indeed

C c 2

are

are of a more intenfe heat than in Virginia, but the winters
are milder and fhorter.   The climate of Carolina, like all
American weather, is fubject to fudden tranfitions from heat
to cold, and from cold to heat ; but not to fuch violent extremities as Virginia.   The winters are feldom fevere enough to
freeze any confiderable water, affecting only the mornings
and evenings ; the frofts have never fufficient ftrength to refift
the noon-day fun ; fo that many tender plants, which do not
ftand the winter of Virginia, flourifh in Carolina, for they have
oranges in great plenty near Charles-Town, and excellent in
their kinds, both fweet and four.

> SOIL, PRODUCE, AND FACE }   In this refpect too there is
>   OF THE COUNTRY.   { a confiderable coincidence

between thefe countries and Virginia : the Carolinas, however, in the fertility of nature, have the advantage ; but
Georgia is not of near fo good a foil as the other provinces.
The whole country is in a manner one foreft, where our planters have not cleared it.   The trees are almoft the fame in
every refpect with thofe produced in Virginia ; and by the different fpecies of thefe, the quality of the foil is eafily known.
The land in Carolina is eafily cleared, as there is little or no
underwood, and the forefts moftly confift of tall trees at a
confiderable diftance.   Thofe grounds which bear the oak, the
walnut, and the hickory, are extremely fertile ; they are of
a dark fand intermixed with loam ; and as all their land
abounds with nitre, it is a long time before it is exhaufted ;
for here they never ufe any manure.   The pine barren is the
worft of all ; this is an almoft perfectly white fand, yet it
bears the pine tree, and fome other ufeful plants naturally,
yielding good profit in pitch, tar, and turpentine.   When
this fpecies of land is cleared, for two or three years together
it produces very good crops of Indian corn and peafe ; and,
when it lies low, and is flooded, it even anfwers for rice.   But
what is moft fortunate for this province is, that this worft part
of its land is favourable to a fpecies of the moft valuable of
all its products, to one of the kinds of indigo.   The low,
rich, fwampy grounds, bear their great ftaple, rice.   The
country near the fea is much the worft, in many parts little
better than an unhealthy falt marfh ; for Carolina is all an
even plain for 80 miles from the fea, not a hill, not a rock,
nor fcarce even a pebble to be met with.   But the country,
as you advance in it, improves continually ; and at 100 miles
diftance from Charles-Town, where it begins to grow hilly,
the foil is of a prodigious fertility, fitted for every purpofe of
human life ; nor can any thing be imagined more pleafant to the
eye than the variegated difpofition of this back country.   Here
                                                            the

the air is pure and wholefome, and the fummer heat much more temperate than in the flat fandy coaft.

In Carolina, the vegetation of every kind of plant is incredibly quick. The climate and foil have fomething in them fo kindly, that the latter, when left to itfelf, naturally throws out an immenfe quantity of flowers and flowering fhrubs. All the European plants arrive at perfection here beyond that in which their native country affords them. With proper culture and encouragement we might have filk, wine, and oil from thofe colonies: of the firft we have feen famples equal to what is brought to us from Italy. Wheat grows extremely well in the back parts, and yields a prodigious increafe.

From what we have obferved of thefe valuable provinces, their productions appear to be, vines, wheat, rice, Indian corn, barley, oats, peafe, beans, hemp, flax, cotton, tobacco, indigo, olives, orange, citron, cyprefs, faffafras, oak, walnut, caffia, and pine trees; white mulberry-trees for feeding filk-worms; farfaparilla, and pines which yield turpentine, rofin, tar, and pitch. There is a kind of tree from which runs an oil of extraordinary virtue for curing wounds; and another, which yields a balm, thought to be little inferior to that of Mecca. There are other trees befide thefe, that yield gums. The Carolinas produce prodigious quantities of honey, of which they make excellent fpirits, and mead as good as Malaga fack. Of all thefe, the three great ftaple commodities at prefent are, the indigo, rice, and the produce of the pine. Nothing furprifes an European more at firft fight, than the fize of the trees here, as well as in Virginia and other American countries. Their trunks are often from 50 to 70 feet high, without a branch or limb; and frequently above 36 feet in circumference. Of thefe trunks, when hollowed, the people of Charles-Town as well as the Indians make canoes, which ferve to tranfport provifions and other goods from place to place, and fome of them are fo large, that they will carry 30 or 40 barrels of pitch, though formed of one entire piece of timber. Of thefe are likewife made curious pleafure-boats.

ANIMALS.] The original animals of this country do not differ much from thofe of Virginia; but in Carolina they have a ftill greater variety of beautiful fowls. All the animals of Europe are here in plenty; black cattle are multiplied prodigioufly: to have 2 or 300 cows is very common, but fome have 1000 or upwards. Thefe ramble all day at pleafure in the forefts; but their calves being feparated and kept in fenced paftures, the cows return every evening to them. The hogs range in the fame manner, and return like the cows; thefe

are

are very numerous, and many run quite wild, as well as horned cattle and horfes, in the woods. It is furprifing that the
cattle fhould have encreafed fo quickly fince their being firft
imported from Europe, while there are fuch numbers of
wolves, tygers, and panthers, conftantly ranging the woods
and forefts. We have already obferved that thefe animals are
lefs ravenous than the beafts of Africa and Afia; they very
feldom attempt to kill either calves or foals in America, and
when attacked, their dams make a vigorous defence.

HISTORY, GOVERNMENT, POPU-⎫ The firft Englifh ex-
  LATION, CHIEF TOWNS, AND ⎬ peditions into Caro-
  COMMERCE.   ⎭ lina were unfortu-
nate. Nothing fuccefsful was done in this way till the year
1663, in the reign of Charles II. At that time feveral Englifh
noblemen, and others of great diftinction, obtained a charter
from the crown, invefting them with the property and jurifdiction of this country. They parcelled out the lands to fuch
as were willing to go over into the new fettlement, and to
fubmit to a fyftem of laws, which they employed the famous
Locke to compofe for them.

They began their firft fettlement at a point of land towards
the fouthward of their diftrict, between two navigable rivers.
Here they laid the foundation of a city, called Charles-Town,
which was defigned to be what it now is, the capital of the
province. In time, however, as no reftriction had been laid
upon the religious principles of thofe who fettled in Carolina,
the difputes between the church of England-men and diffenters caufed a total confufion in the colony. This was rendered
ftill more intolerable by the incurfions of the Indians, whom
they had irritated by their infolence and injuftice. In order to
prevent the fatal confequences of thefe inteftine divifions and
foreign wars, an act of parliament was paffed, which put this
colony under the immediate protection of the crown. The
lords proprietors accepted a recompence of about 24,000 l.
for both the property and jurifdiction ; and the conftitution of
this colony in thofe refpects in which it differed from the royal
colonies was altered. Earl Granville, however, thought fit
to retain his feventh fhare, which is ftill in the poffeffion of
his family. For the more convenient adminiftration of affairs
too, Carolina was divided into two diftricts, and two feparate
governments. This happened in 1728, and from that time,
peace being reftored in the internal government, as well as
with the Cherokees and other Indian tribes, thefe provinces
began to breathe ; and their trade has advanced of late with
wonderful rapidity.

The

The settlement of Georgia was projected in 1732, when several public-spirited noblemen and others, from compassion to the poor of these kingdoms, subscribed a confiderable sum, which, with 10,000 l. from the government, was given to provide in necessaries such poor persons as were willing to transport themselves into this province, and to submit to the regulations imposed on them. In process of time, new sums were raised, and new inhabitants sent over. Before the year 1752, upwards of 1000 persons were settled in this province. It was not, however, to be expected that the inhabitants of Georgia, removed as they were at a great distance from their benefactors, and from the check and controul of those who had a natural influence over them, would submit to the magistrates appointed to govern them. Many of the regulations too, by which they were bound, were very improper in themselves, and deprived the Georgians of privileges which their neighbours enjoyed, and which, as they increased in numbers and opulence, they thought it hard that they should be deprived of. From these corrupt sources arose all the bad humours which tore to pieces this constitution of government. Diffentions of all kinds sprung up, and the colony was on the brink of destruction, when, in 1752, the government took it under their immediate care, removed their particular grievances, and placed Georgia on the same footing with the Carolinas.

The method of settling in Carolina, and indeed in other provinces of British America, was to pitch upon a void space of ground, and either to purchase it at the rate of 20 l. for 1000 acres, and one shilling quit-rent for every 100 acres; or otherwise, to pay a penny an acre quit-rent yearly to the proprietors, without purchase-money: the former method is the most common, and the tenor a freehold. The people of Carolina live in the same easy, plentiful, and luxurious manner with the Virginians already described. Poverty is here almost an entire stranger; and the planters are the most hospitable people that are to be met with to all strangers, and especially to such as by accident or misfortunes are rendered incapable to provide for themselves.

The only town in either of the Carolinas worthy of notice is Charles-Town, the metropolis, in South-Carolina, which for size, beauty, and trade, may be considered as one of the first in British America. I have already mentioned its admirable situation at the confluence of two navigable rivers, one of which is navigable for ships 20 miles above the town, and for boats and large canoes near 40. The harbour is good in every respect, but that of a bar, which hinders vessels of more

than 200 tons burden from entering. The town is regularly
and pretty ftrongly fortified by nature and art; the ftreets are
well cut; the houfes are large and well built, fome of them
are of brick, and others of wood, but all of them handfome
and elegant, and rent is extremely high. The ftreets are wide
and ftraight, interfecting each other at right angles; thofe
running eaft and weft extend about a mile from one river to
the other. It contains about 1000 houfes, and is the feat of
the governor, and the place of meeting of the affembly. Its
neighbourhood is beautiful beyond defcription. Several handfome equipages are kept here. The planters and merchants
are rich and well bred; the people are fhewey and expenfive in
their drefs and way of living; fo that every thing confpires to
make this by much the livelieft, the lovelieft, and politeft
place, as it is one of the richeft too, in all America. It ought
alfo to be obferved, for the honour of the people of Carolina,
that, when in common with the other colonies, they refolved
againft the ufe of certain luxuries, and even neceffaries of
life; thofe articles which improve the mind, enla ge the underftanding, and correct the tafte, were excepted: the importation of books was permitted as formerly.

As South-Carolina has met with infinitely more attention
than the other provinces, the commerce of this country alone
employs 140 fhips, while that of the other two does not employ 60. Its exports to Great-Britain of native commodities,
on an average of three years, amount to more than 395,000 l.
annual value; and its imports at 365,000 l. The exports of
North-Carolina are computed at more than 68,000 l. and its
imports at about 18,000 l. The trade of Georgia is likewife
in its infancy; the exports amount to a little more than
74,000 l. and the imports at 49,000 l.

The trade between Carolina and the Weft-Indies is the
fame in all refpects with that of the reft of the colonies, and
is very large; their trade with the Indians is likewife in a
very flourifhing condition; and they carry Englifh goods on
pack-horfes 5 or 600 miles into the country weft of Charles-
Town.

The mouths of the rivers in North-Carolina form but ordinary harbours, and do not admit, except one at Cape Fear,
veffels of above 70 or 80 tuns. This lays a weight upon their
trade, by the expence of lighterage. Edenton w.s formerly
the capital of North-Carolina, which is no more than a
trifling village; but they are now projecting a town farther
fouth, which is more eccentrical.

Georgia has two towns already known in trade. Savannah,
the capital, is commodioufly fituated for an inland and foreign
trade,

trade, about ten miles from the fea, upon a noble river of the fame name, which is navigable for 200 miles farther for large boats, to the fecond town, called Augufta, which ftands in a country of the greateft fertility, and carries on a confiderable trade with the Indians. From the town of Savannah you fee the whole courfe of the river towards the fea; and on the other hand, you fee the river for about 60 miles up into the country. Here the Rev. Mr. George Whitefield (who ufed to crofs the Atlantic every other year) founded an orphan-houfe, which is now converted into a college for the education of young men defigned chiefly for the miniftry; and through his zeal and pious care, this favourite feminary is at prefent in a thriving condition.

East and West FLORIDA.

SITUATION AND EXTENT.

Miles.		Degrees.
Length 500 }	between {	80 and 91 weft longitude.
Breadth 440 }		25 and 32 north latitude.

BOUNDARIES.] THIS country, which was ceded by Spain to Great-Britain by the late treaty of peace, and includes a part of Louifiana, is now divided into the governments of Eaft and Weft Florida. See the Royal Proclamation.

RIVERS.] Thefe are the Miffifipi, which forms the weftern boundary of Florida, and is one of the fineft in the world, as well as the largeft; for including its turnings and windings, it is fuppofed to run a courfe of 4500 miles; but its mouths are in a manner choaked up with fands and fhoals, which deny accefs to veffels of any confiderable burden; there being, according to Mitchel's map, only twelve feet water over the bar (captain Pittman fays feventeen) at the principal entrance. Within the bar there is 100 fathom water, and the channel is every where deep, and the current gentle, except at a certain feafon, when, like the Nile, it overflows and becomes extremely rapid. It is, except at the entrance already mentioned, every where free from fhoals and cataracts, and navigable for craft of one kind or other almoft to its fource. The Mobille, the Apala-chicola, and St. John's rivers, are alfo large and noble ftreams.

BAYS AND CAPES.] The principal bays are, St. Bernard's, Afcenfion, Mobile, Penfacola, Dauphin, Jofeph, Apalaxy, Spiritu Sancto, and Charles Bay.

4

The

The chief capes are, Cape Blanco, Samblas, Anclote, St. Auguſtine, and Cape Florida, at the extremity of the peninſula, which terminates the Britiſh America ſouthward.

AIR AND CLIMATE.] It is very difficult to reconcile the various accounts that have been given of theſe particulars in this country. The people who have obtained grants of lands in Florida, and are deſirous to ſettle or ſell them, repreſent the whole country as a Canaan, and St. Auguſtine, in Eaſt-Florida, as the Montpelier of America: they tell us, that the climate of Florida is an exceeding agreeable medium betwixt the ſcorching heat of the tropics, and the pinching cold of the northern latitudes; that there is indeed a change of the ſeaſons, but it is a moderate one: in November and December, many trees loſe their leaves, vegetation goes on ſlowly, and the winter is perceived, but ſo mild, that ſnow is never ſeen there; and the tendereſt plants of the Weſt-Indies, ſuch as the plantain, the allegator-pear-tree, the banana, the pineapple, the ſugar-cane, &c. remain unhurt during the winter, in the gardens of St. Auguſtine: that the fogs and dark gloomy weather, ſo common in England, are unknown in this country. And though at the equinoxes, eſpecially the autumnal, the rains fall very heavy every day for ſome weeks together, yet, when the ſhower is over, the ſky immediately clears up, and all is calm and ſerene.

Others have repreſented this very coaſt as the grave and burying-place of all ſtrangers who are ſo unhappy as to go there, affirming as a truth, the well known ſtory propagated ſoon after the laſt peace, That upon the landing of our troops to take poſſeſſion of Florida, the Spaniards aſked them "What crimes have you been guilty of at home?" We ſhall take the liberty to obſerve on this head, that though the air here is very warm, the heats are much allayed by cool breezes from the ſeas which environ and waſh a conſiderable part of this country. The inland countries towards the north feel a little of the roughneſs of the north-weſt wind, which, more or leſs, diffuſes its chilling breath over the whole continent of North-America, carrying froſt and ſnow many degrees more to the ſouthward in theſe regions, than the north-eaſt wind does in Europe.

That the air of Florida is pure and wholeſome, appears from the ſize, vigour, and longevity of the Floridan Indians, who in theſe reſpects far exceed their more ſouthern neighbours, the Mexicans. That when the Spaniards quitted St. Auguſtine, many of them were of great age, ſome above 90. Since it came into the hands of Great-Britain, many gentlemen in a deep conſumption have aſcribed the recovery of their

health

health to that climate; and it is a certain fact, that the ninth regiment, stationed on different parts of the coast, did not lose a single man by natural death in the space of twenty months.

SOIL, PRODUCTIONS, AND ⎱ Many of the disadvantages
FACE OF THE COUNTRY. ⎰ indiscriminately imputed to the soil of the whole country, should be confined to East-Florida, which indeed, near the sea, and 40 miles back, is flat and sandy. But even the country round St. Augustine, in all appearance the worst in the province, is far from being unfruitful; it produces two crops of Indian corn a year; the garden vegetables are in great perfection; the orange and lemon trees grow here, without cultivation, to a larger size, and produce better fruit, than in Spain and Portugal. The inland country towards the hills is extremely rich and fertile, producing spontaneously the fruits, vegetables, and gums, that are common to Georgia and the Carolinas, and is likewise favourable to the rearing of European productions. There is not, on the whole continent of America, any place better qualified by nature to afford not only all the necessaries of life, but also all the pleasures of habitation, than that part of this country which lies upon the banks of the Missisippi.

From the climate of Florida, and some specimens sent home, there is reason to expect, that cotton, sugar, wine, and silk, will grow here as well as in Persia, India, and China, which are in the same latitudes. This country also produces rice, indigo, ambergris, cochineal, amethysts, turquoises, lapis lazuli, and other precious stones; copper, quicksilver, pit-coal, and iron ore: pearls are found in great abundance on the coast of Florida: mahogany grows on the southern parts of the peninsula, but inferior in size and quality to that of Jamaica. The animal creation are here so numerous, that you may purchase a good saddle-horse in exchange for goods of five shillings value prime cost; and there are instances of horses being exchanged for a hatchet per head.

POPULATION, COMMERCE, ⎱ Notwithstanding the luxu-
AND CHIEF TOWNS. ⎰ riancy of the soil, the salubrity of the air, the cheapness and plenty of provisions, the encouragement of the British government, (See the proclamation) and the wise measures taken by the governors sent thither to settle these provinces, the number of English inhabitants are yet very inconsiderable, and, in all appearance, the increase of population will be here extremely slow, and that proceeding from unavoidable causes.

When we consider the long and destructive wars which the mother country has supported by sea and land against the house

of

of Bourbon; the emigrations to our other settlements in North America, the East and West Indies; the numerous manufactures carrying on at home; and the prodigious shipping employed in transporting these to every corner of the globe; it would appear, that, instead of peopling our colonies, we wanted a supply of hands at home; and, of course, the acquisition of a new territory, without people to plant it, must be an incumbrance to the mother country, especially as the civil and military establishments of both Floridas are said to cost the government near 100,000 l. per annum.

If, for this purpose, we look to the northern colonies of America, we shall find them less able, and the people less disposed to relinquish countries which present them with all the comforts of life in vast abundance, and where they live in affluence, ease, and safety. Is any planter able to improve more ground; or, does the increase of his family and stock require 1000 acres more to his estate? the vast regions behind (for, comparatively speaking, little more than the sea coast of North America is yet cleared and inhabited by Europeans) present themselves to his view. For a penny an acre in some places, and a halfpenny in others, annually, he may traverse the forest, chose out the most enchanting situation, upon the banks of a fine navigable river, and fix upon as much ground as he can possibly cultivate. Is he ambitious to become a freeholder? for the value of a suit of clothes he may purchase 500 acres; the fertility of which, in a few years, puts him on a respectable footing with his neighbours, and sometimes gives him a seat in the council of the people.

It has been therefore hinted, that the chief advantage to be derived to Great-Britain from the possession of Florida, arises from its situation; serving as a frontier against the incursions of our enemies: that its ports, situated in the Gulph of Mexico (See the map of North America) will always be a check upon Spain, as it commands the passage between her settlements; for the galeons, and other vessels, in their passage from Vera Cruz in Mexico to the Havannah, are obliged, by reason of their north-east trade winds, to stretch away to the northward, and generally keep as near the coast of Florida as possible. And that in time of war with that nation, or her ally the French, the harbours of Florida are most commodiously situated for a place of rendezvous and refreshment to the royal navy sent to protect our own West-India islands, or attack those belonging to France and Spain.

But these advantages, great as they are, seem totally eclipsed, when we consider the situation of Florida in a commercial view; for though hitherto, while in a wild, uncultivated state,

its

Its productions have entered very little into the general scale of British commerce, we have still a prospect of establishing and carrying on a trade with the Spanish colonies; it being certain that a regular intercourse might be established with them, which would open a vent for the commodities of Great Britain and yield returns for them in gold and silver, the most profitable of all kinds of commerce.

The chief town in West Florida is Pensacola, which is seated within the bay of the same name, on a sandy shore that can only be approached by small vessels. The road is, however, one of the best in all the gulph of Mexico, in which vessels may lie in safety against every kind of wind, being surrounded by land on every side. This place sends, in skins, logwood, dying stuffs, and silver in dollars, to the annual value of 63,000 l. and receives of our manufactures, at an average of three years, to the value of 97,000 l.

St. Augustine, the capital of East Florida, runs along the shore, and is of an oblong form, divided by four regular streets, crossing each other at right angles. The town is fortified with bastions, and enclosed with a ditch. It is likewise defended by a castle, which is called Fort St. John; and the whole is well furnished with cannon. At the entrance into the harbour are the north and south breakers, which form two channels, whose bars, at low tides, have eight feet water. Our exports to St. Augustine amount to little more than 7000 l. per annum; its exports have hitherto been nothing more than the produce of some little trade carried on with the Indians.

The low state of commerce in Florida arises from this, that no European nation had, before the conclusion of the late war, made it an object of attention; but since that period, its importance becomes more known. Its climate and soil are extremely favourable for the raising of silk. Some attempts indeed have been made in Carolina and Georgia, where in one place the raising of silk is become a kind of staple commodity; but there the worms are often injured by the cold mornings, at other times they are benumbed and made sickly for want of warmth, and sometimes actually destroyed; an inconvenience which is also frequently experienced in Italy: but the more southern climate of Florida has placed this tender insect beyond the reach of such disasters; and experience will shew, that the air and climate of this country is as favourable to the silk-worm as it is to the mulberry-tree on which it feeds, and which grows here in its utmost luxuriancy. The numerous vines too, which grow up spontaneously in the forests of this country, seem to invite us to cultivate the grape, and to

prog-

prognosticate, that the produce of Florida may, with proper
cultivation, gladden the heart of Britons in future ages.

We have already mentioned the difficulty of peopling this
country from Great Britain or her colonies, but, with suitable
encouragement from government, foreigners might be invited
thither, such as Germans from the Rhine, Moselle, and other
parts where they cultivate vineyards; protestants from the
south of France, used to the culture of silk, olives, &c. Greeks
from the Levant, who are groaning under the Turkish yoke,
and are an industrious people, well skilled in the cultivation of
cotton, vines, raisins, currants, olives, almonds, and silk-
worms; for which the climate of Florida is so well adapted.
And herein may be perceived the value of this country to
Great Britain; for though from the variety of climates in the
extensive empire of British America, reaching in a direct line
from the frozen wilds of Labrador, where the hardy inhabitants, cloathed in furs, wander amidst eternal snow, to the
sultry regions within the tropics, where, seated in the heart of
a luxuriant soil, the wealthy planter shelters himself from the
scorching sun by the spreading umbrella; we command a much
greater number of articles of commerce and the conveniencies
of life than any nation on earth, yet it is to Florida that we
must look for silk, wine, and some other articles, and these
too of the best sorts, which hitherto we purchased, and do
still purchase in immense quantities, from different powers of
Europe and Asia; nor can a rich and trading nation possibly
be without them, as we daily experience from the quantity of
treasure sent annually to China for silk.

To what has been observed respecting the climate, soil, and
produce of Florida, we shall take the liberty to give the following extracts from some letters of a gentleman who went to
St. Augustine about the year 1764, in a consumptive state of
health.

May 15, 1767. " I am much obliged to you for your
enquiry after my health; I have agreed with Florida extremely
well: indeed this country is in general very healthy, and till
last autumn we had no sick here, and then our sickness was
not mortal, although very much so in every other part of
America. I believe my friends do not know that we are so
near Charles-Town, and that we have not only a water but a
land communication with that place. Sending letters by the
packet is very tedious, as they must go round by the West-
Indies."

April 16, 1768. " You cannot conceive how agreeable it
is for people in such an exotic country as this, to receive a
European letter. This country, in all probability, will make
a figure

a figure foon, as a number of gentlemen of confiderable property, both from England and Scotland, have obtained orders from his majefty for grants of land in this province, and are now bufy in forming plantations. Between 6 and 700 working flaves are already in the colony of Eaft Florida."

And in a third letter, received in 1770, there is the following intelligence. " This goes by a veffel of Mr. ————, which arrived here fome time ago with a cargo of flaves from the coaft of Africa ; fhe fails from this to-morrow directly for your port of London, and carries our firft produce to that market, viz. between 8 and 9000 weight of indigo, fome cotton, rice, and deer-fkins ; likewife fome fhip-timber, by way of trial. This province bids fair to exceed all the other American provinces in the article of indigo, as the plant ftands the winter, that is fhoots up from the old roots in the fpring ; by which means we have a full cutting more than they have to the northward. Our quantity this year is fmall, but the quality remarkably good. Some of our planters have vanity enough to think they are entitled to the medal given by the Society for the Encouragement of Arts, &c. and have applied for it accordingly."

WEST INDIES.

WE have already obferved, that between the two continents of America, lie an innumerable multitude of iflands, which we call the Weft Indies, and which, fuch as are worth cultivation, now belong to five European powers, as Great Britain, Spain, France, Holland, and Denmark. As the climate and feafons of thefe iflands differ widely from what we can form any idea of, from what we perceive at home, we fhall, to avoid repetitions, fpeak of them in general, as well as fome other particulars that are peculiar to the Weft-Indies.

The climate in all our Weft India iflands, is nearly the fame, allowing for thofe accidental differences which the feveral fituations and qualities of the lands themfelves produce. As they lie within the tropics, and that the fun goes quite over their heads, paffing beyond them to the north, and never returning further from any of them than about 30 degrees to the fouth, they are continually fubjected to the extreme of an heat, which would be intolerable, if the trade wind, rifing gradually as the fun gathers ftrength, did not blow in upon them from the fea, and refrefh the air in fuch a manner, as to enable them to attend their concerns even under the meridian sun. On the other hand, as the night advances, a breeze begins to be perceived, which blows smartly from the land, as it were from its center, towards the sea, to all points of the compass at once.

By the same remarkable Providence in the disposing of things, it is, that when the sun has made a great progress towards the tropic of Cancer, and becomes in a manner vertical, he draws after him such a vast body of clouds, as shield them from his direct beams; and dissolving into rain, cool the air, and refresh the country, thirsty with the long drought, which commonly reigns from the beginning of January to the latter end of May.

The rains in the West Indies (and we may add in the East Indies) are by no means so moderate as with us. Our heaviest rains are but dews comparatively. They are rather floods of water, poured from the clouds with a prodigious impetuosity; the rivers rise in a moment; new rivers and lakes are formed, and in a short time all the low country is under water *. Hence it is, that the rivers which have their source within the tropics, swell and overflow their banks at a certain season; and so mistaken were the antients in their idea of the torrid zone, which they imagined to be dried and scorched up, with a continual and fervent heat, and to be for that reason uninhabitable: when in reality, some of the largest rivers of the world have their course within its limits, and the moisture is one of the greatest inconveniences of the climate in several places.

The rains make the only distinction of seasons in the West Indies; the trees are green the whole year round; they have no cold, no frosts, no snows, and but rarely some hail; the storms of hail are, however, very violent when they happen, and the hailstones very great and heavy. Whether it be owing to this moisture, which alone does not seem to be a sufficient cause, or to a greater quantity of a sulphureous acid, which predominates in the air of this country, metals of all kinds, that are subject to the action of such causes, rust and canker in a very short time: and this cause, perhaps as much as the heat itself, contributes to make the climate of the West Indies unfriendly and unpleasant to an European constitution.

It is in the rainy season (principally in the month of August, more rarely in July and September) that they are assaulted by hurricanes; the most terrible calamity to which they are subject (as well as the people in the East Indies) from

---

* See Wafer's Journey across the Isthmus of Darien, in Vol. II. of the Collection of Voyages and Travels, advertised at the end of this book.

from the climate; this deftroys, at a ftroke, the labours of many years, and proftrates the moft exalted hopes of the planter, and often juft at the moment when he thinks himfelf out of the reach of fortune. It is a fudden and violent ftorm of wind, rain, thunder, and lightning, attended with a furious fwelling of the feas, and fometimes with an earthquake; in fhort, with every circumftance, which the elements can affemble, that is terrible and deftructive. Firft, they fee as the prelude to the enfuing havock, whole fields of fugar canes whirled into the air, and fcattered over the face of the country. The ftrongeft trees of the foreft are torn up by the roots, and driven about like ftubble; their windmills are fwept away in a moment; their utenfils, the fixtures, the ponderous copper boilers, and ftills of feveral hundred weight, are wrenched from the ground, and battered to pieces; their houfes are no protection, the roofs are torn off at one blaft; whilft the rain, which in an hour rifes five feet, rufhes in upon them with an irrefiftible violence.

The hurricane comes on either in the quarters, or at the full change of the moon. If it comes at the full moon, obferve thefe figns. That day you will fee the fky very turbulent; you will obferve the fun more red than at other times; you will perceive a dead calm, and the hills clear of all thofe clouds and mifts which ufually hover about them. In the clefts of the earth, and in the wells, you hear a hollow rumbling found, like the rufhing of a great wind. At night the ftars feem much larger than ufual, and furrounded with a fort of burs; the north-weft fky has a black and menacing look; the fea emits a ftrong fmell, and rifes into vaft waves, often without any wind; the wind itfelf now forfakes its ufual fteady eafterly ftream, and fhifts about to the weft; from whence it fometimes blows with intermiffions violently and irregularly for about two hours at a time. The moon herfelf is furrounded with a great bur, and fometimes the fun has the fame appearance. Thefe are figns which the Indians of thefe iflands taught our planters, by which they can prognofticate the approach of an hurricane.

The grand ftaple commodity of the Weft Indies is fugar; this commodity was not at all known to the Greeks and Romans, though it was made in China, in very early times, from whence we had the firft knowledge of it; but the Portuguefe were the firft who cultivated it in America, and brought it into requeft, as one of the materials of a very univerfal luxury in Europe. It is not fettled whether the cane, from which this fubftance is extracted, be a native of America, or brought thither to their colony of Brazil, by the Portuguefe, from India and the coast of Africa (fee Vol. II. page 322) but, however the matter may be, in the beginning they made the moſt, as they ſtill do the beſt ſugars which come to market in this part of the world. The juice within the ſugar-cane is the moſt lively, elegant, and leaſt cloying ſweet in nature; and which, ſucked raw, has proved extremely nutritive and wholeſome. From the molaſſes rum is diſtilled, and from the ſcummings of the ſugar, a meaner ſpirit is procured. Rum finds its market in North America (where it is conſumed by the Engliſh inhabitants, or employed in the Indian trade, or diſtributed from thence to the fiſhery of Newfoundland, and the African commerce; beſides what comes to Great-Britain and Ireland. However, a very great quantity of molaſſes is taken off raw, and carried to New-England, to be diſtilled there. The tops of the canes, and the leaves which grow upon the joints, make very good provender for their cattle, and the refuſe of the cane, after grinding, ſerves for fire ; ſo that no part of this excellent plant is without its uſe.

They compute that, when things are well managed, the rum and molaſſes pay the charges of the plantation, and the ſugars are clear gain. However, by the particulars we have ſeen, and by others which we may eaſily imagine, the expences of a plantation in the Weſt-Indies are very great, and the profits at the firſt view precarious ; for the chargeable articles of the wind-mill, the boiling, cooling, and diſtilling houſes, and the buying and ſubſiſting a ſuitable number of ſlaves and cattle, will not ſuffer any man to begin a ſugar plantation of any conſequence, not to mention the purchaſe of the land, which is very high, under a capital of at leaſt 5000 l. Neither is the life of a planter, if he means to acquire a fortune, a life of idleneſs and luxury ; at all times he muſt keep a watchful eye upon his overſeers, and even overſee himſelf occaſionally. But at the boiling ſeaſon, if he is properly attentive to his affairs, no way of life can be more laborious, and more dangerous to the health ; from a conſtant attendance day and night, in the extreme united heats of the climate, and ſo many fierce furnaces ; add to this, the loſſes by hurricanes, earthquakes, and bad ſeaſons; and then conſider when the ſugars are in the caſk, that he quits the hazard of a planter, to engage in the hazards of a merchant, and ſhips his produce at his own riſk. Theſe conſiderations might make one believe, that it could never anſwer to engage in this buſineſs; but, notwithſtanding all this, there are no parts of the world, in which great eſtates are made in ſo ſhort a time, from the produce of the earth, as in the Weſt-Indies. The produce of a few good ſeaſons, generally provide againſt the ill effects of the worst, as the planter is sure of a speedy and profitable market for his produce, which has a readier sale than perhaps any other commodity in the world.

Large plantations are generally under the care of a manager, or chief overseer, who has commonly a salary of 150 l. a year, with overseers under him in proportion to the greatness of the plantation, one to about thirty negroes, and at the rate of about 40 l. Such plantations too have a surgeon at a fixed salary, employed to take care of the negroes which belong to it. But the course which is the least troublesome to the owner of the estate is, to let the land, with all the works, and the stock of cattle and slaves, to a tenant, who gives security for the payment of the rent, and the keeping up repairs and stock. The estate is generally estimated to such a tenant at half the neat produce of the best years; such tenants, if industrious and frugal men, soon make good estates for themselves.

The negroes in the plantations are subsisted at a very easy rate. This is generally by alloting to each family of them a small portion of land, and allowing them two days in the week, Saturday and Sunday, to cultivate it: some are subsisted in this manner, but others find their negroes with a certain portion of Guinea or Indian corn, and to some a salt herring, or a small portion of bacon or salt pork a day. All the rest of the charge consists in a cap, a shirt, a pair of breeches, stockings and shoes; the whole not exceeding 40 s. a year, and the profit of their labour yields 10 or 12 l. The price of men negroes upon their first arrival is from 30 to 36 l. women and grown boys about 50 s. less; but such negro families as are acquainted with the business of the islands generally bring above 40 l. upon an average one with another, and there are instances of a single negro man expert in business bringing 150 guineas, and the wealth of a planter is generally computed from the number of slaves he possesses.

To particularize the commodities proper for the West-India market, would be to enumerate all the necessaries, conveniences, and luxuries of life; for they have nothing of their own but cotton, coffee, tropical fruits, spices, and the commodities I have already mentioned.

Traders there make a very large profit upon all they sell, but from the numerous shipping constantly arriving from Europe, and a continual succession of new adventurers, each of whom carrying out more or less as a venture, the West India market is frequently overstocked; money must be raised, and goods are sometimes sold at prime cost or under. But those who can afford to store their goods, and wait for a better

market,

market, acquire fortunes equal to any of the planters. All kinds of handicraftfmen, efpecially carpenters, bricklayers, braziers and coopers, get very great encouragement. But it is the misfortune of the Weft Indies, that phyficians and furgeons even outdo the planter and merchant, in accumulating riches.

Before the late war, there were allowed to be in our Weft Indies at leaft 230,000 negro flaves; and, upon the higheft calculation, the whites there in all did not amount to 90,000 fouls. This difproportion between the freemen and negroes, which grows more vifible every day, fome writers have endeavoured to account for, by alledging, that the enterprizing fpirit, which the novelty of the object, and various concurrent caufes, had produced in the laft century, has decayed very much. That the difpofition of the Weft Indians themfelves, who for cheapnefs choofe to do every thing by negroes, which can poffibly be done by them, contributes greatly to the fmall number of whites of the lower ftations. Such indeed is the powerful influence of avarice, that though the whites are kept in conftant terror of infurrections and plots, many families employ 25 or 30 negroes as menial fervants, who are infinitely the moft dangerous of the flaves, and in cafe of any infurrection, they have it more in their power to ftrike a fudden and fatal blow.

The firft obfervation we think is not well founded; that enterprizing fpirit which firft led Britons out to difcovery, and colonization, ftill animates in a very confiderable degree, the people of this nation, but the field is now more ample and enlarged; emigrants have greater fcope whereon to range; the Britifh empire extends with incredible ftrides. Befides the vaft continent of North America, which takes in fuch a variety of climates; difcovers fuch richnefs of foil; where the people live under various modes of religion, laws and government, and all admirably fuited to Britifh tempers; the Eaft Indies, an inexhauftible mine of riches, begins to draw the attention of mankind from that of the Weft. Countries, as well as individuals, attain a name and reputation for fomething extraordinary, and have their day. Thither many of the beft families of this nation, are ambitious of procuring places for their fons in the army, or the compting-houfe. Here is an ample field for all adventurous fpirits, who, difdaining an idle life at home, and ambitious of becoming ufeful to themfelves, their connections, or the community, boldly venture into the immenfe regions of this eaftern world. Others, full as remote from an indolent difpofition, but with lefs conduct and inferior abilities, fet out with the moft sanguine hopes. These are your fiery, restless tempers, willing to undertake the severest labour, provided it promises but a short continuance, who love risk and hazard, whose schemes are always vast, and who put no medium between being great and being undone.

THE islands of the West Indies lie in the form of a bow, or semicircle, stretching almost from the coast of Florida north, to the river Oronoque, in the main continent of South America. Some call them the Caribbees, from the first inhabitants ; though this is a term that most geographers confine to the Leeward Islands. Sailors distinguish them into Windward and Leeward Islands, with regard to the usual courses of ships, from Old Spain, or the Canaries, to Carthagena, or New Spain and Portobello. The geographical tables and maps, distinguish them into the great and little Antilles.

JAMAICA.] The first that we come to belonging to Great Britain, and also the most important, after leaving Florida, is Jamaica, which lies between the 75th and 79th degrees of west longitude from London, and between 17 and 18 north latitude. From the east and west it is in length about 140 miles, and in the middle about 60 in the breadth, growing less towards each end, in the form of an egg. It lies near 4500 miles south-west of England.

This island is intersected with a ridge of steep rocks tumbled by the frequent earthquakes in a stupendous manner upon one another. These rocks, though containing no soil on their surface, are covered with a great variety of beautiful trees, flourishing in a perpetual spring ; they are nourished by the rains, which often fall, or the mists which continually brood on the mountains, and which, their roots penetrating the crannies of the rocks, industriously seek out for their own support. From the rocks issue a vast number of small rivers of pure wholesome water which tumble down in cataracts, and together with the stupendous height of the mountains, and the bright verdure of the trees through which they flow, form a most delightful landscape. On each side of this great chain of mountains, are ridges of lower ones, which diminish as they remove from it. On these coffee grows in great plenty. The vallies or plains between these ridges, are level beyond what is ordinary in most other countries, and the soil is prodigiously fertile.

The longest day in summer is about thirteen hours, and the shortest in winter about eleven; but the most usual divisions of the seasons in the West Indies, are into the dry and wet seasons.

The

The air of this island is, in moſt places, exceſſive hot and un-favourable to European conſtitutions; but the cool ſea breezes, which ſet in every morning at ten o'clock, render the heat more tolerable : and the air upon the high grounds is temperate, pure, and cooling. It lightens almoſt every night, but without much thunder, which when it happens is very terrible, and roars with aſtoniſhing loudneſs, and the lightning in theſe violent ſtorms, frequently does great damage. In February or March, they expect earthquakes, of which we ſhall ſpeak hereafter. During the months of May and October, the rains are extremely violent, and continue ſometimes for a fortnight together. In the plains are found ſeveral ſalt fountains; and in the mountains, not far from Spaniſh Town, is a hot bath, of great medicinal virtues. It gives relief in the dry belly-ach, which excepting the bilious and yellow fever, is one of the moſt terrible endemial diſtempers of Jamaica.

Sugar is the greateſt and moſt valuable production of this iſland. Cocoas were formerly cultivated in it to great extent. It produces alſo ginger, and the piemento, or as it is called Jamaica Pepper; the wild cinnamon tree, whoſe bark is ſo uſeful in medicine; the manchineel, whoſe fruit, though un-commonly delightful to the eye, contains one of the worſt poiſons in nature; the mohogany, in ſuch uſe with our cabi-net-makers, and of the moſt valuable quality, but this wood begins to wear out, and of late is very dear. Excellent cedars of a large ſize and durable; the cabbage-tree, remarkable for the hardneſs of its wood, which when dry is incorruptible, and hardly yields to any kind of tool; the palma, affording oil, much eſteemed by the ſavages, both in food and medicine; the ſoap-tree, whoſe berries anſwer all purpoſes of waſhing; the mangrove and olive bark, uſeful to tanners; the fuſtic and redwood to the dyers; and lately the logwood. The indigo plant was formerly much cultivated; and the cotton-tree is ſtill ſo. No ſort of European grain grow here; they have only maize, or Indian corn, Guinea corn, peas of various kinds, but none of them reſembling ours, with variety of roots. Fruit, as has been already obſerved, grow in great plenty; citrons, ſeville and china oranges, common and ſweet lemons, limes, ſhadocks, pomegranates, mamees, ſourſops, papas, pine-apples, cuſtard apples, ſtar apples, prickly pears, allicada pears, melons, pompions, guavas, and ſeveral kinds of berries, alſo garden ſtuffs in great plenty and good. The cattle bred on this iſland are but few; their beef is tough and lean; the mutton and lamb are tolerable; they have great plenty of hogs, many plantations have hundreds of them, and their fleſh is exceeding ſweet and delicate. Their horſes are

4   ſmall,

small, mettlefome and hardy; and when well made generally fell for 30 or 40 l. fterling. Jamaica likewife fupplies the apothecary with guaiacum, farfaparilla, China, caffia, and tamarinds. Among the animals are the land and fea turtle, and the alligator. Here are all forts of fowl, wild and tame, and in particular more parrots than in any of the other iflands; befides parrokets, pelicans, fnipes, teal, Guinea hens, geefe, ducks and turkies; the humming-bird, and a great variety of others. The rivers and bays abound with fifh. The mountains breed numberlefs adders, and other noxious animals, as the fens and marfhes do the guana and gallewafp; but thefe laft are not venomous. Among the infects are the ciror, or chegoe, which eats into the nervous and membraneous parts of the flefh of the negroes, and the white people are fometimes plagued with them. Thefe infects get into any part of the body, but chiefly the legs and feet, where they breed in great numbers, and fhut themfelves up in a bag. As foon as the perfon feels them, which is not perhaps till a week after they have been in the body, they pick them out with a needle, or the point of a penknife, taking care to deftroy the bag entirely, that none of the breed, which are like nits, may be left behind. They fometimes get into the toes, and eat the flefh to the very bone.

This ifland was originally a part of the Spanifh empire in America. Several defcents had been made upon it by the Englifh, prior to 1656; but it was not till this year, that Jamaica was reduced under our dominion. Cromwell had fitted out a fquadron, under Pen and Venables, to reduce the Spanifh ifland of Hifpaniola, but there this fquadron was unfuccefsful. The commanders, of their own accord, to atone for this misfortune, made a defcent on Jamaica, and having carried the capital St. Jago, foon compelled the whole ifland to furrender. Ever fince it has been fubject to the Englifh, and the government of it is one of the richeft places, next to that of Ireland, in the difpofal of the crown, the ftanding falary being 2,500 l. per annum, and the affembly commonly voting the governor as much more, which, with the other perquifites, make it on the whole little inferior to 10,000 l. per annum.

We have already obferved, that the government of all the American iflands is the fame, namely, that kind, which we have formerly defcribed under the name of a royal government. Their religion too is univerfally of the church of England; tho' they have no bifhop, the bifhop of London's commiffary being the chief religious magiftrate in thofe parts.

About the beginning of this century, it was computed, that the numbers of whites in Jamaica amounted to 60,000, and

D d 4

that

that of the negroes to 120,000. It appears at prefent that Jamaica is rather on the decline, as is the number of inhabitants, the whites not exceeding 25,000, and the blacks 90,000. Befides thefe, a number of fugitive negroes have formed a fort of colony among the blue mountains, independant of the whites, with whom they make treaties, and are in fome refpects ufeful to the inhabitants of the ifland, particularly in fending back run-a-way flaves.

Indigo was once very greatly cultivated in Jamaica, and it enriched the ifland to fo great a degree, that in the parifh of Vere, where this drug was chiefly cultivated, they are faid to have had no lefs than 300 gentlemen's coaches; a number I do not imagine even the whole ifland exceeds at this day; and there is great reafon to believe, that there were many more perfons of property in Jamaica formerly than are now, though perhaps they had not thofe vaft fortunes, which dazzle us in fuch a manner at prefent. However, the Jamaicans were undoubtedly very numerous, until reduced by earthquakes, and by terrible epidemical difeafes, which, treading on the heels of the former calamities, fwept away vaft multitudes. The decreafe of inhabitants, as well as the decline of their commerce, arifes from the difficulties to which their trade is expofed, of which they do not fail to complain to the court of Great Britain: as that they are of late deprived of the moft beneficial part of their trade, the carrying of negroes and dry goods to the Spanifh coaft; the low value of their produce, which they afcribe to the great improvements the French make in their fugar colonies, which are enabled to underfel them by the lownefs of their duties, the trade carried on from Ireland, and the northern colonies, to the French and Dutch iflands, where they pay no duties, and are fupplied with goods at an eafier rate. Some of thefe complaints, which equally affect the other iflands, have been heard, others ftill remain unredreffed. Both the logwood trade, and this contraband have been the fubjects of much contention, and the caufe of a war between Great Britain, and the Spanifh nation. The former we always avowed, and claimed as our right; and was at the laft peace confirmed to us. The latter we permitted; becaufe we thought, and very juftly, that if the Spaniards found themfelves aggrieved by any contraband trade, it lay upon them, and not upon us, to put a ftop to it, by their guarda coftas, which cruize in thefe feas, purpofely to feize and confifcate fuch veffels and cargoes, as are found in this trade. In this manner did the Britifh court argue, till of late, when the politics of this nation, in compliance with the court of Spain, thought proper to fend Englifh cruizers, to the American coaft, coaſt, effectually to cruſh that lucrative trade, of which the whole body of Britiſh ſubjects in America have complained, as it put a ſtop to the principal channel which hitherto enabled them to remit ſo largely to Great Britain.

Port Royal was formerly the capital of Jamaica. It ſtood upon the point of a narrow neck of land, which, towards the ſea, formed part of the border of a very fine harbour of its own name. The conveniency of this harbour, which was capable to contain a thouſand ſail of large ſhips, and of ſuch depth as to allow them to load and unload at the greateſt eaſe, weighed ſo much with the inhabitants, that they choſe to build their capital on this ſpot, though the place was a hot dry ſand, and produced none of the neceſſaries of life, not even freſh water. But the advantage of its harbour, and the reſort of pirates, made it a place of great conſideration. Theſe pirates were called Buccaneers, they fought with an inconſiderate bravery, and then ſpent their fortune in this capital with as inconſiderate diſſipation. About the beginning of the year 1692, no place, for its ſize, could be compared to this town for trade, wealth, and an entire corruption of manners. In the month of June, in this year, an earthquake, which ſhook the whole iſland to the foundations, totally overwhelmed this city, as to leave, in one quarter, not even the ſmalleſt veſtige remaining. In two minutes, the earth opened and ſwallowed up nine-tenths of the houſes, and two thouſand people. The water guſhed out from the openings of the earth, and tumbled the people on heaps; but ſome of them had the good fortune to catch hold of beams and rafters of houſes, and were afterwards ſaved by boats. Several ſhips were caſt away in the harbour; and the Swan frigate, which lay in the dock to careen, was carried over the tops of ſinking houſes, and did not overſet, but afforded a retreat to ſome hundreds of people, who ſaved their lives upon her. An officer, who was in the town at this time, ſays, the earth opened and ſhut very quick in ſome places, and he ſaw ſeveral people ſink down to the middle, and others appeared with their heads juſt above ground, and were ſqueezed to death. At Savannah, above a thouſand acres were ſunk, with the houſes and people in them; the place appearing for ſome time like a lake, was afterwards dried up, but no houſes were ſeen. In ſome parts, mountains were ſplit; and at one place a plantation was removed to the diſtance of a mile. They again rebuilt the city, but it was a ſecond time, ten years after, deſtroyed by a great fire. The extraordinary convenience of the harbour, tempted them to build it once more; and once more, in 1722, was it laid in rubbiſh by a hurricane, the moſt terrible on record,

Such

Such repeated calamities feemed to mark out this place as a devoted fpot; the inhabitants therefore refolved to forfake it for ever, and to refide at the oppofite bay, where they built Kingfton, which is lately become the capital of the ifland. It confifts of upwards of one thoufand houfes, many of them handfomely built, and in the tafte of thefe iflands, as well as the neighbouring continent, one ftory high, with porticos, and every conveniency for a comfortable habitation in that climate. Not far from Kingfton, ftands St. Jago de la Vega, a Spanifh town, which, though at prefent inferior to Kingfton, was once the capital of Jamaica, and is ftill the feat of government, and the place where the courts of juftice are held.

The whole product of the ifland may be reduced to thefe heads. Firft, fugars, of which they exported in 1753, twenty thoufand three hundred and fifteen hogfheads, fome vaftly great, even to a tun weight, which cannot be worth lefs in England than 424,725l. Moft of this goes to London, Briftol, and Glafgow, and fome part of it to North America, in return for the beef, pork, cheefe, corn, peas, ftaves, planks, pitch, and tar, which they have from thence. Second, rum, of which they export about four thoufand puncheons. The rum of this ifland is generally efteemed the beft, and is the moft ufed in Great Britain. Third, molaffes, in which they make a great part of their returns for New England, where there are vaft diftilleries. All thefe are the produce of the grand ftaple the fugar cane. Fourth, cotton, of which they fend out two thoufand bags. The indigo, formerly much cultivated, is now inconfiderable, but fome cocoa and coffee are exported, with a confiderable quantity of pepper, ginger, drugs for dyers and apothecaries, fweetmeats, mohogany, and manchincel planks. But fome of the moft confiderable articles of their trade are with the Spanifh continent of New Spain and Terra Firma, for in the former they cut great quantities of logwood, and both in the former and latter they did drive a vaft and profitable trade in negroes, and all kinds of European goods. And even in time of war with Spain, this trade between Jamaica and the Spanifh Main goes on, which it will be impoffible for Spain to ftop, whilft it is fo profitable to the Britifh merchant, and whilft the Spanifh officers, from the higheft to the loweft, fhew fo great a refpect to prefents properly made. Upon the whole, many of the people of Jamaica, whilft they appear to live in fuch a ftate of luxury, as in moft other places leads to beggary, acquire great fortunes in a manner inftantly. Their equipages, their cloaths, their furniture, their tables, all bear the tokens of the greateft wealth and profufion imaginable. This obliges all the treafure they

receive,

receive, to make but a very short stay, being hardly more than sufficient to answer the calls of their necessity and luxury on Europe and North America.

On Sundays, or court time, gentlemen wear wigs, and appear very gay in coats of silk, and vests trimmed with silver. At other times they generally wear only thread stockings, linen drawers, a vest, a Holland cap, and a hat upon it. Men servants wear a coarse linen frock, with buttons at the neck and hands, long trowfers of the same, and a check shirt. The negroes, except those who attend gentlemen, who have them dressed in their own livery, have once a year Osnaburghs, and a blanket for cloathing, with a cap or handkerchief for the head. The morning habit of the ladies is a loose night-gown, carelessly wrapped about them : before dinner they put off their dishabille, and appear with a good grace in all the advantage of a rich and becoming dress.

The common drink of persons in affluent circumstances is Madeira wine mixed with water. Ale and claret are extravagantly dear ; and London porter sells for a shilling per bottle. But the general drink, especially among those of inferior rank, is rum punch, which they call Kill-Devil, because, being frequently drank to excess, it heats the blood, brings on fevers, which in a few hours sends them to the grave, especially those who are just come to the island, which is the reason that so many die here upon their first arrival.

English money is seldom seen here, the current coin being entirely Spanish. There is no place where silver is so plentiful, or has a quicker circulation. You cannot dine for less than a piece of eight, and the common rate of boarding is three pounds per week ; though in the markets beef, pork, fowl and fish, may be bought as cheap as in London ; but mutton sells at nine-pence per pound.

Learning is here at a very low ebb : there are indeed some gentlemen well versed in literature, and who send their children to Great Britain, where they have the advantage of a polite and liberal education ; but the bulk of the people take little care to improve their minds, being generally engaged in trade or riotous dissipation.

The misery and hardships of th negroes is truly moving ; and though great care is taken to make them propagate, the ill treatment they receive so shortens their lives, that instead of increasing by the course of nature, many thousands are annually imported to the West-Indies, to supply the place of those who pine and die by the hardships they receive. They are indeed stubborn and untractable for the most part, and they must be ruled with a rod of iron, but they ought not to

be

be crufhed with it, or to be thought a fort of beafts, without fouls, as fome of their mafters or overfeers do at prefent, tho' fome of thefe tyrants are themfelves the dregs of this nation, and the refufe of the jails of Europe. Many of the negroes, however, who fall into the hands of gentlemen of humanity, find their fituations eafy and comfortable; and it has been obferved, that in North-America, where in general thefe poor wretches are better ufed, there is a lefs wafte of negroes, they live longer, and propagate better. And it feems clear, from the whole courfe of hiftory, that thofe nations which have behaved with the greateft humanity to their flaves, were always beft ferved, and ran the leaft hazard from their rebellions. The flaves, on their firft arrival from the coaft of Guinea, are expofed naked to fale; they are then generally very fimple and innocent creatures, but they foon become roguifh enough; and when they come to be whipped, excufe their faults by the example of the whites. They believe every negro returns to his native country after death. This thought is fo agreeable, that it cheers the poor creatures, and renders the burden of life eafy, which would otherwife to many of them be quite intolerable. They look on death as a bleffing, and it is furprizing to fee with what courage and intrepidity fome of them meet it; they are quite tranfported to think their flavery is near an end, that they fhall revifit their native fhores, and fee their old friends and acquaintance. When a negro is about to expire, his fellow flaves kifs him, and wifh him a good journey, and fend their hearty good wifhes to their relations in Guinea. They make no lamentations; but with a great deal of joy inter his body, believing he is gone home and happy.

BARBADOES.] This ifland, the moft eafterly of all the Caribbees, is fituated in 59 deg. W. lon. and 13 deg. N. lat. It is 21 miles in length, and in breadth 14. When the Englifh, fome time after the year 1625, firft landed here, they found it the moft favage and deftitute place they had hitherto vifited. It had not the leaft appearance of ever having been peopled even by favages. There was no kind of beafts of pafture or of prey, no fruit, no herb, nor root, fit for fupporting the life of man. Yet as the climate was fo good, and the foil appeared fertile, fome gentlemen of fmall fortunes in England, refolved to become adventurers thither. The trees were fo large, and of a wood fo hard and ftubborn, that it was with great difficulty they could clear as much ground as was neceffary for their fubfiftence. By unremitting perfeverance, however, they brought it to yield them a tolerable fupport;
and

and they found that cotton and indigo agreed well with the
foil, and that tobacco, which was beginning to come into
repute in England, anfwered tolerabiy. Thefe profpects, together with the ftorm between the king and parliament, which
was beginning to break out in England, induced many new
adventurers to tranfport themfelves into this ifland. And
what is extremely remarkable, fo great was the increafe of
people in Barbadoes, 25 years after its firft fettlement, that in
1650, it contained more than 50,000 whites, and a much
greater number of negro and Indian flaves; the latter they
acquired by means not at all to their honour ; for they feized
upon all thofe unhappy men, without any pretence, in the
neighbouring iflands, and carried them into flavery. A practice, which has rendered the Caribbee Indians irreconcilable
to us ever fince. They had begun, a little before this, to
cultivate fugar, which foon rendered them extremely wealthy.
The number of the flaves therefore was ftill augmented ; and in
1676, it is fuppofed that their number amounted to 100,000,
which, together with 50,000, make 150,000 on this fmall
fpot ; a degree of population unknown in Holland, in China,
or any other part of the world moft renowned for numbers.
At this time Barbadoes employed 400 fail of fhips, one with
another of 150 tuns, in their trade. Their annual exports
in fugar, indigo, ginger, cotton, and citron-water, was above
350,000l. and their circulating cafh at home was 200,000l.
Such was the increafe of population, trade, and wealth, in
the course of 50 years. But fince that time, this ifland has
been much on the decline, which is to be attributed partly to
the growth of the French fugar colonies, and partly to our
own eftablifhments in the neighbouring ifles. Their numbers
at prefent are faid to be 20,000 whites, and 100,000 flaves.
Their commerce confifts in the fame articles as formerly,
though they deal in them to lefs extent. Their capital is
Bridgetown, where the governor refides, whofe employment
is faid to be worth 5000l. per annum. They have a college
founded and well endowed by colonel Codrington, who was a
native of this ifland. Barbadoes, as well as Jamaica, has
fuffered much by hurricanes, fires, and the plague.

Sт. CHRISTOPHER's.] This ifland, commonly called
by the failors, St. Kitt's, is fituated in 62 deg. W. lon. and
17 deg. N. lat. about 14 leagues from Antigua, and is 20
miles long, and feven broad. It has its name from the famous
Chriftopher Columbus, who difcovered it for the Spaniards.
This nation, however, abandoned it as unworthy of their
attention; and in 1626, it was fettled by the French and
Englifh

Englifh conjunctly; but entirely ceded to us by the peace of Utrecht. Befides cotton, ginger, and the tropical fruits, it generally produces near as much fugar as Barbadoes, and fometimes quite as much. It is computed that this ifland contains 6000 whites, and 36,000 negroes.

ANTIGUA.] Situated in 61 deg. W. lon. and 17 deg. N. lat. is of a circular form, near 20 miles over every way. This ifland, which was formerly thought ufelefs, has now got the ftart of the reft. It has one of the beft harbours in the Weft-Indies, and its capital St. John's, which, before the fire in 1769, was large and wealthy, is the ordinary feat of the governor of the Leeward iflands. Antigua is fuppofed to contain about 7000 whites, and 30,000 flaves.

NEVIS AND MONTSERRAT.] Two fmall iflands, lying between St. Chriftopher's and Antigua, neither of them exceeding 18 miles in circumference, and are faid each to contain 5000 whites and 10,000 flaves. The foil in thefe four iflands is pretty much alike, light and fandy, but notwithftanding fertile in an high degree; and their principal exports are derived from the fugar cane.

BARBUDA.] Situated in 18 deg. N. lat. 35 miles north of Antigua, is 20 miles in length, and 12 in breadth. It is fertile, and has a good road for fhipping, but no direct trade with England. The inhabitants are chiefly employed in hufbandry, and raifing frefh provifions for the ufe of the neighbouring ifles. It belongs to the Codrington family, and the inhabitants amount to about 1500.

ANGUILLA.] Situated in 18 deg. N. lat. 60 miles north-weft of St. Chriftopher's, is about 30 miles long, and 10 broad. This ifland is perfectly level, and the climate nearly the fame with that of Jamaica. The inhabitants, who are not numerous, apply themfelves to hufbandry, and feeding of cattle.

DOMINICA.] Situated in 15 deg. N. lat. and in 61 deg. 24 min. W. lon. lies about half way between Guadalupe and Martinico. It is near 28 miles in length, and 13 in breadth. It got its name from being difcovered by Columbus on a Sunday. The French have always oppofed our fettling here, becaufe it muft cut off their communication, in time of war, between Martinico and Guadalupe. By the laft treaty of peace, however, it was ceded in exprefs terms to the Englifh; but we have derived little advantage from this conqueft, the ifland being at prefent no better than a harbour for the natives of the other Caribbees, who being expelled
their

their own settlements, have taken refuge here. The soil of this island is thin, and better adapted to the rearing of cotton and coffee than sugar; but the sides of the hills bear the finest trees in the West-Indies, and the island is well supplied with rivulets of fine water.

St. VINCENT.] Seated 13 deg. 30 min. north lat. and in 61 deg. west lon. 50 miles north-west of Barbadoes, 30 miles south of St. Lucia, is about 24 miles in length, and 18 in breadth. It is extremely fruitful, being a black mould upon a strong loam, the most proper for the raising of sugar. Indigo thrives here remarkably well, but this article is less cultivated than formerly throughout the West-Indies. It is at present chiefly inhabited by the Caribbeans, and many fugitives from Barbadoes and the other islands, who are now numerous, and have many villages where they are said to live well.

GRANADA and the GRENADINES.] Granada is situated in 12 deg. north lat. and in 61 deg. 40 min. west lon. about 30 leagues south-west of Barbadoes, and almost the same distance north of New-Andalusia, or the Spanish Main. This island is said to be 30 miles in length, and 15 in breadth. Experience has proved that the soil of this island is extremely proper for producing sugar, tobacco, and indigo; and upon the whole it carries with it all the appearance of becoming as flourishing a colony as any in the West Indies, of its dimensions. A lake on the top of a hill in the middle of the island supplies it plentifully with fine rivers, which adorn and fertilize it. Several bays and harbours lie round the island, some of which might be fortified to great advantage, which renders it very convenient for shipping; and it has the happiness of not being subject to hurricanes. Its chief port, called Lewis, has a sandy bottom, and is so capacious and safe, that 1000 vessels from 3 to 400 tun may ride secure from storms; and 100 ships of the greatest burden may be moored in its harbour. This island was long the theatre of bloody wars between the native Indians and the French, during which these handful of Caribbees defended themselves with the most resolute bravery. In the last war, when Granada was attacked by the English, the French inhabitants, who were not very numerous, were so amazed at the reduction of Guadalupe and Martinico, that they lost all spirit, and surrendered without making the least opposition; and the full property of this island, together with the small islands on the north, called the Grenadines, which yield the same produce, were confirmed to the crown of Great Britain by the treaty of peace.

TOBAGO.] The moſt ſoutherly of all the Britiſh iſlands
or ſettlements in America (except Falkland Iſlands, in the
South-Seas) is ſituated 11 deg. odd min. north lat. 120 miles
ſouth of Barbadoes, and about the ſame diſtance from the
Spaniſh Main.   This iſland is about 32 miles in length, and
nine in breadth.   The climate here is not ſo hot as might be
expected ſo near the equator ; and it is ſaid that it lies out of
the courſe of thoſe hurricanes that have ſometimes proved ſo
fatal to the other Weſt-India iſlands.   It has a fruitful ſoil,
capable of producing ſugar, and indeed every thing elſe that
is raiſed in the Weſt Indies, with the addition (if we may
believe the Dutch) of the cinnamon, nutmeg, and gum copal,
all valuable commodities, and which will undoubtedly render
this iſland of vaſt importance and immenſe benefit to Great
Britain.   It is well watered with numerous ſprings ; and its
bays and creeks are ſo diſpoſed as to be very commodious for
all kind of ſhipping.   The value and importance of this iſland
appears from the expenſive and formidable armaments ſent
thither by European powers in ſupport of their different
claims.   It ſeems to have been chiefly poſſeſſed by the Dutch,
who defended their pretenſions againſt both England and
France with the moſt obſtinate perſeverance.   By the treaty of
Aix-la-Chapelle, in 1748, it was declared neutral ; but by
the treaty of peace in 1763, it was yielded up to Great
Britain.

Theſe three laſt mentioned iſlands were ſince the war erected
into one government.

NEWFOUNDLAND.] Excluſive of the Weſt-India
ſugar iſlands lying between the two continents of America,
Great Britain claims ſome others, that are ſeated at the diſtance
of ſome thouſand miles from each other, upon the coaſt of
this quarter of the globe, of which we ſhall ſpeak according
to our method, beginning with the north.

Newfoundland is ſituated to the eaſt of the Gulph of St.
Lawrence, between 46 and 52 deg. north lat. and between 53
and 59 deg. weſt lon. ſeparated from Labrador or New-Britain
by the Straits of Belleiſle, and from Canada by the Bay of
St. Lawrence, being 350 miles long, and 200 broad.   The
coaſts are extremely ſubject to fogs, attended with almoſt continual ſtorms of ſnow and ſleet, the ſky being uſually overcaſt.
From the ſoil of this iſland we are far from reaping any ſudden
or great advantage, for the cold is long continued and ſevere ;
and the ſummer heat, though violent, warms it not enough
to produce any thing valuable ; for the ſoil, at leaſt in thoſe
parts of the iſland with which we are acquainted, is rocky and
I   barren.

barren. However, it is watered by several good rivers, and hath many large and good harbours. This island, whenever the continent shall come to fail of timber convenient to navigation (which on the sea coast perhaps is no very remote prospect) will afford a large supply for masts, yards, and all sorts of lumber for the West-India trade. But what at present it is chiefly valuable for, is the great fishery of cod, carried on upon those shoals which are called the Banks of Newfoundland. Great-Britain and North-America, at the lowest computation, annually employ 3000 sail of small craft in this fishery; on board of which, and on shore to cure and pack the fish, are upwards of 10,000 hands; so that this fishery is not only a very valuable branch of trade to the merchant, but a source of livelihood to so many thousands of poor people, and a most excellent nursery to the royal navy. This fishery is computed to encrease the national stock 300,000 l. a year in gold and silver, remitted to us for the cod we sell in the North, in Spain, Portugal, Italy, and the Levant. The plenty of cod, both on the great bank, and the lesser ones, which lie to the east and south-east of this island, is inconceivable; and not only cod, but several other species of fish, are caught there in abundance; all of which are nearly in an equal plenty along the shores of Newfoundland, New-Scotland, New-England, and the isle of Cape Breton; and very profitable fisheries are carried on upon all their coasts; from which we may observe, that where our colonies are thinly peopled, or so barren as not to produce any thing from their soil, their coasts make us ample amends, and pour in upon us a wealth of another kind, and no way inferior to that arising from the most fertile soil.

This island, after various disputes about the property, was entirely ceded to England by the treaty of Utrecht, in 1713; but the French were left at liberty to dry their nets on the northern shores of the island; and by the treaty of 1763, they were permitted to fish in the Gulph of St. Lawrence, but with this limitation, that they should not approach within three leagues of any of the coasts belonging to England. The small islands of St. Pierre and Miquelon, situated to the southward of Newfoundland, were also ceded to the French, who stipulated to erect no fortifications on these islands, nor to keep more than 50 soldiers to enforce the police. The chief towns in Newfoundland are Placentia, Bonavista, and St. John; but there do not above 1000 families remain here in the winter.

CAPE BRETON.] This island, seated between Newfoundland and Nova-Scotia, is in length about 110 miles. The soil is barren, but it has good harbours, particularly that of Louisburgh, which is near four leagues in circumference, and has every where fix or feven fathoms water. Since the conqueft of this ifland by Great Britain in the late war, France has not one fea port for the relief and fhelter of her trading fhips, either to or from the Weft-Indies, open to them any where in America, to the northward of the river Miffifippi; and confequently their whole trade in the fifhery muft for the future be expofed to the Englifh privateers from the northern colonies in the time of war; a circumftance which may have fome weight with that nation, in rendering them lefs forward to commence hoftilities with Great-Britain.

ST. JOHN's.] Situated in the gulph of St. Lawrence, is about 60 miles in length, and 30 or 40 broad, has many fine rivers, and though lying near Cape-Breton and New-Scotland, has greatly the advantage of both in pleafantnefs and fertility of foil. Upon the reduction of Cape-Breton, the inhabitants of this ifland, amounting to 4000, fubmitted quietly to the Britifh arms; and to the difgrace of the French governor, there were found in his houfe feveral Englifh fcalps, which were brought there to market by the favages of New-Scotland; this being the place where they were encouraged to carry on that barbarous and inhuman trade. This ifland was fo well improved by th French, that it was ftiled the granary of Canada, which it furnifhed with great plenty of corn, as well as beef and pork.

BERMUDAS or SUMMER ISLANDS.] Thefe received their firft name from their being difcovered by John Bermudas, a Spaniard; and were called the Summer Iflands, from Sir George Sommers, who was fhipwrecked on their rocks in 1609, in his paffage to Virginia. They are fituated, at a vaft diftance from any continent, in 32 deg. north lat. and in 65 deg. weft lon. Their diftance from the Land's end is computed near 1500 leagues, from the Madeiras about 1200, and from Carolina 300. The Bermudas are but fmall, not containing in all above 20,000 acres; and are very difficult of accefs, being, as Waller the poet, who refided fome time there, expreffes it, walled with rocks. The air of thefe iflands, which Waller celebrates in one of his poems, has been always efteemed extremely healthful; and the beauty and richnefs of the vegetable productions is perfectly delightful. Though the foil of thefe iflands is admirably adapted to the cultivation of the vines, the chief and only bufinefs of the inhabitants, who confift of about 10,000, is the building and navigating of light floops and brigantines, which they employ chiefly in the trade between North America and the Weft Indies. Thefe veffels are as remarkable for their fwiftnefs, as the cedar of which they are built is for its hard and durable quality.

The town of St. George, which is the capital, is feated at the bottom of a haven in the ifland of the fame name, and is defended with feven or eight forts and feventy pieces of cannon. It contains above 1000 houfes, a handfome church, and other elegant public buildings.

LUCAY's, OR BAHAMA ISLANDS.] The Bahamas are fituated to the fouth of Carolina, between 22 and 27 deg. north lat. and 73 and 81 deg. weft lon. They extend along the coaft of Florida quite down to the Ifle of Cuba; and are faid to be 500 in number, fome of them only mere rocks; but 12 of them are large, fertile, and in nothing different from the foil of Carolina: all are, however, abfolutely uninhabited, except Providence, which is 200 miles eaft of the Floridas, though fome others are larger and more fertile, on which the Englifh have plantations. Between them and the continent of Florida is the Gulph of Bahama, or Florida, through which the Spanifh galeons fail in their paffage to Europe. Thefe iflands were the firft fruits of Columbus's difcoveries; but they were not known to the Englifh till 1667, when captain Seyle, being driven among them in his paffage to Carolina, gave his name to one of them; and being a fecond time driven upon it, gave it the name of Providence. The Englifh, obferving the advantageous fituation of thefe iflands for being a check on the French and Spaniards, attempted to fettle them in the reign of Charles II. Some unlucky accidents prevented this fettlement from being of any advantage, and the Ifle of Providence became an harbour for the Buccaneers or pirates, who for a long time infefted the American navigation. This obliged the government, in 1718, to fend out captain Woodes Rogers with a fleet to diflodge the pirates, and for making a fettlement. This the captain effected; a fort was erected, and an independant company was ftationed in the ifland. Ever fince this laft fettlement thefe iflands have been improving, tho' they advance but flowly. In time of war, people gain confiderably by the prizes condemned there; and at all times by the wrecks, which are frequent in this labyrinth of rocks and fhelves.

FALKLAND ISLANDS.] Leaving the Bahama and Weft-India iflands, we fhall now proceed along the fouth-eaft coaft of America, as far as the 52d deg. of fouth lat. where the reader, by looking into the map, will perceive the Falkland iflands, fituated near the Streights of Magellan, at the utmoft extremity of South-America. It has been generally believed, that the richeft gold mines in Chili are carefully concealed by the Indians, as well knowing that the difcovery of them would only excite in the Spaniards a greater thirft for conqueft and tyranny, and would render their own indepen-

dence

dence more precarious. King Charles II. of England confidered the difcovery of this coaſt of ſuch conſequence, that
Sir John Narborough was purpoſely fitted out to ſurvey the
Streights of Magellan, the neighbouring coaſt of Patagonia,
and the Spaniſh ports in that frontier; with directions, if
poſſible, to procure ſome intercourſe with the Chilian Indians,
who are generally at war, or at leaſt on ill terms with the
Spaniards; and to eſtabliſh a commerce and a laſting correſ-
pondence with them. Though Sir John, through accidental
cauſes, failed in this attempt, which, in appearance, promiſed
ſo many advantages to this nation, his tranſactions upon that
coaſt, beſides the many valuable improvements he furniſhed to
geography and navigation, are rather an encouragement for
further trials of this kind, than any objection againſt them.
It appeared by the precautions and fears of the Spaniards, that
they were fully convinced of the practicability of the ſcheme
he was ſent to execute, and extremely alarmed with the apprehenſion of its conſequences. It is ſaid, that his majeſty king
Charles II. was ſo far prepoſſeſſed with the belief of the emoluments which might redound to the public from this expedition,
and was ſo eager to be informed of the event of it, that,
having intelligence of Sir John Narborough's paſſing through
the Downs, on his return, he had not patience to attend his
arrival at court, but went himſelf in his barge to Graveſend
to meet him.

    " As therefore it appears (ſays the author of Anſon's
Voyage) that all our future expeditions to the South-Seas muſt
run a conſiderable riſk of proving abortive, whilſt in our
paſſage thither we are under the neceſſity of touching at the
Portugueſe ſettlement of Brazil (where we may certainly
depend on having our ſtrength, condition, and deſigns be-
trayed to the Spaniards) the diſcovery of ſome place more to
the ſouthward, where ſhips might refreſh, and ſupply themſelves with the neceſſary ſea-ſtock for their voyage round Cape
Horn, would be an expedient that would relieve us from theſe
embarraſments, and would ſurely be a matter worthy the attention of the public. Nor does this ſeem difficult to be
effected; for we have already the imperfect knowledge of two
places, which might, perhaps, on examination, prove extremely convenient for this purpoſe; one of them is Pepy's
Iſland, in the latitude of 47, ſouth, and laid down by Dr.
Halley about 80 leagues to the eaſtward of Cape Blanco, on
the coaſt of Patagonia; the other is *Falkland's Iſles*, in the
latitude of 51 and a half, lying nearly ſouth of Pepy's Iſland.
The laſt of theſe have been ſeen by many ſhips, both French
and Engliſh. Woodes Rogers, who run along the north-eaſt
coaſt of theſe iſles in the year 1708, tells us that they extended
                                                            about

about two degrees in length, and appeared with gentle defcents from hill to hill, and feemed to be good ground, interfperfed with woods, and not deftitute of harbours. Either of thefe places, as they are iflands at a confiderable diftance from the continent, may be fuppofed, from their latitude, to lie in a climate fufficiently temperate. This, even in time of peace, might be of great confequence to this nation ; and in time of war, would make us mafters of thofe feas."

Falkland iflands were firft difcovered by Sir Richard Hawkins in 1594, the principal of which he named Hawkins Maidenland, in honour of queen Elizabeth. The prefent Englifh name Falkland, was probably given them by captain Strong, in 1689, and being adopted by Halley, it has from that time been received into our maps.

In the year 1764, the late lord Egmont, then firft lord of the admiralty, revived the fcheme of a fettlement in the South-Seas, and commodore Byron was fent to take poffeffion of Falkland iflands in the name of his Britannic majefty, and in his journal reprefents them as a valuable acquifition. On the other hand, they are reprefented by capt. M'Bride, who in 1766 fucceeded that gentleman, as the outcafts of nature. " We found, fays he, a mafs of iflands and broken lands, of which the foil was nothing but a bog, with no better profpect than that of barren mountains, beaten by ftorms almoft perpetual. Yet this is fummer, and if the winds of winter hold their natural proportion, thofe who lie but two cables length from the fhore, muft pafs weeks without any communication with it." The plants and vegetables which were planted by Mr. Byron's people, and the fir-tree, a native of rugged and cold climates, had withered away ; but goats, fheep, and hogs, that were carried thither, were found to thrive and increafe as in other places. Geefe, of a fifhey tafte, fnipes, foxes, fea-lions, penquins, plenty of good water, and in the fummer months, wild falary, and forel, are the natural luxuries of thefe iflands.

But though the foil be barren, and the feas tempeftuous, we have happily fucceeded in the grand object of a fettlement here, by the difcovery of a fine harbour, capable of containing the whole royal navy of England, and fecured from the fury of the winds by furrounding mountains.

By our having the poffeffion of one good harbour here, and keeping the royal navy on a refpectable footing, we fhall have nothing to fear from all the united force of France, Spain, and Portugal. Whoever turns his eye to the map of America, and obferves the number of our fettlements, and their fituation in refpect to the poffeffions of thofe powers, will fee the impoffibility of their trade efcaping the vigilance of our cruifers,

pouring

pouring out from every corner of this new world. Add to
this, that having hitherto attempted their colonies with suc-
cefs, what may we not expect in a future war, from such
additional ftrength, fo many convenient harbours to refit, or
to fupply our fleets and armies.

PROCLAMATION,

*For regulating the Ceffions made to us in America by
the laft Treaty of Peace.*

GEORGE R.

WHEREAS we have taken into our royal confideration
the extenfive and valuable acquifitions in America,
fecured to our crown by the late definitive treaty of peace,
concluded at Paris the 10th day of February laft ; and being
defirous that all our loving fubjects, as well of our kingdoms
as of our colonies in America, may avail themfelves, with all
convenient fpeed, of the great benefits and advantages, which
muft accrue therefrom to their commerce, manufactures, and
navigation ; we have thought fit, with the advice of our privy-
council, to iffue this our royal proclamation, hereby to publifh
and declare to all our loving fubjects, that we have, with the
advice of our faid privy-council, granted our letters patent,
under our great feal of Great-Britain, to erect within the
countries and iflands, ceded and confirmed to us by the faid
treaty, four diftinct and feparate governments, ftiled and
called by the names of Quebec, Eaft-Florida, Weft-Florida,
and Grenada, and limited and bounded as follows, viz.

Firft, The government of Quebec, bounded on the Labrador coaft by the river St. John, and from thence by a line
drawn from the head of that river through the lake St. John
to the fouth end of the lake Nipiffim ; from whence the faid
line, croffing the river St. Lawrence and the lake Champlain
in 45 degrees of north latitude, paffes along the high lands
which divide the rivers that empty themfelves into the faid
river St. Lawrence, from thofe which fall into the fea ;
and alfo along the north coaft of the Bay des Chaleurs, and
the coaft of the Gulph of St. Lawrence to Cape Rofieres,
and from thence croffing the mouth of the river St. Lawrence
by the weft end of the ifland Anticofti, terminates at the aforefaid river of St. John.

Secondly, The government of Eaft-Florida, bounded to the
weftward, by the Gulph of Mexico and the Apalachicola
river ;

river; to the northward, by a line drawn from that part of the said river, where the Chatahouchee and Flint rivers meet, to the source of St. Mary's river; and by the source of the said river to the Atlantic ocean; and to the eastward and southward, by the Atlantic ocean, and the Gulph of Florida, including all islands within six leagues of the sea-coast.

Thirdly, The government of West-Florida, bounded to the southward by the coast of Mexico, including all islands within six leagues of the coast from the river Apalachicola to Lake Pontchartrain; to the westward, by the same lake, the lake Maurepas, and the river Mississippi; to the northward, by a line drawn due east from that part of the river Mississippi which lies in 31 degrees north latitude, to the river Apalachicola or Chatahouchee; and to the eastward by the said river.

Fourthly, The government of Grenada, comprehending the island of that name, together with the Grenadines, and the islands of Dominico, St. Vincent, and Tobago.

And to the end that the open and free fishery of our subjects may be extended to, and carried on upon the coast of Labrador, and the adjacent islands, we have thought fit, with the advice of our said privy-council, to put all that coast, from the river St. John's to Hudson's Streights, together with the islands of Anticosti and Madelaine, and all other smaller islands lying upon the said coast, under the care and inspection of our governor of Newfoundland.

We have also, with the advice of our privy-council, thought fit to annex the islands of St. John, and Cape Breton, or Isle Royale, with the lesser islands adjacent thereto, to our government of Nova Scotia.

We have also, with the advice of our privy-council aforesaid, annexed to our province of Georgia, all the lands lying between the rivers Alatamaha and St. Mary's.

And whereas it will greatly contribute to the speedy settling our said new governments, that our loving subjects should be informed of our paternal care for the security of the liberties and properties of those, who are and shall become inhabitants thereof: we have thought fit to publish and declare, by this our proclamation, that we have, in the letters patent under our great seal of Great-Britain, by which the said governments are constituted, given express power and direction to our governors of our said colonies respectively, that so soon as the state and circumstances of the said colonies will admit thereof, they shall, with the advice and consent of the members of our council, summon and call general assemblies within the said governments respectively, in such manner and form as is used and directed in those colonies and provinces in America, which are under our immediate government; and we have also given power to the said governors, with the confent of our said councils, and the reprefentatives of the people, fo to be fummoned as aforefaid, to make, conftitute, and ordain laws, ftatutes, and ordinances for the public peace, welfare, and good government of our said colonies, and of the people and inhabitants thereof, as near as may be agreeable to the laws of England, and under fuch regulations and reftrictions as are ufed in other colonies; and in the mean time, and until fuch affemblies can be called as aforefaid, all perfons inhabiting in or reforting to our said colonies, may confide in our royal protection for the enjoyment of the benefit of the laws of our realm of England; for which purpofe we have given power under our great feal to the governors of our said colonies refpectively, to erect and conftitute, with the advice of our said councils refpectively, courts of judicature and public juftice within our said colonies, for the hearing and determining all caufes, as well criminal as civil, according to law and equity, and as near as may be agreeable to the laws of England, with liberty to all perfons, who may think themfelves aggrieved by the fentences of fuch courts, in all civil cafes, to appeal, under the ufual limitations and reftrictions, to us, in our privy-council.

We have alfo thought fit, with the advice of our privycouncil as aforefaid, to give unto the governors and councils of our said three new colonies upon the continent, full power and authority to fettle and agree with the inhabitants of our said new colonies, or with any other perfons who fhall refort thereto, for fuch lands, tenements, and hereditaments, as are now, or hereafter fhall be in our power to difpofe of, and them to grant to any fuch perfon or perfons, upon fuch terms, and under fuch moderate quit-rents, fervices, and acknowledgments, as have been appointed and fettled in our other colonies, and under fuch other conditions as fhall appear to us to be neceffary and expedient for the advantage of the grantees, and the improvement and fettlement of our said colonies.

And whereas we are defirous, upon all occafions, to teftify our royal fenfe and approbation of the conduct and bravery of the officers and foldiers of our armies, and to reward the fame, we do hereby command and impower our governors of our said three new colonies, and all other our governors of our feveral provinces on the continent of North-America, to grant, without fee or reward, to fuch reduced officers as have ferved in North-America during the late war; and to fuch private foldiers as have been or fhall be difbanded in America, and are actually refiding there, and fhall perfonally apply for the fame,

the

the following quantities of lands, fubject, at the expiration of ten years, to the fame quit-rents as other lands are fubject to in the province within which they are granted, as alfo fubject to the fame conditions of cultivation and improvement, viz.

To every perfon having the rank of a field officer, 5000 acres.

To every captain, 3000 acres.

To every fubaltern or ftaff-officer, 2000 acres.

To every non-commiffion officer, 200 acres.

To every private man, 50 acres.

We do likewife authorife and require the governors and commanders in chief of all our faid colonies upon the continent of North-America, to grant the like quantities of land, and upon the fame conditions, to fuch reduced officers of the royal navy of the like rank, as ferved on board our fhips of war in North-America, at the times of the reduction of Louifbourg and Quebec, in the late war, and who fhall perfonally apply to our refpective governors for fuch grants.

And whereas it is juft and reafonable, and effential to our intereft, and the fecurity of our colonies, that the feveral nations or tribes of Indians, with whom we are connected, and who live under our protection, fhould not be molefted or difturbed in the poffeffion of fuch parts of our dominions and territories as not having been ceded to or purchafed by us, are referved to them or any of them as their hunting-grounds; we do therefore, with the advice of our privy-council, declare it to be our royal will and pleafure, that no governor or commander in chief in any of our colonies of Quebec, Eaft-Florida, or Weft-Florida, do prefume, upon any pretence whatever, to grant warrants of furvey, or pafs any patents for lands beyond the bounds of their refpective governments, as defcribed in their commiffions; as alfo that no governor or commander in chief in any of our other colonies or plantations in America, do prefume for the prefent, and until our further pleafure be known, to grant warrants of furvey, or pafs patents for any lands beyond the heads or fources of any of the rivers which fall into the Atlantic Ocean from the weft and north-weft; or upon any lands whatever, which not having been ceded to, or purchafed by us, as aforefaid, are referved to the faid Indians, or any of them.

And we do further declare it to be our royal will and pleafure, for the prefent as aforefaid, to referve under our fovereignty, protection, and dominion, for the ufe of the faid Indians, all the lands and territories not included within the limits of our faid three new governments, or within the limits of the territory granted to the Hudfon's-Bay company; as

also

alfo all the lands and territories lying to the weftward of the
fources of the rivers which fall into the fea from the weft and
north-weft as aforefaid ; and we do hereby ftrictly forbid, on
pain of our difpleafure, all our loving fubjects from making
any purchafes or fettlements whatever, or taking poffeffion of
any of the lands above referved, without our fpecial leave and
licence for that purpofe firft obtained.

And we do further ftrictly enjoin and require all perfons
whatever, who have either wilfully or inadvertently feated
themfelves upon any lands within the countries above defcribed,
or upon any other lands, which not having been ceded to or
purchafed by us, are ftill referved to the faid Indians as aforefaid, forthwith to remove themfelves from fuch fettlements.

And whereas great frauds and abufes have been committed
in the purchafing lands of the Indians, to the great prejudice
of our interefts, and to the great diffatisfaction of the faid
Indians ; In order therefore to prevent fuch irregularities for
the future, and to the end that the Indians may be convinced
of our juftice and determined refolution to remove all reafonable caufe of difcontent, we do, with the advice of our privy-
council, ftrictly enjoyn and require, that no private perfon do
prefume to make any purchafe from the faid Indians of any
lands referved to the faid Indians within thofe parts of our
colonies, where we have thought proper to allow fettlement ;
but that if at any time any of the faid Indians fhould be inclined
to difpofe of the faid lands, the fame only fhould be purchafed
only for us, in our name, at fome public meeting or affembly
of the faid Indians, to be held for that purpofe by the governor
or commander in chief of our colony refpectively, within
which they fhall lie ; and in cafe they fhould lie within the
limits of any proprietary government, they fhall be purchafed
only for the ufe and in the name of fuch proprietors, confor-
mable to fuch directions and inftructions as we or they fhall
think proper to give for that purpofe. And we do, by the
advice of our privy-council, declare and enjoyn, that the trade
with faid Indians fhall be free and open to all our fubjects
whatever ; provided that every perfon, who may incline to
trade with the faid Indians, do take out a licence for carrying
on fuch a trade, from the governor or commander in chief of
any of our colonies refpectively, where fuch perfon fhall refide,
and alfo give fecurity to obferve fuch regulations as we fhall at
any time think fit, by ourfelves or by our commiffaries, to be
appointed for this purpofe, to direct and appoint for the benefit of the faid trade : And we do hereby authorife, enjoyn,
and require the governors and commanders in chief of all our
colonies, refpectively, as well as thofe under our immediate
government,

government, as thofe under the government and direction of proprietaries, to grant fuch licences without fee or reward; taking efpecial care to infert therein a condition that fuch licence fhall be void, and the fecurity forfeited, in cafe the perfon, to whom the fame is granted, fhall refufe or neglect to obferve fuch regulations as we fhall think proper to prefcribe as aforefaid.

And we do further exprefsly enjoin and require all officers whatever, as well military as thofe employed in the management and direction of Indian affairs within the territories referved, as aforefaid, for the ufe of the faid Indians, to feize and apprehend all perfons whatever, who, ftanding charged with treafons, mifprifions of treafons, murders, or other felonies and mifdemeanours, fhall fly from juftice and take refuge in the faid territory, and to fend them under a proper guard to the colony where the crime was committed of which they ftand accufed, in order to take their trial for the fame.

Given at our court in St. James's, the 7th day of October, 1763, in the third year of our reign,

G O D Save the K I N G.

SPANISH DOMINIONS in NORTH AMERICA.

NEW MEXICO, including CALIFORNIA.

SITUATION AND EXTENT.

Miles.   Degrees.

Length 2000 } between { 94 and 126 W. longitude.
Breadth 1600 }   { 23 and 43 N. latitude.

BOUNDARIES.] BOUNDED by unknown lands on the north; by Louifiana, on the eaft; by old Mexico, and the Pacific ocean, on the fouth; and by the fame ocean, on the weft.

Divifions.	Subdivifions.	Chief towns.
North-eaft divifion	New Mexico Proper —	SANTA FE, W. lon. 104. N. lat. 36.
South-eaft divifion	Apacheira	— St. Antonio.
South divifion	Sonora —	— Tuape.
Weft divifion	California, a peninfula—	St. Juan.

. SOIL AND CLIMATE.] Thefe countries lying for the moft part within the temperate zone, have a climate in many places
extremely

extremely agreeable, and a foil productive of every thing, either for profit or delight.   In California however they experience great heats in the summer, particularly towards the seacoaft; but in the inland country, the climate is more temperate, and in winter even cold.

FACE AND PRODUCE OF } The natural hiftory of thefe
    THE COUNTRY.   { countries is as yet in its infancy.
The Spaniards themfelves know little of the matter, and the little they know, they are unwilling to communicate.   Their authority being on a precarious footing with the Indians, who here at leaft ftill preferve their independance; they are jealous of difcovering the natural advantages of thefe countries, which might be an inducement to the other nations of Europe, to form fettlements there.   It is certain, however, that in general the provinces of New Mexico and California, are extremely beautiful and pleafant; the face of the country is agreeably varied with plains, interfected by rivers, and adorned with gentle eminences covered with various kinds of trees, fome producing excellent fruit.   With refpect to the value of the gold mines in thofe countries, nothing pofitive can be afferted. They have undoubtedly enough of natural productions, to render them advantageous colonies to any but the Spaniards. In California there falls in the morning a great quantity of dew, which, fettling on the rofe leaves, candies, and becomes hard like manna, having all the fweetnefs of refined fugar, without its whitenefs.   There is alfo another very fingular natural production.   In the heart of the country there are plains of falt, quite firm and clear as chryftal, which confidering the vaft quantities of fifh found on its coafts, might render it an invaluable acquifition to any induftrious nation.

INHABITANTS, HISTORY, GOVERNMENT, } The Spanifh
    RELIGION AND COMMERCE.   {   fettlements
here are comparatively weak; though they are encreafing every day in proportion as new mines are difcovered.   The inhabitants are chiefly Indians, whom the Spanifh miffionaries have in many places brought over to Chriftianity, to a civilized life, to raife corn and wine, which they now export pretty largely to Old Mexico.   California was difcovered by Cortez, the great conqueror of Mexico; our famous navigator Sir Francis Drake took poffeffion of it in 1578, and his right was confirmed by the principal king, or chief in the whole country. This title however the government of Great-Britain have not hitherto attempted to vindicate, tho' California is admirably fituated for trade, and on its coaft has a pearl fifhery of great value.   The inhabitants and government here do not materially differ from thofe of Old Mexico.

OLD MEXICO or NEW SPAIN.

SITUATION AND EXTENT.

Miles.   Degrees.

Length 2000 } between { 83 and 110 W. longitude.
Breadth 600 }   { 8 and 30 N. latitude.

BOUNDARIES.] **B**OUNDED by New Mexico, or Granada, on the north; by the gulph of Mexico, on the north-eaſt; by Terra Firma, on the ſouth-eaſt; and by the Pacific ocean, on the ſouth-weſt, containing three audiences, viz.

Audiences.	Chief Towns.
1. Galicia or Guadalajarra	Guadalajarra.
2. Mexico Proper ———	MEXICO, W. lon. 102-35. N. lat. 20. Acapulco Vera Cruz.
3. Guatimala —— ——	Guatimala.

BAYS.] On the north-ſea are the gulphs or bays of Mexico, Campeachy, Vera Cruz, and Honduras; in the Pacific ocean, or South-Sea, are the bays Micoya and Amapalla, Acapulco, and Salinas.

CAPES.] Theſe are cape Sardo, cape St. Martin, cape Cornducedo, cape Catoche, cape Honduras, cape Cameron, and cape Gracias Dios, in the North Sea.

Cape Marques, cape Spirito Sancto, cape Corientes, cape Gallero, cape Blanco, cape Burica, cape Prucreos, and cape Mala, in the South-Sea.

WINDS.] In the gulph of Mexico, and the adjacent ſeas, there are ſtrong north winds from October to March, about the full and change of the moon. Trade winds prevail every where at a diſtance from land within the tropics. Near the coaſt in the South-Sea, they have their periodical winds, viz. Monſoons, and ſea and land breezes, as in Aſia.

SOIL AND CLIMATE.] Mexico lying for the moſt part within the torrid zone, is exceſſively hot, and on the eaſtern coaſt, where the land is low, marſhy, and conſtantly flooded in the rainy ſeaſons, it is likewiſe extremely unwholeſome. The inland country, however, aſſumes a better aſpect, and the air is of a milder temperament; on the weſtern ſide the land is not ſo low, as on the eaſtern, much better in quality, and full of plantations. The ſoil of Mexico in general is of a good variety, and would not refuſe any ſort of grain were

2

the

the induftry of the inhabitants to correfpond with their natural advantages.

PRODUCE.] Mexico, like all the tropical countries, is rather more abundant in fruits than in grain. Pine apples, pomegranates, oranges, lemons, citrons, figs, and cocoa-nuts, are here in the greateft plenty and perfection. Mexico produces alfo a prodigious quantity of fugar, efpecially towards the gulph of Mexico, and the province of Guaxaca and Guatimala, fo that here are more fugar mills than in any other part of Spanifh America. But what is confidered as the chief glory of this country, and what firft induced the Spaniards to form fettlements upon it, are the mines of gold and filver. The chief mines of gold are in Veragua and New Granada, confining upon Darien and Terra Firma. Thofe of filver, which are much more rich, as well as numerous, are found in feveral parts, but in none fo much as in the province of Mexico. The mines of both kinds are always found in the moft barren and mountainous part of the country; nature making amends in one refpect for her defects in another. The working of the gold and filver mines depends on the fame principles. When the ore is dug out, compounded of feveral heterogeneous fubftances, mixed with the precious metals, it is broke into fmall pieces by a mill, and afterwards wafhed, by which means it is difengaged from the earth, and other foft bodies which clung to it. Then it is mixed with mercury, which, of all fubftances, has the ftrongeft attraction for gold, and likewife a ftronger attraction for filver, than the other fubftances which are united with it in the ore. By means of the mercury, therefore, the gold and filver are firft feparated from the heterogeneous matter, and then by ftraining and evaporation, they are difunited from the mercury itfelf. Of the gold and filver, which the mines of Mexico afford, great things have been faid. Thofe who have enquired moft into this fubject, compute the revenues of Mexico at twenty-four millions of our money; and it is well known that this, with the other provinces of Spanifh America, fupply the whole world with filver. The other articles next in importance to gold and filver, are the cochineal and cocoa. After much difpute concerning the nature of the former, it feems at laft agreed, that it is of the animal kind, and of the fpecies of the gall infects. It adheres to the plant called Opuntia, and fucks the juice of the fruit, which is of a crimfon colour. It is from this juice that the cochineal derives it value, which confifts in dying all forts of the fineft fcarlet, crimfon and purple. It is alfo ufed in medicine as a fudorific, and as a cordial; and it is computed that the Spaniards annually export

no

no lefs than nine hundred thoufand pounds weight of this commodity, to anfwer the purpofes of medicine and dying. The cocoa, of which chocolate is made, is the next confiderable article in the natural hiftory and commerce of Mexico. It grows on a tree of a middling fize which bears a pod about the fize and fhape of a cucumber, containing the cocoa. The Spanifh commerce in this article is immenfe; and fuch is the internal confumption, as well as external call for it, that a fmall garden of cocoa's is faid to produce to the owner, twenty thoufand crowns a year. At home it makes a principal part of their diet, and is found wholefome, nutricious, and fuitable to the climate. This country likewife produces filk, but not in fuch abundance as to make any remarkable part of their export. Cotton is here in great abundance, and on account of its lightnefs is the common wear of the inhabitants.

POPULATION, INHABITANTS, } We fhall place thefe
GOVERNMENT AND MANNERS. } heads under one point of view, becaufe, the reader will foon be fenfible, they are very nearly connected. We have already defcribed the original inhabitants of Mexico, and the conqueft of that country by the Spaniards. The prefent inhabitants may be divided into Whites, Indians, and negroes. The Whites are either born in Old Spain, or they are creoles, i. e. natives of Spanifh America. The former are chiefly employed in government or trade, and have nearly the fame character with the Spaniards in Europe; only a ftill more confiderable portion of pride; for they confider themfelves as entitled to every high diftinction as natives of Europe, and look upon the other inhabitants as many degrees beneath them. The creoles have all the bad qualities of the Spaniards, from whom they are defcended, without that courage, firmnefs, and patience, which makes the praife-worthy part of the Spanifh character. Naturally weak and effeminate, they dedicate the greateft part of their lives to loitering, and inactive pleafures. Luxurious without variety or elegance, and expenfive with great parade, and little conveniency, their general character is no more than a grave and fpecious infignificance. From idlenefs and conftitution their whole bufinefs is amour and intrigue; and their ladies of confequence are not at all diftinguifhed for their chaftity or domeftic virtues. The Indians, who notwithftanding the devaftations of the firft invaders, remain in great numbers, are become by continual oppreffion and indignity, a dejected timorous and miferable race of mortals. The blacks here, like all thofe in other parts of the world, are ftubborn, hardy, and well adapted for the grofs flavery they endure.

Such

4

Such is the general character of the inhabitants, not only in Mexico, but the greatest part of Spanish America. The civil government is administered by tribunals, called Audiences, which bear a resemblance to the parliaments in France. In these courts the viceroy of the king of Spain presides. His employment is the greatest trust and power, which his Catholic majesty has in his disposal, and is perhaps the richest government entrusted to any subject in the world. The greatness of the viceroy's office is diminished by the shortness of its duration. For, as jealousy is the leading feature of Spanish politicks, in whatever regards America, no officer is allowed to maintain his power for more than three years, which no doubt may have a good effect in securing the authority of the crown of Spain, but is attended with unhappy consequences to the miserable inhabitants, who become a prey to every new governor. The clergy are extremely numerous in Mexico, and it has been computed, that priests, monks and nuns of all orders, make upwards of a fifth of all the white inhabitants, both here and in the other parts of Spanish America. It is impossible indeed to find a richer field, or one more peculiarly adapted to ecclesiastics in any part of the world. The people are superstitious, ignorant, rich, lazy, and licentious : with such materials to work upon, it is not remarkable, that the church should enjoy one fourth of the revenues of the whole kingdom. It is more surprising, that it has not a half.

COMMERCE, CITIES, AND SHIPPING. The trade of Mexico consists of three great branches, which extends over the whole known world. It carries on a traffic with Europe, by la Vera Cruz, situated on the gulph of Mexico or North-Sea; with the East Indies, by Acapulco on the South-Sea, and with South-America, by the same port. These two sea-ports Vera Cruz and Acapulco, are wonderfully well situated for the commercial purposes to which they are applied. It is by means of the former, that Mexico pours her wealth over all the whole world ; and receives in return the numberless luxuries and necessaries, which Europe affords to her, and which the indolence of her inhabitants will never permit them to acquire for themselves. To this port the fleet from Cadiz, called the Flota, consisting of three men of war, as a convoy, and 14 large merchant ships, annually arrive about the beginning of November. Its cargo consists of every commodity and manufacture of Europe, and there are few nations but have more concern in it than the Spaniards, who send out little more than wine and oil. The profit of these, with the freight and commission to the merchants, and duty to the king, is all the advantage which Spain derives from her American commerce.

commerce. When all the goods are landed and difposed of at La Vera Cruz, the fleet takes in the plate, precious ftones, and other commodities for Europe. Sometimes in May they are ready to depart. From La Vera Cruz, they fail to the Havanna, in the ifle of Cuba, which is the rendezvous where they meet the galleons, another fleet which carries on the trade of Terra Firma, by Carthagena, and of Peru by Panama and Porto Bello. When all are collected and provided with a convoy neceffary for their fafety, they fteer for Old Spain.

Acapulco is the fea-port, by which the communication is kept up between the different parts of the Spanifh empire in America and the Eaft Indies. About the month of December, the great galeon, attended by a large fhip as a convoy, which make the only communication between the Philippines and Mexico, annually arrive here. The cargoes of thefe fhips, for the convoy, though in an under-hand manner, likewife carries goods, confift of all the rich commodities and manufactures of the eaft. At the fame time the annual fhip from Lima the capital of Peru comes in, and is not computed to bring lefs than two millions of pieces of eight in filver, befides quickfilver and other valuable commodities, to be laid out in the purchafe of the galeons cargoes. Several other fhips from different parts of Chili and Peru, meet upon the fame occafion. A great fair, in which the commodities of all parts of the world are bartered for one another, lafts thirty days. The galeon then prepares for her voyage, loaded with filver and fuch European goods as have been thought neceffary. The Spaniards, though this trade be carried on entirely through their hands, and in the very heart of their dominions, are comparatively but fmall gainers by it. For as they allow the Dutch, Great Britain, and other commercial ftates, to furnifh the greater part of the cargo of the Flota, fo, the Spanifh inhabitants of the Philippines, tainted with the fame indolence which ruined their European anceftors, permit the Chinefe merchants to furnifh the greater part of the cargo of the galeon. Notwith-ftanding what has been faid of Vera Cruz, and Acapulco, the city of Mexico, the capital of the empire, ought to be confi-dered as the center of commerce in this part of the world. For here the principal merchants refide, and the greateft part of the bufinefs is negotiated. The Eaft India goods from Acapulco, and the European from Vera Cruz, all pafs thro' this city. Hither all the gold and filver come to be coined, here the king's fifth is depofited, and here is wrought all thofe utenfils and ornaments in plate which is every year fent into Europe. The city itfelf breathes the air of the higheft magni-ficence, and according to the beft account contains about 80,000 inhabitants.

Spanifh Dominions in SOUTH AMERICA.

TERRA FIRMA, or Caftilla del Oro.

SITUATION AND EXTENT.

Miles.		Degrees.
Length 1400 ⎱	between	⎰ 60 and 82 W. longitude.
Breadth 700 ⎰		⎱ the equator and 12 N. lat.

BOUNDARIES.] BOUNDED by the north fea (part of the Atlantic ocean) on the north ; by the fame fea and Surinam, on the eaft ; by the country of the Amazons and Peru, on the South ; and the Pacific ocean and New Spain, on the weft.

Divifions.	Subdivifions.	Chief towns.
The north divifion contains the provinces of	1. Terra-firma Proper, or Darien ———	Porto Bello PANAMA, W.lon. 81-52 N. lat. 8-50
	2. Carthagena ——	Carthagena
	3. St. Martha ———	St. Martha
	4. Rio de la Hacha —	Rio de la Hacha
	5. Venezuela ———	Venezuela
	6. Comana	Comana
	7. New Andalufia, or Paria	St. Thomas
The fouth divifion contains the provinces of	1. New Granada —	Santa Fé de Bagota
	2. Popayan ———	Popayan.

BAYS, CAPES, &c.] The Ifthmus of Darien, or Terra-firma proper, joins North and South America. A line drawn from Porto Bello in the north, to Panama in the South-Sea, or rather a little weft of thefe two towns, is the proper limit between North and South America, and here the Ifthmus or Neck of land is only 60 miles over.

The principal bays in Terra-firma are, the bay of Panama, and the bay of St. Michael's in the South-Sea ; the bay of Porto Bello, the gulph of Darien, Sino bay, Carthagena bay and harbour, the gulph of Venezuela, the bay of Maracaibo, the gulph of Triefto, the bay of Guaira, the bay of Curiaco, and the gulph of Paria or Andalufia, in the north fea.

The

The chief capes are, Samblas point, Point Canoa, Cape del Agua, Swart point, Cape de Vela, Cape Conquibacoa, Cape Cabelo, Cape Blanco, Cape Galera, Cape Three Points; and Cape Naffau; all on the north fhore of Terra-firma.

CLIMATE.] The climate here, particularly in the northern divifions, is extremely hot; and it was found by Ulloa, that the heat of the warmeft day in Paris, is continual at Cartha-gena; the exceffive heats raife the vapour of the fea, which is precipitated in fuch rains as feem to threaten a general deluge. Great part of the country therefore, is almoft con-tinually flooded; and this, together with the exceffive heat, fo impregnates the air with vapours, that in many provinces, particularly about Popayan and Porto Bello, it is extremely unwholefome.

SOIL AND PRODUCE.] The foil of this country, like that of the greater part of South America, is wonderfully rich and fruitful. It is impoffible to view, without admiration, the perpetual verdure of the woods, the luxuriancy of the plains, and the towering height of the mountains. This however only applies to the inland country, for the coafts are generally barren fand, and uncapable of bearing any fpecies of grain. The trees, moft remarkable for their dimenfions, are the caobo, the cedar, the maria, and balfam tree. The manza-nillo tree is particularly remarkable. It bears a fruit refembling an apple, but which, under this fpecious appearance, contains the moft fubtile poifon, againft which common oil is found to be the beft antidote. The malignity of this tree is fuch, that if a perfon only fleeps under it, he finds his body all fwelled, and racked with the fevereft tortures. The beafts from inftinct always avoid it. The Habella de Carthagena is the fruit of a fpecies of willow, and contains a kernel refembling an almond, but lefs white, and extremely better. This kernal is found to be an excellent and never failing remedy for the bite of the moft venomous vipers and ferpents, which are very frequent all over this country. There were formerly rich mines of gold in this country, which are now in a great meafure ex-haufted. The filver, iron, and copper mines, have been fince opened, and the inhabitants find emeralds, fapphires, and other precious ftones.

ANIMALS.] In treating of North America we have taken notice of many of the animals that are found in the foutheru parts, it is therefore unneceffary to repeat them hereafter. Among thofe peculiar to this country, the moft remarkable is the floth, or as it is called by way of derifion, the Swift Peter. It bears a refemblance to an ordinary monkey in fhape

and

and fize, but is of a moft wretched appearance, with its bare hams and feet, and its fkin all over corrugated. He ftands in no need of either chain or hutch, never ftirring unlefs compelled by hunger; and he is faid to be feveral minutes in moving one of his legs, nor will blows make him mend his pace. When he moves, every effort is attended with fuch a plaintive, and at the fame time, fo difagreeable a cry, as at once produces pity and difguft. In this cry confifts the whole defence of this wretched animal. For on the firft hoftile approach it is natural for him to be in motion, which is always accompanied with difguftful howlings, fo that his purfuer flies much more fpeedily in his turn, to be beyond the reach of this horrid noife. When this animal finds no wild fruits on the ground, he looks out with a great deal of pains for a tree well loaded, which he afcends with a world of uneafinefs, moving, and crying, and ftopping by turns. At length having mounted, he plucks off all the fruit, and throws it on the ground, to fave himfelf fuch another troublefome journey; and rather than be fatigued with coming down the tree, he gathers himfelf in a bunch, and with a fhriek drops to the ground.

The monkeys in thefe countries are very numerous; they keep together 20 or 30 in company, rambling over the woods, leaping from tree to tree, and if they meet with a fingle perfon, he is in danger of being torn to pieces by them; at leaft they chatter, and make a frightful noife, throwing things at him; they hang themfelves by the tail, on the boughs, and feem to threaten him all the way he paffes; but where two or three people are together, they ufually fcamper away.

NATIVES.] Befides the Indians in this country, who fall under our general defcription, vol. II. page 338, there is another fpecies of a fair complexion, delicate habit, and of a fmaller ftature than the ordinary Indians. Their difpofitions too are more foft and effeminate; but what principally diftinguifhes them is their large weak blue eyes, which, unable to bear the light of the fun, fee beft by moon light, and from which they are therefore called Moon-eyed Indians.

INHABITANTS, COMMERCE,⎫ We have already men-
    AND CHIEF TOWNS. ⎬ tioned how this country fell
into the hands of the Spaniards. The inhabitants therefore do not materially differ from thofe of Mexico. To what we have obferved therefore with regard to that country, it is only neceffary to add that the original inhabitants of Spain are varioufly intermixed with the negroes and Indians. Thefe intermixtures form various gradations, which are carefully diftinguifhed from each other, becaufe every perfon expects to be regarded in proportion as a greater fhare of the Spanifh blood
runs

runs in his veins. The firft diftinction, arifing from the intermarriage of the whites with the negroes, is that of the mulattoes, which is well known. Next to thefe are the Tercerones, produced from a white and mulatto. From the intermarriage with thefe and the whites, arife the Quarterones, who, though ftill nearer the former, are difgraced with a tint of negro blood. But the produce of thefe and the whites, are the Quinterones, which is very remarkable, are not to be diftinguifhed from the real Spaniards, but by being of a ftill fairer complexion. The fame gradations are formed in a contrary order, by the intermixture of the mulattoes and the negroes; and befides thefe, there are a thoufand others, hardly diftinguifhable by the natives themfelves. The commerce of this country is chiefly carried on from the ports of Panama, Carthagena, and Porto Bello; which are three of the moft confiderable cities in Spanifh America; and each containing feveral thoufand inhabitants. Here there are annual fairs for American, Indian, and European commodities. Among the natural merchandife of Terra Firma, the pearls found in the coaft, particularly in the bay of Panama, are not the leaft confiderable. An immenfe number of negro flaves, are employed in fifhing for thefe, and have arrived at wonderful dexterity at this occupation. They are fometimes however devoured by fifh, particularly the fharks, while they dive to the bottom, or crufhed againft the fhelves of the rocks. The government of Terra Firma is on the fame footing with that of Mexico.

P E R U.

SITUATION AND EXTENT.

Miles.		Degrees.
Length 1800	between	the equator and 25 fouth lat.
Breadth 500		60 and 81 weft longitude.

BOUNDARIES.] BOUNDED by Terra Firma, on the north; by the mountains, or Cordeleiria's des Andes, eaft; by Chili, fouth; and by the Pacific ocean, weft.

Divifions.	Provinces.	Chief Towns.
The north divifion	Quito — —	Quito Payta
The middle divifion	Lima, or Los Reyes	LIMA, 77-30 W.lon. 12-15 S. lat. Cufco, and Callao.
The fouth divifion	Los Charcos —	Potofi Porco.

Seas, bays, and harbours.] The only sea which borders on Peru is the Pacific ocean or South-Sea. The principal bays and harbours are Payta, Malabrigo, Cuanchaco, Cosma, Vermeio, Guara, Callao, the port town to Lima, Ylo, and Arica.

Rivers.] There is a river whose waters are as red as blood. The rivers Granda, or Cagdalena, Oronoque, Amazon, and Plate, rise in the Andes.

A great many other rivers rise in the Andes, and fall into the Pacific ocean, between the equator and eight degrees S, Lat.

Petrified waters.] There are some waters, which, in their course, turn into stone; and fountains of liquid matter, called Coppey, resembling pitch and tar, and used by seamen for the same purpose.

Soil and climate.] Though Peru lies within the torrid zone, yet, having on one side the south Sea, and on the other the great ridge of the Andes, it is not so stifled with heat, as the other tropical countries. The sky too, which is generally cloudy, shields them from the direct rays of the sun; but what is extremely singular, it never rains in Peru. This defect, however, is sufficiently supplied by a soft kindly dew, which falls regularly every night on the ground, and so refreshes the plants and grass, as to produce in many places the greatest fertility. Along the sea coast Peru is generally a dry barren sand, except by the banks of rivers, where it is extremely fertile, as are all the low lands in the inland country.

Animal, vegetable, and} There are many gold
   Mineral productions. } mines in the northern part, not far from Lima. Silver too is produced in great abundance in various provinces; but the old mines are constantly decaying, and new ones daily opened. The towns shift with the mines. That of Potosi, when the silver there was found at the easiest expence, for now having gone so deep, it is not so easily brought up, contained 90,000 souls, Spaniards and Indians, of which the latter were six to one. The northern part of Peru produces wine in great plenty. Wool is another article of its produce, and is no less remarkable for its fineness, than for the animals on which it grows; these they call Lamas and Vicunnas. The Lama has a small head, in some measure resembling that of a horse and sheep at the same time. It is about the size of a stag, its upper lip is cleft like that of a hare, through which, when enraged, it spits a kind of venomous juice, which enflames the part it falls on. The flesh of the Lama is agreeable and salutary, and the animal is not only useful in affording wool and food, but also as a beast of
burden.

burden. It can endure amazing fatigue, and will travel over the fteepeft mountains with a burden of 60 or 70 lb. It feeds very fparingly, and never drinks. The Vicunna is fmaller and fwifter than the Lama, and produces wool ftill finer in quality. In the Vicunna too is found the Bezoar ftones, regarded as a fpecific againft poifons. The next great article in their produce and commerce is the Peruvian bark, known better by the name of Jefuits bark. The tree which produces this invaluable drug, grows principally in the mountainous parts of Peru, and particularly in the province of Quito. The beft bark is always produced in the high and rocky grounds; the tree which bears it, is about the fize of a cherry tree, and produces a kind of fruit, refembling the almond. But it is only the bark, which has thefe excellent qualities that render it fo ufeful in intermitting fevers, and other diforders to which daily experience extends the application of it. Guinea pepper, or Cayenne pepper, as we call it, is produced in the greateft abundance in the vale of Arica, a diftrict in the fouthern parts of Peru, from whence they export it annually to the value of 600,000 crowns. Peru is likewife the only part of Spanifh America, which produces quickfilver, an article of immenfe value, confidering the various purpofes to which it is applied, and efpecially the purification of gold and filver. The principal mine of this fingular metal is at a place called Guancavelica, where it is found in a whitifh mafs refembling brick ill burned. This fubftance is volatilifed by fire, and received in fteam by a combination of glafs veffels, where it condenfes by means of a little water at the bottom of each veffel, and forms a pure heavy liquid.

MANUFACTURES, TRADE AND CITIES.] We join thefe articles here becaufe of their intimate connection; for, except in the cities we fhall defcribe, there is no commerce worth mentioning. The city of Lima is the capital of Peru, and of the whole Spanifh empire; its fituation in the middle of a fpacious and delightful valley, was fixed upon by the famous Pizarro, as the moft proper for a city, which he expected would preferve his memory. It is fo well watered by the river Rimac, that the inhabitants, like thofe of London, command a ftream, each for his own ufe. There are many very magnificent ftructures, particularly churches, in this city; though the houfes in general are built of flight materials, the equality of the climate, and want of rain, rendering ftone houfes unneceffary; and befides it is found, that thefe are more apt to fuffer by fhocks of the earth which are frequent and dreadful all over this province. Lima is about two leagues from the fea, extends in length two miles, and in breadth one and a

quarter.

quarter. It contains about 60,000 inhabitants, of whom the whites amount to a sixth part. One remarkable fact is sufficient to demonstrate the wealth of this city. When the viceroy, the duke de la Palada, made his entry into Lima in 1682, the inhabitants, to do him honour, caused the streets to be paved with ingots of silver, amounting to seventeen millions sterling. All travellers speak with amazement of the decorations of the churches, with gold, silver and precious stones, which load and ornament even the walls. The only thing that could justify these accounts is the immense richness and extensive commerce of the inhabitants. The merchants of Lima may be said to deal with all the quarters of the world, and that both on their own accounts, and as factors for others. Here all the product of the southern provinces are conveyed, in order to be exchanged at the harbour of Lima, for such articles as the inhabitants of Peru stand in need of; the fleet from Europe, and the East Indies, land at the same harbour, and the commodities of Asia, Europe, and America, are there bartered for each other. What there is no immediate vent for, the merchants of Lima purchase on their own accounts, and lay up in warehouses, knowing that they must soon find an outlet for them, since by one channel or other they have a communication with almost every commercial nation. But all the wealth of the inhabitants, all the beauty of the situation, and fertility of the climate of Lima, are not sufficient to compensate for one disaster, which always threatens, and has sometimes actually befallen them. In the year 1747, a most tremendous earthquake laid three-fourths of this city level with the ground, and entirely demolished Callao, the port town belonging to it. Never was any destruction more terrible or perfect, not more than one of three thousand inhabitants being left to record this dreadful calamity, and he by a providence the most singular and extraordinary imaginable.—This man, who happened to be on a fort which overlooked the harbour, perceived in one minute the inhabitants running from their houses in the utmost terror and confusion; the sea, as is usual on such occasions, receding to a considerable distance, returned in mountainous waves, foaming with the violence of the agitation, buried the inhabitants for ever in its bosom, and immediately all was silent; but the same wave which destroyed the town, drove a little boat by the place where the man stood, into which he threw himself and was saved. Cusco, the antient capital of the Peruvian empire, has already been taken notice of. As it lies in the mountainous country, and at a distance from the sea, it has been long on the decline. But it is still a very considerable place, and contains above 40,000 inhabitants,

inhabitants, three parts Indians, and very induſtrious in manufacturing baize, cotton, and leather. They have alſo both here and in Quito, which ſhall be mentioned directly, a particular taſte for painting, and their productions in this way, ſome of which have been admired in Italy, are diſperſed over all South America. Quito is next to Lima in populouſneſs, if not ſuperior to it. It is like Cuſco, an inland city, and having no mines in its neighbourhood, is chiefly famous for its manufactures of cotton, wool, and flax, which ſupply the conſumption over all the kingdom of Peru.

INHABITANTS, MANNERS } It would be in vain to pre-
    AND GOVERNMENT.   } tend ſaying any thing deciſive with regard to the number of inhabitants in Peru. The Spaniards themſelves are remarkably ſilent on this head. It has been gueſſed by ſome writers, that in all Spaniſh America, there are about three millions of Spaniards and creoles of different colours; and undoubtedly the number of Indians is much greater; though neither in any reſpect proportionable to the wealth, fertility, and extent of the country. The manners of the inhabitants do not remarkably differ over the whole of the Spaniſh dominions. Pride and lazineſs are the two predominant paſſions. It is agreed on by the moſt authentic travellers, that the manners of Old Spain have degenerated in its colonies. The creoles, and all the other deſcendants of the Spaniards, according to the above diſtinctions, are guilty of many mean and pilfering vices, which a true born Caſtilian could not think of but with deteſtation. This no doubt in part ariſes from the contempt in which all but the real natives of Spain are held in the Indies, mankind generally behaving according to the treatment they meet with from others. In Lima the Spaniſh pride has made the greateſt deſcents, and many of the firſt nobility are employed in commerce. It is in this city that the viceroy reſides, whoſe authority extends over all Peru, except Quito, which has been lately detached from it. The viceroy is as abſolute as the king of Spain, but as his territories are ſo extenſive, it is neceſſary that he ſhould part with a ſhare of his authority to the ſeveral audiencies or courts eſtabliſhed over the kingdom. There is a treaſury court eſtabliſhed at Lima, for receiving the fifth of the produce of the mines, and certain taxes paid by the Indians, which belong to the king of Spain,

C H I L I.

	Miles.		Degrees.
Length	1200	} between {	25 and 45 fouth latitude.
Breadth	500		65 and 85 weft longitude.

BOUNDARIES.] BOUNDED by Peru on the north ; by La Plata on the eaft ; by Patagonia on the fouth ; and by the Pacific ocean on the weft.

Divifions.	Provinces.	Chief Towns.
On the weft side of the Andes	Chili Proper —	St. Jago, W. lon. 77. S. lat. 34. Baldivia. Imperial.
On the eaft side of the Andes	Cuyo, or Cutio	St. John de Frontieræ.

LAKES.] The principal lakes are thofe of Tagatagua near St. Jago, and that of Paren. Befides which, they have feveral falt-water lakes, that have a communication with the fea part of the year. In ftormy weather the fea forces a way through them, and leaves them full of fifh ; but in the hot feafon the water congeals, leaving a cruft of fine white falt a foot thick.

BAYS, SEAS, AND HARBOURS.] The only fea that borders upon Chili, is that of the Pacific ocean on the weft.

The principal bays or harbours are Copiapo, Coquimbo, Govanadore, Valparifo, Iata, Conception, Santa Maria, La Moucha, Baldivia, Brewers-haven, and Caftro.

CLIMATE, SOIL AND PRODUCE.] Thefe are not remarkably different from the fame in Peru ; and if there be any difference, it is in favour of Chili. There is indeed no part of the world more favoured than this is, with refpect to the gifts of nature. For here, not only the tropical fruits, but all fpecies of grain, of which a confiderable part is exported, come to great perfection. Their animal productions are the fame with thofe of Peru, and they have gold almoft in every river.

INHABITANTS.] This country is very thinly inhabited. The original natives are ftill in a great meafure unconquered and uncivilized ; and leading a wandering life, attentive to no object but their prefervation from the Spanifh yoke, are in a very unfavourable condition, with regard to population. The Spaniards do not amount to above 20,000 ; and the Indians, negroes and mulattoes, are not fuppofed to be thrice that number.

COMMERCE.] The foreign commerce of Chili is entirely confined to Peru, Panama, and some parts of Mexico. To the former they export annually corn sufficient for 60,000 men. Their other exports are hemp, which is raised in no other part of the South Seas, hides, tallow, and salted provisions, and receive in return the commodities of Europe, and the East Indies, which are brought to the port of Callao.

PARAGUAY, or LA PLATA.

SITUATION AND EXTENT.

	Miles.		Degrees.
Length	1500	} between {	12 and 37 south latitude.
Breadth	1000		50 and 75 west longitude.

BOUNDARIES.] BOUNDED by Amazonia, on the north; by Brasil, east; by Patagonia, on the south; and by Peru and Chili, west.

Divisions.	Provinces.	Chief Towns.
East division contains	Paraguay —	Assumption
	Parana —	St. Anne
	Guaira —	Cividad Real
	Uragua —	Los Reyes
South division	Tucuman —	St. Jago
	Rio de la Plata	BUENOS AYRES, W. lon. 57-54. S. lat. 34-35.

BAYS AND LAKES.] The principal bay is that at the mouth of the river La Plata, on which stands the capital city of Buenos Ayres; and cape St. Antonio, at the entrance of that bay, is the only promontory. This country abounds with lakes, one of which is 100 miles long.

RIVERS.] This country, besides an infinite number of small rivers, is watered by three principal ones, which united near the sea, form the famous Rio de la Plata, or Plate River, and which annually overflow their banks; and, on their recess, leave them enriched with a slime, that produces the greatest plenty of whatever is committed to it.

AIR, SOIL AND PRODUCE.] This vast tract is far from being wholly subdued or planted by the Spaniards. There are many parts in a great degree unknown to them, or to any other people of Europe. The principal province of which we have any knowledge, is that which is called Rio de la Plata, towards the mouth of the above mentioned rivers. This province, with all the adjacent parts, is one continued level, interrupted by not the least hill for several hundred miles every way; extremely fertile, and producing cotton in great quantities;

tobacco,

tobacco, and the valuable herb, called Paraguay, with a variety of fruits, and prodigious rich pastures, in which are bred such herds of cattle, that it is said the hides of the beasts are all that is properly bought, the carcase being in a manner given into the bargain. A horse some time ago might be bought for a dollar, and the usual price for a beast chosen out of a herd of 2 or 300, was only four rials. But, contrary to the general nature of America, this country is destitute of woods. The air is remarkably sweet and serene, and the waters of La Plata are equally pure and wholesome.

FIRST SETTLEMENT, CHIEF CITY AND COMMERCE. The Spaniards first discovered this country, by sailing up the river La Plata in 1515, and founded the town of Buenos Ayres, so called on account of the excellence of the air, on the south side of the river, fifty leagues within the mouth of it, where the river is seven leagues broad. This is one of the most considerable towns in South America, and the only place of traffic to the southward of Brazil. Here we meet with the merchants of Europe and Peru, but no regular fleet comes here, as to the other parts of Spanish America; two, or at most three, register ships, make the whole of their regular intercourse with Europe. Their returns are very valuable, consisting chiefly of the gold and silver of Chili and Peru, sugar and hides. Those who have now and then carried on a contraband trade to this city, have found it more advantageous than any other whatever. The benefit of this contraband is now wholly in the hands of the Portuguese, who keep magazines for that purpose, in such parts of Brazil as lie near this country. Since the English have got a footing near this coast by their new settlement of port Egmont in the Falkland isles, we may suppose they will make an attempt to a share of this profitable commerce. The trade of Paraguay, and the manners of the people, are so much the same with those of the rest of the Spanish colonies in South America, that nothing further can be said on those articles.

But we cannot quit this country without saying something of that extraordinary species of commonwealth, which the Jesuits have erected in the interior parts, and of which these crafty priests have endeavoured to keep all strangers in the dark.

About the middle of last century those fathers represented to the court of Spain, that their want of success in their missions, was owing to the scandal which the immorality of the Spaniards never failed to give, and to the hatred which their insolent behaviour caused in the Indians, wherever they came. They insinuated, that, if it were not for that impediment, the

the empire of the gospel might, by their labours, have been extended into the most unknown parts of America; and that all those countries might be subdued to his Catholic majesty's obedience, without expence, and without force. This remonstrance met with success; the sphere of their labours was marked out; an uncontrouled liberty was given to the Jesuits within these limits; and the governors of the adjacent provinces had orders not to interfere, nor to suffer any Spaniards to enter into this pale, without license from the fathers. They on their part agreed, to pay a certain capitation tax, in proportion to their flock; and to send a certain number to the king's works whenever they should be demanded, and the missions should become populous enough to supply them.

On these terms the Jesuits gladly entered upon the scene of action, and opened their spiritual campaign. They began by gathering together about 50 wandering families, whom they persuaded to settle; and they united them into a little township. This was the slight foundation upon which they built a superstructure, which has amazed the world, and added so much power, at the same time that it has brought on so much envy and jealousy, to their society. For when they had made this beginning, they laboured with such indefatigable pains, and with such masterly policy, that, by degrees, they mollified the minds of the most savage nations; fixed the most rambling, and subdued those to their government, who had long disdained to submit to the arms of the Spaniards and Portuguese. They prevailed upon thousands of various dispersed tribes to embrace their religion, and these soon induced others to follow their example, magnifying the peace and tranquillity they enjoyed under the direction of the fathers.

Our limits do not permit us to trace with precision all the steps which were taken in the accomplishment of so extraordinary a conquest over the bodies and minds of so many people. The Jesuits left nothing undone, that could conduce to their remaining in this subjection, or that could tend to encrease their number to the degrees requisite for a well ordered and potent society; and it is said that above 340,000 families, several years ago, were subject to the Jesuits, living in obedience, and an awe bordering upon adoration, yet procured without any violence or constraint: That the Indians were instructed in the military art with the most exact discipline, and could raise 60,000 men well armed: That they lived in towns; they were regularly clad; they laboured in agriculture; they exercised manufactures; some even aspired to the elegant arts; and that nothing could equal the obedience of the people of these missions, except their contentment under

it.

it. Some writers however have treated the character of thefe Jefuits with great feverity, accufing them of ambition, pride, and of carrying their authority to fuch an excefs, as to caufe even the magiftrates, who are always chofen from among the Indians, to be corrected before them with ftripes, and to fuffer perfons of the higheft diftinction, within their jurifdictions, to kifs the hem of their garments, as the greateft honour. The priefts themfelves poffefs large property, all manufactures are theirs, the natural produce of the country is brought to them, and the treafures annually remitted to the fuperior of the order, feem to evince that zeal for religion is not the only motive of their forming thefe miffions. The fathers will not permit any of the inhabitants of Peru, whether Spaniards, Meftizos, or even Indians, to come within their miffions in Paraguay. Some years ago, when part of this territory was ceded by Spain to the crown of Portugal, the Jefuits refufed to comply with this divifion, or to fuffer themfelves to be transferred from one hand to another, like cattle, without their own confent. And we are informed by the authority of the Gazette, that the Indians actually took up arms; but, notwithftanding the exactnefs of their difcipline, they were eafily, and with a confiderable flaughter, defeated by the European troops, who were fent to quell them.

SPANISH ISLANDS IN AMERICA.

CUBA.] The ifland of Cuba is fituated between 19 and 23 deg. north lat. and between 74 and 87 deg. weft lon. 100 miles to the fouth of cape Florida, and 75 north of Jamaica, and is near 700 miles in length, and generally about 70 miles in breadth. A chain of hills run through the middle of the ifland from eaft to weft, but the land near the fea is in general level and flooded in the rainy feafon, when the fun is vertical. This noble ifland is fuppofed to have the beft foil, for fo large a country, of any in America. It produces all the commodities known in the Weft Indies, particularly ginger, long pepper, and other fpices, caffia, fiftula, muftic and aloes. It alfo produces tobacco and fugar, but from the want of hands, and the lazinefs of the Spaniards, not in fuch quantities as might be expected. It is owing to the fame caufe that this large ifland does not produce, including all its commodities, fo much for exportation as our fmall ifland of Antigua.

The courfe of the rivers is too fhort to be of any confequence, but there are feveral good harbours in the ifland, which belong to the principal towns, as that of St. Jago, facing Jamaica, ftrongly fituated, and well fortified, but neither populous nor rich.

rich. That of the Havannah, facing Florida, which is the capital city of Cuba, and a place of great ftrength and importance, containing about 2000 houfes, with a great number of convents and churches. It was taken however, by the courage and perfeverance of the Englifh troops in the laft war, but reftored in the fixty-third article of the treaty of peace. Befides thefe, there is likewife Cumberland harbour, and that of Santa Cruz, a confiderable town thirty miles eaft of the Havannah.

HISPANIOLA, or ST. DOMINGO.] This ifland was at firft poffeffed by the Spaniards alone, but by far the moft confiderable part is now in the hands of the French. However, as the Spaniards were the original poffeffors, and ftill continue to have a fhare in it, Hifpaniola is commonly regarded as a Spanifh ifland.

It is fituated between the 17th and 21ft deg. north lat. and the 67th and 74th of weft lon. lying in the middle between Cuba and Porto-Rico, and is 450 miles long, and 150 broad. The face of the country prefents an agreeable variety of hills, vallies, woods and rivers, and the foil is allowed to be extremely fertile, producing fugar, cotton, indigo, tobacco, maize, and caffava root. The European cattle are fo multiplied here, that they run wild in the woods, and as in South America, are hunted for their hides and tallow only. In the moft barren parts of the rocks, they difcovered formerly filver and gold. The mines however are not worked now. The north-weft parts, which are in the poffeffion of the French, confift of large fruitful plains, which produce the articles already mentioned in vaft abundance. This indeed is the beft and moft fruitful part, of the beft and moft fertile ifland in the Weft Indies, and perhaps in the world.

The moft antient town in this ifland, and in all the new world, built by Europeans, it St. Domingo. It was founded by Bartholomew Columbus, brother to the admiral, in 1504, who gave it that name in honour of his father Dominic, and by which the whole ifland is fometimes named, efpecially by the French. It is fituated on a fpacious harbour, and is a large well-built city, inhabited, like the other Spanifh towns, by a mixture of Europeans, creoles, mulattos, muftees, and negroes.

The French towns are, cape St. Francois, the capital, which is neither walled nor paled in, and is faid to have only two batteries, one at the entrance of the harbour, and the other before the town. It contains about 8000 whites and blacks. Leogane, though inferior in point of fize, is a good port, a place of confiderable trade, and the feat of the French government in that ifland. They have two other towns confiderable for their trade, Petit Guaves, and port Louis.

It is computed that the exports of the French, from the above-mentioned places, are not lefs in value than 1,200,000 l. They likewife carry on a contraband trade with the Spaniards, which is much to their advantage, as they exchange French manufactures for Spanifh dollars.

PORTO RICO.] Situated between 64 and 67 deg. weft lon. and in 18 deg. north lat. lying between Hifpaniola and St. Chriftopher's, is 100 miles long, and 40 broad. The foil is beautifully diverfified with woods, vallies, and plains ; and is extremely fertile, producing the fame fruits as the other iflands. It is well watered with fprings and rivers ; but the ifland is unhealthful in the rainy feafons. It was on account of the gold that the Spaniards fettled here, but there is no longer any confiderable quantity of this metal found in it.

Porto Rico, the capital town, ftands in a little ifland on the north fide of the main ifland, forming a capacious harbour, and joined to the chief ifland by a caufey, and defended by forts and batteries, which render the town almoft inacceffible. It was, however, taken by Sir Francis Drake, and afterwards by the earl of Cumberland. It is better inhabited than moft of the Spanifh towns, becaufe it is the center of the contraband trade carried on by the Englifh and French with the king of Spain's fubjects.

VIRGIN ISLANDS.] Situated at the eaft end of Porto Rico, are extremely fmall.

TRINIDAD.] Situated between 59 and 62 deg. weft lon. and in 10 deg. north lat. lies between the ifland of Tobago and the Spanifh Main, from which it is feparated by the ftreights of Paria. It is about 90 miles long, and 60 broad ; and is an unhealthful, but fruitful foil, producing fugar, fine tobacco, indigo, ginger, variety of fruit, and fome cotton trees, and Indian corn. It was taken by Sir Walter Raleigh, in 1595, and by the French in 1676, who plundered the ifland and extorted money from the inhabitants.

MARGARETTA.] Situated in 64 deg. weft lon. and 11-30 N. lat. feparated from the northern coaft of New Andalufia, in Terra-firma, by a ftreight of 24 miles, is about 40 miles in length, and 24 in breadth ; and being always verdant, affords a moft agreeable profpect. The ifland abounds in pafture, in maize, and fruit; but there is a fcarcity of wood

and

and water. There was once, a pearl fishery on its coast, which is now discontinued.

There are many other small islands in these seas, to which the Spaniards have paid no attention. We shall therefore proceed round Cape Horn into the South Seas, where the first Spanish island of any importance is CHILOE, on the coast of Chili, which has a governor and some harbours well fortified.

JUAN FERNANDES.] Lying in 83 deg. west lon. and 33 south lat. 300 miles west of Chili. This island is uninhabited, but having some good harbours, it is found extremely convenient for the English cruisers to touch at and water; and he e they are in no danger of being discovered, unless when, as is generally the case, their arrival in the South Seas, and their motions, have been made known to the Spaniards by our good friends in Brazil. This island is famous for having given rise to the celebrated romance of Robinson Crusoe. It seems one Alexander Selkirk, a Scotsman, was left ashore in this solitary place by his captain, where he lived some years, until he was discovered by captain Woodes Rogers, in 1709; when taken up, he had forgot his native language, and could scarcely be understood, seeming to speak his words by halves. He was dressed in goats skins, would drink nothing but water, and it was some time before he could relish the ship's victuals. During his abode in this island, he had killed 500 goats, which he caught by running them down; and he marked as many more on the ear, which he let go. Some of these were caught, 30 years after, by lord Anson's people; their venerable aspect and majestic beards, discovered strong symptoms of antiquity.

Selkirk, upon his return to England, was advised to publish an account of his life and adventures in his little kingdom. He put his papers into the hands of Daniel Defoe, to prepare them for publication. But that industrious gentleman, by the help of these papers and a lively fancy, transformed Alexander Selkirk into Robinson Crusoe, and returned Selkirk his papers again, after defrauding him, by this piece of craft, of the benefits he was so justly entitled to hope from them.

The other islands that are worth mentioning are, the Gallipago isles, situated 400 miles west of Peru, under the equator; and those in the bay of Panama, called the King's or Pearl Islands.

PORTUGUESE AMERICA;

Containing BRAZIL.

Situation and extent.

Miles.		Degrees.
Length 2500 } between {		the equator and 35 S. latitude
Breadth 700 }		35 and 60 weſt longitude.

BOUNDARIES.] BOUNDED by the mouth of the river Amazon, and the Atlantic Ocean, on the north; by the ſame ocean, on the eaſt; by the mouth of the river Plata, ſouth; and by a chain of mountains, which divide it from Paraguay and the country of Amazons, on the weſt.

On the coaſt are three ſmall iſlands, where ſhips touch for proviſions in their voyage to the South-Seas, viz. Fernando, St. Barbara, and St. Catharine's.

SEAS, BAYS, HARBOURS, } The Atlantic Ocean waſhes
AND CAPES. } the coaſt of Brazil on the north-eaſt and eaſt, upwards of 3000 miles, forming ſeveral fine bays and harbours; as the harbours of Panambuco, All-Saints, Porto-Seguro, the port and harbour of Rio Janeiro, the port of St. Vincent, the harbour of St. Gabriel, and the port of St. Salvador, on the north ſhore of the river La Plata.

The principal capes are, Cape Roque, Cape St. Auguſtine, Cape Trio, and Cape St. Mary, the moſt ſoutherly promontory of Brazil.

FACE OF THE COUNTRY, } The name of Brazil was
AIR, CLIMATE AND RIVERS. } given to this country, becauſe it was obſerved to abound with a wood of that name. To the northward of Brazil, which lies almoſt under the equator, the climate is hot, boiſterous, and unwholeſome, ſubject to great rains and variable winds, particularly in the months of March and September, when they have ſuch deluges of rain, with ſtorms and tornadoes, that the country is overflowed. But to the ſouthward, beyond the tropic of Capricorn, there is no part of the world that enjoys a more ſerene and wholeſome air, refreſhed with the ſoft breezes of the ocean on one hand, and the cool breath of the mountains on the other. The land near the coaſt is in general rather low than high, but exceeding pleaſant, it being interſperſed with meadows and woods; but on the weſt, far within land, are mountains from whence iſſue many noble ſtreams, that fall into the great rivers Amazon

and

and La Plata, others running acrofs the country from eaft to weft till they fall into the Atlantic Ocean, after meliorating the lands which they annually overflow, and turning the fugar mills belongibg to the Portuguefe.

SOIL AND PRODUCE.] In general the foil is extremely fruitful, producing fugar, which being clayed, is whiter and finer than our mufcovado, as we call our unrefined fugar. Alfo tobacco, hides, indigo, ipecacuanha, balfam of Copaibo, Brazil wood, which is of a red colour, hard and dry, and is chiefly ufed in dying, but not the red of the beft kind ; it has likewife fome place in medicine, as a ftomachic and reftringent.

The animals here are the fame as in Peru and Mexico. The produce of the foil was found very fufficient for fubfifting the inhabitants, until the mines of gold and diamonds were difcovered ; thefe, with the fugar plantations, occupy fo many hands, that agriculture lies negle&ted ; and, in confequence, Brazil depends upon Europe for its daily food.

INHABITANTS, MANNERS, AND CUSTOMS.] The portrait given us of the manners and cuftoms of the Portuguefe in America, by the moft judicious travellers, is very far frcm being favourable. They are defcribed as a people, who, while funk in the moft effeminate luxury, pra&tife the moft defperate crimes. Of a temper hypocritical and diffembling ; of little fincerity in converfation, or honefty in dealing ; lazy, proud, and cruel. In their diet, penurious ; for, like the inhabitants of moft fouthern climates, they are much more fond of fhew, ftate, and attendance, than of the pleafures of free fociety, and of a good table ; yet their feafts, which are feldom made, are fumptuous to extravagance. When they appear abroad, they caufe themfelves to be carried out in a kind of cotton hammocks, called ferpentines, which are borne on the negroes fhoulders, by the help of a bamboo, about twelve or fourteen feet long. Moft of thefe hammocks are blue, and adorned with fringes of the fame colour : they have a velvet pillow, and above the head a kind of tefter, with curtains ; fo that the perfon carried cannot be feen, unlefs he pleafes ; but may either lie down or fit up, leaning on his pillow. When he has a mind to be feen, he pulls the curtains afide, and falutes his acquaintance whom he meets in the ftreets ; for they take a pride in complimenting each other in their hammocks, and will even hold long conferences in them in the ftreets ; but then the two flaves who carry them, make ufe of a ftrong well-made ftaff, with an iron fork at the upper end, and pointed below with iron : this they ftick faft in the ground, and reft the bamboo, to which the hammock is fixed,

on

on two of thefe, till their mafter's bufinefs or compliment i
over. Scarce any man of fafhion, or any lady, will pafs the
ftreets without being carried in this manner.

TRADE AND CHIEF TOWNS.] The trade of Portugal is
carried on upon the fame exclufive plan on which the feveral
nations of Europe trade with their colonies of America ; and
it more particularly refembles the Spanifh method, in not
fending out fingle fhips, as the convenience of the feveral
places, and the judgment of the European merchants, may
direct ; but by annual fleets, which fail at ftated times from
Portugal, and compofe three flotas, bound to as many ports
in Brazil ; namely, to Fernambuco, in the northern part ; to
Rio Janeiro, at the fouthern extremity ; and to the Bay of
All-Saints, in the middle.

In this laft is the capital, which is called St. Salvador, and
fometimes the city of Bahia, and where all the fleets rendezvous
on their return to Portugal. This city commands a noble,
fpacious, and commodious harbour ; it is built upon an high
and fteep rock, having the fea upon one fide, and a lake,
forming a crefcent, invefting it almoft wholly fo as nearly to
join the fea, on the other. The fituation makes it in a manner impregnable by nature ; and they have befides added to
it very ftrong fortifications. It is populous, magnificent,
and, beyond comparifon, the moft gay and opulent city in all
Brazil.

The trade of Brazil is very great, and increafes every year ;
which is the lefs furprifing, as the Portuguefe have opportunities of fupplying themfelves with flaves for their feveral works
at a much cheaper rate than any other European power that has
fettlements in America ; they being the only European nation
that has eftablifhed colonies in Africa, and from hence they
import between 40 and 50,000 negroes annually, all of which
go into the amount of the cargo of the Brazil fleets for Europe.
Of the diamonds there is fuppofed to be returned to Europe to
the amount of 130,000 l. This, with the fugar, the tobacco,
the hides, the valuable drugs for medicine and manufactures,
may give fome idea of the importance of this trade, not only
to Portugal, but to all the trading powers of Europe.

The chief commodities the European fhips carry thither in
return, are not the fiftieth part of the produce of Portugal :
they confift of the woollen goods, of all kinds, from England,
France, and Holland ; the linens and laces of Holland,
France, and Germany ; the filks of France and Italy ; filk
and thread ftockings, hats, lead, tin, pewter, iron, copper,
and all forts of utenfils wrought in thefe metals, from England ;
as well as falt-fifh, beef, flour, and cheefe. Oil they have

4

from

from Spain: wine, with some fruit, is nearly all they are supplied with from Portugal.

England is at present most interested in the trade of Portugal, both for home consumption and what they want for the use of the Brazils. However, the French have become very dangerous rivals to us in this, as in many other branches of trade.

Hence it is principally that Brazil is the richest, most flourishing, and most growing establishment in America. Their export of sugar, within 40 years, is grown much greater than it was, though antiently it made almost the whole of their exportable produce, and they were without rivals in the trade. Their tobacco is remarkably good, though not raised in such large quantities as in our American colonies. The northern and southern parts of Brazil abound with horned cattle; these are hunted for their hides only, of which no less than 20,000 are sent annually to Europe.

The Portuguese were a considerable time possessed of Brazil before they discovered the treasures of gold and diamonds, which have since made it so considerable. Their fleets rendezvous in the bay of All-Saints, to the amount of 100 sail of large ships, in the month of May or June, and carry to Europe a cargo little inferior in value to the treasures of the flota and galeons. The gold alone, great part of which is coined in America, amounts to near four millions sterling; but part of this is brought from their colonies in Africa, together with ebony and ivory.

History and Government.] This country was first discovered by Americus Vespusio, in 1498, but the Portuguese did not plant it till 1549, when they fixed themselves at the Bay of All-Saints, and founded the city of St. Salvador. They met with some interruption at first from the court of Spain, who considered the whole continent of South America as belonging to them. However, the affair was at length made up by treaty; and it was agreed that the Portuguese should possess all the country lying between the two great rivers Amazon and Plata, which they still enjoy. The French also made some attempts to plant colonies on this coast, but were driven from thence by the Portuguese, who remained without a rival till the year 1580, when in the very meridian of prosperity, they were struck by one of those blows which instantly decides the fate of kingdoms: don Sebastian, the king of Portugal, lost his life in an expedition against the Moors in Africa, and by that event the Portuguese lost their liberty, being absorbed into the Spanish dominions.

The Dutch, foon after this, having thrown off the Spanifh yoke, and not fatisfied with fupporting their independency by a fuccefsful defenfive war, and flufhed with the juvenile ardor of a growing commonwealth, they purfued the Spaniards into the remoteft receffes of their extenfive territories, and grew rich, powerful, and terrible, by the fpoils of their former mafters. They particularly attacked the poffeffions of the Portuguefe; they took almoft all their fortreffes in the Eaft Indies, and then turned their arms upon Brazil, where they took feven of the captainfhips or provinces; and would have fubdued the whole colony, had not their career been ftopt by the archbifhop, at the head of his monks, and a few fcattered forces. The Dutch were, however, about the year 1654, entirely driven out of Brazil; but their Weft-India company ftill continuing their pretenfions to this country, and harraffing the Portuguefe at fea, the latter agreed, in 1661, to pay the Dutch eight tuns of gold, to relinquifh their intereft in that country; which was accepted; and the Portuguefe have remained in peaceable poffeffion of all Brazil from that time, till about the end of 1762, when the Spanifh governor of Buenos Ayres, hearing of a war between Portugal and Spain, took, after a month's fiege, the Portuguefe frontier fortrefs called St. Sacrament; but, by the treaty of peace, it was reftored.

FRENCH AMERICA.

THE poffeffions and claims of the French before the laft war, as appears by their maps, confifted of almoft the whole continent of North America; which vaft country they divided into two great provinces, the northern of which they called Canada (comprehending a much greater extent than the Britifh province of that name) and in which they included a great part of our provinces of New-York, New-England, and New-Scotland. The fouthern province they called Louifiana, in which they included a part of Carolina. This diftribution, and the military difpofition which the French made to fupport it, formed the principal caufe of the laft war between Great Britain and that nation, the iffue of which is well known to all the world. For while the French were rearing their infant colonies, and with the moft fanguine hopes, forming vaft defigns of an extenfive empire, one wrong ftep in their politics loft them the whole; their imaginary empire, which exifted only upon the face of their maps, vanifhed like fmoke. They over-rated their ftrength; and by commencing hoftilities many years too foon, they were driven

from

from Canada, and forced to yield to Great Britain all that fine country of Louifiana eaftward of the Miffifippi. At the treaty of peace, however, they were allowed to keep poffeffion of the weftern banks of that river, and the fmall town of New Orleans, near the mouth of it; which, in 1769, they ceded to Spain, for reafons unknown to the public.

The French therefore, from being one of the greateft European powers in that quarter, and to the Britifh colonies a very dangerous neighbour and rival; have, in the manner we have feen, loft all footing in North America; but on the fouthern continent they have ftill a fettlement which is called Cayenne, or Equinoctial France, and is fituated between the equator and fifth degree of north latitude, and between the 50th and 55th of weft longitude. It extends 240 miles along the coaft of Guiana, and near 300 miles within land; bounded by Surinam, on the north; by the Atlantic Ocean, eaft; by Amazonia, fouth; and by Guiana, weft. The chief town is Caen.

All the coaft is very low, but within land there are fine hills very proper for fettlements; the French have, however, not yet extended them fo far as they might; but they raife the fame commodities which they have from the Weft-India iflands, and in no inconfiderable quantity. They have alfo taken poffeffion of the ifland of Cayenne, on this coaft, at the mouth of the river of that name, which is about 45 miles in circumference. The ifland is very unhealthy; but having fome good harbours, the French have here fome fettlements, which raife fugar and coffee.

FRENCH ISLANDS IN AMERICA.

THE French were amongft the laft nations who made fettlements in the Weft-Indies; but they made ample amends by the vigour with which they purfued them, and by that chain of judicious and admirable meafures which they ufed in drawing from them every advantage that the nature of the climate would yield; and in contending againft the difficulties which it threw in their way.

They are fenfible that as the mother country is ultimately to receive all the benefit of their labours and acquifitions, the profperity of their plantations muft be derived from the attention with which they are regarded at home. For this reafon, the plantations are particularly under the care and infpection of the council of commerce, a board compofed of twelve of the moft confiderable officers of the crown, affifted by the deputies of all the confiderable trading towns and cities in

France,

France, who are chosen out of the richest and most intelligent of their traders, and paid a handsome salary for their attendance at Paris, from the funds of their respective cities. This council sits once a week, when the deputies propose plans for redressing every grievance in trade, for raising the branches that are fallen, for extending new ones, for supporting the old, and, in fine, for every thing that may improve the working, or promote the vent of their manufactures, according to their own lights, or to the instructions of their constituents. When they are satisfied of the usefulness of any regulation, they propose it to the royal council, where their report is always received with particular attention. An edict to enforce it accordingly issues; and is executed with a punctuality that distinguishes their government, and which alone can render the wisest regulations any thing better than serious mockeries. To this body, the care of the plantations is particularly entrusted.

The government of their several colonies, is a governor, an intendant, and a royal council. The governor is invested with a great deal of power; which, however, on the side of the crown, is checked by the intendant, who has the care of the king's rights, and whatever relates to the revenue : and on the side of the people, it is checked by the royal council, whose office it is to see that the people are not oppressed by the one, nor defrauded by the other: and they are all checked by the constant and jealous eye which the government at home keeps over them; the officers of all the ports of France being charged, under the severest penalties, to interrogate all captains of ships coming from the colonies, concerning the reception they met with at the ports to which they have sailed? how justice was administered to them? what charges they were made liable to, and of what kinds?

That the colonies may be as little burthened as possible, and that the governor may have less temptation to stir up troublesome intrigues, or favour factions in his government, his salary is paid by the crown : he has no perquisites, and is strictly forbidden to carry on any trade, or to have any plantations in the islands or on the continent; or any interest whatever, in goods or lands, within his government, except the house he lives in, and a garden for his convenience and recreation. All the other officers are paid by the crown, out of the revenues of the mother country. The fortifications are built and repaired, and the soldiers paid out of the same funds.

In general, their colonies pay no taxes; but when, upon any extraordinary emergency, taxes have been raised, they were very moderate. The duties upon the export of their
produce

produce at the West India islands, or at its import into France, is next to nothing; in both places hardly making two per cent. What commodities go to them pay no duties at all.

Their other regulations, respecting the judges of the admiralty, lawsuits, recovery of debts, lenity to such as have suffered by earthquakes, hurricanes, or bad seasons; the peopling their colonies, number of whites to be employed by the planters, and, lastly, the management of negroes, cannot be sufficiently admired; and would, doubtless, be of great use, were some of them introduced into our sugar islands, where proper regulations in many respects seem to be much wanted.

We have already mentioned the French colony upon the Spanish island of Hispaniola, or St. Domingo, as the most important and valuable of all their foreign settlements, and which they possess through the indolence of the Spaniards on that island, or the partiality of their court to the French nation. We shall next proceed to the islands of which the French have the sole possession, beginning with the large and important one of

MARTINICO.] Which is situated between 14 and 15 deg. of north lat. and in 61 deg. west lon. lying about 40 leagues north west of Barbadoes, is about 60 miles in length, and half as much in breadth. The inland part of it is hilly, from which are poured out upon every side, a number of agreeable and useful rivers, which adorn and enrich this island in a high degree. The produce of the soil is sugar, cotton, indigo, ginger, and such fruits as are found in the neighbouring islands. But sugar is here, as in all the West India islands, the principal commodity, of which they export a considerable quantity annually. Martinico is the residence of the governor of the French islands in these seas. Its bays and harbours are numerous, safe, and commodious; and so well fortified, that they used to bid defiance to the English, who in vain attempted this place. However, in the last war, when the British arms were triumphant in every quarter of the globe, this island was added to the British empire, but it was given back at the treaty of peace.

GUADALUPE.] So called by Columbus, from the resemblance of its mountains to those of that name in Spain, is situated in 16 deg. north lat. and in 62 west lon. about 30 leagues north of Martinico, and almost as much south of Antigua; being 45 miles long, and 38 broad. It is divided into two parts by a small arm of the sea, or rather a narrow channel, through which no ships can venture; but the inhabitants

bitants pafs it in a ferry-boat. Its foil is equally fertile with that of Martinico, producing fugar, cotton, indigo, ginger, &c. . This ifland is in a flourifhing condition, and its exports of fugar, almoft incredible. Like Martinico, it was formerly attacked by the Englifh, who gave up the attempt; but in 1759, it was reduced by the Britifh arms, and was given back at the peace of 1763.

St. LUCIA.] Situated in 14 deg. north lat. and in 61 deg. weft lon. 80 miles north-weft of Barbadoes, is 23 miles in length, and 12 in breadth. It received its name from being difcovered on the day dedicated to the virgin martyr St. Lucia. The Englifh firft fettled on this ifland in 1637. From this time they met with various misfortunes from the natives and French; and at length it was agreed on between the latter and the Englifh, that this ifland, together with Dominica and St. Vincent, fhould remain neutral. But the French, before the late war broke out, began to fettle thefe iflands; which, by the treaty of peace, were yielded up to Great Britain, and this ifland to France. The foil of St. Lucia, in the valleys, is extremely rich. It produces excellent timber, and abounds in pleafant rivers, and well fituated harbours.

St. BARTHOLOMEW, DESEADA,   }   Are three fmall
      AND MARIGALANTE,   }   iflands lying in
the neighbourhood of Antigua and St. Chriftophers, and are of no great confequence to the French, except in time of war, when they give fhelter to an incredible number of privateers, which greatly annoy our Weft India trade. It would therefore be good policy in Great Britain, upon the breaking out of a war with France, immediately to take poffeffion of thefe iflands, which would feem to be a matter of no great difficulty, as they have been frequently reduced by the Englifh, and as frequently given back to the French; who have often, and upon many occafions, experienced the generofity of the Britifh court.

DUTCH AMERICA.

Containing SURINAM, on the Continent of SOUTH AMERICA.

AFTER the Portuguefe had difpoffeffed the Dutch of Brazil in the manner we have feen; and after they had been entirely removed out of North America, they were obliged to confole themfelves with their rich poffeffions in the Eaft Indies, and to fit down content in the Weft with Surinam; a country once in the poffeffion of England, but of no great value whilft we had it, and which we ceded to them in exchange for New York; and with two or three fmall and barren iflands in the north fea, not far from the Spanifh Main.

Surinam, or Dutch Guiana, is fituated between 5 and 7 deg. north lat. extending 100 miles along the coaft from the mouth of the river Oronoque, north, to the river Maroni, or French Guiana, fouth. The climate of this country is generally reckoned unwholefome; and a confiderable part of the coaft is low and covered with water. The chief fettlement is at Surinam, a town built on a river of the fame name; and the Dutch have extended their plantations 30 leagues above the mouth of this river. The colony is now in the moft flourifhing fituation, not only with Europe, but with the Weft-India iflands. Their chief trade confifts in fugar, a great deal of cotton, coffee of an excellent kind, tobacco, flax, fkins, and fome valuable dying drugs. They trade with our North American colonies, who bring hither horfes, live cattle, and provifions; and take home a large quantity of molaffes; but their negroes are only the refufe of thofe they have for the Spanifh market.

DUTCH ISLANDS IN AMERICA.

ST. EUSTATIA.] SITUATED three leagues north-weft of St. Chriftopher's, and is only a mountain about 29 miles in compafs, rifing out of the fea like a pyramid, and almoft round. But, though fo fmall, and inconveniently laid out by nature, the induftry of the Dutch have made it turn out to very good account; and it is faid to contain 5000 whites, and 15,000 negroes. The fides of the mountain are laid out in very pretty fettlements; but they have neither fprings nor rivers. They raife here fugar and tobacco; and this ifland, as well as Curaffou, is engaged in the Spanifh contraband trade, for which, however, it is not fo well fituated; and it draws the fame advantage from its conftant neutrality. Its fituation renders it the ftrongeft of all the Weft-India iflands, there being but one good landing-place, which may be eafily defended by a few men; and the haven is commanded by a ftrong fort.

CURASSOU.] Situated in 12 deg. north lat. 9 or 10 leagues from the continent of Terra Firma, is 30 miles long and

and 10 broad. It seems as if it were fated, that the ingenuity and patience of the Hollanders should every where, both in Europe and America, be employed in fighting against an unfriendly nature; for the island is not only barren, and dependent upon the rains for its water, but the harbour is naturally one of the worst in America: yet the Dutch have entirely remedied that defect; they have upon this harbour one of the largest, and by far the most elegant and cleanly towns in the West Indies. The public buildings are numerous and handsome; the private houses commodious; and the magazines large, convenient, and well filled. All kind of labour is here performed by engines; some of them so well contrived, that ships are at once lifted into the dock.

Though this island is naturally barren, the industry of the Dutch has brought it to produce a considerable quantity both of tobacco and sugar; it has, besides, good salt-works, for the produce of which there is a brisk demand from the English islands, and their colonies on the continent. But what renders this island of most advantage to the Dutch, is the contraband trade which is carried on between the inhabitants and the Spaniards, and their harbour being the rendezvous to all nations in time of war.

The Dutch ships from Europe touch at this island for intelligence, or pilots, and then proceed to the Spanish coasts for trade, which they force with a strong hand, it being very difficult for the Spanish guarda costas to take these vessels; for they are not only stout ships, with a number of guns, but are manned with large crews of chosen seamen, deeply interested in the safety of the vessel and the success of the voyage. They have each a share in the cargo, of a value proportioned to the station of the owner, supplied by the merchants upon credit, and at prime cost. This animates them with an uncommon courage, and they fight bravely, because every man fights in defence of his own property. Besides this, there is a constant intercourse between this island and the Spanish continent.

Curassou has numerous warehouses, always full of the commodities of Europe and the East-Indies. Here are all sorts of woollen and linen cloth, laces, silks, ribbons, iron utensils, naval and military stores, brandy, the spices of the Moluccas, and the calicoes of India, white and painted. Hither the Dutch West-India, which is also their African company, annually bring three or four cargoes of slaves; and to this mart the Spaniards themselves come in small vessels, and carry off not only the best of the negroes, at a very high price, but great quantities of all the above sorts of goods;
and

and the feller has this advantage, that the refufe of warehoufes and mercers fhops, with every thing that is grown unfafhionable and unfaleable in Europe, go off here extremely well; every thing being fufficiently recommended by its being European. The Spaniards pay in gold and filver, coined or in bars, cacao, vanilla, jefuits bark, cochineal, and other valuable commodities.

The trade of Curaffou, even in time of peace, is faid to be annually worth to the Dutch no lefs than 500,000 l. but in time of war, the profit is ftill greater, for then it becomes the common emporium of the Weft-Indies: it affords a retreat to fhips of all nations, and at the fame time refufes none of them arms and ammunition to deftroy one another. The intercourfe with Spain being then interrupted, the Spanifh colonies have fcarce any other market from whence they can be well fupplied either with flaves or goods. The French come hither to buy the beef, pork, corn, flour, and lumber, which the Englifh bring from the continent of North-America, or which is exported from Ireland; fo that, whether in peace or in war, the trade of this ifland flourifhes extremely.

The trade of all the Dutch American fettlements was originally carried on by the Weft-India company alone: at prefent, fuch fhips as go upon that trade, pay two and a half per cent. for their licenfes: the company, however, referve to themfelves the whole of what is carried on between Africa and the American iflands.

The other iflands, Bonaire and Aruba, are inconfiderable in themfelves, and fhould be regarded as appendages to Curaffou, for which they are chiefly employed in raifing cattle and other provifions.

The fmall iflands of Saba and St. Martins, fituated at no great diftance from St. Euftatia, hardly deferve to be mentioned: the latter is partly inhabited by the Englifh.

DANISH ISLANDS IN AMERICA.

St. THOMAS.] AN inconfiderable member of the Caribbees, fituated in 64 deg. weft lon. and 18 north lat. about 15 miles in circumference, and has a fafe and commodious harbour.

St. CROIX, or SANTA CRUZ.] Another fmall and unhealthy ifland, lying about five leagues eaft of St. Thomas, ten or twelve leagues in length, and three or four where it is broadeft. Thefe iflands, fo long as they remained in the

hands

hands of the Danish West-India company, were ill managed, and of little confequence to the Danes; but that wife and benevolent prince, the late king of Denmark, bought up the company's ftock, and laid the trade open ; and fince that time the ifland of St. Thomas has been fo greatly improved, that it is faid to produce upwards of 3000 hogfheads of fugar of 1000 weight each, and others of the Weft-India commo-dities in tolerable plenty. In time of war, privateers bring in their prizes here for fale ; and a great many veffels trade from hence along the Spanish Main, and return with money in fpecie or bars, and valuable merchandize. As for Santa Cruz, from a perfect defert a few years fince, it is beginning to fettle faft ; feveral perfons from the Englifh iflands, fome of them of great wealth, have gone to fettle there, and have received very great encouragement to do fo.

These two nations, the Dutch and Danes (and we may now add the French) hardly deferve to be mentioned among the proprietors of America ; their poffeffions there are com-paratively nothing. But as they appear extremely worthy of the attention of thefe powers, and as the fhare of the Dutch is worth to them at leaft 600,000 l. a year, what muft we think of our extenfive and valuable poffeffions ? what atten-tion do they not deferve from us ? and what may not be made of them by that attention ?

" There feems to be a remarkable providence (fays an in-genious and polite writer) in cafting the parts, if I may ufe that expreffion, of the feveral European nations who act upon the ftage of America. The Spaniard, proud, lazy, and magnificent, has an ample walk in which to expatiate ; a foft climate to indulge his love of eafe, and a profufion of gold and filver to procure him all thofe luxuries his pride demands, but which his lazinefs would refufe him.

The Portuguefe, naturally indigent at home, and enterpri-zing rather than induftrious abroad, has gold and diamonds as the Spaniard has, wants them as he does, but poffeffes them in a more ufeful, though a lefs oftentatious manner.

The Englifh, of a reafoning difpofition, thoughtful and cool, and men of bufinefs rather than of great induftry, im-patient of much fruitlefs labour, abhorrent of conftraint, and lovers of a country life, have a lot which indeed produces neither gold nor filver ; but they have a large tract of a fine continent; a noble field for the exercife of agriculture, and fufficient to furnifh their trade without laying them under great difficulties. Intolerant as they are of the moft ufeful reftraints, their commerce flourishes from the freedom every

man

tian has of pursuing it according to his own ideas, and directing his life after his own fashion.

The French, active, lively, enterprizing, pliable, and politic; and tho' changing their pursuits, always pursuing the present object with eagerness, are, notwithstanding, tractable and obedient to rules and laws, which bridle their dispositions, and wind and turn them to proper courses. These people have a country (when Canada was in their possession) where more is to be effected by managing the people than by cultivating the ground; where a peddling commerce, that requires constant motion, flourishes more than agriculture, or a regular traffic; where they have difficulties which keep them alert by struggling with them, and where their obedience to a wise government (meaning the excellent regulations already mentioned respecting the French colonies in America) serves them for personal wisdom. In the islands, the whole is the work of their policy, and a right turn their government has taken.

The Dutch have got a rock or two, on which to display the miracles of frugality and diligence, (which are their virtues) and on which they have exerted these virtues, and shewn those miracles."

TERRA-INCOGNITA, or unknown Countries.

In AMERICA.

IN North America, towards the pole, are Labrador or New-Britain, New North and South Wales, New-Denmark, &c. very little known. The inhabitants, like those of Nova Zembla, Greenland, Groenland, and the northern parts of Siberia, are few, and these savage; low in stature, and of an ugly appearance, scarcely resembling any thing human. They live upon the raw flesh of whales, bears, foxes, &c. and go muffled up in skins, the hairy sides next their bodies. In these unhospitable regions, their nights (as may be seen in the table of climates in the Introduction) are from one to six months, and the earth bound up in impenetrable snow; so that the miserable inhabitants live under ground great part of the year. Again, when the sun makes his appearance, they have a day of equal length.

All that vast tract on the back of the British settlements, from Canada and the lakes to the Pacific Ocean, which washes America on the west, is perfectly unknown to us, no European having ever travelled thither. From the climate

and

and situation of the country, it is supposed to be fruitful; it is inhabited by innumerable tribes of Indians, many of whom used to resort to the great fair of Montreal, even from the distance of 1000 miles, when that city was in the hands of the French.

In South America, the country of Guiana, extending from the equator to the eighth degree of north latitude, and bounded by the river Oronoque on the north, and the Amazones on the south, is unknown, except a slip along the coast, where the French at Cayenne and the Dutch at Surinam, have made some settlements; which, from the unhealthfulness of the climate, almost under the equator, and other causes, can hardly be extended any considerable way back.

The country of Amazonia, so called from the great river of that name, has never been thoroughly discovered, though it is situated between the European colonies of Peru and Brazil, and every where navigable by means of that great river and its branches. Some attempts have been made by the Spaniards and Portuguese, but being always attended with vast difficulties, so that few of the adventurers ever returned back, and no gold being found in the country as they expected, no European nation has hitherto made any settlement there.

Patagonia, at the southern extremity of America, is sometimes described as part of Chili; but as neither the Spaniards, nor any other European nation, have any colonies here, it is almost unknown, and is generally represented as a barren unhospitable country. And here in 52½ deg. south lat. we fall in with the streights of Magellan, having Patagonia, on the north, and the islands of Terra del Fuego, on the south. These streights extend from east to west 110 leagues, but the breadth in some places falls short of one. They were first discovered by Magellan, a Portuguese in the service of Spain, who sailed through them, in the year 1520, and thereby discovered a passage from the Atlantic to the Pacific or Southern Ocean. He has been since considered as the first navigator that sailed round the world; but having lost his life in a skirmish with some Indians before the ship's return to Europe, the honour of being the first circum-navigator has been disputed in favour of the brave Sir Francis Drake, who in 1574 passed the same streight in his way to India, from which he returned to Europe by the cape of Good-Hope. In 1616, La Maire, a Dutchman, keeping to the southward of these straits, discovered, in lat. 54½, another passage, since known by the name of Straits La Maire, and this passage, which has been generally preferred by succeeding navigators, is called doubling cape
Horn.

Horn. The author of Anfon's voyage, however, from fatal experience, advifes mariners to keep clear of thefe ftreights and iflands, by running down to 61 or 62 deg. fouth lat. before they attempt to fet their face weftward, towards the South-Seas; but the extreme long nights and intenfe cold in thofe latitudes, render that paffage practicable only in the months of January and February, which there is the middle of fummer.

In A S I A.

TOWARDS the north-eaft, are Yefdo, Kamfchatfka, and other countries or iflands, which the Ruffians are daily difcovering, but are imperfectly known even to that court, and fuppofed to be joined to North-America, or very near that part of the globe.

Below the Molucca ifles, in the Eaft-Indies, are New-Guinea, Carpentaria, New Holland, Dieman's Land, and, a little farther, New Zealand; regions difcovered by the Dutch and Englifh about the middle of the laft century, and are fuppofed to be a vaft continent, entirely feparated from Afia or America; but our knowledge of them, even at this time, is very imperfect, our navigators having only failed along the coafts, which ftretch from the equator to 44 deg. of fouth lat. by whom we learn that the natives are black, go naked, and in fome places are very numerous.

Befides thefe countries, the Europeans are daily making difcoveries of iflands that are fcattered up and down the Pacific ocean; and it is generally believed that there are many large tracts of land towards the fouth-pole, of which at prefent we know nothing.

A NEW GEOGRAPHICAL TABLE,

Containing the Names and Situations of the chief Cities,
Towns, Seas, Gulphs, Bays, Streights, Capes, and other
remarkable Places in the known World. Collected from
the moſt authentic Charts, Maps and Obſervations.

Towns.	Provinces.	Countries.	Quart.	Latitude. D. M.	Long. D. M.
A Berdeen,	Aberdeenſhire,	Scotland,	Europe	57-22N.	1-40W.
Acapulco,	Mexico,	North	Amer.	17-10N.	101-40W.
Adriatic Sea, or G. of Venice,	between	Italy & Turkey,	Europe,	Mediterranean Sea.	
Adrianople,	Romania,	Turkey,	Europe	42-00N.	26-30 E.
Agra,	Agra,	Eaſt India,	Aſia	26-43N.	76-30 E.
Air,	Airſhire,	Scotland,	Europe	55-30N.	4-35W.
Aleppo,	Syria,	Turkey,	Aſia	35-42N.	37-24 E.
Alexandria,	Lower Egypt,	Turkey,	Africa	31-10N.	30-19 E.
Albany,	New York,	North	Amer.	42-48N.	73-30W.
ALGIERS,	Algiers,	Barbary,	Africa	36-50N.	3-16 E.
Amboyna,	Amboyna Iſle,	Eaſt India,	Aſia	4-25 S.	127-25 E.
AMSTERDAM,	Holland,	Netherlands,	Europe	52-23N.	5-04 E.
Annapolis,	Nova Scotia,	North	Amer.	45-00N.	64-00W.
ANNAPOLIS,	Maryland,	North	Amer.	39-00N.	76-50W.
Antioch,	Syria,	Turkey,	Aſia	36-30N.	32-46 E.
Antwerp,	Brabant,	Netherlands,	Europe	51-13N.	4-29 E.
Archipelago,	Iſlands of	Greece,	Europe,	Mediter. Sea.	
Archangel,	Dwina,	Ruſſia,	Europe	64-30N.	40-30 E.
Aſtracan,	Aſtracan,	Ruſſia,	Aſia	47-00N.	52-00 E.
Athens,	Achaia,	Turkey,	Europe	37-58N.	24-05 E.
AtlanticOcean,	ſeparates	Eu. Aſia, Afr.	from America		
AVA,	Ava,	Eaſt India,	Aſia	20-20N.	95-30 E.
BAY of Biſcay	Coaſt of	France,	Europe,	Atlantic Ocean.	
— of Beng.	Coaſt of	India,	Aſia,	Indian Ocean.	
Baltic Sea,	between	Ger. & Swed.	Europe,	Atlantic Ocean.	
Baldivia,	Chili,	South	Amer.	39-35 S.	81-10W.
Balbec,	Syria,	Turkey,	Aſia	33-40N.	37-00 E.
Barcelona,	Catalonia,	Spain,	Europe	42-26N.	2-18 E.
Baſtia,	Corſica Iſle,	Italy,	Europe	42-20N.	9-40 E.
Bath,	Somerſetſhire,	England,	Europe	51-27N.	2-32W.
Bagdat,	Eyraca Arab.	Turkey,	Aſia	33-40N.	45-00 E.
Baſſora,	Eyraca Arab.	Turkey,	Aſia	30-45N.	48-00 E.
BATAVIA,	Java Iſle,	Eaſt India,	Aſia	6-00 S.	107-00 E.
BAZIL,	Bazil,	Switzerland,	Europe	47-40N.	7-40 E.
Belfaſt,	Ulſter,	Ireland,	Europe	54-39N.	6-30W.
Bender,	Beſſarabia,	Turkey,	Europe	46-40N.	29-00 E.
BERGEN,	Bergen,	Norway,	Europe	60-10N.	5-40 E.
BERLIN,	Brandenburg,	Germany,	Europe	52-33N.	13-32 E.
Bern.	Bern,	Switzerland,	Europe	47-00N.	7-20 E.
Berwick,	Berwick,	Scotland,	Europe	55-48N.	1-45W.
Belgrade,	Servia,	Turkey,	Europe	45-00N.	21-20 E.
Bencoolen,	Sumatra Iſle,	Eaſt India,	Aſia	3-55 S.	101-00 E.
Bilboa,	Biſcay,	Spain,	Europe	43-26N.	3-18W.
Birmingham,	Warwickſhire,	England,	Europe	52-30N.	1-50W.

Towns.	Provinces.	Countries.	Quart.	Latitude.	Long.
				D. M.	D. M.
Bombay,	Bombay Ifle,	Eaft India,	Afia	19-00N.	71-30 E.
Bokharia,	Ufbec	Tartary,	Afia	39-15N.	67-00 E.
Bourdeaux,	Guienne,	France,	Europe	44-50N.	00-38W.
Borroughfton-nefs,	Linlithgowfh.	Scotland,	Europe	55-58N.	3-44W.
Bofton,	Lincolnfhire,	England,	Europe	53-10N.	00-25 E.
BOSTON,	Maffachufets,	New England,	Amer.	42-20N.	70-40W.
Breda,	Brabant,	Netherlands,	Europe	51-40N.	4-40 E.
Breft,	Bretany,	France,	Europe	48-23N.	4-25W.
Bremen,	Low. Saxony,	Germany,	Europe	53-25N.	8-20 E.
BRESLAU,	Silefia,	Bohemia,	Europe	51-15N.	16-50 E.
Briftol,	Somerfetfhire,	England,	Europe	51-33N.	2-40W.
Britifh Sea,	between	Brit. & Germ.	Europe,	Atlantic Ocean.	
Black, or Euxine Sea,	Turkey in	Europe and	Afia.		
BRUSSELS,	Brabant,	Netherlands,	Europe	50-50N.	4-06 E.
Bruges,	Flanders,	Netherlands,	Europe	51-16N.	3-05 E.
Brunfwick,	Low. Saxony,	Germany,	Europe	52-30N.	10-30 E.
Buda,	Lower	Hungary,	Europe	47-40N.	19-20 E.
BURLINGTON,	Jerfey,	North	Amer.	40-08N.	75-00W.
BUENOS AYRES,	La Plata,	South	Amer.	34-35 S.	57-54W.
CAIRO,	Lower	Egypt,	Africa	30-00N.	32-00 E.
Cagliari,	Sardinia,	Italy,	Europe	39-25N.	9-38 E.
CACHAO,	Tonquin,	Eaft India,	Afia	21-30N.	105-00 E.
Calais,	Picardy,	France,	Europe	50-58N.	1-54 E.
Cambletown,	Argylefhire,	Scotland,	Europe	55-30N.	5-40W.
Cambridge,	Cambridgefh.	England	Europe	52-15N.	00-05 E.
Cadiz,	Andalufia,	Spain,	Europe	36-33N.	6-01W.
Calcutta,	Bengal,	Eaft India,	Afia	22-00N.	87-00 E.
Canterbury,	Kent,	England,	Europe	51-16N.	1-15 E.
Candia,	Candy Ifland,	Turkey,	Afia	35-19N.	25-23 E.
CANTON,	Canton,	China,	Afia	23-14N.	113-06 E.
CAMBODIA,	Siam,	Eaft India,	Afia	13-30N.	105-00 E.
Carlifle,	Cumberland,	England,	Europe	54-47N.	2-35W.
Carthage ruins,	Tunis,	Barbary,	Africa	36-30N.	9-00 E.
CARTHAGENA	Terra Firma,	South	Amer.	10-28N.	77-00W.
Cardigan,	Cardiganfhire,	Wales,	Europe	52-10N.	4-38W.
Candy,	Ceylone I.	Eaft India,	Afia	7-54N.	79-00 E.
Cafpian Sea,	Ruffian	Tartary,	Afia.		
Caffel,	Heffe-Caffel,	Germany,	Europe	51-20N.	9-20 E.
Cape Clear,	Cork,	Ireland,	Europe	51-10N.	9-40W.
—— Finiftere,	Galicia,	Spain,	Europe	43-12N.	10-05W.
—— Vincent,	Algarve,	Portugal,	Europe	36-53N.	9-06W.
—— Verd,		Negroland,	Africa	14-43N.	17-20W.
—— of Good Hope,	Hottentots,	Caffraria,	Africa	34-07 S.	19-35 E.
—— Comorin,	Hither India,	Mogul Empire,	Afia	7-50N.	77-30 E.
—— Florida,	Eaft Florida,	North	Amer.	24-57N.	80-30W.
—— Horn,	Delfuego Ifle,	South	Amer.	56-35 S.	79-55W.
Cattegate Sea,	between	Swed. & Denm.	Europe	Atlantic Ocean.	
Ceuta,	Fez	Morocco,	Africa	35-54N.	6-30W.

Towns.	Provinces.	Countries.	Quart.	Latitude. D.M.	Long. D.M.
Chefter,	Chefhire,	England,	Europe	53-15N.	3-00W,
CHARLES TOWN,	South Carolina	North	Amer.	32-45N.	79-12W,
Civita Vech.	Pope's Territ.	Italy,	Europe	42-05N.	12-30 E,
COPENHAGEN	Zealand Ifle,	Denmark,	Europe	55-41N.	12-50 E.
Cork,	Munfter,	Ireland,	Europe	51-49N.	8-40W.
Coventry,	Warwickfhire,	England,	Europe	52-25N.	1-25W.
CONSTANTI- NOPLE,	Romania,	Turkey,	Europe	41-00N.	28-56 E.
Conftance,	Swabia,	Germany,	Europe	47-37N.	9-12 E,
Corinth,	Morea,	Turkey,	Europe	37-30N.	23-00 E.
Cracow,	Little Poland,	Poland,	Europe	50-00N.	19-30 E.
Curaffou,	Curaffou Ifle,	Weft India,	Amer.	11-56N.	68-20W.
Cufco,	Peru,	South	Amer.	12-25 S.	70-00W.
DAmafcus,	Syria,	Turkey,	Afia	33-15N.	37-20 E.
Dantzic,	Polifh Pruffia,	Poland,	Europe	54-22N.	18-36 E.
Dacca,	Bengal,	Eaft India,	Afia	23-30N.	89-20 E.
DELLY,	Delly,	Eaft India,	Afia	29-00N.	76-30 E.
Delft,	Holland,	Netherlands,	Europe	52-06N.	4-05 E.
Derbent,	Dagiftan,	Perfia,	Afia	41-40N.	50-30 E.
Derby,	Derbyfhire,	England,	Europe	52-58N.	1-30W,
Derry,	Ulfter,	Ireland,	Europe	54-52N.	7-40W.
Dieu,	Malabar,	Eaft India,	Afia	21-37N.	69-30 E.
Dover,	Kent,	England,	Europe	51-08N.	1-25 E.
DRESDEN,	Saxony,	Germany,	Europe	51-00N.	13-36 E.
Dundee,	Forfar,	Scotland,	Europe	56-26N.	2-48W.
DUBLIN,	Leinfter,	Ireland,	Europe	53-20N.	6-28W.
Durham,	Durham,	England,	Europe	54-48N.	1-25W,
Dumbarton,	Dumbartonfh.	Scotland,	Europe	55-54N.	4-20W.
Dunkirk,	Flanders,	Netherlands,	Europe	51-00N.	2-20 E.
Dunbar,	Haddington,	Scotland,	Europe	55-58N.	2-25W.
Dumfries,	Dumfriesfhire,	Scotland,	Europe	55-08N.	3-25W,
ENgl. Chan.	between	Engl.& France,	Europe,	Atlantic Ocean.	
Ephefus,	Natolia,	Turkey,	Afia	38-01N.	27-53 E.
EDINBURGH,	Edinburghfh.	Scotland,	Europe	55-58N.	3-00W.
Elbing,	Pruffia,	Poland,	Europe	54-15N.	20-00 E.
Embden,	Lower	Germany,	Europe	53-25N.	7-10 E.
Ethiopian Sea,	Coaft of	Guinea,	Africa,	Atlantic Ocean.	
Exeter,	Devonfhire,	England,	Europe	50-44N.	3-30W.
FAlkirk,	Stirling,	Scotland,	Europe	55-58N.	3-48W.
Falmouth,	Cornwall,	England,	Europe	50-10N.	5-20W.
Fez,	Fez,	Morocco,	Africa	33-30N.	6-00W.
Ferrol,	Gallicia,	Spain,	Europe	43-30N.	8-40W,
FLORENCE,	Tufcany,	Italy,	Europe	43-30N.	12-15 E,
Fort St. David,	Coromandel,	Eaft India,	Afia	12-05N.	80-55 E,
GEneva,	Geneva,	Switzerland,	Europe	46-20N.	6-00 E.
GENOA,	Genoa,	Italy,	Europe	44-25N.	9-00 E.
Ghent,	Flanders,	Netherlands,	Europe	51 00N.	3-36 E,
Gibraltar,	Andalufia,	Spain,	Europe	36-00N.	6-00W,
Glafgow,	Lanerkfhire,	Scotland,	Europe	55-50N.	4-05W,
Gloucefter,	Gloucefterfh.	England,	Europe	51-50N.	2-10W.
Goa,	Malabar,	Eaft India,	Afia	15-31N.	74-70 E.

Towns.	Provinces.	Countries.	Quart.	Latitude. D.M.	Long. D.M.
Gombroon,	Farfiftan,	Perfia,	Afia	27-30N.	57-25 E.
Gottenburg,	Gothland,	Sweden,	Europe	58-00N.	11-30 E.
Greenock,	Renfrewfhire,	Scotland,	Europe	55-52N.	4-22W.
Guam,	Landrone Ifles,	Eaft India,	Afia	14-00N.	140-30 E.
G. of Bothnia,	Coaft of	Sweden,	Europe,	Baltic Sea.	
—— Finland,	between	Swed. & Ruf.	Europe,	Baltic Sea.	
—— Venice,	between	Italy & Turk.	Europe,	Mediter. Sea.	
—— Ormus,	between	Perfia & Arab.	Afia,	Indian Ocean.	
—— Perfia,	between	Perfia & Arab.	Afia	Indian Ocean	
—— St. Lawr.	Coaft of	New Scotland,	N. Amer.	Atlantic Ocean	
—— Californ.	between	Calif. & Mexico,	N. Amer.	Pacific Ocean.	
—— Mexico,	Coaft of	Mexico,	N. Amer.	Atlantic Ocean.	
HAGUE,	Holland,	Netherlands,	Europe	52-10N.	4-00 E.
Hamburg,	Holftein,	Germany,	Europe	53-41N.	9-40 E.
Heliefpont,	Med. & Bl.Sea,	Europe and	Afia.		
Hallifax,	Yorkfhire,	England,	Europe	53-45N.	1-52W.
HALLIFAX,	Nova Scotia,	North	Amer.	44-40N.	63-15W.
Hanover,	Saxony,	Germany,	Europe	52-32N.	9-35 E.
Havannah,	Cuba	Ifland,	Amer.	23-00N.	84-00W.
Haerlem,	Holland,	Netherlands,	Europe	52-20N.	4-10 E.
Hughly,	Bengal,	Eaft India,	Afia	21-45N.	87-55 E.
Hereford,	Herefordfhire,	England,	Europe	52-06N.	2-38W.
Hull,	Yorkfhire,	England,	Europe	53-45N.	0-12W.
Hudfon's Bay,	Coaft of	Labrador	N. Amer.	Northern Ocean.	
ISthmus of Suez,	joins	Africa to	Afia.		
—— Corinth,	joins the Morea to	Greece,	Europe.		
—— Panama,	joins	North and S.	America.		
—— Malacca,	joins Malacca to	Further India,	Afia.		
JEDDO,	Japan Ifle,	Eaft India,	Afia	36-20N.	139-00 E.
JERUSALEM,	Paleftine,	Turkey,	Afia	32-00N.	36-00 E.
Indian Ocean,	Coaft of	India,	Afia,	Southern Ocean.	
Invernefs,	Invernefsfhire,	Scotland,	Europe	57-33N.	4-02W.
Irifh Sea,	between	G. Brit. & Irel.	Europe,	Atlantic Ocean.	
ISPAHAN,	Irac Agem,	Perfia,	Afia	32-50N.	51-30 E.
Ivica,	Ivica Ifle,	Italy,	Europe	38-50N.	1-40 E.
KElfo,	Roxboroughfh.	Scotland,	Europe	55-38N.	2-12W.
Kilmarnock,	Airfhire,	Scotland,	Europe	55-38N.	4-30W.
Kinfale,	Munfter,	Ireland,	Europe	51-32N.	8-20W.
KINGSTON,	Jamaica,	Weft India,	Amer.	17-40N.	77-00W.
KONINGSBERG,	Pruffia,	Poland,	Europe	54-43N.	21-35 E.
LAncafter,	Lancafhire,	England,	Europe	54-05N.	2-55W.
Levant Sea,	Coaft of	Syria,	Afia,	Mediterranean Sea.	
Lahor,	Lahor,	Eaft India,	Afia	32-40N.	75-30 E.
Leith	Edinburghfh	Scotland	Europe	55-58N.	2-2W.

Towns.	Provinces.	Countries.	Quart.	Latitude. D. M.	Long. D. M.
Limerick,	Munſter,	Ireland,	Europe	52-35N.	8-48W.
LISBON,	Eſtramadura,	Portugal,	Europe	38-42N.	8-53W.
LIMA,	Peru,	South	Amer.	12-15 S.	77-30W.
Litchfield,	Staffordſhire,	England,	Europe	52-43N.	1-40W.
LOUISBURG,	Cape Breton I.	North	Amer.	45-54N.	59-30W.
Loretto,	Pope's Territ.	Italy,	Europe	43-15N.	14-15 E.
LONDON,	Middleſex,	England,	Europe	51-30N.	firſt Mer.
London Derry,	Ulſter,	Ireland,	Europe	55-00N.	7-40W.
Lubec,	Holſtein,	Germany,	Europe	54-00N.	11-40 E.
Lyons,	Lyons,	France,	Europe	45-46N.	4-55 E.
Luxemburg,	Luxemburg,	Netherlands,	Europe	49-40N.	5-40 E.
MAcao,	Canton,	China,	Aſia	22-13N.	113-51 E.
Majorca,	Majorca Iſle,	Spain,	Europe	39-30N.	3-03 E.
MADRID,	New Caſtile,	Spain,	Europe	40-30N.	4-15W.
Mancheſter,	Lancaſhire,	England,	Europe	53-30N.	2-22W.
Malta,	Malta Iſle,	Mediterranean,	Europe	35-53N.	14-32 E.
MANTUA,	Mantua,	Italy,	Europe	45-20N.	10-47 E.
Malacca,	Malacca,	Eaſt India,	Aſia	2-12N.	101-00 E.
Madraſs,	Coromandel,	Eaſt India,	Aſia	13-11N.	80-32 E.
Manilla,	Philippine I.	Eaſt India,	Aſia	14-20N.	118-00 E.
Marſeilles,	Provence,	France,	Europe	43-15N.	5-20 E.
Medina,	Arab. Deſerta,	Arabia,	Aſia	25-00N.	39-53 E.
MECCA,	Arab. Deſerta,	Arabia,	Aſia	21-45N.	41-00 E.
Mediter. Sea,	between	Europe and	Africa,	Atlantic Ocean.	
Mequinez,	Fez,	Barbary,	Africa	34-30N.	6-00 E.
MESSINA,	Sicily Iſland,	Mediter. Sea,	Europe	38-30N.	15-40 E.
MEXICO,	Mexico,	North	Amer.	20-00N.	103-00W.
Milford Haven,	Pembrokeſhire,	Wales,	Europe	51-45N.	5-15W.
MILAN,	Milaneſe,	Italy,	Europe	45-25N.	9-30 E.
MOCHO,	Arabia Felix,	Arabia,	Aſia	13-40N.	43-50 E.
MODENA,	Modena,	Italy,	Europe	44-45N.	11-20 E.
Montreal,	Canada,	North	Amer.	45-35N.	73-11W.
Montpelier,	Languedoc,	France,	Europe	43-30N.	3-50 E.
Montroſe,	Forfar,	Scotland,	Europe	56-34N.	2-20W.
MOROCCO,	Morocco,	Barbary,	Africa	30-32N.	6-10W.
Moscow,	Moſcow,	Ruſſia,	Europe	55-45N.	37-51 E.
Munſter,	Weſtphalia,	Germany,	Europe	52-00N.	7-10 E.
NANCY,	Lorrain,	Germany,	Europe	48-44N.	6-00 E.
Nanking,	Nanking,	China,	Aſia	32-00N.	118-30 E.
NAPLES,	Naples,	Italy,	Europe	41-00N.	14-19 E.
NARVA,	Livonia,	Ruſſia,	Europe	59-00N.	27-35 E.
Newcaſtle,	Northumber-land,	England,	Europe	55-03N.	1-24W.
Nice,	Piedmont,	Italy,	Europe	43-42N.	7-05 E.
Newport,	Rhode Iſland,	North	Amer.	41-35N.	71-06W.
NEW YORK,	New York,	North	Amer.	40-40N.	74-00W.
NINEVEH,	Aſſyria,	Turkey,	Aſia	36-00N.	45-00 E.
Nottingham,	Nottinghamſh.	England,	Europe	53-00N.	1-06W.
Northampton,	Northamp-tonſhire,	England,	Europe	52-15N.	00-55W.
Norwich,	Norfolk,	England,	Europe	52-40N.	1-25 E.

3

Towns.	Provinces.	Countries.	Quart.	Latitude.	Long.
				D. M.	D. M.
OLympia,	Greece,	Turkey,	Europe	37-30N.	22-00 E.
OLMUTZ,	Moravia,	Bohemia,	Europe	49-30N.	16-45 E.
Oporto,	Duoro,	Portugal,	Europe	41-10N.	9-00W.
Ormus,	Ormus Ifle,	Perfia,	Afia	26-50N.	57-00 E.
Oran,	Algiers,	Barbary,	Africa	36-30N.	0-05 E.
Oftend,	Flanders,	Netherlands,	Europe	51-15N.	2-45 E.
Oxford,	Oxfordfhire,	England,	Europe	51-45N.	1-15W.
PAcific or	between	Afia and	America.		
Oriental O.					
Padua,	Venice,	Italy,	Europe	45-30N.	12-15 E.
Paifley,	Renfrewfhire,	Scotland,	Europe	55-48N.	4-08W.
PALERMO,	Sicily Ifle,	Mediterranean,	Europe	38-30N.	13-43 E.
Palmyra,	Syria,	Turkey,	Afia	33-00N.	39-00 E.
PANAMA,	Darien,	Terra Firma,	Amer.	8-50N.	81-52W.
PARIS,	Ifle of France,	France,	Europe	48-50N.	2-25 E.
PARMA,	Parmefan,	Italy,	Europe	44-45N.	10-51 E.
Patna,	Bengal,	Eaft India,	Afia	25-45N.	83-00 E.
PEGU,	Pegu,	Eaft India,	Afia	17-00N.	97-00 E.
Pekin,	Pekin,	China,	Afia	40-00N.	116-28 E.
Pembroke,	Pembrokefhire,	Wales,	Europe	51-45N.	4-50W.
Penzance,	Cornwall,	England,	Europe	50-08N.	6-00W.
PENSACOLA,	Weft Florida,	North	Amer.	30-22N.	87-20W.
Perth,	Perthfhire,	Scotland,	Europe	56-22N.	3-12W.
Perthamboy,	New York,	North	Amer.	40-30N.	74-20W.
Perfepolis,	Irac Agem,	Perfia,	Afia	30-30N.	54-00 E.
PETERSBURG,	Ingria,	Ruffia,	Europe	60-00N.	30-25 E.
PHILADELPHIA	Penfylvania,	North	Amer.	40-00N.	75-20W.
Pifa,	Tufcany,	Italy,	Europe	43-36N.	11-15 E.
PLACENTIA,	Newfound. Ifle,	North	Amer.	47-26N.	55-00W.
Plymouth,	Devonfhire,	England,	Europe	50-26N.	4-15W.
Plymouth,	New England,	North	Amer.	41-48N.	70-25W.
Pondicherry,	Coromandel,	Eaft India,	Afia	12-27N.	80-00 E.
Portfmouth,	Hampfhire,	England,	Europe	50-48N.	1-06W.
Portfmouth,	New England,	North	Amer.	43-10N.	70-20W.
Porto Bello,	Darien,	Terra Firma,	Amer.	10-00N.	82-00W.
Port l'Orient,	Bretany,	France,	Europe	47-42N.	3-15W.
Port Royal,	Jamaica Ifle,	Weft India,	Amer.	18-00N.	77-00W.
Potofi,	Peru,	South	Amer.	21-00 S.	67-00W.
PRAGUE,	——	Bohemia,	Europe	50-00N.	14-20 E.
Prefton,	Lancafhire,	England,	Europe	53-45N.	2-50W.
PRESBURG,	Upper	Hungary,	Europe	48-20N.	17-30 E.
QUEBEC,	Canada,	North	Amer.	46-55N.	69-48W.
Quito,	Peru,	South	Amer.	0-30 S.	78-00W.
RAgufa,	Dalmatia,	Venice,	Europe	42-45N.	18-25 E.
Ratifbon,	Bavaria,	Germany,	Europe	48-56N.	12-05 E.
Revel,	Livonia,	Ruffia,	Europe	59-00N.	25-07 E.
Rheims,	Champagne,	France,	Europe	49-14N.	4-00 E.
RHODES,	Rhodes Ifland	Levant Sea,	Afia	36-20N.	28-00 E.
Riga,	Livonia,	Ruffia,	Europe	56-55N.	24-00 E.
ROME,	Pope's Territ.	Italy,	Europe	41-54N.	12-45 E.
Rofetto,	Egypt,	Turkey,	Africa	31-10N.	41-35 E.
Rotterdam,	Holland,	Netherlands,	Europe	51-55N.	4-30 E.

Towns.	Provinces.	Countries.	Quart.	Latitude. D. M.	Long. D. M.
Rouen,	Normandy,	France,	Europe	49-26N.	1-10 E.
St. Augus-tin,	East Florida,	North	Amer.	29-45N.	81-12W.
— Domingo,	Hispaniola I.	West India,	Amer.	18-20N.	70-00W.
— Helena,	St. Helena,	Island,	Africa	16-00 S.	6-36W.
— Jago,	Chili,	South	Amer.	34-00 S.	77-00W.
— Salvador,	Brazil,	South	Amer.	13-00 S.	38-00W.
Sallee,	Fez,	Barbary,	Africa	34-00N.	6-20W.
Samarcand,	Usbec	Tartary,	Asia	40-40N.	69-00 E.
Salisbury,	Wiltshire,	England,	Europe	51-06N.	1-45W.
Santa Fe,	New Mexico,	North	Amer.	36-00N.	104-00W.
Savannah,	Georgia,	North	Amer.	31-55N.	80-20W.
Sayd, or Thebes	Upper	Egypt,	Africa	27-00N.	32-20 E.
Samaria Ruins,	Holy Land,	Turkey,	Asia	32-40N.	38-00 E.
St. George's Channel,	between	Engl. & Irel.	Europe,	Atlantic Ocean.	
Scarborough,	Yorkshire,	England,	Europe	54-18N.	0-10W.
Scone,	Perthshire,	Scotland,	Europe	56-24N.	3-10W.
Sea of Asof,	Little Tartary,	Europe &	Asia,	Black Sea.	
— Marmora,	Turkey in	Europe and	Asia,	Black Sea.	
— Kamf-chatka,	Coast of	Kamschatka,	Asia,	Pacific Ocean.	
— Korea,	Coast of	Korea,	Asia,	Pacific Ocean:	
Shrewsbury,	Shropshire,	England,	Europe	52-43N.	2-46W.
Shields,	Durham,	England,	Europe	55-02N.	1-15W.
Sheerness,	Kent,	England,	Europe	51-25N.	00-50 E.
Schiras,	Farsistan,	Persia,	Asia	29-30N.	53-00 E.
Seville,	Andalusia,	Spain,	Europe	37-15N.	6-05W.
Siam,	Siam,	East India,	Asia	14-18N.	100-55 E.
Sidon,	Palestine,	Turkey,	Asia	33-33N.	36-15 E.
Smyrna,	Natolia,	Turkey,	Asia	38-28N.	29-00 E.
Southampton,	Hampshire,	England,	Europe	50-55N.	1-25W.
Spaw,	Liege,	Germany,	Europe	50-30N.	5-40 E.
Sound,	between	Denm. & Swed.	Europe,	Baltic Sea.	
Stafford,	Staffordshire,	England,	Europe	52-50N.	2-00W.
Sterling,	Sterlingshire,	Scotland,	Europe	56-10N.	3-50W.
Stralsund,	Pomerania,	Germany,	Europe	54-23N.	13-22 E.
Strasburg,	Alsace,	Germany,	Europe	48-38N.	7-51 E.
Stockholm,	Uplandia,	Sweden,	Europe	59-30N.	18-08 E.
Streights of Dover,	between	Eng. & France,	Europe,	Eng. Channel.	
— Gibraltar,	between	Europe and	Africa,	Mediter. Sea.	
— Babel-mandel,	between	Africa and	Asia,	Red Sea.	
— Ormus,	between	Persia & Arab.	Asia,	Persian Gulph.	
— Malacca,	between	Malac.&Sumat.	Asia,	Indian Ocean.	
— Magellan,	in Patagonia	South	Amer.	Atlant. & S. Sea.	
— La Maire,	in Patagonia	South	Amer.	Atlant. & S. Sea.	
Suez,	Suez,	Egypt,	Africa	29-50N.	33-27 E.
Sunderland,	Durham,	England,	Europe	54-55N.	1-10W.
Surinam,	Surinam,	South	America	6-00N.	55-30W.
Surat,	Cambaya,	East India,	Asia	21-10N.	72-25 E.

Towns.	Provinces.	Countries.	Quart.	Latitude. D. M.	Long. D. M.
Syracufe,	Sicily Ifle,	Mediterranean,	Europe	37-04N.	15-05 E.
TAngier,	Fez,	Barbary,	Africa	35-42N.	5-45 W.
Tanjour,	Tanjour,	Eaft India,	Afia	11-27N.	79-07 E.
Tauris, or Ecbatana,	Medea,	Perfia,	Afia	38-20N.	46-30 E.
Teflis,	Georgia,	Perfia,	Afia	43-30N.	47-00 E.
Tetuan,	Fez,	Barbary,	Africa	35-40N.	5-18W.
Thorn,	Regal Pruffia,	Poland,	Europe	52-56N.	19-00 E.
TOBOLSKI,	Siberia,	Ruffia,	Afia	58-00N.	69-00 E.
Toledo,	New Caftile,	Spain,	Europe	39-45N.	4-12W.
Toulon,	Provence,	France,	Europe	43-07N.	6-00 E.
Trapefond,	Natolia,	Turkey,	Afia	41-50N.	40-30 E.
Trent,	Trent,	Germany,	Europe	46-05N.	11-02 E.
Troy Ruins,	Natolia,	Turkey,	Afia	39-30N.	26-30 E.
TRIPOLI,	Tripoli,	Barbary,	Africa	33-30N.	14-30 E.
Tripoli,	Syria,	Turkey,	Afia	34-30N.	36-15 E.
TUNIS,	Tunis,	Barbary,	Africa	36-47N.	10-00 E.
TURIN,	Piedmont,	Italy,	Europe	44-50N.	7-30 E.
Tyre,	Judea,	Turkey,	Afia	32-32N.	36-00 E.
UTrecht,	Holland,	Netherlands,	Europe	52-07N.	5-00 E.
VEra Cruz,	Old Mexico,	North	Amer.	18-30N.	97-48W.
Verfailles,	Ifle of France,	France,	Europe	48-40N.	2-15 E.
VIENNA,	Auftria,	Germany,	Europe	48-20N.	16-20 E.
WArwick,	Warwickfhire,	England,	Europe	52-18N.	1-32W.
WARSAW,	Warfovia,	Poland,	Europe	52-15N.	21-05 E.
Waterford,	Munfter,	Ireland,	Europe	52-12N.	7-16W.
Whitehaven,	Cumberland,	England,	Europe	54-38N.	3-36W.
WILLIAMS- BURG,	Virginia,	North	Amer.	37-12N.	76-48W.
Wells,	Somerfetfhire,	England,	Europe	51-12N.	2-40W.
Winchefter,	Hampfhire,	England,	Europe	51-06N.	1-15W.
Worms,	Lower Rhine,	Germany,	Europe	49-38N.	8-05 E.
Worcefter,	Worcefterfhire,	England,	Europe	52-10N.	2-15W.
YArmouth,	Norfolk,	England,	Europe	52-45N.	1-48 E.
York,	Yorkfhire,	England,	Europe	54-00N.	1-03W.

F I N I S.

DIRECTIONS to the *Binder* for placing the MAPS.

The Binder is defired to beat the Book before he places the Maps.

BOOKS printed for, and sold by J. KNOX, Nᵒ 148, near SOMERSET-HOUSE, in the STRAND.

A NEW EDITION, being the third, of this Book, neatly printed in one large Octavo Volume, illustrated with a Set of small Maps, by Mr. Kitchin. Price bound 6 s. *See the English and foreign Reviews of this Book.*

	l.	s.	d.		l.	s.	d.
Anson's Voyage, 4to. —	1	1	0	Middleton's Cicero, 3 V. 8vo.	0	15	0
——— 8vo.	0	6	0	Murray on Ship-Building, 4to.	1	1	0
——— 12mo.	0	3	0	Nelson's Festivals, 8vo. —	0	5	0
Arbuthnot's Works, 2 V. 12mo.	0	6	0	New Collection of Voyages and			
Burkitt on the New Test. fol.	1	1	0	Travels, 7 V. 8vo. with 49			
Ditto with Plates	1	5	0	Plates	2	2	0
Brown's (Thomas) Works, 4 V.				Otway's Plays, 3 V. 12mo. —	0	9	0
12mo. — —	0	12	0	Pamela, 4 V. 12mo. —	0	12	0
Bailey's Dictionary, 8vo.	0	6	0	Paradise Lost, 12mo. —	0	3	6
Bacon's Works, 5 V. 4to.	5	5	0	—Ditto, with Newton's Notes,			
Biographia Britannica, 7 V. fol.	10	10	0	2 V. 8vo. —	0	12	0
Biographical Dict. 12 V. 8vo.	3	12	0	Paradise Regain'd, 12mo. —	0	3	0
Boyle's Works, 6 V. 4to.				—Ditto, with Newton's Notes,			
Beaumont and Fletcher, 10 V. 8vo.	2	10	0	2 V. 8vo. —	0	10	0
Chalmers's Dict. 4 V. fol.				Patoun's Navigation, 8vo. —	0	5	0
Cambden's Britannia, 2 V. fol.				Pope's Works, 9 V. 8vo. —	2	14	0
Campbel's Lives of the Adm.				——— 9 V. small 8vo.	1	7	0
4 V. 8vo. —	1	4	0	——— 6 V. 12mo.	0	18	0
Clarissa, 8 V. 12mo. —	1	4	0	Postlethwayt's Dictionary,			
Cruden's Concordance, 4to.	1	5	0	2 V. fol. —	4	4	0
Don Quixote, by Smollet, 4 V.				Prior's Poems, 12mo. —	0	3	6
12mo. — —	0	12	0	Rambler, 4 V. 12mo. —	0	12	0
Dictionary of Arts and Sciences,				Roderic Random, 2 V. 12mo. —	0	6	0
8 V. 8vo. —	2	8	0	Rabelais, 5 V. 12mo. —	0	15	0
Dodd's Sermons to Young Men,				Rollin's Roman Hist. 10 V. 8vo.	3	0	0
3 V. 8vo. —	0	10	6	——— Ant. Hist. 7 V. 8vo.	2	2	0
Francis's Horace, 4 V. 12mo.	0	12	0	——— Arts and Sciences 3 V. 8vo.	0	18	0
Farmer's Kalendar, 8vo.	0	5	0	——— Belles Lettres, 3 V. 8vo.	0	18	0
Gill Blas, by Smollet, 4 V. 12mo.	0	12	0	Rowland's Antiq. of the Isle of			
Glass's Cookery, 8vo.	0	5	0	Anglesey, 4to. —	0	18	0
Guthrie's History of the World,				Seed's Sermons, 2 V. 8vo. —	0	10	0
12 V. 8vo. — —	3	12	0	Shaw's Travels, 4to. —	0	18	0
Henrietta, 2 V. 12mo. —	0	6	0	Smollet's History, 7 V. 8vo.	2	2	0
Hervey's Medit. 2 V. 12mo.	0	6	0	Sully's Memoirs, 6 V. 12mo.	0	18	0
Harris's Voyages, 2 V. folio	4	4	0	Turkish Spy, 8 V. 12mo. —	1	1	0
Johnson's Dictionary, 2 V. fol.	4	10	0	Temple's Works, 4 V. 8vo,	1	4	0
——— 2 V. 8vo.	0	10	0	Wood's Conveyancing, 3 V. fol.	5	10	0
Locke's Works, 4 V. 4to.	4	4	0				

Where may be had, a complete Assortment of the best English and foreign Authors; various Editions in different Bindings, and an Allowance to those who purchase for Sale.

www.ingramcontent.com/pod-product-compliance
Lightning Source LLC
Chambersburg PA
CBHW031347290326
41932CB00044B/358